COLLECTED PAPERS ON SCHIZOPHRENIA AND RELATED SUBJECTS

Harold F. Searles, M.D.

with a Preface by
Robert P. Knight, M.D.
Director of the Austen Riggs Foundation

K A R N A C
LONDON   NEW YORK

Reprinted in 1986 with permission
of Hogarth Press Ltd. by
H. Karnac (Books) Ltd.
6 Pembroke Buildings
London NW10 6RE

Second Impression 1993
Third Impression 2005

British Library Cataloguing in Publication Data

A C.I.P. for this book is available from the British Library

ISBN: 0 946439 30 3

www.karnacbooks.com

*To My Mother and
to the Memory of
My Father*

CONTENTS

CONTENTS

8

ACKNOWLEDGEMENTS

SINCE each of these papers endeavours to show, as conscientiously as is within my power, where any ideas considered by me to be original fit into the mosaic of the existing literature, I have not duplicated such acknowledgement in the Introduction. The reader will note how frequently there occur, among these papers, such names as Michael Balint, Bion, Brodey, Bowen, Mabel Blake Cohen, Erikson, Heimann, Hill, Knight, Lidz and Lidz, Little, Loewald, Mahler, Milner, Rosenfeld, Sèchehaye, Werner, Whitaker and Malone, Winnicott, Wynne, and various others, a frequency which suggests something of the stimulation I have gained from their writings.

To go further back, when as an interne in internal medicine I was attracted, extracurricularly so to speak, to Freud's writings, I realized without the need for any teacher or interpreter to tell me that here was an authentic and towering genius, and this provided me one of my earliest incentives to go into psychoanalysis. From Sullivan's teachings, later on, I derived an indelible emphasis upon the interpersonal viewpoint in approaching all psychological phenomena, and I benefited also from the viewpoint implicit in his teachings that schizophrenic persons are not essentially and awesomely different from the rest of us, but only more difficult to deal with than are most of us. Drs Edith Weigert, Robert A. Cohen, and Winifred G. Whitman were supervisors, early in my analytic training, from whom I learned a great deal; Dr Cohen, Director of Psychotherapy at Chestnut Lodge during the first three years of my work there, was a superb supervisor of my work with my first 'Lodge' patient.

From Dr Frieda Fromm-Reichmann I drew, as did all of us at the Lodge, a great deal of knowledge and inspiration. I especially value her insights into the schizophrenic patient's own experience of his world; her steady focus upon the flowingly dynamic process of the therapeutic relationship rather than one's focusing too much upon, and becoming lost in, the content of the patient's words; and her personal example of the essential place which not only intuitive tenderness but also unflinching toughness have in the treatment of schizophrenic individuals.

ACKNOWLEDGEMENTS

I hope that my introduction has given some hint, at least, of the unparalleled debt of gratitude which I feel towards my 'training' analyst, the late Dr Ernest E. Hadley.

It would be presumptuous of me to try to convey briefly how much I have learned from the dozens of colleagues with whom I have shared, at Chestnut Lodge over nearly fifteen years, this difficult work, day by day, of the intensive psychotherapy of schizophrenic patients. Always my proudest moments have come when various of these colleagues have found merit in one or another of the concepts which these papers present. Dr Donald L. Burnham, Director of Research at Chestnut Lodge throughout the period when all but the first five of these papers were written, was a strong source of support to me in many regards. Dr Dexter M. Bullard, Medical Director of Chestnut Lodge, possesses among other admirable qualities the courage and breadth of mind to permit his staff members to publish their concepts irrespective of whether or not they depart from his own; further, I leave it to the reader to guess how many hospital directors there are in the world, with the heavy responsibilities which such persons carry, who would permit the members of their staff to publish articles as candid as are many of those contained here.

To the extent that these papers contain valid insights, they are a measure of the degree to which I have been able to relinquish any preconceptions and allow my patients to convey these insights to me. And I wish to add here that, as much as the late Ernest Hadley and all my patients, my wife Sylvia and my children David, Sandra, and Donald have helped me to grow some.

Mr M. Masud R. Khan, Associate Editor of the *International Psycho-Analytical Library*, became interested, without any application from me, in the publishing of this volume of my collected papers, and I am lastingly grateful to him in the same special sense that I am grateful to Dr Mabel Blake Cohen, who was Editor of *Psychiatry* in the era when that journal accepted my first two papers for publication.

Mrs Verdelia Scott and Mrs Grace Ennis have provided me with outstandingly competent secretarial assistance.

The fourth and fifth of these papers were the outgrowth of studies financed by a research grant from the Foundations' Fund

ACKNOWLEDGEMENTS

for Research in Psychiatry, disbursed by the Washington School of Psychiatry. The sixth paper and all subsequent ones are the product of work supported by a grant to the Chestnut Lodge Research Institute from the Ford Foundation.

The following journals have generously permitted me to include in this volume the various papers which (as shown in the Bibliography) originally appeared in these publications: *Psychiatry – Journal for the Study of Interpersonal Processes*, the *Journal of the American Psychoanalytic Association*, the *International Journal of Psycho-Analysis*, the *British Journal of Medical Psychology*, and the *Psychiatric Quarterly*.

I am also grateful to The Williams & Wilkins Co., Baltimore, for permission to reprint 'The Schizophrenic's Vulnerabiity to the Therapist's Unconscious Processes' and 'Integration and Differentiation in Schizophrenia' from the *Journal of Nervous and Mental Disease* (vol. 127 (1958), pp. 247–62, and vol. 129 (1959), pp. 542–50, respectively).

Basic Books have kindly permitted me to include my paper, 'The Evolution of the Mother Transference in Psychotherapy with the Schizophrenic Patient', which appeared in *Psychotherapy of the Psychoses*, edited by Arthur Burton, Basic Books, 1961. Harper & Row have been similarly kind in allowing me to include 'The Contribution of Family Treatment to the Psychotherapy of Schizophrenia', which appeared in *Family Treatment of Schizophrenia*, edited by Ivan Boszormenyi-Nagy and James L. Framo, Harper & Row, 1964. 'Problems of Psychoanalytic Supervision', which originally appeared on pp. 197–215 of *Psychoanalytic Education*, edited by Jules H. Masserman, Grune & Stratton, 1962, is included here by permission of Grune & Stratton.

'Schizophrenic Communication' and 'Scorn, Disillusionment and Adoration in the Psychotherapy of Schizophrenia' are reprinted from *Psychoanalysis and the Psychoanalytic Review* (Vol. 48, No. 1, Spring 1961; and Vol. 49, No. 3, Fall 1962 respectively) through the courtesy of the Editors and the publisher, National Psychological Association for Psychoanalysis, Inc.

To a number of authors, and to the journals or publishing houses which have published their work, I am indebted for their unfailingly generous permission to quote, in various of my articles, particularly long passages from these authors' writings: *Philosophy in a New Key*, by Susanne K. Langer, Harvard University Press, 1942; *The Sane Society*,

ACKNOWLEDGEMENTS

by Erich Fromm, published by Holt, Rinehart and Winston, Inc., 1955; 'Management and Psychotherapy of the Borderline Schizophrenic Patient', by Robert P. Knight, *Bulletin of the Menninger Clinic*, **17**: 139–150, 1953; 'On Basic Unity', by Margaret Little, *Int. J. Psycho-Anal.*, **41**: 377–84, 1960; 'Notes on the Psycho-Analysis of the Superego Conflict of an Acute Schizophrenic Patient', by Herbert Rosenfeld, *Int. J. Psycho-Anal.*, **33**: 111–31, 1952; and *The Roots of Psychotherapy*, by Carl A. Whitaker and Thomas P. Malone, Copyright 1953 by McGraw-Hill Book Company, Inc. International Universities Press has kindly permitted me to quote passages from the following volumes: *Dementia Praecox or the Group of Schizophrenias*, by Eugen Bleuler, 1950; 'Some Aspects of Psychoanalytic Psychotherapy with Schizophrenics', by Frieda Fromm-Reichmann, in *Psychotherapy with Schizophrenics*, edited by E. B. Brody and F. C. Redlich, 1952; and *Symbolic Realization*, by M. A. Sèchehaye, 1951.

EDITOR'S FOREWORD

IN recent decades an increasing number of psycho-analytic investigators have tried to fathom the nature and origin of schizophrenia 'from within'. Unlike other psychiatric methods, psycho-analytic investigation of these seriously disturbed patients imposes intense stresses on the investigator–there are the primitive emotions released, the painfully slow process in which anxiety-laden changes can be attempted by the patient, and there is the constant struggle for the analyst to elucidate a pattern of significance within the at times baffling phenomena. For the pioneer, these endeavours are heroic and it is little wonder that few psychiatrists have ventured into these realms.

In keeping with his approach, Dr Searles has not done things *to* a large number of patients. Provided with a suitable setting in his hospital, his intensive studies from working *with* a few, however, illuminate this tragic 'illness' in a way that must preclude for the thoughtful psychiatrist many of the current over-simplified views about it. And because the pathological behaviour of the schizophrenic patient appears to relate to developmental failures at critical early phases of the structuring of the personality as an independent human being, this work has a significance far broader than for the conditions it studies. Its implications for the psychotherapist in a wide range of psychiatric disorders are profound; its contribution to our hopes for treatment and prevention is no less.

The bringing together of Dr Searles' papers makes available what in my view is a seminal volume. It will inspire and strengthen many to pass from what has hitherto been a bewildering and discouraging task to the rich rewards of deep understanding for both patient and therapist.   J. D. Sutherland

PREFACE

D R HAROLD F. SEARLES was one of those young physicians who, as a result of their military medical experience during or at the end of World War II, turned from a previously chosen speciality–in his case, internal medicine–to psychiatry and psycho-analysis. Now, sixteen years later at the age of 45, he has become probably the most widely read and respected authority in the world on the psychotherapy of chronic schizophrenics. For a good many years the sections at which he has read his papers at psychiatric and psycho-analytic conventions in America have had overflowing crowds, and reprints of those that have been published have been in great demand (some 2,000 requests, he has told me, have been received). In addition to his having read most of these papers before professional groups, he has published them in a wide variety of journals–five in the *International Journal of Psycho-Analysis*, five in *Psychiatry*, four in the *British Journal of Medical Psychology*, two each in the *Journal of the American Psychoanalytic Association*, the *Journal of Nervous and Mental Disease*, and *Psycho-analysis and the Psychoanalytic Review*, and one in the *Psychiatric Quarterly*. Three others have been included in multi-authored volumes–Vol. 5 of *Science and Psychoanalysis, Psychotherapy of the Psychoses*, and *Family Treatment of Schizophrenia*. Four from the list have been translated into German and published in *Psyche*. It is, therefore, not only a tribute to Dr Searles but also a great service to psycho-analytic psychiatry that the editors of the *International Journal of Psycho-Analysis* and the Publications Committee of the Institute of Psycho-Analysis, London, have undertaken to publish this series of twenty-four papers in the chronological order in which they were written.

Dr Searles has a great many gifts, among which at least four stand out to the reader of his papers: a remarkable dedication to long, hard, energy-draining, often unrewarding hours of work; a great capacity for empathic perceptiveness; a talent for clear, readable reporting and exposition; and, finally, a uniquely high degree of candour and personal humility. To comprehend the hard work aspect of his clinical research over fourteen years, one must know some facts that I obtained from him by specific questions.

15

Practically all the 18 patients (11 women, 7 men) in the study were chronic schizophrenics of six months to 26 years' duration of illness (average 9 years 2 months), of an age range from 22 to 58 (average 35), and with previous hospitalization of zero to 9 years 4 months (average 2·3 years). 8 patients had had no EST (electroshock treatment), and 11 had had no insulin comas, but 10 had had an average of 25 EST (highest numbers, 60), and 7 had had an average of 54 insulin comas (highest number, 136). For one patient Dr Searles was the first therapist; the other 17 had had from one to five previous therapists (average 1·9). To any psychiatrist who has treated schizophrenics these data spell difficult cases, yet Dr Searles regularly carried six such patients at four 50-minute sessions per week over the fourteen-year period, in addition to several other patients who were psychoneurotic or were training analysands, or both. Duration of treatment of the 18 chronic schizophrenics ranged from 3 months to over 14 years, with treatment hours numbering from 40 to 2,650 (average 900). According to the author's estimates of therapeutic success, 13 were remarkably improved (though 7 of these are still hospitalized), 1 was considerably improved, 2 were slightly improved, 1 was unchanged, and 1 committed suicide. Half of the patients in the study were seen in the therapists' office, the other half mostly in the patient's hospital room. Two patients used the analytic couch regularly, two others most of the time, three others a small fraction of the total hours, and eleven not at all. In addition to his own clinical work, as delineated by the above data, the author had to keep extensive records for research purposes, and he also supervised 19 fellow therapists with 25 of their patients at the Chestnut Lodge Sanatorium (where 15 of his own 18 patients were hospitalized), and participated in formal and informal staff conferences on a total of some 600 patients. Certainly this represents a wealth of direct and indirect experience with schizophrenic patients.

The wealth of Dr Searles' experience in terms of numbers is matched by the richness of his empathic observations. Readers of his papers are accustomed to seeing a collection of clinical episodes, encounters between patient and therapist, revealing or insightful quotations from patients, and ruthlessly honest self-revelations by the therapist, all of these representing the empirical observations on which he then constructed his theoretical formulations and his therapeutic technique. There is no armchair flavour in these papers, and the reader often feels that he is being permitted to be a genuine observer of clinical work.

Fortunately this dedicated and skilful therapist can also write clear English–understandable both as one listens to him reading a paper, and as one reads the paper when published. There is relatively little use of psychiatric and psycho-analytic jargon, and a welcome absence of new terminology, or of old terms with new definitions and connotations. While it is true that Dr Searles rather often makes use of very long sentences, yet he keeps his clauses, phrases, and parenthetical remarks well under control with appropriate punctuation, and it is almost impossible for an attentive reader to get lost. Even in this stylistic idiosyncrasy, he is able to make the complex clear.

The fourth and last quality that stands out in these papers is the author's candour, honesty, and personal humility. Dr Searles learned early in his work that all therapy, but probably especially modified psycho-analytic psychotherapy with schizophrenics, consists of deeply significant emotional experience in *each* of the two parties to the therapeutic relationship, and that progress toward a good outcome requires ruthlessly honest self-awareness on both sides. He has exemplified this trait in his writing, perhaps progressively so as he realized the exacting demands of intensive psychotherapy with psychotic patients, who, as Fromm-Reichmann once said, readily forgive mistakes of the head but not those of the heart. Thus we see again and again the candid description of his personal feelings, impulses, fantasies as these were evoked during the stress of hearing the patient's own productions. The reader who is unaccustomed to seeing such highly personal revelations may now and again be startled. My guess is, however, that he will wind up with a heightened respect for, and perhaps even a little envy of, the therapist-author.

Dr Searles has written a remarkable introduction to the series of papers after reading them himself, for the first time, in sequence one after the other. His statements regarding how certain ideas developed, how some early concepts were abandoned and superseded by others, and how he now feels about these earlier formulations, all tend to pull the papers together, to highlight the themes on which he has been working, and to illustrate

PREFACE

again the fourth quality noted above—this time in the perspective of fourteen years of work, the early therapy and writing being co-ordinated with his own stages of emotional development as his own training analysis with the late Dr Ernest Hadley proceeded. The author's Introduction is such a remarkably illuminating addition to this series of twenty-four papers that I recommend that it be read twice—first and last.

13 November, 1963
Robert P. Knight, M.D.
Stockbridge, Massachusetts

INTRODUCTION

DURING the course of my undergraduate years I came to experience anxiety of such proportions as to leave in me an enduring fascination with, and desire to understand, the wondrously intangible thing which is human personality and the mysterious forces which keep it functioning coherently or cause its dissolution or enable it to pull together again and continue growing. When, nine years later, it finally became possible for me to find psychotherapeutic help in the form of a training analysis, I was well aware that I needed this for more than purely didactic purposes, and the benefit which I derived from the analysis, conducted by the late Dr Ernest E. Hadley, was proportionately great.

The first three of the papers that follow were written during the course of my analysis, and not only these three but all the others represent, of course, what I regard as advancing insight into not only my patients' but also my own workings. I present the papers chronologically so that one can see the development of my ideas over the years. On reading them all together for the first time, I have been gratified to find that there is none which I myself regard as being out of date, or as having been largely superseded by a later one.

The following are the major themes which run through these papers and link them together.

Autism and Symbiosis

This is the context in which I now think of the material in the first paper, on 'Incorporation' (1951).* Mutual incorporation I now think of as an aspect of symbiosis, and one's feeling oneself to be totally outside the other person well expresses, I now feel, the subjectively autistic state. I still regard as valid this paper's portrayal of such modes of relatedness as being utilizable unconsciously as defences against various emotions; but I was far from having discovered here, the nuclear growth-potential, in terms of primitive ego-development, which they also hold.

I recall that during one lunch hour, shortly after the paper had

* I abbreviate the titles of the papers here.

appeared I felt weighed down by depression, for which, of course, I could not account. Then I had a sudden fantasy of making gashes in my analyst, tearing out the pages of the paper and stuffing them savagely into the wounds, and thereupon my feeling of depression was instantly gone. This incident was in line with my several-years'-long castigating and reproaching and belittling of him for, as I felt, not being responsive to me, not acknowledging me emotionally. I noticed later, after I had undergone much change, that I visualized the core of myself as being, none the less, like a steel ball-bearing, with varicoloured sectors on its surface, which of course would not change. This too eventually changed; it dissolved in grief, and I came to know that all my several years of craving for him to feel, or to feel more, had actually represented my determined effort to make *him* feel *my* feelings – the feelings repressed in me which I myself had been afraid to experience. So heavily defended an analysand was not prepared to discover yet, in his work with schizophrenic patients, the nuclear role of therapeutic symbiosis.

It is noteworthy that the 'Dependency' paper (ch. 3) is couched throughout in whole, object – genuinely interpersonal – terms, as though in dealing with the schizophrenic person one were dealing with a whole ego; but that paper, a step in the acknowledgement of the patient's emotional significance to the therapist and vice versa, is a step towards my later seeing the therapeutic significance of part-object relatedness and symbiosis.

The 'Vulnerability' paper (ch. 6), emphasizing the effect upon the patient of the therapist's unconscious processes, is another step towards the concept of therapeutic symbiosis, in that it describes an aspect of the deep confluence of feeling between the two participants. But the emphasis here is primarily upon the potentially destructive, rather than potentially curative, aspect of such a confluence; and only as a kind of afterthought, near the end of the paper, do I mention that there is an invaluable communicational aspect to these phenomena of the patient's introjecting various unconscious personality attributes and processes of the therapist.

In the 'Positive Feelings' paper (ch. 7) I emphasize the significant role of symbiotic relatedness in both the child-mother relationship and the patient-therapist relationship; but I have yet to discover any but a predominantly ambivalent, anxiety-arousing variety of symbiosis, as the following passage shows:

> It seems to me that one of the great reasons . . . for its requiring [so long a time to help the patient become free of chronic schizophrenia] . . . . is that the 'good mother' transference-relatedness has a basically symbiotic quality which is anxiety-provoking to both patient and therapist . . . which carries with it into the transference . . . this same charge of anxiety, strong enough to be schizophrenigenic.

I describe only moments of whole-hearted adoration on the patient's part, and repeatedly mention my own anxiety in reaction to such adoration. I stress the importance of the therapist's having the courage to recognize the existence of the mother-infant symbiosis which tends to become re-experienced in the patient's relatedness with the therapist; but I have yet to find that this symbiosis can be so anxiety-free that one can luxuriate in its gratifications. This paper has come far, none the less, from the 'Incorporation' paper's view of *'status quo* relatedness' between patient and therapist as consisting simply in mutually incorporative processes. Such relatedness does indeed involve those processes; but by now I have come to see–though still more than a little anxious about what I see–the deeply though unconsciously gratifying aspects of the symbiotic relatedness which both patient and therapist are reluctant to relinquish. Also, it can be said that I have yet to see here how deeply *curative* it is for the patient to become quite free to enjoy these gratifications in the oneness with the therapist.

'The Effort to Drive the Other Person Crazy' (ch. 8), written just before chapter 7 but published after it, likewise dwells upon what I would now call the ambivalent phase of the symbiosis in the transference; although I comment that the symbiotic transference relatedness 'despite its torments, affords precious gratifications also', that paper is occupied mainly with the torments, and the gratifications are shown as being in the nature of the Lorelei of whose siren-songs we must beware. That I am moving very near the therapeutic-symbiosis concept, however, is shown in this passage: '. . . what the therapist offers the patient which is new and therapeutic, in this regard, is not an *avoidance* of the development of symbiotic, reciprocal dependency upon the patient, but rather an *acceptance* of this . . .'

21

INTRODUCTION

Finally, in the first of the 'Integration and Differentiation' papers (Chs. 10, 11), I introduce the term 'therapeutic symbiosis', and state that '. . . a symbiotic relatedness . . . constitutes a necessary phase in psycho-analysis or psychotherapy with either neurotic or psychotic patients . . .'

In the second 'Integration and Differentiation' paper (ch. 11), in 'Anxiety Concerning Change' (ch. 15), in 'Anxiety in Paranoid Schizophrenia' (ch. 16), and in 'Inevitability of Death' (ch. 17). I discuss various aspects of therapeutic symbiosis, and then in the 'Phases' paper (ch. 18) I come to see the therapeutic symbiosis phase of the transference evolution as being divisible into two sub-phases: an earlier phase of ambivalent symbiosis, and a later (i.e., occurring later in therapy, but representative of a developmentally earlier) phase of pre-ambivalent–or full, or therapeutic–symbiosis. In the last-mentioned paper I trace the patient's movement, from an initially autistic or 'out-of-contact' phase, through these symbiotic phases and on into individuation as a whole person.

'Problems of Psycho-Analytic Supervision' (ch. 20) is concerned in part with the supervisor's contributions during the ambivalently symbiotic and preambivalently symbiotic phases of the treatment; 'Family Treatment' (ch. 24) centres upon family symbiosis; and 'Transference Psychosis' (ch. 23) describes the patient's transference as being in essence a symbiotic infant-mother relatedness.

The Etiologic Role, and the Role in Therapy, of Various Feelings

The earlier phases of my analysis were occupied, not surprisingly, with my hostility and my fear of it, and only later did I come to terms with my feelings of love and grief. Thus, in my first paper there are many clinical data concerning hostility and very little about fondness; and while the incorporative mode of relatedness is shown to be serving as an unconscious defence, in the patient, against hostile feelings and feelings of rejection, I had not yet come to see its grief-repressing function. But in the 'Dependency' paper (ch. 3) I dwell, of course, upon dependency feelings, and the 'Vengefulness' paper (ch. 5) shows vengefulness to be serving as a defence against repressed grief and separation-anxiety.

INTRODUCTION

'The Effort to Drive the Other Person Crazy' (ch. 8) was written, as I have mentioned, just before the 'Positive Feelings' paper (ch. 7), and so vigorously highlighted the significance of the patient's, and my own, capacity for malevolence that it was somewhat in a spirit of contrition that I wrote 'Positive Feelings' (ch. 7), a portion of which, because of its length, had to be published later as the 'Mother Transference' paper (ch. 12). While I still had on hand both those long papers ('The Effort' (ch. 8) as originally written was also much longer than the later published version), the one highlighting the hateful aspect of the therapy of schizophrenic patients and the other the loving aspect, I for a time had it in mind to publish them as a monograph under the title, 'Love and Hate in the Psychotherapy of Schizophrenic Patients', to be headed by a beautifully pertinent quote from Freud's *The Ego and the Id* (1923): '. . . human nature has a far greater extent, for both good and for evil, than it thinks it has . . .' (p. 52).

The 'Oedipal Love' paper (ch. 9) is occupied with feelings of both love and loss; 'Anxiety Concerning Change' (ch. 15) and 'Anxiety in Paranoid Schizophrenia' (ch. 16) discuss the forms of anxiety which their titles indicate; 'Inevitability of Death' (ch. 17) is primarily concerned with grief; and 'Scorn, Disillusionment, Adoration' (ch. 21) focuses upon those particular feelings.

Love and Hate

After several of my papers had been written I discovered, with deep pleasure, areas of coalescence among the various fields of interest, previously felt as diverse, with which I had been successively occupied, and my interest in a variety of feelings, one after another—hostility, dependency, grief, and so on—became more coherently an interest in love and hate and the interrelatedness between them. All my discussions of symbiosis centre, of course, about these latter feelings. In the 'Family Treatment' paper (ch. 24) I mention '. . . the central tragedy in these families: the extent to which the family-members are being crippled and paralyzed by their inability to face the fact that they *both* intensely hate *and* deeply love one another.' Comparably, at the time when I had just written 'The Effort to Drive the Other Person Crazy' (ch. 8) and 'Positive Feelings' (ch. 7), my clinical work with schizophrenic patients had not yet given me to know – as both my analysis and my personal life had given me to know, over and over – that even here, too, in one's relationship with the chronically schizophrenic patient, love proves not only to be stronger than, but to exist at the very heart of, hate. At that juncture, when I was contemplating the publication of the monograph I have mentioned, I felt that love and hate in schizophrenia, and in the psychotherapy of schizophrenia, were equal in power. The later papers which describe therapeutic symbiosis show that I had found, by then, that hatred is subsidiary to – that, as the intensity of the relationship deepens, hatred dissolves into – love.

On the one hand, work with schizophrenic patients holds before the therapist the lure of a durably hate-free love; nothing is more characteristically schizophrenic than the patient's manifesting, in his relatedness with another person, of this beautiful will-o'-the-wisp which unfailingly evokes a poignant yearning, sooner or later, in any human heart. The intensity of my own conflict about this matter is expressed in chapter 18 ('Phases'), written after a dozen years of this work: '. . . I have come reluctantly to conclude that there is no sure criterion by which one can know, for long periods of time, whether one is involved in a genuinely preambivalent symbiosis with the patient, or rather in a predominantly paranoid symbiosis which is a defence against hatred. . . .'

But it is still my best judgement that, as 'Sexual Processes' (ch. 14) phrases it, a basically Good Mother-thriving infant relatedness, in which the lustful and destructive feeling-components of the Bad Mother have become largely transformed into, and in any event safely subordinated to, a feeling of boundless love, is the only soil from which the patient's healthy ego-differentiation and maturation can subsequently grow. And I would still say that, as chapter 18 states it in describing the phase of preambivalent symbiosis, 'One comes to see that, at this level of dedifferentiation, "love" and "hate" are one, and that any intense and overt relatedness is, in effect, love.'

Awesome as is the intensity of the hatred which one discovers in oneself and in the patient during the course of the long work with him, still more awesome to me has been the power of the basic lovingness which is unfailingly revealed if both participants find the courage to keep going forward in the face of the anxiety and despair. Especially memorable to me in this regard have been such experiences as 'Vengefulness' (ch. 5) details, which have shown me that such an ugly emotion as vindictiveness is basically a reaction against such positively-oriented emotions as separation-anxiety and grief; and such experiences as 'Transference Psychoses' (ch. 23) describes, which have revealed to me that the so-castrative paranoid patient, for example, is basically concerned not with trying to castrate me, over and over, but rather with the achievement and maintenance and growth of his own individuality.

As I have become more and more deeply convinced that I, in keeping with my fellow human beings, am a basically loving and constructively oriented person rather than a basically malevolent and destructive one, I feel increasingly free to interact, whether in a subjectively loving or subjectively malevolent, manner with my patients. I would no longer find it necessary to inveigh quite so strongly against love-replacement therapy as I did in 'Dependency' (ch. 3), for example, and would no longer take pains to caution, as I did there, that 'It is well for the therapist to maintain . . . a degree of emotional distance between himself and the patient.' And whereas it was in a spirit of lingering guilt that I confessed, in 'The Effort to Drive the Other Person Crazy' (ch. 8), that 'I discovered conclusive proof of such a character-trait in myself, to my great dismay, late in my personal analysis (about seven years ago) . . .', now, by contrast, I find a generous place in psychotherapy for all the sadism I can muster—for example, to needle and infuriate the apathetic or 'out-of-contact' patient into more overt relatedness, or to pay him back for the hurts he has been inflicting upon me. With an abundance of this kind of interaction between us, he has good reason to know that I am in no wise a saint, and we can deal with his own problems about sadism in a person-to-person fashion.

The Interrelatedness between Emotions on the one Hand and Ego-Structure, such Ego-Functions as Perception and Thinking and Communication, and the Technique of Psychotherapy, on the other

At the outset I was not drawn to explore such subjects as egostructure, thinking, and perception, and I mistrusted any endeavour to formulate technique as such. It was only in the realm of feeling that I found aliveness and interest and, on the basis of too many years of personal experience with thought and personality-structure as being defences against spontaneous emotion, I reacted to these as being basically inert and hostile to life.

But as time went on I found, as my 'Perplexity' paper (ch. 2) indicates, that various mental states such as perplexity, confusion, and suspicion represent a most dynamic unconscious striving to keep various feelings out of awareness—represent, that is, most valuable clues, in the psychotherapeutic interaction, to various repressed feelings. Similarly, the realm of thinking in general became of lively interest to me as I saw its indissoluble linkage to the realm of emotion; as chapter 19 points out,

> ... These [ego-] boundaries can become established only by degrees as the patient becomes able to face the intense and conflictual *emotions* against which the schizophrenic illness system was designed to shield him. Thus we discover some evidence that the modes of thought characteristic of the healthy adult are founded upon the awareness of emotion.

Likewise such subjects as communication, and early ego-formation by primitive identification, become of interest to me as I saw how steeped in feeling are these processes. Both 'Vulnerability' (ch. 6) and 'The Informational Value of the Supervisor's Emotional Experiences' (ch. 4) centre upon processes of unconscious communication which consist in the patient's or the therapist's or the supervisor's unconsciously identifying, in an atmosphere of intense feeling, with various processes at work in the other participant in the therapy or the supervision respectively. This kind of unconscious-communication-via-the-displaying-of-unconscious-identification remains to me the most interesting area in the field of communication.

When it comes to psychotherapeutic technique, no matter whether I am describing particular areas of the subject (as in chapters 3, 13, 15, 16, 19, and 23), or attempting to cover the whole subject of technique in working with the chronically schizophrenic patient, always I find the therapist's openness to various *feelings*, of whatever sort, to be the key to the situation. For example the 'Phases' paper (ch. 18), originally planned as a

26

study of technique, at its beginning expresses my having come to realize that

> . . . the 'technique' of psychotherapy of schizophrenia is best spelled out in terms of an evolutionary sequence of specific, and very deep, feeling-involvements in which the therapist as well as the patient becomes caught up, over the course of . . . the 'normal' and predictable over-all course of psychotherapy with the chronically schizophrenic person.

The first 'Integration and Differentiation' paper (ch. 10) focuses, more than any of those that precede it, upon structural matters in contrast to my earlier absorption with various feelings; and it is probably no coincidence that in this paper, where for the first time I am able to express my acceptance of therapeutic symbiosis, I am able also for the first time in my work to get some grasp of the over-all process of treatment. That is, I am no longer caught up in defending myself against, and finally discovering the important role of, this or that *feeling*, and can now attend to such matters as emerging ego-structure over the course of the treatment.

Thus my frame of reference in viewing various clinical data shifts, from a focus upon feelings to a focus upon ego-formation; this newer frame of reference, while not invalidating the former one nor the concepts which sprang therefrom, is none the less more comprehensive and therefore more adequate. For example, the kind of patient-therapist interaction which is presented in documentation of 'The Effort to Drive the Other Person Crazy' (ch. 8) is described, in chapter 11, as being essential to the patient's advancing ego-integration and differentiation. The latter paper points out that 'The therapist's capacity to endure such a barrage of fragmentation-fostering experiences . . . is essential in his helping the patient to become better integrated through identification with the therapist whose personal integration can survive this onslaught.' And still later, in the 'Phases' paper (ch. 18), such interaction is located in the ambivalently symbiotic phase of the over-all evolution of the treatment.

Chapter 16 states, in its opening paragraph, that 'I shall endeavour to demonstrate how affective phenomena and structural phenomena are interrelated'–'structural' referring here to ego-structure, ego-fragmentation, and ego-dedifferentiation.

INTRODUCTION

Like-wise, one of the keynotes of the 'Phases' paper (ch. 18) is a quotation from Spitz in which he emphasizes that emotion plays a leading role in the formation of the 'organizers of the psyche' (which he defines as emergent, dominant centres of integration) during the first eighteen months of life.

'Non-Human' Phenomena, the Issue of Therapist Neutrality, and Feelings Concerning Change and Death

In 1951 I became interested in the role of the non-human environment in my work with schizophrenic patients, and in human living as a whole, and over the next eight years I worked, somewhat apart from the writing of my successive papers on schizophrenia, on a monograph concerning this subject which eventually appeared in 1960. Two among its several theses are that the human infant is, early in his ego-development, subjectively undifferentiated from either the human *or the non-human* ingredients of his surroundings, and that the non-human environment is, in its own right, of much significance to him. I continue today to regard this monograph as being filled with valuable clinical data; but one of my early dissatisfactions with the published work consisted in a feeling that the second thesis began like a kind of golden thread which somehow became lost in the interpersonal intricacies which the book goes on to detail.

Among these papers, my interest in the non-human environment first shows itself in 'Vengefulness' (ch. 5), in the description of a patient who related herself to various inanimate objects in a vindictive fashion. 'Anxiety in Paranoid Schizophrenia' (ch. 16) contains many 'non-human' data in my expanding upon the point that 'If there is any single most basic threat to the paranoid schizophrenic person, it is . . . the threat that he will cease to exist as a human individual.' Chapter 19 conveys, in its lengthy descriptions of my work with each of the two illustrative patients, a great deal of data having to do with 'non-human' aspects of their experience and behaviour; and the 'Family Therapy' paper (ch. 24) includes some mention, as the following passages indicate, of the impact upon the child of his family's forcing him into, or keeping him in, the essentially non-human role of a projected part-object:

One of my paranoid patients, telling how in high school his brother

28

had condemned him as being a 'force of evil', gave me some glimpse of how devastating it must be, for a child who has no solid whole-person relationships to which to cling, to be thus reacted to as a part-object–as, in this instance the embodiment of the brother's repressed and projected hostility.

. . . So the patient finds himself progressively deprived of any real and accessible person to whom to relate; this in turn throws him more and more back upon functioning, toward the other family members, as a projected part-object [which would foster in him, of course, a non-human self image].

In chapter 22, which appeared in 1963, I presented a major revision in the development of my thinking about the 'non-human' realm. After first noting that in my monograph I had included many separate instances of the schizophrenic patient's reacting to the therapist as being an inanimate object, I go on to say that

. . . It is, I have come to see, in this phase [of therapeutic symbiosis] that the whole of the patient's former 'realty', including the whole non-human realm in aggregate, is as it were poured into the symbiosis with the therapist, and it is out of this symbiosis that the patient's 'reality' becomes more deeply cathected with feeling and with, therefore, a genuine sense of reality, and he correspondingly becomes more able to distinguish among such realms as human and non-human, animate and inanimate, through rediscovering them in the therapist-mother.

In other words, what I had thought to be the regrettably lost 'golden thread' of the second-mentioned of my monograph's themes, namely that which emphasized the importance of the non-human environment in its own right (i.e. over and beyond, or apart from, the influence of any other person in the normal child's, or schizophrenic adult's, environment), now appears as a displacement–of some increment of the child's essentially mother-directed feelings (of love, dependency, and so on) over to the non-human realm–a displacement which cannot be sustained as one pushes on into a deeper personal understanding of this subject. I added in the same paper that 'I can now fully believe Spitz's comment that "The child . . . learns to distinguish animate objects from inanimate ones by the spectacle provided by his mother's face in situations fraught with emotional satisfaction".' 'Scorn, Disillusionment, Adoration' (ch. 21) traces my increasing acceptance of my patients' adoration of me, viewed by them in the evolving transference-situation as the adored mother who comprises the whole world of the infant, which enabled me to accept this revised view of the significance of the non-human realm.

I still do not feel, of course, that the last word about this so-important subject has been said. It might be thought that ideally the mother would 'humanize' the whole of the maturing infant's and young child's inner and outer reality; but child-rearing conditions are in no actual instance ideal, so that every child will be confronted with something of the struggle to differentiate human from non-human and animate from inanimate in his perceptual inner and outer worlds—every child will have to engage, that is, in this struggle which the schizophrenic patient found to be overwhelming in its difficulty. Moreover, if the mother were somehow capable of doing all this differentiating *for* the child, he presumably would never achieve individuality, for the unceasing struggle to make such differentiations may well be essential to the achievement and maintenance of human individuality.

To return to a further noting of the place, in my over-all theory about the treatment process, of this revised concept of the significance of the non-human realm, chapter 23 points out that

. . . the therapist must become able to function as a *part* of the patient and to permit the patient to be genuinely, at a deep level of psychological functioning, a part of himself [which is another way of saying that the therapist must become unanxious at either his own, or the patient's, functioning in a 'non-human' fashion in the relationship].

And towards the end of chapter 18, I emphasize that

. . . each of these patients—and, I think, this is true to a lesser degree of the neurotic patient also—needs in the course of the therapy to project upon the therapist the subjectively unfeeling, nonhuman and even inanimate, aspects of himself, and thus to see his therapist, in the transference, as the representation of the parents who were, to the child's view, incapable of human feeling, as has been the patient himself in his own view. Only by thus re-externalizing his pathogenic introjects can the patient make contact with his own feeling-capacities and come to know, beyond any further doubt, that he is a human being. . . .

The above quotation, having to do with the therapeutic-symbiosis phase of therapy, shows how integrally related are the subject of symbiosis and that of the 'non-human' realm; they really make up a single subject.

The 'Transference Psychosis' paper (ch. 23) shows that the kind of 'non-human' data which are presented in my monograph, from the work with schizophrenic patients, is particularly typical of the first of the four varieties of transference psychosis which this paper describes, namely that found in 'transference-situations in which the therapist feels unrelated to the patient'. It will be seen, further, that such data found their place in the 'Phases' paper (ch. 18) in my description of the initial or 'out-of-contact' phase.

Just as I have come to see that the healthy need for therapeutic symbiosis is at the heart of the 'mutual incorporation' which my first paper describes, so I have come to understand that the clinical processes having to do with what is generally called autism, at that early time no less frightening to me than were the prospects of symbiotic involvement, likewise are expressive of a basically healthy need–in this instance, a need for the kind of primitive part-object relatedness–'non-human' relatedness–which must become established in order that subsequent individuation and whole-object–genuinely interpersonal–relatedness may be achieved.

As I became comfortable in the 'non-human' transference-role of a part-object for the patient, subjectively unemotional therapist-participation no longer rested upon the 'Dependency' paper's (ch. 3) rather strict and therefore anxious assertion that it is well for the therapist to maintain, for the most part, a degree of emotional distance between himself and the patient, but rather upon the recognition (ch. 18) that it is in the nature of the therapeutic process that the therapist will find himself feeling, most of the time, a calm, neutral, investigative orientation–a point which forms the essential thesis of chapter 22.

The more we see how healthy and energetic is the striving which is at work behind a patient's so 'inanimate' or otherwise 'non-human' demeanour–behind, that is, his modes of inter-personal participation–the more we come to reject the commonly-held

31

picture of him as being the broken and inert victim of schizophrenia. I make this point explicitly in several of the papers, including chapters 19, 22, and 23, and implicitly in all the others. 'Thinking' (ch. 19) for, example, points out

. . . his unconscious defensive use of this very instability of ego boundaries, and similar use of the 'concrete' thinking which that instability permits.

Thus we find that the dissolution of ego boundaries is not merely a tragic end result of the schizophrenic process, but one of the formidably energetic defence mechanisms comprising that process.

The more free the therapist becomes to experience 'non-human' ego-states, the more he can sense – the more he can know at first hand – what is presumably the schizophrenic patient's own subjective experience, a topic with which each of my papers is concerned. Similarly, the two papers which focus most explicitly upon forms of anxiety which clearly are common in some degree to all human beings, namely the papers entitled 'Anxiety Concerning Change' (ch. 15) and 'Inevitability of Death' (ch. 17), are intended further to dissolve the supposed qualitative distinctions which by tradition have separated schizophrenic patients from their non-schizophrenic fellow human beings.

The Distinction and Interaction between Intrapsychic Processes and Interpersonal Processes

In chapter 1 ('Incorporation'), I cite various instances in which ostensibly genuine object-relatedness (interpersonal relatedness) is found to consist predominantly in intrapsychic processes and to amount mainly, therefore, to *intra*personal relatedness. For example, I noted, concerning one patient's relationship with his mother, that

. . . The patient's interpersonal relations with her have consisted to a large extent in an *intra*-personal process of relatedness between the patient's very underdeveloped ego and a 'mother' within which he has kept his ego incorporated. This 'mother' has not been the real mother, not the mother who exists in the reality outside himself, but rather a fantasy figure constructed largely of repressed and projected aspects of his personality which are as yet intolerable to the ego.

Similarly in my description of '*status quo* interaction' – stalemate characterized by mutual-incorporation processes–between a paranoid patient and myself, I mentioned that '. . . there appeared many indications that the "personality" of the other, within which each of us had been keeping his functioning personality incorporated, was actually in large part a fantasy personality formed of his own repressed and projected feelings'.

The two 'Integration and Differentiation' papers (chs. 10, 11) likewise describe my finding basically intrapsychic processes at work in ostensibly interpersonal relationships, in the clinical vignettes which describe the patient's advancing integration-and-differentiation as occurring first outside himself, in the therapist or among the persons who surround him on the ward, before, by his identifying with these others, the increments of increased ego-maturation become part of the patient himself. For example, in my comments about the ward-situation, I comment that

Look at it from the vantage point of the patient, each of the significant other persons in this group-symbiosis represents not only a transference-figure, but also an externalized fragment of his own ego. In this sense, the complex, previously unsorted-out, unintegrated fragments of his own self become painted on the canvas which the ward situation presents to him. . . .

Likewise, the 'Family Treatment' paper (ch. 24) endeavours mainly to emphasize how prone are the family members to confuse intrapsychic processes with interpersonal processes, and that, in family therapy, '. . . it is extraordinarily difficult, however essential, for the therapist to keep clear that it is not basically the mother or father, for example, who is central to the patient's illness, but rather the patient's introject, distorted and unintegrated into his ego, of that parent'.

And the intense competition, in these families, between intrapsychic processes and 'interpersonal' processes is further emphasized:

. . . The spuriousness of the manifestations of 'object-relatedness' in these families consists . . . in the fact that . . . they are defensive and premature. Specifically, they are a defence against the threat of symbiotic undifferentiatedness, and they are premature because such undifferentiatedness needs to hold sway, at a deep level, between any two persons . . . before genuine object-relatedness can mature from this . . .
. . . there is a basically healthy need, therefore, for undifferentiated

relatedness, but a correspondingly great anxiety lest their tenuous object-relatedness, which is so largely spurious and ill-established, be dissolved into such primitive undifferentiatedness.

Whereas some of my papers endeavour, as I have said, to demonstrate that in many instances an ostensibly interpersonal relatedness (an ostensible object-relatedness) is found to be not really such but rather an instance of basically *intra*psychic processes at work, on the other hand nearly all my papers stress the opposite side of the matter. Specifically, one of my main endeavours, throughout, is to show that the schizophrenic patient is reacting in a therapeutic relationship which is to a greater degree genuinely interpersonal – to a greater degree a product of real contributions from both patient *and* therapist – than we have been given to believe from the more traditional portrayals of the 'crazy' schizophrenic patient, whose 'purely delusional' experience was depicted as being based only intrapsychically and not at all upon any real contribution from the therapist. This interpersonal emphasis in my papers reaches deepest in the 'Transference Psychosis' paper's (ch. 23) concept of delusional identification: 'In summary, . . . even the most other-worldly, even the most "crazy", manifestations of schizophrenia come to reveal meaningfulness and reality-relatedness not only as transference-reactions to the therapist, but, even beyond this, as delusional identifications with real aspects of the therapist's own personality. . . .'

And chapter 17 gives some glimpse of the mutuality of genuine object-relatedness which eventually develops in therapy, in my experience:

. . . any successful, long-range psycho-analysis or psycho-therapy comes to involve the patient and the doctor in facing life's most basic issues together, even though the doctor may be participating little in an overt, verbal fashion. Each emerges, when the treatment is over, with a deepened and enriched understanding of life's meaning. . . .

The Over-All Process of Therapy

Only after a number of years, as various of my patients had come sufficiently far toward health, could I begin to achieve some grasp of the whole course of therapy with schizophrenic patients. 'Positive Feelings' (ch. 7), containing a description of what I had come tentatively to regard as the typical evolution of the transference, and chapters 10 and 11, are my earliest discussions of this subject, going on to the elaboration of my current concepts about it in chapters 18, 21, 22, and 23.

But again, it was change in myself which enabled me to see these clinical experiences differently as these years went on. More than anything, I have been impressed with the degree to which the over-all transference evolution, in the therapy of a schizophrenic individual, both requires that the therapist possess or develop a reasonably sound self-esteem and, by the same token, helps him to develop this. Early in my analysis, the pathological quality of my own self-regard was manifested by such symptoms as self-loathing on the one hand, and a considerable degree of subjective omnipotence on the other. The former became one of the most completely and durably resolved among my symptoms, and the latter was gradually relinquished with many prolonged pangs; one thing that helped me to reach some healthy perspective on the latter was a dream in which a witty and perceptive close friend and colleague, standing across the room and looking at me thoughtfully, raised the question, 'Harold, I wonder whether what you have is *omnipotence*, or *ominous impotence*?'

At any rate, it may be noted that in my first paper, I said of my intensive psychotherapy with a paranoid schizophrenic individual that 'His . . . delusional ideas . . . had subsided after a few months of hospitalization, apparently largely because of the security which he had found in a locked-ward hospital environment'. This was typical of my early underestimation of my significance to the schizophrenic patient as his therapist; and I recall feeling quite disconcerted when the supervisor, Dr Robert A. Cohen, pointed out to me, on one occasion when I was feeling quite futile in the face of the patient's denial of any need for therapy, that the man had evidently found the relationship with me to be important and useful enough to him for him to have been able to climb back out of psychosis through its agency.

My self-esteem was simply not yet sound enough to feel so worthwhile as that to any one, and when a little later in the 'Dependency' paper (ch. 3), I comment concerning patients' feelings of awe and adoration toward the therapist, 'In my patients I have seen these . . . much less frequently than I have found competitiveness or contempt', I had yet to realize that the

35

faulty state of my self-esteem was tending to perpetuate the expression of the latter feelings by my patients, and to forestall the kind of undisguised adoration which is reported in the 'Positive Feelings' paper (ch. 7), the various papers which describe the phase of therapeutic symbiosis and, most fully, in chapter 21. Surely it is no coincidence that, as I have become relatively comfortable with feelings of adoring and being adored, I have become much freer to express and make therapeutic use of previously suppressed scornful feelings towards patients, finding that these do not destroy, but rather help to activate, the therapeutic relatedness.

A number of persons expressed to me the opinion, when the 'Positive Feelings' paper (ch. 7) appeared, that it did not do full justice to the positive contributions which the therapist makes to the patient's progress. I still do not concur with that view; but it would have been, indeed, like me at that time to underestimate the extent of my own original contribution to the treatment. Later papers, notably 'Mother Transference' (ch. 12) and 'Phases' (ch. 18), present my conceptions of the evolution of the reality-relatedness between patient and therapist over the course of the treatment. I feel that the nature and significance of the therapist's own contribution is implicit, if not focused upon explicitly, throughout all the papers except perhaps the first few.

It was an increasingly sound self-esteem which permitted me, as the years went on, to notice and accept the wishes of various other persons—whether my children or my younger colleagues or my patients—to identify with me, and to discern the 'delusional identification' aspect of schizophrenia. And it was a hard-won freedom from the need to employ the unconscious defence of infantile omnipotence which enabled me to work through the disillusionment phase with the patient, and, still more essentially, to see the extent to which both patient and therapist, as my later papers describe, become immersed in and swept forward by the current, the *process*, of treatment. As chapter 18 puts it,

> . . . not only the patient but he [the therapist] also is in the grip of a process, the therapeutic process, which is comparable in its strength to the maturational process in the child, . . . which . . . is far too

powerful for either the patient or himself to be able at all easily to
deflect it . . . away from the confluent channel which it is tending . . .
to form for itself.

Some of these papers depict the therapist as functioning, when
one thinks about it, as in a sense the creator of the patient's
personality to a startling degree–for example, chapters 10 and 11,
which describe the patient's advancing integration and differentiation as occurring increment by increment first in the
therapist before these increments become part of the patient
himself; or chapter 22, which describes the whole of the patient's
'reality', including the so-called non-human realm of experience, as being poured into the symbiosis with the therapist-mother
in the transference, and as being reformulated into healthy
reality-relatedness through the agency of this symbiotic relatedness.

But the therapist finds that all this provides no real food for
arrogance, for subjective omnipotence, since he is repeatedly
faced not only with the overarching and pervasive power of the
therapeutic process in which both he and the patient are immersed, but also with the fact that, if he emerges as a kind of
God the Creator in the formation of the patient's healthily
developing self, the patient emerges as no less a God the Creator
in the therapist's development. Our most deeply ill patients are
predominantly attuned to the healing of our most primitive, and
therefore most important, areas of hurt–in structural terms,
areas of fragmentation and undifferentiation–and nothing is
more difficult for us than the acceptance, with gratitude rather
than humiliation, of their help to us.

For example, near the end of the very last and most recent of
these papers, I describe the successive changes, over the years, in
my understanding of a previously hebephrenic woman's references to, variously, her head or my head as being something
inanimate. The final view presented there has to do with an
incident when she asked, 'Is it all going to fall off?–Is it that
bad?', rubbing her forehead and the top of her head as she spoke,
in such a way as to convey the idea that these areas of her body
were all crumbling, like something inanimate. Thereupon, as the
paper states, I realized that she was trying to point out, in a
semi-amused way, a long-familiar tendency of mine to be over-

concerned. But upon reading the paper over again, prior to writing this introduction, I realized that she was helping me, at a much more basic level, with my residual anxiety lest I lose my humanness and aliveness through regression into the 'non-human' realm; and with this discovery I realized in retrospect how much she had helped me in this so basic regard over all the preceding years of our work together.

Chapter 1

DATA CONCERNING CERTAIN
MANIFESTATIONS OF INCORPORATION
(1951)[1]

INCORPORATION will here be discussed as a mode of interpersonal relationship in which a person feels himself to be at
one with the person with whom he is in interaction, and is
unaware of any sense of separateness between his personality and
the personality of the other. He equates interpersonal relatedness with a process of engulfment, in which his personality is in
the process of devouring or being devoured by the personality of
the other participant in the interaction.

This particular mode of interpersonal relationship is a universal phenomenon, since it is for everyone the earliest mode of
relationship with other people. If the child's personality development follows a relatively unimpeded course, this mode of interaction decreases in intensity and frequency as he matures. In
such patients as those here under discussion, however, the process
of maturation has somehow been interfered with during the
early months or the very early years of life, so that this mode of
interaction remains predominant in their behaviour.

Certain passages from Fenichel's *The Psychoanalytic Theory of
Neurosis* (1945) pertaining to incorporation and introjection
–terms which he seems to use interchangeably–may be taken as
an augmented introduction to this subject:

By incorporating objects one becomes united with them. The 'oral
introjection' is simultaneously the executive of the 'primary identification'. The ideas of eating an object or of being eaten by an object
remain the ways in which any reunion with objects is thought of
unconsciously (p. 63).
[Regarding the primitive ego] . . . since the psychological separation of the ego from the external world is still incomplete, through
comprehending the outside world or parts of it within itself, the ego
comes to feel itself omnipotent. . . . There always remain certain

[1] First published in *Psychiatry*, Vol. 14 (1951), pp. 397-413.

traces of the original objectless condition, or at least a longing for it ('oceanic feeling'). Introjection is an attempt to make parts of the external world flow into the ego. . . . When the child is forced through experiences to renounce his belief in his omnipotence, he considers the adults who have now become independent objects to be omnipotent, and tries by introjection to share their omnipotence again (pp. 39–40).

Of course, the idea of being eaten is not only a source of fear but under certain circumstances may also be a source of oral pleasure. There is not only a longing to incorporate objects but also a longing to be incorporated by a larger object. Very often, the seemingly contradictory aims of eating and of being eaten appear condensed with each other (p. 64).

It is hoped that the material here adduced will be found useful in showing how frequently, and in what limitlessly varied fashions, one can find incorporative processes in action during analytic hours. Above all, if this paper can help other therapists to become alert to any tendencies in themselves towards the incorporation–and hence the thwarting of self-growth, of individuation –of their patients' personalities, it will have served its main purpose.

These data have been derived chiefly from the analyses of outpatients whose psychiatric conditions, in so far as it is possible to apply psychiatric labels to them, fall under the standard classifications of (a) one or another of the psychoneuroses, or (b) 'schizoid personality'. This chief body of the data consists in direct quotations, written down as the material was being expressed during the course of analytic hours. A relatively small portion of the data, consisting largely of retrospective descriptions of analytic situations, stems from work with schizophrenic patients.

The material which is to be presented bears upon the following aspects of incorporation: (i) those factors operative in the patient's early environment which hindered his recognition of himself as a separate human entity, distinct from the personalities of his parents, or, to put it another way, the tracing of the patient's early failure to mature beyond a conception of himself as being incorporated with the parent figure(s); (ii) the continuing use of this incorporative method of interaction in chronologically adult persons, to ward off anxiety; and (iii) manifestations of

40

incorporative processes within the transference-countertransference relationship.

One final preliminary word regarding the data: it is recognized that other psychodynamic processes, in addition to incorporation, will be apparent, particularly in the longer passages. These other processes will not be discussed, and hence there will be no endeavour to achieve comprehensive psychodynamic formulations of the various data presented, since the focus of this paper is limited to the process of incorporation.

The Factors Operative in the Patient's Early Environment

In essence, the parent's need for security cannot allow him or her to feel the child as a separate entity, and the parent therefore cannot give indication to the child that the child is capable of emotionally affecting the parent. It is presumed that most of the parents of the patients under discussion are basically schizoid, afraid of feeling any intense emotions – whether tenderness, libidinal desire, anger, envy, jealousy, or whatever – and therefore unable to react save with anxiety in response to strong expressions of feeling by the child.

The child, finding himself unable to evoke appropriate emotional responses from the parent, is thereby denied the experience of feeling himself to be an individual human entity, distinct from but capable of emotional contact with the parent. Instead, the child feels himself to be either completely outside the *impenetrable* parent or completely incorporated within the parent – that is, unable to utilize his (the child's) feelings effectively either in establishing a feeling-contact with the parental ego or in breaking off such a contact, respectively.

Such a child experiences existence as an oscillation between two extreme states. In one, he finds that no activity, however daringly conceived, can carry him beyond the confines of, so to speak, his mother's tolerant smile and forgiving arms. In the other, he finds himself completely shut out of his mother's awareness, out in the cold, with a highly anxious sense of non-existence, of not being really alive, and no move on his part can insure re-entry into his mother's favour, into the realm of the really living. Most importantly, the child feels that the oscillation between one state and the other is a process which is only to a

41

very limited extent affected by his emotions; it is conditioned much more by the level of his mother's anxiety, and hence by the breadth of her sphere of awareness, at the moment.

Were the child able repeatedly to evoke feeling, other than anxiety, from the parent, he would gain simultaneously a sense of liberation from the confines of the parental ego, and a sense of existence as a separate ego capable of affective contact with another ego. But the parental anxiety by which his efforts are actually met creates in him an empathized anxiety which demands the repression of his own feelings; not having had the experience of being able to exist separately from the parent, he dare not make the parent anxious.

The parental anxiety is presumably the one all-important environmental influence which tends to keep the child from advancing beyond the infantile sense of union with the mother to a mature awareness of the self as a separate individual. The parental *behaviour*, verbal and non-verbal, which points towards such anxiety, is protean in its manifestations. Most commonplace and well known, perhaps, are the signs of parental overprotection – admonishing Johnnie to be sure to wear his rubbers, to be exceedingly cautious in crossing the street, to stay out of all sorts of situations in which he could conceivably receive injury, and, in short, the constant conveying to Johnnie of a picture of the world as a nightmarishly frightening place peopled with limitless dangers, from which he will be safe only so long as he stays within his mother's precepts.[2]

Some of the ways in which parents behave incorporatingly are reflected in the following words of patients:

Patient A, a 22-year-old man, said, 'When I grew up I never expressed myself much. It seemed to hurt their [mother's and father's] feelings when I expressed my own opinion, because it was so different from theirs. . . . They didn't have much use for other people elsewhere in the United States. . . . She [mother] had a tendency to feel that people far away like that was no good, so to speak. She read so much in the paper and heard so much on the radio about killing, rape, stealing, and things like that, that she didn't have much use for people she didn't know about. . . .

[2] For a particularly valuable description of such incorporative behaviour on the part of the mother, see Hilde Bruch's 'Psychological Aspects of Obesity' (1947).

'On furloughs I used to tell her about the Army, and my grandmother even wrote her a letter about what a good boy I was; but she never discussed it [his 4 years' Army experience, including much overseas duty]. . . . I spent a lot of time right up till her death, trying to convince her that there were people far away just as good as people she knew.'

(Therapist: ' "It seemed to hurt their feelings" – how did they show that?') 'Well, that's hard to put into words. The way they'd look at me; that's about all I can say.

'I think where the credit – wouldn't be exactly credit, but the *excuse* for me being so different was that I left home, went so far away in the Army, for four years. . . . I crossed the United States twice, went around the world once. . . . Something else they'd never do: they'd never ask me about my Army life, where I'd been, what I'd saw. In comparison to my mother and father I'd been around a lot more than they had – one hundred per cent, maybe even more than that. . . . Seemed to wait for *me* to do the talking, if I done any.'

(Therapist: 'Had your father travelled much?') 'No, I wouldn't think so. He had an opportunity one time when he was a young fellow that I wished I'd had when I was a young fellow. He'd been a fatherless boy since he was 4 or 5 years old, helped his mother making a living, worked in a textile mill – where he does now, as a matter of fact. . . . Well, a man and a woman who stayed overnight at his mother's offered to take him with them to South Africa as a companion, on a wild animal hunt, stand his doctor bills, and all like that. But he didn't go.

'Course, he didn't like to leave his mother. But she was healthy. . . . Very nice of him to take his mother into consideration. . . . I give him credit for that. But that was quite an opportunity.'

(Therapist: 'Did he urge *you* to take opportunities?') 'Yeah, one time he did. . . . He mentioned me going out west and follering a wheat harvest. Well, the reason I didn't do that was because my mother was always talking about how hard it was to be away from home, out on your own, no mother, no father, no home to turn to. I guess I didn't have faith in myself.

'That's the way they kept me out of the Army [for a time]. I don't know till this day what accident made me go into the Army. Just decided one day, "I'm going in the Army." Looks like I *could* have gone out west and follered the wheat harvest, but I never did.

'I bought my first car. I wanted a motor-cycle, but my father didn't have a car, and I couldn't afford both, so I got a car. . . .

'All along since I've been on the job, making my own money, from time to time I'd mention paying the grocery bill or the rent, but they wouldn't accept my money. I think I mentioned before–little responsibilities that was so obvious, like buying groceries and paying rent. . . . The way I understand it, that sorta cramped my style as far as foreseeing opportunities, for example. . . .

'I know my mother used to kid me a lot, right up till her death, about the way I'd dress. I'd try to keep clean. . . . She used to kid me about taking so much time with my clothes.'

The incorporating effect of the mother who represses her own id-impulses and projects them upon the outer world, and of the parents who cannot give recognition to their son's individual achievements lest they feel the full impact of their own inferiority feelings, seems evident here.

Patient B, a 38-year-old man, in speaking of his aunt who served as mother surrogate to him from early childhood, says: 'One of the things that angered me most was when I'd try to be especially pulverizing to her, mean to her–try to really *get inside her**[3]–she would chuckle and chuckle as though she got a big kick out of it. She seemed to enjoy the strength of my reaction. I guess that she didn't believe that there was any real anger behind what I said, thought that it was sort of evidence of my love for her.'

Later, complaining that the chairman of his social club talks too much, he says, 'He reminds me of my father in his *complete imperviousness** when he was talking. When my father was talking about his profession, he'd stare right past me; I might as well not be there.'

Here, in the described experiences both with the mother surrogate and with his father, the patient seems to have felt himself to be *totally* outside the parent figure, without any real emotional contact between them. It appears that, to the patient, one could

[3] In these verbatim passages, all words which I have italicized for emphasis are followed by an asterisk (*). All other italics in these passages are words which the patient stressed as he spoke.

be only completely outside or completely inside ('really get inside her') the parent figure. Generalizing from this, he seemed to view all interpersonal relations as fundamentally a matter of either incorporating, or being incorporated by, the other person. His own incorporating tendencies were much in evidence during the course of his therapy. For example:

'A man is coming to see me about a hot-shot routine they use in another department. I was amused at how enthusiastic he was, and I felt like saying "There, there." His work engulfs his life.'

(Therapist: 'Let's see what "There, there" brings to mind.') 'I've had an urge to say that lots of times, when I've felt superior to an enthusiasm of somebody's else's. I've had an urge to say that to you sometimes. Sometimes you get all in a stew about things and I feel like saying, "Oh, it doesn't matter that much." '

Patient C, a 34-year-old woman, in speaking of her relationship with her husband (which bears much similarity to her relationship with her mother), says, exasperatedly: 'If I snap at him about something that's perfectly legitimate, he'll say, "You're acting like a baby." What do you do then? If you go on, you're just acting more like a baby. If you go on, he's right—you know? You still haven't won your argument. You still haven't got any place.'

It seems that this woman, like Patient B, felt incapable of having any real emotional impact upon another person—or, to put it another way, she apparently had no awareness of herself as being emotionally *outside* any person with whom she was dealing at all closely.

Patient D, a 40-year-old man, says during free association: 'I always felt guilty about getting money from my mother, especially when it came to getting clothes—I'd never start the idea —somebody else in the family would—I'd never make any demands—my troubles with buying clothes nowadays—I still feel more or less at sea—like to get someone's opinion about them— sort of afraid of buying something freakish.'

(Therapist: 'Something freakish?') 'The clothes I've been talking about—loud shirts, poor style in the suits—my mother comes up, for some reason—her exaggeration—small differences of opinion were likely to seem freakish to her.'

The patient's mother seems to utilize, as one of her techniques of incorporating the son's personality, the ridiculing of any deviations from her attitudes, her tastes, her values. The son, in his efforts towards individuation, towards self-realization, tends to be driven back into the fold–into his mother's personality–by the potent weapon of ridicule.

The Continuing Use of the Incorporative Method of Interaction

ITS USE TO AVOID FACING THE REALITY OF THE OUTER WORLD

The process of incorporating one's self into another's personality –the substitution of another person's ego-boundaries for one's own–has as one of its most common functions the denial that one's own ego has any limits–that is, the perpetuation of the infantile feeling of omnipotence, the denial that there is any reality outside one's self. This process of incorporation by another ego allows one to retain the unconscious conviction that one can do everything–even more, that one *is* everything.

How often, for instance, one encounters the patient who, burdened with impossibly grandiose self-expectations, bitterly or self-righteously says that he could have realized his aspirations but for the personality limitations of a parent, a wife, or a problem child! He reports that as it is his achievements have remained relatively humble, solely because of his enslavement within these family ties.

Patient E, a 26-year-old man, on several occasions during his analysis, while describing various reality problems, thus depreciates outer reality: 'It's the *reaction to* these things that's important, rather than the *things themselves*. It's the *viewpoint* you take toward the things that's important.'

In referring to some of his problems with his job, for instance, he said: 'And I know the trouble is inside *me*. It's not traceable to any of the guys I work with. . . . It's my own *viewpoint toward* these problems.' [This patient expresses this same idea in slightly different words later on in the paper.]

Normally in late infancy there develops an awareness of separateness from the mother. I suspect that in this patient – and very possibly in all such patients with a predominantly incorporative interpersonal orientation–this process failed to occur, and that it failed largely because it would have entailed the recognition of an intolerably great hostility on the part of the mother towards the infant, and vice versa. Whether or not this 'cause' be correct, there were many data concerning Patient E to indicate that the relationship between patient and mother was characterized by a remarkably close identification by the patient with his mother, coupled with a high degree of repressed hostility towards the mother.

Moreover, it is concerning his relationship with his mother that one finds his comments most vividly portraying his incorporative tendency – his tendency to deny the individuality of the other person:

'It's hard as *hell* to distinguish between what her ideas are and what mine would be if I were in her position. In fact, I can't do it. I can't distinguish between myself and her, whereas I can do so as far as my father is concerned, and I can with my sister. . . .

'I pity her, as I'd pity myself if I were in her place – pity her *very* much. But I'm blasted if I can distinguish – *she just doesn't have a definite personality other than the one I attribute to her, with my attitudes and feelings* [tone of amazed discovery].'

It would be difficult to conceive of a more complete denial, a more complete erasure from awareness, of the real mother. The patient's interpersonal relations with her have consisted to a large extent in an *intra*-personal process of relatedness between the patient's very underdeveloped ego and a 'mother' within which he has kept his ego incorporated. This 'mother' has not been the real mother, not the mother who exists in the reality outside himself, but rather a fantasy figure constructed largely of repressed and projected aspects of his personality which are as yet intolerable to the ego.

He continues: 'So the feeling of identity with her is awfully strong. Maybe I can figure it out by seeing what sort of person she actually is. Maybe I can do it by trying that. She is – she wants affection a great deal and – uh – that may be a repetition of my own – '

This patient, whose tendency to intellectualize is obvious in the quoted passages, spent several analytic hours largely in an attempt to figure out intellectually in what respects his own personality differed from that of his mother. It is particularly interesting to note the feelings he reports having had at times when he was trying to differ from the mother, trying to establish a difference of viewpoint which presumably neither of them could tolerate—because of the need of each to deny the individuality of the other:

'Aside from that business of obliviousness to the other person, she [mother] is quite *intelligent* about the situation—*infuriatingly* so, in things that I've opposed her on. It's a hell of a job to show that she's wrong in anything, and when I attempt to do so I get all tied up in knots.

'Probably part of my trouble there comes from this problem of identifying myself with her, so that assuming that she has the same viewpoint I have, it's just about like arguing against yourself, because I go on the assumption that her answers are going to be just what my own answers would be if I were in her place [laughs]. So that's probably why it practically makes me tear my hair out.

'And the few times when I've been very confident of my argument and have licked her, then she's always done something that stops me completely: she starts to weep. Then I think of how I'd feel if I were in her shoes; I'm hurt and I feel pity for her.'

And in an hour about seven months later: 'I guess I have the inclination to attribute more intelligence to her than she actually has—in fact, I'm sure that's what happens. Then I get all up in the air when she doesn't show that much intelligence—that was when I used to get so exasperated. . . . I guess I didn't wanta see that she is pretty narrow-minded about these things [various intellectual problems], and when I'm faced with ironclad evidence that she is narrow-minded, I get mad at her and mad at myself.[4] I get very tense and unhappy.[5]

'I get that way with my sister, too. She's being untrue to me in terms of what I've expected her to be able to do. . . .

'My mother's inability to grasp some of these things drives me nuts. So there we have an overestimation of my mother in my mind,[6] an overestimation of her abilities, an overestimation of her affection.

[4] This indicates one of the great difficulties with resolving such close identifications: the identification serves to keep hostility out of awareness, and resolving the identification necessitates the bringing into awareness of hostility *against one's self* as well as against the parent figure (that is, against that area of one's self which heretofore has been identified with the parent). In this connexion, see also Patient G's material in the section on the use of incorporation to avoid feelings of rejection.

[5] This situation disturbs his cherished belief in the omnipotence not only of his mother, but of himself.

[6] The 'in my mind' is accurate; this mother is truly in the patient's mind rather than existing in outer reality.

'And it's a good thing to get these things said. That's a beginning, and I have to say these things over and over to really get a feel of them. It's a tremendous job for me to see her as she really is in reality, as distinguished from the things I've attributed to her in my own mind.'

This patient's tendency to develop the same incorporative relationship with his girl friend as that which he had with his mother is clearly reflected in the following excerpts from one of his analytic hours. Note the many remarks which point towards his feeling increasingly incorporated within the personality of his girl friend:

'I've found in the last day or two a lack of interest in everything . . . and along with that, a kind of irritability with other people and with myself. I feel as though there is a lot of anger beneath this apathetic feeling. . . . I get angry very easily, and curse. . . .

'I think part of the anger grows out of my being in the backwash of things, from the feeling that I'm not really in the swim, and I do have the capacity to get into the swim. Part of my staying out of the swim is due to my fear of pushing out from the shore and getting my teeth into things. . . .

'Speaking of marriage, the way of life I foresee in it frightens me. I would have very little time for my hobbies. I would have very little opportunity to meet interesting, stimulating people. And there's this driving feeling that I must decide damned soon about it [about marriage], that I must get a move on. . . .

'I just seem to be going around in circles. And with this attitude toward my work I'm not healthy as far as my body is concerned; I have headaches and indigestion, and I know they're psychosomatic. It's probably due to frustration. . . . It's a matter of getting exhausted with constantly trying to get out of a squirrel cage that hasn't any door.' [Note how frequently the patient's choice of descriptive words and phrases reflects his incorporative tendencies.]

'And I know the trouble is mine alone. It's not something I can trace to any one of the guys on the job. . . . It's my viewpoint toward these things.' [Note the denial of the importance of outer reality.]

'And part of this apathy is related to Judy [his sweetheart], and feeling that in some ways I'm getting on more intimate terms with her and finding her more desirable. And there's some God-damned response *to* that. It's tied up somehow with that business of being scared of women, that we talked about a while back. . . . I wouldn't be surprised if a hell of a lot of this apathy is due to the nearness I've gotten in my own mind to Judy as a choice, as someone I may marry; then comes a reaction, like pulling your hand away from a hot stove [from, one might surmise, projected hostility]. And then comes a scared feeling that any chance for me to become an individual, to achieve my intellectual goals, will go by the board. . . .

'It's a bitch of a job with her to get an hour or two to work on my novel. I was with her all the time during my Christmas vacation. I have to raise hell and really put my foot down in order to get an hour to work on my novel. So my reaction is to feel apathetic, and it goes back to a fear of being swallowed up [the first use of this phrase, by either of us, in his analysis]. And I suppose the fear itself is based on a lack of sureness about my relationship with women. . . .

'I realize that's absurd, but that's my feeling about it. And ya see, that traces back to my mother who was so domineering, who ruled the roost so much, that I musta got sold on the idea that all girls are that way. But what concerns me is that my reaction to Judy is not one of saying what I want to say and doing what I want to do, but it's a bird-caught-in-a-cage sort of thing. In my relationship with Judy, *I* am not really the boss. I'm not the leader—and it's not her fault so much as mine. I've got some queer lack of sureness myself, otherwise Judy wouldn't be so domineering.

'It has nothing to do with my being *scared* of being the boss, either—though it may. But it's a matter of intellectual uncertainty, and emotional uncertainty.

'Now the thing that hasta be worked out is, how can I get to be free, so I can do things because *I wanta* do them, not because somebody told me when I was a kid that it is my moral obligation to do them, or because I'm afraid that this would happen or that would happen if I didn't do them? . . .'

(Therapist: 'Any thought as to why one might be *scared* of being the boss?') 'Yeah, I don't have enough confidence in myself.

'And I know *why* I don't feel surer of myself, too. I think that

50

can be traced back to my family. The fact that my mother was always so absolutely *positive* of her point of view that whenever I'd bring up an opposing idea she'd blast it to pieces. With that going on, over and over and over again, she musta undermined my confidence in my own ideas. . . . So that, no matter how many times my ideas have turned out to be good ones, from an objective standpoint, I don't have enough of a *feeling* of confidence in them. I didn't have confidence in myself when I went out for football, and the reason I didn't was that nobody fostered any confidence in myself when I was growing up. . . .

'And this lack of interest I have right now is a result of that. It's a matter of not feeling confident. . . .

'Judy doesn't particularly like opera, and I do. That's a real difference – ya can't deny that. I never listen to my records when she's over at my place. I'll bet I haven't listened to my records more than two or three times since I started dating her, six months ago.' [Note here the patient's own intolerance of difference, of separateness.]

'. . . The few times when I've tried to listen to an album of records when she was over there, she'd sit there looking at me. I felt like a heel – she was obviously wanting me to pay attention to her.'

In the above excerpts, we clearly see that the patient's incorporation within the personality of his girl friend serves (1) to place upon the girl friend the blame for his not fulfilling his own fantasied omnipotence, and (2) to keep largely repressed his hostility towards her. In a sense, the incorporation by the personality of the girl friend serves to keep the patient's anxiety-laden hostile feelings contained; he is apprehensive lest they burst forth. Unfortunately, the frustration attendant upon his feeling himself to be so greatly restricted by her is undoubtedly a major source of the hostility.[7]

From the very outset of his analysis – not only in the single hour cited above – it was evident that this patient had a view of himself as being omnipotent, and there were various indications that his tendency to become incorporated within the personality of his girl friend was in part traceable to his need to feel omnipotent. For example, he found himself unable to ignore her frequent

[7] See the next section for other material concerning this hostility-repressing function of incorporation.

periods of mute resentment; he had to 'get her out of' them. Shortly after such an incident he came to his hour and reported:

'My trouble is I know *I can do anything** [momentary pause] I really wanta do– . . . I can get her out of those spells where she won't say anything and looks so surly. I resent the need in me that makes me feel I *hafta* haul her out of them.'

Presumably his compulsion to 'haul her out of them' stems, at least in part, from his need to demonstrate to himself, over and over again, that he is really omnipotent–that he *can* dissipate his girl friend's resentful moods.

ITS USE TO KEEP HOSTILE FEELING UNDER REPRESSION

It has already been noted that Patient E's need to become incorporated within another's personality is based partially upon his inability to tolerate the full admission into awareness of his hostile feelings. Next, in order further to portray this function of incorporation as a defence against hostile feelings, I shall present excerpts from an analytic hour of Patient F, a man of 32. At the beginning of the hour he handed to me the following written description of a dream (the two sections of which were labelled 'A' and 'B' by the patient) which had occurred several nights previously, and which was dealt with by free association during the analytic hour:

(A) I was alone on a vast plain. I looked up and saw a globular spaceship, brilliantly white and far above in the sky. I had a bow and arrow with me, and shot an arrow at the spaceship, and watched the arrow as it sped through the sky. It was astonishing to see the arrow hit the ship, after having gone through many erratic curves and turnings, in various directions, on the way.

Then, strange things happened in the sky. First, the spaceship turned from white to deep purple. Then part of it seemed to disengage itself from the main ship, and become a small ship hovering close to the mother ship.

I felt terrified, and people everywhere showed terror also. The mother ship gradually became darker and darker in colour. I tried to think; an arrow could only go so far up into the sky, and no further. How could it have gone so high? Was all this phenomenon really my fault?

Then it seemed we were being invaded, perhaps by enemies

from the mother ship. Everyone started packing their belongings to flee. Before I fled, however, I had tᴏ rush into my room in a building for my own clothing. I chose a heavy sweater and an overcoat, having a feeling it would be very cold where I was going. I had to hurry in order to escape the danger, and not be left alone.

When I came out I tried to find someone I could join but everybody had gone and I was alone.

(B) I went to a hotel in some city to stay for a few days; but the desk clerk told me they had no room available at the moment. I knew there were other hotels within easy walking distance, and started back out to find a room at one of them, but before I got to the door, the hotel manager accosted me, said he'd overheard that I was looking for a room and that he'd be glad to have one cleaned up and prepared for me promptly in order to save me the trouble of going elsewhere. He lisped, and he was very elegantly dressed, and I felt sure he was homosexual. I made a promise to him that I'd see him that night and repay him for the favour he had done for me.

That evening, as I was getting ready to retire, there came a knock on my door and when I opened it the hotel manager was there. He asked me if there were anything further he could do for me. I knew he was making sexual advances to me, but I declined and shut the door. I knew he was frustrated at this, but I didn't feel bothered about my refusal. He hadn't done anything which made me feel under any strong obligation to him— he'd merely saved me a few blocks' walk to another hotel.

(Therapist: 'Let's just see what comes to mind.') 'The tearing loose from the mother spaceship of this subordinate ship–somewhere in there I get the idea of birth–changing of the mother ship from usual colour, white, to threatening purple colour carried with it menace, threat.

'The arrow's winding up on ship itself after zigzag course. I get idea of resenting the idea or the appearance of the other body. . . .

'I can see where the round ship could very easily represent a breast, a female breast–how easy it must have been to suck milk from Mother's breasts, with no brothers, at that time, to compete with me, no need to hurry–I get impression somehow of her refusing to feed her baby any longer–I do know she soon put me

53

on a formula–all this pandemonium in the sky reminds me of this pent-up anger–which I have right now, as a matter of fact, had a bad night–I've been terribly impatient to have intercourse with my wife.

'Her sister is staying at our house, and I feel that I can't have sex with my wife because of her damned sister–although I *did* feel last night that we had an opportunity to have relations without her sister's hearing us, but Margaret [his wife] said good night, and I lay awake for hours, burning with anger and sexual frustration.'

(Therapist: 'What is childish about wanting your wife sexually and feeling frustrated?') 'The intense rage, and I didn't *tell* her of my desire–just kept it all inside–yet, I swear, when I get in one of those rages I can no more knock on the door and ask for a favour than I can piss from here to San Francisco–so, feeling about this spaceship thing is intense hate and resentment–I lack the self-confidence to go to my wife and ask her, "Honey, can't we have intercourse?" instead of bottling up all my feelings –it's so much like situations in Westport, where when Mother and Dad had been fighting and had taken certain attitudes, nothing I said had any effect. . . .'

(Therapist: 'Its being very cold where you were going?') 'This idea of aloneness–uncertain prospects of where I may wind up–whether my going to a cocktail party will be another matter of feeling entirely alone, and anxious as hell–the question of how will I get along with the people–how will they like *me*, how will they accept *me*–whether I'll be overcome with anxiety and hafta try to dominate them, rather than being casually friendly, or whether they'll dominate me–a cake of ice covered with sawdust and locked in an icehouse–when people want ice they unlock the door, shovel off the sawdust, and take out the cake of ice in order to melt it.

'Right now I get a tremendous desire for revenge against the whole world–at least the world back home–mother and father, brothers, sister–but the coldness is this feeling of not being in touch with anyone. . . . The thing that constantly confounds me is how *my wife* can be so sweet and lovable with guests–we had guests last evening, including this second cousin of hers, Ed– how she can be so warm toward them–and when it comes to *me*, it's the cold treatment.

'It's the same sort of two-faced stuff I used to hate down home in Louisiana—my mother could be so nice around people. . . . When we'd go visiting, people would say, time after time, "What an adorable mother you have!"—but, Christ! the *moment* we started back home, up would come the usual situation, in which everything revolved around Mother, everything had to be designed to please Mother—I know that's one reason why I strongly mistrust people—I *know* they don't really feel as friendly toward me as they appear to be.'

(Therapist: 'The hotel manager who had done nothing for you beyond saving you a few blocks' walk?') [Patient pauses a few seconds.] 'The thought that came to me was not so much the identity of the person as the terribly distorted sense of gratitude —that is, someone who's ready to offer his *body* just because he's had a little favour done for him—I can see myself acting in a similar way in so many situations.

'Another thought was, why was it so necessary for me to make so *very* much of the favour he'd done for me? It's similar in a way to this business of intercourse, where having intercourse with my wife has developed such a tremendous importance to me— here in the dream you have this homosexual combination man and woman—again this idea of putting on a show—Mother had the very same habit or character trait—whatever might be done for her or the family, she would overflow with gratitude, however slight the thing might be which the person had done for her. If somebody would send her a Christmas card, for instance, she would practically go into orgasms of gratitude. If I can be as hypocritical as my mother, I can put on as big an act as she does —and in a way it's getting revenge on her; I don't know how— I think if I go into these terrific twists of effusiveness with other people. . . .'

(Therapist: 'Terrific twists of effusiveness?') 'Mental picture I got was of a python, twisting and writhing around limbs—not very relevant picture.' (Therapist: 'Well, what else?') 'Squeezing the life out of its victim, a deer, for instance, or a boar—not so irrelevant after all, is it? Bore—that's the one thing in life I fear more than anything else, is boring people—bore also has a sexual association—boring into my wife—I'd like to satisfy her so *tremendously* that she'll say she never enjoyed anything half as much in her whole life.

55

'I've often wondered if I do satisfy her sexually—her having been married twice before makes me feel that I have to make up to her what she didn't get in her first two marriages—with Mother, too, the feeling I had to make up to her what she didn't get from my father. . . .'

(Therapist: 'Hotel manager?') 'My first thought was that when I was a kid I used to want to become a smooth, suave type of hotel manager who could butter up people in all sorts of subtle ways—people used to say, too, about my mother, that she'd have made a fine hotel manager—and I can see why—wonderful smile, wonderful approach—really some of the most skilful play-acting you yourself have ever seen—and it's a superb way to win esteem from people, and yet keep them at a distance.

'But her real self, that she showed to me, without the fancy dressing—naturally it made me feel badly—I felt I deserved her compliments, her favours, as much as the outside world did, the people *outside* the family.'

His associations suggest that the dream may be interpreted as follows:

(1) The mother spaceship represents his mother, and the disengaging small ship represents the patient's self. We have a pictorial representation of disincorporation, the resolution of an identification with the mother.

(2) The particular personality trait, formerly operating out of awareness, as an unconscious identification with the mother, and now emerging into awareness, is that of effusiveness.

(3) The patient's own effusiveness is seen to be a manifestation of his hostility towards his mother. Anxiety has prevented his recognizing the full intensity of his anger at his mother's effusiveness; instead, he has unconsciously identified with her in this regard—he has been acting out a similar effusiveness without having been aware of doing so.

(4) The effusiveness has served not only to repress, but also to act out, his hostility towards his mother: compare the 'erratic curves and turnings' of the arrow which he shoots at the mother spaceship with the 'terrific twists of effusiveness' by which 'I can put on as big an act as she does—and in a way it's getting revenge on her. . . .'

(5) The patient's anxiety concerning his 'identification-bound' hostility is depicted in the dream: 'I felt terrified, and people

56

everywhere showed terror also. . . . Then it seemed we were being invaded, perhaps by enemies from the mother ship.' The hostility which he has 'kept out of awareness by transforming it into identification-with-mother, is released and is felt as directed not only towards mother but also towards one's self, towards that aspect of one's self which is identified with mother. The patient is faced with the prospect of having to deal not only with rage towards his mother for being insincerely effusive, but also with rage towards himself for having the same trait. His need to attribute a fantastic power to his anger causes him to feel that 'people everywhere' are threatened by its liberation.

It is worth noting that, in not only the content of his communications, reproduced above, but also in their feeling-tone, the patient was giving evidence in this hour of much progress in therapy, in terms of markedly increased freedom of emotional expression and markedly increased self-assurance.

ITS USE TO AVOID FEELINGS OF REJECTION

The above material concerning Patient F is presented to illustrate the manner by which patients with incorporative tendencies deal with tabooed hostility: namely, by indentification with the hated person, or, to phrase it differently, by incorporation within the hated person. In F's dream, he portrays his disincorporation from the hated person, his mother (using the dream symbols of a small spaceship disengaging itself from the 'mother ship'), with respect to the particular personality trait under consideration – namely, effusiveness. Presumably a comparable disincorporation with regard to many other unconscious identifications will be needed in order that the patient may achieve the goal of analysis – the state of freely functioning as a highly self-aware person, as an individual in his own right.

Again, this material from the case of Patient F can readily be interpreted, in terms of his prior need to remain incorporated within his mother in order to avoid facing the feelings of rejection which would be attendant upon the recognition of himself as an entity separate from the mother. The element of repressed rage was so conspicuous, however, that the material was presented mainly to depict the rage-binding function of incorporation.

In the following excerpts from analytic hours with three patients we see incorporation used in order to avoid feelings of rejection:[8]

(1) Patient G, a 34-year-old man, while free associating, thought of 'having a woman suck my penis-. . . . That story Randall told of that girl in France-Lucy and Norma-Lucy, who wanted to do that more than anything else, and Norma, who used to do it because *I* wanted it-and yet-I begin to see something there -both times, they couldn't get me to really relate myself to them -it's confusing; it's [tone of discovery] the *one way* I can cast them off *definitely* and know at the same time that they're not fooling me about their feelings, that they feel fond of me and I can push them away.

'I see now what I'm afraid of pouring out my feelings to a girl, or to *any* one: they might do the same thing to me. . . . they might say, "You're of no use to me any more! Get out!" . . .'

(Therapist: 'Aren't you reversing some role you have played with a woman?') [G is silent for a few seconds and I start to repeat this, but he interrupts me with:] 'Having difficulty in saying it-I thought that I tried to go down on Edna once and she refused, calmly, without raising hell at all about it-it didn't satisfy me, her refusing so calmly-I wanted her to blow her top, give me the devil about it-

[No break in G's reporting] 'and-I thought of Mother and her breasts-but I don't go any further with that-as though I were right here [places right hand a few inches in front of his chest, looking flushed and very anxious]-*as though I were my mother**- and as though I were right near her breasts but not quite *at* her breasts.'

(Therapist: 'Did you know that you said, "As though I were my mother"?') 'Yeah-I guess *it made me more comfortable to say that I, being my mother, was rejecting me.'**

To be precise, the process of G's incorporating himself within his mother is used to avoid the return of repressed and projected feelings on his own part *towards* the other person, originally the mother, as well as to avoid any real rejection *by* the other person.

---

* It might well be thought inappropriate to separate the function of incorporation as a defence against the awareness of hostile feelings from the function of incorporation as a defence against the awareness of feelings of rejection, since rage is such an integral component of, or sequela to, feelings of rejection. This separation is made only in the hope that it will more clearly delineate the functions of incorporation.

The intensely rejecting quality which is the source of his anxiety here is not evidenced by Edna, for example, but is under repression in the patient himself.

(2) Patient H, a 24-year-old man, during an analytic hour reported the following associations:

'Once at a Boy Scout meeting–I was about twelve–someone else was elected patrol leader, something I'd been hoping for–guess I resented it, because I became a big hell-raiser–the meeting was a farce, largely due to my efforts–the Scoutmaster made me stay away from the next meeting–*painful thing, and when I was allowed to come back to the meeting after that, I cried**–brings up a vacation, when I stayed for a few days of it with friends, and there again, *feeling like crying on leaving them**–I was about nineteen–again there, sort of *the feeling that I wish someone would make me stay.'** [Note here the wish to be incorporated into his Boy Scout group, or into the home of his friends, in order to avoid feeling rejected by them.]

'Wanting to be controlled in general–always the limits that I automatically place–want to use the word "exoskeleton", am having trouble doing it–in any case, I wanted to say I'm always contained within an exoskeleton that someone else forms around me, even here–the process of testing out how much elbowroom I have–nothing is done that's a complete separation from the process that seems to be determined by an outside source, nothing that would push through the exoskeleton and slough it off, nothing that would, so to speak, free me from the eggshell that's around me. . . .'

(Therapist: 'Exoskeleton?') 'I say I have difficulty in saying the word because I wasn't sure you'd understand immediately what it means. I know doctors have some zoology as part of their education, but I thought you might not recall that term right away–uh, the exoskeleton is the calcareous sheath covering certain forms of animal life, particularly the crustaceans–I suppose my not wanting to use that word was due to fear of your not understanding it, and retaliation–that it would anger you that I should use a word you wouldn't understand–the idea of a container, being contained within certain rules and values of other people. . . .

'A novel–one I just read last evening–guess this is a good time to read it–symbolism in the novel–house–these Mexican peons-conflict with the law-just the whole situation of being in a house where the limitations of these people are being shown, and at the end the hero of the novel breaks through these limitations and leaves the family. . . .

'Idea of dependency comes up-and in general the acceding-the acceding to innumerable demands as payment for certain things you need-of course, the things I'm talking about are acceptance, love-like Marge [his wife]-the idea of fearing any conflict with her, lest it destroy the rest of the relationship-that's pretty persistent. My brother comes to mind-again, my siding with my mother against him-and there's the-uh-fear that he'd learn that I was taking that role-of course, the difficulty there, the difficulty of conforming both to my mother's wishes and to my brother's [patient is referring to an elder brother who served as father surrogate to him throughout much of his developmental period]. . . .'[9]

Here one sees that H feels he must be 'always contained within an exoskeleton that someone else forms around me' (incorporated within the other's personality) lest he become completely rejected by the other person. The prospect of being without their acceptance and love, and subject to their retaliation for his differing with them, is intolerable to him.

Again, as with Patient G, the need of H to imprison himself, to incorporate himself, within the personality of the other person is presumably in large part traceable to his inability to tolerate within awareness the full intensity of his *own* feelings of actively rejecting *other* persons. Instead, he projects such feelings upon other persons and considers himself to be constantly in imminent danger of being totally rejected by them. It is not they, or certainly not they alone, who cannot endure his differing from them and freely expressing his individuality. It is his *own* re-

---

* This 'difficulty of conforming both to my mother's wishes and to my brother's' is worth a brief additional note. It is one of the many problems encountered by one who endeavours to ward off by incorporative defences the anxiety which he experiences in relations with many different persons. He comes more and more to feel unconsciously as though he were bearing innumerable personalities within himself, not integrated within his own ego, but rather existing 'undigested' like foreign bodies. Particularly among psychotics one not infrequently hears the patient equating himself to an overloaded train or to Noah's ark, for instance, and he may act out these various incorporated personalities in a quite bewildering fashion, behaving now as though he were his father, now as though he were his aunt, and so on. The terror experienced by a patient who is living in such a state beggars description.

pressed feelings which command the *other* person, 'Be like me, be *me*, or suffer total rejection by me!'

(3) Patient H, while free associating in a later hour, again gave evidence of his use of the process of incorporating himself within the personality of another person in order to avoid feeling totally rejected: 'The possibility of being rejected–brings up a class in grammar school a long time ago–and expressing an opinion– somebody else, a girl, said an opinion and I was called on and I said *exactly* the same thing she had said, word for word. I felt very un-comfortable about it, and had a great deal of general animosity toward everyone there–seemed as though I were compelled to do that–I had a great deal of anxiety when I was called on to say something–I certainly had nothing in particular I wanted to say, anyhow–everyone was asked to say something.

'I'm thinking of my mother, and–her sharp manner of speaking at times, often–and the possibility of her cutting me off when I said something–I don't know what–she speaks sharply, and im-pulsively, and–uh–in general doesn't give the other person a chance to say much, especially if she has any disagreeing ideas....'

Here we get a clue pointing towards the original interpersonal relationship–that is, that with his mother–within which H de-veloped his view of interpersonal relationships as involving only two possibilities: (a) mutual incorporation or (b) total rejection. The clue is found in his reference to his mother's 'cutting me off when I said something'. In another hour he described how, at any one time, one or another of the several siblings in the family would be completely in the mother's favour and all the others would feel completely excluded. The aspect of *total* 'acceptance' (incorporation) and *total* rejection was prominent in all his des-criptions of his intrafamilial life in childhood.

Note H's reference to his having felt 'a great deal of general animosity toward everyone there'. We may surmise that a major source of this hostility is H's conviction that the others in the classroom will not tolerate his expressing himself. He hates them because he feels that they will not allow him to be an individual. To pursue this line of thought, one might wonder to what extent murder which occurs within an intense interpersonal relation-ship is an attempt on the part of the murderer to free himself, to burst the bonds supposedly imposed by the personality of the murdered person–not being aware of the fact that this 'personality' of the murdered person has been composed in large part of the murderer's own repressed and projected feelings and attitudes.

Undoubtedly one can find incorporative processes to serve a number of functions in addition to these three on which data have been presented above. It is by no means presumed that the possibilities as regards its functions have been fully dealt with in this paper.

Manifestations of Incorporative Processes within the Transference-Countertransference Relationship

It is obviously desirable for the therapist to be alert to any indications that the transference-countertransference relationship has an incorporative quality. Not only is incorporation a state representative of anxieties which need clarification and resolution, but incorporation is a defence-against-anxiety which is the very antithesis of a major goal of psycho-analytic therapy – namely, the development of the patient's self as a freely functioning entity.

To the degree that the patient needs to keep his personality incorporated within what he conceives (largely through projection) to be the personality of the analyst, or to the degree that he needs to utilize the personality of the analyst (again, as the patient perceives that personality, distorted by many projections of his own repressed self-images) as a nucleus for his own functioning self, to that degree the patient's efforts towards individuation are unsuccessful. And in so far as the therapist himself needs to keep the patient's personality incorporated within his own, or to keep his own personality incorporated within that of the patient, he is hampering the patient's efforts to achieve the goal of an independently functioning self.

The following three manifestations of an incorporative transference-countertransference relationship have been particularly useful as clues to the writer, although undoubtedly there are many additional clues which would prove similarly useful. The sample situations which are used to illustrate these three manifestations are presented, for the sake of simplicity, from a unilateral point of view – as though only one of the two participants were carrying on the incorporation process. It is to be emphasized that in any transference-countertransference relationship in which personality incorporation is present, it will be found to be a mutual process, with each participant, therapist and patient, showing tendencies both to incorporate the personality of the other and to become incorporated within the personality of the other.

CONSUMING ENTHUSIASM

Occasionally one finds one of the participants enveloping the other with what one might call a consuming enthusiasm. I vividly recall one analytic hour, for example, in which the patient, an extraordinarily fluent and enthusiastic talker, began talking about modern art, of which I know very little. As he talked, in what might be described as a torrent of words, he waxed more and more enthusiastic. He kept gazing intently at my face, and whenever I opened my mouth to speak – either to express some of my relatively lukewarm enthusiasm about modern art or to endeavour to find out what was going on here as regards the transference situation – he would pour out words with renewed rapidity and succeed in stifling me. I became increasingly anxious, feeling more and more overwhelmed and unable to express myself in any direction, until by the end of the hour I felt as though I had been tied up within a package and sent tumbling over and over into a void.

Another patient, a salesman by occupation, spoke with relish of how, when he was in the mood, he was capable of 'talking the customers deaf, dumb, and blind'. I had the opportunity of experiencing the effect of this at first hand: once while he was showing me a sales item, which he carried around with him, and describing it with voluble enthusiasm and immense persuasiveness, I could literally feel my hand being strongly drawn down towards the pocket where I carried some money, as though by his volition rather than my own. The hypnotic quality of his performance is clearly suggested by this description. One wonders whether in hypnosis there is a personality incorporation of the subject by the hypnotist – or, to put it another way, with the focus upon the activity of the subject, whether in hypnosis the subject incorporates himself within the personality of the hypnotist.

The particular examples given above portray the consuming enthusiasm as it is expressed by patients, although such enthusiasm

63

when voiced by a therapist is presumably no less suggestive of an incorporative process.

PREMATURE AND OVER-ABUNDANT INTERPRETATIONS

It is my impression that one of the most common ways in which a therapist unwittingly attempts to keep his patient's personality incorporated within his own, is by the offering of premature and over-abundant interpretations. A number of patients have called my attention to a tendency of mine to add to their feelings of discouragement and futility by giving little or no recognition to the forward steps which they themselves are currently achieving, but rather by smothering, so to speak, these achievements of theirs within a network of verbose interpretations concerning that which is still to be worked through.

For example, in one particular hour a patient had been achieving, with very little verbal participation on my part, insight at an unusually rapid rate, and insight into personality areas which I had explored to only a very limited extent in myself. During the hour, while listening to him, I was having a sense of discovering new areas of my own personality, with attendant feelings of anxiety and thoughts that he was getting beyond me. At the end of the hour I made some lengthy, pedantic remarks which gave only brief reference to the insight he had achieved during the hour, and which dealt at length with hypothetical areas which he might now be distantly approaching, but which might as easily have been figments of my own associational processes and projection mechanisms, for he had produced extremely few data in support of them.

When my dissertation drew to a close, he was silent for a few seconds, then slowly sat up on the couch, and said in a let-down, uncertain, unhappy tone, '*I* think what I've said tonight is important, and rather new.' I hastily assured him that I thought so, too—without, of course, ameliorating the unfortunate effect of my incorporative manner of reacting to the insight which he had been achieving during that hour.

It seems that when a therapist's anxieties cause him to engage in incorporative behaviour towards the patient, he is particularly likely to find himself making not only premature and over-abundant but also extremely general, all-embracing interpretations. Thus, no matter how significant are the insights at which the

64

patient subsequently arrives, he will find that he is still operating within the incorporative analyst's I-told-you-so.

There is nothing novel in suggesting that it is unconstructive for the therapist to endeavour to help the patient to get feelings expressed by exhorting the patient to do so. It is well known that for the therapist to say, in one way or another, 'Come on and tell me how much you hate me,' is about as effective as anything could possibly be towards insuring the patient's bottling up of his hostile feelings. What I want to suggest here is only that such exhortations can be representative of a therapist's unconscious effort to incorporate the personality of the patient. In the face of such urging, the patient can achieve no awareness of functioning as an emotional entity, regardless of how intensely he responds either negatively or positively to the therapist's exhortations; only to the degree that he can ignore the exhortations of the therapist, can he function as an entity.

I refer here, of course, not to a calm, unanxious encouragement by the therapist of the patient's expression of feeling, but rather to the type of anxious exhortation – in whatever fashion, whether verbal or non-verbal – which conveys to the patient a therapist's plea to 'hurry up and get aired and dissipated those feelings which are filling me with anxious suspense'.

STATUS QUO INTERACTION

The incorporative aspects of a transference-countertransference situation characterized largely by the maintenance of what one might call a status quo interaction can perhaps best be pointed out by a rather extreme example of such a situation:

The patient is a 42-year-old man who had been through a number of paranoid schizophrenic episodes. This was his first admission to the hospital at which I was employed. His verbose expression of rather lurid delusional ideas and quite free acting-out of them had subsided after a few months of hospitalization, apparently largely because of the security which he had found in a locked-ward hospital environment. He had been on an out-patient status for several months, and for some time had re-established the modes of personality functioning which had characterized his previous behaviour between psychotic episodes: he was excessively neat in his personal appearance; he was tremendously overcontrolled in his physical movements and in his verbal expression; and he maintained a vigorous denial of any importance that I, or his illness, might possess in relation to him.

In a typical hour during the period when our relationship was at its most incorporative level, our chairs were placed so that they faced one another, but he usually stared stonily at one wall and I stared woodenly at another. He might venture, early in the hour, a few brief references to a lecture he had heard or a play he had seen recently. My response to this would be to direct half-hearted efforts–efforts of a sort which had been defeated by him upon dozens or even hundreds of occasions in the past–towards encouraging him to expand on this material and to relate it to his own life situation. In a few remarks, usually delivered with consummate scorn, he would pulverize my efforts as being ridiculously inappropriate.

We would then lapse into silence. Thoughts of saying this or that, which might promise to break the stalemate, would occur to me, only to be quickly dismissed by some counterthought which said, 'This suggestion would only hurt his feelings,' or 'That idea would only make him more anxious,' or, most often, 'I've already said that at least a hundred times before, and he always knocks it down with his scorn.'

As for the patient, his facial expression would gradually change during the minutes of silence, from one expressive of some degree of interest and responsiveness to one expressive, by turns, of restrained disappointment, restrained impatience, and restrained irritation, disgust, and hopelessness.

Both of us would change position seldom, go on smoking casually and very heavily, and in general, endeavour to give one another the impression that we were able to tolerate this sort of thing quite comfortably for years, at the current frequency of five hours per week. I felt fairly certain that I was being successful in indicating to him that I by no means had any feeling that I might explode at any moment, and he would behave as though he felt similarly certain of his own outward equanimity, although he would often appear at the same time to be on the point of exploding.

After about ten minutes of silence on one occasion, two other patients began playing tennis on a court outside the window. When another five minutes or so had passed, in which the stillness had been broken only by the sound of the tennis ball, the patient looked at me for a few moments and said, in a flat voice, 'I think tennis is a monotonous game, don't you?'

On another occasion, again after about ten minutes of silence, he looked at me for a long moment and observed, calmly, 'You look monotonous.'

After such hours, which generally came in the late morning, just before lunch-time, it was my custom to go home feeling enchained by depression, and snarl to my wife that, for instance, 'we lead a *petit bourgeois* life of the worst type!' (The patient's scorn towards me often contained reminders of the fact that he had travelled about the world a great deal, in contrast to myself, and had far higher socioeconomic origins than I.)

This stalemate changed rapidly and promptly into one of relatively free interaction between the patient and me as soon as I was able to recognize in myself a quite intense degree of anger towards him. Although I expressed it quite directly to him on more than one occasion, the important ingredient was that I had become able to *feel* it very strongly and without attendant anxiety. Previously, I had been aware of feeling exceedingly tense, but not of feeling angry.

In the ensuing several months, the therapy with this patient was characterized by an increasingly varied and spontaneous expression of feeling by both the patient and myself, with a concomitantly increasing ability on his part to explore wider and wider areas of his personality functioning.

It is worth noting that the feelings expressed after the stalemate had been broken included not only anger but disappointment, hurt feelings, libidinal feelings, and fondness–feelings which during the stalemate I had been largely unaware of in myself and which he had given little indication of recognizing in himself.

Much evidence then accumulated which suggested that during the stalemate, the incorporative phase of the treatment-relationship, each of us had been incorporating his own personality within the 'personality' of the other in order to avoid recognizing the full intensity of inner feelings which disincorporation, or functioning as separate individuals, subsequently caused us to recognize within ourselves.

Moreover, there appeared many indications that the 'personality' of the other, within which each of us had been keeping his functioning personality incorporated, was actually in large part a fantasy personality formed of his own repressed and projected feelings.

Thus, the so-called patient within whom I was maintaining my personality in a state of incorporation, was to only a limited degree the real patient himself: the 'patient' was to a larger degree a fantasy construct of my own repressed and projected feelings of anger, scorn, hurt, and so on. So long as my own anger, hurt feelings, scorn, and so on, could not be tolerated within my awareness, I functioned as though *his* similar feelings must not be touched off. I behaved as though he, not I, were unable to tolerate such feelings in consciousness.

Contrariwise, the evidence was that the patient had been projecting on to me his own intense scorn, for example, so that he felt powerless to express himself freely lest *my* (actually his own projected) scorn be mobilized against him—which is not to deny that in actuality I did feel scorn towards him.

Particularly until the resolution of the stalemate, for this patient—and, of course, this was true of myself to a fortunately somewhat lesser degree—any other person to whom he related himself at all closely constituted a prison, within which the patient's feelings were frustratedly incarcerated. The bars of this prison were constituted by the patient's own repressed and projected feelings.

To him, the other person appeared not as that person actually was, but rather as a 'personality' constituted to a large degree of, for example, the patient's own great tendency to express scorn, his own great intolerance of his hurt feelings, his own intolerance of his capacity for anger, and so on. Thus, the other person became the *one* whose feelings the patient must be extraordinarily careful not to wound, whose scorn was greatly to be feared, whose anger was to be avoided. And, as the relationship between the patient and that other person (the therapist, for example) grew closer and closer, the patient's feelings became mobilized in greater and greater intensity; but, since these feelings still had to be repressed and projected, they caused the patient to see the other person as being ever more constricting, ever more on the verge of expressing these tabooed feelings towards the patient. Thus the patient felt that he had to be increasingly wary lest these forbidden feelings enter into the situation.[10]

With this patient, I continued to note, following the resolution of the stalemate, an incorporative type of relationship developing in the treatment situation at times when our mutual anxiety became relatively intense; but the incorporation process grew increasingly infrequent and transitory, so that it came to serve largely as a valuable indicator of anxiety rather than constituting a block to the analytic collaboration.

I shall not endeavour to elaborate further upon evidences of incorporative processes within the transference-countertransference relationship, or try to draw up any inclusive list of them. Surely they could be found to be almost innumerable, and present in many treatment situations. It is my own belief that when a patient comes to a therapist complaining of feeling that he is 'in a rut', or 'going around in circles', or 'tied down' by someone, or 'feeling as though I'm going to explode', one is very likely to find that he uses incorporative processes, among other defence mechanisms, to ward off anxiety, and one can in all likelihood find these incorporative processes operating within the transference-countertransference relationship.

[10] The progressively destructive nature of an incorporative relationship between two 'lovers' is brilliantly portrayed in the form of a novel by William Faulkner: *The Wild Palms* (1939).

Chapter 2

CONCERNING A PSYCHODYNAMIC FUNCTION OF PERPLEXITY, CONFUSION, SUSPICION, AND RELATED MENTAL STATES (1952)[1]

THIS paper will attempt to delineate a function common to the mental states of perplexity, confusion, suspicion, and the related conditions of feeling, which might, for instance, include bafflement and uncertainty.[2] I will not attempt any accurate and comprehensive delineation of the psychodynamic boundaries, so to speak, of these states; the endeavour is rather to point out a function that runs as a common thread throughout all of them. I believe that all these states represent a striving to keep out of awareness an intensity, or a type, of affect which is sensed as intolerable to the ego–as threatening to overwhelm the ego and disrupt the interpersonal relatedness. In essence, these states are considered for the purposes of this paper to function as defences against the awareness of repressed affects. Although this is not by any means the only psychodynamic or interpersonal function of these mental states, this paper will exclusively focus on this function as being a distinctly important one.

Survey of Previous Literature

Freud (1909) made brief mention of the function of uncertainty and doubt in obsessional neurosis in his 'Notes Upon a Case of

---

[1] First published in *Psychiatry*, Vol. 15 (1952), pp. 351–76.
[2] *Webster's New International Dictionary* defines all five terms in a way which is quite satisfactory for the present purpose. *Perplexity* is defined as 'the agitated or confused mental condition occasioned by a disturbing, vexing, or puzzling situation or state of affairs; . . . bewilderment; distracting doubt or uncertainty'. To *baffle* means 'to check or defeat by perplexing; to disconcert; frustrate; thwart; foil', and *bafflement* means 'the state of one who is baffled, confused, or bewildered'. *Uncertainty* refers to 'lack of certainty, doubt', or the state of 'not having certain knowledge', of being 'not assured'. *Confusion* is defined as 'a mental state characterized by unstable attention, poor perception of present reality, disorientation, and inability to act coherently'. Finally, *suspicion* is defined as the 'imagination or apprehension of something wrong or hurtful, without proof, or on slight evidence; also, the mental uneasiness aroused in one who suspects'.

Obsessional Neurosis'. His viewpoint is thoroughly dynamic; his portrayal of these states as manifestations of an energetic striving on the part of the personality has never been developed in subsequent literature as far as I know. After discussing superstition in obsessional neurosis, Freud observes:

> Another mental need, which is also shared by obessional neurotics and which is in some respects related to the one just mentioned, is the need for *uncertainty* in their life, or for *doubt*. . . . The creation of uncertainty is one of the methods employed by the neurosis for drawing the patient away from *reality* and isolating him from the world—which is among the objects of every psychoneurotic disorder. Again, it is only too obvious what efforts are made by the patients themselves in order to be able to avoid certainty and remain in doubt. . . . The predilection felt by obsessional neurotics for uncertainty and doubt leads them to turn their thoughts by preference to those subjects upon which all mankind are uncertain and upon which our knowledge and judgements must necessarily remain open to doubt. The chief subjects of this kind are paternity, length of life, life after death, and memory—in the last of which we are all in the habit of believing, without having the slightest guarantee of its trustworthiness (1909, pp. 232–3).

It has been surprising to find how little has been written concerning the mental states under discussion here.[3] This paucity of literature may be due to a fairly prevalent attitude that each of these mental states may arise from such a large number of diverse psychiatric conditions as to make it inappropriate for the particular mental state in question to be regarded as a symptom-entity.

Of the mental states under discussion the one most frequently dealt with in the literature is *confusion*. Only rarely do such papers deal with the psychodynamics of confusion; instead they deal with it as a manifestation of, for example, exophthalmic goitre or typhoid fever, of acute cholecystitis or alcoholism, or with the therapy of confusional states by shock therapy or penicillin or other physical measures. Writings which have to do with the psychodynamics of confusion, or of any of the other states under discussion, are few indeed.

[3] The literature prior to 1944 has been searched with only moderate thoroughness, since Fenichel's *The Psychoanalytic Theory of Neurosis* (1945) was regarded as presenting a reasonably comprehensive statement of the psycho-analytic thought on this subject which was then current. But the literature in English, in both psychoanalysis and general psychiatry, was thoroughly reviewed for the period January 1944 to August 1951 inclusive.

The few publications concerned with the psychodynamics of such states portray them solely as a relatively static, inert, troublesome *product* of failure in personality-maturation or, when examined more closely, as the again relatively inert *result* of various underlying *causes* having to do with disordered personality-functioning. Nowhere, except in the previously mentioned paper by Freud, have I found presented a viewpoint which regards them as being representative not only of a failure in maturation but also of a very active striving on the part of the personality to cope with quantities of anxiety which threaten to disrupt the interpersonal situation.[4]

Thus Bleuler, in his monograph on dementia praecox, expressed these thoughts regarding confusion:

Confusion itself must not be considered as a symptom, sui generis. It is *the result of* [5] the various elementary mental disturbances which have finally reached such a degree of intensity that the connections and relationships have been completely lost for the patient or for the observer or for both. . . . In schizophrenia, the confusion is at times the *consequence* of a sort of dissolution of ideas, at other times *the result of* a 'blocking' by newly emerging ideas, at still other times the suppression of single associative determinants with inroads by secondary associations; or again it may be *the result of* a pressure of thoughts, of a real flight of ideas, of hallucinations, or even several of these factors acting together (Bleuler, 1911, p. 31).

Confusion is an *end-symptom* which can be *caused by* a variety of disturbances if they are sufficiently intense. The manic, epileptic, hysterical, delirious, and catatonic patients may occasionally show confusion (p. 274).

Similarly, Fenichel deals with *perplexity* solely by postulating its *causation*, in schizophrenia:

The beginning of the schizophrenic process is a regression to narcissism. This brings with it an increase in the 'libido tonus' of the

---

[4] Since writing this paper, I have had an opportunity to read the chapter on paranoia from a book of Sullivan's posthumous writings (Sullivan, 1953b). In this chapter, Sullivan discusses self-pity, envy, and hypochondriacal preoccupations, as types of what he calls substitutive processes. He describes substitutive processes as 'primarily addressed to minimizing or avoiding anxiety. . . . Substitutive activity, in contrast to indirect exploitative attitudes, is not addressed primarily to an audience; instead it is addressed primarily to avoiding certain conscious clarity about one's own situation, one's own motivations, and so on.' This seems an interesting parallel to the theme of this present paper.
[5] In these quotations, all italics are mine unless otherwise indicated.

body (either of the whole body or, depending on the individual history, of certain organs). . . . [Sometimes] the ego . . . succeeded in warding off these sensations by means of a countercathexis, and the result is . . . estrangement. [Fenichel uses the term 'estrangement' to refer to 'a feeling of lack of sensations'.]

. . . What has been said of the feelings of estrangement and de-personalization, that is, that they represent a reaction of the ego to the perception of the increase in narcissistic libido, can also be said of the schizophrenic's general *perplexity*, of his feeling that everything has changed. All these initial symptoms are *due to* an inner percep-tion of the narcissistic regression and of the accompanying libidinal displacements (Fenichel, 1945, pp. 418–20).

An extremely interesting article by Rosenfeld (1950) deals with the psychopathology of confusional states in chronic schizo-phrenia. He also treats confusion in no terms other than its causation and its consequent appearance in the analytic situation as an end-symptom, but his thoughts concerning its causation are very interesting.

Feelings of confusion are part of normal development. . . . We may assume that in earliest infancy the baby lives in a state of unintegra-tion . . . Where perception is incomplete and where external and internal stimuli, external and internal objects and parts of the body *can often not be differentiated*. This confusion due to unintegration is normal and gradually disappears during development. We also have to keep in mind here that any developmental progress may lead temporarily to some confusion until a new adjustment is made.

. . . I suggest that [in the infant] under certain external and internal conditions when aggressive impulses temporarily predominate, states may arise in which love and hate impulses and good and bad objects *cannot be kept apart* and are thus felt to be mixed up or confused. These infantile states of confusion are states of disintegration and are related to the *confusional schizophrenic states of the adult* [italics Rosen-feld's] which I am describing in this paper. The confusional state is associated with extreme anxiety, because when libidinal and destruc-tive impulses become confused, the destructive impulses seem to threaten to destroy the libidinal impulses. Consequently the whole self is in danger of being destroyed.

In concluding, Rosenfeld says:

In observing confusional states during the analyses of chronic schizophrenic patients I was particularly impressed by the fact that the patients were *unable to differentiate* between their libidinal and

73

aggressive impulses and their good and bad objects. Both the impulses and objects were felt by the patients to be in a state of confusion. . . .

As can be gathered from the above quotations, Rosenfeld consistently regards confusion exclusively as an *outgrowth* of *inability* to achieve a more harmonious personality integration. To be sure, it does represent such an inability; but in addition I believe that it is an expression of an active striving on the part of the personality within the immediate interpersonal situation.

Method

The following case material illustrative of the theme of this paper will be presented within a *context*-in so far as that is feasible-not of the personality of either of the two participants in the therapeutic relationship, patient or therapist, but rather of the relationship between them.

This material points towards a general statement that, in order that any one of these five mental states may be utilized defensively in an interpersonal relationship, that particular state need not itself be prominently shared by both persons in the relationship; it may be prominent in only one. Thus, material concerning perplexity shows the perplexity to be prominent in both patient and therapist; the material concerning uncertainty shows this mental state to be prominent only in the patient; and, in the material concerning bafflement, the bafflement is prominent only in the therapist. As the following material indicates, both of the participants can be seen, in each case, to be *contributing to* the production of the particular mental state under consideration, whether that mental state is prominent in both, or in only one, of the participants.

In keeping with the endeavour to portray these mental states as relationship processes-particularly in dealing with bafflement, which is prominent only in the therapist-the countertransference will accordingly be described at relatively great length. It is my impression that any major contribution which the therapist makes towards the fostering, in the therapeutic relationship, of one or another of these mental states is traceable to countertransference processes.

With each of the patients presented in the data, psychoanalytically-oriented intensive psychotherapy was used on a basis of four or five hours a week.

PERPLEXITY, CONFUSION, SUSPICION

Clinical Material

PERPLEXITY

Patient A, 32 years old at the time of my first interview with her, was a single woman of Scots-Irish descent who had been trained as a nurse. She had just been transferred from a private sanatorium in her home city on the West Coast, where she had been admitted following the appearance of schizophrenic symptoms with less prominent manic features. Her prepsychotic personality had been basically schizoid with, in addition, many obsessional character traits.

During her stay of several months at the first sanatorium she was found to be socially isolated and preoccupied with reading works on Jungian psychology. She showed, according to the sanatorium's report, 'inappropriateness of affect, pressure of speech and flight of ideas'; she manifested temper-tantrum-like behaviour at times; and she was intensely and openly hostile to her parents and to her two brothers when they visited her.

Following her arrival at the new hospital, at which time I became her therapist, the ward personnel found her capable of adjusting quite readily to the patient-personnel group in a superficially adequate and inconspicuous social manner. But during her therapeutic hours her behaviour reflected much anxiety. During the first several weeks, she sat utterly motionless and mute throughout the greater portion of each hour—and, on several occasions, throughout the entire hour. At intervals during the hours there was much smiling punctuated by sudden, brief outbursts of weeping. Her speech came, for many months, in sudden outpourings so that many words were unintelligible. Its content reflected highly critical feelings about the parts which her parents and brothers had played in various intrafamilial relationships.

Very near the onset of my work with her, as she verbalized more and more concerning these intrafamilial relationships, she began showing, week after week, more and more frequent *perplexity* concerning the *meanings* of the recollections she was having—*why* this or that member of the family had said or done this or that to her, what they had *meant* by it—and the purpose of the therapeutic situation. She would wonder aloud (less to me than to herself) what we were about, look perplexed, and then

75

quickly give a shrug and go on pouring out critical thoughts. Her appearance portrayed, more and more often, perplexity. Her head was cocked to one side and her brow was furrowed into a perplexed frown. For some months her perplexity was in evidence almost constantly.

Then, as so often happens in therapy with a defence,[6] the *defensive function* of the perplexity, in this case, became more and more readily apparent, once the perplexity became sporadic in its appearance. It became more and more clear that this perplexity in the patient was serving to keep under repression an intensity of affect, which at the moment seemed intolerable for her to experience within awareness. I began to see that it was a defence against the awareness of feeling-states of *various* sorts—grief, scorn, anxiety, anger, and so forth.

A particularly illuminating situation took place in the fourteenth month of my treatment with her, in which her perplexity was manifestly serving as a defence against *anger*. The patient had started to express perplexity as to why her elder brother, who had persuaded the parents to place her in the former sanatorium very much against her conscious wishes, had told her, while he was bringing her to this new hospital, that, as she put it, 'he could have persuaded Mother and Father to send me on a trip to Europe instead, but that it wouldn't have been fair to me'. She said this in a perplexed but unusually vehement tone, although apparently without awareness of anger. She said, without either anger *or* vehemence, only with perplexity, 'I don't understand why he said that. Everyone in the family respects his judgement'; and then she suddenly burst out, openly angry, 'It just *burns* me!'

An instant later, her tone and facial expression changed back to perplexity, devoid of either anger or vehemence, as she puzzled, 'It would have been easier to ask, but I didn't think of it. I just sat there and tried to figure out what he meant.' It seemed clear that the patient still had to keep under repression, through the (unconscious) utilization of perplexity as a defence, some degree of her anger.[7]

[6] An extremely interesting paper dealing with this subject is Herbert Staveren's 'Suggested Specificity of Certain Dynamisms in a Case of Schizophrenia' (1947).
[7] Her anxiety concerning the anger within her had been particularly well revealed in an hour during the first month of therapy; she had reported, during that hour, that she had felt afraid of letting her thoughts go, lest she become so angry that she

I would like to emphasize, particularly during the first several months, perplexity was being engendered not only within the patient, but also within myself. It was as though perplexity from *two* sources was serving to damp down or dilute the intensity of conscious affect in the transference-countertransference interaction to a level which enabled the interpersonal relationship to continue. The patient 'made' me perplexed in manifold ways. Her speech was often unintelligibly rapid and sometimes inaudible. Very often, her response to a comment from me would not even be verbal, but would consist only in a barely perceptible movement of her head in assent or dissent. If the movement was not definitely visible to me, I might ask again for her response, whereupon she would generally utter a one-word response with such curtness as to have a distinctly discouraging effect upon my subsequent striving for clarification.

She would frequently start a sentence and then stop midway through it, start smiling in a secretly amused or embarrassed way, and be either unable or unwilling to complete the sentence when I showed an interest in hearing the whole of it. Again, in referring to persons whom she had not previously mentioned, she habitually used only the first name and never sketched in any identifying information–for instance, whether this person were a child she had known in her very early years or a classmate from nursing school.

Whenever she utilized an associational method of reporting, she switched subjects so rapidly that I very soon began to experience a frustrating, anxiety-provoking, and above all perplexing impression of glimpsing, time after time, an important thread in the association which needed to be focused upon and pursued in therapy, but which quickly vanished into the developing fabric of the associational content, to be succeeded by numerous other important-looking threads, which, in turn, vanished as quickly.

Although it is apparent from the above that the patient's perplexity was serving a function in her personality and that some aspects of her behaviour tended to produce perplexity in me, we need also to examine what function my perplexity was serving in my personality within the context of the interpersonal relationship,

should start hitting me and find that neither she nor I could stop her and she would 'just keep on hitting and hitting'.

and in what respects my behaviour was such as to promote a feeling of perplexity in the patient. It would be difficult to believe that the tone of a relationship characterized so prominently, and for so long, by perplexity could have been engendered and maintained to meet the needs of one of the participants alone.

Here, even long after the termination of the interpersonal situation in question, I feel myself to be upon much less sure ground than I am when looking at the personality-functioning of the patient. Presumably one never reaches a stage of self-awareness which permits one to see oneself quite as clearly as one can see the other person. But concerning a few of the aspects of my personality-functioning in this transference-countertransference interaction I feel at least reasonably sure.

I can see in retrospect that in at least two ways I was operating in a fashion which tended to engender such perplexity. First, I proposed the use of the free associational procedure in the second hour of therapy, and encouraged its use as her main form of verbal participation in the relationship subsequently, even though her history gave much evidence of proclivity towards scattering of her ego-functioning – such as her running from one interpersonal relationship to another in rapid succession, her rapid change of interest from one hobby or career to another, and so forth. A far wiser course would probably have been to devote a very considerable number of hours, at the beginning of the therapy, to history-taking and quite active verbal participation on my part.

Secondly, not until a good many months after the beginning of the therapy did I endeavour to define for her in some fashion what, in general, psycho-analytically-oriented psychotherapy is about, what it consists of, what in general it is designed to accomplish. For this particular patient, some such explanation might well have been helpful much earlier in therapy. My failure to provide it at or near the beginning of my work with her may well have fostered her tendency to become perplexed.

My reasoning at the time had been that for me to discourage use of the free associational procedure, and to carry on, instead, a quite active verbal participation in the relationship with her (in, for example, making prolonged efforts to get historical material and to explain to her what psychotherapy is about), would only activate her clearly intense defiance. I considered that this defiance would only greatly increase the difficulty in our building up a usefully collaborative relationship. In retrospect, the course I pursued was actually determined, however, much less by any conscious choice than by my own unconscious emotional needs.

Indeed my own perplexity functioned in such a way as to keep under repression certain of my feelings in the transference-countertransference interaction. The first previously repressed feeling which I glimpsed in myself was an intensely anxious sensation of having no part whatsoever in the patient's life. This particular sensation I had never had before. The feeling had probably been there unconsciously for a considerable time but maintained under repression by various defences, including that of perplexity. This took place during one hour in the period of several months when perplexity was so prominent a characteristic of the treatment situation. I experienced this feeling, for a period measured only in seconds, after she had been utilizing, with unprecedented vigour, various of her customary measures designed to shut me out of any felt participation with her.

Some months later a second previously repressed feeling broke through my defensive perplexity. This second feeling was one of anger. The patient had been unusually defiant, whereupon I suddenly found myself suffused with anger, which I promptly ventilated to her. Prior to this incident I had frequently experienced an intense feeling of frustration, so much so that at times I felt like beating my fists upon the floor and walls of the office; but never had I experienced anger towards her—never had I felt a desire to, for example, hit *her*. Following this incident I experienced anger towards her not infrequently, and was freely able (without anxiety) to feel like hitting her either verbally or physically. Significantly, the occasion of my experiencing this second previously repressed affect coincided very closely in time with the resolution of the perplexity in myself. Thereafter, I felt increasingly confident of my ground and increasingly able to make firm suggestions, pursuing unwaveringly one or another important theme and being relatively undeterred by her expressions of defiance and contempt.

In retrospect, the indications are that during these relatively early months of therapy, countertransference processes were operative in the form of unconscious dependency towards the patient as a mother-representative. Apparently I felt anxious lest her defiance be mobilized by a firmer, more active therapeutic approach on my part, and anxious (before the second occasion mentioned above) lest I experience the full intensity of my anger towards her. In both cases the prospect of possible dissolution of our relationship, with consequent thwarting of my unconscious dependency needs, was too disturbing for me to risk.

In the later months of therapy, I found myself experiencing both tender feelings and libidinal feelings of a much greater intensity than any such emotions which had previously entered my awareness during the therapeutic hours. Conceivably they had not previously been stimulated in me to an equal degree, even at an unconscious level; but I strongly surmise that they had been, and that since they were so anxiety-laden as to be for the most part inadmissible to my awareness, perplexity, among other defences, had supervened in order to keep these feelings largely out of my consciousness.

BAFFLEMENT

Patient B, a married man of German descent, was 40 years of age at the time I became his therapist. He had been admitted to two psychiatric hospitals previously—once for a period of one and a half years, and the second time for a period of six months. His symptomatology during his stay at each of the two previous hospitals had been, as it was when I first saw him, typical of paranoid schizophrenia.

During the first few interviews with me, he allowed silences of no more than a second or two. He kept up an almost incessant stream of conversation, consisting in a mélange of references to books he had read, interspersed with comments reflecting self-misidentification, such as, 'Of course I'm Cortez. . . . I died in 1910 as Tolstoy. . . . I was Esther Williams in [name of a motion picture]. . . .' He apparently considered himself to be, from one moment to another, a limitless number of prominent persons, present and past, including Alexander the Great, Pericles, General Lee, Lincoln, Goethe, Senator Vandenberg, various movie actors and actresses, and so on, and made references to various supernatural powers which he possessed. He frequently displayed his knowledge of Latin and Greek.

He appeared flushed, very tense, and restless, and often

laughed in a pent-up fashion. He muttered a good deal to himself. Much of the conversation ostensibly directed towards me was unintelligible because of its low volume and rapidity. He changed subjects so rapidly that it was impossible to achieve any exchange of conversation. From time to time he would pause fleetingly, glance at me and ask, impatiently, 'Is there anything you want to ask?' or 'Is there anything you had in mind?' I would generally then repeat, verbatim, some comment he'd made, in a questioning way designed to encourage his elaborating upon this subject. Almost before I had started to speak, however, he would glance away again and resume verbalizing the same sort of miscellany as before. Then, after about a minute of this, during which he had touched on many other subjects, he would turn his gaze back upon me and say with raised eyebrows, very contemptuously, condescendingly, and impatiently, 'What was that?' I would thereupon repeat my verbatim quotation of his own words, and he would look as though he had no idea as to what in God's name I was talking about–as though he had never heard such a thing before. Sometimes he would make some curt, condescending comment in which he would deny the significance of my remark before looking away and resuming his rapid-fire, miscellaneous talking.

Although he kept indicating that he wanted me to participate–wanted, particularly, that I should ask him questions–I felt at the same time warded off by his behaviour.

By the fifth hour of therapy, the patient's behaviour and reporting had changed markedly. The uninterrupted flow of such warding-off conversation, which characterized his behaviour during the first few hours of therapy, was by then so sporadic that one could see both its defensive function and some of the areas of his personality involved. He was appearing much less tense and spending a much greater part of the hour in talking sequentially about persons whom I could assume to be important to him in his actual life–including, particularly, his wife, his mother, an uncle (who had served as a father-surrogate to him), his two sisters, and various of his fellow patients.

During this hour, it became apparent that his voicing of delusional material regularly followed immediately upon my touching on some area of his history which was associated with his disturbing feelings, such as feelings of inferiority. At one point during this hour he mentioned that he had not been invited to join the college fraternity he preferred. When I started inquiring about this, he suddenly interjected into the conversation, 'Of course, I'm Aristotle and Confucius and Jonathan Swift, and I died in 1865 as Lincoln. And I control the movements of the planets in the solar system–you don't believe it [resentfully], but I *do*.'

In another hour two days later, we were in the midst of an exchange about his relationship with his elder sister, dealing with material which was charged with intense feelings, when he suddenly said, 'I was Winnie-the-Pooh in those books by A. A. Milne.' This kind of thing occurred many times during each of the hours thereafter for some weeks. My notes on the tenth hour describe accurately the effect which this defence of his regularly had upon me:

'I noticed today that when I would become interested in some one comment of his and would start inquiring along this specific line, after a few moments of this questioning he would throw up a cloud of, "Of course I'm (so and so and so and so, etc.) and I died in 1852 as the Duke of Wellington." Thereupon, I'd become stopped in my intensive "pursuit", would feel stymied, buffaloed, baffled. I commented to him about this. He merely looked bored and mildly amused.'

In an hour during the seventh week of therapy, while we were in the middle of a conversation about the terror he'd been going through in the several months before his present hospitalization, he suddenly commented, 'Of course I'm King Amenhotep of Egypt, who ruled in the second millennium B.C.'. I felt this definitely as a distance manoeuvre. Its manifest absurdity so baffled me that I didn't know what to say or do; he suddenly seemed to have put himself thousands of miles and thousands of years away from me, and completely stopped me in my efforts to push further into the subject we had been dealing with.

A typical example of this manoeuvre occurred during the eighth week of therapy, by which time this defence was appearing relatively seldom. The patient went through approximately the first half of the session talking entirely rationally about real figures and events in his life. He then commented that he hadn't heard from his wife for a week. 'So perhaps my last letter [a distinctly cool one, as he had described it to me] had the right effect.'

82

He went on to say that in her last letter she had demanded to know if he planned to divorce her after discharge from the hospital, as he had evidently intimated to her some time prior to his admission. He added, in response to my inquiry, that he had not said 'yes' to this question, except perhaps in a disguised way.

'It's better to avoid arousing her anger,' he explained. 'She might come down here with a knife and try to stab me,' he said with an obviously very forced grin, as though this were a joke. I took this up, however, and he said seriously that he actually feared violence on her part; he said that he had never seen her behaving violently, but that she did have a violent temper at times.

Shortly after this, I asked, 'These quarrels that went on between your mother and your elder sister–did they take merely a verbal form?' He replied, 'Not always,' and went on to say that his mother had struck the sister sometimes; '–but not very often', he added as though to close the subject.

I then said, 'In spite of logical evidences to the contrary, in spite of such facts as, for example, your being a reasonably strong adult man, probably much stronger than your mother, still one can carry with one the fear of a little child at seeing a much larger person, his mother, in a state of rage.'

He replied, with obviously forced amusement, 'You'll pardon me if I'm amused at what you've said.' I asked him, 'Do you think it absurd that you might have felt physically afraid of your mother?'

It was at this point, interestingly enough, that he referred for the first time–more than halfway through the hour–to his being anyone other than himself. In reply to my question, he asked me very promptly, 'Have you read *Anthony Adverse?*' Feeling momentarily baffled, I said, 'Yes.' He continued, 'Of course I wrote that novel, as Hervey Allen,' and added sardonically, 'I'm sorry to befuddle you and make you sceptical by mentioning that.'

I replied, 'Yes, that sort of thing does confuse me.[8] I'd like to

---

[8] This illustrates the impossibility of making any thoroughly sharp differentiation among such related psychic states as bafflement, confusion, perplexity, and the others under discussion in this paper. I present this material from Patient B to illustrate the use of *bafflement* as a defence because the *predominant* psychic state which I detected in myself, in connexion with this defence, was bafflement, although there were overtones of, for instance, confusion, perplexity, and uncertainty.

report to you what I've been aware of in myself when you bring up that sort of thing. I've noticed that at times I become very much interested in some particular aspect of this situation, such as your feeling that psychiatry has nothing to offer you. I'll get pursuing that very persistently, and then when you mention being various different people, it serves to stop me, to make me mentally sink back, baffled. Very probably you do need to shut me up in that fashion so that you can get expressed something you want to express.'⁹ He replied, 'Yes, I do need to discourage these petty trifles you bring up, such as the vexatious matter of your referring to Dorothy [his younger sister] as my sister.'

At this point I wish to delineate more clearly the particular emotions which were so charged with anxiety in this patient as to require him to keep them to a greater or lesser degree out of his awareness through the employment of various defences, including that of bafflement. In general, what I most often saw him trying to keep out of awareness in this early phase of the therapy were feelings of inferiority, futility, and anger. One could see particularly clearly that he had great anxiety in the face of his repressed anger. During the early weeks of therapy he mentioned, at one point, very seriously, that his uncle had said to him, when he was a child, that one should never hate anybody. In one hour while talking about his years in public grammar and high schools, he said, 'I didn't fight, ever – I stayed away from fights.'

In another hour during the eighth week, he mentioned, 'I felt ineffectual during my hours with Dr X [his therapist at one of the previous hospitals].' I suggested that perhaps he felt futile during the hours with me also, and he agreed. I then suggested that one finds life enjoyable, unmonotonous, unboring, 'to the extent that one can let oneself *feel* strongly about things – feel anger, for instance – rather than having to stay at a distance from people so one won't have strong feelings.'

He observed, scornfully, 'Typical manly point of view.' I said, 'I hadn't thought of it as a *manly* point of view.' He then looked serious and thoughtful as he said, 'Perhaps women have that attitude, too,' and went on, with flushed face and averted eyes, 'One has to be cautious.'

I repeated, interestedly, 'One has to be cautious – about

⁹ It would have been more accurate to have said, 'so that you can get away from some subject about which you have much anxiety'.

84

what?' He explained, 'About people.' I said, 'Otherwise, what?' He replied, 'Otherwise there's dissension and resentment. I keep out of things; that's the way *I* like to operate.' I said, curiously, 'What is there about resentment that is so intolerable?' He replied, 'It leads to violence.'

I pressed further with, 'What is there about violence that one must avoid – is it the possibility of being killed, or of killing somebody, or of breaking furniture?' He replied, uncomfortably, 'All those.'

In the work with Patient A both patient and therapist showed perplexity. With Patient B, however, I was unaware that bafflement was at all prominent among the patient's feelings; so far as I could discern it was prominent only in myself.

But here again, as with Patient A, abundant evidence accumulated which indicated that I was playing a very active part in fostering this defensive use of bafflement in the therapy situation.

Late in the eighth hour of therapy, having felt unusually frustrated with the way the hour had been going, I suddenly became aware that I had been sitting far forward in my chair throughout most of the hour, feeling very impatient, wearing a worried frown on my face, and smoking incessantly, whereas the patient, as was usual during that period of the therapy, was sitting back in his chair, smoking very casually and affecting great boredom and lack of interest. With this recognition, I felt distinctly that I had been taking upon myself the quite total responsibility for 'curing' him, and that he seemed to be enjoying my concern, which relieved him of responsibility for actively participating in the investigation of his problems.

On the following morning, while walking alone between two buildings in the grounds of the sanatorium, I suddenly had a triumphant feeling that actually he would have to come to *me*, that I was keeper of the keys, that I held the reins, and that if he wanted to get out of the sanatorium he would have to come begging, or, in other words, would have to get down to business in his therapy; I could afford to wait, I realized. This distinctly gloating feeling was, I noticed, one which I felt to be strongly reprehensible, one which I felt to be precisely the opposite of the Christlike attitude which I felt a therapist should have towards his patients. It would thus seem that my earlier, more superficial, attitude of a worried having-to-get-him-well was designed to repress this deeper attitude which, although far more comfortable than my former one, was distinctly offensive to my superego.

It thus appears that my bafflement was serving the function of keeping me to some degree out of an interpersonal relationship in which I tended to assume a total responsibility, which made me very susceptible to feeling intense anxiety, guilt, and resultant rage towards the patient for his supposedly creating such uncomfortable feelings in me. My bafflement held me back, so to speak, from feeling so deeply into his situation that my anxiety, guilt, and rage would have become overwhelmingly intense.

My bafflement also served as a rather direct expression of my deeper attitude of feeling that he had to come begging to me and of gloating over it. So long as I was holding myself out of the situation in this state of bafflement, he was required to stew in his own juice, or to make intense efforts to get me to participate with him in some way far more useful than my impatient pushing of him.

My notes following the eleventh hour are pertinent to this aspect of the countertransference:

'Much the same as yesterday. He rarely mentions his delusions of being thus and so any more, except when I get asking about interpersonal relations with people toward whom he presumably has disturbing feelings. . . .

'Seems evident how he uses this to make me desist from asking about anxiety-laden topics. I really should behave toward him in such a way (by not pushing him) as to make it unnecessary for him to do this very often. Seems clear I'm still much too impatient, too pushing.'

Another aspect of the countertransference manifested itself in relation to the intense scorn which he so frequently expressed to me. During the interval between his fifth and sixth hours, in an effort to become clearer and more comfortable about the countertransference, which I sensed to be already quite intense and poorly formulated by myself, I tried something new which proved quite illuminating to me; I let myself free associate on the typewriter for about ten minutes, beginning with this patient and deliberately returning to him whenever I found my thoughts straying far off on to other subjects; in this way my associations were considerably more directed, of course, than free association ordinarily is. This procedure brought to light much material on the significance of this patient in my feelings. Most prominent in this material were associations indicating that he represented my father to me, particularly as he seemed to me when I was between about 5 and 10 years old, a period which involved much admiration on my part towards him, and much feeling of being scorned by him. In addition, and probably even more importantly, my associations indicated that I had a hitherto unrecognized, intense degree of scorn towards my father during those years, and towards this patient currently.

It is interesting in this connexion that, during the night between the seventeenth and eighteenth hours of therapy with the patient, I had a dream in which I saw myself walking up a flight of stairs, while the patient was sitting in a chair near the foot of the stairs and looking up at me in a scornful way. In the dream I felt inferior and uncomfortable. I cannot at this time recall my associations to that dream; but even taken by itself it would seem to represent additional evidence of my proclivity for feeling either scorned or scornful in my relationship with him. Here, we may presume, was another function of my bafflement: my bafflement apparently stopped me from going so deeply into the investigation of any particular subject under discussion as to evoke from him a degree of defensive scorn which would be intolerably anxiety-provoking to me. Simultaneously, it apparently prevented me from seeing too deeply into his problems in living, problems which I tended to react to with scorn; and this scorn in turn was intolerable to my superego.

My notes following the twenty-third hour reflect my anxiety about feeling too deeply into the treatment relationship:

'At a time when the patient was manifesting anxiety about projected hostility—making various references to atomic bombs, wars, and volcanoes—I started giving some little lecture, beginning, "Fears like that are often actually fears of internal excitement, from one's emotions. . . ." In the middle of a subsequent remark, I suddenly got the feeling that I was pushing him too much, that I was in much too great a hurry for him to come on and express his presumably cataclysmic fears. A few minutes previously I had gotten some inkling of what a terribly frightening world he may be living in.

'I think it becomes clear that the way I write this—"frightening world", for instance—does not differentiate between "frightening to him" and "frightening to me". I think it is fairly clear that my pushing him, or trying to push him, into hurrying up and expressing his fears, his anger, etc., stems from my being afraid of his feelings, my wanting therefore to get these "threatening", apprehension-tinged feelings out in the open.'

In this, again, we see something of the anxieties in myself which bafflement, among other defences, served to keep to some degree out of my awareness.

In approximately the 110th hour, the patient began expressing an unprecedentedly intense scorn ostensibly about his uncle (who, in retrospect, may well have been serving also as a screen for the therapist), practically hissing such scornful statements as, 'He's just *nothing*; he's a *nonentity*.' I felt awed and unable to say anything about this. I clearly realized that this was too strong for me to tolerate.

During later phases of the therapy he came to deal with very intense anger, grief, hopelessness, and so on. I distinctly recall, however, that bafflement played no prominent part whatsoever in the transference-countertransference relationship after about the second month of therapy, by which time his expression of delusional ideas had ceased.

During the first two months of therapy, closely paralleling the gradual subsidence and, finally, the disappearance of the element of bafflement in the treatment relationship, there developed more and more evidence of decreasing anxiety and increasing spontaneity in the relationship.

For example, during the fourth week of therapy he began verbalizing anger as well as scorn quite openly to me, angrily calling me 'stupid', 'an infant', and so forth. Likewise in this fourth week he became able to tolerate silences of several minutes without having to fill them in with conversation, and his talk assumed a leisurely pace.

My notes on an hour during the fifth week of therapy are as follows:

'Patient spent the whole hour in an almost entirely spontaneous account of various past incidents from his life with mother, uncle, and sisters. He seemed much more relaxed, showed almost none of his usual scorn, looked serious [in contrast to his former, frequently flippant manner].'

The notes concerning an hour in the sixth week report that

'He began the hour by practically *growling* his anger about being here–same old content but much more expressed impatience, anger, and scorn. This went on for some minutes, then gradually he developed as relaxed and friendly a manner as he's ever shown toward me, talked spontaneously and at length about various things which evidently were of much emotional importance in his past life.'

By the end of the second month, his voicing of delusional ideas, and along with that the element of bafflement in the transference-countertransference situation, had ceased. By the end of the fourth month he had achieved so much freedom of emotional expression that he was able to express himself in the fashion shown in my notes concerning an hour in that period of the work:

'Patient showed increasing impatience with me, during the hour, when I kept returning to some subject he'd brought up [earlier in the hour] in which I was interested. Finally, he said, very angrily, "Why don't you keep up with me? You're always behind. If you would keep up with me I wouldn't be here in the hospital. I've tried for the past fifteen minutes to change the subject to something that interests *me*." '

These evidences of progress early in the therapy are not meant to imply, however, that there were no further major difficulties. Some of the abundant difficulties which became manifest in later phases of the therapy of this patient will be described in the next section of this paper.

UNCERTAINTY

Material to illustrate the defensive utilization of this mental state will be drawn from the therapy with the patient referred to in the above section on bafflement, namely, Patient B.

Near the end of the third month of therapy with Patient B, about one month after the virtual disappearance of the element of bafflement from the transference-countertransference relationship, I became aware of how *uncertain* he seemed to be feeling hour after hour, about some aspects of his life-situation. He first expressed uncertainty about whether the Bureau of Internal Revenue would grant him a large refund, which he had long been seeking. He very frequently expressed uncertainty about this question, for many weeks.

He first used the word uncertainty himself near the end of the third month of therapy: 'I don't like the uncertainty about the tax refund. I don't like uncertainty about things.'

From then on, for a period of approximately six months, he presented himself as being, during a large proportion of his hours, in a very uncomfortable state of uncertainty about one or another aspect of his current life-situation. He voiced uncertainty about the following questions: whether his wife would visit him during the coming weekend; when the administrator would permit him to move from the locked building to an un-locked building at the sanatorium; when he would be permitted to visit his home in the Midwest; when he would be permitted to move to outpatient status; whether, before moving out of the sanatorium, he would be able to acquire an apartment of the sort he desired; whether his application for enrolment in a night course at a local university would be accepted; whether, as time went on, his family would become insistent upon his taking a position in a branch of the family business.

My initial inner reaction to his expression of uncertainty was one of identification with him on the basis of my own past experiences of uncertainty, so that my conscious response to him was one of pity.

Near the end of this six-month period, during an hour in which he was voicing uncertainty about one of the situations mentioned above, I suddenly had the thought, 'Well, what the hell? *Everybody* has a lot of uncertainty in his life!' This thought was accompanied by an access into awareness of irritated, impatient feeling at the patient for his uncertainty which I had previously 'pitied'.

I did not tell him about this changed reaction of mine; but from that point on I had an entirely different, much more objective attitude towards his uncertainty. I now began seeing it, more and more clearly, as an unconsciously-utilized defence on his part, resorted to at moments during his hours when he felt threatened with the access into awareness of feelings which were laden with intolerably great anxiety.[10]

Thus, towards the end of the first and during the second year of my therapy with him, when he would start to become very

[10] We see here that his uncertainty presumably had additional functions of causing me to 'pity' him and causing me to feel guilty. Such additional functions of the various mental states under discussion I shall not go into here.

angry about not having been permitted by his administrator to move to outpatient status, the patient would suddenly switch off this feeling with the reflection that this was a matter of uncertainty–that he might, after all, be able to move out fairly soon, since the administrator had not, of course, set any date when the move would be permissible.

Similarly, when he began to have feelings of grief and nostalgia about persons and places in his past, he damped down the intensity of these feelings by the consideration that there was, after all, uncertainty as to how long he would have to stay at the hospital; he might soon, it occurred to him, be able to return to the Midwest and visit old friends again, so perhaps it made no sense to have strong feelings about this.

This same defensive use of uncertainty enabled him to defer for a long time the exploration of his feelings about women, feelings which, as it later became clear, involved heavily anxiety-laden hatred, envy, and tender feelings which exposed him to painful emotions of rejection and grief. He kept these feelings out of awareness for many months, partially by his uncertainty as to whether he would ever be able to live again outside a psychiatric institution, where he would have an opportunity to live with a woman.

Later, when he started to think about acquiring a job, he was able to postpone an exploration of the welter of very intense feelings which this involved, by reflecting that it was, after all, a matter of uncertainty whether his therapy would require his residing in this area long enough to make it advisable for him to seek employment here. (He could overlook in this way his feelings of resentment towards his parental family and dependence upon them, of inferiority as to his capabilities, of apprehension about becoming part of any working group, and so on.)

My relatively scanty notes upon the therapy during this second year of the work contain a few of his remarks bearing upon this defensive use of uncertainty:

Once he spoke of his lack of concern as to what ill fortunes his younger sister had, even though she was estranged from the family and had very little money. The patient seemed to feel quite guilty as he said this. He then said, 'I think I *would* be quite concerned about her, and feel quite responsible for her welfare, if I weren't having to stay in a psychiatric hospital.' Thus his uncertainty as to when, or whether, he would again be living outside a sanatorium, served to postpone his becoming conscious of the full intensity of his feelings of inadequacy, resentment, and guilt about his sister's welfare.

In an hour near the middle of the second year of therapy, after he had moved out of the sanatorium, he said, 'I would like to get a grand piano for my apartment. I feel that the spinet I have is not pretentious enough [broad smirk] for me. But of course, getting a grand piano is out of the question as long as the distinguished scientists out here decree that this incredibly expensive nonsense called psychotherapy is still vital to my metabolism.'

This touched upon conflictual feelings in himself which numerous other indications, before and after that hour, showed to be very intense: feelings of pride in appearing dignified and conservative, and of scorn towards persons who appeared undignified, ostentatious, and 'flashy'; in conflict with strong desires to be exhibitionistic and most undignified. Again, as long as he could focus his awareness upon the uncertainty of how long he would have to go on paying for psychotherapy, he could to some degree avoid awareness of these intensely conflictual feelings which would be mobilized by his coming face to face with the decision whether to replace his relatively modest piano with what he considered a pretentious new one.

In another hour, he mentioned that shortly after his discharge from one of the previous hospitals, he had got into an argument with his uncle regarding the family business. Interestingly, in describing this he mentioned that he had tried to remain as calm as possible during the argument, lest he be rehospitalized. Here again, it would seem that uncertainty as to whether he were going to be rehospitalized (an uncertainty which he showed also for some months following his move from our hospital to outpatient status) served to keep under repression some of the intensity of his anger towards his uncle.

As might be expected, concomitantly with my recognizing more and more clearly the defensive function which the patient's uncertainty had, his uncertainty became less and less something which weighed upon the relationship and hampered the therapeutic investigation, and more and more a valuable indicator of areas of anxiety which needed further exploration. As this change took place, his uncertainty played a less and less prominent part in the transference-countertransference relationship.

In this particular instance, uncertainty was prominent only in the patient. At least, I was not aware of feelings of uncertainty as being particularly prominent in myself at any phase of the therapy with Patient B. But even though I was not conscious of any prominent feelings of uncertainty in myself, there were various indications that certain countertransference processes were contributing to the production of the patient's uncertainty.

I shall mention only three such countertransference processes which apparently fostered uncertainty on his part. First, as mentioned earlier, for some six months my conscious reaction to his expressed uncertainty was one of pity, on a basis of identification with him. It later became clear that his uncertainty had been serving a function for me of enabling me to give expression to my own self-pity—to give expression to it in such a vicarious way as to be acceptable to my superego.

Secondly, we have seen that my anxiety about his expressions of intense scorn in reference to his uncle (the latter often serving, undoubtedly, as a screen for myself) continued after the termination of that phase of the therapy when his use of bafflement was a prominent defence; my anxiety in reaction to such scorn continued for some time into the phase of therapy when he was utilizing uncertainty as a defence, and this anxiety of mine had a distinct correlation in timing with his use of the latter defence. Thus, at such times his (always, I emphasize, more or less completely unconscious) utilization of uncertainty as a defence had a function not only for himself but also for me: it damped down my anxiety by moderating his expression of scorn, which, whether directed towards his uncle or towards myself, tended to arouse anxiety in me.

Thirdly, subsequent events made clear to me that my 'pity' towards him had served, as one might surmise, as a disguised expression of feelings of scorn on my part towards the patient. I distinctly found that as this particular brand of 'pity' towards him was resolved, I felt a much more solid respect for him as a capable adult.

CONFUSION

Patient C, a 35-year-old unmarried woman of Swedish descent, had developed a schizophrenic illness several years before her admission to the hospital where I was employed, and her symptoms had been so severe as to require hospitalization throughout most of the intervening time. Her experience at a state hospital in the Northwestern United States had included a total of about two hundred insulin coma treatments and an indeterminate number of electro-shock treatments. She had received her most recent electro-shock treatment within three days before her transfer.

From the first, confusion was the keynote of her behaviour during the hours with me, and this remained one of her major defences against anxiety, although later diminishing in degree, throughout the many months of my subsequent work with her. I found in the early hours of the therapy that although she was overtly willing to participate in a therapeutic relationship, she regularly presented a markedly confused, preoccupied appearance, with eyes gazing into space oscillating irregularly back and forth, with mouth slightly parted, and with an entranced smile on her lips.

During the first hour, she began by outlining quite rationally the few months of psychotherapy she had had at the previous hospital. But she spent the rest of the hour in expressing great confusion about various incidents in her past life: *why* one male acquaintance had not responded to her greeting when she had seen him walking on the opposite side of the street, why another had shown no eagerness to play golf with her, and so on. Although these incidents were such as to lead one to presume that during them she had *tended* to feel rejected, humiliated, grieved, or angry, such affects were quite lacking from her tone. Instead I heard, in both the content and the affective tone of her speech, only a confused wondering.

For example, she mentioned several times in this first hour that one of her male acquaintances, Paul, had not invited her to play golf with him when she had seen him at a golf course in her home city. In this connexion she said, in a confused way, 'Clara [a friend of the patient] told me that he didn't go much for women, but I know he does. . . . And it couldn't be because of my looks, because the women he dated didn't look any better than I did.' She continued to muse over this same incident several times during the hour.

At no time did she come to grips with the basic fact that the incident *had happened* and thus allow herself to experience and express the feelings (of hurt, or anger, or whatever) attendant upon the fact. It was as though she kept warding these feelings off from her awareness, through a ceaseless search for an explanation *why* the incident had occurred.

It is this same process, repeated over and over in relation to various areas of her living, past and present, that shows up in the subsequent material from her therapy. In my notes concerning the second hour I mentioned that

'Nearly all the hour was spent in discussion about Paul, during which she showed extreme confusion with slow, reflective, ruminative thinking. She referred to a bridge party at which a younger woman at the table had "glanced down twice at a fraternity pin she [the younger woman] was wearing". The patient asked me, "Did she do it to confuse me, or as a compliment, or what?" '

As far as I was able to determine, the younger woman's glancing down at the fraternity pin in the presence of the patient was either a chance occurrence which was misinterpreted by the patient as directed to herself, or an attempt of the younger woman to flaunt before the patient this symbol of success with the other sex. But again, one heard in the patient's tone as she reported this no envy or irritation, only confusion.

By the fifth hour, her time was spent almost exclusively in confused wondering as to why Paul had said or done this or that, years previously in her distant home city. I mentioned in my notes after that hour, 'It seems clear now that she is *using* preoccupation with her relationship with Paul as a way of avoiding spontaneous living with people *near* her *currently*.'

The observations of the nurses and attendants indicated that she was meeting with repeated rebuffs in her anxious, awkward efforts to strike up acquaintances with other patients on the floor. All their observations pointed towards her finding her current life in the hospital to be an extremely disappointing, unhappy existence, which was presumably too painful for her to focus directly upon during her hours with me.

In the sixth hour I fully broached to her my impression that her preoccupation with Paul might represent an escape from the complexities of establishing relationships with people currently

95

around her. In answer to this she said, 'But the people here aren't interesting.' Later in the hour, however, she said concerning the other patients on the ward, '*They* aren't interested in *me*,' and cited as an example her having asked another patient where the latter's home was; 'She didn't answer me,' she said in an unhappy tone.

I was left at the end of this hour with a distinct impression that her confused wondering about various aspects of her (to a small extent real, to a much larger extent autistic) relationship with Paul–who was now thousands of miles away and whom she had not seen for many months–was serving the function of keeping out of awareness various painful or otherwise distressing emotions arising from her interpersonal relations on the hospital ward.[11]

In my notes following the tenth hour, I said that

'The general motif of this hour, as of all the others, was great confusion in the patient. As before, she kept trying to figure out things, looked often in front of her, with wide, confused-looking eyes, would say again and again, "I don't know whether . . ." and "That's the trouble; I wasn't *sure*–" and similar expressions reflective of her trying to figure things out.'

In the fourteenth hour, in reference to certain frightening misinformation her brother had conveyed to her about sex during the patient's adolescence, she asked me, 'Why did Bill scare me– is it supposed to be good for you, or something?' Subsequent material indicated that on such occasions her brother had thus misinformed the patient in a cruel attempt to retaliate for the fact that she had arrived upon the scene at a time when he had been enjoying an only-child status in the family for five years, and had then usurped most of the parental attention which he had been receiving. Rather than allow herself to experience the hurt feelings, grief, and rage presumably associated with her brother's hostile behaviour towards her, she tried instead to figure out some friendly motive on the part of the brother, so as to spare herself from experiencing in awareness these unwelcome

---

[11] It was not until several months later that I began to realize how much this confusion was a function of *immediate* interpersonal processes in relation to the transference-countertransference relationship. I thus came belatedly to realize that this had been one of her major ways of keeping out of awareness various disturbing emotions arising in response to numerous rejections and disappointments, some fancied and some real, at my own hands.

emotions. Many times in subsequent hours she engaged in such a search for a friendly motive on the part of the other person whom she was discussing; and since it was frequently by no means easy for her to find some plausible friendly motive, she often followed a very devious, illogical path in her reasoning. Occasional examples of this twisted type of logic will be presented in what follows.

It was this patient who first enabled me to recognize, clearly enough for me to formulate, the general psychodynamic phenomenon I am describing in this paper—namely, the defensive utilization of confusion and related mental states as a means of warding off intolerably intense emotions. In her thirty-second hour she made a statement in reference to Paul's never having asked her out on a date. She said, now with beginning anger in her tone, 'There must have been a reason. *Otherwise it would be an affront*' [italics mine].

I repeated what she had said, 'You say that there must have been a reason, that otherwise it would be an affront?' She replied, vehemently, 'Yes, there must have been a reason. Otherwise I'd feel affronted.' Interestingly, it was somewhat later in this same hour that she was able to express, more undisguisedly than ever before, angry feelings towards Paul.

In the fortieth hour, at the end of the second month of therapy, the patient seemed still to be trying to 'figure out' reasons for unhappy past events in such a way as to avoid experiencing the painful or disturbing emotions unconsciously associated with the events. In particular she kept trying to convince herself and me that Paul's refusal to see her, when she had gone uninvited to his office one afternoon with the conscious intent of getting reassurance of his love for her, had been due to *fear* on his part that *she* would rebuff *him*.

In the forty-first hour, on the following day, she was again showing the same devious reasoning, trying confusedly but persistently to interpret certain incidents in her past life (particularly in relation to Paul)—incidents that would seem almost certainly to have been rebuffs to her—as somehow indirectly representing compliments or signs of affection from the other person. Finally, late in the hour, I said something similar to what I had said several times in the previous few hours, but this time more firmly: 'Note how you keep trying to avoid facing the other

97

possibility–that Paul *wasn't* as much interested in you as you wished. It seems to me idle for us to keep trying to find out why things happened, or exactly what happened. Our important problem seems to be to find out why you at present cannot tolerate facing the uncomplimentary possibility.'

She replied, seriously and thoughtfully, 'That's a good point,' which seemed a quite significant response, coming as it did from a patient who regularly before had either immediately brushed aside my comments or ignored them entirely. But in a few moments she went back to her efforts to arrive at a self-complimentary consensus with me as to the meaning of what had been actually rejecting actions on Paul's part towards her.

I persisted, however, in asking her, 'What has been your experience with disappointments in the past?' She replied, with a wave of her hand (a gesture which seemed to say, 'Oh, *that* stuff that I've always lived with like the air I've breathed'), '*Nobody's* been through what I've been through. Coming back home [after having spent many months in a psychiatric hospital some distance away] assuming Clara was going to share an apartment with me again, and then finding I was crazy, was an awful jolt to me.'

On the following day (forty-second hour), she continued to express more of this same feeling of shock, which had apparently been kept more or less completely out of awareness by her confused but persistent search for a more comfortable interpretation of these past incidents. She spoke again of the 'terrible shock when I came back home expecting to be invited into the Literary Club [a ladies' club whose membership represented the cream of local society] and found out that the idea was crazy.' She went on to say that for some time thereafter she felt like committing suicide, 'realizing that my social chances were *nil*'.

But then she went on (later in this same hour) to say that after a period of feeling intensely depressed and humiliated, 'I had another jolt, and realized that Paul [who was one of the most socially eligible of local bachelors in her home city] loves me.' She agreed that the second 'jolt' marked the beginning of her current view of the relationship with Paul–that she was going to marry him. Thus it was clear that, at this stage of the therapy, her optimistic delusion about Paul had by no means been resolved. But it seemed similarly clear that her so frequent confusion, which had been momentarily relinquished, enabling one to see what lay underneath, possessed the function of keeping out of her awareness feelings of, for instance, grief and despair.[12]

In the forty-fourth hour, she again manifested the twisted logic which, in an effort to circumvent feelings of rejection or some other variety of repressed affect, permeated her confused thinking generally. She was again describing having gone, uninvited, to Paul's office. 'He didn't see me when I went into the outer office. That was because he didn't think I was interested in him.'

But, by a week later, in the forty-eighth hour, she had become able to withdraw much of her confusion from this particular area of her living, and let herself see and experience much of the anger which had lain underneath: she said very angrily, 'Paul had his secretary kick me out! It was a God-damn sleazy trick! . . .' She then went on to refer, still, to future marriage to Paul, but in a fashion which was now a far cry from her former starry-eyed anticipation: 'If the marriage were unhappy I could get a

[12] In dealing with the case material concerning this patient, I have not attempted to show how confusion was serving a defensive function *in our relationship*, rather than exclusively in the patient herself. Certain points should be mentioned, however, regarding this more pervasive functioning of confusion in the transference-countertransference relationship:

(1) On many occasions I was aware that confusion was prominent not only in the patient but also in myself during the hours with her, although my confusion was at no time so subjectively overwhelming as hers frequently appeared to be.

(2) In retrospect I can see that the element of confusion in the transference-countertransference relationship was serving to protect not only the patient but also myself from the full awareness of, as examples: (*a*) the poignancy of some of the material she was expressing (such as that concerning her shock, upon returning to her home city from a distant psychiatric hospital, at finding that her long cherished expectation of acceptance into local society was a groundless delusion); and (*b*) the guilt, embarrassment, and remorse which I experienced much later on perusing my notes concerning this early part of the work with her, when it became apparent to me how often my participation in the therapy had a hostile motivation and a discouraging effect upon the patient's striving to get well.

(3) I was able to see in retrospect that my manner of participation in the relationship with her was of such a sort as to engender, or at least maintain, confusion in her. In particular, I think here of how often I felt under great pressure, because of her extraordinarily intense anxiety and her insistence upon my giving her reassurance to allay her anxiety, so that I found myself going much too fast with interpretative comments, touching upon many deeper lying conflicts which only served to increase her confusion and anxiety. I shall later make further comments on this last error, which the therapist who is dealing with a confused patient is liable to make.

Thus it seems clear how much the confusion under discussion here was a function of the *relationship* between the patient and myself, rather than a purely intrapsychic phenomenon within the patient. It is chiefly because of the extraordinary difficulty inherent in any attempt at a written description of relationship phenomena, that I am presenting the material from the work with Patient C in the admittedly fragmentary and much distorted, but far more simply utilizable, frame of reference in which her confusion is viewed as an intrapsychic phenomenon.

divorce. I think I could. I don't know. How do I know whether I'd be happy with him? I don't know much about Paul; I've never been with him very much.'

In the fiftieth hour she again evidenced her increasing ability to tolerate the feelings of anger which had been underlying her confusion. In reference to various of the socially prominent women in her home city, whom she had previously considered eager to have her join their ranks, she now said angrily, 'Well, to hell with those women if they don't want me in their club!'

In the ensuing several months, as she became more and more able to admit freely into awareness her feelings of hostility, disappointment, and grief, the confusion was less and less in evidence. Her increased freedom in expressing feelings of, for example, hostility is indicated by her angrily telling the charge nurse, during the ninth month of therapy (about six months after the fiftieth hour, mentioned above), 'Get away or I'll kill you!' During the same month, she said angrily to me on one occasion, 'I hate you!' and during her hours she often glared at me, with fists doubled, angrily demanding that I allow her to leave the sanatorium.

Her confusion was usually in evidence however, to some degree, and remained one of her major defences against intolerably great anxiety during particularly stressful phases of the therapy. Much later, in the twenty-fifth month of therapy, an unusually clear-cut instance of this functioning of her confusion occurred. She was lying quietly on the couch (which she had started to use sporadically many months previously), looking unprecedentedly calm and composed. I myself was feeling very close and tender towards her. After a few minutes of silence, she said quietly, 'I feel very near to my best friend [a term which – though she never could elucidate it specifically – was regularly used in a context which indicated that it referred to me], and yet Mr Smith [an attendant of whom she was both envious and fond] is very, very beloved to me, too.' She then turned her head towards the wall for several seconds, during which time I heard two distinct sobs. Not for many months – and then only very briefly – had she been able to express such feelings of grief and tenderness as seemed to be conveyed by these sobs.

She then turned her head back, again gazing at the ceiling with a quite composed, reflective expression, and began ruminating aloud in a tone devoid of any grief or tenderness, and reflective only of perplexity or moderate confusion, 'I was wondering how I'd feel if I worshipped two men equally – they say diametrically different things attract – and it's attractive to be cosmopolitan. . . . I don't like to be the subordinate. . . . I don't like to be the object of compassion – I wonder why that is? – You aren't supposed to tell anybody you have compassion for them –'

In the twenty-sixth month of therapy, she began to show more anxiety and agitation than she had shown in many months, often went out of the office on one excuse or another, and in one particular session seemed very hard put to it to keep from attacking me with a heavy bookend. On this occasion, she picked up the bookend from the bookcase in my office and held it for a while, silently examining its design with distinctly forced casualness. Many years before, she had threatened to kill her mother with a bookend; and there were abundant indications during this period of the therapy that she was largely engaged in trying to cope with highly ambivalent feelings towards me as a representative of her mother. I commented, 'You feel like hitting me with it. Let's hear about that.'

In reply, she said something about 'an earthquake shaking the ground – a fit of shaking – I had a lot of fits of shaking at home'. Presumably she was referring to fits of rage

At the next hour she came in, showing much the same degree of tension and agitation, immediately lay on the couch, and began pouring out, under great pressure and in a loud voice, an unceasing stream of ruminative statements whose content had to do with the qualities of various people's manner of walking. Often before, in periods of unusually intense anxiety, she had filled the hour with an unceasing, confused, and confusing salad of ruminations having to do with this subject – a salad containing so many neologisms and unusually constructed phrases that I was never able to note them down at any length after the session.

On this occasion, she had talked on this subject for about ten minutes – speaking in a tone which sounded as though she were trying to figure something out, and saying such things as, 'the left foot turned outward very slightly whenever it was put down, and this plus the very tiny roll of the right hip made things equal' – when she suddenly said in a hasty aside, her tone now not ruminative but desperate, 'I can't *tolerate* it here!' She then rapidly went on with her former salad of associations.

I asked, 'You can't tolerate it here?' having to speak loudly, for she did not pause. She replied, very intensely, 'This place frightens me and makes me feel wretched,' and immediately went on with her confusing associations. I asked, 'It frightens you and makes you feel wretched – any other thoughts about that?' She replied, 'They don't have any interest in me.' Several times during previous months she had been able to reveal a feeling that I was indifferent about her welfare. 'I used to think Bill [her brother] was interested in me,' she said, and went on to describe her brother as the only person she had talked to during her childhood; and she said something of how relieved she had felt upon being reassured by him.

Again she quickly went on with the musing about various persons' gaits. I said, 'You say Bill *used* to be interested in you, but you feel he lost interest in you? You mentioned a couple of days ago that Bill hasn't shown much interest in you recently.' This I had to half shout, and only in fragments, because she was now voicing her confusing ruminations very rapidly and in a very loud voice. Several times while I was saying the fragments of these last two sentences, she ordered me to be quiet and wait until she had finished. Refusing to listen to any other comments from me, she went on unceasingly for the remaining ten or fifteen minutes of the hour.

Here again the patient seemed to be utilizing the confused and confusing ruminations about the symbolism of various features of different persons' gaits, as a defence against any full and prolonged awareness of certain intolerable feelings (feelings, in this instance, presumably having mainly to do with her relationship with me). Significantly, when she was doing this ruminating, her full attention seemed to be taken up with it; I had the definite impression that this was a defence operating very largely at an unconscious level, rather than one consciously utilized to confuse me.

In concluding, I wish to emphasize that all the above-quoted remarks of Patient C were among the more rational and readily comprehensible of her verbal communications, which in far greater part were so replete with symbolically-used words, unusually constructed phrases, and neologisms that, as mentioned previously, I was never able to remember any lengthy samples of them after the hours. Since she objected strenuously to my proposed use of a recording machine, I never employed one. Fortunately, late in the period of my work with her she wrote a few letters to the attendant mentioned above. From one of these (written in the twenty-third month of therapy) I shall quote briefly, in order to convey more adequately how very confused was the ideation which had characterized her more anxious periods during the whole course of the therapy:

> . . . my side I advanced myself fawning did I show myself to good advantage about being GN child. there was focus only on PL hip from distance, was it very courtly of them not to chase me, or were they getting themselves stimulated for me now, shoes, etc., dont mean chase me in gender mean exhil., not assumed by them, LP backwards for pl. I don't see it, where does the return of what I've endured come, people were refined, so should I be angry at them for not discarding the thing, was it expected from you of them. I never then was assertive enough with PL, didn't give him the nod when should have, how could I help it if I thought I was doing the wise thing, not just to me. Lousy tramps if that true. What is the now, dont think they are really tramps. Ronald Coleman think related to son. so I guess focus on them. Please tell me what the now is. This is physically concerns me. I get exhilarating quiver from doing something considerate for people I worship, 2 why couldn't I forget RC. or wouldn't he allow it, was it essential. . . .

Repeated psychological tests during the period of my work with this patient indicated the presence of an organic element in addition to her schizophrenic illness; this was not surprising, in view of the abundance of insulin coma therapy (and the probable abundance of electro-shock therapy) which this patient had undergone in the past. It none the less seems clear that her confusion, even though possibly based partially upon organic changes, was serving a psychodynamic function. In this connexion, it may be useful to mention that my experience with patients who have purely functional illness, whether psychosis or neurosis, has borne out the thesis that confusion, in such cases also, serves the same general psychodynamic function as that portrayed in the case of Patient C.

Patient D was a 32-year-old single man of Italian descent who worked as a bricklayer. I saw him over a period of only about five months. He was an extremely suspicious person who, throughout his waking hours, perceived the outer world as intensely threatening by reason of his projecting upon it his own unconscious murderous feelings, and who divulged, in the course of the therapy, a number of typically paranoid delusions of persecution.

This man had an extremely unkempt, neglected appearance. He lived an extraordinarily isolated existence, in the scantily furnished attic of an uncle's home. He felt himself to be almost totally deprived of love and friendship; but he himself vigorously (though largely unconsciously) discouraged any social contacts between himself and the uncle or uncle's wife and two small children who lived on the floor below. Both at home and at his job, contacts between himself and other people were few indeed, and these few were looked upon by him at the time with great suspicion; he made a persistent attempt to find in the other person's behaviour evidence of hidden motivations, rather than allowing himself to participate in the contacts at all spontaneously.

I shall give only one clinical example of his suspicion, since I believe that this example will suffice to show that his suspicion served the same function as the other states I have described.

At the beginning of one hour, he was silent and extremely tense for a few moments and then said, in a low voice, 'Something happened the other day: my aunt's little girl called me "Smelly Joe". I started wondering where she had learned that name. I knew my aunt must have taught it to her. I don't like to go downstairs very much, because there are always a lot of people down there; so at night sometimes I piss in a bottle beside my bed. I wondered if that was the reason why my aunt called me that.'

I inquired, 'So your first reaction, when the little girl called you that, was that it set you to wondering?' He replied, 'Yes.'

I went on, 'You didn't first feel like swatting her?' He looked abashed and shocked at this, and said uncomfortably, 'No, I wouldn't want to swat a little girl.' Since on two or three occasions earlier in therapy he had been able to reveal some annoyance in relation to this little girl and her brother for pounding on his door, I asked, 'You *never* feel like swatting her?' He replied, quite emphatically, 'No.'

This seems to be a rather clear example of how his suspicion—his 'wondering'—served to keep under repression a degree of anger which he was unable to admit into his awareness. All the indications had pointed to the likelihood that his niece's calling him 'Smelly Joe' stirred up anger, which however remained unconscious. Rather than, for example, feeling immediately angry and telling her sharply that he did not like that name, he experienced promptly a suspicious wondering as to what had led her to call him by that name. From there he went on to construct an assumption that his aunt had taught the little girl that name, followed by an idea as to *why* his aunt had presumably taught her the name, so that he then was apparently able to reach, finally, a state of intrapsychic equilibrium in response to the original stimulus (namely, the cousin's addressing him by the offensive name).

Whereas an emotionally well-integrated person would have reached much earlier and much more satisfactorily a state of equilibrium by admitting into full awareness the feelings called up by the stimulus, this man reached a state of equilibrium only after a more or less complicated, uncomfortable process of suspicious 'figuring out why' the little girl had addressed him as she did. Moreover, the fact that his equilibrium was an incomplete one was indicated by his evidencing in an hour with me, at least a day later, a considerable degree of uncomfortable feeling about the incident.

Implications Regarding Psychotherapeutic Technique

The foregoing clinical material would seem to contain some general implications regarding psychotherapeutic technique. My own experience with approaches which have been useful, and approaches which have proved either useless or detrimental to the therapeutic process, has borne out the implications which I shall now touch upon.

First, the clinical material which has been presented above indicates that each of these several mental states represents a largely intellectual defence, with a conscious affective tone which is of low degree, serving to keep under repression various affects of intolerable intensity. It follows that if the therapist endeavours to deal with his patient's confusion, for example, by trying intellectually to 'figure out' some supposed order within the confusion itself, he will inevitably not only fail to achieve such a goal, but will in this effort miss what far more importantly needs his attention–the affect which is striving to break through the defence into the patient's awareness. In my own experience, I have repeatedly found that not until I had ceased to try to analyse intellectually the content of what a confused or perplexed patient was saying, and allowed myself to be emotionally receptive to the nuances of feeling conveyed by the patient (often in nonverbal ways), was I able to direct my efforts towards the patient's affect.

In dealing with these particular mental states, as with any other defence against anxiety, one may come to the point in therapy when one is able to discern that the patient's uncertainty, for example, is no longer constantly present and of relatively constant degree but is intermittent and distinctly fluctuating. It is at this point that the *timing* of its recrudescence or subsidence deserves primary attention. It can be an extremely valuable indicator of areas of remaining anxiety in the patient (or in the therapist, or in both participants).

The therapist's limiting his attention to the particular mental state itself, rather than allowing himself to relate to the underlying affect in the patient, can be not merely useless but can harmfully increase the feelings of futility with which so many neurotic and psychotic people are already heavily burdened. For example, in Patient B's oft-expressed uncertainty regarding the question of whether the Bureau of Internal Revenue would grant him a refund, the patient was clearly experiencing severe feelings of futility. It seemed evident that he had already made every possible effort to convince the Bureau of the justice of his case, and now felt he could do nothing but wait for their decision. At this stage of the therapy he was quite unable to recognize and explore the ambivalence of his wishes as to what their decision would be. As a result, whenever he brought up this matter he seemed to be feeling quite futile about it. Before I became relatively clearly aware of the defensive function of his uncertainty, I distinctly augmented his feelings of futility. When he would bring up this topic of the possible tax refund, rather than attending to the timing of its appearance during the hour and endeavouring to help him uncover the affects against which he was thus defending himself, I confined my remarks solely to this topic which was laden with uncertainty and futility for him. Then, as he and I went on dealing with this subject, which in reality must remain one of uncertainty until the Bureau reached a decision about it, we got repeatedly into a mutual state of futility, a final 'so what?' feeling of having reached a blind alley.

As I gradually became more and more aware that these topics appeared in the patient's reporting when he seemed to be approaching the recognition of some unconscious affect related often to the transference relationship, our talking ourselves into these blind alleys subsided.

On the other hand, one can press too vigorously towards the underlying affect, without sufficient regard for the anxiety which is being stirred up in the patient through the confrontation of his ego by this affect. In the following instance I paid not too much but rather too little attention to the defence in failing to recognize how urgently the patient needed to maintain that defence.

The patient with whom I found myself making this technical error (undoubtedly due in part to my own anxieties) was C. Within the first few weeks of therapy she began manifesting an unusually intense degree of overt anxiety along with her confusion, which latter had been prominent from the very beginning of my work with her. Hour after hour, she began pleading for, and finally more and more insistently demanding, reassurance from me that no harm would come to her. Then, with the conscious motive of endeavouring to relieve her intense anxiety, I entered into what I later realized to be the error of making interpretative remarks concerning various emotions which were detectable in her but were wholly or largely unconscious. For example, I repeatedly indicated, early in therapy when she was conscious of only positive feelings towards her boy-friend, how much rage and disappointment she must presumably be feeling in relation to him.

I did this with the idea in mind that her persistently mounting anxiety would subside if she only could admit into awareness these unconscious affects which were, I presumed, the major source of her anxiety. But my efforts had, as I later realized, quite the opposite effect, causing her anxiety to increase and her confusion (at the time her major defence against anxiety) to increase concomitantly.

It was not until several months of this had gone on that I came to recognize the anti-therapeutic effect of my 'pushing' her in this fashion. Now I began to respond to her confused but insistent demands for reassurance neither by offering verbal reassurance (which I had attempted a few times very early in the therapy, to no avail) nor by the 'pushing' which I have just described. Instead, I calmly sat silent much of the time, speaking only to encourage her to go ahead and express her feelings.

This changed kind of participation on my part had a distinctly beneficial effect: she went on, over the course of several hours, to get an increasingly strong anger expressed towards me for not reassuring her, and then began getting expressed the hurt and angry feelings, in relation to the boy-friend, which had been previously maintained under repression.

Incidentally, it can be seen from what has just been said that if the patient's confusion (or suspicion, uncertainty, and so on) is found to be increasing during the course of therapy, this may be an indication that the therapist is 'going too fast' in the manner I have just described. Thus, here again, the particular mental state in question is to be looked upon not as an inert or entirely useless or harmful product of the patient's psychopathology, but rather as a dynamic indicator of the quality of the therapist's current interpersonal integration with the patient.

Theory Concerning a Mode of Psychogenesis of Delusions

Lastly I shall introduce a subject which, in contrast to all the above material, I regard as more or less highly theoretical. This, namely, is a theory concerning one mode of psychogenesis of delusions.

In essence, I suggest that a delusion may represent an end result of a process in which the patient has previously been utilizing, as his major defences against anxiety, various of the mental states under discussion in this paper (perplexity, bafflement, uncertainty, confusion, suspicion), which defences in turn have required, in their functioning, such an intolerably complex pressure of thoughts that some form of relief through simplification of the thought processes is called for. This relief comes, I suggest, through the emergence of a delusion.

This process might be likened to the formation of a dream. That is, the relatively few elements which comprise a dream actually represent the condensed expression of a vast number of unconscious determinants. A second analogy is the emergence of a typical conversion symptom, which in the course of a long analysis can be found to represent the expression of remarkably numerous and complex intrapsychic conflicts.

But here, in contrast to the process involved in the evolution of the dream and to that involved in the genesis of the conversion symptom, there ensues (prior to the appearance of the delusion) *in awareness* a sense of intolerable complexity of thought, relief from which is desperately needed.

To see how this comes about, let us see what transpires in a patient whose major defence against anxiety is *suspicion*. The process which I shall now outline is, I believe, essentially the same in patients whose major defence is any one of the other four mental states under discussion in this paper.

It appears that the suspicious patient is unable to let himself spontaneously feel in awareness, from moment to moment in his living, anything like the full intensity of those affects which are engendered within him by either internal or external stimuli. Instead, when, for example, someone directs towards him a remark which would (if he were a better integrated person) stir up quick anger, the suspicious patient manages greatly to delay and dilute his own affective response–manages consciously to experience little or no anger, and at most to feel it very belatedly–by immediately focusing his attention in an intellectual way upon the remark made to him, searching for nuances and implications in an effort to find out 'why he said it' or 'what he meant by it'.

This process, if it leads at all to any feeling in the suspicious patient of having reached a satisfactory intellectual conclusion about the remark, takes at best a relatively long time to do so– days, months, or even years–by contrast to the probably few moments it would have required an emotionally well-integrated person to let himself experience in awareness the full intensity of the anger engendered by the remark and thereby to be able to move freely on past that particular interpersonal experience, unencumbered by it.

The suspicious patient, moreover, will undoubtedly be far from having achieved his complex and laborious 'resolution' of this particular interpersonal experience when his personality, now even somewhat less ready and resilient than it was before that experience, is confronted by a second stimulus. Let us say that this second stimulus comes, like the first, from without, but that this time it comes in the form of a sincerely fond look directed towards him by some third person, a few minutes after the previous interpersonal experience.

Now, unable to let himself admit into awareness the fond feelings which are (let us assume) responsively stirred up within him by the fond glance from this third person, and already busily engaged in trying to wall off by a meshwork of suspicion the affect engendered in his unconscious by the first experience, he has to become engaged simultaneously in a second complex network of suspicious thoughts concerning why the third person looked at him 'that way'.

Then, since life flows on, however incapable he is of letting himself emotionally flow with it, his personality will shortly have another external stimulus with which to cope, and then still another, and so on, with very likely many of these ensuing before even that which was first described has been successfully 'resolved'.

The suspicious patient is unable to escape such stimuli. No matter how isolated a life he lives, at least occasional interpersonal experiences, which confront him with external stimuli, are inevitable. And the threat of eruption into awareness of inner stimuli, in the form of repressed affects which continually seek entrance into his awareness, is ever present. Could the patient but realize it, his salvation lies in the full admission into awareness of these very affects, which are like outcasts who desire not only to be accepted but also to be useful. But to the suspicious patient they, like the outer stimuli, are felt as threatening, and the same bulwarks of suspicion are directed against them. Thus if our suspicious patient is quite schizoid indeed, or openly schizophrenic, he will meet the threatened awareness of sexual excitement with suspicions that someone is mysteriously, from a distance, causing him to experience electrical stimulation, localized in his genitals, for purposes which are in turn mysterious and therefore grounds for further suspicion.

If the patient is so openly disturbed as to have been admitted to the disturbed ward of a psychiatric hospital, the external stimuli which he encounters are now particularly copious and diverse. Even the relatively well-integrated person on the staff may at times find himself close to feeling overwhelmed on such a ward by the manifold evidences of grief and despair, of rage and hatred, of intense yearning to love and be loved. The suspicious patient, unable to let himself respond to these outer stimuli through conscious recognition of the feelings which they stir up in his unconscious, finds his major defence (his suspicion) very heavily taxed indeed.

It is well to note at this point the effect upon the patient if (say, in addition to his having to reside, because of the severity of disturbance of his behaviour, on the disturbed floor) he is so unfortunate as to have a therapist who does not realize how weak is the ego he possesses, in relation to the overwhelming power of the emotions which the patient is striving to keep under repression. Such a therapist, perhaps feeling impatient with the patient's relatively affectless verbalized suspicions, will attempt to go to the heart of the matter by questioning, commenting, and interpreting about repressed emotions in such a way that the inner stimuli with which the patient has defensively to cope are greatly increased. The result will be that the patient's suspicions will have to increase.

I might also remind the reader, as regards the external stimuli, that the patient is barraged (whatever his environment) not only with 'real' emotogenic stimuli–that is, stimuli which would stir up emotion in a psychologically healthy person–but also with stimuli which are emotogenic to the patient alone, by reason of symbolic values with which he endows them. For example, one patient whom I saw for some time on a disturbed ward found cause for anxious suspicion not only in the innumerable 'real' external stimuli coming to him from the patients and staff about him, but also in such ordinarily non-emotogenic circumstances as the particular timing of a patient's footsteps, the relative position of the dishes on his own food tray, the singing of birds in a distant tree, the shapes and relative positions of clouds in the sky, and so on *ad infinitum*. It appeared that to this patient's tortured thinking, *everything* his sense organs perceived had some anxiety- and suspicion-provoking significance.

In the literature, the best description I have seen of this sort of pressure of thought, which I consider likely to result from a snowballing of the defence of suspicion (or of any one of the other four mental states discussed in this paper), is found in Bleuler's monograph, *Dementia Praecox or the Group of Schizophrenias* (1911, p. 33). He reproduces a quotation from a patient of Forel:

> In my mind there ran like an endless clockwork a compulsive, torturing, uninterrupted chain of ideas. Naturally, they were not too sharply defined or clearly developed. There were joined idea upon idea in the most remarkable and bizarre series of associations although there was always a certain definite or inherent connexion from link to link. There was sufficient coherence or system to the whole so that I could always differentiate the light and shadowy side of things, people, actions, or spoken words which struck my interest. What ideas, what images have not tumbled around in my head! ... I always seemed to come back again and again to certain conceptions, to certain images which, now, however, I can hardly remember, e.g. France's Divine Right! Barbera! Rohan! They did seem to constitute steps in that racing train of thoughts; and I would speak out loud rapidly, like a pass word, the idea which my restless thoughts had just reached. I also used this means in order not to lose the threads and to maintain a certain control over the overwhelming, maddening, rushing train of thoughts. This was particularly necessary at certain periods of my daily life[13]—such as coming into a room, or when the door was opened, or on going to eat, when someone met me in the hall, etc.

In one who is experiencing such a pressure of thought, there is an increasingly intense need for simplification of the thought-processes. This need is satisfied, finally, by the emergence of the delusion (or, more often, of a number of delusions), for now the patient can feel '*This* [the delusion] is *so*; the rest is unimportant and can therefore be disregarded'. Later on, he may refer to this as the occasion when 'everything fell into place'.

Actually not 'everything' falls into place, not all the myriad thoughts which were rushing through his mind prior to the formation of the delusion. But the delusional pattern, having emerged like an island out of the sea of his confused thoughts, now provides something definite upon which his formerly scattered attention can be focused. Henceforth, he consciously registers only those external and internal stimuli which can

[13] Very probably at times of increase in the number of external emotogenic stimuli.

readily form ideational accretions to the delusional island. It is common clinical experience that those stimuli which do not 'fit in with' the delusion are consciously disregarded by the patient so that he is – at least consciously – quite untroubled by them.

The advent of the delusion results in a decrease in the former pressure of thought not only by the screening-out process just described, but also, and more importantly, by the fact that the pressure of thought is decreased through the patient's concomitant relinquishing of those formerly predominant defences in the form of confusion, suspicion, and so on – defences which by their very nature had given rise to the pressure of thought, in the fashion outlined above. Now, to the degree that these defences have been replaced by the delusion, the former wellspring of chaotic ideas has been turned off.

I do not suggest that the mode of psychogenesis of a delusion outlined above – with at first the utilization of such defences as confusion, suspicion, perplexity, and so on, then the consequent development of an increasingly disturbing pressure of thought, and finally the emergence of the delusion as a means of relieving this pressure of thought – holds true for all delusions. It may be that in many instances, particularly in acute psychoses, the ego is threatened with the sudden access into awareness of an overwhelmingly great intensity of affect, so that a delusional defence is immediately erected, without there having been utilized any preliminary defences in the form of suspicion, confusion, and so on, and hence without the patient's having experienced any such pressure of thought as that described above. But at least in my experience, it appears that the theoretical mode of formation of a delusion as outlined here does apply to those delusions which are manifested in the majority of patients with chronic psychoses.

Chapter 3

DEPENDENCY PROCESSES IN THE PSYCHOTHERAPY OF SCHIZOPHRENIA (1955)[1]

THERE is widespread agreement concerning the fundamental importance of dependency processes in schizophrenia.[2] For the patient who is involved in a schizophrenic illness, probably nothing is harder to endure than the circumstance of his having intense dependency needs which he cannot allow himself to recognize, or which if recognized in himself he dare not express to anyone, or which are expressed by him in a fashion that, more often than not, brings an uncomprehending or actively rejecting response from the other person. For the therapist who is working with such a patient, certainly there is nothing that brings more anxiety, frustration, and discouragement than do these processes in the schizophrenic person with whom he is dealing. This paper endeavours to delineate these processes in a fairly comprehensive fashion.

The dependency on which this paper is focused throughout is that which has its closest analogue, in terms of normal personality development, in the experience and behaviour of the infant or of the young child. The dependency needs, attitudes, and strivings which the schizophrenic manifests may be defined in the statement that he seeks for another person to assume a total responsibility for gratifying all his needs, both physiological and psychological, while this other person is to seek nothing from him.

Of the *physiological* needs which the schizophrenic manifests, those centring about the oral zone of interaction are usually most prominent, analogous to the predominant place held by nursing

---

[1] This paper is a product of my collaboration with Drs Frieda Fromm-Reichmann, Alberta B. Szalita-Pemow, Marvin L. Adland, and Donald L. Burnham in a weekly research seminar concerning the intensive psychotherapy of schizophrenia, during a period of ten months in 1952-3. To these four people I am indebted for many of the views which are expressed in this paper. It was first published in the *Journal of the American Psychoanalytic Association*, Vol. 3 (1955), pp. 19-66.

[2] See, for example, the work of Abrahams and Varon (1953), Brody and Redlich (1952), Bychowski (1952), Duhl (1951), Eissler (1943), Federn (1952), Knight (1946, 1953), Nunberg (1948), Rosen (1953), Schwing (1954), Sèchehaye (1951a), Steinfeld (1951), Sullivan (1925, 1953a), and Whitaker and Malone (1953).

in the life of the infant. Desires to be stroked and cuddled, like-wise so characteristic of the very early years of normal develop-ment, are also prominent in the schizophrenic. In addition, desires for the relief of genital sexual tensions, even though these have had their advent much later in the life history than have his oral desires, are manifested on much the same level of an early, infantile dependency. That is, such genital hungers are manifested in much the same small-child spirit of 'you ought to be taking care of this for me' as are the oral hungers.

The *psychological* needs which are represented among the schizophrenic's dependency processes consist in the desire for the other person to provide him with unvarying love and protection, and to assume a total guidance of his living.

In the course of this paper, further characteristics of the schizophrenic's dependency processes will be defined much more fully.

The points which will be offered here in regard to schizo-phrenia refer, with rare and specified exceptions, to schizo-phrenia in general, irrespective of diagnostic subtypes. That is, in my own experience the points which are to be put forward here possess validity in work with schizophrenic patients, whether of catatonic, paranoid, hebephrenic, or other diagnostic sub-divisions.

It is to be emphasized further that no one of the dependency processes here described is characteristic only of the schizo-phrenic, or qualitatively different from processes operative at some level of consciousness in persons with other varieties of psychiatric illness and in normal persons. With regard to de-pendency processes as well as with regard to other aspects of per-sonality functioning, we find that research in schizophrenia has its greatest potential value in the fact that the schizophrenic shows us in a sharply etched form that which is so obscured, by years of progressive adaptation to adult interpersonal living, in human beings in general. Thus I hope that this paper may be useful not only to workers in the field of the psychotherapy of schizophrenia, but in some degree also to other students of human experience and behaviour.

1. Sources of the Patient's Anxiety about His Dependency Needs

(*a*) As nearly as can be determined, the patient is unaware of pure dependency needs; for him, apparently, they exist in consciousness, if at all, only in the form of a hopelessly conflictual combination of dependency needs *plus* various defences–defences which render impossible any thoroughgoing or sustained gratification of these needs. These defences (which include grandiosity, hostility, competitiveness, scorn, and so forth) have so long ago developed in his personality, as a means of coping with the anxiety attendant upon dependency needs, that the experiencing of pure dependency needs is, for him, lost in antiquity and to be achieved only relatively late in therapy after the various defences have been largely relinquished.

Thus it appears to be not only dependency needs *per se* which arouse anxiety, but rather the dependency needs plus all these various defences (which tend in themselves to be anxiety-provoking) plus the inevitable frustration, to a greater or less degree, of the dependency needs.[3]

Hostility was mentioned above as one of the defences against awareness of dependency needs. Certainly repressed dependency needs are one of the most frequent bases of murderous feelings in the schizophrenic; in such instances the murderous feelings may be regarded as a vigorous denial of dependency. What frequently happens in therapy is that both patient and therapist become so anxious about the defensive murderous feelings that the underlying dependency feelings long remain unrecognized.

Every schizophrenic possesses much self-hatred and guilt which may serve as defences against the awareness of dependency feelings ('I am too worthless for anyone possibly to care about me'), and which in any case complicate the matter of dependency. The schizophrenic has generally come to interpret the rejections in his past life as meaning that he is a creature who wants too much and, in fact, a creature who has no legitimate needs. Thus he can accept gratification of his dependency needs, if at all, only if his needs are rendered acceptable to himself by reason of his becoming physically ill or in a truly desperate

---

[3] So far as I have been able to determine, this principle applies to other repressed affects as well as dependency needs—namely, that what is anxiety-provoking is the repressed affect *plus* the attendant defences. Szalita-Pemow (1952) touched upon this principle in a limited sense in saying, 'While the term regression is used primarily to designate a definite defence mechanism, I consider that regression in its main structure is what we defend ourselves against.'

emotional state. It is frequently found that a schizophrenic is more accessible to the gratification of his dependency needs when he is physically ill, or filled with despair, than at other times. Thus, because of the presence of self-hatred, and guilt, one ingredient of the patient's over-all anxiety about dependency needs has to do with the fact that these needs connote to him the state of feeling physical illness or despair.

In essence, then, we can see that the patient has a deep-seated conviction that his dependency needs will not be gratified. Further, we see that this conviction is based not alone on unfortunate past experience of repeated rejections, but also on the fact that his own defences, called forth concomitantly with the dependency desires, make it virtually certain that his dependency needs will not be met.

(b) The dependency needs are anxiety-provoking not only because they involve desires to relate in an infantile or small-child fashion (by breast- or penis-sucking, being cuddled, and so forth) which is not generally acceptable behaviour among adults, but also, and probably more importantly, because they involve a feeling that the other person is frighteningly *important*, absolutely indispensable to the patient's survival.

This feeling as to the indispensable importance of the other person derives from two main sources: (a) the regressed state of the schizophrenic's emotional life, which makes for his perceiving the other as being all-important to his survival, just as in infancy the mothering one is all-important to the survival of the infant; and (b) certain additional handicapping features of his schizophrenic illness, which render him dependent in various special ways which are not quite comparable with the dependency characteristic of normal infancy or early childhood.

I shall now mention a number of points in reference to source (b) above.

First, we can perceive that a schizophrenic who is extremely confused, for example, is utterly dependent upon the therapist (or other significant person) to help him establish a bridge between his confusion and reality.

Second, we can see also that the patient who is in transition between old, imposed values and not-yet-acquired values of his own, has only the relationship with his therapist to depend upon.

Third is the consideration that, in many instances, the schizophrenic appears to be what one might call a prisoner in the present. He is so afraid both of change and of the memories which tend to be called forth by the present that he clings desperately to what is immediate. He is in this sense imprisoned in immediate experience, and looks to the therapist to free him so that he will be able to live in all his life, temporally speaking—present, past, and future.

Fourth, it might be surmised that an oral type of relatedness to the other person (with the all-importance of the other which this entails) is necessary for the schizophrenic to maintain, partly in order to facilitate his utilization of projection and introjection as defences against anxiety. Bychowski (1952, p. 79) says, 'The separation between the primitive ego and the external world is closely connected with orality; both form the basis for the mechanism which we call projection' (and, I would add, for introjection). Stärcke (1921) earlier commented, 'I might briefly allude to the possibility that in the repeated alternation between becoming one's own and not one's own, which occurs during lactation, there lies . . . a path for the later psychic process of projection . . . the situation of being suckled plays a part in the origin of the mechanism of projection.'

(c) The patient has anxiety lest his dependency needs lead him either to take in harmful things, or to lose his identity.

The schizophrenic does not have the ability necessary to tolerate the frustration of his dependency needs so that he can, once they emerge into awareness, subject them to mature discriminatory judgement before seeking their gratification. Instead, like a voraciously hungry infant, his tendency is to put into his mouth (either literally or figuratively) whatever is at hand, whether nutritious or harmful. This tendency is thus at the basis of some of his anxiety concerning his dependency needs, for he fears that they will lead him blindly into receiving harmful medicines, bad advice, electro-shock treatment, lobotomy, and so forth. Schizophrenic patients have been known to beg, in effect, for all these, and many a patient has been 'successful' in obtaining a remarkably long series of such supplies in response to his dependency desires. A need for self-punishment is, of course, an additional motivation in such instances.

A statement by Fenichel (1945, p. 39) is relevant here: 'The pleasure principle, that is the need for immediate discharge, is incompatible with correct judgement, which is based on consideration and postponement of the reaction. The time and energy saved by this postponement are used in the function of judgement. In the early states the weak ego has not yet learned to postpone anything.'

The paranoid position, in which the environment is seen as totally rejecting, has as one of its functions that it enables one to avoid seeing the totally devouring quality of one's dependency needs. This urge to devour is anxiety-provoking not only because it threatens to lead one to destroy other people,[4] but also because one fears that if one takes in too much, one will no longer be oneself—one's identity will be lost. And this anxiety is augmented, moreover, by the schizophrenic's tendency to identify unconsciously with other persons in the environment as a way of keeping out of awareness various emotions stirred up by those other persons. It should be noted that, in so far as the patient utilizes this latter type of defence against anxiety, his fear that he will lose his identity if he comes too close, emotionally, to another person (and dependency needs tend, of course, to bring one closer to the other person) is a realistic fear. It is common to find schizophrenic patients helplessly identifying with various behaviour traits of people around them.[5]

In the same vein, one finds that to the extent that the schizophrenic projects on to other persons his own needs to suck and to devour, he feels threatened with being devoured by these other persons.

To elaborate now in a somewhat different direction upon this fear of loss of identity: the schizophrenic fears that his becoming dependent on another person will lead him into a state of conformity to that other person's wishes and life values. A conformer is almost the last sort of person the schizophrenic wishes to become, since his sense of individuality resides in his very eccentricities. He assumes that the therapist (for example) will not allow him to enter into a state of dependency without, in the process, requiring him to give up his individuality. All too often,

---

[4] A variation of this is the anxiety of the patient lest he pull the therapist into his own dangerous world. Fromm-Reichmann has presented material about this (1952, p. 105).
[5] Robert Bak (1949) has presented some interesting material concerning the dissolution of the ego boundaries in schizophrenia.

this is the kind of price which the parental figures in his past have attempted to exact from him, and whatever healthy ego he has been able to salvage has refused to pay this price.

Many schizophrenics are all the more ready to assume that dependency entails such a kind of automaton-like conformity because they confuse genuine dependency with a kind of pseudo-dependency, based largely on unconscious hostility, in which the person manifests a puppet-like obedience in lieu of becoming aware of hostility towards the other person. Many schizophrenics have had the experience either of finding themselves engaged in such behaviour, or of seeing such behaviour manifested by one or another parent. They tend then to label such behaviour as dependency and to avoid it like the plague. They cannot conceive of the dependent state as being one in which they can retain the ability to exercise discriminatory judgement and to initiate action.

(*d*) The other person – the object of the dependency strivings – is perceived as hostile and rejecting. There are several bases for this, in addition to the obvious consideration that the parental figures in the schizophrenic's past life have often met his dependency manifestations with hostility.

First, the schizophrenic commonly projects upon the other person (the therapist, let us say) his own hostility. When we consider that frustrated dependency needs are probably the major source of hostile feelings, we can see how much the working through of the dependency needs is complicated by this element of projection. If the dependency needs are deeply repressed, the frustration anger is likewise so successfully repressed that it need not be dealt with by projection on the therapist, and the patient can succeed in viewing the therapist as being of about the same order of importance to him as a spot on the wallpaper. But as the dependency needs come, in the course of therapy, closer to the patient's awareness, the frustration anger associated with them also comes to the fore, and in so far as this latter has to be projected upon the therapist, the latter is then viewed as a hostile person on whom it would be folly to depend. This sequence of processes is often reflected in the course of psychotherapy in which the patient commonly brings his dependency feelings into the open precisely after a particularly stormy period during which he had been convinced that the therapist was oriented thoroughly against him.

In actuality, it is probably more accurate to say that the schizo-phrenic tends to project, at any one moment during the thera-peutic hour, either his hostility *or his positive feelings* (tender, friendly, loving feelings) upon the therapist. The ambivalence of the schizophrenic is so great, and the need so great to keep the hostile feelings and the positive feelings from coming into aware-ness simultaneously, that the schizophrenic tends to perceive the therapist as being in the nature of someone approximating to either a devil or a saint, depending upon whether the hostile or the positive side of the ambivalent feelings is being projected.

Rosenfeld (1950), writing of confusional states in chronic schizophrenias, says, 'The confusional state is associated with ex-treme anxiety, because when libidinal [positive] and destruc-tive impulses become confused, the destructive impulses seem to threaten to destroy the libidinal impulses. Consequently the whole self is in danger of being destroyed.'

In my experience, the schizophrenic is equally afraid that the hostile side of his ambivalent feelings will be destroyed by the positive (libidinal) side. When we consider that the patient's potentially healthy self-assertiveness is bound up in the hostile feelings, this fear becomes quite understandable.

So then, the schizophrenic's ambivalence, his need to keep his hostile feelings and his positive feelings from simultaneous aware-ness lest either destroy the other and so destroy the self, is one source of his anxiety about his dependency needs. He cannot expect to gain satisfaction for his human dependency needs from someone so distant and other-worldly as either a devil or a saint.

A second basis for the schizophrenic's perceiving the therapist as hostile and rejecting is to be found in the patient's suspicion. He has such a degree of suspicion that he cannot believe that the therapist will give him anything without there being an ulterior motive behind the gift. He fears that this suspicion, accompany-ing his dependency needs, will be perceived by the therapist and reacted to with resentment.

Third, to the schizophrenic there is no distinction between feel-ing and acting, in the sense that he assumes that a dependency desire on his part, for instance, to suck the therapist's breasts or penis will inevitably lead him to attempt this in action. He senses that the therapist would react with hostility to such a move.

Fourth, he projects upon the therapist his own tendency to

reject dependency needs. It is to be emphasized that the schizophrenic is a person who has a tendency to be severely rejecting of dependency needs not only in himself but also in others, for various reasons: (a) the other person's dependency needs are so reminiscent of his own that he has to react against them with hostile rejection, because of the anxiety they create in him; (b) he often feels so starved and empty himself that he cannot bear to give; (c) he assumes the other person's gain to represent, automatically, a loss to himself; and (d) throughout his life he has felt his position to be so insecure that he has been afraid to release hostility except when the other person has been dependent upon him—so, at least with many schizophrenics, the rejection of a dependent other person has been the most frequent means of consciously discharging hostility. This rejectingness of his own the schizophrenic projects upon the therapist; hence he assumes that if he allows himself to become dependent, the therapist will vengefully reject him.

Fifth, and closely related to the factor just described, the schizophrenic projects on to the therapist his own undependability in interpersonal relations. There is probably no person more undependable than the schizophrenic, who for a variety of excellent reasons (having to do with his ambivalence and his great anxiety about interpersonal intimacy) cannot be depended upon to make consistent and determined efforts towards the maintenance of an interpersonal relationship. The schizophrenic attributes to the therapist, by projection, his own undependability and assumes that the therapist will let him down.

Sixth, the schizophrenic has so much guilt feeling associated with his hostility that, in order to justify the hostility, he strives to prove that the therapist is depriving, neglectful, and generally hostile towards him. This striving, of course, interferes greatly with his dependency strivings.

Seventh, he assumes that his own dependency needs on the one hand, and the therapist's on the other, are mutually exclusive; he cannot conceive of a collaborative relatedness from which both persons derive satisfaction simultaneously. He assumes that anything he obtains from the therapist will foster feelings of deprivation and hostility in the therapist.

Eighth, he (particularly if he is strongly paranoid) cannot let himself be aware that he really needs anything from anyone, cannot allow himself to feel that he gets anything really valuable from anyone, and hence anything which the therapist (for example) asks of him makes him feel that he is being exploited. This same feeling has an additional basis in the total, or almost total, absence of any sense of personal worth. The latter quality, strongly characteristic of all schizophrenics, makes it impossible for one to entertain the possibility that the therapist has one's *own* welfare in mind.

Ninth, he is likely to be so unable to communicate his thoughts and feelings, in general, in a sufficiently understandable fashion so as to make his need known to the other person. In such an instance, satisfaction for the need is impossible and, even more painful to him, its very existence will go unacknowledged despite his efforts to communicate it.[6]

(*e*) His repressed dependency needs are closely associated with his repressed feelings of loneliness; so his recognition of the dependency needs brings with it a devastating realization of how terribly alone he is.

Probably there is no greater threat to the schizophrenic than the repressed knowledge of his aloneness, the realization that he, who yearns so strongly for oneness with another person, not only has the same inevitable aloneness as every human being, but in addition is even more completely cut off from his fellow human beings by reason of his isolation within his schizophrenic illness.

A deeply psychotic young male patient was able to tell his therapist after several months of intensive psychotherapy, 'I feel as though I'm on a deserted frontier.' One might speculate that, earlier, he had felt not even this tenuous contact with civilization, so to speak – had felt even more alone; still earlier, his schizophrenic symptoms (delusions, hallucinations, and so on) may have protected him from the awareness of his loneliness.

I have never found a more moving expression of the loneliness within the schizophrenic who is overtly convinced that he needs nothing from anyone, than is conveyed in a poem composed at about the age of eighteen, during a schizophrenic illness, by Eithne Tabor (1950):

> Break, crested waves;
> On the sheer cliff of onyx break
> In wild foam – and fall back, powerless.

---

[6] This point has been found to be of much operational importance in the management of a disturbed ward, as reported by Schwartz, Schwartz, and Stanton (1951).

Lash, O wild winds,
'Gainst the unbending oak, aye, lash
In high fury—it is feelingless.

Beat, O deep drums,
Thunder your message fearsome—beat
Your dark rhythms—into soundlessness.

Speak, O strong Voice,
Speak peace, security—aye, speak!
Only You can fill this loneliness.

(f) In so far as the schizophrenic becomes aware of his dependency needs, he must relinquish the fantasied omnipotence which serves as a defence against manifold anxieties, and provides him with tremendous gratification in itself. The importance of this gratification (even though it lies within the realm of fantasy), and the importance of the very real feelings of loss which the patient must undergo in the relinquishing of his infantile omnipotence, should not be underestimated. This position of infantile omnipotence is untenable when the patient reaches an awareness of the intensity of his dependency needs; an omnipotent god does not have needs.

Certain speculations concerning the early development of the future schizophrenic are rendered highly plausible by the evidence which intensive psychotherapy with schizophrenics produces in regard to the relationships between dependency needs and fantasied (i.e. infantile) omnipotence.

In normal development, it appears that gradually, during infancy and very early childhood, the subjective omnipotence which seems to exist in that phase of life is gradually relinquished, concomitantly with a fortunate, continuing experience of reasonable gratification and reasonable frustration of the dependency needs, such that the child grows towards a fairly accurate awareness of his own real power and of the limitations upon it. It is as though he can clearly see that he is not omnipotent, specifically because of the fact that he has *needs* for which he is *unable*— impotent—to acquire instant and full gratification.

It is widely accepted that, in normal development, the phase of infantile omnipotence is succeeded, in infancy or very early childhood, by a conception of the mothering person as being omnipotent.[7] Silverberg (1953) has emphasized that this provides for a continuing subjective feeling of omnipotence on one's own part: in so far as one can manipulate this omnipotent mothering figure, one is omnipotent.

Now, as regards the early development of the future schizophrenic, it seems likely that the infantile omnipotence is perpetuated and elaborated as later development proceeds, for two main reasons. (a) The normal dependency needs of infancy and early childhood meet with unendurably intense and prolonged feelings of frustration, so that the needs themselves have to become more or less repressed, and the initially normal feeling of omnipotence is greatly strengthened to form a defence against the awareness of dependency needs–in effect, a denial of the needs. (b) The mothering figure has never relinquished her own infantile omnipotence, feels therefore that she should be able to satisfy all the child's needs, feels guilty whenever she does not do so, and thereby conveys to the child the impression that the mothering figure is omnipotent and that he, as her child, an extension of her, is also potentially omnipotent if he could only 'get the combination'.

In relation to (b) above, we can see how the 'omnipotent', guilt-ridden parent fosters in the child an expectation of receiving, in effect, the whole world as his rightful due. Thus the patient's normal dependency strivings have had added to them limitless grandiose demands for which, in the light of his own upbringing, he has a quite reasonable right to expect gratification.

Such a parent has, by the same token, behaved possessively towards the child, has given the child to feel that he must turn his dependency strivings towards no one other than this parent. The parent who has not relinquished her (or his) own infantile omnipotence cannot bear to find that the child's dependency needs can be better fulfilled by someone other than herself, as would inevitably be seen if the child felt free to turn his dependency needs towards all available persons in his environment. A more emotionally secure parent would assume that other persons in her child's life are often better equipped, or in a better position, to meet the child's dependency needs, and would help the child to feel that it is thoroughly acceptable to turn to them.

[7] See Fenichel (1945, p. 40).

But as regards the child of this other kind of parent previously described, we see that the infantile omnipotence is perpetuated and becomes firmly entrenched for the additional reason that it serves as a defence for the child against the anxiety engendered by the parent's possessiveness. Save for this fantasied omnipotence, the child might feel utterly at the mercy of the possessive parent.

With such a child, as later in the adult schizophrenic, the dependency demands and strivings which are manifested are probably voiced much more in the service of the pathological grandiosity–which is, of course, insatiable–than in the service of such basically normal dependency needs as those for physical closeness, for gratification of physiological hungers, for guidance, and so forth. It is as if the schizophrenic were saying, 'If you would only give me enough, then I could assume my rightful position of omnipotence in the Universe,' rather than simply, 'I need you as a little child needs its mother.'

It should be clearly seen how very much the fantasied omnipotence interferes with the patient's obtaining whatever gratification is available for his ordinary, normal human dependency needs. He is so caught up in grandiose expectations of himself and of the therapist (for example) that his basic, normal dependency needs are very thoroughly warded off, as either being of no importance or posing a great threat to his fantasied omnipotence. Many an aloof schizophrenic patient, caught up in grandiose fantasies, seems to be conveying by his manner, 'What need could *I* have for closeness with *you*, a mere human being?' We can often find abundant evidence that such a patient has had, during his developmental years, a relationship with a parent in which each was so involved in grandiose conceptions, of himself and of the other person, that the relationship involved very little gratification for the basic dependency needs of either individual.

So, in the therapy of the adult schizophrenic, we find that as his dependency needs become manifested they (*a*) can be found to include not only basically normal dependency strivings, but also, and very prominently, grandiose strivings (demands for the therapist to help one become the world's greatest scientist, or painter, or what not); and (*b*) all these strivings (those referable to normal dependency needs plus those having an infantile-omnipotence basis) become focused exclusively upon the therapist. To be sure, the patient actually does receive partial gratification of his dependency needs from other people, but from the viewpoint of his infantile omnipotence he strives to make the therapist alone gratify all of them, because were he to face the facts that he is *unable* to make the therapist gratify all of them and that the therapist is inherently *unable* to gratify all of them, his conception of both himself and the therapist as omnipotent would have to be relinquished.

2. The Patient's Ways of Dealing with his Dependency Needs in Therapy

In an effort further to delineate the processes under discussion, let us now examine them in terms of how the patient deals, in the therapeutic relationship, with his dependency needs. In what follows, it is assumed that his 'dealing with' them operates at a level which is completely, or very largely, unconscious.

What perhaps deserves first mention is the schizophrenic's very prevalent *projection* of his dependency needs upon the therapist. The patient functions much of the time in such a way as to make it clear that he feels the therapist, not himself, to be the one who has the greater, or even the only need. He may behave solicitously towards the therapist, offer sympathy, exhibit the manner of a host towards a guest, or–very often–show great anxiety at what he feels to be the therapist's demands upon him. His ego boundaries are so very fluid that if the therapist, in an effort to encourage him to express his dependency needs, speaks of such needs in the patient, the patient is very prone to assume that it is the therapist's needs which are being expressed and may then anxiously shy away from the subject. I wish to emphasize that all this may, and very often does, hold true by reason of the schizophrenic's innate psychopathology, without being in any major part attributable to countertransference–although, as will be pointed out in the next section of this paper, all this will be greatly complicated if the therapist is actually largely repressing his own dependency needs and the schizophrenic is then responding, not so much projectively as realistically, to these needs in the therapist.

In line with the above considerations about projection, a schizophrenic may maintain a vigorous, incessant demandingness towards the therapist as a means of defending himself from supposed (i.e. patient-projected) demands by the latter.

Second to be mentioned are the patient's *competitiveness and contempt* towards the therapist, both of these feeling states often functioning as unconscious defences against the dependency needs. For instance, rather than consciously experiencing how greatly he needs the therapist, the patient may strive to prove that he is a better therapist (better mother or father) than the therapist.[8] Or he may exhibit such intense scorn towards the therapist as to make it clear that he feels the latter to be beneath competition. Such scorn serves to help him keep his dependency needs under repression, for who could possibly feel any need for so worthless a creature as the therapist? Incidentally, a very full awareness of the prevalence of this defence can be extremely helpful to the therapist's maintenance of his own self-esteem in the face of the persistent and prolonged buffeting to which it is subjected in the course of therapy with schizophrenic patients.

To the same category belong *awe* and *adoration* of the therapist, which may serve the same function for the schizophrenic as does contempt, placing the therapist at such a distance that the patient's dependency needs are hindered from being consciously directed towards the therapist. In my patients I have seen these latter two defensive feeling states much less frequently than I have found competitiveness or contempt.

In the history of many a schizophrenic patient, we find evidence that he reacted to severe frustration of his dependency needs by the development of a secondary, defensive grandiosity, which in turn led him, as his development proceeded, into esoteric and highly learned hobbies and career activities. These activities were of a sort in which the parent figures, so important in terms of his repressed dependency needs, could not possibly be expected to be able to participate with him. There has been, such a history shows, a progressive process of his isolating himself

---

[8] One wonders whether the term 'competitiveness' is accurate here. Perhaps what feels to the therapist like competitiveness is, from the viewpoint of the schizophrenic, more a matter of his being unable to conceive of any other than two possible roles in living, that of infant and that of mother, so that in so far as he strives to avoid or to grow beyond the role of infant, he must operate as a mother. There is in the background of so many schizophrenic patients such a close symbiotic relationship between patient and mother person, that this explanation seems more likely.

in such activities more and more, feeling consciously more and more scornful of his benighted parents, and unconsciously becoming more and more starved as regards his basic dependency needs towards them. In such a case, the defensive grandiosity finally has to become so predominant that a frank schizophrenic psychosis ensues.

To return to the therapeutic relationship, a third consideration to be emphasized is that the schizophrenic patient is unable to conceive of gratification (for his dependency needs) in terms of long-range, adult, experiential (emotional-intellectual) gratification; what he feels a need for instead is immediate, concretely tangible gratification of his infantile (largely physiological) hungers. It is inevitable, then, that he will quickly find that the awareness of needs will lead to intense dissatisfaction with the therapist, for the therapist's major potential usefulness lies in the realm of very long-range gratification of an impalpable and relatively abstract sort. Specifically, psychotherapy is not a tangible thing, it is not easy for anyone to develop a clear conception of what it actually is—and it is quite impossible for a schizophrenic to perform such a conceptual feat; and psychotherapy is, finally, a process which generally takes a long time to yield major results in terms of the gratification of the patient's urgent dependency needs.

One pertinent consideration here is that many a schizophrenic possesses, certainly at the beginning of psychotherapy, far too much hopelessness about himself for him to be able to perceive the therapist as someone who holds out any strong hope that he, the patient, may be able, with the therapist's aid, to establish a far more satisfying way of life. He can believe that the therapist may give him a cigarette or a key to the door, or may side with him against the persecutors, but of this other he cannot conceive.

Fourth, the patient may keep his greatest needs under repression by means of experiencing in awareness, and expressing, other needs which are thus of a defensive nature and which one might call irrelevant. Often a patient will, for instance, make numerous requests for the therapist to perform for him various functions which he, the patient, is quite able to do himself (such as finding an ashtray, or asking the nurse for some fruit juice), whereas the same patient will vigorously resist becoming dependent upon the therapist's therapeutic functions which he, the patient, is unable to carry out himself.[*] The former kind of requests do not carry the threat of any real dependency of the kind which would be connoted by his conscious recognition of the therapist's therapeutic importance to him. Of course, at times these requests by the patient may represent tentative, preliminary efforts to bring forward more important but at least partially *conscious* needs for the therapist's therapeutic functions. Only a therapist's intuition can help him to know, in any given situation, whether the satisfying of a patient's request for a concrete gratification would further the expression of the deeper-lying needs, or whether on the other hand it would turn the focus away from them. This matter will be dealt with more fully in the final section of this chapter.

In other instances, the deeper-lying (repressed) need may be of a relatively infantile nature, and hidden behind an overt request for an adult type of gratification. For instance, the patient may beg the therapist to allow him to return home and take up an (overtly) adult life, while at the moment he is striving to keep under repression a desire to sit on the therapist's lap and be cuddled.

Fifth, whenever the patient does consciously express dependency needs, he tends to present them in some fashion which precludes their gratification by the therapist. For instance, he may beg the therapist to do something which it is not within any human being's capacity to do; or he may present a request just at a time when he has been making the therapist so infuriated with him that he is vigorously disinclined, at that moment, to accede to any request from the patient; or he may plead with the therapist to do something for him which, if done, could only have the connotation that the patient is, in the therapist's estimation, a less capable person than he actually considers him to be. A frequent example of the last-mentioned type is when the patient asks the therapist to bring some near-lying item to him, just at a moment when the therapist feels it important for the patient to find within himself the capability to do this. At such a moment, then (and only the therapist's intuition can tell him what is useful to do at a particular moment), the therapist may find that

[*] The patient has especially intense anxiety at recognizing how dependent he is upon the therapist's sheer *presence*.

to serve the best interests of the patient's therapy, he must refuse the request.

This matter of soliciting rejection serves several functions for the patient. (a) It reassures him that life is, for him, just as he has always—or at any rate for a very long time—known it to be. We must not forget that whereas new experience tends to be disconcerting to a neurotic, it tends to be frightening to a schizophrenic. (b) In at least one respect it would be a greater source of anxiety to the schizophrenic to obtain some gratification than to obtain none. Any gratification he might get would be only partial, since no human needs are ever gratified both thoroughly and consistently, and certainly the schizophrenic's dependency needs, with the grandiose elements which complicate them, are not. So a little gratification is all too apt to affect the schizophrenic as a crumb would affect a starving man, making him even more keenly aware of the intensity of his hunger. Thus a total rejection is, to the schizophrenic, in a sense more tolerable. (c) Any conscious conflict about dependency is temporarily put out of mind by a rejection from the therapist. This I shall immediately explain.

The patient may be in a state of conscious, extremely distressing conflict between desires to be dependent upon the therapist and strong desires to avoid this at all cost. If he can then 'succeed' in feeling rejected by the therapist, the distressing conflict is, at least for the moment, no longer occupying his conscious thoughts: he is now fully absorbed in wholehearted, consciously unambivalent, resentment or hurt feeling about the therapist.

3. Manifestations of Anxiety in the Therapist with Regard to His Own and the Patient's Dependency Needs[10]

Up to this point we have been discussing the *patient's* anxiety with regard to his dependency needs, and his unconscious defences against this anxiety as we find them operative in the therapeutic relationship. We shall now concern ourselves with the *therapist's* anxiety about the dependency needs in the patient and, basic to this, his anxiety about his own infantile and early childhood dependency needs.

While the following comments pertain especially to the therapist

[10] This section, modified and somewhat abbreviated, was read at the Midwinter Meeting of the American Psychoanalytic Association, New York, December 1953.

who has had little or no personal analysis and who has had little experience in the therapy of schizophrenics, I wish to emphasize that any therapist, however well analysed and long experienced in this field, is likely to evidence, at some phase in the course of his work with one or another of these difficult patients, some of the characteristics of the anxiety-ridden therapist to be described below.

For a number of reasons, therapy with schizophrenic patients tends, even more than does the analysis of neurotic patients, to stimulate anxiety in the therapist with regard to dependency needs.

First, both the schizophrenic's dependency needs and his anxiety about them are greater than are those of the neurotic.

Second, the schizophrenic has, usually, very strong identifications with the early mother. These identifications become manifest in therapy as strong maternal qualities which tend to call forth infantile dependency feelings in the therapist.[11] If the therapist is prone to experience anxiety with regard to such feelings in himself, he is then particularly likely to undergo such anxiety in this field of psychotherapeutic endeavour.

Third, the schizophrenic has such an inability to make distinctions among thinking, feeling, and acting that he tends to express his dependency needs in seeking for physical contact. This is much more likely to stir up anxiety in the therapist than is the neurotic's *verbalized wish*, for instance, to suck the analyst's penis or breast.

Fourth, because the therapy of a schizophrenic usually requires a much longer time than does the analysis of a neurotic, the therapist is faced with a relationship in which the patient's dependency will be not only more intense but also longer-lasting, even if the therapy goes well.

Fifth, if the therapy is taking place within a hospital setting,

[11] Ruth W. Lidz and Theodore Lidz (1952) offer an interesting discussion of the symbiotic needs of schizophrenic patients in relation to therapy. A portion of their summary shows the theme of the article: 'A developmental problem common to many schizophrenic patients, the symbiotic relationship to a parent who utilizes the patient to complete her own life, has been related to some of the problems of maintaining a therapeutic relationship in a manner that can lead to a successful outcome. The problems stressed revolve around the passive seeking for a new protecting figure who is not only necessary to the patient but for whom the patient is essential.' Abrahams and Varon (1953), in their volume describing the course of events in a therapeutic group comprised of schizophrenic daughters and their mothers, describe this same symbiotic relatedness in rich detail.

the therapist is under a special kind of pressure: the patient's level of daily-life interpersonal functioning is clearly there for all his colleagues, upon whose esteem he is to a degree realistically dependent, to see. This situation often places a considerable burden upon the therapist in the process of working with a patient who is loudly proclaiming (often most effectively in non-verbal ways) how utterly uncaring his therapist is.

Now I shall mention briefly those vulnerabilities which the therapist himself brings into the relationship with his schizophrenic patient, vulnerabilities to anxiety about dependency needs. My main effort is to describe various indicators of the presence of such anxiety in the therapist, rather than to explain why this anxiety is present in him. Very briefly, then, it can be said that the therapist is vulnerable to experiencing such anxiety in proportion as (a) he has to maintain under repression his own infantile and early-childhood dependency needs; (b) he has to retain the fantasied omnipotence which dates from the same early period of his life as do his repressed dependency needs, namely, infancy and early childhood; and (c) he has not yet developed confidence in his therapeutic technique in this field.

The therapist's own difficulty here possesses, on the other hand, a most valuable facet. There is much evidence to indicate that it is this very problem with regard to infantile and early-childhood dependency needs which forms one of the strongest motivations, in therapists, for undertaking this kind of work and for persisting in it.[12]

The manifestations of anxiety in the therapist will be presented in two categories: his compulsion to be helpful, and his failing to hear, or actively discouraging, the patient's expression of dependency needs.

THE THERAPIST'S COMPULSION TO BE HELPFUL

He has a compulsion to be helpful to the patient, experiencing chronic anxiety and guilt in relation to a feeling that he is not helping him, or not helping him as much as he should. This compulsion is very likely to have, at least as one of its bases, the

[12] Whitaker and Malone (1953, p. 101) point out that 'The enthusiasm and elation felt when contemplating the possibility that schizophrenic patients may be amenable to psychotherapy may reflect a perception that some residual needs can perhaps be answered only in therapeutic experience with the schizophrenic'.

projection of his own dependency needs upon the patient. In such an instance, failure to satisfy 'the patient's' (actually the therapist's own, projected) needs carries with it the threat of his having to recognize his own repressed needs.

He experiences a frequent, uncomfortable feeling of 'not knowing what to say' in response to the patient's communications. He feels called upon to make immediate responses, does not allow the patient time to come forth with elaborative statements, nor time for himself to allow his own associational processes to operate with the freedom necessary to a useful intuitive response. He tends, therefore, to adhere to the literal content of the patient's productions, for his intuition is not operating freely enough to bring to light their symbolic content.

In this connexion, we can often see that the therapist's overabundant interpretations represent his way of anxiously trying to satisfy the patient's oral needs, much as if he were plying the patient with cigarettes or milk. The more panicky and ego-fragmented a schizophrenic is, the more likely he is to meet with this kind of thing from some therapists. In such instances, the patient may well be sensing that he is being called upon to satisfy the therapist's dependency needs (which the therapist is repressing and projecting upon the patient), and the anxiety which this causes the patient may have much to do with prolonging or augmenting the panic.

The therapist is particularly anxious whenever the patient is silent and withdrawn. He may try desperately somehow to keep the patient from going out of contact, rather than focusing upon what sequence of events leads to the patient's doing this.

His 'therapeutic curiosity' may assume a voracious aspect.[18] This is all the more important when we consider that the most essential attitude for a therapist to maintain is one of therapeutic curiosity. Such voracity in the anxious therapist (who is consciously experiencing merely a very eager concern to get more data from the patient in order to be more helpful to him) strongly reinforces the schizophrenic's anxiety about closeness, with the

[18] In this connexion a statement of Fenichel (1945, p. 491) is of interest: 'By displacement of the constellation "hunger" to the mental field, curiosity may become an oral trait of character, and under certain conditions assume all the voracity of the original oral appetite.'

threat which that always poses to him, namely, the loss of his ego boundaries.

The therapist experiences guilt in connexion with his not meeting the patient's dependency needs fully – even those needs which could not possibly be fully satisfied by anyone. The therapist's need to retain, at an unconscious level, his own fantasied infantile omnipotence, is a potent source of such guilt: he cannot accept his human limitations. He tries unduly much to help the patient by giving advice and reassurance, by manipulation of his environment in order to shield him from anxiety and frustration, by having extra hours with him on an emergency basis, and so forth.

He gets into frequent tangles with administrative and nursing personnel, feeling that they should be doing more for the patient. In so far as his protests are successful, his own repressed and projected needs are more fully satisfied, in a vicarious fashion. It should be noted, however, that the schizophrenic's psychopathology places great pressure upon any therapist to get into such tangles; the patient generally presents his needs-towards-the-therapist in such an indirect and obscure fashion that it is easy to misinterpret the needs as being directed towards better administrative and nursing care.

He may greatly underestimate the patient's ego strength, as contrasted with the estimates of other personnel members who are working closely with the patient. This is likely to be in the service of his maintaining a relationship with the patient in which the therapist's own repressed dependency needs can be un-wittingly gratified; so long as he can perceive the patient as having an extremely weak ego, as being utterly dependent upon him, then he need not fear that he will lose the patient. Real progress on the patient's part poses, of course, a great threat to such a therapist and he is likely, therefore, to be much slower to see this progress than are the other personnel members.

THE THERAPIST'S FAILING TO HEAR, OR ACTIVELY DISCOURAGING, THE PATIENT'S EXPRESSION OF DEPENDENCY NEEDS

Paradoxically, this same therapist who has a compulsion to help the patient often fails to recognize the patient's expression of dependency needs, or actively – though unconsciously – discourages such expression. It is as though he unconsciously keeps himself preoccupied with his compulsion to help the patient in order not to let himself see and hear the patient's actual expression of need for help. It appears that there are two main bases for his unreceptivity to such communications by the patient.

First, the patient's expression of dependency needs would, if heard, sound too uncomfortably close, so to speak, to the expression of his own repressed needs. Second, when he hears these communications from the patient, the therapist's unconscious fantasy of omnipotence is threatened. If he were omnipotent, the patient could not possibly be hungering for more from him than he can provide. This same unconscious fantasied omnipotence causes him to feel guilt: since there are no limitations on what he, the therapist, can do, he *should* be satisfying all the patient's needs.

So, then, he often fails to recognize his patient's disguised, indirectly expressed pleas for help. He unwittingly fosters the patient's continued use of highly disguised language in the expression of dependency needs, because such direct, simple statements from the patient as, for instance, 'I missed you over the week-end,' make him feel anxious and guilty.

He does not recognize how tremendously important he is to the patient. When (as so often happens in any therapist's work with schizophrenics) the patient treats him with scorn, he is too ready to accept this as a reality evaluation rather than looking upon it as being, very probably, an unconscious defence in the patient against the recognition that the therapist is of tremendous importance to him.

He seldom, if ever, finds his patients expressing any desire for a change of therapist; this kind of material he unconsciously discourages, on the basis of his own repressed, fantasied omnipotence and of his repressed dependency upon the patient. He tends, likewise, either to disrupt the relationship prematurely, in order to avoid a state of prolonged dependency between himself and the patient, or to prolong it beyond the time when it would be in the patient's own interest for it to be terminated.

Although he at times underestimates the patient's ego strength, he as often overestimates it. This is often representative of the striving of his repressed infantile needs towards an omnipotent parent to lean upon. Hence, he is slow to realize how very confused, in how very poor contact with reality, his schizophrenic patients are. He is likely to react, when his patients express fragmentary and highly symbolic communications, as though he were being personally abused, as though the patients really have it within their ability to speak more intelligibly if they so desired. Moreover, it may well be that this very confusion, which the therapist is overlooking, constitutes the patient's most urgent problem, the symptom for which he most desperately needs help.

The therapist reacts with dismay, discouragement, irritation, or scorn to the patient's conscious expressions of dependency feelings, rather than welcoming them. He interprets them as signs of increasing pathological regression, as indications that the patient's clinical state is worsening and the prognosis is growing gloomy. He does not realize, or keep in mind, that the patient's dependency needs were largely subjected to repression at a very early age and have not, therefore, had the opportunity to mature along with other areas of the personality. Thus, when they emerge into the patient's awareness during the course of therapy, they are bound to appear in a very early state of development. The patient himself is so prone to meet this emergence with great dismay and humiliation, that it is all the more important for the therapist to see clearly the positive quality of this therapeutic development.

Lest I give the impression that it is easy to avoid the kind of antitherapeutic attitude described here, consider how difficult it may be to encourage the patient's expression of such a feeling as was expressed to me on one occasion in the following words: '*I go to the trouble to want* to see Miss R. [a nurse to whom the patient was intensely attached],' he said in an outraged tone, 'so I should see her all I want!' To be sure, what at times may be needed in therapy, in response to such a statement, is the therapist's firm pressure upon the patient to help him see the unreasonableness of his demands. But at other times, the patient may instead need encouragement towards the further expression of such feelings, which a portion of the therapist's self tends to react to as being intolerably presumptuous. This patient made it clear, with this and other statements, that he felt that the environment should meet his needs without his having to *want* anything, let alone having to *ask* for it. We can without animosity visualize an infant's having some such feelings, but it may be genuinely difficult to avoid reacting against a chronologically adult person when he voices them.

To return to the hypothetical therapist under discussion, we find that he tends to become preoccupied with the patient's *defences against* dependency needs, rather than perceiving the *needs themselves* as the centrally important focus at the moment. Thus, he may become preoccupied for a long period of time with the patient's scorn in itself, or murderous feeling in itself, or genital-libidinal interest in itself, at a time when the affect in question is functioning in a predominantly defensive capacity, in the service of keeping dependency needs under repression.[14]

He may become anxious at relating in a person-to-person fashion with the patient, may endeavour to present himself to the patient, scrupulously, in some limited doctor role, may need to maintain a limited view of the patient as being only a patient rather than basically a person who bears the label, so to speak, of patient.

In summary, let me emphasize that all those unconscious defences against anxiety in the therapist, described above, interfere with the free exercise of his therapeutic intuition. Because of his having to maintain his own dependency needs under repression, he cannot let himself freely experience his own desire to receive. Thus his *receptivity*, both to the patient's communications and to messages from his own unconscious intuition, is greatly interfered with.[15] Further, his awareness of what is transpiring in the therapeutic relationship is clouded by his preoccupation with the compulsion to help the patient. One can see, in seminars or supervisory hours, that as a therapist becomes freer from this compulsion, he becomes increasingly aware of significant sequences in the patient's reporting, of the timing of increases in the patient's anxiety, and of the nuances of his own varying inner responses to what is going on between himself and the patient. His intuition is

[14] I do not mean to imply here that I consider the dependency needs to be the central issue always; in fact, it is common enough to find repressed murderous feeling, for example, disguised within overt infantile-dependent behaviour.

[15] In such an instance, the therapist's inability freely to receive (verbal and non-verbal communications, gifts, and so forth) from the patient tends to perpetuate the patient's feeling that he himself has nothing worth while to offer. Moreover, the schizophrenic feels so worthless, and so hopeless about himself, that he often has to participate in therapy on a basis of doing it for the therapist's sake; he cannot conceive of doing something for his own sake. If the therapist is so anxious about his own dependency needs that he must insist that therapy takes place for the sake of the patient, this is then a major hindrance to the therapeutic process.

now freer to function in the service of the therapeutic relationship.

4. Therapeutic Technique in dealing with the Patient's Dependency Needs

One cannot formulate detailed rules which are applicable to the complex and changing conditions of a therapeutic relationship, rules by which one can know when to help a patient to become aware of a need which he has been acting out, when to offer gratification for his dependency needs, when firmly to pursue an investigative path, or when bluntly to refuse a demand as being unreasonable and presumptuous.

But there are several general principles which I have found to be consistently useful guides. Moreover, each of these principles is valid, in my experience, in both the early phase of therapy during the development of a workable psychotherapeutic relationship and in the later phases, when therapist and patient are working towards the final goal of the patient's recovery with insight–recovery based upon the patient's own personal integration rather than upon the shaky foundation of an unresolved transference dependency towards the therapist.

The therapist's major task is not to attempt to make up to the patient for past deprivations, but rather to help the patient to arrive at a full and guilt-free *awareness* of his dependency needs (in the course of which process he must help the patient to recognize a variety of feelings about the past deprivations–feelings of rage, disappointment, grief, anxiety, and so forth).

In the literature, one often finds statements which imply that the primary requisite of successful therapy is for the therapist to be a superhumanly loving individual, a person so endowed with love as to be able to make up for the lack of love in the patient's relationship with the mother of his infancy and early childhood. This hypothesis is seldom stated so explicitly as by Rosen (1953):

> The governing principle of direct analysis is that the therapist must be a loving, omnipotent protector and provider for the patient. Expressed another way, he must be the idealized mother who now has the responsibility of bringing the patient up all over again. This duty must be undertaken because the patient has been forced, under heavy psychic threat, to become again for the most part an infant. Since direct analysis holds that this catastrophic collapse is the

consequence of unconscious malevolent mothering, it could have been predicted, even in the absence of overwhelming clinical evidence, that the antidote would have to be a benevolent mother . . . (pp. 8–9).

He [the therapist] must make up for the tremendous deficit of love experienced in the patient's life. Some people have this capacity for loving as a divine gift. But it is possible to acquire this the hard way—by psychoanalysis. It is the *sine qua non* for the application of this method in the treatment of schizophrenia (p. 73).

To be sure, Rosen also emphasizes that 'Being an indulgent parent when deprivation is indicated does no service to the patient and may undermine successful treatment' (p. 152). But he still leaves an over-all impression that he is advocating a type of therapy in which the therapist is somehow omnipotent and possessed of a healing love towards the patient.

My own experience indicates, by contrast, that to the very degree that the therapist can freely accept his own human limitations, he can help the patient to relinquish his infantile omnipotence and accept his human dependency needs. Once the therapist has been able to help the patient to reach a full awareness of the dependency needs, the latter is now able to turn to any suitable figures in his environment for such gratification as it may be possible to acquire, and he will undoubtedly find other figures better able than the therapist to gratify many of his needs. Even this process, however, cannot possibly make up for past deprivations; they can only be integrated by the patient as irretrievable losses to which the therapist has helped him to become reconciled.

Special emphasis needs to be placed upon the importance of helping to resolve the *guilt* which is regularly associated, in the schizophrenic, with dependency needs.

In my own work, when a patient expresses a dependency need to me, I seldom find it indicated for me to set about trying to gratify the need, even though I may promptly feel sympathetic with the need and may feel that I could, without going far out of my way, supply gratification for it. Instead, what repeatedly seems to be more helpful to the patient is for me either to encourage him to express his feeling of need as fully as he can, or to convey to him by a brief comment my acknowledgement of his feeling of need, often adding something to the effect that I can see how, under the circumstances, he of course does feel that way.

In this response, I believe, one is doing more for the patient than when one gives gratification for the need itself: one is helping the patient to become free from the guilt which has imprisoned his dependency needs, so that he can see them more clearly, accept them into his conscious personality functioning, and henceforth seek gratification for them from persons in his daily life.

I find it unfeasible for the therapist to fulfil the function which I have just described and, at the same time, to do very much in the way of trying to gratify the dependency needs. To a considerable degree these two modes of functioning are incompatible. What often happens, as described in Section 3, is that the therapist sets about trying to gratify the patient's need in an unconscious effort to avoid looking, with the patient, at the full intensity of the ungratified need.

Oftentimes when a patient is being most obnoxiously demanding, he is trying to express a basically valid and understandable need about which he, however, feels guilt and self-hatred. Here again, then, the therapist's effort should usually be directed neither towards gratifying the need nor towards chastising the patient for being so obnoxious, but rather towards uncovering the guilt and self-hatred, and helping the patient to see the irrational quality of these affects which are causing him to express his need in such an alienating manner.

Next I shall turn to a consideration of the work of Sèchehaye, since this is pertinent to the matter of the schizophrenic's guilt in relation to his dependency needs.

In 1951 appeared the English translation of her important book, *Symbolic Realization* (1951a), in which she described her method, of the same name, for the psychotherapy of schizophrenia. With it appeared the very interesting companion volume (1951b) containing an account by the patient, in whose therapy Sèchehaye had developed her method, of her illness and of her treatment by Sèchehaye.

Sèchehaye's own conception of the essence of her symbolic realization technique, and of its rationale in terms of the pathogenic early experience of the schizophrenic, is most clearly expressed in the following passages:

The tragedy of the situation is that maternal love is indispensable to the baby, and its deprivation leads to hopeless clinging of the child, who does not want to die; there results a fixation to this stage which he cannot outgrow. Deprivation in this case [i.e., that of Renée] had fastened our patient to this stage of her evolution and thus kept her ego from growing, from becoming distinct from that of her mother's.

Renée could not recover, because, between the unaccepted facts [of psychological trauma in her infancy] and the delirium [i.e. the psychosis] there was a legitimate desire, the insatiability of which caused the fixation, the aggressiveness and the guilt.

The whole problem consisted in realizing this desire, so that it would not be compensated any more by the delirium, and permit a normal development of dynamic growth.

Direct realization, however, was impossible: Renée could not return to the infant stage in order to satisfy the needs of this age. It was necessary to take a substitute, the symbol, since she asked for satisfaction in this form (1951a, pp. 136–138).

Here, then, Sèchehaye has been pointing to the *deprivation* of maternal love, and the *insatiability* of the patient's desire for maternal love, as the central problems. She refers to *guilt* only as one of the products of the insatiability. She then goes on to state, 'The whole problem [in therapy] consisted in realizing this desire. . . .' Most unfortunately, she never makes entirely clear what she means when she uses the term 'realization'. Her very strong implication in the above passages, and in others, is that she means *gratification*.

But in other passages, she seems to consider – more correctly, in my opinion – that the guilt is the central problem, and that gratification by the therapist is therapeutic not in terms of any making up for past deprivations of maternal love, but rather in the sense that the act of gratification helps, at crucial moments, to relieve the patient's guilt and so helps him to experience his needs as being legitimate and no longer, therefore, requiring repression:

I constantly came up against a feeling of indomitable guilt which enclosed Renée in a vicious, impassable circle. . . . This guilt feeling, attached to the primitive stage of moral realism, was certainly the most difficult to uproot. At this stage, the estimation of feelings and acts usually can be traced to the mother's judgements: what mother gives is good, what she refuses is bad. Deprivation is a refusal; therefore, a desire which was refused is bad: the desire for maternal love, which seemed to have been refused, became a guilty tendency; it is forbidden to desire love (1951, pp. 135–6).

[Sèchehaye has just described a calming of Renée's agitation upon her being put to bed, to the accompaniment of a sedative and of soothing, permissive comments by the therapist, in a green room.] I understood suddenly why Renée was relieved by the 'green setting'. The retreat into autism, which is a refusal of life's responsibilities, comprises a violent feeling of guilt. And this guilt of the autism, like all unconscious guilt feelings, keeps one from detaching oneself from a fixation of this state. In order to remove guilt feeling, it is necessary to give permission to do the thing. One must therefore be authorized to retreat into autism, in order to be rid of this guilt feeling and thus get out of it. The reason is simple: there follows guilt in retreating into the maternal body, since the mother wants to force the child to live and does not want her in her body.

I had to go with Renée to the ultimate regression – autism – and grant her in this way, symbolically, the right to take refuge at the maternal bosom, when she suffered too much (pp. 73–4).

In my opinion, Sèchehaye places far too much stress on gratification, and far too little on the often equally therapeutic value of timely, judicious frustration coupled with a primarily investigative approach.

Whitaker and Malone (1953), in their highly unorthodox but, like Sèchehaye's book, thought-provoking volume on psychotherapy, speak much of symbolic gratification by the therapist:

[In the 'core stage' of the psychotherapeutic process] the patient demands complete symbolic gratification. [As the 'core stage' proceeds into the ending phase of the process, the patient] has satisfied some of his more fundamental infantile needs and begins to have more mature and real needs. Part of his testing of the relationship results from a loss of interest in a symbolic relationship and a demand for a real, adult relationship with the therapist. The mature therapist responds to this by a rejection of these real demands, leaving the patient with the need and opportunity to end the symbolic relationship constructively. This frees the patient to secure these gratifications in other areas. In the transition from the core stage to the ending phase, the motivations of the patient toward ending increase almost geometrically as he secures more and more satisfaction in his real-life experience (1953, p. 103).

Their most detailed description of what they refer to by the phrase 'symbolic gratification' is contained in the following passages:

Behaviourally, at any rate, silence comprises the framework within which regression occurs and core satisfactions are achieved. The authors have found that regression may, at times, be facilitated by certain props or auxiliaries. Thus, the therapists have used bottle feeding, physical rocking of patients, and other aids which stimulate in both theraptist and patient the requisite affect for infantile satisfaction of the patient. It reproduces in therapy aspects of the mother-child relationship. More recently, the authors have found that if aggression is utilized at this point of therapy it most appropriately takes the form of spanking. These, however, are auxiliary techniques which compensate for the therapist's inadequacy by inducing the deep affect which the patient seeks for the satisfaction of his infantile and dependent needs. Theoretically, the authors are convinced that these regressive and core satisfactions can be provided without any props or auxiliary techniques since the process of therapy is essentially an intra-psychic one. Technical implementation must only reflect certain immaturities in the intra-psychic functioning of the therapist.

In the core stage of therapy, the experience is primarily a non-verbal shared fantasy experience. . . . The forced joint fantasy may, in its inception, be verbal. It is presented by the therapist as an experience in the present tense in which he relates to the patient with feeling and affect appropriate to the nursing mother who responds to a hungry child. The fantasy need not seek refuge in metaphor or allegory. The fantasy forced at this point becomes direct and primitive. If the patient is ready for the core experience in therapy, and the therapist is capable and sufficiently involved, the forced fantasy proceeds easily from the verbal presentation of it to the non-verbal experience itself. The verbal inception, or precipitation into the feeding experience, may be further implemented by techniques involving physical contact, changes in body posture, and a very frank, face to face relationship (pp. 211–12).

Here again, as in the volume by Sèchehaye, an impression is given that the nucleus of the therapeutic technique is the *gratification* of the patient's infantile dependency needs. It is interesting that even Whitaker and Malone do not consider, apparently, that the patient achieves *full* gratification of these needs: in the 'core stage', they say, 'the patient demands complete [N.B.] symbolic gratification', but that as the ending phase ensues, the patient has satisfied only 'some of' his more fundamental infantile needs. In their way of phrasing it, however, they do imply that at least these needs which he has satisfied are *permanently* satisfied.

In my opinion here, as in reference to Sèchehaye's work, the therapeutic effect of the technique described lies in the patient's having acquired, partly through timely symbolic gratifications, a fuller *awareness* of the infantile dependency needs as being legitimate, rather than their being a continuing source of guilt and requiring repression. The needs themselves are never permanently satisfied, or otherwise eradicated, so long as life goes on; but the patient is now freer to experience these needs and to seek their satisfaction, either in a direct form if the situation at the moment allows for infantile behaviour, or in a reformulated form adapted to adult modes of behaviour. An excellent case could probably be made for the hypothesis that it is these very basic, primitive needs which constitute the wellspring of energy that enables human beings to accomplish their most highly complex, adult personality functions.

In therapy with schizophrenics, just as in analysis with neurotics, the therapist's most consistently appropriate 'gift' to the patient is his psychological presence, alert and with an ever-alive therapeutic curiosity. Material gifts have a very limited place in the analysis of neurotics, and an only somewhat less limited place in the therapy of schizophrenics. The therapist helps the schizophrenic patient to deal with infantile dependency needs much less by material gifts, however timely, than by his consistent, attentive, receptive psychological presence with the patient during the therapeutic hour.

I hope that this will not be taken as suggesting that the therapist's thoughts, during the long periods of silence that occur from time to time in the work with any schizophrenic, should be clearly centred always on the patient. I have heard a number of therapists express guilt at finding their thoughts 'straying far away from the patient'. The free use of the therapist's intuition in the service of the patient requires that he be as open as possible to free-associational processes within himself throughout the hour, during both silences and periods of verbal communication.

The position in which the therapist finds himself, in either being asked to gratify the patient's dependency needs or being offered dependency supplies by the patient, is often an inherently, inevitably conflictual position.

Oftentimes, for instance, when a patient offers the therapist some candy, the therapist may sense that if he declines it the patient will feel rejected, but that if he accepts it, this will substantiate the patient's fantasy that the therapist is totally, frighteningly dependent upon the patient. Thus, there is no action which the therapist can take which will meet the patient's over-all needs at the moment, since these needs are basically ambivalent.

I do not mean, of course, that for the therapist to participate in either receiving from or giving to the patient is always so conflictual a business. Very frequently, the therapist's intuition will quickly tell him what is clearly the appropriate thing to do at the moment. But often the patient's own desires in this regard are so very ambivalent that the therapist senses this ambivalence and feels that neither activity – declining or accepting – is appropriate at the moment.

This is equally true, of course, as regards the patient's requests for dependency supplies from the therapist. Frequently, the therapist senses that if he does not grant a patient's plea (for advice, for information, for orange juice, or what not), a genuine hunger in the patient will go unsatisfied, but that if he supplies what is asked for, on the other hand, then the patient's self-esteem will be further lowered by the implication that the patient cannot meet this need adequately himself.

My main point here is that whereas a therapist may oftentimes, upon finding himself feeling conflictual in answer to a patient's request or proffered gift, feel that his conflictual state is an indication of inadequacy as a therapist, actually this state in which he finds himself is very often inevitable, in view of the patient's own conflictual feelings about dependency. This observation ties in with the emphasis which I shall place, shortly, upon the importance of the investigative response as the one which it is most consistently appropriate for the therapist to make, in such situations.

But in returning for the present to this matter of the patient's conflictual feelings about dependency, I shall mention a few relevant items from the literature.

Sullivan described these feelings in the patient quite accurately · (1953), in a chapter entitled, 'The Later Manifestations of Mental Disorder: Matters Paranoid and Paranoiac'. Of what he terms the 'indirect exploitative attitude', he says,

. . . there is a sort of continuous offer that one can be found to be dependent. It suggests to me the expression 'come-on'; one offers, but one does not quite deliver. One cannot bear to be regarded as dependent . . . (p. 352).

In my experience, we see this quality in many schizophrenic patients in general, not merely in those whose illness is predominantly paranoid in nature.

The schizophrenic patient's ambivalence about his dependency needs is probably one factor which makes for the striking lack of agreement, among therapists who work with schizophrenics, as to how far the therapist should endeavour to go on gratifying or frustrating the patient's dependency needs.[16]

Rosen and Schwing may be cited as therapists who represent (markedly though their techniques differ in many respects) one end of the scale of this disagreement, so to speak, in advocating the therapist's actively assuming the position of an omnipotent, loving figure to the patient. Some of Rosen's comments in this respect have already been quoted. Brody and Redlich (1952) describe Schwing's therapy as follows:

. . . As she put it, she gave the patients instinctively what had been lacking in their child-mother relationship; motherliness. Sometimes this involved long hours of sitting in silence, permitting a patient to proceed at her own rate in establishing contact. She often brought her patients bits of candy or fruit. Sometimes she offered substitute gratifications – small heaps of chocolate substituted for eating faeces, and the manipulations of plasticine substituted for faecal smearing. When circumstances required she would comb her patient's hair, and wipe their perspiration, and when a patient asked her for a kiss she gave it (pp. 49–50).

Schwing is clearly in accord with the following statement by Federn (1952): '. . . with psychotics one must preserve the positive transference and avoid provoking a negative one' (p. 171).

Certain other therapists – and it is these with whom I myself agree – advocate much more moderation on the part of the therapist as regards the gratifying of the patient's dependency needs, and place considerable emphasis upon the patient's anxiety about closeness and need for firmness from the therapist. From some of these therapists I shall quote in the section immediately following.

---

[16] For an interesting survey of the same disagreement in the field of analysis with neurotics, see Berman's article (1949).

It is well for the therapist to maintain, for the most part, a degree of emotional distance between himself and the patient. This is important for three main reasons. First, it is essential to his fulfilling the observer portion of his over-all function as a participant observer. Secondly, although the patient's dependency needs are intense, his anxiety about them is likewise intense, for the numerous reasons which were given in Section 1 of this paper. Thirdly, the therapist must remain, most of the time, at a sufficient emotional distance to allow the patient freedom to express hostility as it arises and to meet such expressions by the patient with firmness.

The therapist who is afraid of the patient's hostility, and of his own counterhostility, is likely to function in an overindulgent, smothering manner which is repetitive of the schizophrenic's pathogenic early experience with the original mother person.

In addition, as Eissler (1943) has pointed out, an overindulgent approach by the therapist may increase the guilt which, as mentioned before, is associated with dependency needs. In commenting upon Schwing's therapeutic approach, Eissler says,

Getrud Schwing leaves no doubt that she considers love as the main road to get access to the schizophrenic personality. . . . Schwing's work with schizophrenics deserves greatest appreciation. [But he then adds:] I should like to mention some factors which may contribute to an appraisal of her work with schizophrenics. Schwing worked at a hospital in which the utter lack of consideration and love for the patient was the outstanding feature. I surmise that in such an environment a loving attitude as recommended by her has the best chance of success. The patient, after having been mistreated and exposed to severe mishandling, will take the loving stroke as the gesture of a saviour and react favourably to such gestures. However, I wonder if this approach would be equally successful in a hospital of more affectionate and understanding background. . . .

Schwing's patients had gone through a kind of treatment which, I surmise, had relieved them from feelings of guilt due to the punishing attitude of nurses and physicians. Hence, they were prepared for love, and they could accept it without guilt reaction. But it is safe to say that loving indulgence may drive schizophrenics into deeper withdrawal if it increases feelings of guilt (1943, pp. 386–7).

Knight, in his extraordinarily moving account of his successful therapy with a 17-year-old catatonic youth (1946), emphasizes not only the importance of the therapist's optimism and affection for the schizophrenic but also

... the necessity, in such a case as this, of active firmness on the part of the therapist in breaking through the barriers of the [catatonic] trance and defiance. Firmness has further values. It makes the patient feel more secure from his own 'bad' impulses if he can count on the therapist's adding his considerable strength in the struggle against the 'bad' impulses. Thus a too permissive or indulgent attitude on the part of the therapist may lead the patient to feel that he is without an ally, helpless against his own overwhelming hates, defiant feelings, and primitive erotic wishes, and a prey to the intolerable anxiety they cause him. The protective strength of the therapist may thus be experienced by the patient as reinforcement of his own enfeebled ego, making it possible for him to contemplate eventual success in his struggle if this good ally will stay in the fight (1946, p. 339).

Similarly, in a recent paper on borderline schizophrenic states, Knight (1953) says that of the three pitfalls which are likely to be encountered in psychotherapy, one is the 'unwise employment of an overpermissive therapeutic attitude'.

Fromm-Reichmann's comments (1952) in this regard are so useful that I shall quote extensively from them:

Violence in action should be prohibited, and verbalized hostile outbursts should be first listened to and then responded to with a therapeutic investigation of their causes. Silent acceptance of violence in word or action is inadvisable, not only in self-defence, but also in pursuit of the respect due to patients, and in protection of their self-respect. Retrospectively, schizophrenic patients loathe themselves for their hostile outbursts, and do not respect the therapist who lets them get away with it (p. 94).

In our therapeutic endeavours we [referring to herself and her associates at Chestnut Lodge] try to address ourselves, if it is at all feasible, to the adult part of the patient's personality, regardless of how disturbed he is. . . .

Trying to initiate or facilitate treatment of a schizophrenic by making friends with him, or by other attempts at turning the strictly professional relationship into a pseudosocial one, may, according to our experience, turn into a serious threat to successful psychotherapeutic procedure. As we know from psychoanalytic work with neurotics, such attempts are inacceptable there. They may destroy the central core of psychoanalytic psychotherapy, which is to utilize the vicissitudes of the doctor-patient relationship as a mirror of patients' patterns of interpersonal relationships at large, hence as the most informative therapeutic means of investigating and understanding their pyschopathological aspects. In the case of schizophrenics, there are several additional serious difficulties connected with any falsification of the professional character of the doctor-patient relationship. This must be definitely kept in mind in the presence of the temptation to try to reach a very disturbed psychotic schizophrenic by offering closeness, friendship, or love.

. . . my suggestion of elimination of nonprofessional contacts in psychoanalytic treatment is not intended to imply a repudiation of all the very valuable attempts to create an atmosphere of acceptance, comfort, understanding, or elimination of anxiety-arousing factors from these patients' environment. Such efforts are most commendable as means of speeding patients' emergence from acute psychotic states, and, if administered by persons other than the psychoanalyst, as most useful adjuncts to the psychoanalytic treatment proper (pp. 101–4).

[She continues, regarding] the specific reasons for our warning against offering nonprofessional warmth to a schizophrenic patient in the setting of psychoanalytic treatment—first, the schizophrenic is afraid of any offer of closeness. Closeness in the present entails the danger of rebuff in the future to the early traumatized schizophrenic. Also, he will not be able to hide his 'ugliness', his 'meanness', his hostile and destructive impulses, from a person who comes close to him. . . .

Again, closeness increases the schizophrenic's ever-existing fear of having lost or of losing his identity, of losing the sense of the boundaries between himself and the outside world [–a fear which is a quite rational one, since an unconscious, uncontrollable process of identifying with the other person is one of the schizophrenic's major defences against anxiety–H. F. S.].

There is one last reason, which makes me warn against the attempt to start psychotherapy with a schizophrenic on the basis of any relationship other than the realistic professional one, that is his alert sensitivity to and rejection of any feigned emotional experience. As one patient bluntly expressed herself upon being offered friendship in an initial interview by a young psychoanalyst, 'How can you say we are friends? We hardly know each other' (p. 105).

It is interesting to see described, in a paper by Fromm-Reichmann (1948), the evolution which had taken place in the psychotherapeutic approach at Chestnut Lodge since a paper by her in 1939. In the earlier paper she had stressed the importance of the therapist's approaching the schizophrenic patient with extreme delicacy, permissiveness, and caution so as to avoid causing the patient to feel rejected. By 1948, she indicates, she and her colleagues had come to feel that 'this type of doctor-patient relationship addresses itself too much to the rejected child in the schizophrenic and too little to the grown-up person before regressing'.

She went on to give additional reasons for the changed orientation, an orientation which now substantially coincides with that described in her 1952 article, quoted at length immediately above.

In intensive psychotherapy with schizophrenics, as in analysis with neurotics, the most consistently useful therapeutic approach with respect to the patient's dependency needs is one of neither gratification nor rejection but rather investigation. In general, the therapist's effort should be towards helping the patient to recognize and explore dependency feelings.

For instance, although upon occasion the therapist may sense that at the moment it is therapeutic for him to extend some oral gratification (such as a cigarette or a glass of fruit juice), he will much more often be giving the patient a far more valuable gift if he holds firm in exploring the patient's need with him, and the frustration rage which is attendant upon the therapist's investigating rather than gratifying. It is well to note that a simple rejection *per se* (of a patient's request for a cigarette or what not) is not what I am recommending here; the therapist's focus should be upon investigating the patient's need, rather than either simply gratifying or simply frustrating it.

Quite regularly, both patient and therapist find it less uncomfortable when the patient is blaming the therapist for failing to satisfy infantile needs, than when both patient and therapist are clearly seeing the naked needs as such, for this latter process carries with it a realization of their mutual helplessness to satisfy the needs at all fully. Yet it is precisely in the therapist's helping the patient to recognize clearly the intensity of the patient's own infantile needs, unalleviated by protective feelings of blame and angry demandingness, that he is being of most real service as a therapist.

Again, a therapist may often become preoccupied with the question, 'Should I or shouldn't I acquiesce in the patient's request?' rather than maintaining an investigative attitude, focusing upon the sequence of events in the hour which led up to the patient's making this particular request. Once more, the probability is that the therapist can be of most use to the patient by neither granting nor declining the request as such, but rather by helping to uncover its meaning in their relationship. Oftentimes, the patient most urgently demands an answer just when he is trying (unconsciously) most vigorously to avoid an area of anxiety which needs investigation, and for which his request is a defence.

The therapist's own intuition, his sensing of what need the patient is expressing and what is therapeutic for him to do or say in response at the moment, is his most reliable guide as to whether to meet the patient's dependency needs with gratification, frustration, or investigation.

The more inexperienced a therapist is in this field, and the less aware he is of his own feelings, attitudes, and interpersonal processes, the more he will need to rely upon rules as to what to say or do in response to his patients' manifestations of dependency needs. For him, such rules are necessary and thoroughly legitimate. I refer here, for instance, to such a rule as never to accept a gift from a patient without first investigating what the giving of the gift means to the patient.

But gradually, through experience in psychotherapy with schizophrenics and through increasing ability to trust his own unconscious processes, the therapist finds that he can dispense with such rules and utilize his intuition as a much more dependable guide to his therapeutic functioning. In his doing this, he will undoubtedly find that the patient will complain that the therapist is being inconsistent—that he does this or that one way now, and another way at another time. But, as Fromm-Reichmann says, 'There is one point where you are consistent, namely, that you try to do always and by all means that which you consider therapeutically valid in any given situation with any given patient. The realization of this principle may, at times, result in the most glaring psychotherapeutic "inconsistency" any psychiatrist could dream of. We must have the courage to be "inconsistent", if need be, without developing anxiety, pangs of conscience and conventional guilt feelings.'[17]

[17] Personal communication.

152

DEPENDENCY IN SCHIZOPHRENIA

Rosen (1953, pp. 8–9), with some of whose therapeutic philosophy and technique I strongly disagree, none the less makes some comments which are very well put and are relevant here:

The conscious, tangible needs of the patient which anyone can recognize, such as food, warmth, and protection, are the easiest for the therapist to provide. Much more difficult is providing the proper instinctual response which the benevolent mother must make to the unconscious needs of the patients. For this response, the therapist's own psyche must be in order. His instinctual drives of love, hate and aggression must have come into such a balance that, as he relates himself to the patient, the patient will thrive. This balance . . . cannot be forced by conscious effort alone. . . .

Steinfeld (1951, pp. 103–4) likewise emphasizes the central importance of the therapist's intuition:

. . . wherever any results are achieved [in psychotherapy], creative efforts, consciously or unconsciously, must be combined with scientific understanding. The therapist must allow himself to be guided by an intuitive or 'sympathetic' understanding of the patient, while he also uses the intellect and its systematized body of abstract knowledge as a complementary tool. The intellect alone in psychotherapy is as inadequate as Bergson would have it in all dealings with the living, creative stream of all reality.

Knight's statements on this subject merit quotation at length. In an article (1953) concerning borderline schizophrenic patients (pp. 149–50), he makes some comments which may be considered to apply to the more severely ill schizophrenic patients as well:

With the borderline schizophrenic patient, the therapist often has some difficult decisions to make regarding what is the proper attitude to take with respect to firmness and permissiveness. Put another way, this is the question of need gratification versus need frustration, the frustration being a preliminary step to interpretation. In psychoanalysis, need gratification is at a minimum, and definite limits are set by the technique *per se*. Length of appointments is maintained fairly strictly, the patient may not even face the therapist, extra-analytic remarks at the beginning and end of each hour are minimal, extra appointments are rare, physical contact is ruled out, and communication is through verbal channels primarily. We know that many psychiatric patients are too ill to adapt themselves to these technical strictures and must have a preliminary period of greater or lesser duration in which certain needs are gratified. For example, the patient is permitted to sit up and face the therapist, supportive and encouraging remarks are made by the therapist, some active advice may be given, and the like. The borderline schizophrenic patient especially cannot tolerate the isolation of the analytic couch, and needs visual as well as increased auditory demonstrations of support and understanding. He needs *proofs* of emotional support, of trusting and trustworthiness, and of genuine human interest rather than merely detached professional interest.

It becomes necessary, therefore, for the therapist to gauge these needs qualitatively and quantitatively with some accuracy, and to make judicious decisions as to what needs should be met and what needs may be frustrated by limit setting followed by interpretation. The overmaternal, overpermissive therapist may encourage regressive tyranny in the patient by meeting too many needs, while the over-rigid detached therapist may put his patient on what, for this patient, is a starvation diet. Such attitudes in the therapist are partly temperamental, partly a matter of difference between the sexes, and partly a matter of training. Ideally a therapist should be capable of considerable flexibility in his responses so that he can adapt himself with genuineness and spontaneity to the widely varying therapeutic situations arising in work with different patients.

Eissler (1943, p. 387) sums it up in an excellent statement: 'The entire gamut of emotions from hatred to love should be at the psychiatrist's disposal and applied in accordance with the patient's instantaneous needs.'

In my own work with schizophrenic patients, I have frequently found that my response to a patient's expression of dependency needs and demands may usefully range from tender solicitude to harshness to imperturbability, all within the same hour.

Berman (1949, pp. 164–5) places an extremely valuable emphasis upon the positive aspect of the circumstance that the analyst will inevitably fail at times to supply a therapeutic response. Although Berman is writing of analysis with neurotics, his remarks are applicable to therapy with schizophrenics also:

The 'analytic attitude' varies considerably as regards how much warmth and subtle 'giving' is blended with the simultaneous remaining 'outside' of the patient and his problems. Probably, analysts intuitively try to hit the appropriate dosage of genuine 'giving' and of proofs of their friendliness and dedication with each patient according to the point each has reached in the analysis. There are many indirect ways in which this is effectively done. The analyst may vary the amount of friendly discussion of some real life problem or interest–for example, the patient's work. There may be more or less laxity in allowing a session to run beyond its official end. There may be a greater or lesser deviation from a previously agreed upon statement as to when the patient would be charged for a missed session, and so on. However, it seems it is not really possible for the analyst to be consistently so keenly attuned to the patient as to achieve an accurate dosage of what the patient needs all the time. This 'failing', if it does not become too marked, probably also plays a part in the therapeutic process. The patient has occasion to experience the reality of a person who dedicates himself to the task of helping him to grow up and who comes through reasonably well in spite of obvious difficulties.

Lidz and Lidz (1952, p. 173) comment on this same point: 'The strength in the therapist that must be conveyed to the patient may well derive from sufficient integrity not to need to be infallible.'

My own experience has indicated that as therapy with a schizophrenic patient progresses, he becomes increasingly able to assume responsibility for discerning his own needs, for seeking satisfaction for them, for dealing with his feelings of frustration when satisfaction is not forthcoming, and for redirecting his needs into more adult or symbolic channels when circumstances require this. The therapist finds it less often appropriate, as therapy proceeds, to extend the gratifications which he may have felt it therapeutic to extend earlier in the treatment. But this process can advance to a successful outcome, in which the patient can come to accept both himself and the therapist as human beings rather than omnipotent beings, only in so far as the therapist can accept his own human needs–most importantly, his own infantile dependency needs.

In closing, I wish to emphasize that this subject is one which we need to investigate much more fully. This paper, representative of an effort to deal fairly comprehensively with the subject, probably constitutes in actuality no more than the beginning of such a task, in view of the complexity and pervasive importance of dependency processes in the psychotherapy of schizophrenia.

Particularly in the matter of relevant therapeutic technique there is, at present, a striking lack of agreement among reports in the literature. Among the authorities with long experience in psychotherapy with schizophrenic patients, there is no subject about which there is a wider dispersal of viewpoints than this one, the psychotherapeutic approach to the schizophrenic's dependency needs. Currently there are nearly as many different technical approaches as there are psychotherapists reporting them.

We have as yet insufficient evidence to demonstrate convincingly that there is any one teachable psychotherapeutic approach which yields better, more durable results than do other approaches. To fill this void in our knowledge, we need careful studies of the psychotherapeutic process as participated in by therapists utilizing somewhat the approach of, for instance, Schwing or Rosen or Whitaker and Malone, with, for comparison, similar studies of the psychotherapeutic process as participated in by therapists using approximately the approach recommended by, for example, Fromm-Reichmann, Knight, and myself. Such studies should throw much light upon the actual quality of the two contrasting therapeutic relationships, the quality of the personality integration effected in the patients, and the comparative long-range treatment results, including the quality and durability of recoveries.

Chapter 4

THE INFORMATIONAL VALUE OF
THE SUPERVISOR'S EMOTIONAL
EXPERIENCES (1955)[1]

THE emotions experienced by a supervisor—including even his private, 'subjective' fantasy experiences and his personal feelings about the supervisee—often provide valuable clarification of processes currently characterizing the relationship between the supervisee and the patient. In addition, these processes are often the very ones which have been causing difficulty in the therapeutic relationship and, because heretofore unrecognized by the supervisee, have not been consciously, verbally reported by him to the supervisor. This thesis is undoubtedly well known to many persons engaged in supervision, and in everyday use by them in this work; but my own experience indicates that it is far from universally recognized, and it has not, to the best of my knowledge, been presented in the literature.

It would be at least equally valid to express the principle in the following fashion: the processes at work currently in the *relationship between* patient and therapist are often reflected in the *relationship between* therapist and supervisor. But it makes for simplicity of presentation to present this material from the viewpoint of the supervisor.

Until recent years, published articles on supervision have portrayed the supervisor as a dispassionate mentor, whose useful participation in the supervisory session is limited mainly to his carefully attending to the therapist's verbal report and making suggestions regarding improved handling of the material which the patient has been producing. Beyond this, the supervisor has been generally considered to be in a position to point out to the

[1] An abbreviated version of this paper was read, as part of a symposium on intuitive processes in psychotherapy, before a joint meeting of the Washington Psychiatric Society, the Washington Psychoanalytic Society and the Medical Society of St Elizabeth's Hospital in October 1954. Another such version was read before the meeting of the American Psychoanalytic Association in May 1955. It was first published in *Psychiatry*, Vol. 18 (1955), pp. 135–46.

therapist, to a greater or lesser extent, evidences of counter-transference phenomena, and perhaps to function to a degree as an auxiliary analyst in exploration of their sources. But the basic view was, apparently, long held that any emotional reactions which the supervisor felt towards the therapist, other than those of a friendly teacher-and-colleague variety, were merely incidental to their collaborative effort or, more often, an active deterrent to it. (See, for instance, Kovacs [1936]; Bibring *et al.* [1937]; Balint [1945]; Fleming [1953].)

Within the past two years, however, a different light has been shed upon the supervisory relationship by Meerloo (1952), Blitzsten and Fleming (1953), and Ackerman (1953), who describe the supervisor as having a considerable degree of emotional involvement in the situation. They present him as being subject to feelings of competitiveness with the therapist and with the therapist's personal analyst, and to anxiety, hostility, and various feelings of a countertransference origin towards the therapist. But they imply that the supervisor's emotional involvement is largely determined by certain reality aspects of the supervisory relationship, such as the matter of the fee, the matter of present and future competitor status between supervisor and therapist, and so on. Any emotions experienced by the supervisor outside this narrow realm are considered, apparently, to be quite extraneous to the supervisory process *per se*, and due to unwelcome countertransference difficulties in the supervisor.

Thus, while these authors depart from the classical conception of the supervisory relationship, they stop considerably short of the conception here presented. In my view, the supervisor experiences, over the course of a supervisory relationship, as broad a spectrum of emotional phenomena as does the therapist or even the patient himself–although, to be sure, the supervisor's emotions are rarely so intense as those of the therapist, and usually much less intense than those of the patient.[2] Moreover, the supervisor can often find that these emotions within himself do not represent foreign bodies, classical countertransference phenomena, but are highly informative reflections of the relationship between therapist and patient.

[2] Incidentally, I am not advocating the supervisor's emoting, in an overt fashion, to the supervisee. I am focusing upon the supervisor's 'subjective' emotional experience in the supervisory situation.

I shall refer to this phenomenon as *the reflection process*. I use this term, first, for the sake of brevity, and, second, in an attempt to emphasize the particular *source* of the emotions which I am here considering. When a supervisor notices any certain feeling in himself, this, taken by itself, might be an indication of something primarily in *himself* which calls for analytic investigation, or of something primarily so in the *therapist*, or of some area of difficulty primarily in the *patient*. I am here focusing upon the last of these possibilities; but I am not suggesting that this should always be assumed to be the case. Rather, I believe that it is a possibility which is often overlooked.

I have not used the classical term *countertransference* because it tends to focus attention on the first of these possibilities – to imply that the supervisor's emotions flow from a repressed source in his own childhood. Certainly the supervisor is subject to such emotions; he may react to the supervisory relationship less in terms of the reality of the immediate situation than in terms of some long-past relationship in which certain feelings on his own part had to be repressed, have since then remained under repression, and are now experienced not as pertaining to that early relationship, but rather as if they were a reality-reaction (which they are not) to the supervisory relationship.

But when the supervisor finds himself experiencing some emotion during the supervisory hour, he should be alert not only to the possibility that the source of this emotion may lie chiefly in his own repressed past, in which case he is experiencing a classical countertransference reaction to the therapist; he should be alert also to the possibility that the source of this emotion may lie chiefly in the therapist-patient relationship and, basically, chiefly in the patient himself. If the latter is found to be the case, then we may say that the supervisor's emotion is a *reflection* of something which has been going on in the therapist-patient relationship and, in the final analysis, in the patient. This reflection process is by no means to be thought of as holding the centre of the stage, in the supervisory situation, at all times. Probably it comprises, in actual practice, only a small proportion of the events which occur in supervisory hours. Yet its part is a vital one, for it may offer clues to obscure difficulties besetting the patient-therapist relationship.

In turning from the literature on supervision to that on

countertransference in the therapeutic (or analytic) relationship, we find three recent articles expressing a view regarding the emotional experience of the therapist which is quite analogous to my view regarding that of the supervisor. Each of the writers – Heimann (1950), Mabel Blake Cohen (1952), and Weigert (1954) – emphasizes how much the analyst can learn about the patient from noticing his own feelings – tenderness, sympathy, resentment, rage, or whatever – in the analytic relationship.

Clinical Material

INDIVIDUAL SUPERVISION

Example 1. – The patient is a man with a severe obsessive-compulsive neurosis, and the therapist a person whom I had known and respected for a relatively long time prior to my undertaking this supervision with him. In the first supervisory hour I was surprised to hear him describe, throughout the greater portion of the hour, a recent incident in which he had engaged in some conscious role-playing with the patient, and which he obviously thought had probably represented poor technique on his part. While describing the incident, he looked at me searchingly, as if expecting adverse criticism. I felt, indeed, most critical of him, particularly since I knew him to be a much more competent therapist than this occurrence would seem to indicate, and I was open in expressing the criticism.

I would have thought such an incident to be most exceptional in this therapist's work, and was therefore troubled to find that in the second supervisory hour, also, he started describing in detail another situation in which he had participated in a fashion which, again, he seemed now to recognize as having been distinctly anti-therapeutic, and was showing again an expectation of being criticized by me. After hearing the details of this second incident for about twenty minutes, during which I had been feeling a strong sense of condemnation towards the therapist, I began to realize that the feeling-tone of my relationship with him was very similar to that of our first hour. I immediately felt concern as to what this would lead to if it went on week after week: such growing resentment between us that the supervision would hamper, rather than facilitate, the therapy.

Just as this was occurring to me, the therapist went on to say, 'Another thing that I've noticed with B is that he keeps presenting to me material that might be called ugly–perverse sexual material, things about faeces, and so on.' I immediately felt that in so doing, the patient was functioning, as regards the feeling tone he was fostering in the therapist, similarly to the manner in which the therapist had been functioning in the supervisory relationship, despite the difference in verbal content. That is, in each instance material was reported which had a repellent, or distancing, effect.

The therapist continued, uninterruptedly, to describe this 'ugly' material, and I privately felt that it was, indeed, extraordinarily ugly and repellent. He mentioned that the patient, while reporting this, 'looks searchingly [n.b.] at me'. It was at this point that I described to the therapist what I felt to be the similarity between this kind of reporting from the patient, and the therapist's own manner of reporting to me. I suggested that perhaps the patient was thus trying to maintain distance between himself and the therapist.

The therapist seemed most receptive to these comments,[3] and seemed subsequently to find them useful. In response to that mode of reporting from the patient he had previously been focusing too much upon the content and had not clearly seen the interpersonal process to which the content was subservient– that is, the patient's maintaining emotional distance in the relationship. My own 'personal' feeling towards the therapist, in response to his manner of reporting the predominantly highly criticizable material, thus provided valuable data which helped to bring to light that aspect of the therapeutic relationship.

What I observed and was emotionally responsive to was, I believe, less an aspect of the therapist's own personality than a transitory unconscious identification occurring as a function of his relationship with the patient. Following this second supervisory hour, he no longer manifested such an approach to me in the supervisory hours. Since then, he has been better able to present his work with the patient in a way which, for all the difficulties that the therapy still poses, allows for much greater mutual regard, and better collaboration, between us.

[3] Subsequent experience has shown me, however, that pointing out to the therapist what appear to be similarities between the patient's mode of functioning and his own is likely to foster self-consciousness and defensiveness. Expressing one's remarks exclusively in terms of suggestions as to what the patient seems to be doing brings about the same result without straining one's relationship with the therapist.

Example 2.–The therapist is another male colleague, and the patient a male latent schizophrenic, hospitalized, whom most of the personnel find to be intimidating in his oral demandingness which he reinforces by chronically threatening physical assault.

I began the supervision with anxious misgivings, not only because of the difficult therapeutic problem which the patient inherently represented, but also because of my long-standing feelings of disapproval towards this therapist's approach to patients–an approach which, I felt, was based upon a need to deny hostile feelings in himself and in his patients. Also, he had shown no spontaneous interest in seeking help from me; he came for supervision merely in obedience to the wish of a higher authority. I surmised that the therapist must resent the supervisory situation, and I felt uneasy about the intensity of my own disapproval of his therapeutic technique. In retrospect, it is evident that I myself had more resentment at finding myself in this situation than I realized at the time.

It was therefore a relief to me to find, as the first supervisory hour progressed, that I was able to experience a fair degree of approval of his therapy, and to voice it. Early in the hour he commented in passing that he felt greatly burdened by the patient's dependency demands; but neither of us pursued this and he quickly turned to reporting data which were more agreeable to us both. These data consisted in an enthusiastic description of how 'closely' he and the patient often collaborated, with his often thinking of what the patient was about to say, and the patient's often anticipating, lo and behold, just what the therapist was about to say.

To this I reacted with approval; yet my approval felt, to myself, somewhat forced, and before the hour was up I brought myself to comment delicately, one might say in passing, that *sometimes* the kind of relatedness he described *may* serve a defensive function, as an unconscious way of warding off awareness of mutual hostility in the relationship. I gently and casually added that a criterion of whether the 'closeness' he described was being used as an unconscious defence would be whether he found himself feeling constricted in the therapeutic relationship. His statement early in the hour, as to the burdensome effect of the patient's dependency, we both pleasantly ignored, and the hour ended on a note of mutual enthusiasm which felt to me just a bit intoxicating in quality, rather than solid and convincing. This 'enthusiasm', I now know, had the same whistling-in-the-dark quality as did the 'closeness' between patient and therapist.

A number of supervisory hours might have been spent in this kind of mutual anxious assurance that the supervision and the therapy were proceeding happily, had it not chanced that the therapist gave a previously scheduled presentation of this case to the hospital staff only two days later. During the discussion following the presentation, the other staff members expressed striking and forthright agreement that the therapist had been, indeed, unaware of the patient's massive hostility (and, one may add in retrospect, unaware of his own hostility towards the patient). The 'closeness' was clearly, they felt, a defence against the recognition of this hostility.

In subsequent supervisory hours, taking courage from this view expressed frankly by the other therapists, I ceased the kind of pussyfooting with him which he himself had been engaging in with the patient; when I felt critical of his approach, I said so quite directly. He responded well to this, and the tenor of the supervisory relationship became much healthier, more basically friendly and collaborative, from then on. The therapeutic relationship showed, concomitantly, a favourable change in the same area.

Example 3. – A therapist was working with a very difficult female schizophrenic patient who had left the hospital and was leading a precarious outpatient existence, her relatives having refused to finance further in-patient therapy. She showed an aggressive demandingness; while earlier the hospital personnel had helped to cope with this, the therapist now felt required to meet the problem alone. Because of the pressure on him to try to meet her needs sufficiently for her to manage to stay out of the hospital, he felt largely at the mercy of her demands for him to take over, in effect, the management of her daily life.

This was the situation at the beginning of the supervision, some months after the patient had left the hospital, and, decreasingly, for several months thereafter. One major factor which made for beneficial change was my own experiencing at first hand the kind of pressure which the therapist was evidently experiencing in the therapeutic situation. Week after week in each supervisory hour, I felt under uncomfortable pressure from him to supply him with something that would somehow relieve his chronic anxiety about this patient. He did not verbalize any complaints about the supervision, but in non-verbal ways conveyed his demand for more from me.

My own emotional response gave me a clearer realization of the pressure he was feeling than I could have obtained from his words alone. Moreover, my eventual way of responding proved to be of value to the therapeutic relationship. After extending myself uncomfortably much to meet his unverbalized demands, I gradually came to stick reasonably firmly to a line of giving as much assistance as I felt able to supply without, for example, extending the supervisory hour over time, or pouring out sympathy, or trying desperately to contribute brilliant ideas, as I had done previously to some degree. After several weeks of this latter kind of participation by me, there ensued an outburst of anger from the therapist towards me, related to my, as he put it, taking my leisure in the face of the torment he was enduring.

We both weathered this well, and there were indications subsequently that this episode contributed to his gradually becoming less afraid of his own anger in response to the frequently presumptuous demandingness of the patient, able to function with more firmness and self-assurance, and able to meet more firmly the occasional presumptuous interventions by the relatives which, all along, had interfered with the therapy.

Example 4.–In this instance, the reflection process helped me to become more fully aware of a previously rather obscure sexual element in the transference-countertransference relationship between a female schizophrenic patient and her male therapist. After several months of supervision, the therapist was one day quoting some remarks of the patient which, as usual, we both found quite confusing. Suddenly, as the therapist was talking, I fantasied his asking me for a declaration of love to him. I immediately dismissed this as being utterly irrelevant, and presumably representative of one of those aberrant desires which one may chance to experience from time to time and must learn to put up with, without gratification.

I was therefore startled a few minutes later to hear him quote the patient as saying something that sounded to me like a disguised expression of romantic love for her therapist. Had I not experienced the fantasy a few minutes before, I might easily have missed the disguised meaning in these remarks. When I suggested this interpretation to him, he was able to get a clearer view of the sexual nature of the current transference-countertransference situation, and in subsequent hours with the patient he validated my surmise. My impression is that he, too, had seen glimmerings of this element in his relationship with the patient, but, like myself, had dismissed his 'hunches' as groundless or irrelevant.

Example 5.–In this example, a supervisory relationship proceeded to an unsuccessful outcome, partly because I failed to recognize the importance of the phenomenon here under discussion. Only later, in looking back ,over my work with the therapist, did I realize how important this phenomenon had become, largely unnoticed by me, in the supervisory hours.

The therapist had been working for about two years with a male schizophrenic patient before I began supervising the therapy. A previous therapist had discontinued work with this patient after two years of discouraging results. The patient's intense, chronically-acted-out pressure upon the therapist to assume total initiative and responsibility for the course of the relationship had been proving resistive to the efforts of this second therapist; it had proved insoluble in the relationship with the former one. This second therapist, upon coming to me for supervision, made clear that he was having great difficulty with the patient's long silences, during which an intense demandingness was conveyed to the therapist. The patient concomitantly expressed, by facial expression and by occasional words, a taunting, derisive attitude, as if daring the therapist to try to do anything for him.

The supervision went on for six months, on the customary once-a-week basis. I found the therapeutic situation with which we were concerned a difficult, 'problem' one from the first, felt under chronic pressure from the therapist to contribute more towards the resolution of his difficulties with the patient, and found him to be meeting my repeated, earnest efforts with much the same derisive, taunting negation that the patient exhibited in response to the therapist's own efforts. I worked hard in the supervisory situation, just as the therapist clearly did in the therapeutic situation; and just as he had long been embittered by the patient's lack of utilization of his therapeutic efforts, I grew increasingly embittered in feeling that the therapist was consistently rejecting, rather than accepting and using, my supervisory efforts. Our relationship proceeded inexorably in this manner until, by mutual agreement, we terminated our work together.

During the considerable time we had worked together as colleagues before the supervisory relationship began, there had been major and undisguised differences between our approaches to psychotherapy in general. It was my impression, as the supervision went on, simply that our usual differences were becoming increasingly a hindrance to our collaborative effort. But when I privately reviewed the course of our work together, a few hours after we had had the final supervisory hour, I realized how probable it was that, all along, I had to a considerable degree been blinded by what I felt to be innate personality differences between us, such that I had failed to realize how considerable a part of these consisted in–I now surmised–temporary unconscious identifications by the therapist, and by myself, with the patient's defences against anxiety. In looking back over the six months of work, I found that each one of five problem-areas which I had perceived in the supervisory relationship had its corollary problem-area in the therapeutic relationship. This gave me a new attitude towards the therapist: I now felt that in much of his behaviour which I had regarded as personally antagonizing he had been in actuality attempting, unconsciously, to show me the kind of behaviour which the patient was exhibiting, concerning which he, the therapist, was most in need of assistance from me.

My realization of this did not yield enough of friendly and confident feelings to lead me to seek a resumption of the supervisory relationship which had been so discouraging and frustrating to me over so many weeks. But viewing this discovery from a longer perspective, I still felt sure of its validity, and believed that if it had been made earlier the supervision would have proceeded more successfully.

Although the main focus of this paper is upon the emotional experience of the supervisor, I should now like briefly to describe two complementary experiences from the supervisee's point of view.

Example 6.–For several years I analysed a man whose aggressive oral-demanding qualities I found intimidating, and reacted to, for a long time, by a strong identification on both conscious and unconscious levels. This patient kept trying tenaciously and threateningly to force me to function as an all-providing mother to him. Concomitantly, throughout the early and middle phases of the analysis, I went regularly for supervision and tried in various ways to coerce the supervising analyst into functioning as an all-providing mother to me. These efforts the supervisor met with much more firmness than I felt able to muster towards the patient; I felt the supervisory hours to represent ice-cold 'reality baths', and I protested, from time to time, that the supervisor was exhibiting an unduly harsh attitude in regard to the patient (and, I felt privately, towards me). Gradually, however, I worked through my resentment about this and came to accept the insatiability of many of my own demands, to share the supervisor's general attitude towards the patient's demands, and to be able to work firmly and eventually successfully with these previously intimidating demands from the patient.

Example 7.–I was analysing a schizoid female patient who, for many months, was so anxious about any interpersonal closeness that she consistently prevented me from participating with her in any but the most distant manner, repeatedly rejecting my remarks and being very intolerant of my saying anything at all. Concomitantly, for almost as many months I functioned in a very similar way in relation to the supervising analyst, going through what amounted, as nearly as I could ensure, to a soliloquy. I became most uncomfortable whenever the supervisor presented to me, in any one hour, several suggestions which my intellect regarded as valuable, but which emotionally I could not accept because of my having to keep at a great distance in the supervisory relationship. Like the patient with me, I was most impatient with the supervisor's saying anything; this always felt to me like an interruption. When this was brought out consciously between the supervisor and myself, the difficulty was sufficiently resolved for me to be better able to deal with the analogous difficulty in the analytic situation.

GROUP SUPERVISION

I shall now present some examples of this same process which occurred in a group supervisory situation, a hospital research seminar, in its second year at time of writing. During the first year of the research project, five investigators met weekly, for two hours, to explore the recorded psychotherapy of one member with a chronic schizophrenic patient. The therapist would tell the other members what he considered to have transpired in the therapy during the preceding week, and would play a sample portion of a recorded hour with the patient. The members, including the patient's therapist, would then discuss the therapeutic relationship, general problems in the therapy or dynamics of schizophrenia, and the interpersonal processes we detected among ourselves in the group. One of the areas of interest was the interrelationship between the psychodynamic processes in the therapeutic relationship and the psychodynamic processes in the weekly research seminar.[4]

We were impressed not only with the influence of the seminar on the therapeutic relationship (an influence which came to be clearly beneficial), but also with the striking influence which the current mode of relatedness between patient and therapist exerted upon the mode of relatedness among the members of the seminar. The influence in this latter direction was effected, apparently, both by the therapist's verbal and non-verbal communications to us and, very importantly, by our hearing the patient's and therapist's own affect-laden voices from the recordings. Most impressive of all was the capacity of the schizophrenic patient, whose anxiety was generally so much more intense than our own, to influence the therapist's functioning and, in turn, our relatedness within the group.[5]

[4] As so often happens in research projects, this was not the initial area intended for exploration, but an area which proved so fruitful that it has been given prolonged attention. The research group set out originally to attempt to formulate, in communicable and therefore teachable terms, the processes which promote or inhibit the development of therapeutic intuition; and this problem continued to be of interest in the project. The members, all therapists on the Chestnut Lodge staff, were, during the first year, Drs Frieda Fromm-Reichmann (who has been, throughout, the head of the research project), Alberta Szalita-Pemow, Marvin L. Adland, Donald L. Burnham, and myself. The members in the second year were Drs Fromm-Reichmann and Adland, and myself.

[5] During the second year, the patient's therapist was no longer a member of the group, and we no longer listened to recordings. Yet we found, when we investigated together transcripts of some of the material from the previous year—portions of the therapeutic hours and the associated discussions among the group members—that our current interpersonal relatedness was considerably influenced by the therapeutic situation, even at that distance.

The following three examples demonstrate the process under discussion here:

Example 1.–At the beginning of the project, the therapist mentioned that one of his reasons for selecting his work with this particular patient as the subject of our research, was that he had long been finding this case a particularly difficult one. One indication of the difficulty was that he often found himself feeling sleepy in the hours with this patient.

Interestingly, during the next four weeks of seminar meetings, an evolution occurred in which the group relatedness among the members of the seminar–including the therapist, in his presentations of each week's therapy–had a distinctly somnolent tenor at first, which became so replaced by a livelier interest, before the end of that month, that the changed atmosphere was commented upon by one of the members and attested to by each of the others. The therapist mentioned that he was finding himself no longer sleepy in the hours with the patient, and expressed the belief that this was at least in part because of his having 'confessed my sins in that regard to the group'. At this same time the therapist reported finding that he was having more courage, in his hours with the patient, to let his own associational processes range freely in response to what the patient was saying and doing. This latter change, which all members of the seminar agreed to be at least in part a result of the research group's participation with the therapist–participation which often opened his mind to new lines of thought about the patient–apparently had much to do with the resolution of the therapist's sleepiness.

Thus, the group had experienced at first hand a difficulty which had been hampering the therapeutic relationship and were able to deal with this difficulty in a here-and-now fashion. We came to see that this difficulty was traceable to the patient's own highly anxiety-charged, ambivalent feelings, which had been so anxiety-provoking to the therapist that he found himself resorting unconsciously to an unaccustomed defence, sleepiness. It appeared that the therapist had been communicating this anxiety to the group so that, for a time, the group as a whole manifested this same unconscious defence against anxiety.

Let me interject at this point that my experience in hearing numerous additional therapists present cases before groups (analytic training seminars and hospital staff conferences) has caused me to become slow in forming an unfavourable opinion of any therapist on the basis of his presentation of a case. With convincing frequency I have seen that a therapist who during an occasional presentation appears to be lamentably anxious, compulsive, confused in his thinking, or what not, actually is a basically capable colleague who, as it were, is trying unconsciously, by this demeanour during the presentation, to show us a major problem-area in the therapy with his patient. The problem-area is one which he cannot perceive objectively and describe to us effectively in words; rather, he is unconsciously identifying with it and is in effect trying to describe it by way of his behaviour during the presentation.

Example 2.–In one of the therapeutic hours soon after our research project had been set up, the patient was describing his constant striving for integration within himself and for integration (that is, good communication, emotional closeness) between himself and other people, his repeated failure, and his consequent feelings of anxiety and despair. He felt helpless and hopeless about the fragmentation of his self into various isolated islands, and about the isolation of his over-all existence from that of other human beings. His words were fumbling, imprecise, often strange, and yet at times couched in poetically beautiful allegory; and he gave one an unforgettably poignant impression of a person who was striving against despair. After each member of the seminar had read a transcript of this interview, the group listened to a recording of part of it, and also heard from the therapist a résumé of the entire week's therapy. The focus of the group discussion was intended to be upon this particular therapeutic hour.

It is therefore striking, in examining a transcript of this therapeutic hour alongside a transcript of the seminar which then ensued, to see how closely our group interaction paralleled, in its conspicuous uncoordination, the very lack of intrapsychic and interpersonal integration which the patient himself had portrayed so vividly. Almost two-thirds of our discussion time had elapsed before we brought our attention to bear upon the interview. Meanwhile, there had been a very long and quite generalized, theoretical discussion about despair, without mention of the despair which the patient himself had voiced so movingly. Both before and after our listening to the recorded excerpt of the hour, there was an extraordinary lack of integration in the seminar's functioning. This is indicated, on perusing the transcript, by numerous instances of one member's failing to hear another member's words, one member's misconstruing the point of another's remarks, and one member's interrupting with a new subject when another was talking; and by additional evidences of irritation and impatience among the members, including the sleepiness referred to in the first example.

Thus when transcripts of the therapeutic hour and of this associated seminar meeting are studied together, it is apparent that the temporary disintegration of the seminar members' inter-relationships was, at least in part, a consequence of the lack of integration in the patient himself and in his interpersonal relationships (including his relationship with the therapist). While the seminar was taking place, our temporarily great difficulty in working with one another was experienced, apparently, in terms of, 'I never could work with So-and-so' (that is, some other seminar member), or 'So-and-so always thinks he knows more than anybody else.'

Example 3.—An especially clear-cut example of this process occurred in the eighth month of our research. For about the first third of the particular session we worked together with the reasonably good collaboration which had by this time become customary. Then, for a few minutes, we listened to the recording of a portion of one of the therapeutic hours, which was outstanding for a kind of poignant complexity which the patient expressed. In the main, he was describing, in a laboured way, the confusion he had felt as a child as to whether he was loved and accepted in the family, and as to how his father's mind and his own mind worked, and his confusion, after the onset of his psychosis, as to why he did some of the strange things he found himself doing—as to 'whether I'm really me or not. . . . whether it is my personality or who I was'.

Immediately after listening to this recording, we began to relate to one another quite differently. We became, in essence, all tangled up: a long and complicated wrangle occurred over one member's having interrupted another, and as soon as this subsided, another complicated wrangle developed as to whether one member had been critical towards the therapist in a remark about this recorded excerpt.

At the end of about ten minutes of this strikingly tangled inter-relatedness, one of the members finally said, 'This is really fascinating. We've just heard from R [the patient] what to me was a very stressful thing to hear, about how terribly *complex* his childhood relations were, and what happens is that within ten minutes we get all tangled up to hell in a very *complicated* kind of present interaction. I wonder if it's a way of trying to keep from feeling with R this early childhood material.'

Within a few moments, three of the other four members agreed to this point (the fifth member being noncommittal), and the collaboration among all five seminar members pursued, through-out the remainder of the session, the productive course which it had been following until we had listened to the recording.

In this instance again, it would have been easy for all five of us to dismiss our wrangling with one another as purely due to a flaring up of long-known personal 'allergies' towards one another. Our recognition of the connexion with the therapeutic situation enabled us to derive meaningful therapeutic data from the incident. It led us on, during the remainder of the seminar, to a deeper understanding of the interaction between patient and therapist, and a deeper realization of the stresses to which the patient had been subjected during his upbringing.

By precisely what mechanism or mechanisms the reflection pro-cess occurs, I feel most unsure and cannot, therefore, do more than tentatively suggest. As has been indicated, I believe that uncon-scious identification is one of the nuclear processes involved.

It appears that the reflection process is initiated when the therapy touches upon an area of the patient's personality in which repressed or dissociated feelings are close to awareness, so that he simultaneously manifests anxiety and some defence against this anxiety. The therapist then, being exposed to the patient's anxiety, experiences a stirring up of his own anxiety with regard to the comparable area of his own personality. The therapist now, it seems, unconsciously copes with this anxiety in himself by either identifying with the defence-against-anxiety which the patient is utilizing, or by resorting to a defence which is complementary to that which the patient is utilizing.[6] Next,

[6] An example of the therapist's identifying with the patient's defence: the patient experiences confusion; the therapist also experiences confusion. An example of the

when the therapist comes for supervision about this therapeutic relationship, the supervisor may intuitively realize, in the way that I have repeatedly illustrated, that the therapist, in the anxiety and defence-against-anxiety which he is exhibiting, is unconsciously trying to express something about what is going on in the patient—something which the therapist's own anxiety prevents him from putting his finger on and consciously describing to the supervisor. It is as if the therapist were unconsciously trying, in this fashion, to tell the supervisor what the therapeutic problem is.[7]

The anxiety shrouded within this problem-area is presumably most intense within the patient himself, is somewhat less intense as 'shared' in the relationship between patient and therapist, and comes to the supervisor in a still more attenuated form. This attenuation is due not only to the circumstance that, among the three participants, *self-awareness* is usually least in the patient and greatest in the supervisor, but also to the fact that the *depth of emotional involvement* in the therapeutic situation is usually greatest in the patient, and least in the supervisor.

Thus the supervisor and the therapist are enabled to deal with the problem-area therapeutically, in a here-and-now context. After a therapeutic process has been set in motion on this, so to speak, miniature scale, the therapist is in a position to carry over the therapeutic process into his relationship with the patient, and eventually the patient is thereby enabled to accomplish an intrapsychic resolution of the problem.

Perhaps the reflection process is an extension of a process which the therapist commonly encounters, in his work with patients, in which the patient while manifesting some difficult kind of behaviour is, as it were, unconsciously telling the therapist,

---

therapist's utilizing a defence which is complementary to the patient's defence: the patient's defence-against-anxiety takes the form of his becoming accusing towards the therapist; the therapist in response, to keep his own anxiety out of awareness, feels accused and guilty.

[7] M. Cohen comments upon instances '. . . in supervised analyses, where the supervisee communicates to the supervisor that he is in an anxiety-arousing situation with the patient, not by the material he relates, but by some appearance of increased tension in his manner of reporting' (Cohen, 1952, p. 239). One sees that she stops short of attributing to such communicated anxiety the high degree of specificity which I find in it. That is, in my experience the supervisee often communicates not only that he is in an anxiety-arousing situation with the patient, but also specifically what *kind* of anxiety-arousing situation it is, or, in other words, what the anxiety is *about*.

'The way you are feeling now, in response to my behaviour, is the way I so often felt in response to my mother (or father, or whomever) when she treated me the way I am treating you.' In this kind of transference the patient relates to the therapist as though the therapist were the patient's earlier self, and the patient now were, say, the patient's mother or father.[8] It is in very much this fashion that the therapist is, so frequently, unconsciously saying to the supervisor, 'The way you are feeling now is the way I feel much of the time during my hours with this patient', or, 'The way you are feeling now is the way the patient himself feels during the hours, which is just as he used to feel towards his mother (or father, or whomever) as a child.'

The objection may be raised that if a therapist unconsciously identifies with a patient in the fashion I have outlined, this must mean that an area of dissociated or repressed feeling is present in the therapist's personality, and that he must be incompletely analysed – that this reflection process would be of negligible importance among experienced and well-analysed therapists. I quite agree that such unconscious identification presumably occurs less often, in any troublesome intensity, as a therapist grows in self-awareness and psychotherapeutic experience. But I would emphasize that this is a matter of degree. My own experience strongly suggests that no therapist ever reaches such a high degree of self-awareness and technical competence as to be consistently free from important involvements of the kind I have been describing, when he is exposed to intense anxiety in his patient.

I do not doubt that there is occasionally a distribution of anxiety quite different from that described above as being typical – that is, there may be situations in which the therapist's, or even the supervisor's, anxiety is more intense than that of either of the other two participants, at least for a limited period of time. Under these circumstances, the disturbing processes in the therapeutic relationship, and the inner emotional responses in the patient, will be, in part, reflections of anxiety in the supervisor-therapist relationship.

At this point, let me emphasize that it is not only 'negative'

[8] Another way of describing this, psychodynamically, is to say that the patient is manifesting an unconscious identification with a traumatizing personality trait of, for example, his mother or father.

elements, anxiety-laden processes, which are carried over from the patient-therapist relationship to the therapist-supervisor relationship, or vice versa. Positive elements (fondness, pleasure derived from a collaborative effort which is bearing fruit, and so forth) may likewise be carried over. For example, if a supervisor finds in himself an especial fondness for a therapist during a particular phase of their work, this may be in part traceable to the circumstance that patient and therapist are currently very fond of one another.

As I have suggested, other processes instead of, or in addition to, the reflection process may lead a supervisor to perceive similarities between the supervisor-therapist relationship and the therapist-patient relationship. To describe only a few:

The supervisor may be projecting an important area of his own personality on to both therapist and patient. This would cause him to perceive therapist and patient as being strikingly similar in their modes of operation.

The therapist may be projecting similarly on to both supervisor and patient. This would cause him to behave similarly towards each of them, and would thus cause the supervisor to perceive similarities between the therapist's mode of functioning in the supervisory relationship and the therapist's mode of functioning in the therapeutic relationship.

The therapist may be involved in countertransference attitudes (in the strict, classical sense of the term) with regard to the patient and the supervisor alike, or the supervisor may be involved in countertransference attitudes towards the therapist and the patient alike. In either of these two instances, again, the supervisor would then find strikingly similar patterns in the supervisory relationship when compared with the therapeutic relationship.

As has been pointed out by Gitelson (1948, p. 209), the therapist who is himself under analysis may utilize his patient's conflicts as defences in his own analysis and, I would add, in the supervisory relationship also. This, too, would lead the supervisor to perceive major parallels between the supervisory relationship and the therapeutic relationship. Ackerman (1953) has dealt at some length with a number of these and other related complexities in an informative article.

Despite such possible complicating circumstances as these, the

175

reflection process is, in my experience, very important and frequently occurring, yielding rich dividends when one is alert to it and utilizes it in the general fashion which has been described. My experience in certain long-term supervisory relationships suggests that the further the supervisor and therapist advance in self-awareness and clinical experience, the more their *relationship* becomes free from such complicating circumstances as those just mentioned, and the more sensitively this relationship becomes attuned to the therapeutically useful reflection process. This may be regarded as quite analogous to the evolution which a therapist or supervisor undergoes as an *individual*, wherein as he becomes (through personal analysis, therapeutic experience, and general experience in living) progressively free from countertransference difficulties and from tendencies to projection, the more he can trust his inner emotional responses as being sensitive indicators of what is actually happening in the immediate interpersonal relationship.

Finally, let me emphasize that there would seem to be great value in studying exhaustively the interplay between the patient-therapist relationship and the therapist-supervisor relationship, since this total situation is without a parallel anywhere else among human relations, in that each relationship includes at least one expert in the study of intrapersonal and interpersonal processes. Thus this area offers unique possibilities for research. The results of such research might well be applicable not only to psychotherapy and to the supervision of psychotherapy, but to human relationships in general.

Chapter 5

THE PSYCHODYNAMICS
OF VENGEFULNESS (1956)[1]

IN psychiatric and psycho-analytic literature, vengefulness is customarily described merely as one form of hostility. Only in occasional papers is it noted that the striving for revenge can serve, in addition, important defensive functions–that is, as a defence against the awareness of anxiety-laden, repressed emotions. This paper will emphasize the defensive functions of vengefulness, particularly with regard to repressed grief and separation-anxiety–two affects which have been given little cognizance as being among the basic determinants of chronic vindictiveness.

One might accurately say, perhaps, that vindictiveness–or, for that matter, any one of the other forms of hostility–may serve as a defence against any repressed affect whatsoever. But vindictiveness seems to lend itself particularly well to the repression of grief and separation-anxiety. It enables the person to avoid or postpone the experiencing of both these affects, because he has not really *given up* the other person towards whom his vengefulness is directed: that is, his preoccupation with vengeful fantasies about that person serves, in effect, as a way of psychologically *holding on to* him.

In my experience, patients do not become free from a crippling thirst for revenge merely by working through the hostility residing therein. Not until the therapy has gone on to achieve a working-through of the deeper-lying grief and separation-anxiety is the foundation for vengefulness eradicated, and the patient's approach to his fellow men governed instead by genuine friendliness.

The ubiquitous importance of a revenge motive among both neurotic and psychotic patients is portrayed well by Izette DeForest in an article (1950), entitled 'The Self-Dedication of the Psychoneurotic Sufferer to Hostile Protest and Revenge'.

[1] First published in *Psychiatry*, Vol. 19 (1956), pp. 31-9.

Although vengefulness is but one among the many twisted channels into which the neurotic or psychotic patient's life has become diverted, I have been impressed with the number of patients, of all diagnostic types, in whom, in Karen Horney's words, therapy or analysis brings to light 'the compulsive drive towards revenge', which, she says, is 'the governing passion of a lifetime to which everything is subordinated, including self-interest. All intelligence, all energies, then, are dedicated to the one goal of vindictive triumph' (Horney, 1948, p. 5).

As to the origin of vindictiveness in the course of the patient's early development, various writers have offered different hypotheses. DeForest ascribes it to thwarting, by the parents, of the growing child's individuality, with resultant vengefulness on his part for having been forced to mould himself to their values. August Stärcke, in his classic paper (1921) on the castration complex, in which he identifies weaning with a primal castration, seems to suggest that vindictiveness first appears in the form of a desire in the infant to retaliate upon the mother–in particular, upon the mother's breasts–for her having robbed him of this erstwhile precious part of himself, as he has experienced it. Gustav Bychowski, in his book on the psychotherapy of psychosis (1952), points to this weaning situation as the origin of the depressive patient's desire to 'revenge himself on his mother, either by taking away her breast or her imaginary penis' (p. 260). None of these three writers has pointed out the importance of separation-anxiety and grief; vengefulness is presented as consisting, rather, merely in retaliatory hostility.

Karl Abraham, in a paper (1924) on the oral character, hints at the importance of separation-anxiety in such persons, who, he implies, possess much vengefulness as part of their character. And Otto Fenichel (1945) in his book *The Psychoanalytic Theory of Neurosis*, clearly acknowledges the importance of separation-anxiety in the vengefulness evident in many schizophrenics. Otherwise, so far as I have been able to determine, the thesis presented here has not been dealt with in the literature. In particular, apparently no one has previously stressed the role, here, of grief.

The question of what functions vengefulness serves in the economy of neurosis or psychosis has been dealt with only by Horney, so far as I know. In a stimulating article on this subject

(1948) she states that vindictiveness serves (i) to provide a form of self-protection to the person against the hostility from without, as well as against the hostility from within (by 'self-protection . . . against the hostility from within', I understand her to mean that vengefulness is experienced by the person not as hostility *per se*, but rather as righteous wrath); (ii) to restore injured pride; and (iii) to provide the hope for, or sensation of, a vindictive triumph. She also suggests that it may serve (iv) to keep under repression feelings of hopelessness about one's life.

It appears, then, that the thirst for revenge has had a multi-determined origin in the neurotic or psychotic person's early development, and that it likewise serves multiple functions in his chronologically adult personality. The following clinical examples will highlight only two functions of vengefulness: its unconscious utilization by the patient as a defence against the awareness of, first, repressed grief and, second, repressed separation-anxiety. These affects appear, however, to constitute two of the deepest-lying roots of vengefulness.

In placing these examples in two separate categories to illustrate these two functions, I am employing an artificial device for the sake of this presentation. In actual practice, one is likely to find that both grief and separation-anxiety are importantly present in the patient who exhibits the defence of chronic vengefulness. Certain of the following examples show both these affects quite prominently, and the categorization in two sets of examples is based simply upon my finding that in certain patients, grief seemed to be of *predominant* importance as compared with separation-anxiety, whereas the reverse was true of the other patients described.

The Role of Grief

Example 1.–A man in his late twenties had been hospitalized for several years with paranoid schizophrenia, and had had some years of intensive psychotherapy before coming to Chestnut Lodge Sanitarium, when I became his therapist. For nearly a year after his transfer to the Lodge he was–as he was reported to have been for years–vengefulness personified. He apparently spent most of his waking hours in plotting revenge upon numerous figures, now including me. In his therapeutic sessions he viciously described the terrible retaliation that would be wrought upon all who had abused him. His facial expression was usually one either of tautness, with narrowed eyes, as he directed vengeful warnings to me, or of vindictive triumph as he bellowed a vivid description of the destruction that would be brought upon me and his other tormentors when the tables were finally turned.

But from the very beginning of my contacts with him, there were indications that all this vindictiveness was mainly serving to shield him from grief—grief which he was terrified of facing. It seemed that as long as he could perceive all other persons as being inhumanly abusive to him, he was able to keep his feelings of love under repression, and as long as he could do this latter, then there were no conscious grounds for grief: as he saw it, no one had ever been kind to him; no one had ever, therefore, been the object of his fondness; so there were no conscious feelings of loss, of grief, concerning either past or present experiences.

After nearly a year of work with me, however, he finally started experiencing his grief and began weeping openly. He was even able to say of his mother, who had died late in his childhood and whom, in his illness, he had vilified more intensely than anyone else, 'She liked me.' As he made this simple statement his voice was full of love and grief. This, I think, one would regard as a landmark in the therapy of any person suffering from paranoid schizophrenia.

Of particular interest is the fact that then, for a time, he recoiled from this by a redoubling of his venomous, vengeful utterances, with especial regard, as usual, to delusionally distorted mother-figures. His vengefulness had never found more frank expression. He said at this time, among other things, 'In order to crush them you have to crush them *financially*, and that's what I'm going to do! That is my vow!' This was declared with a steely intentness of purpose, and he was clearly serving notice on *me*; this was one of the many times in the therapy when I was in the transference position of a malevolent mother.

Then about a month later he experienced an upsurge of fondness towards a nurse on the ward, one who had long been a prominent object of his venom as another evil mother-figure. Near the beginning of one hour he started to tell, fondly, of something this nurse had just been saying or doing, but had hardly begun when he broke into tears, clutched his side—where he had often complained of feeling pain – and said in anguish, 'I can't stand it.' I replied, 'The grief?' and he said, 'Yes.'

But then, in the course of a very few moments, he pulled himself together and began talking vengefully in both tone and content, asserting that he could start a riot, and that he could prove how wrong are the authorities who speak over the radio. (These authorities were a frequent target of his vindictiveness.) Such vengeful expressions, in the customary unending stream, took up the remaining two-thirds of the hour, although this time they were not openly directed towards me. At the end of the hour, after having weighed the question of whether to do so, I said to him reassuringly, 'Grief is painful; but it's important for you to go ahead and feel through it.'

He replied, in a triumphant, vindictive spirit, 'All right! *Now I know where you stand!*' and he hurled at me, '*Now I know where you stand!*' two or three more times as I left the room.

Not only upon these two occasions which I have described, but upon numerous subsequent ones in my work with this man, I saw his vengefulness in action as a defence against the underlying grief – and linked with it, of course, his likewise-repressed love – which was so frightening and painful to him by contrast to the long-accustomed, relatively comfortable thirsting for revenge.

Example 2. – The patient, a 25-year-old premedical student, whom I saw in an out-patient clinic for a total of twelve interviews scattered over the course of six months, was, like the patient just described, overtly one of the most vengeful, bitter persons whom I have ever seen. He began the initial interview by voicing intense hostile feelings, and continued to spend the majority of the time in this and the subsequent interviews expressing vindictiveness, bitterness, and scorn about various people. These feelings were most often directed at his wife, as a nagging, domineering mother-surrogate, but frequently also towards the people in his home town in Wisconsin, which he had left five years previously. Towards these latter people he felt vengeful because of their having freely let him know that he, as he put it, 'came from the wrong side of town'.

This man had experienced an extraordinarily traumatic upbringing. While he was still a small child, his only sibling, a younger brother, died a violent death, and soon after this his parents were divorced. Throughout his upbringing, he lived in economic poverty in a home which suffered social ostracism in the small community where he grew up.

It was in his fifth hour with me that he volunteered the statement that in attending college, which he was then doing, 'I am trying to get revenge—revenge on the people back in Wisconsin.' He said this in a way which, in contrast to his usual tone, was only half-heartedly bitter and vindictive; he seemed somewhat ashamed and embarrassed. He then fell to recounting, bitterly, some of the incidents which he had described before, about how various of the townspeople used to ridicule him for having a prominent nose, and for coming from the wrong side of town. He said that if he could get through college he would feel 'gleeful' at 'proving to them that I can become somebody'. 'They all expected me to stay on the wrong side of town and grow up pushing a plough', he explained, sarcastically.

'I suppose', he went on, 'that the fellows out there who were the idols of the town when I was a kid are pushing a plough now.' But significantly he then said, no longer with sarcasm but with regret, 'I suppose they're happy; but that life is not for me.' I got the impression here, as I did many times during this hour, that he inwardly felt that he really had no choice—that he felt unable to go back there to live, however much he might yearn to do so. Material from this and other hours indicated that this feeling stemmed from various sources, including his need to keep under repression some of his feelings about his life there, and his compulsive loyalty to his mother, who had smarted under the social ostracism there and had put pressure upon her son to go elsewhere and make good in order to 'show them'.

Later in the course of this fifth interview, he described further the rejections he had suffered from the townspeople. His tone was different now. Before, it had been bitter and vengeful, tending to impress one with the callous hostility of those who had rejected him, whereas he spoke now in a tone of grief, so that I could see, more clearly than before, how much real hurt he had suffered and how intensely he longed to be accepted in his home town.

I inquired whether he had noticed even transitory desires, from time to time, to return there to live. He promptly disclaimed any such wish, adding, 'I have thought I would like to live in Ohio, or Minnesota, or Illinois; but I would never want to go back to that town to live.' This he said determinedly; but it is interesting that two of the states he mentioned border Wisconsin on two sides! He later mentioned that he enjoyed going back there to visit with a few good friends, said that he liked to 'shoot the breeze' with them, and, when I asked if he perhaps missed them, he agreed, 'I do miss them.' Simple though this may appear, it represented a quite striking change in this man who had appeared, initially, so confirmedly bitter and vengeful about his home town.

Example 3.–Several years ago I undertook intensive psychotherapy with a married but childless Southern woman, then 35 years of age, who had just been admitted to Chestnut Lodge in a depressive condition. During the first several therapeutic hours, she spent each session almost exclusively in trying to remember the names of various members of the personnel at the Lodge, including my own, and the gross outlines of her own life history, and in castigating herself for her inability to remember. Repeatedly she would start to say something, forget what she had started to say, develop an increasingly worried and finally very exasperated facial expression, berate herself as being 'worthless . . . just a numbskull, that's all!', burst into tears, and then become doubly exasperated and condemnatory towards herself for weeping without, so far as she could see, any rational reason for doing so. Although the bulk of the evidence came to indicate that hers was a severe neurotic rather than a psychotic condition, the self-castigation initially seemed psychotic in its degree of harshness; and although she eventually proved to be of normal intelligence and free from organic mental impairment, her initial difficulty in thinking seemed so marked as to indicate either mental deficiency or organic brain disease.

The history–as it was obtained from relatives, from a hospital where she had been treated five years previously, and increasingly from herself as her memory improved slowly after about the first two weeks of therapy–showed that a sister had died at age 3, four years before the patient's own birth. The mother had been in a depression from the time of the death of this older daughter– that is, before the patient was born. When the patient was 9, the mother finally had to be hospitalized, and subsequently committed suicide in the psychiatric hospital. The mother had always related herself to the patient in a solicitous, overprotective fashion, and now the child was suddenly left as the sole surviving female in a family which included four older brothers and an emotionally remote, rigidly domineering father. Only two of the brothers were at all close to her in age, and both rapidly outdistanced her in social and intellectual achievements. She was chronically regarded as 'the stupid one' in the family, and her first breakdown occurred at the age of 20, while she was enrolled in a small teacher's college where she was not making the grade either socially or academically. The details of this breakdown are unknown, save that she was said to have been 'disturbed and unmanageable'. Significantly, a period of five months' rest in the company of a female nurse, at a mountain resort, enabled her to recover without hospitalization, and even to return home a markedly more warm and outgoing person than she had been previously.

At the age of 25 she married a lumber dealer, a man regarded by her family as being socially and intellectually much inferior to themselves. Towards her husband she maintained, from the first, a clinging dependency, masked behind an almost incessant henpecking of him. Five years later an aunt died, who in the words of her husband, had been 'like a mother to her'. He said that his wife thereupon showed a marked accentuation of her anxious, clinging behaviour towards him, and began to awake often at night, weeping, without knowing why she was weeping. Her condition rapidly increased in severity so that, one month after the aunt's death, she was admitted to a psychiatric hospital. There she was found to be 'Confused, disoriented, incoherent. Delusional, hallucinatory, continuously weeping without tears.' In the course of a period of electroshock therapy followed by a long series of insulin coma treatments, she reached an inactive, apathetic state in which, 18 months after admission, she was released from the hospital.

During the next few years at home, she improved slowly. But then, in a setting – as she eventually brought out in the therapy with me – of increasing anxiety lest she lose her husband, who had never tried to have children by her and who was under increasing pressure from his own family to divorce her, she gradually developed the depressive symptomatology which necessitated her hospitalization at the Lodge. She had evidently not let herself recognize the anxiety as having to do with the threatened dis-

184

solution of her marriage; she had only noticed with mounting concern, over the months, that she was gradually losing weight.

As the therapy progressed, it became increasingly clear that her tendency was to relate herself to other persons, and even to aspects of her own self and to various inanimate objects, in a vindictive, railing fashion. As she had excoriated herself initially for her poor memory and her tears, she later castigated the nasal discharge which, for a time, supplanted the tears, and frequently reviled, for example, her arm, in which she still experienced pain following a severe burn some years before, her menstruation, and her brain ('It's a hell of a brain!'). It was as if her conscious ego resided, at different times, in varying parts of her psycho-physical being and railed against one or another part of herself as being an offensive, hatefully unsatisfactory foreign body. She also directed the same kind of vituperation towards various in-animate objects—towards a powder-compact which, as it were, refused to work, towards various items which she purchased from time to time and which proved to be unsatisfactory to her, and so on.

As the months of therapy went by, her deeper-lying feelings of fondness began to emerge—fondness towards her husband, her father, various nurses, certain other patients, and me. Interestingly, her growing intimacy towards me was spearheaded by the same vindictive kind of feelings. After a few months she had improved sufficiently, symptomatically, to move to out-patient status.

Gradually indications appeared that a long-buried grief about the loss of her mother was at the root of her illness. In an hour during the fourteenth month of therapy this came out in the clearest form in which I ever perceived it. After having wept copiously throughout much of the hour, in a spirit now not of self-condemnation but of genuine grief, she spoke of missing her husband and of wanting to be at home with him. I asked if she had ever missed anyone as strongly as this before. She replied hesitantly, in a childlike, naïve way, 'I miss my mother; but I know she can never return, so I think about George [her husband] instead.' 'I think he's all right', she added in an uncertain, anxious tone.

It was during the month following this hour that she dis-continued her therapy here and returned to her home. The indications were that what she was fleeing from, in therapy, was primarily the ancient grief about the loss of her mother. My belief now is that I, too, contributed to the dissolution of the therapy, on the basis of my own anxiety about grief from my early life–an area which, at the time, I had not yet explored at all thoroughly in my personal analysis.

The Role of Separation-Anxiety

Example 1.–A man in his middle thirties, under analysis for a compulsive neurosis, mentioned in one of his hours that on the previous evening, while at a girl friend's apartment waiting for her to get ready to go out with him, he had felt like smashing up her furniture to 'make her pay' for keeping him waiting like this so often. When I asked for associations to 'making someone pay', he smiled embarrassedly and said, 'Sometimes I feel that I'm making all the doctors–all the doctors I've ever known–pay, when I come in here and never let on that I feel at all fond of you.' I asked, 'Making them pay for—?' He replied, 'For always treating me so impersonally.'

But significantly, within a few seconds after this he was telling about how, from preparatory school onward, in his relationships with each one of a long series of girl friends, he would try to endear himself to the girl and then if he succeeded, and she began to show fondness for him, he would 'drop her like a hot potato'.

This last comment suggests that although there was, in the analytic hours, a conscious vengeful feeling in his withholding the expression of fondness towards me, at an unconscious level this was based upon separation-anxiety–anxiety lest I drop him if he ventured to express his fond feelings, just as he himself had dropped his girl friends. Material in subsequent hours established that this was indeed the case.

Example 2.–A 31-year-old government official, the father of three children, had a character-structure in which one prominent component was vengefulness. Throughout approximately the first two-thirds of his analysis, he chronically ventilated bitterness about how little he had received from his parents in the past and how little he was receiving from me at present, and asserted his determination to wrest the desired–basically oral– supplies from these unjust persons while wreaking a long-sought revenge upon them at the same time. His vengefulness was so intense, and his all-round capability to back it up was so formidable, that for a long time I felt quite intimidated by it.

It was little more than halfway through his analysis that the functioning of his vengefulness, as a defence against anxiety-laden repressed feelings, began to reveal itself to me. It gradually became evident that separation-anxiety, particularly referable to his very early relationship with his mother, was one of the most important of these repressed feelings. The following material from the 416th analytic hour, a little over two years following the start of the analysis, is a sample of the data concerning this point:

At the beginning of this hour, I mentioned to him that I would not be working on the following Monday. He replied, rather nastily, 'Oh?' and was silent for about three minutes, then spent nearly half an hour castigating me for 'just announcing' this. He ended by protesting irately that *he* had to come regularly for the hours or to ask my permission to stay away, whereas *I* 'simply announced it without asking me if it would be okay with me'.

It was next that he revealed, in a succinct statement, a clear view of the defensive function of his vindictiveness. He began, in a threatening, vengeful tone, 'Wait until the Monday after that—*I'll* take *that* Monday off', but then added in an anxious, very weakly sarcastic voice, 'I'm sure I'll still *be* here then.' He had recently been making such good analytic progress in other areas that he evidently felt threatened—as he had repeatedly felt before in reaction to similar phases of progress—that I might abruptly terminate the analysis.

Later in this same hour he spoke of his anxiety about an alcoholic filing clerk, a very unstable person, whose work the patient was supervising. 'I think the main fear that was gnawing at me', he said in referring to a recent altercation between them, 'is the fact that here is a fellow who does lose control of himself when he's been drinking, and beats people up. I'm afraid that the way I'm telling him what to do will make him real vengeful.' When I asked for associations to 'vengeful', he paused shortly and said, 'Well, *I* feel quite vengeful, I think mostly when situations like this [my taking the following Monday off] come up. . . .'

Next, he reported a dream of the previous night which clearly portrayed his being separated from a mother-figure—a female co-worker, considerably older than himself, who had recurrently, throughout the analysis, emerged in dreams and associations as an early mother-figure—and his feeling of anxiety about this separation. He went on to spend the remainder of the hour in expressing a wealth of free associations having to do with separation-anxiety involving a series of five mother-figures, including his actual mother and me. In the course of this he said, in a tone of anxious exasperation, 'I just feel so *alone* from time to time, and it just seems that when I'm feeling nice and friendly I don't have any difficulty with these people; but other times I do have trouble, and I don't know what it is.'

In response to this I asked for associations to 'feeling alone', and he replied that, at such times, 'I wanta sock people in the teeth—everything feels hateful.' He added, 'At other times, when I'm feeling friendly, other people are, too.' 'But what can I *do* about it? I don't know what's going on', he stressed, in the same anxious, exasperated manner.

When I then suggested for association, 'something you couldn't do anything about', he replied, 'Well, there've been so many things, of course, that I've felt for so long that I couldn't do anything about, like wanting to get people by the throat and strangle them till they're black in the face. . . .'

This last statement he made in the vengeful spirit which had been so characteristic of him throughout the analysis thus far. Here it seemed reasonably clear that his vindictiveness was serving a defensive function, to ward off the awareness of some degree of his anxiety about separation—from, originally, his mother early in his childhood—and his anxiety about the feeling of aloneness associated with that state of separation.

Example 3.—The patient was a 32-year-old married man with a severe and chronic conversion neurosis, who was treated at Chestnut Lodge by Margaret J. Rioch.[2] The patient's major complaint was of a persistent backache.

This man had been given to feel, during his upbringing, that his life was to be devoted wholly to the welfare of his parents and other family members. To this he had acquiesced wholeheartedly, on a conscious level; but in the course of psycho-analysis he came to realize that the expectation had been building up within him,

[2] I wish to express my appreciation to Dr Rioch for her kind permission to use this material.

all along, that some day he would be rewarded for all this devotion. He married, a number of years before undertaking analysis, a woman who promised complete devotion to him, but who, as it turned out, did not meet his emotional needs at all satisfactorily. In the course of his analysis he became aware that his conversion symptom represented an effort on his part to force her – and others – to provide more satisfactorily for these needs.

For a long time after he had begun psycho-analysis, his parental family members kept up their usual reproachful barrage that he should come home and take care of his mother, who was old and sick, or of his wife, who was not, they insisted, able to manage the marital home without him. Meanwhile, as analysis progressed, he became aware that he was tired of *giving* and realized that now, as he put it, 'I just want to *take*'. This new feeling was, at first, laden with strong self-reproach.

It gradually became clear that the strong repression of his dependency needs, with the severe deprivation which this entailed, had long been giving rise to various feelings which were frightening to him. Among these feelings was an intense thirst for revenge.

His family had always attached tremendous importance to the acquisition of money. He considered, with apparently considerable justification, that he had dragged his family up out of the slums. Now, he felt, in the course of his expensive psychiatric treatment he was using up all the money. On the one hand he felt very guilty about taking any of it; but on the other hand, he now realized, he would like to take it all. He came to express vengeful feelings quite openly, saying he would just like to grab all the money, in retaliation for their not wanting to *give* him any. He went on to express revenge-fantasies about various parent figures in current life who, he felt, were depriving him. His fantasies had to do with a retaliatory depriving of each of these persons of his or her livelihood.

Much of his vindictive feeling was traceable, in particular, to his early relationship with his mother who, the patient was bitterly convinced, had chronically usurped the role of child and forced the patient to mother *her*.

But it developed that this vengefulness was screening deeper feelings of both grief and separation-anxiety. One day when his psychiatric administrator at the hospital had refused to inform him what his liquid sedation contained, he came into his analytic hour and burst out crying, very much like a sobbing infant, and said, 'I want to go home to my mother,' and went on in that vein for some time. In the following hour he expressed both grief and separation-anxiety about the death, several years previously, of an uncle who had been like a father to him, and about the recent death of a nurse at the hospital, clearly a good mother-figure of whom he had been very fond. He expressed anxiety that he himself might die imminently; an anxiety which seemed based, in part, upon his equating death with a terrifyingly complete deprivation of his dependency needs.

In the same hour he reported a dream in which he had no analyst and was trying to find one. A great number of people he knew were in the dream, but as he turned to each for help, each one was unable to help him or, in one instance, vengefully refused to help. The dream was confused and reflective of a feeling of being cut off from other persons. One may take it as portraying, among other things, his separation-anxiety.

These deeper insights were followed by relief, for a time, from his conversion symptom, the backache, which had been more or less incapacitating for years. He found himself freer now in ventilating his feelings to people, and the occasions of his doing so coincided with remissions in his painful symptom. Further, he now for the first time started planning to go home for a visit to see his wife, his mother, and other members of his parental family. He had never spoken of this before except in terms of a flight from analysis; but now he showed a genuine desire to see them again.

I shall conclude by quoting a passage written about 350 years ago by Shakespeare, one which beautifully portrays how the repression of grief can give rise, in extreme instances, to a literally insane striving for revenge. In this passage, King Lear has just experienced the shock of feeling that the two elder of his beloved three daughters have turned against him. In the presence of a court fool, he cries out,

You heavens, ...
. . . .
. . . . . . touch me with noble anger,

VENGEFULNESS

And let not women's weapons, water-drops,
Stain my man's cheeks! – No, you unnatural hags,
I will have such revenges on you both
That all the world shall – I will do such things, –
What they are, yet I know not; but they shall be
The terrors of the earth. You think I'll weep;
No, I'll not weep.
I have full cause of weeping; but this heart
Shall break into a hundred thousand flaws,
Or ere I'll weep. – O, Fool! I shall go mad!
                    (*King Lear*, Act II, scene 4.)

This he proceeds to do.[3]

---

[3] I referred to this as an example of repression. Strictly speaking it is, of course, an instance of suppression, a conscious rather than an unconscious process. But Shakespeare presented here, as if it were on a conscious basis, a process which in clinical practice one finds in actuality occurring at an unconscious level – a matter, that is, not of suppression but of repression.

Chapter 6

THE SCHIZOPHRENIC'S
VULNERABILITY TO THE
THERAPIST'S UNCONSCIOUS
PROCESSES (1958)[1]

AFTER several years of doing intensive psychotherapy with schizophrenic patients, I began to realize that schizophrenic experience and behaviour consists, surprisingly frequently, in the patient's responding to other people's unconscious processes. I had long been aware of the tremendous importance of *projection* in such patients' illnesses; but I was slower to see the great—perhaps equally tremendous—part which *introjection* plays, too, in schizophrenia and, hence, in the psychotherapy of schizophrenia. On theoretical grounds one can readily think, concerning any patient whose ego-boundaries are so incomplete as to facilitate massive projection, that by the same token he will be profoundly susceptible, also, to introjection. But in actual clinical work, introjection is a process which is in most instances much more subtle, much less conspicuously displayed, than is projection, and its detection in the arena of the therapeutic relationship tends to call for a higher degree of self-awareness in the therapist than the noticing of the patient's projection generally requires.

The schizophrenic patient's so frequent delusion of being magically 'influenced' by outside forces (radar, electricity, or what-not) is rooted partially in the fact of his responding to unconscious processes in people about him—people who, being unaware of these processes, will not and cannot help him to realize that the 'influence' comes from a non-magical, interpersonal source.

For two reasons I shall limit this study to an examination of the impact of the *therapist's* unconscious impulses and attitudes upon the schizophrenic patient. First, it is in the setting of the therapeutic relationship that I as a therapist have had my best

[1] First published in the *Journal of Nervous and Mental Disease*, Vol. 127 (1958), pp. 247–62.

opportunities to see this mechanism operating. Secondly, no matter how greatly this mechanism pervades a patient's relationships with everybody else, it must be regarded as having especially crucial significance when it occurs in the therapeutic relationship, both because this relationship is of unparalleled importance in the patient's current experience, and because it is essential that the therapist, and eventually the patient, become as aware as possible of the forces at work in their therapeutic investigation. The potential influence, for good or ill, of the therapist's personality upon the schizophrenic patient is even more awesome than that of the analyst in relation to the neurotic patient; hence it is especially incumbent upon the therapist, here, to be as fully aware as possible of the processes at work in him, and of their impact upon the patient.

I shall not attempt to trace out the presumable countertransference element in these unconscious processes in the therapist; rather, I wish only to show various of the *effects* which they have upon the patient's subjective experience and outward behaviour. The data I shall present derive solely from the psychotherapy of schizophrenia; but my experience with non-schizophrenic patients has led me to surmise that the relatively dramatic phenomena to be presented here have analogues, less dramatic and less easily detectable but of much importance none the less, in other varieties of psychiatric illness. In short, I surmise that it is in the *therapist's* relationship with a *schizophrenic* patient that he can see most readily certain introjective processes which are actually at work, in some form or other, in *any* relationship involving a patient with any type of neurotic or psychotic illness.

Survey of Relevant Literature

In psycho-analytic literature, it is in papers concerning countertransference, of course, that the analyst's unconscious processes have been described, and in actuality this whole vast segment of the literature is relevant to my present subject, a segment which had its historical point of origin in a paper by Freud (1910), in which he wrote, '. . . We have become aware of the "countertransference", which arises, in [the physician] as a result of the patient's influence on his unconscious feelings and we are almost inclined to insist that he shall recognize this countertransference in himself and overcome it' (1910, pp. 144–5).

From the subsequent flow of papers concerning countertransference in the analysis of neurotic patients, three recent articles are of the greatest relevance here. Little (1951) noted that '. . . Unconsciously we may exploit a patient's illness for our own purposes, both libidinal and aggressive, and he will quickly respond to this.'

Schroff (1957) gave an account of the analysis of a man with a character disorder of which sexual acting out was a prominent feature. He mentioned that, during a period of treatment with an earlier therapist, the man had acted out some of the therapist's unconscious impulses; and Schroff found, in his own work with the patient, that his countertransference problems influenced unfavourably the man's acting out, until late in the eventually successful analysis. This kind of mechanism, incidentally, had been described in a paper by Johnson and Szurek (1952), in which these authors reported their finding of children's acting out the parents' unconscious antisocial impulses. Barchilon (1957), in a paper concerning 'countertransference cures', reported a number of examples of analytic 'cures' which he showed to be based precariously upon not only transference but also countertransference, and he commented that 'In more extreme cases, the therapist forces the patient to act out his own unconscious solutions with little relevance to the patient's needs. . . .'

Turning now to the literature concerning schizophrenia, we find many papers which have emphasized the schizophrenic's powerful tendency towards incorporation or introjection;[2] a tendency which renders him vulnerable to the kind of phenomena which I shall describe. A few examples of such papers, concerning incorporation or introjection in schizophrenia, are those by Nunberg (1921), Abraham (1927), Bychowski (1930), and Allen (1935). In 1945 Fenichel commented that

> . . . it is possible to demonstrate in persons suffering from delusions of persecution the presence of the pregenital aim of incorporation which was the undifferentiated forerunner of both love and hate. Projection as such is based on a vagueness of the borderline between ego and non-ego. Ideas of incorporation also correspond to this vagueness. The incorporated object has become a part of the subject's ego . . . (Fenichel, 1945, p. 428).

[2] In this paper the terms 'incorporation' and 'unconscious identification' will be regarded as synonymous with the term 'introjection'. If these three terms refer to different psychodynamic processes, I have failed, despite careful perusal of the literature concerning them, to discern any such differences.

THE SCHIZOPHRENIC'S VULNERABILITY

Hill, in his volume, *Psychotherapeutic Intervention in Schizophrenia* (1955), described the parent's unconscious as playing an integral role in the development of schizophrenia in the child. Hill stressed the etiological importance of what one might call the introjection, into the child's super-ego, of the mother whose own personality-integration is under severe assault from her unconscious affects:

> . . . [The patient's] life has been severely restricted, limited, and invaded by the requirements of his parents' conscious and unconscious conflicts and drives. Anything in the unconscious of the parent which would produce anxiety must become a preoccupation of the patient in order to keep down parental anxiety and thereby reduce his own distress . . . (Hill, 1955, p. 53).

> . . . one meaning of the futility of the dependence-independence struggle of the schizophrenic . . . is his belief, based upon his observations, that, if he should improve and become well . . . , his mother would become psychotic . . . (*ibid.*, p. 127).

> [Concerning 'the mother as a presence in the superego' of the patient –] . . . his superego is to him a very real person within him, who not only advises and threatens or opposes but actually dominates his life with crippling restrictions and interdictions supported by the threat that the superego itself will go crazy . . . (*ibid.*, p. 156).

> . . . there is danger constantly of invasion of primitive superego demands which will disorganize the ego into a psychosis . . . (*ibid.*, p. 153).

Limentani, in a paper (1956) concerning symbiotic identification in schizophrenia, made, in passing, the following reference to a patient's sensitivity to his therapist's unconscious processes:

> . . . Richard was so keenly aware of his therapist's mood and reproduced it so closely that the therapist at times gained, from the interviews with the patient, awareness of how he himself felt.

Bowen also, in a preliminary report (1956) concerning his findings in a research project involving concomitant psychotherapy of schizophrenic patients and their parents, with the latter being housed on the hospital ward with their children, likewise portrayed the schizophrenic's vulnerability to the parent's unconscious affects:

> The more we have worked with these family groups at close range, the more we can see the interchangeability of anxiety and symptoms.

When we hear a mother express a worry about something that is outside the local setting, and when we get some feel of the intensity of the mother's worry with no expression of the worry in the mother, but at the very same time we see the patient's psychosis increase, it makes us more and more inclined to believe that schizophrenia is a process that exists within the family constellation rather than a problem in the patient alone (Bowen, 1956).

In Chapter 1 of this book concerning various manifestations of incorporation (which I am here terming introjection) in the therapeutic relationship, I described a number of instances in which mutual incorporation was found to be present; one of these examples was from my work with a schizophrenic patient. In Chapter 3 I pointed out that the schizophrenic's fear that he will lose his identity if he comes too close, emotionally, to another person, is a realistic fear in so far as he utilizes the mechanism of unconscious identification with (i.e. introjection of) the other person as a means of keeping out of awareness the anxiety-laden affects which interpersonal closeness stimulates in him. And in a 1957 paper (now Chapter 8 below) I presented the concept that one significant factor in the causation, and maintenance, of schizophrenia in any given individual consists in the impact upon him of other persons' efforts – largely or wholly unconscious efforts – to drive him 'crazy'. In support of this concept I presented data from patients' intrafamilial relationships, ward-group relationships, and intensive psychotherapeutic relationships; and I reported the finding that the motivation of the other person, who integrates with the patient in such a fashion, seems most often to consist in an unconscious desire to maintain a symbiotic relatedness with him.

Clinical Material

There now follow clinical data illustrative of three different ways in which a patient may respond to the therapist's unconscious processes. The patient may (a) experience the therapist's unconscious processes as being facets of his own personality; or (b) experience them in the form of hallucinations; or (c) compulsively act them out in behaviour which he himself finds incomprehensible.

THE SCHIZOPHRENIC'S VULNERABILITY

The Patient's Experiencing the Therapist's Unconscious Processes as being Facets of his own Personality

In illustrating this first phenomenon material from only one therapist-patient relationship will be presented, because it is essentially the same phenomenon, I think, as that which one finds so commonly and characteristically in depressive states. I present it here solely because I realized only shortly before writing this paper how frequently this can be detected among schizophrenic patients also. With these latter patients, *projection* is so conspicuous that one may fail to detect the more subtle, but perhaps equally important, place of this type of *introjection* among the patient's psychotic defences.

Three months before writing this paper I began working with a 26-year-old schizophrenic woman whose previous therapist had left the Chestnut Lodge staff. I had seen this woman, in passing, innumerable times in the course of her several years' stay there, and had always thought of her behaviour as outstandingly dominated by paranoid projection. She made almost incessant accusations to me and other passers-by, of this kind: 'I know what you're thinking! You're thinking that I shouldn't have drunk that coffee at 2 p.m. yesterday', or 'I know what you're going to say – you're going to say that I should have visited longer with my aunt over the telephone last week.' She would go, actually, into endless detail, and with innumerable variations, quite unwittingly displaying before the public eye the most private areas of her own unconscious, in this projected form. And in her psychotherapy with my predecessor, she evidenced projection in a similarly prominent fashion, as I learned from him in my capacity as supervisor during about 18 months of their work together.

It therefore came as a great surprise to me, when I began having therapeutic sessions with her, to find that although her long-known projection continued to be prominent, there were fascinatingly subtle evidences that introjection was at work with something like equal frequency.

During the first months of work with her I did not find this operative with respect to truly *unconscious* processes in myself, the kind of processes with which this paper is especially concerned, although I had little doubt that the future course of our work would bring such connexions to light. What I did find, rather,

197

were dozens of evidences of her introjecting aspects of myself which were preconscious in me at the moment and readily accessible to my consciousness. Had they not been so, I could not so quickly have discerned that she introjected them.

For example, in one of the first week's sessions, as she was prattling on in a self-depreciating and rather absent-minded fashion, I took my ease by tilting my head over, at a sharp angle, against the wall. She continued rambling on, but apparently taking in, with her eyes, this shift in my posture; one of the features of her behaviour which had impressed me during these early sessions was her apparently taking sharp visual note of every least thing about my appearance and bodily movements, but never making any verbal comments about these—never expressing any opinions about, or direct reactions to, them. In this instance, what I heard within a few seconds, in the midst of her prattling, was, 'I know I looked awkward on the tennis court', whereupon it occurred to me that this unusual, head-tilted posture of mine might well look awkward to her. In another session soon thereafter, the day was so hot that I removed my coat and loosened my tie; within a few seconds I heard, in the midst of her self-critical prattle, the statement, 'I'm a very slovenly person.' Thereupon I realized that in the eyes of this woman who had come from a highly genteel background and even in her illness was generally neatly groomed, I might well appear slovenly, sitting there in shirt sleeves and loosened necktie. But the fascinating thing was that she evidently genuinely experienced these traits as being aspects of herself and was quite unable to perceive them as traits of mine. I had already heard from her, within these first few hours, enough about her relationships with her parents to surmise that she had had largely to repress any critical feelings experienced towards either of her parents, both being people with unresilient and defensive character-structures, during her upbringing.

One might look at it that, in each of these instances I have described, this woman reacted, in keeping with her low self-esteem and intense self-criticism, to my actions as being non-verbal communications to her, communications designed to convey to her my opinion that she was awkward and slovenly. This would be quite a true viewpoint, I think, but would not negate the fact of her genuinely introjecting these behaviour-traits of mine. Incidentally, it should be noted that what she introjected were, apparently, not only my behaviour-traits themselves, but, even more clearly, my preconsciously *low opinion of* these behaviour-traits in myself. This I regard as an example of one of the mechanisms by which the schizophrenic patient expresses his unconscious endeavour to relieve the parent's own anxiety–by, namely, introjecting the parent's intrapsychic conflicts.

In subsequent hours, I found her to be referring to herself variously as 'smug', 'swaggering', 'blah', 'sleepy', and so on, at times when I realized, after hearing her say each of these things, that I was feeling thus and that I was no doubt appearing thus to her, but so appearing at a level of perception which was unconscious in her. It was evident that at a conscious level she genuinely perceived only *herself* as being thus and so, as, to be sure, she indeed was at times; but she seemed quite unable to perceive, consciously, that *I too* was being smug (or what not), and being so, oftentimes, when she showed nothing in her demeanour which would warrant her self-accusation along this line.

Perhaps partly as a result of my perceiving this tendency towards introjection on her part, and my therefore encouraging her to experience, and express, critical feelings to me as these became roused in her by the things I said and did, it required only a few weeks for her to begin expressing annoyance to me about my looking smug, or 'blah', or what not, at times when I was indeed feeling so. The relative ease with which this introjective mechanism could be relinquished suggests that her perception of these various behaviour-traits of mine had been taking place at, actually, a preconscious rather than fully unconscious level. And this consideration ties in with my general impression that this particular type of introjective phenomenon which I have just described is found in schizophrenic patients whose ego-functioning is at least somewhat more intact than that of the patients who manifest the other two types of introjective phenomena which I shall illustrate. These latter, more deeply-disorganized patients leave one with little doubt that these phenomena are taking place in them at a deeply unconscious level–deepest of all, I believe, as regards the third type of phenomenon to be described.

Before going on to the second type of phenomenon, however,

let me call attention to the general point, touched upon at the beginning of this paper, that–as can be seen in the brief data already given–introjective phenomena are less easily perceptible, and their detection calls for a higher degree of self-awareness in the therapist, than is the case with projective phenomena. A simple example will indicate this contrast. If a patient looks suspiciously at the therapist and says with hostility, 'I know what you're thinking–you're just figuring out a way to kill me!' and if this comes at a time when the therapist has no such thought or feeling in his awareness, he is at once alerted to the possibility that the patient is *projecting* some murderous intent upon him. But if a patient says, instead, with the self-disparagement that one finds so frequently among schizophrenic patients, 'I'm just a fat slob who can't even speak English!', it takes a bit of doing for the therapist, who probably at the moment is not having the thought that he himself is a fat slob who doesn't speak English in any outstandingly cultured way, to let his own trend of thought open up to just this rather unpleasantly jolting new reflection: namely, that much as he prefers to view himself otherwise, he *is* somewhat corpulent and his use of grammar *isn't* the best. Not until the therapist has traversed this relatively roundabout and difficult path does the thought occur to him, now, that *introjection* may have been involved in the statement which the patient has just made.

The Patient's Experiencing the Therapist's Unconscious Processes in the Form of Hallucinations

Until about a year before writing this paper I considered hallucinations to be, without exception, essentially projective phenomena. That is, I found that my clinical experience substantiated the usual textbook descriptions of them as being due to projection. I refer, here, to such descriptions as the following one by Fenichel (1945): of hallucinations he says that '. . . Inner factors are projected and experienced as if they were external perceptions . . .' (p. 425)

But in the course of my work with a certain schizophrenic man I discovered that, in at least some instances, to understand why a patient is hallucinating we must see this as having to do with not only *pro*jection but also *intro*jection. To be specific, in this particular instance I found that the patient's evident hallucinating of

murderously threatening figures connoted not only his projecting, in the form of hallucinatory figures, his own unconscious
murderous impulses, but connoted also his struggle against the
introjection of *my* own unconscious murderous impulses towards
him.

A 32-year-old man, he had been hospitalized constantly for
nearly ten years (including a five-year stay at another hospital
prior to his admission to the Lodge), and had had nearly five
years of intensive psychotherapy with a succession of therapists,
before I undertook therapy with him. He proved, soon after I
had begun seeing him, to be a most intensely frustrating and
threatening person. For about two and a half years his behaviour
during my sessions with him was limited almost exclusively to
(*a*) sitting in slovenly torpor, dropping cigarette ash on my rug,
picking his nose and wiping the yield therefrom upon his
trousers, and making no sound except for belches and the extremely frequent and quite unrepentantly loud passage of flatus;
and (*b*) infrequent vitriolic outbursts at me, in which he would
give every evidence of being barely able to restrain himself from
attacking me physically, and would say such things as, 'You
black, slimy son of a bitch! Shut up or I'll knock your teeth out!'
As the months wore on, I felt under increasing strain because of
his massive resistance to psychotherapy, and increasingly afraid
of his tenuously-controlled rage. There were many evidences,
which need not be detailed here, that his rage was largely dissociated; so I had reason to feel that this man, who outweighed
me by at least twenty pounds, had a great deal of rage which
neither I, nor he himself, could reliably contain.

Meanwhile, he had evidently begun to respond to hallucinatory voices, both in his daily life on the ward and, at times,
during his psychotherapeutic sessions. For several months he
gave every indication, in the content and tone of his responses to
them, that these were contemptuous, taunting voices; he would
talk back to them in a furiously angry way. Only in retrospect
did it occur to me that maybe these hallucinations had some
connexion with the contempt which had developed in me towards him, contempt which in that phase of our work remained in
an unconscious, dissociated state in me, erupting into my awareness only at brief moments with an intensity which I found
shocking. For example, once when I saw him passing through the

far end of the corridor I had a startlingly new thought and feeling about this man whom I had been consciously regarding predominantly as a desperately suffering, psychotic individual, no matter how discouragingly and frighteningly so. My thought was, 'There goes that crazy son of a bitch!', accompanied by a most intense feeling of contempt towards him.

During still later months in this two-and-a-half-year period, it seemed that the hallucinatory figures to which he frequently responded were predominantly frightening ones; his responses to them were not so much angry as frightenedly defiant, as if he were trying to keep his courage mustered in the face of them. In one of the sessions, while I was feeling, as usual, more intensely 'strained' than anything else, I noticed that as he came in and sat down he said to himself in a hushed, quavering, very frightened voice, 'Careful!', as if he sensed an ominous presence in the room. It was only a few sessions after this that an incident occurred which showed me how much dissociated rage there had been in me, presumably for a long time, and presumably fostered by my having been labouring under so much discouragement and, still, threat of physical injury for so long. In this particular session to which I now refer, he had been leafing through one of the magazines from a nearby table in my office, as he had taken to doing occasionally, with my whole-hearted approval. But after finishing with it he tossed it desultorily towards my couch; it fell short and lay on the floor. At the end of the hour, he left without bothering to pick it up. As he was walking out of the door I stooped down to pick up the magazine, still feeling only a sense of great strain. But as I lifted it up I suddenly became overwhelmed with fury, and smashed the magazine down on to the table with all my strength, sending a glass ash-tray flying. It was at this moment that I realized the probability that he had long been sensing, and responding hallucinatorily to, this rage in me which had heretofore been dissociated.

It required several more months for me to become accustomed to feeling such an intensity of rage towards him. Meanwhile, over this period of several months, this feeling would come into my awareness only fleetingly and then return, presumably, to an unconscious level. One of these subsequent occasions of my momentarily increased awareness involved a magazine again. When this time he slung one of my more prized magazines into a nearby chair, rumpling and tearing it somewhat with the force of the throw, I found myself saying to him in a balefully threatening, even tone, 'Go easy on the magazines. You're not in a pigpen.' On another occasion when he had been contributing to the session nought but occasional belches and flatus and a kind of insolently contented appearance, and then took out a cellophane-wrapped package of crackers and ate them, it was at the point when he nonchalantly tossed the cellophane on to the floor that I found myself filled with quick fury and said, 'Listen!–Don't do that in my office! Don't throw paper on my floor!', at which he looked flustered and immediately picked up the cellophane. On another occasion, when I was discussing his psychotherapy with a number of colleagues in a seminar, telling them that I had recently begun sitting over in a corner away from the door so that he would have ready access to the door in case he became terrified of his murderous rage towards me, I realized that I had been unconsciously manœuvring the seating arrangement so that, in case he attacked me physically, I would now have a legitimate excuse–since I would now be unable to get to the door–to enter into a knock-down-drag-out fist fight with him for which, I now knew, I had been yearning for weeks. And it was within a few days of this time that when someone asked me, at lunch, how this patient was getting along, I found myself grating, 'Well, he's alive, and that's not doing badly, considering how I feel towards him.' More than once I had felt lucky to get out of our sessions alive; but I had not realized before that he could be looked upon as being fortunate in this same sense.

The most memorable of these incidents when this usually dissociated rage came into my awareness was when, one night, I dreamed that he and I were fighting, and I was reacting to him as being–as I in waking life was then considering him to be–a dangerous, uncontrollable person. In the course of this dream-struggle he got his hands on a knifelike letter-opener. But what then happened, as I was astonished to recall upon awakening, was that *he* took *me* into custody; he, functioning as a kind of sheriff's deputy, was marching me out to turn me over to the authorities when the dream ended. Upon awakening I realized that my chronic fear of his attacking me was based, in part, upon a fear of my own largely dissociated and therefore poorly controlled rage. On the following day this instructive dream yielded good dividends: when, while sitting in an upholstered chair in my office, he suddenly passed flatus of an unusually gurgling sort, I was able to have, with no attendant anxiety, this furious thought, 'You son of a bitch, if you shit in that chair I'll massacre you!'

It was both fascinating to me in a research sense, and deeply gratifying to me as a therapist, to find that, by the end of two and a half years of both his, and my own, becoming more fully and consistently aware of our respective feelings of intense contempt and rage, his hallucinating had now all but disappeared from our sessions. One way of describing what had happened is to say that my increasing recognition, and acceptance, of my own feelings of contempt and rage towards him served to arm me sufficiently for me to be able to step in and interact with him at the furiously vitriolic level at which he had often 'interacted' with his hallucinations, previously, while I had sat by, paralysed with anxiety at the extraordinarily intense rage and contempt which his behaviour was arousing in me at an unconscious level. I had come to realize that it actually relieved me greatly when he shunted the most intense portion of his rage, for example, off to one side, towards an hallucinatory figure, and disclaimed that he was having any such feeling towards me. But there came a certain memorable session in which I felt sufficiently furious about what was going on, and sure enough of my ability to meet both my own rage and his, to be able to step into the shoes, as it were, of the hallucinatory figure or figures at whom he was directing his greatest fury, and from that day on it was as though there were less and less 'need' for these hallucinatory figures in our interaction with one another. What I did, specifically, in that crucial session was to insist, with unyielding fury–despite his enraged threats to assault me–that these vitriolic tirades, such as he had just now been ventilating while denying repeatedy that they were meant for me, were really directed towards me.

Midway in all this long development, it occurred to me that the emotional wavelength, or level of 'interaction', upon which he participated with the hallucinatory figure(s) provided me with a clue to the level at which he needed *me* as his therapist to be interacting with him; namely, this same level of vitriolic contempt and rage. I still feel that this was true enough, and that this can be looked upon as a valid general principle in one's therapy with a patient who is hallucinating. But during the subsequent months of this development which I have described, I realized in retrospect that I *had already been* participating with him at this emotional level, but had been dissociating my feelings which were invested at this level of interaction.

Following my experience with this man, I have seen a number of times this same mechanism at work in patients' hallucinatory experiences. I shall mention briefly only two of these additional examples. One occurred in the course of my work with a 35-year-old woman suffering from paranoid schizophrenia, a woman who for years–even before I became her therapist–had been indicating, frequently, her involvement in an hallucinatory experience of being raped and impregnated; pregnancy she considered to take place not in the uterus but in the 'stomach'. I came to see in retrospect, during my own work with her, that this experience of hers bore quite possible correlations with my then dissociated desires to impregnate her. The likelihood of this came to my attention when the following two events occurred in close sequence. (1) In one of our sessions, in which she was not being her usual antagonistic self, but in which there was, rather, predominantly a feeling-tone in the hour which I experienced as mutual, warm friendliness, with considerable sexual undertones, she suddenly looked anxious and demanded, insistently, 'Did you just put something from your stomach into my stomach? *Did* you?' I reacted–correctly, I think–to this question as being equivalent to, 'Did you just impregnate me?', and her anxiety was so great that, rather than making an analytically investigative response, I assured her flatly and simply that I had not. (2) But only a relatively few nights later, I had a dream in which I was impregnating her. Prior to this I had been unaware of this specific desire towards her, although I had felt many times before, in response to her frequently seductive behaviour, an erotic urge in which this specifically reproductive aim did not show itself. I cannot, of course, prove that her subjective impregnation experience was indeed in part a reaction to such dissociated desires in myself. But it is my impression that there was such a connexion, and I am quite ready to believe that her similar experiences in past years, prior to my own work with her, had involved similar links with dissociated processes in other people who at that time were important to her.

The third and final example is from my supervisory work with a therapist who was undergoing personal analysis and who was seeing me for the supervision of his work with a schizophrenic young man. After the therapy–and likewise the supervision–had been under way for several months, I noticed that two new developments had appeared at approximately the same time. Firstly, the patient began showing, in the therapeutic sessions, clear-cut evidence of hallucinatory experiences; specifically, there were strong suggestions, in the way that the patient giggled in a sexually titillated fashion, and murmured verbal responses in the same vein, that he was experiencing some sexually teasing hallucinatory figure in the room. Secondly, I noticed that the demeanour of the therapist himself had changed very appreciably; he had previously appeared to me to be quite a sexually repressed person, but now was showing many non-verbal indications of seductiveness. He described, at this time, a single instance of his verbally teasing the patient; but I had the impression that the therapist was quite unaware of the probable erotic element in this teasing. My belief was, and is, that the patient was hallucinatorily responding not only to projected desires to tantalize sexually, but also to similar desires in the therapist, which latter desires were being brought towards the surface, but not yet into conscious awareness, by, I thought most likely, his own personal analysis. Again, I realize that these data fall far short of constituting solid proof for such an hypothesis. But it is my distinct impression that such was the case; for, in summary, I found the therapist to be evidencing a newly-revealed sexually teasing quality towards me, and there were hints that he was evidencing–unwittingly, as seemed to be the case in his relationship with me–a similar quality towards the newly-hallucinating patient.

It is valid, I think, to consider any hallucination as a manifestation of some affect, or combination of affects, which is being warded off from acceptance into the individual's conscious ego. Hence it is indeed correct–no matter how curious it may sound –to look upon the above patients' hallucinations, resultant from both their own and their therapists' dissociated feelings, as representing not only a *projection* of certain feelings of the patient's own, but also a struggle against the *introjection* of the therapist's dissociated feelings of this same variety. A paper by Greenson (1954) entitled 'The Struggle Against Identification', provides clinical data which form an interesting comparison with the data I have just presented. Greenson's data were derived from neurotic rather than psychotic patients, and reveal their struggle against identifications with *parents* from the *past*, whereas my material shows the patient's struggle against identifying with–introjecting –the *therapist*, or more specifically certain unconscious elements in the therapist, in the *present*. A sufficiently searching investigation of the transference-connexions between the present and past in the experience of the patient would, I feel sure, show how integrally related are Greenson's material and my own; but such an inquiry is beyond the scope of this paper.

One last theoretical point should be made before going on to the third and final clinical category. This is a point which pertains to each of these three categories of clinical phenomena, but it can be seen most clearly, perhaps, in connexion with such hallucinatory phenomena as have been described. That is, one may say in general, I think, that an individual must have a relatively healthy ego in order to remain convinced of the reliability of his perceptions of the other person, in the absence of any *consensual validation* from the latter; validation which, if forthcoming, would reassure him that he is indeed perceiving realistically. A therapist, for instance, must possess a relatively healthy ego to be able to carry on his daily work, relying heavily upon his own perceptions of patients in the usual absence of much corroboration from the patients, corroboration of, for instance, the therapist's perception of preconscious or unconscious hostility, or guilt, or friendliness, or what not, in the patient. Therapists can, and much of the time in their daily work do, successfully meet this ego-challenging experience. But the psychotic patient's ego is too weak to meet a similar challenge without his suffering a temporarily increased ego-fragmentation: if he senses that his therapist is murderously inclined, for example, towards him, but if he gets no conscious validation from the therapist that this perception is a correct one, the patient is then likely to experience an hallucination of a murderously-inclined figure; since, we might phrase it, the therapist has refused to accept the perception as being truly applicable to himself, as 'belonging here upon me'.

Acting Out as a Response to, or Vicarious Expression of, the Therapist's Unconscious Processes

For several years I have had the impression that some instances of a patient's acting out may be due partially to the therapist's own unconscious strivings in this same direction; may represent, that is, a vicarious, compulsive expression of, or a response to, the therapist's unconscious desires. Since this general concept has already been described by Schroff (1957) and Barchilon (1958), and the identical mechanism as taking place in the patient's intrafamilial relationships has been described by Johnson and Szurek (1952), Hill (1955), Limentani (1956), and Bowen (1956), I shall give only brief examples of this general mechanism before turning to a more specific type of manifestation of it which, so far as I know, has not been mentioned in the literature.

It was about eight years ago that I discovered evidence, in work with a hebephrenic woman, that the acting out in which one's patient is involved may consist partially in a response to one's own unconscious desires. Relatively early in my work with this woman, she began to evidence, both during her therapeutic sessions and in her daily life on the ward, an intense fear lest she be raped. In the words of her administrative psychiatrist, she was 'crawling with terror' in this regard; her life on the ward was largely taken up with her insistently demanding reassurance against this from one and all about her. It was only after several months of this that I became aware, I think very belatedly, of powerful urges to rape her. These urges I found so frighteningly powerful, in fact, that I confided to the Director of Psychotherapy my concern lest I be unable to control them. I might add that he only laughed in mild amusement, a response which I found vaguely belittling; but the life of a director of psychotherapy is doubtless a difficult one. I realized, thus in retrospect, that the patient's anxiety lest she be raped was probably, at least in part, a response to these powerful, and at that time dissociated, desires in me. There were many data at hand to suggest that her transference to me was predominantly coloured by her earlier relationship with her father who, her history strongly indicated, had long struggled against just such unconscious desires towards her.

In later months of my work with her she began showing a

sexually provocative behaviour towards some of the male staff and after this had gone on for many weeks, I gained from my personal analysis the realization that erstwhile unconscious homosexual desires in myself had been quite possibly a factor in this particular acting out; the realization, that is, that she had been vicariously expressing, in her behaviour, my unconscious desires to make sexual overtures to these men. And still later on in her therapy I found various clues pointing towards a connexion between, on the one hand, her beginning now to start fires on the ward and, on the other hand, largely dissociated urges of a similar kind on my own part. The group of nurses on her ward at this time reacted to me as being quite directly responsible for the patient's fire-setting; on one occasion, for example, when I went up to her ward for the therapeutic session, the charge nurse bluntly let me know this. She met me with an accusing, 'Edith just set a fire in one of the wastebaskets', and when I protested, 'The way you nurses react to me about this sort of thing, anybody would think *I* had set the fire in the wastebasket!', she retorted, '*Well*–?' Later on, as I became more fully conscious of my own similar desires, and of the very probable influence these desires had had upon this phase of the patient's illness, I realized that the nurses' accusations had not been totally unfounded and unfair.

Now I wish to describe, in greater detail, a specific kind of phenomenon of this same general third sort–a specific kind which, as I mentioned, I have not seen described in the literature, and which has come to my attention within the past three years. This phenomenon consists in the (schizophrenic) patient's evidencing, in the therapeutic session itself, pathological and often puzzlingly grotesque behaviour which arises partially from this same source; an acted-out behavioural response to, or expression of, unconscious elements in the therapist.

I first became aware of this 'introjective acting out' psychodynamic basis of such grotesque behaviour in the course of my work with a deeply ego-fragmented schizophrenic woman, 28 years of age at the time when I became her therapist. During the first two years of our work together, she incessantly manifested a striking variety of bizarre, changing physical postures; looking thoroughly bewildered and acting as though the sudden and discoordinate movements of her limbs, head, and torso were taking place *via* a puppeteer's strings quite outside her control. And such verbalizations as she uttered were, for the most part, similarly discoordinate and confusing to, it appeared, herself as well as to the therapist.

Then, over a subsequent period of approximately six months, a series of incidents suggested to me that a considerable portion, at least, of her strange behaviour (as strange in her daily ward-life as in her sessions with me) rested partially upon the psycho-dynamics – the combination of introjection and acting out – which I have described.

One of these incidents occurred during a session in which I was sitting, as I often did, slumped far down in a chair and with my knees crossed in a way which, I realized in retrospect, may well have looked grotesque to an observer. But all I was aware of at the time was that I was feeling comfortably seated and that she, in a nearby chair, began muttering something to the effect that 'He comes in here and tears off my arms and legs.' She then asked me, twice, to put my leg down, which I declined to do. Then, after a considerable interval, she half rose and stood with a leg extended before her, awkwardly crooked and unsupported in the air; the leg gave a peculiar impression of dismemberment from the rest of her body. I asked, astounded at this thought, 'Is that the way my leg looks to you?' She agreed, convincingly. I think it valid, too, to look upon such an incident in the following terms: she reacted to my assuming a dismembered-looking posture (a posture which I had experienced simply as being a comfortable one) as being my way of serving notice upon her that I intended to dismember her. But I am quite ready to believe, in terms of my long experience with this unusually deeply ill woman, that she may indeed have felt dismembered on the basis of an introjective reaction to my grotesque posture.

My better judgement tells me that, as regards the communicational facet of this incident, what she was responding to, in me, were unconscious desires to dismember her, desires which my posture betrayed; but this I can only conjecture, for I have not recognized such desires towards her in our still-continuing work. I have clearly discerned such desires on her part, and have no doubt that *projection*, as well as introjection, was playing a part in this incident as in all these other incidents which I have been describing.

THE SCHIZOPHRENIC'S VULNERABILITY

By the time this phase in our work had been reached, the patient was now able, as the above material shows, *consciously to let me know* that her bizarre posture was a response to her perception of my own posture. But by now her air of bewilderment had greatly diminished, as had her grotesque and dissociated-looking physical movements. My belief is that in this earlier, two-year phase, when her ego-functioning had been clearly more profoundly impaired, she herself had been quite unable to realize that the puzzling movements of her body had any connexion with her perceptions of my own movements.

On subsequent occasions she was able to let me know, similarly, that her assuming the posture of a model on a surfboard was her way of showing me how I, draped narcissistically, I now realized, in my chair, appeared to her; and that her (now only occasional) use of verbal gibberish was a representation of the way my own speech often sounded to her. For years she had plucked hair from her scalp and had picked her clothing to pieces, and now, in one of the sessions, as she went through the gestures of pulling the flesh of her hands to pieces, she communicated to me the point that she experienced me as picking and pulling her, with horrifying cruelty, into pieces. In each of these instances, I was able, with deep dismay at times, to find a kernel of reality in her perceiving me thus. And when late in one of our sessions I saw a horrid grimace, a grotesquely taut kind of diabolical smile, slowly come over her face as if of its own accord, I was at first baffled, and then reached the jolting realization that this 'smile' was a representation of the way in which a hypocritical, forced, and undoubtedly rather cruel smile which I had turned on, early in this session, and appeared to her.

In most such instances—and I have found many like examples in my own work with other patients, and in my supervision of other therapists' work with their schizophrenic patients—the patient's response is such a grossly exaggerated caricature of the therapist's actual behaviour, as to add to the therapist's unreadiness to recognize this connexion. That is, the therapist is hampered not only by the fact that he has been manifesting something which he would prefer not to find in himself, but also by the fact of the patient's portraying this in so extremely exaggerated a form. Here it must be remembered that the patient's perception is grossly warped by the factors of both projection and transference. But it is very important for the therapist to be able to recognize the nucleus of *reality*-perception which lies in the patient's response, for it is by encouraging the growth of such fragments of reality-relatedness that he can be of greatest value to these deeply ill patients.

I shall mention only a second and brief example of this same phenomenon before proceeding to discussion. This example is from my work with the 32-year-old schizophrenic man whose hallucinatory phenomena were described at length in the preceding clinical material. This incident occurred during that phase of our work in which intense rage and contempt towards him had developed within me, but had not yet come fully into my awareness. At the end of one of the very many sessions throughout which he had remained mute save for belching and the passage of flatus, I said, with forced 'friendliness' and 'politeness', 'Well, the time's up for today.' To this he responded with a growlingly hostile, dissociated-sounding, 'Go to hell, you son of a bitch!' I recognized this, later on, as constituting not only a presumable expression of the way he felt towards me, but also a quite accurate expression of my own genuine, but repressed or at least heavily suppressed, feeling of rejectingness towards him at this moment.

Eissler (1943) made a comment which is relevant to this last-mentioned clinical incident:

. . . The . . . [therapist's] communication, so far as it is verbal, will frequently contain more aggression than the schizophrenic's sensitivity can stand. Actually language contains innumerable terms which have changed their original meaning, so far as they have lost their primary connotations of local or physical reference in favour of a more spiritual meaning. The background of the schizophrenic's language regresses to those original meanings of a cruder, even brutal coloring. Hence, ordinary language tends to hurt the schizophrenic.

But, evidently unlike Eissler, I do not believe that it is simply that the schizophrenic *reads into* the content of the therapist's words an archaic meaning, a brutal meaning, which is not there in actuality. I believe, rather, that here again there is a kernel of reality in the schizophrenic's response; there is genuinely conveyed by the words, in such instances, brutality which is present in the therapist's unconscious, no matter how greatly the patient's response is exaggerated through such mechanisms as projection and transference.

Discussion

This paper does not represent an effort to describe all possible types of introjective manifestations which schizophrenic patients exhibit, but rather to describe only those having to do with *unconscious* processes in the *therapist*. One sometimes finds, for example, a patient expressing the conviction that persons whom he knows or has known in the past are literally inside him now—in his stomach or in his leg or his foot, or what not; or he may be convinced that his bodily parts are those of some other individual.[3] But such material is outside the scope of this particular study.

And I do not mean to imply that the patient introjects only those processes in the therapist which are *unconscious*, or preconscious, in the latter. I surmise that it is indeed such processes in the therapist, or some other person, that the schizophrenic patient is more prone to introjecting, than is the case with the other person's *conscious* affects and ideation – for the reason, having to do with the absence or presence of consensual validation, mentioned earlier. But I consider this particular facet of the matter to be, likewise, beyond the focus of my effort here.

A third point is already implied in this paper, and needs to be made explicit only briefly: the *therapist* not uncommonly has introjective experiences vis-à-vis the *patient*. In my own sessions with schizophrenic patients, I have had, not infrequently, feelings and fantasies which seemed distinctly alien to my usual experience, which I experienced as foreign bodies in my consciousness, and which I regard as instances of introjection on the part of the therapist. And I have heard, many times, fellow therapists describe similar experiences.

This, in turn, brings up the therapeutically *constructive* side of

[3] A few days ago, for instance, I read the following item in the daily nurses' report concerning one of my female schizophrenic patients. This item was written by a middle-aged female attendant who has an excellent relationship with the patient: '. . . Called me to rub her back. Says she has my knees. "Why, Ruth?" "Because my knees hurt." "How did you know my knees hurt, Ruth?" "Last week you walked funny and this week you don't." I told her that was because I was wearing my arch supports. "I'm glad for you; but every time you get a new body they give me your old one, and you change bodies so often." I told her it was the same old body but just bulged more in some places. She had a good laugh over that one and laid her head over against my arm. Says there are people in her legs and their heads are the hips.'

this whole matter. The therapeutic usefulness of these last-mentioned experiences, experiences of introjection by the therapist, is, I believe, very great; they seem to me to constitute the essence of the therapist's emphatic sensing of what is transpiring in the patient. And as I indicated in Chapter 4, this same process, carried one interpersonal link further, helps the supervisor to sense what is occurring at a deep level in the therapeutic relationship which is being described to him by the therapist in the supervisory session.

And, as regards the therapeutic relationship itself, although I have utilized here the frame of reference of the patient's *vulnerability* to the therapist's unconscious processes and, in keeping with this emphasis, have presented examples of disturbances in patients' behaviour in this connexion, one can see on the other side of the coin an invaluable communicational aspect to this. It is as if the patient were trying to tell the therapist, in all three of the varieties of introjective manifestations which I have described, 'See, this is the way you look to me', or, 'See, this is what is going on between us, below the surface.'

I believe that the constructive aspect of these introjective processes in the therapeutic relationship resides not only in this furtherance of *communication*, but resides also in–to present a formulation, now, at which informal discussions with John L. Cameron, a colleague on the Chestnut Lodge staff, have helped me to arrive–a process which is even more directly therapeutic. I refer here to the seeming circumstance that the therapist, at the deepest levels of the therapeutic interaction, temporarily introjects the patient's pathogenic conflicts and deals with them at an intrapsychic, unconscious as well as conscious, level, bringing to bear upon them the capacities of his own relatively strong ego, and then, similarly by introjection, the patient benefits from this intrapsychic therapeutic work which has been accomplished in the therapist. Incidentally, I believe that the patient, on not infrequent occasions, gives the therapist the same kind of therapeutic help with the latter's intrapsychic conflicts. Concerning the benefits which the patient obtains by introjection from the therapist, the following comments by Hill (1955) are of interest:

... schizophrenic patients ... differ conspicuously from hysterical patients in their lack of immoderate admiration, affection, love, and so on, for their physician. ...

That the patient does not mention those qualities of his physician which he admires does not mean that he fails to note them. What he does with them is characteristically schizophrenic. *He takes them in as if they were mother's milk, thereby incorporating some of the goodness which comes to be his own and upon which his ego feeds and grows* [italics mine] ... He is good, and the badness is left with the doctor ... (pp. 205–6).

Wexler (1952) and Hoedemaker (1955) have also published valuable clinical examples of, and theoretical observations about, schizophrenic patients' recoveries as being facilitated by introjective responses to the therapist. Both these writers have overlooked, however, the *mutual*, two-directional, nature of this process, and have taken little note of the fact–in my experience–of the therapist's participation here upon unconscious, as well as conscious, levels.

My final observation is directed towards those therapists who have not yet relatively thoroughgoing personal analysis, and lengthy clinical experience, behind them; to others this comment will be superfluous. I would regard this paper as having been harmful rather than helpful, if it accentuated a therapist's irrational feeling of responsibility for what occurs in the therapeutic session, and in the over-all course of the patient's illness. The therapist has a responsibility, to be sure, and it is a large one; but it is shared with many other persons, including the patient himself, and it does not go to the irrational extent of requiring one to be free from the influence of one's own unconscious. I have long ago become convinced that, quite on the contrary, psychotherapy with schizophrenic patients requires that the therapist become able to rely, more and more readily, upon his unconscious as being in the nature of a friend, a friend indispensable both to himself and to his patients. Among such clinical incidents which I have described from my own experience, even those which at the moment caused me the greatest dismay proved subsequently to be of inestimable value in illuminating the nature of the transference as well as the countertransference.

Chapter 7

POSITIVE FEELINGS IN THE RELATIONSHIP BETWEEN THE SCHIZOPHRENIC AND HIS MOTHER (1958)[1]

M Y experience in the psychotherapy of chronic schizophrenic patients has convinced me that, in the patient's relationship with his mother, the basic feelings, those which more than any others determine the structure of the relationship and the development of the patient's illness, are positive—fondness, adoration, compassion, solicitude, and loving loyalty and dedication. In this relationship, which is regarded by many psychodynamically-oriented researchers as being of central importance in the aetiology of most cases of schizophrenia, I have found that it is not the often-emphasized mutual hatred and rejection and self-seeking dependence which forms its foundation, but rather genuine love for one another—love largely maintained in the unconscious through intense denial mechanisms, and love which finds extremely warped expression, but love none the less. Further, I have found that it is essential for the patient to become aware of the presence of this love between his mother and himself, in order to develop both a healthy self-esteem and a thorough-going resolution of his schizophrenic illness.

This concept, to which I also allude in Chapter 8 below concerning another aspect of schizophrenia, is rooted partially in a personal communication made to me about four years before writing this paper by the late Ernest E. Hadley. He helped me to realize that the potentiality for a loving relatedness between a mother and a child is in no instance totally absent, and that it is essential for any patient's self-esteem that he make contact with this area of feeling between himself and his mother.

The views I shall present grew out of, in addition, (a) eight years of work devoted predominantly to the intensive psycho-

[1] First published in the *International Journal of Psycho-Analysis*, Vol. 39 (1958), pp. 569–86.

therapy of schizophrenic patients at Chestnut Lodge; (*b*) interviews with the parents of schizophrenic patients, occurring sporadically during these eight years, and in relatively great number during one year when I served as admitting physician at the Lodge; (*c*) observations of the work of the many colleagues with whom I worked during this time; and, last but very important, (*d*) my family-life experience with my wife and our three–I believe relatively normal–children.

REVIEW OF THE LITERATURE

There is a great deal of literature on this subject, the bulk of it in agreement as to the predominantly and basically hateful nature of the relationship in question–a view from which this paper marks a sharp departure.

A paper by Suzanne Reichard and Carl Tillman (1950) provides an exhaustive review of the then existing literature concerning this and closely related subjects; it includes a summary of about thirty previous writings. There is a total emphasis here –not only in the authors' report of their own work, but also throughout the earlier reports of other writers which their paper summarizes–on parental hostility, with no mention whatever of any genuine love on the part of the parent towards the child. Reichard and Tillman stress, in particular, their concept of a 'schizophrenogenic mother' who covertly rejects the child while simultaneously battening parasitically upon him, through maintaining towards him a symbiotic relationship designed solely to meet her own selfish personality-needs.

Ruth W. Lidz and Theodore Lidz (1952) describe the child as being basically motivated by a (selfish) concern for his own security in the face of a mother who battens parasitically upon him and is striving primarily to express her malevolence towards him. Lewis B. Hill (1955) likewise sees the mother-child relatedness as being motivated, on the part of each of the two persons, by a basically selfish concern for one's own security. Davide Limentani also (1956) describes the symbiotic mother-child relatedness as based primarily on hostility and fear; there is a total lack of recognition that love exists at all in such a relationship.

Gregory Bateson and his associates (1956) introduce the concept that a 'double bind' relationship–one in which the child is trapped by hopelessly conflicting injunctions from the mother–

is of specific aetiological importance in schizophrenia. While brilliantly describing the negative affects at work in the mother-child relationship, the authors do less than justice, I believe, to the positive ones. I would put it, by contrast, that the child is trapped in such a relationship by, more than anything else, his own ambivalence, in which there are powerful ingredients of genuine solicitude, devotion, and loyalty, towards his tragically-enmeshed mother, who is in reality fully as much a 'victim' of the double bind as is the child himself. Moreover, while Bateson *et al.* brilliantly describe the complexity of the incessant jockeying for position that goes on between patient and mother, they seem unaware that this jockeying can involve an element of covert, but intensely and mutually pleasurable, playfulness, with this endlessly fascinating, complex 'game', as I have repeatedly discovered with my patients, relatively late in the course of therapy. The authors dwell upon this as being solely in the nature of anguished, conflictual, desperate relatedness.

A pair of articles written by a Mayo Clinic research-group headed by Adelaide M. Johnson (1956), report experiences in, and draw theoretical conclusions from, the intensive study of 27 acutely schizophrenic patients by means of collaborative psychotherapy–that is, concomitant treatment of patients and their parents. It appears that this research study, involving a considerable number of investigators and an exhaustive collection of data during an unspecified time-span, unearthed no evidence of fondness as a significant ingredient in the relationship between the child and his parents. What the authors perceived in the parent was, evidently, simply thoroughgoing hatred rather than ambivalence, and they found that the child was rendered helpless not by intense ego-splitting affects of love and hatred within himself, engendered as a function of an ambivalent relationship with the parent, but simply by something quite outside himself: an overwhelmingly hateful and threatening parent.

In the literature, despite its very predominant emphasis upon the negative aspects of the mother-child relatedness, we occasionally come upon a paper which pays somewhat greater heed to the positive factors involved. For example, Margaret S. Mahler (1952) says that a symbiotic mother-infant relatedness is essential to healthy infancy, and reports that the more severe of two types of psychosis found in young children, the autistic type, occurs in those who have never shared such a mother-infant symbiosis. Carl A. Whitaker and Thomas P. Malone (1953) at least convey the implication that there is, as a part of the schizophrenic patient's personality, a genuine wish and need to give personal help to the (parent-figure) therapist. A book by Abrahams and Varon (1953) presents, with very detailed clinical data, a most unusual and valuable portrayal of the positive, as well as the negative, ingredients in the relationship between the schizophrenic patient and the mother. The authors report their work at St Elizabeth's Hospital with a therapeutic group made up of seven female patients with very severe and chronic schizophrenia (including four hebephrenics), their mothers, and the senior author as therapist.

L. Murray Bowen is conducting at the National Institute of Mental Health in Bethesda, Maryland, a research project involving concomitant psychotherapy of schizophrenic patients and their mothers, the mothers being housed in the hospital ward with their children and carrying out with them, in so far as feasible in this setting, their usual parental functions. He, too, evidently finds the mother-child relationship to comprise not only destructive but also constructive affective ingredients, as indicated in the following passage from his preliminary report. After detailing a certain patient's remarkably rapid improvement in therapy, Bowen (1956) says:

In summary, we feel that this patient has made a rather marked response, and that the things primarily responsible for it were the presence of the mother and our fairly good success in preserving the relationship between the patient and her mother.

Still, to the best of my knowledge, no one has gone so far as I am going here in stressing the importance of the positive feelings in this mother-child relationship—in portraying such feelings as its most powerful determinants, and in regarding the overlying intense, mutual hostility as consisting in unconscious, mutual denial of these deeply-repressed positive feelings. The crucial data supporting my theoretical concepts have come from transference phenomena, often of a non-verbal nature, encountered in very long-range psychotherapy with schizophrenic patients. It is the evolution of the transference which reveals, usually only after a duration of intensive psychotherapy which in most institutions is utterly unfeasible, that behind what has appeared for literally years to be rock-bottom hatred and rejection towards the therapist as a parent-figure, there exist very deep-lying, very powerful and utterly genuine feelings of love towards the parents –including, as is seen last of all but entirely convincingly, the mother. The schizophrenic illness now becomes basically revealed as representing the child's loving sacrifice of his very individuality for the welfare of the mother who is loved genuinely, altruistically and with the wholehearted adoration which, in the usual circumstances of human living, only a small child can bestow.

My Own Views on this Subject

The formulation which I shall present must inevitably emerge as an over-simplification of the relationship between the schizophrenic patient and the mother, for two reasons. First, I am trying to generalize, and generalizations can never do justice to the manifold individual differences between any one such patient-parent relationship and another. Secondly, I am focusing upon the *love-element* in that relationship, a relationship which comprises various other important ingredients. But, in the latter connexion, I must emphasize that I consider this love-element to be the most influential among all these various ingredients. That is, I think that the whole relationship between the patient and his mother can be described most adequately as a function not of mutual efforts at warding off anxiety, or of a mutual conflict between dependence needs and efforts towards individuation, but rather as a function of both persons' efforts to express love towards one another. My whole conceptual structure rests upon a conviction that the most powerful driving force in human beings, including schizophrenic patients and their mothers, is nothing so negative as an effort to avoid anxiety, but rather is the effort to express himself or herself in a loving, constructive way.

I shall describe first the psychodynamics in the mother, as I understand them, with respect to the expression of love; thus I hope to portray the kind of readiness for interpersonal relatedness which the newborn infant finds in his mother. Then I shall touch upon the needs, as regards loving relatedness, which the normal newborn infant brings into the relationship with the mother. Next I shall discuss the ensuing relationship between mother and infant (child), and, lastly, the developments in the patient-therapist relationship which result from this early-life experience of the patient.

THE PSYCHODYNAMICS IN THE MOTHER

First I wish to note her evident *fear of her own love-feelings*, her reacting to them as being the most destructive component within herself, that which requires the most vigorous repression. It appears that this fear developed primarily as a result of her having found, in childhood, that her expressions of love rendered her mother anxious and psychologically withdrawn. Further, in many instances, tragic early-life experiences of beloved persons dying, or otherwise departing permanently from the scene, tended to confirm the child's fear that her own love had an annihilating effect upon others.

In consequence, her love-feelings became subjected to growingly complete repression, so early in the child's life that these feelings were still in a relatively primitive form, poorly differentiated – in line with the immaturity of her young ego – from other, potentially quite different, affects, such as murderous feelings, dependence feelings, and so on, which became largely repressed along with the love-feelings, in a poorly-differentiated complex of what one might call the child's deepest passions. This repressed feeling-complex, being largely cut off from the conscious ego, failed to mature[2] and to become more fully differentiated into qualitatively very distinct feelings, by contrast to personality-ingredients which are more fully in consciousness. Thus when the mother's love does at times succeed in breaking through the repression and emerging into awareness, it surges up in a frighteningly primitive form (often an oral-incorporative form, as is chronically acted out in these mothers' 'smothering' maternal behaviour), and associated, moreover, with frustration-rage and various other primitive emotions from which the love-feelings have never become clearly differentiated.

The mother of a schizophrenic young man, in the course of an unusually illuminating two-hour interview with me, poignantly revealed her anxiety concerning her feelings of maternal love – anxiety which had evidently operated with regard not only to her schizophrenic son, but to her other two children, a few

[2] The general principle expressed in the first part of this sentence was conveyed to me several years ago by Dr Edith Weigert.

years older than he, both of whom were functioning well, apparently quite free from schizophrenic symptoms. She said, with regard to all her children as infants, that she had wanted intensely to hold them; but, knowing that she herself had been nervous in childhood and adolescence, she had been afraid that her holding them would cause them to become nervous. 'I enjoyed it so intensely, holding them, that I wondered if there were something wrong with me. You know—having a baby's head on your shoulder, and cuddling it.' She said this in a tone of unmistakably genuine yearning to express her love. She went on, in a pathetically uncertain way, 'Over the years I've wondered' about the feeling, wondered whether it were a normal feeling. She said that in recent years she had been pleased to find that she had felt this same feeling towards her grand-children while holding them; these experiences, occurring several years after her own reproductive life was over, she had found reassuring, for 'I felt it was *me*, and not because of my glands, like a mother kitten.'[3] It seemed that she regarded her own maternal feelings as being subhuman, and threatening, therefore, to have a dehumanizing effect upon her babies.

Another mother helped me to realize that the love-feelings may be sensed as dangerous to the child because these feelings are so capricious: since they are not reliably available to the mother herself, she cannot make them dependably available to her child; hence her expression of them, fleetingly, to the child, inflicts upon him the hurtful experience of feeling loved momentarily, only to find himself, suddenly and unexpectedly, being hated or rejected by the mother who only a moment ago was being warm and loving to him. This woman was the mother of two children, towards each of whom she had a classically 'schizophrenigenic mother' attitude of individuality-thwarting possessiveness. She herself was a paranoid schizophrenic patient, and had then been in therapy with me for $1\frac{1}{2}$ years, during which time a great deal of intensely hateful transference-feelings had been resolved, such that she had recently been moving more and more into the area of her fond feelings towards me as being in the transference, more often than not, a loved and loving son.

[3] Her use of the curious phrase 'mother kitten', rather than 'mother cat', is significant: this woman, like other mothers of schizophrenic patients whom I have seen, had much about her that was touchingly childlike. The typical mother of the schizophrenic is, in my experience, a kind of mother-child (mother-kitten).

With this development, she took to warning me repeatedly that there would be nothing but tragedy in store for me if I let myself become fond of and dependent upon her, since, as she put it, 'I don't know where I'm going to be from one moment to the next.'

One element in her delusional system was her conviction, still continuing, that she was repeatedly knocked out and moved about, while unconscious, over the face of the earth, being supplanted at her former location by a double of herself, a double–and there were, she had been convinced for years, several of these–who would do and say things which then would be attributed, by other persons, to herself, but which she was convinced she had not done. This was one among various schizophrenic defences against her becoming aware of her tenderness, her hatred, and other feelings unacceptable to herself. This delusion had been present throughout her marriage.

In one session during this same phase of the therapy, her anxiety with regard to her tender feelings was evidenced not only in the transference to me, but also, on this particular occasion, in expressed recollections of her past experiences with her children. She said, in reference to her maternal feeling, that it had been 'thwarted' throughout the years of her taking care of her children, for she had felt it essential to restrict herself to merely 'making a gesture of being maternal', without letting her deep, genuine maternal love come forth. I asked her if she had felt it necessary, for some reason, to protect her children from her genuine maternal feeling. She agreed that this had indeed been so, and protested movingly, 'What would you want me to do–tell them when I tucked them into bed at night, "Now, I may not be here when you wake up in the morning; someone else may be here in my place"? ' Thus she had striven–unsuccessfully, of course; many data showed that her real maternal feeling had leaked through such defences, to the children, on innumerable occasions–to protect her children from experiences of loving relatedness with her, relatedness which would then be torn through, without warning to either child or mother, by the supervening of previously-dissociated hatred and rejectingness in the mother. In the session which I have just touched upon, she expressed heart-rendingly intense, long-denied grief and anguish over the several-years-long separation from her two children.

So far, as regards the mother's psychodynamics which are

relevant in this paper, I have been dealing with her fear of her own love-feelings. The second factor which I wish to mention is her *low self-esteem*. This is no doubt based, in any one individual mother, upon a variety of causes; but there are at least two causes, I believe, operative generally in these mothers: (*a*) early-life experience of her feeling unaccepted, unloved, by her own mother; and (*b*) the consequent repression of her own lovingness, which I have described above. These two circumstances result in her regarding herself, in adult life, as a being unworthy of being loved and devoid of genuine love to offer to other persons, including her children.

Her low self-esteem will come to have, as I shall shortly show, traumatic effects upon her relationship with her child, on at least two scores. It will interfere with her receptivity of the child's loving solicitude and helpfulness, so that the child will be hampered in the development of a sense of personal worth in relation to the most important individual in his life; he will tend to feel worthless to, and unneeded by, his mother. And the mother's low self-esteem will interfere also with the child's idolizing of her–with the development and maintenance of the kind of relationship which the young child needs to have with his mother in order to develop constructive identifications with her. The young child–of, say, 2 to 8 years of age–needs to be able to adore his parents, to worship them, for the sake of his own healthy ego-building. But the mother who has an inner sense of profound worthlessness cannot tolerate her child's worship.

The third factor, unlike the two foregoing, is operative towards the pre-schizophrenic *one(s)* of her children in *particular*. It is a factor which sets these mothers somewhat further apart from the general run of human beings, in nearly all of whom one can find, I believe, evidences of at least some degree of anxiety with respect to their own love-feelings, and some impairment of self-esteem. And this factor, in its effect upon the personality of the particular child(ren) 'selected' for schizophrenigenic relatedness, comes to set him very much apart from his siblings.

This third factor is discernible, I believe, when we see that, in one mother-child relationship after another, the mother's view of the child as a genuinely new individual is obscured, persistently and with few if any breaks, by a peculiar combination of unconscious perceptions which the mother has of this particular child. She perceives him, on the one hand, as the embodiment of a galaxy of repressed concepts of herself: to her he represents her lonely, isolated self, or her hopelessly stupid self, or her hopelessly hostile, rejectable self, or her appallingly animal-like, lustful self, and so on. On the other hand, as I have found with astonishment, she reacts to this same child as an omnipotent mother-figure whose acceptance she (the actual mother) recurrently seeks, in a self-abasing fashion, while despairing of ever obtaining it.[4]

The more I have thought about this peculiar combination of attitudes which these mothers clearly demonstrate towards their pre-schizophrenic or schizophrenic children, the more it appears to me to point to the mother's having reconstituted, with her young child, a symbiotic relatedness such as had existed, I believe, in the mother's own early childhood, between herself and her own mother. That is, I hypothesize that the well-known symbiotic relatedness now existing between the child and the mother is fostered by *a transference to this child, on the mother's part, of feelings and attitudes originally operative in a symbiotic relationship which obtained between herself as a small child and her own mother.* At what phase in the patient's life his mother brings these transference feelings to bear upon him I do not know. My impression is that the timing may vary considerably in various instances; for some children it is in late infancy, for others in early infancy, for others at birth, and for not a few, I believe, before birth.

I do not mean to exclude the possibility of the mother's transference to the child of feelings from others of her own early-life relationships, in addition to that which existed between herself and her mother. One woman whom I saw over a course of four months, in interim therapy of her mixed psychoneurosis, was the mother of a six-year-old schizophrenic boy. Whenever she spoke of him, it was remarkably easy to see that her perceptions of him coincided with either (a) aspects of her personality of which she was unaware and apparently was projecting upon him, or (b) her perceptions of *various* figures from her own childhood, including her mother, father, and two siblings. As I went on with her, session after session, I tried to discern what was so harmful

[4] Abrahams and Varon (1953) present very detailed clinical material showing the mothers' dependence upon their schizophrenic children, and report their astonishment at coming upon this factor, unsuspected at the outset of their research.

to this boy in his relatedness with his mother, who in various respects (not here detailed) seemed to me to be considerably open to her own feelings. I became growingly convinced that it was this factor which I have just described: the boy, it seemed to me, despite the mother's showing a considerable richness of feeling-response in the situation, rarely if ever had reason to feel that she was responding to *him* as an individual in his own right; she seemed to be responding incessantly either to a projected part of herself, or to some figure from her early life.

To add another hypothesis, I think it valid to regard the mother's transference, here, as an unconscious defence against her moving into loving relatedness with her son as an individual in his own right. Such a development is unconsciously sensed, I believe, by the mother–and eventually by the child also–as tantamount to mutual annihilation. For example, a schizophrenic young woman whose relationship with her mother was characterized by a tremendous degree of overt effusiveness–appearing to myself and other observers as saccharine pseudo-love –led me to feel convinced, as the transference to me as a mother-figure progressed through such a saccharine phase into a more direct, genuinely fond relatedness, that this saccharinity had been one of her, and her mother's, unconscious defences against their deeper-lying, *genuine* love for each other. The patient expressed to me, in the transference, her anxiety concerning such genuine fondness: 'I'm afraid if we got together we might kill one another.' There was abundant evidence of murderous feeling in herself, her mother, and me; but various therapeutic developments dispelled any doubt in my mind that the ingredient in the patient-mother relatedness which had been most severely repressed, most intensely anxiety-provoking to both of them, was not their murderous rage but their genuine fondness for one another. I shall give a detailed account of my work with this patient in a later section of this paper.

THE NEEDS OF THE NORMAL INFANT AND CHILD

Throughout most of the literature concerning the aetiology of schizophrenic illness–and in fact that concerning the psychogenesis of *any* variety of psychiatric illness–there is an almost exclusive emphasis upon the infant's (and child's) need to *receive* love, and upon the failure of those about him to *give him* the love he needed. What is usually overlooked is the fact that the infant and child has an equally great need, from the first, to express his own love to others. Much of this literature portrays the newborn baby, for example, as being totally receiving, as though those in his environment – including his mother – received nothing of value from him.

My belief, by contrast, is that the infant and child normally gives, and *needs to give*, at least as much as he receives. For example, the lactating mother whose breasts are painfully swollen with milk has a need to be nursed which is no less urgent than is the hungry infant's need to nurse. Here we see, in this basic situation, that genuine receptiveness (as personified by the nursing infant) bestows, in the same process, a gift – a joy, a relief, an enriching experience – on the giver. And in many other ways the newborn infant offers rich rewards to the parent. He provides one with an object whom one can wholeheartedly love with a simplicity, a relative freedom from ambivalence, which is most difficult, if not impossible, of attainment in the more complex relationships which exist between two many-faceted adults. One can have the self-enriching experience of worshipping him with much the same devotion and joy which a really devout Christian may feel towards the Christ-child; the latter can be seen as, in this connexion, a symbol of the radiant joys which a newborn baby bestows upon those who love him and welcome his arrival.

I share with W. R. D. Fairbairn (1954) and Melanie Klein (1955) the conviction that the infant is object-related from the very beginning; but I do not adhere to Klein's concept of an innate death instinct, as paraphrased here by Paula Heimann.

... the infant from the beginning of life is under the influence of the two primary instincts of life and death. Their derivatives in the form of self-preservative and libidinal impulses on the one hand and of destructive and cruel cravings on the other are active from the beginning of life (Heimann, 1955, p. 35).

I am convinced, from daily-life observations of infants and young children, and from psycho-analytic and psychotherapeutic work with neurotic and psychotic adults, that lovingness is the basic stuff of human personality, that it is with a wholehearted openness to loving relatedness that the newborn infant responds to the outside world, with an inevitable admixture of cruelty and destructiveness ensuing only later–being deposited on top of the basic bedrock of lovingness–as a result of hurtful and anxiety-arousing interpersonal experience.

Freud himself pointed out that

> . . . the child is capable long before puberty of most of the psychical manifestations of love–tenderness, for example, devotion . . . except for his reproductive power, a child has a full-developed capacity for love long before puberty . . . (1907, p. 134).

But Freud made this point primarily to demonstrate that the child was not nearly so much a stranger to matters sexual as was thought to be the case by the psychiatrists of that day. Freud did not give us a picture of the infant and child as *having a need to* give love; but, for the most part, a picture of the newborn infant as wrapped in wholly self-preoccupied primary narcissism, as in subsequent months and years primarily oriented towards wresting from the environment supplies for his own selfish needs, and only with the advent of adult genitality being able to participate in anything resembling an altruistic loving relatedness. Sullivan, somewhat similarly, indicated in his writings (1947) that a capacity for true givingness, truly altruistic love, does not begin to appear until preadolescence; prior to that, he regarded the child as capable of no more than co-operation and collaboration with another person:

> Around the age of 8½, 9½ to 12, in this culture, there comes what I once called the quiet miracle of preadolescence. . . . I say 'miracle' of preadolescence because now for the first time from birth, we might say even from conception, there is a movement from what we might, after traditional usage, call egocentricity, toward a fully social state (1947, p. 19).
>
> . . . The capacity to love in its initial form makes appearance as the mark that one has ceased to be juvenile and has become preadolescent. What this means in the outline of situations which it brings about is this: at this point the satisfactions and the security which are being experienced by someone else, some particular other person, begin to be as significant to the person as are his own satisfactions and security (p. 20).

It seems to me that lovingness is at its most pure, its most wholly pervasive, in the personality of the newborn infant, and that the adult is loving in proportion as he can effect contact with the loving infant and young child in himself. That the infant and the young child express lovingness in not only warmly receptive, but also in actively outgoing, behaviour is something which, I believe, any thoughtful and observant parent can attest, once he has set about seeing how much he *receives from* his children.

THE RELATIONSHIP BETWEEN MOTHER AND INFANT (CHILD)

As regards the aspect of the child's *receiving* love from the mother, what is traumatic is not a total lack of love coming from her, which would be easier to endure. Instead she expresses love to him, love which emerges through her chronic repression in a form, I believe, which fleetingly is that of the wholehearted lovingness which the young child seeks to express to others. But this love, particularly intense, is expressed capriciously, as I have already said–is unexpectedly and suddenly replaced by rejection. The child's experience in this is, I surmise, closely comparable with experiences which I have had repeatedly with schizophrenic patients who have become half well. Able now to emerge fleetingly from a former relatively unbroken emotional isolation, they express towards one, momentarily, a radiant warmth, unpredictably replaced by an utter withdrawal which leaves one feeling most painfully aware that a warm person is there in them, but completely helpless to make contact with that person. This phase of therapy is, in my experience, harder for the therapist to endure than the earlier phase, when the deeply regressed patient is at least showing much more consistent, dependable, predictable behaviour. If one is left chronically on one's own, one can make do; but to be caught up, unpredictably, in an intensely warm relatedness, and then as unpredictably to find oneself psychologically utterly alone, constitutes a deep assault upon one's personal integration.

And in some instances one even finds oneself reacting to such a patient upon two quite unrelated levels simultaneously–a distinctly ego-splitting experience. I have discussed this kind of relatedness in chapter 8. Only a week before I write, for example, a schizophrenic woman was simultaneously (*a*) mounting a vicious assault upon me, with incessant, stinging, infuriating accusations, like a most formidable prosecuting attorney; and

(b) revealing a very-small-child-like confusion and fearfulness. I have found many data, both from transference-developments in the therapy itself and from historical material given by the patient's three siblings, to indicate that the patient's mother, a highly schizoid person as seen in our staff-members' interviews with her, had presented to the child a double-barrelled behaviour qualitatively identical with that which the patient was exhibiting towards me.

Another schizophrenic woman brought to my attention an additional traumatic aspect of the mother's capricious expression of love; when the mother's lovingness is replaced by emotional withdrawal, it leaves the child filled with love and with no object on whom to pour out his love. One might compare him with a lactating mother who has no infant into whom to pour out, relievingly, the milk from her swollen breasts. This particular patient, who after the resolution of much of her paranoid symptomatology was rapidly becoming a warmly friendly person and was having extreme difficulty in warding off her own awareness of this change, protested, after enumerating various persons about her in the hospital – persons towards whom she expressed fondness which she could not yet admit to herself – that there would be 'no point' in feeling fond, because 'there would be no one to put it on'. The anxiety in her tone as she said this made me realize that there is a kind of anxiety in human beings the existence of which I had not previously suspected: the anxiety of feeling filled with love and with no one towards whom to express this love. I realized, in retrospect, that this accurately described my own unbearable feelings at moments when this woman, and other schizophrenic patients at a similar stage of their psychotherapy, had suddenly become psychologically remote from me after having been, just before, in warmly fond relatedness with me.

As regards the forces which hold the child in the symbiotic relatedness with the mother, I have already, in presenting a review of the literature, touched upon some of my views. In essence, the child cannot grow beyond this kind of relatedness, which is normal only in infancy and very early childhood, until he has had the experience of consciously loving another person and of finding that other person able to acknowledge, consciously to accept, his love. In other words, it is not simply a matter of his failing to receive enough love *from* the other person (the mother).

What happens in such a mother-child relationship as I am describing is that the normal child-love towards the mother is accentuated and, at the same time, blocked in its direction, and turned into complex, indirect channels. That is, the child of a normal mother often feels, I believe, a desire to express help-fulness and solicitude towards his mother, especially at times when she is anxious, fatigued, sorrowful, or when she is simply showing a pleasureful readiness for his helpful participation in her work and life. But the pre-schizophrenic child detects in *his* mother—no matter how unable he is to formulate it thus—a tragically unintegrated and incomplete person. To his mother, tragically enmeshed in her own personality-difficulties, he re-sponds with an intensity of compassion, loyalty, solicitude, and dedication which goes beyond that which a child would have reason to feel towards a relatively well mother.

It is these feelings, blocked from direct expression except on rare occasions, and their importance to the mother largely denied by her, which are primarily responsible for the child's remaining locked in the symbiotic relatedness with the mother, with disas-trous consequences to himself. It is not basically that the mother locks him there with hateful 'double bind' injunctions; it is rather that he cannot bear to grow out of the relationship and leave her there, tragically crippled—much as a therapist finds it excruciatingly difficult to leave in midstream a therapeutic en-deavour with a patient who is grievously ill with schizophrenia. One sees this phenomenon expressed by schizophrenic patients, over and over again, with regard both to the therapist and to fellow-patients, all being responded to as tragically ill mothers. It takes the patient a long time to reconcile himself to getting well while fellow-patients remain ill in the ward; he feels that he must cure them before he can accept health and, as the end of his therapy draws still nearer, he finds it unbearable to go away well, leaving his therapist (at this point a mother transference-figure to him) enmeshed, as the patient perceives him, in hope-less schizophrenia. This latter phenomenon, although without the formulation which I have given as to its transference-aetiology, has been described by Hill (1955).

Melanie Klein's writings suggest that she would regard such

filial love-feelings as I have just described (i.e. solicitude towards the mother, and a struggling to relieve her personality-difficulties) as being secondary to destructive feelings towards the mother. I regard these as evidences of basic love, whereas Klein refers to 'making reparation' in apparently this same regard, as one sees in these passages:

> ... the leading female anxiety situation: the mother is felt to be the primal persecutor who, as an external and internalized object, attacks the child's body and takes from it her imaginary children. These anxieties arise from the girl's phantasied attacks on the mother's body, which aim at robbing her of its contents, i.e. of faeces, of the father's penis, and of children, and result in the fear of retaliation by similar attacks. Such persecutory anxieties I found combined or alternating with deep feelings of depression and guilt, and these observations then led to my discovery of the vital part which the tendency to *make reparation* plays in mental life ... it includes the variety of processes by which the ego feels it undoes harm done in phantasy, restores, preserves, and revives objects. The importance of this tendency, bound up as it is with feelings of guilt, also lies in the major contribution it makes to all sublimations, and in this way to mental health (Klein, 1955, p. 15).

It is my impression that the tragedy in the child's relationship with his mother becomes crystallized, leaving his personality ripe for the development of schizophrenia, in that phase of his childhood when a child normally experiences a 'crush on' each of his parents. The age-limits of this developmental phase, in normal children, I do not know. It is my belief that it begins around 1½ to 2 years, when each parent has emerged, in the child's awareness, as a distinct personality, and that it shades off at something like 6 to 8, when the child has succeeded in developing richly meaningful relationships with adults outside the home. During this phase, his two parents are of tremendous importance to his ego-building through his identifying with them, as regards their admirable personality traits. This process of identification, quite different from unconscious, neurotic identification with the other's objectionable traits as a means of warding off anxiety in the relationship, needs to proceed in a medium of the child's consciously idolizing the parent, and of the parent's welcoming the child's admiration of, and desire to be like, him or her.

To focus again, now, solely upon the *mother's* relationship with the child, since that is the area of interest here: the evidence is that it is in this 'crush' phase of childhood that the child's relationship with the mother comes most to its grief. For several years now I have become growingly impressed by the evidence that the chronically schizophrenic adult is a person fixed in a state of black disillusionment—a person who once saw only good in the world, then became completely disillusioned so that he could now see nothing good in the world, and has not yet succeeded in integrating the disillusioning experience so that he can realize that there is both bad and good in the world. Clinical data which space does not allow my presenting have indicated to me that the primary disillusionment occurred in the relationship with the mother, in the childhood-phase which I have just described, and that it is no coincidence that frequently the overt schizophrenia, later in life, is precipitated by some 'crush' which has an outcome injurious to the individual's self-esteem.[5] Such an experience reactivates the feelings of anxiety, rage, worthlessness, despair, and grief which were kindled originally in the prototype experience with the mother.

The childhood disillusionment involves the mother's failing the child, because of her low self-esteem and fear of loving relatedness, just when he particularly needs to perceive her as admirable and worthy of emulation. She reacts to his adoration with heightened anxiety and, presumably, loosening of her precarious ego-integration. The child is thus faced with an object for his identificatory strivings who is both low in self-esteem and somewhat ego-fragmented, and the child does identify with her, with disastrous results to his own developing ego. He emerges from this phase, naturally enough, not strengthened but profoundly weakened by his introjection of a mother-figure who is pervaded by a sense of worthlessness and whose ego-integration is precarious.

He introjects her not primarily out of hatred or anxiety but out of genuine love and solicitude for his mother whom he has found, upon the close inspection which this 'crush' phase entails, to be not a person admirably stronger than he, but a pathetically

---

[5] Abrahams and Varon mention that 'In the cases of several of the daughters, the daughter seemed to have the experience of overwhelming anxiety, the schizophrenic break, and the subsequent reshuffling of her ways, following an experience attended by a "crush"...' (1953, p. 198).

crippled one who desperately needs relief from the burden of her own personality-difficulties. He introjects her primarily in an effort to save her by taking her difficulties, her cross, upon himself. One schizophrenic woman who, I became convinced after several years of work with her, had gone through such a process in her childhood, phrased it that 'I was crushed at the age of eight'. Such an experience with this 'crush' phase of childhood is quite literally crushing to the developing personality.

A major reason, I think, for our slowness to recognize the genuine love which exists in the relationship between the schizophrenic patient (or the pre-schizophrenic child) and the mother is that these two, afraid to be aware of their love for one another, express it unwittingly, in most unconventional ways – in behaviour towards one another which can readily be construed, by themselves and others about them, as indicating only antagonism or indifference, or what not, towards one another.

The longer I have worked with schizophrenic patients the more fascinated have I become with their idiosyncratic modes of expressing love. One man who repeatedly threatens, in no uncertain terms, to knock my teeth out, while calling me the most abusive, filthy names, is sometimes expressing thereby primarily antagonism towards me; but, as I have come slowly to realize, he is sometimes expressing his love for me in this fashion. I was astounded when this realization first dawned on me, though I immediately saw it to dovetail with the fact of his father's having often expressed warmly personal passions towards his wife and children by beating them, and with the fact that the patient had been disappointed, many times in life, when homosexual partners left him after he had got into fist fights with them – just when, that is, he had begun to express in his own idiosyncratic, childhood-family-patterned fashion, his love for them.

In other instances, I have found that patients express genuine love towards me, or towards fellow-patients, nurses, or relatives, by what seems merciless picking on the other person, or thoroughly contemptuous verbal outpourings, or wholly brutal bullying, or various other modes of expression which are equally far removed from conventional expressions of tenderness. As another example, it took me a long time to realize that a female patient with whom I had been working for a number of years, and who had taken to behaving – upon passing me in the corridors, as well as during much of the time in therapy sessions–as though I did not exist, was thereby often expressing passionate love to me. All these *forms* of behaviour are not, after all, so very far removed from what one sees in 'normal' living; but with the adult schizophrenic patients these modes of interaction, following the patterns set in earlier family life, take place at a *level of intensity* which makes it extraordinarily difficult for one to realize that they are often disguised expressions of love.

With one woman patient who expresses her fondness–a fondness which she herself is still largely afraid to recognize–towards me by bellowing ostensibly contemptuous insults and threats of brutal physical violence, I have long ago come to realize that, increasingly often, she is thereby expressing warmly fond feelings towards me, and I bask in them at such times, and am amused when colleagues, nurses, or neighbouring patients marvel at my ability to endure such rough treatment. It was not many years ago when I used to wonder how a colleague in an adjoining office could endure similarly 'rough' treatment from a patient of his, and I more than once expressed my sympathy to him. But now I know better. I read with amusement the following passage, in which, I feel sure, reference is being made to this same phenomenon, but without its being seen as such by the authors. After describing the intensity of the therapist's own emotional involvement in the group situation, the writers note that:

. . . This involvement was present in all the professional people who visited the group, to a varying extent. In some, it was so severe that they had to leave the room because of mounting fury or psychosomatic symptomatology. Most asked, after the session, 'How could you stand it?' or, 'Why didn't you do something to stop that mother from doing that to her poor daughter?' (Abrahams and Varon, 1953, p. 177).

I have already mentioned, in connexion with the comments regarding the reports by Bateson *et al.* (1956), my conception of the desperately ambivalent and complex relationship between mother and child as involving an element of genuinely enjoyable playfulness, however mutually denied. And in my repeated experiences of this ingredient in the transference-relationship with schizophrenic patients, this carries with it a quality of genuine pleasure which goes beyond a flavour of one's simply making the best of a tragic situation. This enjoyable-game quality usually does not come to light until after many months of therapeutic work, and even then is likely to go undetected if the therapist feels too burdened with the responsibility of helping the patient to resolve the latter's genuinely tragic difficulties. When one comes to realize that part of the tragedy resides in the very fact that the patient and his mother were rarely free to play together *openly* and *consciously*, then it becomes somehow more acceptable, as well as more understandable, to the therapist to see this denied playfulness going on behind a wholly tragic mask.

More often than not, I have found that the histories of schizophrenic patients, whether male or female, describe the father as being by far the warmer, the more accessible, of the two parents, and the patient as having always been very much attached to the father, whereas the mother was always a relatively cold, rejecting, remote figure. But I have repeatedly found that, disguised behind the child's idol or inseparable chum, is a matter of the father's transference to the child as being a mother-figure upon whom he, the father, makes insatiable demands. It seems that the father, in these instances, is an infantile individual who reacts both to his wife and to his child as mother-figures, and who, by striving to be both father and mother to the child, unconsciously seeks to intervene between mother and child in such a way as to have each of them to himself. I have seen abundant evidence of this by now, in a considerable number of cases, both in the transference-developments with the patients and in interviews with the parents.

My point here is that the mother and child allow this interposition by the father to happen, because of their anxiety about their fondness for, their wish to be close to, one another. I have found, in the psychotherapy with the now-adult child, that the transference development follows, in the main, this sequence: the patient reacts to the therapist initially, and, usually, for a number of months, as being mainly a relatively warm father-figure, while the mother-transference is difficult or impossible to locate; then as being a hostile, remote, frightening mother-figure; then as being a desirable mother-figure of whom the patient is fond, but a mother-figure who exasperatingly allows an infantile, 'King Baby', kind of father to keep intervening, placing impossible demands for mothering upon the patient; finally comes a phase of the patient's responding to the therapist as a mother with whom he can share an unashamedly fond relatedness, no longer burdened by the father's scornfully and demandingly coming between them. One of the discoveries which patient and therapist make, in this transference-evolution, is that behind the patient's enjoyment of hiking, swimming, golfing, talking for hours, or what not, with the chum-and-idol father, has been an impatience to get this boring, demanding infant off one's neck and get back to the much more fascinating and complex game of relating with the mother, a game quite beyond the ken of this 'square' of a father.

It might well be considered absurd to describe any type of transference-evolution as being of general validity for schizophrenic patients. But I believe that, in very broad outlines, the above sequence occurs more often than not.

THE PATIENT-THERAPIST RELATIONSHIP

This has been touched upon repeatedly in the foregoing pages; but I shall now focus centrally upon it.

The transference-evolution found in the work with the majority of schizophrenic patients, in my own experience and in my observations of the work of my colleagues, has been described above. The time-span involved in this evolution, in the work with chronically schizophrenic adults, may be great indeed. More than once I have had to sweat through approximately two years of being responded to, by the patient, as a 'bad (hateful, cruel, rejecting) mother' before this atmosphere gradually shifted to my finding myself in a 'good (loving and beloved) mother' transference position in the therapy.

It seems to me that one of the great reasons for this long time-span—one of the great reasons, that is, for its requiring such a prolonged period of intensive psychotherapy to help a chronic schizophrenic patient to become free of his schizophrenia—is that the 'good mother' transference relatedness has a basically symbiotic quality which is anxiety-provoking to both patient and therapist and therefore arouses great resistance in each of them, which takes many months to resolve. That is, this symbiotic relatedness involves an intensity of mutual love and need for one another which is found, normally, only between mother and infant; which was too anxiety-provoking to this patient and to his mother for them to allow themselves to recognize its presence in the relationship; and which carries with it into the transference-re-enactment this same charge of anxiety, strong enough to be schizophrenigenic.

In chapter 8 I put forward the concept that this symbiotic mother-infant relatedness tends, inevitably and valuably, to become re-experienced in the transference relationship, and that the therapist's job is not to avoid its establishment, but rather to have the courage to recognize its presence once it has become established, as in successful therapy it inevitably does. What the therapist can here bring into the patient's life which is new and therapeutic is something which the mother, with her low self-esteem and her anxiety in the face of loving interaction, could not provide: an awareness of how greatly the patient loves and needs oneself, and of how greatly one loves and needs the patient.

In this symbiotic form of relatedness, the patient's and therapist's feelings towards one another fluctuate so that now the latter, now the former, is in an omnipotent-mother position; thus the therapist must be as open as possible both to his own infantile dependency needs and to his feeling subjectively omnipotent in relationship to his needful-infant patient.

And, in my experience, it can be at first distinctly anxiety-provoking to find that the patient feels, with his infantile needfulness directed towards oneself, a wholehearted adoration towards oneself also. I have come to believe that, not only in me but in many other therapists, it requires a sounder sense of self-esteem to be exposed to the patient's genuine admiration, of this degree of intensity, than to face his contempt towards oneself. One is likely to feel, that is, unworthy of this adoration, and therefore uncomfortable in the face of it.

Similarly with the patient's solicitude towards oneself, when he detects, for example, anxiety or sadness in one and evidences a genuine wish to assuage such feelings, it may not be a comfortable thing to recognize this solicitude. One is likely to feel, with guilt and embarrassment, something like this: 'What right have *I*, who am supposed to be the therapist helping the *patient*, to be *accepting* help from *him*?' We tend to be too concerned lest this amount to exploitation of the patient, not realizing that one of the patient's own great needs – and this, I think, is especially true with those most deeply ill – is to find that he can be genuinely needed, can be found genuinely and personally useful, by other persons.

One desperately ill, deeply regressed schizophrenic woman, after I had declined a number of proffered gifts, to which I mistakenly reacted as expressive primarily of contempt towards me, said in a deeply troubled tone, 'You mean I have no potentiality for giving?' We need to become quite free from the prevalent misconception that the patient is totally needful of receiving, so similar to the misconception of the normal infant as being totally receiving.

In chapter 3, I described some of the common manifestations of therapists' anxiety in connexion with their own infantile-dependency needs, needs which the psychotherapy with these patients tends strongly to bring into one's awareness. I agree with the concept of Whitaker and Malone that one of the therapist's motivations for pursuing this work consists in a search for therapeutic help for himself; my own impression is that he is unconsciously seeking for help for that aspect of himself which is like a lonely, frightened, confused, hungry small child or infant. And it is not surprising that he might gravitate towards work with schizophrenic patients, for such persons have powerful strivings to make contact with, and bring relief to, the similarly isolated, frightened (and so on) child in the parent. Thus the therapist's own need for therapeutic help—the therapist's 'patient-vectors', in the phrase of Whitaker and Malone—tends to be evoked in work with schizophrenic patients, to a greater degree, I think, than is the case in the work with neurotic patients, because the schizophrenic's childhood experience was such as to imbue him with more powerful strivings to 'cure' his parents. My main point here is that the less embarrassed, anxious, and guilty the therapist feels upon finding such needs in himself, in the transference relationship with the schizophrenic patient, the more able he is to remain available, receptive, and helpful to the patient.

Just as, in the naturally reconstituted symbiotic relationship between the patient and therapist, the therapist tends to find the patient's adoration and solicitude somewhat anxiety-provoking, so too he tends to react with anxiety to his own feelings, equally natural in this transference relatedness, towards the patient as being an omnipotent, adored mother. He almost inevitably experiences considerable embarrassment, dismay, and anxiety upon finding himself experiencing what he may think of as a 'crush on' the patient, whom he now finds incredibly precious and important to him; in this phase of the work it is by no means uncommon, I think, for the therapist to regard the patient, now and again, as being the dearest person in his life. This may make one feel especially awkward if the patient is of one's own sex, for now even prolonged past experience in personal analysis may not protect one fully from the culturally inspired fears lest so powerful feelings of fondness, in this context, mean that one is homosexual. And even if the patient is of the opposite sex, one tends to get into uncomfortable comparisons of one's fondness for the patient over against that for one's wife or husband and children.

In short, then, as the symbiotic relationship between patient and therapist oscillates between the therapist's being now in the position of an omnipotent mother, and now in that of an adoring infant, on either hand he is apt to experience anxiety in the face of the intense, unaccustomed feelings which the position involves. It requires much courage for him to allow these feelings into his awareness. But such courage is amply rewarded, for there is no more crucial phase in the transference resolution of the schizophrenic illness.

In order to make quite clear that what I am describing and advocating is not some variety of 'love therapy' (in which the therapist manages to convince himself that he has towards the patient, from the very outset, a kind of superlative, healing love with which only he and the angels are endowed), I wish to emphasize that it takes a great deal of time, and a great deal of working through of mutual hostility in the therapeutic relationship, before the establishment and recognition by the therapist of the symbiotic relatedness in the transference.

In my work with one extraordinarily deeply and chronically ill paranoid schizophrenic man, for example, I spent the first two years in an ostensibly fully interested and dedicated meeting with him for the sessions, consciously making every effort to be useful to him, but, as I realized near the end of this period, without his really *meaning enough* to me, personally, for me to come fully to grips with the extremely intense feelings at the root of his illness.

Not many months later, however, I found that I now cared so deeply for him that I was no longer greatly concerned, for example, with his long-repeated, furious threats to knock my teeth out; I kept moving, psychologically, towards him, or one might say remaining psychologically available to him, despite these threats. My thought, in retrospect, is that he had come to mean more to me than did my own teeth. And it is not surprising that this recognition of how very much he meant to me came hand in hand with my recognition of how very much I meant to him. I recall so well the feelings with which I came away from an hour with him having seen unusually clear evidences of his fondness for me. Concerning this same man towards whom, for about two years, I had often felt a great deal of contempt, fear, and hatred, I now felt suffused with the radiant discovery, 'He loves me!' And it was not many months later when I realized that the genuine and deep dedication which enables one to hold to these long and difficult therapeutic endeavours is of a piece with the small child's devotion to his mother.

A hint as to the length of time required for the development of deep and genuine fondness in the patient-therapist relationship, and an allusion to the ineffectiveness of what one might call 'love therapy', are to be found in the following passage from a paper by Frieda Fromm-Reichmann (1952).[*]

There is one last reason, which makes me warn against the attempt to start psychotherapy with a schizophrenic on the basis of any relationship other than the realistic professional one, that is his alert sensitivity to and rejection of any feigned emotional experience. As one patient bluntly expressed herself upon being offered friendship in an initial interview by a young psychoanalyst, 'How can you say we are friends? We hardly know each other.'

CLINICAL EXAMPLE

A 38-year-old, single woman was admitted to Chestnut Lodge because of a schizophrenic illness which had begun insidiously only three years previously, but had progressed to an extra-ordinarily profound level of ego-fragmentation and regression. During my first psychotherapeutic session with her, on the day following her admission, I found her to have a shockingly non-human appearance; a nurse had independently formed and noted down a similar opinion, namely that 'this woman looks at times like a demon'; and the administrative psychiatrist, a man with

---

[*] This passage was quoted previously in ch. 3 above, p. 150.

decades of experience in work in state hospitals, recalled in a later staff conference his initial impression of her: 'Katherine was one of the most repulsive-looking things I've ever seen when she first came in here. She looked more like some sort of tamed wild animal or something.'

For several years after her admission, her illness required her to be housed on a maximum-security ward. Only very slowly and gradually was there an improvement in her deeply delusional and hallucinatory state, a state involving profound disturbances in her body-image and a chaotic fragmentation of her intrapersonal and interpersonal experiences.

Her history (as provided by her parents on her admission) indicated that she had always openly idolized her father, with whom, on innumerable occasions, she had gone horseback riding, hiking, and swimming, and had played tennis and golf. To the social worker who obtained a portion of the history, the father expressed undisguised pride in the fact that his daughter had compared each of her boy friends, in a series of broken romances, unfavourably with himself; and to me he expressed his satisfaction about her not having married any of these men (clearly indicating that he would rather that she were in her present, tragically psychotic, state than married to a man whom he considered rather a playboy, or low-bred, or what not).

In my interview with the father, I was impressed with a kind of easy friendliness with which he spoke of his daughter, much as one might speak of a good pal. For all his difficulties, I found him an overtly warmer, more approachable person than his intensely compulsive wife, who spoke about her daughter in a loud, flat, strident voice. The patient had been hospitalized elsewhere for six months prior to her admission here; and the comments made by her former therapist, who accompanied her during the transfer, substantiated my initial impression that the father had, despite all his possessiveness, a warmer, more friendly relationship with the daughter than did the mother. This therapist described how relatively relaxed and communicative the patient had been during her father's frequent visits, and how, during the mother's less frequent ones, the two women had regularly evidenced a most brittle, ungenuine effusiveness towards one another.

In my initial interview with the mother, it was with a startlingly violent emphasis that she said, in describing the patient's having had a severe napkin-rash at the age of five months, 'It was just *ravaging!*' Her way of uttering this last word betrayed a truly savage hostility towards the daughter. And I was rather dazed at the remarkable number of *non sequiturs* involved in many of the remarks which the mother uttered in her characteristic flat, strident, staccato voice; these clearly betrayed a precarious ego-integration.

As the patient's hospitalization went on, it continued to be difficult to perceive any indication of genuine fondness in the mother towards her daughter. I had an interview with the parents during each of the visits they made, every month or two, to their daughter. During a visit by the mother and a sister-in-law of the patient 16 months after the patient's admission (the father being away on a business trip), I was shocked at the chillingly matter-of-fact, offhandedly casual manner in which the mother interjected, 'Oh, by the way, we've sold her motor-boat. We haven't told her about it. We thought if she ever got out, we could get her another one anyway.' The boat had been literally one of the patient's last meaningful links with life outside the hospital. Later in this session, I was amazed to hear the mother report, with a brittle laugh, concerning the visit which she and the patient's sister-in-law had just had with the patient, 'She just kept us in stitches!' by, the mother explained, various pantomimes; I had often seen the patient to be pantomiming in a grotesque, dissociated, intensely anxious way. The sister-in-law, a much more perceptive person and present during this interview, told me how the patient had fallen on the floor, during their visit to her, 'sobbing her heart out' and begging her mother, 'Don't scold me, Mother – don't laugh at me!'

At a still later interview, it was with a nakedly gleeful tone that the mother told me of the 'good blow' which the patient had received on the head, some years before, in an automobile accident – an injury which involved several minutes' loss of consciousness.

As for the patient's feelings towards her mother in past years, it should be mentioned that not only had she conspicuously preferred her idol-and-pal father; but also, as her psychosis developed, she became openly harsh, contemptuous, and (verbally) violently resentful towards her mother. In short, one had little reason to think that there was any significant degree of mutual fondness in this mother-daughter relationship.

During the first 2½ years of my work with the patient, her unfolding transference to me was such as to provide most convincing evidence that her relationship with her mother had been an extraordinarily malevolent one.

For the first few months, she reacted to me oftentimes with a gushy effusiveness which compared closely with that shown by both herself and her mother during the latter's visits. Her effusiveness towards me had an impact of contempt and hostility which became less heavily disguised as the months wore on and the effusiveness slowly dropped away. Meanwhile she often grabbed at one or another of my garments, demanding that I give them to her; her history showed that she and her mother had often worn one another's clothing and jewellery, and her mother had been surprised when the patient, with the advent of the psychosis, antagonistically refused to continue this practice.

By the end of the first few months, the patient and I had become locked in what I increasingly felt to be an extraordinarily malevolent relationship. In ways which were becoming steadily more stereotyped, she was expressing what I felt as an erodingly persistent rejectingness, contempt, and suppressed but violent antagonism towards me; at times I would see her as a tragically, pathetically needful person, but would find that my efforts to be of use met only with seemingly intense dissatisfaction, contempt, or lack of interest on her part. Judging from her facial expressions and from her fragmentary verbal comments, I had every impression that she was immersed oftentimes in fantasies of subjecting me to physical violence, and on many occasions she gave me to feel that, but for my meeting her hostility firmly, she would indeed attack me physically. By far the most frequent target of her hostility was my head.

My own feelings towards her, as these early years wore on, came more and more to consist in a sense of helpless dissatisfaction both with myself and with her, and, above all, a feeling of being helplessly enmeshed in the relationship with her. I found my feelings varying at the mercy of the responses she was showing towards me. When she appeared rejecting, I felt hurt and discouraged and often violently hateful towards her; I felt shocked on many occasions at the vividness of my fantasies of smashing in her skull. When she was showing contempt and loathing towards me, I often experienced similar feelings towards her, at a level of intensity which dismayed me. When she gave me glimpses into the depths of her own despair and profound anxiety, I felt deeply moved, guilty, and even more profoundly helpless. Ever more subtle non-verbal communications became charged with significance to each of us, as I felt it; I hungered for even the tiniest signs of receptiveness on her part, felt profoundly grateful for the most fragmentary and obscure verbalizations from her, and felt murderous rage in reaction to tiny indications of her unexpected withdrawal. Later on, when this long period had come to an end, I realized that my ego-boundaries in the relationship with her had become very indistinct, so that I was feeling about as helplessly caught up in ambivalent feelings as she herself was; I had become, in a sense, deeply immersed in the patient's illness. But at the time, not yet having broken through to a realization that I, a therapist over here, was dealing with a deeply ill patient over there, I could experience it, in summary, only as a growing fear that maybe my hatred was, after all, more powerful than my love–a fear that, on balance, I was basically evil and basically destructive in all my relationships with people.

I have seen, over and over again, in a convincing succession of instances, not only in my own work but in the work of my colleagues, that this kind of profound soul-struggle is resident in the very nature of work with schizophrenic patients; I doubt whether any deeply ill patient has gone on to recovery without his or her therapist's having to undergo, in a phase of the work, this kind of inner doubt and struggle. But, even given this knowledge as to the nature of such work, when one is involved in the struggle it is real and immediate and of desperate personal significance.

I would put it now, also, that the patient and I had developed a symbiotic relationship with one another in which we were conscious almost exclusively of the negative side of our mutual feelings, and were subjecting our positive feelings to a severe, unconscious denial.

Throughout these 2½ years there was a second and much minor theme: the gradually more direct, though never very frequent, expressions of her fondness, and even adoration, towards me as a

245

beloved father. In touching ways, sometimes verbally but more often non-verbally, she let me know that she loved me as being the reincarnation of her beloved father. These expressions came fleetingly, and in one of them she let me know that her life with her mother had been 'hell', worse than life in the disturbed ward where she was now living.

But finally, in the latter part of the third year of our work, our main mode of relatedness began, little by little, to shift. She revealed feelings of guilt for having let her mother down, and consequent feelings of worthlessness and self-hatred. These were at first expressed in a displaced fashion, with regard to the woman who owned the dancing school where she had been working at the time when the schizophrenic illness was becoming overt. She let me know, with this, one reason why she had been so rejecting of the contributions which I had tried to give to her: 'I was told I wasn't supposed to have anything here.' Within a few weeks she confided to me, too, her fear of genuine closeness with me: 'If we got together, we might kill one another.' Hearing this, I felt a little clearer as to why we had been so persistently out of phase with one another (I giving at a moment when she could not receive; she asking for something at a moment when I had withdrawn into sullen resentment or rage; and so on) – why, for $2\frac{1}{2}$ years, we had had no more than an occasional, fleeting moment of contentment with one another.

As the third year drew to a close I felt that my emotional position towards the patient had changed qualitatively, from a former predominantly 'bad mother' position to a present predominantly 'good mother' position. I inferred this from my finding her able to show me relatively freely her feelings of needfulness, anxiety, and discouragement, and from my finding myself aware of her as a separate person, a person over there, a person who was deeply troubled and in need of help, a person with an illness which existed apart from me. I now realized that the fact of her being grievously ill was not *per se* a sign of evilness in me; in short, I realized that *I* was not her illness.

A few weeks later, just before the beginning of the fourth year, there occurred in one of the sessions a break-through of intense feelings on her part towards me as being a father-figure who was maddeningly on her neck and in her hair, a father who had kept her burdened interminably long with his small-boy demands, like a small boy who makes insatiable demands on his mother. I now saw clearly the other side of the I-want-to-be-with-constantly-and-go-everywhere-with-my-idolized-father situation. And I saw this without experiencing any feelings of guilt or self-doubt whatsoever; although she expressed these feelings with the most frantic intensity, I was able to see clearly their transference origin, as a result of having recently achieved a resolution of the counter-transference problem which I have described.

It was two months after this session, in the second month of the fourth year, that she began showing open fondness towards me as a mother-figure to her. Until now, she had been in constant motion of some sort or other throughout our sessions, constantly swaying about from one foot to the other, or glancing away, or assuming grotesque postures, or what not. But now, about two-thirds of the way through a session in which she had been going through this customary avoidance behaviour, she came over and stood behind and a little to one side of my chair, and stood quietly for a minute or two. This in itself was something quite new. Then she came round, sat on the end of her bed immediately in front of me, with her face no more than two feet from mine, and said simply, while looking me full in the eyes in a direct and undisguisedly friendly way, 'I'm tired of running away.'

When another month had passed, she had come to be, in occasional sessions, an attractive, likeable, relatively well-groomed girl—a very marked shift from the persistently subhuman appearance she had always presented before, since her admission over three years earlier. In this same month she let me know that 'my [hallucinatory] daughter and me' were relating to one another, and that I should stop interfering. She still communicated in largely a fragmentary, obscure way, but when I commented, 'It seems to me you're saying that you and your daughter have a relationship with one another that you want me to keep out of, and I keep interfering,' she emphatically, but in a not unfriendly tone, said, '*That's right.*' This was an unusual and most welcome consensus which we had thus reached, and I felt that it clearly spoke of her feeling that her father had interfered grossly and persistently in her relationship with her mother, although she was not yet able to make this point in a more direct and conventional fashion.

Six weeks later (in the fifth month of the fourth year), however, she was able to make it very clear indeed that she felt her father had always been primarily interested in going on trips or spending time at his club, that he had spent little time at home, and that he had been neither interested in the home nor appreciative of the efforts she and her mother had made to keep it looking attractive for him. All this came out in the transference, with my being in the position of the father, in one of the sessions. She kept asking me, sarcastically, if I did not want to travel here and there; she put her bedspread on the floor as a rug, and put another bedspread over her chest of drawers as a tablecover, and in other ways endeavoured to make her room look as attractive as possible for me, indicating meanwhile that she found me thoroughly unappreciative of these efforts.

Later in this same month, when the parents visited her, the mother let me see, for the first time in my experience with her, depths of subjective worthlessness and self-despair which I had never perceived before, and which moved me to see her in a friendlier light. I now realized that this well-groomed, intelligent, and in many ways successful woman had within her a sense of profound worthlessness which was of much the same awesome depth as that which I had long seen in her daughter who had been leading a more or less animal-like existence in a disturbed psychiatric ward for years. The mother revealed enough of this for me to see that it had roots in her own early childhood. I now saw in the mother, too, an unmistakably genuine devotion to her daughter which, as I now realized, had lain behind the artificial effusiveness.

A month later (fourth year, sixth month), the patient was able to express more directly than ever before a feeling of adoration towards me. Looking towards the window at first, she said, 'Wait until you see him!' in a tone of breathless admiration, as if some 'dreamboat of a guy', as I then thought of it, were coming; she had long been hallucinating breathlessly admired figures during our hours, while overtly subjecting me to her usual contempt, antagonism, or disregard. I felt like saying something sardonic, such as, 'Quite a dreamboat, eh?', but held my tongue. Then in the next moment she turned to me and blurted out, 'Have I ever told you you're brilliant?' This she said in a wholly sincere, idolizing tone, as if avowing love for me which she had long kept from revealing.

248

Then, almost without pausing for breath, she turned on some of the old, saccharine, pseudo-admiring talk towards me, of the kind which I had so often heard before. But that moment had been enough to convince me of the presence of this deeper, genuine adoration in her, and to convince me, too, that this genuine adoration actually was more disconcerting to me than was her long-accustomed, saccharine pseudo-admiration. Just as her mother's self-esteem was too low to allow her to endure open expressions of genuine adoration from the daughter, I too found such expressions, at first, productive of anxiety in me. I regarded this, at the time, as a breakthrough, before my very eyes, of the defensive adoration towards her father – a breakthrough, that is, into her deeper adoration towards the mother.

Three months later (fourth year, ninth month), during an interview with the mother, I felt deeply moved both by her profound doubts as to her own worth (doubts such as I had felt so often in my own work with her daughter) and by her genuine devotion to her daughter, when she suddenly revealed to me, weeping profusely, an evidently long-pent-up welter of feelings: 'Do you think it would be all right if I said to Kathy, "Kathy, I'd like to go out to dinner with you. Would you like to go with me?" Do you think she *would* want to go with me or do you think she'd say, "I don't want to go with that old thing!"?'

Then in my session with the patient on the day following this visit, Katherine began evidencing some of the old, spurious effusiveness towards me. At this I asked her, comfortably and rather amusedly, 'Katherine, do you suppose you'll *ever* get over that phony kind of pseudo-admiration, that contemptuous kind of pseudo-admiration, that you give out towards me?' She laughed warmly. Following some intervening comments back and forth between us, she looked at me, while sitting close beside me, and said, 'I'm crazy about you,' in a low, shy, unmistakably genuine way. I replied, simply and unanxiously, 'That's a very nice thing for you to say, Katherine, and I appreciate it.' I then added, 'Perhaps that's the kind of thing you've never been able to say to – I don't know, your mother – your father –', with equal emphasis on each.

She replied, promptly and seriously and emphatically, but without anger, 'Mother.' Then in the next few moments she stood up, meandered over to the window and then moved back to a spot near me–meanwhile, in returning, going through circles backward, looking like an unutterably touching and precious, shy little child who is head over heels in love. I commented, fondly, 'I've got you going around in circles, eh?', feeling this as a clear-cut, non-verbal means of her showing me how crazy she was about me. I felt certain that this was a measure of her fondness not only for me but also for her mother–fondness which she dared not express openly to the mother because the latter's anxiety, based in such low self-esteem as I had seen revealed in the mother only the day before, forbade it. I now saw the mother's and daughter's saccharine effusiveness towards one another as not primarily a manifestation of submerged hatred towards one another, but rather a pathetic and tragic sign of their inability to express openly their genuine love for one another.

With this patient, the ground which had been won initially–the replacement, in the developing transference, of mother-daughter hatred by mother-daughter love–seemed, in several subsequent phases of our work, to be irretrievably lost again, only to be rewon in a larger and deeper form after much hard struggle. In the subsequent months I found, as the recurrent mutual denial of fondness receded, not only new depths of fondness in the patient towards me, but a deeper realization of how very fond and dependent I felt towards the patient; sometimes I regarded her with parental fondness as being a very dear child, and at other times I regarded her as a supremely warm and loving mother person. Time after time I found, sometimes through conferences with fellow-therapists on the Lodge staff, that I had been clinging fast to a deniedly cherished relationship with the patient, consciously most dissatisfied and discouraged and resentful about what seemed like an endless *status quo*, but–as I now would come to see–having been struggling unconsciously with might and main against any threatened change in this profoundly gratifying symbiotic mode of relatedness to her. There were at least three major occasions on which I felt that this problem had been put, once for all, behind us so that I would now be able wholeheartedly to help her to become well.

This struggle went on within me, and in my relationship with the patient, for approximately one full year after the events which I have detailed above. My knowledge of my fellow-therapists' work with their patients convinces me that such a prolonged and recurrent struggle to free oneself from this symbiotic mode of relatedness is not primarily a function of some glaringly unusual susceptibility to counter-transference in myself on this score, but rather is primarily a function of the inevitable course which is followed in the transference evolution of such a deeply and chronically ill schizophrenic patient.

In the tenth month of the fourth year, at the end of a session in which we had been able to communicate much more satisfactorily than usual with one another (during this she had been able to express to me, among other things, her own sense of fragmentation into six or eight pieces), she said shyly, but warmly and appreciatively, as I started to leave, 'She said she had a good time.' I replied in the same feeling-vein, 'I had a good time, too, Katherine,' to which she said, 'Thank you.' This simple exchange is for me of memorable significance, as an indication of our hard-won ability to acknowledge, to ourselves and to one another, how deeply fond of each other we had become.

A month later, she was again able to verbalize an awareness of the ego-fragmentation which had been acted out, in behaviour, throughout the years of her hospitalization; she spoke of being 'broken' into 'eight pieces', and later in the same session expressed it as 'broken into four pieces'. With this last phrase she then added, insistently and pleadingly, 'Don't let it happen to Mother!' Her tone unmistakably conveyed her genuine solicitude and protectiveness with regard to her mother; it was now that I realized, more deeply than ever before, that one facet of her illness consisted in her own enduring this grievously profound ego-fragmentation in order to shield her beloved mother from suffering this same experience herself.

The patient had made this plea, 'Don't let it happen to Mother!', with the demeanour of a little child. I now understood better how it was that the mother had been able to come down from a visit with her tragically ill daughter, with the report which, as I have mentioned, astonished me at the time: 'She kept us in stiches!' I now realized, that is, something of the extent to which the patient had been protecting her mother from seeing the full extent of the ego-fragmentation with which the patient had been grappling here in the hospital. She had thus shielded the mother above all, I think, from seeing the fullness of the mother's *own* ego-fragmentation; she had helped to keep the mother's loose ego-structure stitched together. A few months later, when the patient had improved a good deal more, the mother for the first time seemed to become aware of how tragically disturbed her daughter's experience had long been, and asked with obvious anxiety and anguish what it must be like to experience what Katherine was (still in some measure) going through. The mother evidenced, now, something of the same kind of deep, stony desolation and intense anxiety as had been heretofore so very prominent in her daughter, but which now had given way to measurably improved integration in the patient herself.

It was near the end of the fourth and early in the fifth year of my work with Katherine that I became aware of a pleasurable-game element in our relationship—an element which, I now realized, had long been there but which had been submerged under the realistically, pressingly tragic aspects of her illness and because of the truly desperate importance of the psychotherapy. Now, when I came into the ward for the session with her, I realized that the minute indications of a cold reception from her —indications highly private to our relationship with one another —were not something for me to feel discouraged about, as I had often felt before at seeing or hearing them; they were, I now realized, all part of our playing a complex and mutually fascinating game with one another. A colleague, having an hour at the ward-porch while Katherine was near by, later told me how much he had been impressed by Katherine's absorption in doing an amazingly complex solo dance to the radio music coming over the loudspeaker; this helped me to realize further the extent of her love for complexity. I noticed that she now referred time and again to our relationship as 'a crossword puzzle', in a tone of absorbed interest, and once when she sensed discouragement in me, she said in a touchingly serious tone, as I was leaving at the end of the session, 'Don't stop playing the game.'

By the beginning of the fifth year this young woman, who had manifested so unhuman an appearance upon her admission to the Lodge and for so discouragingly long a time thereafter, had come to show, more and more frequently, the growingly healthy and attractive human being in her. It was at this time that I was most gratified when a fellow-therapist, who had been seeing Katherine for many months, in passing, while having hours with one of his patients in the same ward, spontaneously told me of his astonishment at seeing how different Katherine was now appearing. He said that always before he had seen her looking 'grotesque', and today, by contrast, on going up to the ward he had found her to be well dressed and 'looking like a very pretty girl from a good Eastern school!' She had come over to him and said something of a rational, appropriate sort, which had further endeared her to him.

Katherine and I had a long way yet to go; but the hardest part of the work – the deepest part of her illness – was now behind us, and I am convinced that it was the de-repression of her fondness for her mother, first experienced in terms of myself as the transference-mother, which was most responsible for her improved integration and her acceptance of herself as a female human being.

COMMENTS

An earlier version of this paper, which proved too lengthy for publication, contained not only a much more detailed scrutiny of the literature than does this, but also three clinical examples instead of the single one which I have given above. In condensing the original version I decided that it was wiser to delete two of the examples entirely and thus be able to retain one in its original length, than to try to retain all three, or even two, of the examples, which would then have to be given in so abbreviated a form that they would not, I felt, convey the flavour of what I am here trying to convey.[7]

My work with approximately fourteen additional hospitalized schizophrenic patients, including a number of male patients – work averaging about three years in each case – has contributed to my forming the concepts which I have here presented.

[7] These other two cases are included in ch. 12.

Chapter 8

THE EFFORT TO DRIVE THE OTHER PERSON CRAZY–AN ELEMENT IN THE AETIOLOGY AND PSYCHOTHERAPY OF SCHIZOPHRENIA (1959)[1]

AMONG all the factors in the aetiology of schizophrenia, factors which are undoubtedly complex and, further, considerably variable from one case to another, there appears to be one specific ingredient which can often – and even, I believe, regularly – be found to be operative. My clinical experience has indicated that the individual becomes schizophrenic partly by reason of a long-continued effort, a largely or wholly unconscious effort, on the part of some person or persons highly important in his upbringing, to drive him crazy.

I well know that it would be inane to reduce the complex aetiology of schizophrenia to a simple formula stating that an individual becomes schizophrenic because some other individual drives him crazy. Such a formula would not do justice to the individual's own psychological activity in the situation, to the complexity of that particular interpersonal relationship, to the complex group-processes of the family situation, or to the larger socio-dynamic processes in which the family plays but a part – often a part in which the family as a whole is helpless to deal with large and tragic circumstances quite beyond any family's capacity to control or avert.

Previous Literature

The only writings about this subject which I have found in the professional literature are statements by Arieti (1955), and by that group of researchers at the Mayo Foundation which is headed by Johnson (Beckett *et al.*, 1956; and Johnson, Giffin, Watson & Beckett, 1956), and these statements have done little more than touch upon the subject, without exploring it in detail.

[1] First published in the *British Journal of Medical Psychology*, Vol. 32 (1959), pp. 1–18.

DRIVING THE OTHER PERSON CRAZY

Arieti describes what he terms 'acted-out' or 'externalized' psychoses, explaining that: '. . . These persons often create situations which will precipitate or engender psychoses in other people, whereas they themselves remain immune from overt symptoms.'

Johnson and her co-workers, reporting upon the concomitant psychotherapy of schizophrenic patients and the members of these patients' families, emphasize that this experience confirmed the authors' initial impression that '. . . in some cases parental expression of hostility through a child might both determine psychosis in the child and protect the parent from psychosis' (Beckett *et al.*, 1956). In many instances they found a history of psychological assault by the parent(s) upon the child, assault of a type which was specifically reflected in the patient's earliest delusions. It is of special interest here that among the various types of assault they describe were '. . . threats that insanity may develop in the patient'.

Hill (1955), while nowhere formulating the particular concept which I am here describing, presents a picture of a symbiotic patient-parent relationship which constitutes a conceptual background into which my concept fits, I believe, precisely. He says that the mother (or in occasional instances the father): '. . . Makes the conditions for [the child's] security in living those which meet her own defensive and aggressive requirements to avoid psychosis.' '. . . One meaning of the futility of the dependence-independence struggle of the schizophrenic. . . is his belief, based upon his observations, that, if he should improve and become well in the normal sense, his mother would become psychotic. . . .'

Bowen (1956), as a result of concomitant psychotherapy of schizophrenic patients and their families, has reached conclusions similar to those of Hill. Reichard and Tillman (1950), Lidz and Lidz (1952), and Limentani (1956) are among the other writers whose discussions of symbiotic relatedness are relevant to my paper.

My theoretical formulations will be presented, with such brief samples of clinical documentation as space will allow, in the following categories: *modes* of one's driving the other person crazy; *motives* behind the effort to drive the other person crazy; and this mode of interaction in the *patient-therapist relationship*.

255

Modes of Driving the Other Person Crazy

In trying to delineate the modes or techniques which are employed in one person's effort to drive another person crazy—or, in our professional terminology, schizophrenic—I cannot overemphasize my conviction that the striving goes on at a predominantly *unconscious* level, and my conviction that this is but one ingredient in a complex pathogenic relatedness which is well beyond the capacity of either one, or both, of the participants to control fully.

In general one can say, I think, that *the initiating of any kind of interpersonal interaction which tends to foster emotional conflict in the other person—which tends to activate various areas of his personality in opposition to one another—tends to drive him crazy (i.e. schizophrenic).*

For example, a man in analysis is reported by his wife to be persistently 'questioning the adjustment' of her younger sister, an insecure young woman, until the girl becomes increasingly anxious; he does this, evidently, by repeatedly calling her attention to areas of her personality of which she is at best dimly aware, areas which are quite at variance with the person she considers herself to be. The repressions which have been necessary for the maintenance of a functioning ego are thereby weakened (without actual psychotherapy being available to her), and increasing conflict and anxiety supervene. Quite similarly, it can be seen that the inexperienced or unconsciously sadistic analyst who makes many premature interpretations is thereby tending to drive the patient psychotic—tending to weaken the patient's ego rather than, in line with his conscious aim, to strengthen that ego by helping the patient gradually to assimilate previously repressed material through more timely interpretations.

Or a person may stimulate the other person sexually, in a setting where it would be disastrous for that person to seek gratification for his or her aroused sexual needs; thus, again, a conflict is produced. We see this in innumerable instances from schizophrenic patients' histories, in which a parent behaved in an inordinately seductive way towards the child, thus fostering in the latter an intense conflict between sexual needs on the one hand, and rigorous superego retaliations (in line with the taboo of the culture against incest) on the other. This circumstance can also be seen as productive of a conflict in the child between, on the one hand, his desire to mature and fulfil his own individuality, and on the other his regressive desire to remain in an infantile symbiosis with the parent, to remain there at the cost of investing even his sexual strivings–which constitute his trump card in the game for self-realization–in that regressive relationship.

The simultaneous, or rapidly alternating, stimulation-and-frustration of other needs in addition to sexual ones can have, I believe, a similarly disintegrating effect. One male patient, emerging from a psychosis in which his intense ambivalent feelings towards his mother played a central part, became able to describe something of his childhood relationship with her. The mother's rejecting attitude was highlighted by his recollection that he had never seen her kiss his father, whom the mother had dominated and nagged mercilessly. The patient remembered that there was one occasion when the mother had *started* to kiss her husband. This was at a time when, late in the son's childhood, his father was being rolled into the operating room of a hospital, for a major operation following a car accident. The mother leaned down as though to kiss her husband and the patient saw his face become suffused with joyous anticipation. Then the mother thought better of it, and straightened up. The patient described this with a desolate feeling-tone, as though he himself had experienced this kind of frustration at her hands many times in his own life.

Similarly, with the child's desire, as well as felt duty, to be helpful to (for example) a parent: frequently we find in the histories of schizophrenic patients that one or both the parents made chronic pleas for sympathy, understanding, and what we would call in essence therapeutic intervention, from the child, while simultaneously rejecting his efforts to be helpful, so that his genuine sympathy and desire to be helpful became compounded with guilt, rage and perhaps above all a sense of personal helplessness and worthlessness. In this connexion, Bateson and his colleagues (1956) have described parental injunctions of a mutually contradictory or 'double bind' nature as being important in the aetiology of schizophrenia.

Another technique, closely related to the stimulation-frustration technique just described, is that of one's dealing with the other person upon two (or perhaps even more) quite unrelated levels of relatedness simultaneously. This tends to require the other person to dissociate his participation in one or another (or possibly both) these levels, because he feels it to be so crazily inappropriate that he should find himself responding in terms of that particular level, since it seems to be utterly unrelated to what is going on at the other, more conscious and overt, level.

For example, on one or two occasions in my years-long work with a physically attractive and often very seductive paranoid schizophrenic woman, I have felt hard put to it to keep from going crazy when she was simultaneously (a) engaging me in some politico-philosophical debate (in which she was expressing herself with a virile kind of forceful, businesslike vigour, while I, though not being given a chance to say much, felt quite strongly urged to argue some of these points with her, and did so); and (b) strolling about the room or posing herself on her bed, in an extremely short-skirted dancing costume, in a sexually inflaming way. She made no verbal references to sex, except for charging me, early in the hour, with having 'lustful', 'erotic' desires; from there on, all the verbal interaction was this debate about theology, philosophy, and international politics, and it seemed to me that the non-verbal interaction was blatantly sexual. But–and here is, I think, the crucial point–I felt no consensual validation (at a conscious level) from her about this more covert interaction; this non-verbal sexual interaction tended to appear as simply a 'crazy' product of my own imagination. Even though I knew there was a reality basis for my responding on these two unrelated levels, I still found it such a strain that I felt, as I say, as though I were losing my mind. An insecure child engaged in such a broadly divided interrelatedness with a parent would, I think, suffer significant personality trauma in an oft-repeated situation of this kind.

Another technique, closely akin to that of relating to the other person upon two or more disjointed levels at once, is the sudden switching from one emotional wavelength to another, such as one finds so very frequently among the parents of schizophrenic patients. For example, one deeply schizophrenic young man's mother, a very intense person who talked with machine-gun rapidity, poured out to me in an uninterrupted rush of words the following sentences, which were so full of *non sequiturs*, as regards emotional tone, that they left me momentarily quite dazed: 'He was very happy. I can't imagine this thing coming over him. He never was down, ever. He loved his radio repair work at Mr Mitchell's shop in Lewiston. Mr Mitchell is a very perfectionistic person. I don't think any of the men at his shop before Edward lasted more than a few months. But Edward got along with him beautifully. He used to come home and say [the mother imitates an exhausted sigh], "I can't stand it another minute!" '

The patient, for several months prior to his hospitalization, had spent most of his time at home in the company of his mother, and I thought it significant, in this same connexion, that during the early months of his hospital stay he showed every evidence (in his facial expressions and so on) of being assailed by upsurging feelings which changed in quality with overwhelming suddenness and frequency. For example, one moment his face would show a mixture of hatred and loathing, then he would suddenly jerk as though struck by some massive object, while his face now showed an intense grief.

My implication, that this phenomenon was partly a result of his long-continued exposure to his mother's poorly integrated personality, is not intended to rule out the possibility that the process worked in the reverse direction at the same time. On the contrary, I was impressed with the mother's evidencing a better integration after the patient had been out of the home for some time, and thought it entirely likely that during my above-mentioned interview with her, at the time of her son's admission, she was showing some of the after-effects of years-long exposure to an extremely poorly integrated, psychotic person, with whose capacity to assault one's own integration I myself became most uncomfortably acquainted in the course of my work with him. All this touches upon the matter of struggle, between child and parent or between patient and therapist, to drive one another crazy; I shall go into this matter later on.

The now deceased mother of another schizophrenic man was described by the patient's siblings as having been completely unpredictable in her emotional changeability; for instance, she would return from the synagogue with a beatific expression on her face, as though she were immersed in some joyous spiritual experience, and two minutes later would be throwing a kitchen-pot at one of the children. At times she was warm and tender to the patient, but would suddenly lash out at him with virulent

259

accusations or severe physical beatings. The patient, who at the time of my beginning therapy with him had been suffering from paranoid schizophrenia for some years, required more than three years of intensive psychotherapy to become free of the delusion that he had had not one mother but many different ones. He would object repeatedly to my reference to 'your mother', protesting that he never had *one* mother; once he explained, seriously and utterly convincingly: 'When you use the word "mother", I see a picture of a parade of women, each one representing a different point of view.'

A continual, unexpected switching from one conversational topic to another without, necessarily, any marked shift in feeling-content is in itself a mode of interpersonal participation which can have a significantly disintegrating effect upon the other person's psychological functioning, as can be attested by any therapist who has worked with a patient who shows prolonged and severe confusion.

Each of these techniques tends to undermine the other person's confidence in the reliability of his own emotional reactions and of his own perception of outer reality (a formulation for which I am indebted to Dr Donald L. Burnham). In one of the previously mentioned papers by Johnson et al. (1956) we find the following pertinent description of the schizophrenic patients' childhood relationships with their parents: '. . . When these children perceived the anger and hostility of a parent, as they did on many occasions, immediately the parent would deny that he was angry and would insist that the child deny it too, so that the child was faced with the dilemma of whether to believe the parent or his own senses. If he believed his senses, he maintained a firm grasp on reality; if he believed the parent, he maintained the needed relationship, but distorted his perception of reality. Repeated parental denial resulted in the child's failure to develop adequate reality testing.[2]

The subject about which I am writing in this paper ties in with one from a quite different field of human activity: international

---

[2] One of my patients, who throughout his childhood was told, 'You're crazy!' whenever he saw through his parents' defensive denial, became so mistrustful of his own emotional responses that he relied heavily, for years, upon a pet dog to let him know, by its reaction to this or that other person whom he and his pet encountered, whether the person were friendly and trustworthy, or hostile and one to be on guard against.

politics and warfare. I refer to the subject of brainwashing and allied techniques. In reading a recent and valuable book upon this subject by Meerloo, *The Rape of the Mind* (1956), I was repeatedly impressed with the many similarities between the conscious and deliberate techniques of brainwashing which he describes, and the unconscious (or predominantly unconscious) techniques of thwarting of ego-development, and undermining of ego-functioning, which I have found to be at work in the experiences, both current and past, of schizophrenic patients. The enforced isolation in which the brainwashed person exists – isolated from all save his inquisitor(s) – is but one example of these similarities; in the life of the schizophrenic-to-be child, a regular accompaniment of the parent's integration-eroding kinds of behaviour is an injunction against the child's turning to other persons who might validate his own emotional reactions and assure him against the parent-inspired fears that he must be 'crazy' to have such 'irrational' reactions to the parent.

Meerloo's book describes brainwashing and allied techniques as occurring in the form of (*a*) deliberate experiments in the service of totalitarian political ideologies; and (*b*) cultural undercurrents in our present-day society, even in politically democratic countries. My paper portrays much these same techniques as occurring in a third area: the lives of schizophrenic patients.

Motives behind the Effort to Drive the Other Person Crazy

A mode of interpersonal participation which tends to drive the other person crazy can be based, seemingly, upon any one of a wide variety of motives; in any single instance, probably a complex constellation of various motives are at work. These motives range all the way, apparently, from intense hostility at one end of the scale to desires for a healthier, closer relatedness with the other person, and desires for self-realization at the other. I shall start with those more obvious motives at the former end of the scale.

(i) The effort to drive the other person crazy can consist, predominantly, in the psychological equivalent of murder; that is, it can represent primarily an endeavour to destroy him, to get rid of him as completely as if he were physically destroyed. In this connexion, it is interesting to note that whereas our legal system reserves its severest punishment for him who commits physical murder, it metes out no–or at most negligible–punishment for psychological 'murder', for destroying another person psychologically by driving him 'crazy'. In the knowledge of the average person who is unacquainted with the details of legal procedure, the only legal penalty in this area is the tangentially relevant and entirely unfrightening legal charge of 'mental cruelty' which, he knows, is not infrequently conjured up as an excuse for a high percentage of divorces.

I do not mean to imply that I wonder at this legal state of things, or suggest any change in the law in this regard; I think it would be impracticable to set out to prove, legally, that one person had contributed significantly to another person's 'going crazy'. My point is that this state of things does exist in our legal system, so that whereas one has a reason to feel deterred, by law, from physical murder, one has practically no reason to feel similarly deterred from what might be thought of as psychological murder.

It should be noted, further, that a psychosis severe enough to require years-long hospitalization does indeed serve to bar the patient from continued participation in the life of, for instance, a family, almost as effectively as would death itself. It is not unheard of for the parents of a long-psychotic, hospitalized child to let it be known that the child has died, and it is much more frequent for the family members still at home to avoid making references to the patient, in their everyday life with friends and associates, and to avoid consulting or informing the patient concerning family crises, very much as though he had 'passed away'.

As an example of this kind of motive, I shall cite certain data from my work with a young woman who had been hospitalized for more than three years for a schizophrenic illness, and who by this time had become able to tell me some details about her life in her family before its onset.

She had one sibling, a sister two years younger than herself. Both girls were good looking; both had been strongly indoctrinated with the view, from their mother and father, that a girl's only *raison d'être* is the acquisition of a socially prominent and wealthy husband; both were much involved in fantasies of being the wife of the father, since their mother accepted a much-derogated role in the family. They were therefore intensely and openly competitive with one another.

DRIVING THE OTHER PERSON CRAZY

My patient, in one of her psychotherapeutic sessions, reminisced about a time (not more than two years prior to her first hospitalization) when her sister had been jilted by a boy friend whom the sister had introduced to a supposed friend, named Mary. She said that for about a year after that, her sister wore dark glasses and 'went around the house talking about suicide', and weeping. The patient said that the glasses 'were driving her [i.e. the sister] crazy'. She also added, 'My sister used to say she read a lot so that she wouldn't go nuts', and commented to me that 'the jealousy and hatred . . . and all the teasing . . . make a person wild'. She spoke of 'how jealous Sarah [the sister] was of Mary', giving me to think that she was about to say 'of me', but shifted to 'of Mary'; I got the distinct impression, from other things she said, that the jealousy between herself and her sister was intense during that period. I noticed that when she spoke, from time to time, of the suffering her sister had evidenced, a sadistic smile repeatedly came over her face. She said at one point that 'If two people each want the same thing' they are bound to have hatred and jealousy towards one another, and later spoke of how much hatred and jealousy one has towards somebody who is standing in the way of something or somebody one wants. I commented, here, casually, that naturally one feels like killing the other person, getting rid of them. She replied, 'Killing–that isn't allowed–', as if she had already considered that but had come up against the fact that, for some reason incomprehensible to her, this was forbidden.

Parenthetically, this girl's case history describes her having verbally threatened to murder her sister–'I'll get you in the back when you're not looking'–and having picked up a hammer and threatened to kill her mother with it. The sister, who had been married a few months after the patient's initial hospitalization, was afraid to let the patient visit her for fear the latter would kill the sister's small baby; in short, the family took her threats of murder quite seriously.

Now when she said thoughtfully, during this therapeutic session, 'Killing–that isn't allowed–', she added significantly, '–but there are other ways'. On another occasion, while telling of her sister's depressive symptoms, she fell to reciting the words of the nonsense song 'Mairzy Doats', which had been popular during that era. She puzzled, in her chronically confused way, over the word 'Mairzy', saying twice that sometimes the word is 'Mairzy' and sometimes it is 'Mary', giving me every impression that during the sister's depression she had tormented the sister by asking her about this song, often using the hated word 'Mary', the name of the sister's former friend who had taken from her, and eventually married, her steady boy friend.

This material is too long to reproduce in full here; but in essence it should be reported that the patient had evidently felt herself to be in a desperate struggle with the sister as to which would drive the other crazy first. On one occasion the patient recalled, with obvious anxiety, 'Sarah said I had something to do with it', the 'it' referring to Sarah's depression, and she quoted Sarah as saying, 'I hope you never get this', which evidently had an ominously threatening connotation to the patient. I got the strong impression that she felt guilty about the sister's illness, felt that the sister blamed her for it, and feared that the sister would vengefully cause her to be similarly ill, in retaliation.

This touches upon the subject of what I call 'psychosis wishes', entirely analogous to 'death wishes'. On several occasions, when working with patients who have had an experience, earlier in life prior to their own illness, of a parent's being hospitalized because of a psychotic illness, I have found that the patients show guilt about repressed 'psychosis wishes', entirely similar to 'death wishes' which are productive of guilt in persons who have lost a hated parent through death. The patients who show this guilt over 'psychosis wishes' show every evidence of feeling that they were once successful in a mutual struggle with the parent, in which each was striving to drive the other crazy, and the subsequent appearance of their own psychosis seems to be attributable in part to guilt, and fear of the parent's revenge, stemming from that duel in previous years. In the case I have been describing, the sister was not actually hospitalized; but in other respects the circumstances were those which I have just outlined as regards patients whose mother or father, in their childhood, had been hospitalized with psychosis.

In this girl's family life, the particular mode of interpersonal participation with which I am dealing in this paper–the effort to drive the other person crazy–seems to have been a customary mode, over the years, of the various family members' interaction with one another. I shall cite but one more portion of the available data. During childhood and adolescence, she had experienced a great deal of anxiety about her teeth, partly because she had lost some of them in a playground accident. Her father used to frighten her, time and again, by telling her teasingly, 'I'm going to take your teeth out and use them for golf tees.' For the first several months after her admission to Chestnut Lodge she was, in the words of the psychiatric administrator, 'crawling with terror', incessantly demanding reassurance that no harm would come to her teeth and to various other body parts. After several years of therapy she made clear to me her conviction that her family members, each of them possessing much hatred and envy of her, had acted in concert to drive her crazy and thus rid their home of her presence, and although this is by no means an accurate total picture, it is, I believe, an accurate description of a part of what had happened.

(ii) The effort to drive the other person crazy can be motivated predominantly by a desire to externalize, and thus get rid of, the threatening craziness in oneself. It is well known that the families of schizophrenic patients have a proclivity for dealing with the patient as being 'the crazy one' in the family, the repository of all the craziness among the various other members. Hill's previously mentioned book (1955) contains some valuable observations which help us to grasp the concept that the patient's craziness consists, to a significant degree, in an introjected crazy parent (usually, in Hill's experience as in my own, the mother), a parent who now, introjected, comprises the predominance of the patient's own irrational and cripplingly powerful superego. To the extent to which this process takes place in the mother's relationship with her child, she succeeds, in effect, in externalizing upon him her own 'craziness'. My concept of one's striving to drive the other person crazy emerges naturally, as I mentioned earlier, from many of the interesting formulations at which Hill has arrived.

I have presented in chapter 7 my view that a most important ingredient in the above-described mother-child relatedness is the child's genuine love and solicitude for the mother, love and solicitude of such a degree as to impel him to collaborate with her in this pathological integration. He loves her so deeply, in short, that he sacrifices his own developing individuality to the symbiosis which is so necessary to her personality-functioning.

(iii) Another motive behind this effort which I am describing is, in many instances, the wish to find surcease from an intolerably conflictual and suspenseful situation. If one's mother, for example, recurrently holds before one the threat that she will go crazy, with the implication that it will be catastrophic for oneself if this indispensable person were thus to remove herself from the situation, one may well be tempted to do one's utmost to *drive* her crazy and thus to cut, oneself, the thread that holds this sword of Damocles over one's head; if it is so apt to fall in any case, one can at least salvage the satisfaction of feeling that it is one's own hand which has effected the unavoidable catastrophe.

We see every day in our psychiatric work that patients tend to bring upon themselves any catastrophe which is sensed as being inevitable, in their effort to diminish intolerable feelings of helplessness and suspense in the face of it.

The tormentingly insecure nature of the ever-ambivalent symbiotic relatedness which existed between the schizophrenic, in infancy and childhood, and his mother or father, has been described by Hill (1955), Arieti (1955), Bowen (1956) and myself (above, chapter 1). Anyone who has participated in a long-continued therapeutic endeavour with a schizophrenic patient has experienced at first hand, re-enacted in the transference relationship between the patient and himself, the intensely ambivalent—*mutually* so—relatedness which existed between the patient and the pathogenically more significant parent.

(iv) With surprising frequency one finds, both in patients' histories and, much more impressively, in the unfolding of their childhood relationships with the parents in the evolution of transference phenomena, that they had come to the discovery, over the course of the years of their childhood, that one or another of the parents was, so to speak, a little crazy. They felt—often rightly, I think—that the evidence of the parent's craziness was so subtle, or so hidden from public display and released only in their own relationship with the parent, that only the child himself was aware of the full extent of it. In these circumstances, this knowledge remains as a guilt-laden secret in the child; he strongly tends to feel somehow responsible for the fact of the parent's craziness, and heavily burdened by both the craziness—since the parent seeks satisfaction for the psychotically expressed needs from this child in particular–and by his own knowledge of its existence.

Thus the setting is ripe for his becoming tempted to foster the parent's becoming sufficiently openly psychotic–tempted, that is, to drive the parent into craziness which will be evident to others beside himself–so that the family and the larger community will share his own burden. The patients one encounters who have had this kind of pre-psychotic experience are much more numerous than those who have had the experience of one or another parent's becoming openly psychotic and requiring hospitalization.

In my presentation of this formulation, I do not lose sight of the likelihood that a patient who is himself struggling against a developing psychosis will project his own threatening 'craziness' on to one or another parent. This happens often and even, I believe, regularly. But the process which I have described occurs, not infrequently, in addition.

(v) One of the most powerful and frequently encountered of the motives behind the effort in question is a desire to find a soul-mate to assuage unbearable loneliness. In the case of every one of the schizophrenic patients with whom I have worked long and successfully enough to perceive the childhood relationships relatively clearly, this motive evidently had been at work in whichever parent had integrated a symbiotic relatedness with the child. The precariously integrated parent is typically a very lonely person who hungers for someone to share her or his private emotional experiences and distorted views of the world.

The following report by an attendant, concerning his conversation with a 28-year-old male schizophrenic patient, shows this motive at work:

Carl had been quiet–seemingly depressed all morning–when he suddenly started to talk about his mother's illness. Said he envied his older sister because she didn't have to bear the brunt of his mother's illness. (The sister is not sick.) Said that his mother 'tried out' her paranoid ideas on him. Would go around the house, pull down the blinds, check to see if anyone were near, then tell him what apparently were full-blown paranoid ideas about the neighbours and friends. [He] very philosophically announced that he felt she needed company in her illness–that she felt so lonely that she had to use him

267

in this way. . . . [He] has ideas people are talking about him, and voices these ideas in a naïve, forthright manner.

This parental motive is reflected in patients' fanatical loyalty to the parent, a loyalty which gives way, in the psychotherapy of chronic schizophrenia, only after years of arduous work by patient and therapist. One finds evidence of it, too, in the frequency with which deeply ill patients hallucinate this parent in an idealized form, an idealized parent often, from what I have discerned in my own work, split into two, one the personification of evil and the other the personification of loving protectiveness. With the most deeply ill patients it may require many months of stressful therapeutic labour before the therapist begins to assume, in the patient's view of him, a degree of libidinally cathected reality which can compare with that of the hallucinatory, but to the patient immediately and vividly real, parent-images. And one finds evidence of it, of course, as has been indicated earlier, in the parent's fighting tooth and nail, by every means at his or her disposal, against the patient's and therapist's collaborative effort towards the patient's becoming free from his magically 'close', magically 'mutually understanding', two-against-the-world relatedness with the parent.

In what I have just said, no acknowledgement has been paid to the parents' contrasting, and healthy, desire to help their child reach true maturity, a fulfilment so at variance with the kind of subjectively mutually omnipotent and celestially loving, but in actuality intensely ambivalent and psychotic, relatedness which I have described. Parents are never devoid of such a healthy parental desire and often, in my experience, that desire is strong enough to enable them to make indispensable contributions to the endeavour in which patient and therapist are engaged. But it remains true, none the less, in my experience, that this infantile-omnipotent relatedness between the 'sickest', least mature areas of the parent's personality on the one hand, and the patient's personality on the other, constitutes the greatest obstacle to the patient's becoming well.

All this becomes reproduced in the transference-development of an ongoing patient-therapist relationship, and the therapist inevitably becomes deeply immersed in the subjective experience of magical closeness and shared omnipotence with the patient.

The enthralling nature of this phase accounts in many instances, I believe, for the great length of time consumed by the over-all treatment of these patients. The therapist gets at least one foot into the psychological process in which the patient himself is engaged, namely the process of maintaining a split between his 'good self' and his 'bad self', as well as a split between the 'good other person' and the 'bad other person'; generally, in fact, the therapist gets both feet into this process, for X months. Then both he and the patient spend much time basking in a purely 'good' experience of himself and of the other person, while the 'bad' elements in the relationship are maintained in a state of repression and projection on to the world outside the nest. The therapist, in experiences of this sort, learns at first hand how strong was the lure offered to the patient in childhood by the parent, the lure to share the delights of being 'crazy' along with the parent.

(vi) Something of the complexity which exists in an interpersonal relationship, the complexity of the true state of affairs which renders any attempt to describe that relationship (such as I am attempting here) a crude oversimplification, becomes evident when we consider this next motive.

A mode of interpersonal participation which bears all the earmarks of an effort to drive the other person crazy may be powerfully motivated, in actuality, by a conscious or unconscious desire to encourage the other person into a *healthier* closeness, a better integration both interpersonally, with oneself, and intrapersonally, within himself. In fact, successful psychotherapeutic intervention often takes on precisely this outward form.

Here, that is, the conscious or unconscious effort is to activate dissociated or repressed elements in the other's personality, not with the goal of his ego's becoming overwhelmed by their accession into awareness, but rather with the goal of his ego's integrating them. I do not mean, of course, that the initiator of this kind of participation conceptualizes all this, plans it all out in his mind in any such detail.

This fostering of the other person's intrapersonal and interpersonal integration or self-realization is a part of the essence of loving relatedness as defined by the philosopher-theologian Martin Buber (Friedman, 1955). He refers to this as 'making the other [person] present' and, when it occurs mutually, as 'mutual confirmation': and he expresses his conviction that '. . . The help that men give each other in becoming a self leads the life between men to its height . . .'

To put it in other words, it seems to me that the essence of loving relatedness entails a responding to the wholeness of the other person—including often (particularly in relating to a small child or to a psychiatrically ill adult, but to a lesser degree in relating to all other persons also) a responding in such fashion to the other person when he himself is not aware of his own wholeness, finding and responding to a larger person in him than he himself is aware of being.

Thus, to focus again more specifically upon the seeming effort to drive the other person crazy, we find that this effort can be very close to, and can even be comprised of, an effort to help the other person towards better integration, which latter effort can be considered the essence of loving relatedness. A genuine effort to drive the other person crazy—to weaken his personal integration, to diminish the area of his ego and increase the area of dissociated or repressed processes in his personality—can be considered, by contrast, precisely the opposite of the kind of loving relatedness which Buber describes.

I surmise that in many instances of a parent's fostering his or her child's 'going crazy', the psychosis in the offspring represents a miscarriage of the parent's wish, conscious or unconscious, to help the child towards better, more mature integration. One cannot always know the precise ego-capacities of the other person, as any therapist can attest, and it may well be that parents often perform acts analogous with those interventions of a therapist which are ill-timed or otherwise ill-attuned to the needs of the patient's ego, and which have, instead of the desired effect of further integration in the patient, a disintegrating effect.

I think it significant in this regard that, in very many instances of the outbreak of psychosis, the precipitating circumstances, whatever they may be, have led the patient to become aware of truths about himself and his relationships with others in the family, truths which are actually precious and long-needed, truths which could provide the basis for rapid ego-growth, rapid personality-integration. But they come too fast for the patient's ego to assimilate them and the ego regresses, recoiling from what is now, in its effect, an opened Pandora's box. Thus what could have become–and what in probably a great many instances does become, in persons who never get to a psychiatrist–a valuable, creative, integrative growth experience, becomes an experience of developing psychosis, as various pathological defences (delusions, hallucinations, depersonalization, and so on) become erected against the awareness of those truths.

In psychotherapy the therapist is often called upon to contribute, in skilfully dosed and skilfully timed increments, the very kind of participation which would, if given less skilfully (whether by reason of inexperience or by reason of his orientation towards the patient being a predominantly hateful rather than a predominantly loving one), have an effect precisely opposite to that therapeutically desirable. For instance, premature interpretations may have a disintegrating rather than an integrating effect upon the patient.

(vii) The next motive which I shall discuss can be seen in connexion with a point made prominently by Hill, the point that the mother of the schizophrenic keeps before the child the threat that she will go crazy if he becomes an individual by separating himself, psychologically, from her.

The relevant motive, then, is this: the child's own desire for individuation may be experienced by him as a desire to drive the mother crazy. The mother reacts to his desire for individuation as an effort to drive her crazy; so it seems to me entirely natural that the child himself should be unable to distinguish between his own normal and precious striving towards individuation, on the one hand, and on the other hand a monstrous desire–which latter the mother repeatedly reacts to him as evidencing–to drive his mother crazy.

Such a state of psychodynamic affairs is entirely analogous, I think, to that which obtains in a situation where the mother indicates that if the child really grows up, it will kill her; there, as one finds in clinical work, the child comes to experience his normal desires to become an individual, as being monstrous desires to murder his mother. Hill makes this latter point in his volume.

If, in looking a bit further into the child's relation with such a mother as Hill describes, we shift the frame of reference to visualize the *struggle between* mother and child to drive one another crazy, another interesting point emerges: the mother's ostensible efforts to drive the child crazy can be seen as containing, probably, a nucleus of laudable motivation, though unformulated as such by her, to help her child become an individual. It is probable that, in the mind of such a mother, the concept of psychological separateness, of individuality, is to such an extent equated with craziness, that she cannot conceptualize this motive as a wish to help her child to become an individual. But it may well be that some bit of healthy mother in her senses that the child needs something which she is not providing, something utterly essential, and that it is this part of her which ostensibly tries to drive the child crazy–tries, in actuality, to help the child to become an individual.

In the psychotherapeutic relationship we find that, as a natural consequence of this past experience of the patient, he tends to react to his own developing individuality, his own ego-growth, as anxiety-arousing craziness; and the therapist (in the transference position of the mother at this phase of the work) tends to experience this anxiety also. Thus both participants tend unconsciously to perpetuate a symbiotic relatedness with one another, out of mutual anxiety lest the patient 'go crazy' completely–lest, in truth, he emerge from the symbiosis into a state of healthy individuality. This formulation is in line with Szalita-Pemow's comment (in a personal communication) that 'The [schizophrenic] patient's individuality resides partly in his symptoms'.

(viii) The final motive is actually, in my experience, most often the most powerful of all these motives; my mention of it at this juncture is brief because it has already been touched upon in discussing motive (v) above, and because so much of this chapter's final pages will be devoted to it. This motive is the attainment, perpetuation, or recapture of the gratifications inherent in the symbiotic mode of relatedness. More often than not, the effort to drive the other person crazy, or to perpetuate his craziness, can be found to rest primarily upon both participants' unconscious striving for the gratifications which the 'crazy' symbiotic mode of relatedness, despite its anxiety- and frustration-engendering aspects, offers.

I shall not attempt to discuss other possible motives behind the effort to drive the other person crazy. Others can undoubtedly be found, and some of them may be of as widespread importance as those I have described. But the eight which I have mentioned are, in my experience at least, the most frequently occurring and powerful.

The Patient-Therapist Relationship

A considerable portion of the clinical experience which has led to this paper's central hypothesis has consisted in reports about, and observations of, patients' relatedness with their parental family group and with the group of patients and personnel on their hospital ward; if space allowed, I could present data indicating that in each of these areas, the patient's integration with the group takes the form, in many instances, of a mutual struggle to drive the other person crazy.

But, since I consider that fundamentally the same psycho-dynamic processes are at work there, the only fundamental difference being that they are there operative in a group rather than a dyadic setting, and because my main interest is in individual psychotherapy, I shall confine my remaining remarks to the context of the patient-therapist relationship.

In my experience, it is in the patient-therapist relationship that we can discern most clearly this mode of interaction, the effort to drive the other person crazy. Specifically, we can find this type of relatedness predominating during one particular phase of the schizophrenic patient's evolving transference to the therapist, a phase in which there is reconstituted, between patient and therapist now, an earlier *struggle between* patient and parent to drive each other crazy. From my own therapeutic work, and from what I have observed of other therapists' work at Chestnut Lodge, I have obtained the impression that any successful course of psychotherapy with a schizophrenic patient includes such a phase. During it the therapist becomes, in most instances I believe, deeply involved in this struggle, so that he does indeed feel that his own personal integration is in real jeopardy of a greater or lesser degree. The therapist's necessary participation in this phase of the transference-evolution is one of the main elements in psychotherapy with schizophrenics which make this work at times so stressful to pursue.

One of my male schizophrenic patients expressed his conviction to me, for more than two years, that, as he put it, 'You're kind of *strange*, Dr Searles'; 'You're crazy, Dr Searles'; 'You think peculiarly'; and he would say knowingly, 'You don't express yourself to other people the way you do to me, do you?' In the development of this man's transference to me as a mother-figure, there was beautifully revealed the fact that, in earlier years, he had repeatedly tested his mother's sanity by leading her into various situations and then seeing whether she reacted in a normal or abnormal fashion. The mother, who had died a few years before the patient's hospitalization, had been a highly schizoid individual with whom he had been involved, over many years, in a typically symbiotic relationship. The other family members, highly prestige-conscious people, had maintained a barrier of protectiveness and scorn around the eccentric mother and this son, so like the mother in that eccentricity.

In my work with this man, the struggle to drive one another crazy was re-enacted with unusual intensity. He did an almost incessant amount of testing of me, such as he evidently had done in earlier years with his schizoid mother, in such a way as to bring out evidence to support his persistent suspicion that I was slightly, or more than slightly, cracked. He reiterated, for years, maddeningly bland stereotypes, labelling himself as thoroughly healthy and good, and myself as warped and evil, with a kind of eroding tenacity; and at times he picked on me in the same baiting, sarcastic, accusing way that his mother evidently had employed towards him, to such a degree that I could scarcely make myself remain in the room. He accused me, time and time again, of driving him crazy;[3] after my having gone through a number of hours with him in which I had to struggle with unaccustomed effort to maintain my own sanity, it began to occur to me that this oft-reiterated accusation of his—that *I* was trying to drive *him* crazy—might involve some projection.

In the course of an hour with a 24-year-old schizophrenic woman I became assailed with feelings of confusion and unreality, when she, a luxuriantly delusional person, was reading to me from an instruction book concerning the Japanese game of

[3] A schizophrenic man, after several months of mutism, when he began talking to his therapist said, repeatedly, in anxious protest, 'You talk too queer. . . . You're too crazy.' Following a visit from his mother, he anxiously asserted that his mother wanted to kill him, and declared that his mother had made him sick and had driven the patient's brother (a monk) to the monastery. A few months later on, the same feelings came out in accusations to the therapist. 'You wanted to kill me. You made me sick . . . crazy thoughts. You talk too queer.'

'Go'. She appeared to find some hidden meaning in almost every word and even in almost every syllable, looking at me significantly, with a sarcastic smile, very frequently, as though convinced I was aware of the secret meanings which she found in all this. The realization came to me, with a temporarily quite disintegrating impact, of how threatened, mistrustful, and isolated this woman was. What she was doing with me compares very closely with her mother's taking her to movies, during her childhood, and repeatedly commanding her, 'Now, *think!*' which the patient took–correctly, I believe–as the mother's command for the daughter to perceive the same secret, special meanings in the course of the movie which the mother, an actively psychotic person throughout the girl's upbringing, found in it. The patient had been quite unnerved by this impossible task (whose 'successful' accomplishment would have meant her sharing her mother's psychosis), just as I felt unnerved during that session with her reading. Also on a later occasion she described how she had read to her mother in exactly such a fashion for hours on end while the mother was doing housework, and it was evident to me that she had derived much sadistic satisfaction from having been able to drive her mother to distraction by that method. Many times, similarly, I saw her sit back with a triumphant smile after she had succeeded in making me thoroughly bewildered, and more than a little insecure, with her chaotic verbalizations of delusional material.

This woman had been told over and over again, by various members of her family ever since she was a small child, 'You're crazy!'–whenever, as she herself remembered it, she pressed any one of them for information to resolve the confusion which, to some extent, all children often experience when they are exposed to unfamiliar and complex situations. She said to me once that: 'Whenever I'd open my mouth, six or eight of them [i.e. other members of her unusually large family] would jump down my throat and tell me I was crazy, until I began to wonder whether I really was losing my mind.' It became quite clear that a mutual struggle to drive one another crazy had gone on between her and other family members. It had ensued with particular intensity between herself and her mother, an extremely change- able person (as corroborated by one of the patient's brothers) whom the patient was convinced, for years after beginning therapy with me, was not one person but many. Of this mother, she once made to me this statement, significantly indicative of the kind of struggle I have described: 'They used to say, "You're psychosomatic! If you don't watch out, you'll wind up in a mental hospital!" That's the way *they* were and they wouldn't admit it.'

There were hints in my work with this woman, however, that her efforts to drive me (as a mother-figure in the transference during this phase of the therapy) crazy were motivated at times not primarily by sadistic pleasure in rendering me more or less disorganized, or by a need to externalize upon me her own psychosis, but rather by genuine solicitude for me. At such moments the interaction between us was such as to make clear that I was in the position, as she saw me, of a mentally ill mother who needed treatment which she herself felt helpless to provide for me–entirely similar to the situation which had obtained during her childhood, in her relatedness with a psychiatrically ill mother who never obtained the benefit of professional treatment for her chronic 'ambulatory' schizophrenia.

On one occasion when this facet of the transference was in evidence, the patient protested, late in a session in which we had been exchanging views quite actively: 'Why don't you *go* to a state hospital?–that's what you've been asking for, all the time you were talking.' She said this in a tone not of hostility but of solicitude and helplessness, as if she were being held responsible for placing me in a state hospital, and felt utterly helpless to carry out this obligation. In another hour two weeks later she demanded, 'When are they going to send you to a state hospital? ... I know you're trying to get to one.' In these instances, I assume that one factor at work was a projection of her own unconscious desire to be sent to a state hospital. None the less, all this fits in so precisely with the relatedness which had obtained between herself and her mother, and moreover there were such numerous additional indications that she was responding to me as being her mother from her childhood, that I was convinced of the above-described transference significance of her responses.

The above examples are predominantly illustrative of *patients'* efforts to drive their therapist crazy. My clinical material, from both my own therapeutic work and my observations of that of fellow-therapists, indicative of the *therapist's* own comparable effort, suggests that therapists utilize (largely unconsciously, I again emphasize), just as do patients, the whole gamut of modes or techniques which I have described earlier in this paper; and the range of underlying motives is seemingly as wide for therapists as for patients.

In any single instance, the therapist's striving in this direction can be found, I believe, to arise from two sources: (a) the nature of the patient's transference–namely, a driving-and-being-driven-crazy type of relatedness–to him, such that he is inevitably drawn, to some degree, into a state of feeling, and a mode of overt relatedness, which is complementary to that transference; and (b) a character-trait in the therapist, transcending his relationship with this particular patient, in the form of an unconscious tendency (of, undoubtedly, widely varying strength among various therapists, but probably not totally absent from the enduring constellation of personality-traits of any therapist), to drive the other person crazy–*whatever* other person, that is, with whom he establishes a significantly close relationship.

So then, when we find, upon examining any particular patient-therapist relationship, that it is characterized at this stage predominantly by a mutual struggle between the two participants to drive one another crazy, it is probable that the therapist's behaviour of this kind is based partially–and, I think, in most instances predominantly–on the first-described kind of 'normal' therapist-responsiveness to the patient's transference.

But in, I think, a significant percentage of such instances, the second of the sources which I have mentioned–sources for the therapist's behaviourally participating in this struggle–also plays a greater or lesser part. I discovered conclusive proof of such a character-trait in myself, to my great dismay, late in my personal analysis (about seven years before I write)–a trait which I found to be in operation not only with regard to one or two of the patients with whom I was working at the time, but with regard to all of them, as well as with regard to innumerable other persons–relatives, friends, and acquaintances. The following general considerations are suggestive of a fairly wide distribution of such a character-trait among psychotherapists and psycho-analysts:

(i) An obsessive-compulsive type of basic personality structure is certainly not rare among therapists and analysts. I am not convinced that such a personality structure predominates among us; but anyone's informal observations suggest that it is probably to be found at least as frequently among us as among the members of the general population, in our culture which places so many premiums upon such obsessive-compulsive character-traits as orderliness, competitiveness, intellectualization, and so on.

It is well known that one of the major defence mechanisms of the obsessive-compulsive is reaction formation. It should not be surprising, then, to find that the choice of a profession, on the part of a significant number of psychotherapists and psychoanalysts, has been founded partially on the basis of reaction formation against unconscious wishes which run precisely counter to the conscious endeavour which holds sway in their daily work. That is, just as we would not be surprised to find that a surgeon brings forth, in the course of his psycho-analysis, powerful and heretofore-deeply-repressed wishes physically to dismember other people, so we should be ready to discern the presence, in not a few of us who have chosen the profession of treating psychiatric illness, of similarly powerful, long-repressed desires to dismember the personality structure of other persons.

(ii) To extend the line of–admittedly hypothetical–reasoning which has been presented in (i) above, it is understandable that in the training analyses of persons who have chosen psychotherapy or psycho-analysis as a profession, the analysand would encounter great resistance to the recognition in himself of such desires as those in question here–desires to drive other persons crazy–since these desires run so directly into conflict with his genuine and powerful interests in helping to *resolve* psychiatric illness. Hence such unconscious desires–such a personality-trait, that is–might understandably tend to escape detection, and thoroughgoing resolution, in the training analysis, and the choice of a profession might never be revealed as constituting part of the analysand's struggle against his unconscious wishes to foster personality disintegration in other persons.

I think all this might be described most accurately as follows: desires to drive the other person crazy are a part of the limitlessly varied personality constellation of emotionally healthy human beings; therapists' and analysts' choice of a profession is suggestive that, at least in some instances where the personality structure is of an obsessive-compulsive type, the individual is

278

struggling against more than normally strong unconscious desires of this particular kind; and finally, because therapists and analysts are engaged in the particular life-work to which they are devoting themselves (the relief of psychiatric illness), it is especially difficult for *them* to allow themselves to recognize the presence, in themselves, of these *qualitatively normal* desires.

(iii) So many of us show a persistent readiness to regard this or that kind of functional psychiatric illness, or this or that particular patient, as 'incurable'—in the face of, by now, convincingly abundant clinical evidence to the contrary—that one must suspect that this proclivity for the adoption of an unscientifically 'hopeless' attitude may mask, in. actuality, an unconscious investment in keeping these particular patients fixed in their illnesses. In raising this point, I do not wish to minimize the very great difficulties which stand in the way of recovery for many psychiatric patients; on the contrary, it is my first-hand experience with facing such difficulties, in work with chronically psychotic patients, that makes me feel it all the more important for us to bring into this formidable task as few additionally complicating factors of our own as possible.

I have seen, by now many times over (in my work with chronically psychotic or neurotic patients, in my supervisory experience with approximately twenty other therapists at Chestnut Lodge and elsewhere, and in listening to staff or seminar presentations by many additional therapists), how very prone we are to the development of an attitude of hopelessness in the course of our work with a patient, as a means of unconsciously clinging to the denied, but actually profoundly valued, gratifications which we are obtaining from a symbiotic mode of patient-therapist relatedness. In this phase, we tend to fight tooth and nail, however unwittingly, against the patient's making a major step forward—a step which something in us senses to be in the offing. Time after time, a major forward move in therapy is preceded by such a phase of hopelessness on the part of both patient and therapist, a hopelessness which can now be seen, in retrospect, as a matter of their mutual clinging to their symbiotic mode of relatedness with one another.

Many articles and books have been written which emphasize the pathogenic significance of such a mode of relatedness in the patient's—especially the schizophrenic patient's—upbringing; but

I think we have underestimated the intensely gratifying elements of that mode of relatedness, a kind of relatedness which allows each participant to luxuriate in feelings of infantile satisfaction as well as in omnipotent-mother fantasies. I think that one of the great reasons why schizophrenia is so difficult to resolve is that the therapist finds so much inner resistance against helping the patient to move out of the reconstituted patient-parent symbiotic relatedness in the transference. Not only the patient, but the therapist also, tends to find the prospective fruits of a more mature relatedness *just barely*—if even that—worth the relinquishment of the symbiotic relatedness which, despite its torments, affords precious gratifications also.

Whenever I have been able to acquire up-to-the-minute, detailed data about these situations I have found, as one might expect, that the mutual struggle between patient and therapist to drive one another crazy occurs on the threshold of what, as later events prove, is an unusually big forward step for the patient in therapy. It is as though both of them fight, via a recrudescence of their mutual driving-crazy, symbiotic techniques, against the upsurge of this favourable step in the therapy.

I do not wish to leave the impression that the therapeutic road, after one such break-through, is nothing more than a straight, wide, smooth home-stretch. In the working through, in the transference, of the patient's symbiotic relatedness with the mother, this same struggle has to be gone through again and again. Although in subsequent repetitions it tends to occur with less disruptive severity, the therapist regularly finds himself susceptible to feeling the same black despair, the same sensation of being driven utterly mad by this impossible patient, time after time at the thresholds of successive stages in the loosening of the symbiotic relatedness. This may be compared with the foetus' becoming anatomically separate from the mother: not merely one, but a long series of labour pains is necessary before the baby fully emerges. Of tangential interest, here, are the following remarks by Margaret Little in a paper entitled 'Counter-Transference and the Patient's Response to it' (1951).

Consciously, and surely to a great extent unconsciously too, we all want our patients to get well, and we can identify readily with them in their desire to get well, that is with their ego. But unconsciously we tend to identify also with the patient's superego and id, and thereby with him, in any prohibition on getting well, and in his wish to stay ill and dependent, and by so doing we may slow down his recovery. Unconsciously we may exploit a patient's illness for our own purposes, both libidinal and aggressive, and he will quickly respond to this.

A patient who has been in analysis for some considerable time has usually become his analyst's love object; he is the person to whom the analyst wishes to make reparation, and the reparative impulses, even when conscious, may through a partial repression come under the sway of the repetition compulsion, so that it becomes necessary to make that same patient well over and over again, *which in effect means making him ill over and over again in order to have him to make well* [italics mine – H. F. S.].

Rightly used, this repetitive process may be progressive, and the 'making ill' then takes the necessary and effective form of opening up anxieties which can be interpreted and worked through. But this implies a degree of unconscious willingness on the part of the analyst to allow his patient to get well, to become independent and to leave him. . . .

In my own experience (see chapter 3 above), by contrast to that of Reichard and Tillmann (1950), Lidz and Lidz (1952), Limentani (1956), and many other writers, I find that what the therapist offers the patient which is new and therapeutic, in this regard, is not an *avoidance* of the development of symbiotic, reciprocal dependency upon the patient, but rather an *acceptance* of this – an acceptance of the fact that the patient has come to mean a great deal to him personally. It is this acceptance of one's own dependency upon him that the mother had not been able to offer him.

I believe that in the great majority of instances where a patient and therapist have worked together long enough for this symbiotic relatedness to become well established, and where we find that both are feeling hopeless about the work, we can find much evidence that each is unconsciously struggling to drive – or perhaps, more accurately, to keep – the other person crazy, so that he can cling to this highly immature and therefore 'sick', but deeply gratifying, symbiotic mode of relatedness with the other.

It may well be that the need – widespread not only among schizophrenic patients but also among the professional persons who treat them – to deny the gratifying aspect of the symbiotic relatedness, accounts for some of the persistent viability of the irrational, name-calling 'schizophrenogenic mother' concept. That is, it may be that we are so powerfully drawn, at an unconscious level, towards the gratifications which such a mother offers, with her symbiotic mode of relatedness, that we have to deny our regressive urges in that direction, and thus consciously perceive, and in scientific writings describe, her as a quite totally unappealing 'schizophrenogenic mother' with whom it would be pure hell to relate oneself closely.

(iv) So many therapists' and analysts' personally characteristic ways of responding to patients' communications sound, not infrequently, as if calculated to drive the patient crazy (or crazier), that it is difficult to attribute this phenomenon entirely to lack of clinical experience, skill, and perceptivity. That is, I surmise that many instances of awkward therapeutic technique, technique which fosters further disintegration rather than integration in the patient, may be due to chronically repressed (and therefore chronically present) desires in the therapist to drive the other person crazy.

As one frequently encountered example, we therapists have a strong tendency to react to only one side of a patient's ambivalent feelings. Thus when a hospitalized schizophrenic patient, for instance, is evidencing grossly disturbed behaviour such that we are given to know that he has an unconscious need for the security of continued hospitalization, but he is *consciously* expressing to us a strong, verbalized demand that he be allowed to move out, we may reply, 'I realize that you *really want* to *stay* in the hospital, and are *afraid* of moving out,' in a reassuring tone. This example involves a crudity of therapist technique which we do not encounter with extreme frequency in quite so stark a form, although I have observed, not uncommonly–and retrospectively have realized that I was using in my own work with patients– just as crudely untherapeutic a technique as this. But lesser degrees of this kind of untherapeutic therapist participation (throughout this paper, the points made are considered as applying in psycho-analysis as well as in psychotherapy, although with especial prominence in the latter) are observable with very great frequency indeed. Surely many a neurotic patient in analysis, for example, finds himself maddened on frequent occasions by his analyst's readiness to discount the significance of the patient's conscious feelings and attitudes and to react to preconscious or unconscious communications as though these emanated from the only 'real' and 'genuine' desires and attitudes.

The therapist's or analyst's growing out of such ways of responding is not simply a matter of his learning a technique more appropriate to the patient's genuinely ambivalent, poorly integrated state. To become more useful to his patients he must in addition be prepared to face his own conflict between desires to help the patient to become better integrated (that is, more mature and healthy) and desires, on the other hand, to hold on to him, or even to destroy him, through fostering a perpetuation or worsening of the illness, the state of poor integration. Only this kind of personal awareness prepares him for being of maximal use to patients–above all, to schizophrenic and borderline-schizophrenic patients–and, particularly, for helping them through the crucial phase of the transference which I have been describing here.[4]

[4] The following therapists have given me their kind permission to use data concerning their patients: Drs Cecil C. H. Cullander, Jarl E. Dyrud, John P. Fort, Leslie Schaffer, Roger L. Shapiro, Joseph H. Smith, and Naomi K. Wenner. For the theoretical formulations concerning these data, I alone am responsible.

Chapter 9

OEDIPAL LOVE IN THE COUNTERTRANSFERENCE (1959)[1]

THIS paper will advance three hypotheses which, as will be shown, are interrelated: (a) in the course of a successful psycho-analysis,[2] the analyst goes through a phase of reacting to, and eventually relinquishing, the patient as being his oedipal love-object; (b) in normal personality development, the parent reciprocates the child's oedipal love with greater intensity than we have recognized heretofore; and (c) in such normal development, the passing of the Oedipus complex is at least as important a phase in ego-development as in superego-development.

Since I began doing psycho-analysis and intensive psychotherapy, I have found, time after time, that in the course of the work with every one of my patients who has progressed to, or very far towards, a thoroughgoing analytic cure, I have experienced romantic and erotic desires to marry, and fantasies of being married to, the patient. Such fantasies and emotions have appeared in me usually relatively late in the course of treatment, have been present not briefly but usually for a number of months, and have subsided only after my having experienced a variety of feelings–frustration, separation anxiety, grief and so forth–entirely akin to those which attended what I experienced as the resolution of my Oedipus complex late in my personal analysis.

As I shall detail later, with the first few patients towards whom I found myself having such feelings, I reacted with much anxiety,

[1] A condensed version of this paper was presented at the meeting of the American Psychoanalytic Association in New York in December 1957. It was first published in the *International Journal of Psycho-Analysis*, Vol. 40 (1959), pp. 180–90.

[2] Throughout this paper I shall frequently use the terms 'analyst' and 'analysis' in reference both to psycho-analysis of neurotic patients, and psychotherapy of psychotic patients. I do this for two reasons: first, I wish to avoid awkwardly repetitious qualifications, and second, I have found that in the relatively late stages of treatment with which I am concerned here, psychotherapy with a psychotic patient gradually takes on the characteristics of psycho-analysis, as the various special conditions which obtained in earlier phases (i.e. non-utilization of the couch; severe limitations on the use of free association and analysis of the transference, and dream-analysis, etc.) diminish and typically psycho-analytic interaction emerges.

embarrassment, and guilt. My training had been predominantly such as to make me hold rather suspect any strong feelings on the part of the analyst towards his patient, and these particular emotions seemed to be of an especially illegitimate nature. My observations of colleagues' work with their patients, observations made in the course of listening to case-presentations or during informal chats with colleagues about our work or, later on, while doing supervision, strongly suggested to me that these colleagues were not insusceptible to experiencing such feelings themselves. But it was only a rare one who openly acknowledged the presence of them in himself; so I remained, until not long before writing this paper, largely convinced that I had an unusual propensity for exploiting analytic patients for the purpose of grappling with my own unresolved Oedipus conflicts.

And psycho-analytic literature is, in the main, such as to make one feel more, rather than less, troubled at finding in oneself such feelings towards one's patient. As Lucia E. Tower (1956) has recently noted,

... Virtually every writer on the subject of countertransference ... states unequivocally that no form of erotic reaction to a patient is to be tolerated . . .

But in relatively recent years, an increasing number of writers, such as P. Heimann (1950), M. B. Cohen (1952), and E. Weigert (1952, 1954), have emphasized how much the analyst can learn about the patient from noticing his own feelings, of whatever sort, in the analytic relationship. Weigert (1952), defining counter-transference as emphatic identification with the analysand, has stated that

. . . In terminal phases of analyses the resolution of counter-transference goes hand in hand with the resolution of transference . . .

In some respects this chapter may be regarded as complementing the paper by Weigert from which I have just quoted. These additional passages from her article show her view of counter-transference, in the special sense in which she defines it, as being an innate, inevitable ingredient in the psycho-analytic relationship, and they show, in particular, the feelings of loss which the analyst experiences with the termination of the analysis. But I wish to point out that the particular variety of countertransference with which she is concerned here, is evidently that of the analyst's reacting as a loving and protective *parent* to the analysand, reacted to as being an *infant*:

There are plausible reasons why in the last phase it is especially difficult to achieve and maintain analytic frankness. The termination of analysis is an experience of loss which mobilizes all the resistances in the transference (and in the countertransference too), for a final struggle ... Recently Adelaide Johnson (1951) described the terminal conflict of analysis as fully reliving the Oedipus conflict in which the quest for the genitally gratifying parent is poignantly expressed and the intense grief, anxiety, and wrath of its definitive loss are fully reactivated. . . .[3] Unless the patient dares to be exposed to such an ultimate frustration he may cling to the tacit permission that his relation to the analyst will remain his refuge from the hardships of a reality that is too competitive or too frustrating for him. By attuning his libidinal cravings to an aim-inhibited, tender attachment to the analyst as an idealized parent, he can circumvent the conflicts of genital temptation and frustration.

. . . the resolution of the countertransference permits the analyst to be emotionally freer and spontaneous with the patient, and this is an additional indication of the approaching end of an analysis.

. . . When the analyst observes that he can be unrestrained with the patient, when he no longer weighs his words to maintain a cautious objectivity, this empathic countertransference as well as the transference of the patient is in a process of resolution. The analyst is able to treat the analysand on terms of equality; he is no longer needed as an auxiliary superego, an unrealistic deity in the clouds of detached neutrality. These are signs that the patient's labour of mourning for infantile attachments nears completion. . . .

In my paper I am stressing the point that before an analysis can properly terminate, the analyst must have experienced a resolution of his countertransference to the patient as being a deeply

<hr>

[3] I was interested to read a second reference, this time by L. E. Tower (1956), to this same paper by Johnson. Tower notes that

'. . . A paper presented to the Chicago Psycho-analytic Society four years ago [in 1951] by Adelaide Johnson touched tangentially on this problem [of countertransference affect] and evoked the most massive anxiety and countercathexis in the audience I have observed in many years of psycho-analytic meetings. This reaction seemed all out of proportion to the valid objections which could be raised against the argument of the paper.'

Johnson's paper, entitled 'Some Heterosexual Transference and Countertransference Phenomena in Late Analysis of the Oedipus', has not been published, and I was unable to obtain a copy of it. But Johnson informs me that some of her more recent concepts about this subject are contained in the paper entitled 'The Incest Barrier', by M. J. Barry, Jr, and herself (1957), which I shall discuss later.

beloved, and desired, figure not only on this *infantile* level which Weigert has emphasized valuably, but also on an *oedipal-genital* level. Weigert's paper, which helped me to formulate the views which I am setting down here, might be put with mine, that is, as expressing the total point that a successful psycho-analysis involves the analyst's deeply felt relinquishment of the patient both as being a cherished infant, and as being a fellow adult who is responded to at the level of genital love.

The paper by L. E. Tower (1956) comes similarly close to the views which I advance here. Unlike Weigert, she limits the term countertransference to those phenomena which are transferences of the analyst to his patient. It is all the more striking, therefore, that she finds even this classically defined countertransference to be innate to the analytic process:

. . . It is my belief that there are inevitably, naturally, and often desirably, many countertransference developments in every analysis (some evanescent–some sustained), which are a counterpart of the transference phenomena. Interactions (or transactions) between the transferences of the patient and the countertransferences of the analyst, going on at unconscious levels, may be–or perhaps always are–of vital significance for the outcome of the treatment. . . .

. . . Virtually every writer on the subject of countertransference . . . states unequivocally that no form of erotic reaction to a patient is to be tolerated. This would indicate that temptations in this area are great, and perhaps ubiquitous. This is the one subject about which almost every author is very certain to state his position. Other 'countertransference' manifestations are not routinely condemned. Therefore, I assume that erotic responses to some extent trouble nearly every analyst. This is an interesting phenomenon and one that calls for investigation. In my experience, virtually all physicians, when they gain enough confidence in their analysts, report erotic feelings and impulses toward their patients, but usually do so with a good deal of fear and conflict. . . .

In our selection of candidates for training, we are disposed to pay close attention to the libidinal resources of the applicant, on the theory that large amounts of available libido are necessary to tolerate the heavy task of a number of intensive analyses. At the same time, we deride almost every detectable libidinal investment made by an analyst in a patient . . . various forms of erotic fantasy and erotic countertransference phenomena of a fantasy and of an affective character are in my experience ubiquitous and presumably normal. . . .

I have for a very long time speculated that in many – perhaps every – intensive analytic treatment there develops something in the nature of countertransference structures (perhaps even a 'neurosis') which are essential and inevitable counterparts of the transference neurosis. These countertransference structures may be large or small in their quantitative aspects, but in the total picture they may be of considerable significance for the outcome of the treatment. I believe they function somewhat in the manner of a catalytic agent in the treatment process. Their understanding by the analyst may be as important to the final working through of the transference neurosis as is the analyst's intellectual understanding of the transference neurosis itself, perhaps because they are, so to speak, *the vehicle for the analyst's emotional understanding of the transference neurosis*. Both transference neurosis and countertransference structure seem intimately bound together in a living process and both must be taken continually into account in the work which is psychoanalysis. . . .

. . . I doubt that there is any thorough working through of a deep transference neurosis, in the strictest sense, which does not involve some form of emotional upheaval in which *both* patient and analyst are involved. In other words, there is both a transference neurosis and a corresponding countertransference 'neurosis' (no matter how small and temporary) which are both analysed in the treatment situation, with eventual feelings of a substantially new orientation on the part of both persons toward each other.

While I was writing a preliminary draft of this paper, there was presented at the May 1957 meeting of the American Psychoanalytic Association, in Chicago, a paper which is highly relevant to this one. That paper, entitled 'The Incest Barrier', was written by M. J. Barry, Jr, and A. M. Johnson (1957). The authors kindly provided me with a copy of it, for my purposes here. In their paper, they set out to elucidate the nature of the incest barrier, both as it exists in the family and as it exists in the analytic relationship. They present evidence that the barrier against mother-son incest is universally and rigorously present, in contrast to the barrier against father-daughter incest which is not universally present in all cultures, and of which the authors were able to find many instances of transgression in our own culture, whereas in their own material they encountered no instance of mother-son incest. In directing especially detailed scrutiny, then, to this especially rigorous incest barrier – that having to do with mother-son incest – the authors present a detailed examination of the terminal phase of the analysis of a male patient by a woman, a situation which they regard as being suited to show us the nature of the mother-son incest barrier.

It is in their study of this analytic situation that Barry and Johnson make observations which are of closest relevance to the present paper. Although they do not link the analyst's feeling-responses, as I do, to her own Oedipus complex, they describe these responses with a candour which I consider courageous and badly needed; they leave the clear impression that the patient's experiencing of, and eventual relinquishment of, his oedipal strivings are met, in the analyst, by deeply felt reciprocal responses. The spirit of the paper, as well as its conclusions, are adequately conveyed by the authors' final paragraph:

A study of the terminal phase of analysis of a patient by an analyst of the opposite sex provides some insight into the nature of the [mother-son incest] barrier. Even after analysis of castration anxiety in the classic sense is meticulously pursued, there still is a deterrent to incestuous genital fulfilment. Sensitive, subtle, and frank examination of this last barrier indicates that it is mutually set up by both participants. It arises from the recognition that there is no compelling desire to bind the participants together in any relationship historically rooted in infantile dependency. There always persists the unconscious memory of the transference dependency. Real maturation and necessary growth derive from renunciation of incestuous goals by both protagonists. Renunciation comes about by recognition of the separate individualities of the protagonists and the deeply felt acknowledgement of mutual love and respect for the individualities concerned. From this separation comes realization of the capacity for feeling loved but unbound. The recognition of one's capability for being loved when one is not helpless and dependent forecasts the seeking of a new adult love object outside of the analysis.

In presenting now, from my own work, clinical examples of the concepts which I am putting forward here, I shall be brief, and not only because discretion makes it difficult to go into great detail; I think a few brief examples will be quite sufficient for my purpose.

One of my earlier experiences with what I think of as oedipal love in the countertransference occurred in the course of the analysis, several years ago, of a woman in her middle twenties. Initially, she had manifested a poorly established sexual identity;

her femininity was considerably repressed, with an overlay of much penis envy. But over the course of four years of an unusually successful analysis, she developed into a woman whom I found very likeable, warm and sexually attractive. I found myself having, particularly during about the last year of our work, abundant desires to be married to her, and fantasies of being her husband. As in each of these clinical instances which I shall recount, there was an abundance of 'carry over' of such responses on my part, into both waking life after the analytic sessions, and into dreams as well. I reacted to such feelings with considerable anxiety, guilt, and embarrassment; and when the end of the analysis drew near, there occurred an incident, somewhat amusing to me in retrospect, which stressed how guarded I felt about such responses in my overt behaviour in the sessions.

At the end of one of the sessions near the close of our work, she made some statement which feelingly expressed her sense of sadness and loss at the prospect of our approaching separation. I replied with a comment which felt to me, in the making of it, inappropriate; which she reacted to as being inappropriate; and which in retrospect I well know to have been inappropriate: I laughed rather anxiously and indicated to her that I felt, about this coming separation, much as did the Mrs Gilbreth, of *Cheaper by the Dozen* fame, whom I had recently seen quoted as having said to her husband, when the youngest of their twelve children was now passing out of the phase of early infancy, 'It surely will be strange not to be waking up, for the first time in sixteen years, for the two-o'clock feeding!' Although I believe my tone conveyed the sense of genuine loss which had been conveyed in Mrs Gilbreth's own statement to her husband, I noticed that the patient looked uncomfortably startled, and murmured something about thinking she had become older than that. This incident helped me to realize to what an extent I had been continuing, over-long, to highlight her *infantile* needs and desires–which had been, indeed, legitimately a prominent part of her analysis earlier–in order to avoid frankly seeing how desirable an adult woman she had become, an adult woman who could never be mine.

With her I never became, at this relatively early stage of my analytic career, as free to experience, and openly to allow the patient to see, such feelings, as I have become in more recent years. But she was well enough aware that I had such responses to her, as she let me know before the close of her analysis, when she brought me a magazine cartoon which served nicely to spoof me about having such feelings while acting as though I were interested only in intellectual matters.

Repeatedly, since then, I have had comparable experiences in the analysis of neurotic patients, whether women or men, and I have grown successively less troubled at finding such responses in myself, less constrained to conceal these from the patient, and increasingly convinced that they augur well rather than ill for the outcome of our relationship, and that the patient's self-esteem benefits greatly from his sensing that he (or she) is capable of arousing such responses in his analyst. I have come to believe that there is a direct correlation between, on the one hand, the *affective intensity* with which the analyst experiences an awareness of such feelings–and of the unrealizability of such feelings–in himself towards the patient, and, on the other hand, the depth of maturation which the patient achieves in the analysis.

As usual, it seems that the analyst's own *inner awareness* is the main thing here; when one recommends his doing much along the line of *overtly expressing* such feelings to the patient, one is on dubious and shaky ground. An analyst who is relatively undisturbed at experiencing such feelings will not make any particular point of expressing them to the patient; and the patient, when he or she has achieved sufficient ability to recognize and accept the analyst as a real person, will sense that the analyst has such feelings and that he is able to cope safely with them.

The schizophrenic patient, with his relatively poor contact with reality, needs oftentimes for the therapist to be more open in frankly expressing his feelings, including those which arise from the particular area which I am describing here, than the analyst who is working with a neurotic patient need ever become. I shall now make a few more observations about the work with schizophrenic patients in this regard.

For the past eight years I have devoted the greater portion of my time to intensive psychotherapy with patients suffering from chronic schizophrenia, and I have found that in this kind of work it is more difficult, but even more important, to be able to allow into one's awareness such responses to the patient as I have been describing, than is the case in the analysis of neurotic patients.

That is, it is at least somewhat less disconcerting to find oneself feeling romantically and erotically responsive to a neurotic patient who, late in analysis now, is realistically a desirable marital partner, than it is to find oneself feeling thus towards a schizophrenic patient whom one's fellows might perceive as being, more than anything else, grossly ill and anything but attractive. But, for at least three reasons, I have found it essential to the patient's recovery that his (or her) therapist be 'susceptible' to experiencing such responses to him, and preferably with as little as possible of accompanying anxiety, guilt, and embarrassment.

The first reason is that when the schizophrenic moves, in the course of his therapy, into the phase of the Oedipus conflict, he makes erotic and romantic demands upon the therapist with a tenacity, and an often truly astonishing obliviousness of incest taboos (and of the realities of his own and his therapist's life-situations), which require from the therapist, for their resolution, something other than a repression of responsive romantic and erotic feelings and fantasies which the analyst, in working with the neurotic patient who has a relatively strong ego, may be able to get by with. I do not knowingly practise, and am distinctly opposed to, a therapist's entering into any form of erotic behaviour with any patient, schizophrenic or otherwise, or departing from his basic analytic role by expressing romantic love to a patient. But I have repeatedly found it beneficial, rather than harmful, in the therapy with my schizophrenic patients candidly to allow them to see that they do move me deeply in this respect, when such feelings are genuinely present in me – acknowledging this at times which are appropriate to the interaction of the moment, and acknowledging it in a fashion which leaves me clear in my own mind, even if it is perhaps not yet clear in the mind of the patient, that I remain the therapist rather than becoming the patient's lover or would-be wife or husband. The beneficial effect of such acknowledgements resides in the investigative freeing-up which they foster – the resolution of what had become a stereotyped situation of the patient's being absorbed in making incestuous appeals to, or demands upon, the therapist, in a fashion which had been throttling the mutual investigation of the patient's difficulties. Some acknowledgements do not magically work this result, but they constitute *one* of the therapeutic measures which are valuable here. When, on the other hand, a therapist dare not even recognize such responses in himself–let alone expressing them to the patient–the situation tends all the more to remain stalemated at this level.

The second reason why the therapist needs to have much inner freedom in this regard, a reason integrally related with the first one, is that the schizophrenic patient's abysmally low self-esteem is nourished by whatever emotional responses, whether romantic or erotic or angry or whatever, the patient is able to arouse in his therapist; his self-esteem is too low to tolerate the degree of unconscious denial or repression of feeling which the neurotic patient can tolerate on the part of an analyst. And a third reason is that the intensive psychotherapy of schizophrenia tends so greatly to drive a therapist away in discouragement that *any* basis for his feeling drawn to his work with the patient, whether an erotic basis or any other, is precious and to be welcomed as providing a foundation-stone for the further elaboration of a constructive therapeutic relationship.

One of my first experiences, of the kind under discussion here, with a schizophrenic patient, occurred about the end of the second year of my work with a hebephrenic woman in her middle thirties. In the course of one of the therapeutic sessions with this woman, who was mute and dishevelled and whose behaviour was conspicuously bizarre, I was extremely startled to find myself having fantasies of being married to her, fantasies which were accompanied by powerful affects of romantic love. For many months thereafter, on innumerable occasions both during and between the sessions, I found myself feeling similarly about her, oftentimes with strong erotic impulses; and during this period I had at least a dozen romantic-and-erotic dreams about her. I let her know, on a number of appropriate occasions, in response to various communications from her in our hours, that I had such feelings towards her; and on at least two occasions I frankly admitted that I felt jealous in response to her very conspicuously showing a romantic preference for another male therapist on our staff. The subsequent course of her therapy firmly convinced me that my freedom to experience, and even to express to her, such feelings was one essential factor in the relatively successful outcome of my work with this woman who had been, at the beginning of our work, unusually deeply ill.

Another early experience of this kind with a schizophrenic patient occurred in approximately the twelfth month of my work with a 50-year-old, single woman who was suffering from schizophrenia with marked depressive features. Thus far I had seen her as a drab, colourless, wraithlike individual devoid of any capacity to arouse romantic or erotic feelings in anyone. I was therefore astonished upon awakening, one morning, to remember that I had had a sexual dream about her. From now on I began seeing her with new interest, and it was not long before I began to discern previously unnoticed little evidences of seductiveness on her part. In the ensuing several months, she progressed to the point where she was so attractively feminine a person that it would not be difficult for any man to think of her in sexual terms, and sexual conflicts which had played an integral role in her schizophrenic breakdown now came into the therapeutic investigation. I found every evidence, subsequently, that my sexual dream about her had constituted a most valuable landmark in a deepening, and eventually successful, therapeutic relationship.

When experienced towards a patient of one's own sex, such feelings as these are likely to be particularly anxiety-provoking. During my first two years of work at Chestnut Lodge, I was seeing a paranoid schizophrenic man in his middle thirties, a sensitive, highly intelligent, physically handsome man who manifested a gratifying improvement over the course of our work. But after about eighteen months, I began growing uneasy at the intensity of the fond and romantic feelings which I had come to experience towards him, and particularly alarmed during one of our sessions, while we were sitting in silence and a radio not far away was playing a tenderly romantic song, when I suddenly felt that this man was dearer to me than anyone else in the world, including my wife. Within a few months I succeeded in finding 'reality' reasons why I would not be able to continue indefinitely with his therapy, and he moved to a distant part of the country. To be sure, he had been voicing a persistent desire to make this move, all through our work together; but I am certain that it was my anxiety about these recently recognized responses in myself that caused me to find, now, that it somehow made excellent sense for him to leave here. Subsequently, upon carefully examining the detailed notes I had kept concerning his case, I saw many indications that I had fled from going further, with him, into the exploration of the intense fondness which had prevailed, behind a screen of mutual rejection, between himself and his mother. For many months I had endured from him such sarcasm, scorn, and rejection as he and his mother had characteristically directed at one another; but I was unable to brave the fondness which now came up in the transference.

At that time I had not yet worked through such feelings in my own analysis. Four years later, after the completion of my personal analysis in which I had become relatively at ease about such feelings, in the course of my work with a paranoid schizophrenic man in his early forties I was gratified to find myself able to go ahead constructively in a situation which was much more challenging in this regard than that with the former man had been. This second patient was much more deeply ill than the first, and by ordinary standards so unattractive in his physical person and his mode of dress that it would seem incredibly embarrassing, and even frightening, to find oneself feeling any significant degree of personal attraction towards such an individual. Whereas the first man had been predominantly heterosexually oriented in his sexual history, this man had been exclusively, and very conspicuously, homosexually oriented. My work with him came to involve my exposure to a remarkably intense combination of both poetically tender feelings and sexual feelings (as well as, of course, comparably intense murderousness). After an initial two-year period in which negative feelings seemed clearly to predominate in the transference and the countertransference, I began finding myself feeling surprisingly fond of him, and to be having not infrequent dreams of a fond and sexual nature about him. One morning, as I was putting on a carefully selected necktie, I realized that I was putting it on for him, more than for any of the several other patients I was to see that day.

He referred to us, now in the third and fourth years of our work, as being married, and at other times expressed deeply affective fantasies of our becoming married. When I took him out for a ride in my car for one of the sessions, I was amazed at the wholly delightful fantasy and feeling I had, namely that we were lovers on the threshold of marriage, with a whole world of wonders opening up before us; I had visions of going upon innumerable rides with him, going to look at furniture together, and so on. When I drove home from work at the end of the day

295

I was filled with a poignant realization of how utterly and tragically unrealizable were the desires of this man who had been hospitalized continually, now, for fourteen years. But I felt that, despite the tragic aspect of this, what we were going through was an essential, constructive part of what his recovery required; these needs of his would have to be experienced, I felt, in however unrealizable a form at first, so that they could become reformulated, in the course of our work, into channels which would lead to greater possibilities for gratification. And I felt a solid sense of personal satisfaction that I was able, now, to go through feeling-experiences with a male patient which years before, even in much lesser degree than this, would have scared me away.

Not only my work with patients but also my experiences as a husband and a parent have convinced me of the validity of the concepts which I am offering here. Towards my daughter, now eight years of age, I have experienced innumerable fantasies and feelings of a romantic-love kind, thoroughly complementary to the romantically adoring, seductive behaviour which she has shown towards her father oftentimes ever since she was about two or three years of age. I used at times to feel somewhat worried when she would play the supremely confident coquette with me and I would feel enthralled by her charms; but then I came to the conviction, some time ago, that such moments of relatedness could only be nourishing for her developing personality as well as delightful to me. If a little girl cannot feel herself able to win the heart of her father, her own father who has known her so well and for so long, and who is tied to her by mutual blood-ties, I reasoned, then how can the young woman who comes later have any deep confidence in the power of her womanliness?

And I have had every impression, similarly, that the oedipal desires of my son, now eleven years of age, have found a similarly lively and wholehearted feeling-response in my wife; and I am equally convinced that their deeply fond, openly evidenced mutual attraction is good for my son as well as enriching to my wife. To me it makes sense that the more a woman loves her husband, the more she will love, similarly, the lad who is, to at least a considerable degree, the younger edition of the man she loved enough to marry.

Freud, in his descriptions of the Oedipus complex (1900, 1921, 1923), tended largely to give us a picture of the child as having an *innate*, *self-determined* tendency to experience, under the conditions of a normal home, feelings of passionate love towards the parent of the opposite sex;[4] we get little hint, from his writings, that in this regard the child actually enters into a *mutual relatedness* of passionate love with that parent, a relatedness in which the parent's feelings may be of much the same quality and intensity as those in the child (although this relatedness must indeed be of considerably more importance in the life of the developing child than it is in the life of the mature adult, with his much stronger, more highly differentiated ego and with his having behind him the experience of a successfully resolved oedipal experience during his own maturation).

But in the very earliest of his publications concerning the Oedipus complex, namely *The Interpretation of Dreams* (1900), Freud makes a fuller acknowledgement of the parent's participation in the oedipal phase of the child's life than he does in any of his later writings on the subject:

> ... a child's sexual wishes—if in their embryonic stage they deserve to be so described—awaken very early, and ... a girl's first affection is for her father and a boy's first childish desires are for his mother. Accordingly, the father becomes a disturbing rival to the boy and the mother to the girl ... The parents too give evidence as a rule of sexual partiality: a natural predilection usually sees to it that a man tends to spoil his little daughters, while his wife takes her sons' part; though both of them, where their judgement is not disturbed by the magic of sex, keep a strict eye upon their children's education. The child is very well aware of this partiality and turns against that one of his parents who is opposed to showing it. Being loved by an adult does not merely bring a child the satisfaction of a special need; it also means that he will get what he wants in every other respect as well. Thus he will be following his own sexual instinct and at the same time

---

[4] My whole paper is written, purely for the sake of simplicity of presentation, on the assumption that the child's Oedipus complex is normally a 'simple' one, whereas actually we know that it is really a 'complete' one, as Freud pointed out in 1923 in the first edition of *The Ego and the Id*. He mentioned here that
'... one gets an impression that the simple Oedipus complex is by no means its commonest form, but rather represents a simplification or schematization which, to be sure, is often enough justified for practical purposes. Closer study usually discloses the more complete Oedipus complex, which is twofold, positive and negative, and is due to the bisexuality originally present in children; that is to say, a boy has not merely an ambivalent attitude towards his father and an affectionate object-choice towards his mother, but at the same time he also behaves like a girl and displays an affectionate feminine attitude to his father and a corresponding jealousy and hostility towards his mother ...' (p. 33).

giving fresh strength to the inclination shown by his parents if his choice between them falls in with theirs (1900, pp. 257–8).

Theodor Reik, in his accounts of his coming to sense something of the depths of possessiveness, jealousy, fury at rivals, and anxiety in the face of impending loss, in himself with regard to his two daughters, conveys a much more adequate picture of the emotions which genuinely grip the parent in the oedipal relationship than is conveyed by Freud's sketchy account, given above. Reik's deeply moving descriptions occupy a chapter in his *Listening with the Third Ear* (1949), written at a time when his daughters were twelve and six years of age; and a chapter in his *The Secret Self* (1952), when the older daughter was now seventeen.

Returning to a further consideration of the therapist's oedipal-love responses to the patient, it seems to me that these responses flow from four different sources. In actual practice the responses from these four tributaries are probably so commingled in the therapist that it is difficult or impossible fully to distinguish one kind from another; the important thing is that he be maximally open to the recognition of these feelings in himself, no matter what their origin, for he will then be in the best position to discern, in so far as is possible, whence they flow and what they signify, therefore, concerning the course of the patient's analysis.

First among these four sources may be mentioned the analyst's feeling-responses to the patient's transference. That is, when, as the analysis progresses and the patient enters into an experiencing of oedipal love, longing, jealousy, frustration, and loss with regard to the analyst as a parent in the transference, the analyst will experience, to at least some degree, responses reciprocal to those of the patient–responses, that is, such as were present within the parent in question, during the patient's childhood and adolescence, but which the parent presumably was not able to recognize relatively freely and accept within himself. Some writers apply the term 'countertransference' to such analyst-responses to the patient's transference; but I prefer not to do so.

The second source consists in the countertransference in the classical sense in which this term is most often used: the analyst's responding to the patient in terms of transference-feelings carried over from a figure out of the analyst's own earlier years, without awareness that his response springs predominantly from this early-life source, rather than being based mainly upon the reality of the present analyst-patient relationship. It is this source, of course, which we wish to reduce to a minimum, by means of thoroughgoing personal analysis and ever-continuing subsequent alertness for indications that our work with a patient has come up against, in us, unanalysed emotional residues from our own past. This source is so very important, in fact, as to make the writing of such a paper as this a somewhat precarious venture; its author must expect that some readers will charge him with trying to portray, as natural and necessary to the analytic process generally, certain analyst-responses which in actuality are purely the result of an unworked-through Oedipus complex in himself, which are dangerously out of place in his own work with patients, and which have no place in the well-analysed analyst's experience with his patients.

I surmise that although this source may play a *relatively* insignificant role in the responses of a well-analysed analyst who has conducted a number of analyses through to completion – to a completion deep enough to include a thoroughgoing resolution of the patient's Oedipus complex – it is probably to be found, in some measure, in every analyst. That is, it seems to me that the nature of analytic work presents to the analyst such a peculiarly powerful and conflictual feeling-experience in this regard – a fostering of his deepest love towards the fellow human being with whom he participates in such prolonged and deeply personal work, and a simultaneous, unceasing, and rigorous taboo against his behavioural expression of any of the romantic or erotic components of this love – as to necessitate almost any analyst's tending to relegate the deepest intensities of these conflictual feelings to his own unconscious, much as were the deepest intensities of his oedipal strivings towards a similarly beloved, and similarly unobtainable and rigorously tabooed, parent. I believe that our time-honoured horror of such classical countertransference feelings has only served to increase the likelihood of their remaining in the analyst's *unconscious*, and I hope that this paper will help analysts – in particular, the less experienced analysts – to a readier awareness, and therby diminution, of these countertransference feelings, just as I have been helped, in dealing with other kinds of countertransference feelings, by such papers as those written by P. Heimann (1950), M. B. Cohen (1952), and E. Weigert (1952).

A third source is to be found in the appeal which the gratifyingly improving patient makes to the narcissistic residue in the analyst's personality, the Pygmalion in him. He tends to fall in love with this beautifully developing patient, regarded at this narcissistic level as his own creation, just as Pygmalion fell in love with the beautiful statue of Galatea which he had sculptured. This source, like the second one which I have just mentioned, can be expected to hold *relatively* little sway in the well-analysed practitioner of long experience; but it, too, is probably never absent, and I think it is much more powerfully present, even in analysts of great experience and professional standing, than we may like to think. Particularly in articles and books which describe the author's new technique or theoretical concept as an outgrowth of the work with one particular patient, or a very few patients, do we see this source very prominently present in many instances.

The fourth source, based on the genuine reality of the analyst-patient situation, consists in the circumstance that the nearer a patient comes to the termination of his analysis, the more he becomes, *per se*, a likeable, admirable, and basically speaking lovable, human being from whom the analyst will soon become separated. If he is not himself a psychiatrist, the analyst may very likely never see him again; and even if he is a professional colleague, the relationship with him will become in many respects far more superficial, far less intimate, than it has been. This real and unavoidable circumstance of the closing analytic work tends powerfully to arouse within the analyst feelings of painfully frustrated love which deserve to be compared with the feelings of ungratifiable love which both child and parent experience in the oedipal phase of the child's development. Feelings from this source cannot properly be called countertransference, for they flow from the reality of the present circumstances; but they may be difficult or impossible to distinguish fully from countertransference.

There are, then, four more or less powerful sources tending to promote feelings of deep love with romantic and erotic overtones, and with accompanying feelings of jealousy, anxiety, frustration-rage, separation-anxiety, and grief, in the analyst with regard to the patient. These feelings come to him, like all feelings, without tags showing whence they have come, and only if he is relatively open and accepting of their emergence into his awareness does he have a chance to set about finding out their origin and thus their significance in his work with the patient.

Finally, in line with the considerations which I have presented so far, I shall make a few remarks concerning the passing of the Oedipus complex in normal development and in successful psycho-analysis.

In *The Ego and the Id* (1923) we find italicized a passage in which Freud stresses that the oedipal phase results in the formation of the superego; we find that he stresses the parents' opposition to the child's oedipal wishes; and, lastly, we see this resultant superego to be predominantly a severe and forbidding one:

The broad general outcome of the sexual phase dominated by the Oedipus complex may, therefore, be taken to be the forming of a precipitate in the ego . . . This modification of the ego . . . confronts the other contents of the ego as an ego ideal or super-ego.

. . . The child's parents, and especially his father, were perceived as the obstacle to realization of his Oedipus wishes; so his infantile ego fortified itself for the carrying out of the repression by erecting this same obstacle within itself. It borrowed the strength to do this, so to speak, from the father, and this loan was an extraordinarily momentous act. The super-ego retains the character of the father, while the more powerful the Oedipus complex was and the more rapidly it succumbed to repression (under the influence of authority, religious teaching, schooling and reading), the stricter will be the domination of the super-ego over the ego later on–in the form of conscience or perhaps of an unconscious sense of guilt. . . . (1923, pp. 34–5).

I shall not enter into the subject of pre-oedipal origins of the superego, a subject which has been dealt with by M. Klein (1955), E. Jacobson (1954), and others. My point here is that, aside from that subject, I regard Freud's above-quoted description as more applicable to the child who later becomes neurotic or psychotic, than to the 'normal' child. Since we assume that there is no adult who is wholly free from at least some neurotic difficulties, I assume that Freud's formulation holds true to some degree in every instance. But I believe that *to the extent that* a child's relationships with his parents are healthy, he acquires the strength to accept the unrealizability of his oedipal strivings, not mainly through the identification with the forbidding rival-parent, but mainly, rather, through the ego-strengthening experience of finding that the beloved parent reciprocates his love – responds to him, that is, as being a worthwhile and lovable individual, as being, indeed, a conceivably desirable love-partner – and renounces him only with an accompanying sense of loss on the parent's own part. The renunciation is, I think, again something which is a mutual experience for child and parent, and is made in deference to a recognizedly greater limiting reality, a reality which includes not only the taboo maintained by the rival-parent, but also the love of the oedipally desired parent towards his or her spouse – a love which antedated the child's birth and a love to which, in a sense, he owes his very existence.

Out of such an oedipal situation the child emerges, with no matter how deep and painful a sense of loss at the recognition that he can never displace the rival parent and possess the beloved one in a romantic-and-erotic relationship, in a state different from the relatively ego-diminished, superego-dominated state which Freud described. This child emerges, rather, with his ego strengthened out of the knowledge that his love, however unrealizable, is reciprocated; and strengthened, too, out of the realization, which his relationship with the beloved parent has helped him to achieve, that he lives in a world in which any individual's strivings are encompassed by a reality much larger than himself. My views here represent, I feel, not an attempted contradiction of, but rather a shift of emphasis from, those of Freud; where he stressed that the oedipal phase normally results *mainly* in the formation of a forbidding superego, I think of it as resulting *mainly* in enchantment of the ego's ability to test both inner and outer reality.

All my experience with both neurotic and psychotic patients has indicated to me that, in every individual instance, in so far as the oedipal phase was entered into in the course of their past development, it led to ego impairment rather than ego growth primarily because the beloved parent had to repress his or her reciprocal desire for the child, *chiefly through the mechanism of unconscious denial of the child's importance to the parent.* More often than not, in these instances, I find indications that the parent would unwittingly act out his or her repressed desires in the form of unduly seductive behaviour towards the child; but then, whenever the parent came close to the recognition of such desires within himself, he would unpredictably start reacting to the child as being unlovable, undesirable.

In the cases of many of these parents, it appears that, primarily because of the parent's own unresolved Oedipus complex, his marriage proved too unsatisfying, and his emotional relationship to his own culture too tenuous, for him to dare to recognize the strength of his reciprocal feelings towards his child during the latter's oedipal phase of development. The child is reacted to as a little mother or father transference-figure to the parent, a transference-figure towards whom the parent's repressed oedipal-love feelings are directed. If the parent had achieved the inner reassurance of a deep and enduring love towards his wife, and a deeply felt relatedness with his culture including the incest taboos to which his culture adheres, he would have been able to participate in a deeply felt, but minimally acted out, relationship with the child in such a way as to foster the healthy resolution of the child's Oedipus complex. Instead, what usually happens in such instances, I think, is that the child's Oedipus complex remains unresolved because the child stubbornly–and not unnaturally– refuses to accept defeat within these particular family circumstances, where the acceptance of oedipal defeat is tantamount to the acceptance of irrevocable personal worthlessness and unlovability.

And it seems to me clear enough, then, what this former child, now a neurotic or psychotic adult, requires from us for the successful resolution of his unresolved Oedipus complex: not such a repression of desire, acted-out seductiveness, and denial of his own worth as he met in the relationship with his parent, but rather a maximal awareness on our part of the reciprocal feelings which we develop in response to his oedipal strivings. Our main job remains always, of course, to further the *analysis* of his transference; but what I have just described seems to me to be the optimal feeling background in the analyst for such analytic work.

Chapter 10

INTEGRATION AND DIFFERENTIATION IN SCHIZOPHRENIA (1959)[1]

FROM a purely descriptive viewpoint, schizophrenia can be seen to consist essentially in an impairment of both *integration* and *differentiation*-which are but opposite faces of a unitary growth-process. From a psychodynamic viewpoint as well, this malfunctioning of integration-and-differentiation seems basic to all the bewilderingly complex and varied manifestations of schizophrenia.

Taking first the matter of *integration*; when we assess the schizophrenic individual in terms of the three classical structural areas of the personality-id, ego, and superego-we discover these to be poorly integrated with one another. The id is experienced by the ego as a Pandora's box, the contents of which will overwhelm one if it is opened. The ego is, as many writers have stated, severely split, sometimes into innumerable islands which are not linked discernibly with one another. And the superego has the nature of a cruel tyrant whose assaults upon the weak and unintegrated ego are, if anything, even more destructive to it than are the accessions of the threatening id-impulses, as Szalita-Pemow (1951), Hill (1955), and others have emphasized. Moreover, the superego is, like the ego, even in itself not well integrated; its utterances contain the most glaring inconsistencies from one moment to the next. Jacobson (1954a, b) has shown that there is actually a dissolution of the superego, as an integrated structure-a regressive transformation back into the threatening parental images whose conglomeration originally formed it.

Differentiation is a process which is essential to integration, and vice versa. For personality structure-functions or psychic contents to become integrated, they must first have emerged as partially differentiated or separated from one another; and differentiation

[1] First published in the *Journal of Nervous and Mental Disease*, Vol. 129 (1959), pp. 542–50.

in turn can emerge only out of a foundation of more or less integrated functions or contents.

When we look at this process of differentiation in the schizophrenic person, we find it to be, similarly, severely impaired. It is difficult or impossible for him to differentiate between himself and the outer world. He often cannot distinguish between memories and present perceptions; memories experienced with hallucinatory vividness and immediacy are sensed as perceptions of present events, and perceptions of present events may be experienced as memories from the past. He may be unable to distinguish between emotions and somatic sensations; feelings from the emotional sphere often come through to him as somatic sensations, or even as variations in his somatic structure (changes in the size, colour, and so forth, of bodily parts).

He cannot distinguish between thoughts and feelings on the one hand, and action on the other; thus if the therapist encourages him to explore thoughts and feelings of a sexual or murderous nature, for example, he feels that the therapist is trying to invite him into sexual activity, or incite him to murder. He may be unable to differentiate, perceptually, one person from another, so that he is prone to misidentify them.

In the conduct of his daily life and in his communicating with other persons, he is unable, as Bateson *et al.* (3) have reported, to distinguish between the symbolic and the concrete. If his therapist uses symbolic language, he may experience this in literal terms; and on the other hand the affairs of daily life (eating, dressing, sleeping and so on) which we think of as literal and concrete, he may react to as possessing a unique symbolic significance which completely obscures their 'practical' importance in his life as a human being.

I have stressed how interwoven are the growth processes of integration and differentiation, and it follows that the impairments of both are likewise interwoven. But in the schizophrenic these two processes tend to be out of step with one another, so that at one moment a patient's more urgent need may be for increased *integration*, whereas at another he may more urgently need increased *differentiation*. And there are some patients who show for months on end a more urgent need in *one* of these areas, before the alternate growth-phase comes on the scene. Thus there is a modicum of validity in speaking here of two different 'types' of schizophrenic patients. This distinction is largely artificial, but it is useful for purposes of exposition.

The 'Non-Integrated Type' of Patient

The predominantly 'non-integrated type' of patient, then, can be further described as characteristically being several, or even many, different persons to the various nurses and aides on his ward. In extreme instances, he fosters marked dissension among them, as each responds to a different fragment of his poorly integrated ego. Each staff member, regarding this fragment as the patient's whole ego, feels sure that he or she knows the 'real' Mr Smith, and becomes violently at odds with fellow staff members who are equally convinced of the total validity of the other ego fragments to which they are relating.

In his psychotherapeutic hours, he shows extreme changeability from one moment to the next. One woman, for example, suddenly pauses in the midst of vicious paranoid tirades at me, to ask me in a calm and friendly way for a light for her cigarette. Or he may relate to the therapist on two quite different levels of feeling simultaneously. For instance, a hebephrenic young woman, in trying to sit on one's lap, may be at once a lustful woman and a pathetic little child.

As to such a patient's subjective experience of this non-integration, we find above all that his experience, as regards both current living and memories of the past, is lacking in continuity. Because his ego is too weak to tolerate in awareness his intense, poorly integrated or ambivalent feelings, these are largely dissociated or repressed, and projected on to the outer world which is therefore experienced as chaotically changing; thus an intolerable experience of chaotically changing feelings within is averted. One such woman told me, seriously and convincingly, after I had repeatedly tried to learn something from her about her mother, 'Whenever you use the word mother, I see a whole parade of women, each one representing a different point of view.' This same woman, for approximately the first three years of our work, felt innumerable gaps in her own consciousness of current living; was sure that there were thousands of different Chestnut Lodges among which she was constantly shifted, all over the world; and was sure that there were several different Dr Searleses, one being replaced by another from one day and even from one moment to the next. When her fragmentation was at its height, she was convinced even that her body was only a conglomeration of anatomical parts from various other people; and other people's bodies, including mine, were perceived in the same way.

Two other women I have treated gave me to realize that, over the course of many months, my face was perceived by them as constantly changing, from something beautiful to something monstrous, and so on. One hebephrenic man sat for months, in our sessions, watching my face entirely as if he were watching a fascinating movie, grunting often in astonishment, pleasure, or awe, and on rare occasions verbalizing his experience of seeing, at the moment, a beautiful rose, a dilapidated Cape Cod house, a sex fiend, or what not.

One hebephrenic woman, after many months of showing anxiety and antagonism in response to my moving about, or changing posture, finally let me know that when, for example, on a warm day I got up and shifted my chair round to the opposite side of her bed, to be closer to the open window, she now experienced the presence of two of me in the room, much as if, in watching a motion picture, one saw it not as one continuous motion, but as broken up into a series of 'stills'; in this patient's instance, moreover, the 'stills' remained on the scene, and accumulated. I now understood better why she had complained anxiously, in session after session earlier in her therapy, that there were 200 or 300 doctors in the room. She let me know also, on another occasion, that whenever I changed posture she misidentified me as some different person from her past.

In turning now to the therapist's typical feeling-responses in sessions with such patients, let us acknowledge first the gratifications which he finds in an often dramatic experience of finding the wide gamut of his feeling capacities played upon, in fascinatingly unpredictable ways, over the course of the therapeutic session, in response to the amazingly varied part-persons, so to speak, of which the unintegrated patient is made up.

But all too frequently any such gratification is erased by the anxiety and helplessness, the threat to his own personal integration and his own sense of identity, which he feels upon experiencing suddenly changing, intense emotional responses to the poorly integrated patient, or upon finding himself feeling, even, on two different levels simultaneously towards the patient—levels of powerful affect without any felt connexion between these levels. Thus he may find his feelings unpredictably switching, in response to the patient's deeply fragmented modes of expression, from intense fury at one moment to deeply moved compassion the next, and back again. Or he may feel simultaneously aroused sexually in response to the patient's seductiveness, and utterly incongruously maternal towards the infantile needfulness which she is at the same time evidencing in another area of her behaviour.

Further, such a patient tends naturally and healthily to identify wholeheartedly with the therapist, as a refuge from the fragmentation which overwhelms him—as a means of finding, in symbiotic relatedness to the mother-therapist, a sufficient island of wholeness for him now to turn, to put it in an oversimplified way, and integrate the dissociated components of his personality, one by one, until such time as he has enough ego of his own to endure the resolution of this symbiosis. Benedek (1949, 1952a, b, 1959), Mahler (1952), and Michael Balint (1952, 1955) have pointed out that a symbiotic relatedness, which many earlier writers had described as *per se* pathological, is actually necessary to normal infancy. My experience indicates, further, that such a relatedness constitutes a necessary phase in psycho-analysis or psychotherapy with either neurotic or psychotic patients respectively, and that this phase is especially important in the therapy of schizophrenic patients, for in their histories even that very early life-stage was severly distorted.

Such a symbiotic relatedness involves not only intense gratifications for the therapist, but intense anxiety also; on occasion his sense of identity may be severely threatened by his felt oneness with a deeply fragmented schizophrenic person. I cannot overemphasize, however, the importance of the therapist's being as open as possible to the whole gamut of feeling-responses which such a deeply fragmented patient tends to arouse in him. This is essential to the development of the 'therapeutic symbiosis' I have just described; by contrast, a patient cannot deeply identify with —become subjectively at one with—a therapist whose own feelings are kept largely under repression. Further, one of the major functions of this symbiosis is, in my experience, that it enables the patient's increasing integration to occur as it were *external* to him-

308

self, in the intrapsychic experience of the therapist, as a prelude to its development at an intrapsychic level within the patient himself. Mystical though this sounds, it is based upon logically understandable clinical phenomena.

In one case, for instance, I repeatedly reacted to a schizophrenic woman as being a combination of murderous woman and appealingly needful child. Towards the murderous woman in her I felt fear and anger; towards the child, I felt friendliness, tenderness, and compassion. Moreover, in varying degrees I inevitably *expressed* such feelings, both verbally and non-verbally, to each of these two so-called persons in her. This phase in the evolution of my view of her, this kind of feeling-response on my part towards her, was a necessary prelude to the development which finally came next, after many months; namely, I suddenly realized, in the course of one session with her, that she was a single person whose personality contained both these widely different aspects.

Such a feeling realization, such a felt 'knowing', is not easy to come by; more than once I have heard therapists, in staff presentations, describe their relationship with a schizophrenic patient in such a manner as to make it clear that they are not really describing a person, but a conglomeration of symptoms or personality fragments. But once the relationship has progressed far enough–once, to put it another way, the patient's integration has proceeded far enough–for the therapist to achieve such an integrated inner picture of the patient, from then on he inevitably responds to the patient in this vein, namely, as *a person*, and in accordance with long-known theories of the development of the self, the patient, in finding himself persistently so responded to by the therapist (and, increasingly thenceforward by others in his environment), comes in course of time to the feeling realization that he is a person, comes to such an image of himself at an unconscious as well as a conscious level.

My technical suggestions concerning work with this 'type' of patient relate to what has just been said concerning the growth process involved in the therapeutic relatedness. A patient cannot identify with a therapist who is running off in all directions after the patient's various personality fragments; instead, the therapist will find that, very frequently, the most useful move is to 'stay put' psychologically, simply acknowledging the feeling or feelings which the patient is endeavouring to convey. Such responses from the therapist, when well timed, foster the gradual building up of consensually validated accretions to the patient's conscious ego.

Equally important is it for the therapist to keep in as close touch as possible with the location of what we might call the patient's conscious ego, where his sense of identity resides. If the therapist responds to a personality fragment which is dissociated – that is to say, one of which the patient is unaware – the patient is likely to feel entirely out of touch with, and grossly misidentified by, him. When one has had oneself the experience of being repeatedly, or even constantly, misidentified by a patient in session after session – being responded to as myriad persons other than oneself – one knows how intense is the anxiety aroused by this experience of feeling misidentified.

And when a patient is expressing two affects simultaneously, it is important that the therapist acknowledge both, if both seem to be in the patient's awareness, or acknowledge more emphatically that of which the patient is more fully aware. Suppose, for example, a patient is consciously and verbally demanding to be allowed to leave the hospital, and simultaneously in non-verbal ways is revealing a dissociated desire to be kept in the hospital. If, now, the therapist responds only by saying, 'That's all right; I know you *really* want to stay here. Rest assured that I realize this,' one can see how maddening this is to the patient, how likely it is to increase his anxiety and his feeling of helplessness. If one says instead, 'I know that you're determined to leave, and that you feel you can't stand it here another day; but I wonder if such-and-such behaviour suggests, too, that something in you feels very differently about it?' this is, in my experience, at least less likely to be traumatic. And most frequently, I find it wisest to make *no* comment about the such-and-such behaviour unless I see some indication that the patient is at least partially aware of it himself.

The final technical point I wish to make with regard to the non-integrated 'type' of patient concerns the usefulness of transference interpretations. We see that in the work with such a patient, transference interpretations may have a specifically therapeutic effect, for they may help to focus into the therapeutic relationship itself the patient's multiple ego fragments which are tending to fly off in all directions and remain attached to innumerable disparate persons outside the therapeutic relationship. Transference interpretations may facilitate, that is, the patient's becoming whole *via* his recognizing all these diverse experiences of his as consisting, in part, in reactions to the therapeutic relationship, and specifically to the wholeness of the therapist's personality. But here a note of caution is needed, for, as Lidz and Lidz (1952) have pointed out, premature or over-abundant interpretations of this sort tend to make the patient feel–correctly, I believe (see chapter 1)–that the therapist is trying to incorporate him, as did one or another of his parents in earlier years. And I have seen that he may react with an increase in his personality fragmentation, as an unconscious defence against the incorporatively oriented therapist's transference interpretations.

The 'Non-Differentiated Type' of Patient

This patient, in marked contrast to the one just discussed, has a relatively static, unvarying relatedness with the various staff members on the ward; he has a relatively fixed social role which changes but little over months or even years. Rather than the staff being, as with the former type of patient, in a state of marked dissension as to who this person is, their views of him coincide all too closely. And with this stereotyped social role on the ward, he fosters also a markedly stereotyped relationship with the therapist, such that the therapist as well feels him to be a relatively little differentiated personality. In his therapeutic sessions he is often mute and motionless, and such verbalizations or physical movements as he exhibits are stereotyped, relatively unvarying month after month.

The patient's subjective experience of his poorly differentiated state is, of course, difficult for us to know, for in most such instances he is mute, or nearly so. One such man told me, in a rare moment of verbal communication, that his thoughts would often flicker down, like a candle flame, and be extinguished; another said that it was as though a giant hand were squeezing down his inner experience, more and more constrictingly. A number of such patients have let me know that their perhaps more usual experience was of being alone in a dead, empty world; one man phrased it that he was 'in a mist'. Most of the time, from what I have seen, they feel themselves to be dead.

In so far as they are aware of the world around them, they see this world in global or homogeneous terms, with little if any differentiation. The therapist, for instance, if he emerges at all into their awareness as something distinct from his background, is perceived as but one head in a many-headed mass which includes everybody else in the surroundings, as if he were but one of the many heads of the Hydra of Greek mythology. And the patient's family is not perceived as a group of differentiated individuals, but as 'The Family', entirely comparable with 'The Hospital' of which the therapist is perceived as but an indistinguishable part. In many instances, so far as I have been able to determine, the patient feels himself to be a similarly indistinguishable part of The Family or of The Hospital.

One patient felt herself to be coterminous with the bed in which she lay, and perceived me as being a part of the chair in which I sat next to her bed, very similarly to the perceptions which Savage (1955) and others have described as typical of subjects with LSD-induced psychoses. One of my patients said, 'I'm wrapped up in this building,' and when she first began coming to my office, she let me know that she was filled with a sense of anxious apartness from her self, this self being thoroughly bound up with the hospital room in which she had long been housed.

One comes to realize, in working with such a patient, how premature have been one's efforts to find out what feelings the patient is experiencing or what thoughts he is having; one comes to realize that much of the time he has neither feelings nor thoughts differentiated as such and communicable to us.

Such differentiation as the patient possesses tends to crumble when intense emotion enters his awareness. A paranoid man, for example, may find that when his hatred towards another person reaches a certain degree of intensity, he is flooded with anxiety because he no longer knows whether he hates, or instead 'really loves' the other individual. This is not based, I believe, primarily upon the mechanism which Freud (1911) outlined in his classical description of the nature of paranoid delusions of persecution, a description in which repressed homosexual love played the central role. The central difficulty is rather that the ego is too poorly differentiated to maintain its structure in the face of such powerful affects, and the patient becomes flooded with what can only be described as *undifferentiated passion*, precisely as one finds

312

an infant to be overwhelmed at times with affect which the observer cannot specifically identify as any one kind of emotion.

As for the feelings which the therapist himself experiences in working with this second 'type' of patient, we find, here again, a persistent threat to the therapist's sense of identity. But whereas in the first instance the threat was felt predominantly as a disturbance of one's personal integration, here it is felt predominantly as a weakening of one's sense of differentiation. In this instance, the 'therapeutic symbiosis' which I mentioned before is also, in my experience at least, a necessary development, and I belive that it tends to occur earlier here, for this patient's predominant mode of relatedness with other persons, at the developmental level at which we find him at the very beginning of our work, is a symbiotic one. I have already described how the symbiotic relatedness, with its subjective absence of ego-boundaries, involves not only special gratifications but anxiety-provoking disturbances of one's sense of personal identity.

The comparatively rapid development of symbiotic relatedness is facilitated by the patient's characteristically non-verbal, and physically more or less immobile, functioning during the therapeutic sessions. In response, the therapist's own behaviour becomes more and more similar, so that each participant is now offering to the other, hour after hour, a silent, impassive screen which facilitates abundant mutual projecting and introjecting. Thus a symbiotic state is likely to be reached earlier than in one's work with the typically much more verbal type of patient whom I first described, for in that instance the patient's and therapist's more abundant verbalizations tend persistently to stress the ego-boundaries separating the two persons from one another.

In working with the predominantly non-differentiated patient, the therapist's sense of identity as a complexly differentiated individual entity becomes further eroded, or undermined, as he finds the patient persistently operating on the unwavering conviction, hour after hour, that the therapist is but an undifferentiated aspect of the whole vague mass of The Hospital, but one head of the Hydra which, in psychodynamic terms, is in actuality the patient's projection of his own poorly differentiated hostility, but which, in the patient's tenaciously held view, is the way the world around him really is.

Further, since the patient typically verbalizes little but a few

313

maddeningly monotonous stereotypes, the therapist tends to feel, over the course of time, with so little of his own intellectual content being explicitly tapped in the relationship, that his richness of intellect is progressively rusting away—becoming less differentiated, more stereotyped and rudimentary. Moreover, the patient presents but one of two emotional wave-lengths to which the therapist can himself tune in, rather than a rich spectrum of emotion which calls into response a similarly wide range of feelings from the therapist himself. Thus not only the therapist's intellectual resources, but his emotional capacities too, become subjectively narrowed down and impoverished, as he finds that, month after month, his patient evokes in him neither any wide range of ideas, nor any emotion except, for example, rage, or contempt, or dull hopelessness.

This feeling experience on his part, anxiety-provoking and discouraging though he finds it, is a necessary therapeutic development. It is necessary, that is, for him thus to experience at first hand something of the patient's own lack of differentiation; for, as in the therapy with the non-integrated patient, here again the healing process occurs external to the patient, as it were, at an intrapsychic level in the therapist, before it becomes established in the patient himself. That is, the therapist's coming to view the patient, his relationship with the patient, and himself in this relationship, all as being largely non-differentiated, is a development which sets the stage for the patient's gradually increasing differentiation. Now the therapist comes to sense, time after time, newly emerging tendrils of differentiation in the patient, before the latter is himself conscious of them. In responding to these with spontaneity as they show themselves, time after time, the therapist helps the patient to become aware that they are a part of him.

The nuances of newly emerging differentiation which creep into the patient's stereotyped modes of behaviour are sometimes clearly perceptible to the eye or ear; for example, a long-clenched hand may look a bit more relaxed, a fleeting smile may pass over a stonily antagonistic face, a slow and mechanical walk may momentarily reveal a flash of tripping gaiety. But there are times when a therapist can only say that he feels a new response in himself in reaction to behaviour which objectively seems as stereotyped as ever. A hebephrenic laugh which has always sounded to him clearly derisive and therefore offensive, may now sudddenly make him feel like crying. Or the same verbal stereotype may be sensed as conveying, on landmark occasions over the passage of months, entirely different feelings from those it once conveyed. For example, a nearly mute and motionless woman used to punctuate the long silences, scores of times over the months, by saying to me, 'What about the getting well?' This stereotype, which at first posed a maddening and discouraging barrier between her and myself, a barrier of conveyed reproach and hopelessness, came to be clearly translatable, on one occasion, as a warmly fond 'Speak to me of love' and, on a later occasion, this overtly the same 'What about the getting well?' clearly meant, 'I want to have a baby by you.' And a hebephrenic man has come to use the stereotyped sentence, 'I understand', to convey to me, variously, the following meanings: 'I am completely confused'; 'My worst suspicions are now confirmed'; 'Be quiet, on pain of violence'; 'There, there, little idiot'; and other assorted ones.

Thus a heavy reliance upon one's intuition is a technical point which I have found useful. A second point concerns the relatively sparing use of transference interpretations—perhaps more sparing than in one's work with the predominantly non-integrated, or fragmented, patient. In the instance of that first 'type' of patient, we saw that transference interpretations may have a specific value in fostering the patient's wholeness, his integration, by focusing his disparate personality fragments into the context of the patient-therapist relationship. But the predominantly non-differentiated patient, who is above all trying to branch out, in his interpersonal relationships and in his intrapsychic content, beyond the immediate, symbiotic situation with the therapist, may feel his precarious new differentiation to be destroyed by premature transference interpretations which tend to bring it all back to the relationship with his therapist—which tend, that is, to reduce divergent ramifications of meaning to this one meaning.

The third and last technical point is, like the others, a function of the growth process I have been describing, a process which involves both patient and therapist. The patient's differentiation is fostered not only by the therapist's sensing, and responding to, an increasingly differentiated person in him, but also by the therapist's permitting his own personality differentiation, his own complex individuality which was to a large degree already firmly established before beginning work with this patient, to come more and more freely into play in the therapeutic relationship. At crucial points, for example, he must have the courage to act upon the course that his own intuition directs, in *differing* sharply from the patient–to be the person he knows himself to be and to address the person he knows to inhabit the patient's body, no matter how sharply this conflicts with the patient's own image of himself and of his therapist. Whereas it was essential earlier to allow the anxiety-arousing symbiosis to develop, now the therapist must find similar courage to help determinedly in its resolution. In asserting increasingly his own complex individuality, he provides the patient with an increasingly clearly differentiated person with whom to identify, and over against whom to become conscious of his own separate self.

In conclusion, I wish to stress once again the large element of artificiality in the divisions which I have set up in this paper, for the sake of a theoretical exposition of phenomena which in clinical practice are usually closely intertwined. For example, when a patient says to his therapist, 'I don't know, when I talk to you, whether I'm having an hallucination, or a fantasy about a memory, or a memory about a fantasy,' he is evidencing in the same breath a gross impairment of both integration and differentiation.

I want to emphasize, too, that the growth-processes of integration and differentiation occur, in any prolonged and successful psychotherapeutic endeavour, not only in the patient, but also to a significant degree in the therapist himself; the growth process is a genuinely mutual one.

And lastly, the states of what I have called non-integration and non-differentiation should be thought of as not merely rather fixed *levels of maturation or regression* at which a patient exists over a long period of time, but as *flexible defences of the ego against overwhelming anxiety.* Thus, from noticing at what moments in the therapeutic session, or at what junctures over the long course of treatment, a patient's characteristic non-integration or non-differentiation notably increases or notably lessens, we can tell when areas of particularly severe anxiety have been encountered in his personality investigation, and chart the resolution of this anxiety as growth proceeds.

Chapter 11

INTEGRATION AND DIFFERENTIATION IN SCHIZOPHRENIA: AN OVER-ALL VIEW (1959)[1]

FROM a phenomenological viewpoint, schizophrenia can be seen to consist essentially in an impairment of both *integration* and *differentiation*, which, as I shall attempt to show, are but opposite faces of a unitary process. From a psychodynamic viewpoint as well, this malfunctioning of integration-differentiation seems pivotal to all the bewilderingly complex and varied manifestations of schizophrenia, and basic to the writings on schizophrenia by Bleuler (1911), Federn (1952), Sullivan (1947, 1953, 1956), Fromm-Reichmann (1950, 1952), Hill (1955), and other authorities in this field.

The term 'integration' is used here in an inclusive rather than highly limited sense; I shall discuss integration as a process which pervades multiple personality levels and personality areas. This paper is intended to be relevant to integration of the self-image, integration of one's experience of the surrounding object-world, integration of ideational content with affective impulses, and so on. The term 'differentiation' is employed here in a similar general sense and I am interested in differentiation as taking place in these same numerous areas of personality structure and personality functioning.

The term 'differentiation' is intended to bear the dual connotation conveyed, as I understand it, in common psychoanalytic and psychiatric usage. It connotes, as in biology, the elaboration of distinctive, specialized characteristics of structure and function as well as an ability to distinguish between, or to discriminate, fundamentally different objects and experiences. To take an example, this dual connotation operates when we say

[1] First published in the *British Journal of Medical Psychology*, Vol. 32 (1959), pp. 261-81.

that a relatively mature person is capable of achieving a highly differentiated conception or image of another person. This would imply both that he is relatively well able to grasp the highly complex, special ramifications of the personality of the other, and also to distinguish between that personality and other personalities with whom he has had experience.

Taking the matter of *integration* first, we find that when we assess the schizophrenic individual in terms of the three classical Freudian 'compartments' of the personality–id, ego, and superego–we discover these three personality areas to be poorly integrated with one another. The id is experienced by the ego as an intensely inimical foreign body, which threatens to be overwhelming. In the more normal person it is rather a repository of primitive drives towards which one can maintain a basically friendly and receptive attitude, and which represents priceless wellsprings of energy. The ego itself is severely split in the schizophrenic, as many writers have described, sometimes into innumerable islands which are not linked discernibly with one another. The superego, rather than being, as in the normal person, in the relation of a firm but friendly and helpful guide to the ego in the latter's efforts to cope with the id-impulses and with the outer world, stands in the nature of a cruel tyrant whose assaults upon the weak and unintegrated ego are, if anything, even more destructive to it than are the accessions of the threatening id-impulses (Szalita-Pemow, 1951). Moreover, the superego, even in itself, is not well integrated. Its utterances contain the most glaring inconsistencies from one moment to the next, entirely comparable with a parent who is not only punitive but bewilderingly inconsistent. Jacobson (1954*a*, 1954*b*) has shown that there is actually a dissolution of the superego as an integrated structure, and a regressive transformation back into the threatening parental images whose conglomeration originally formed the superego.

With this structural state of things existing in the personality of the schizophrenic, it naturally follows that he functions in a poorly integrated fashion. When we perceive him in a temporal dimension, we find that he cannot integrate his life-experiences over a span of time as being all part of a continuing, unbroken pattern. Instead, his present and past experiences become all jumbled up, in the way which Federn (1952) has pointed out in his description of the phenomenon of regression to earlier ego-states. When we perceive him in the dimension of immediate interpersonal experience, we find that rather than his having an integrated over-all emotional orientation towards the other person, his reactions to the latter are, instead, an uncoordinated welter of ambivalent feelings–feelings which suddenly erupt, or as suddenly become unavailable to him through repression, in a fashion which severely limits the possibility of his developing a continued, integrated interpersonal relationship.

Differentiation is a process which is essential to integration, and vice versa. And when we look at this process of differentiation in the schizophrenic person, we find it to be similarly severely impaired. It is difficult or impossible for him to differentiate between himself and the outer world; his ego-boundaries are unstable and incomplete. He often cannot distinguish between memories and present perceptions. Memories experienced with hallucinatory vividness and immediacy are sensed as perceptions of present events, and perceptions of present events may be experienced as memories from the past (which may account for many instances in which schizophrenic patients speak of events in the immediate situation in the past tense). He may be unable to distinguish between emotions and somatic sensations; feelings from the emotional sphere often come through to him as somatic sensations, or even as variations in his somatic structure (changes in the size, colour, and so forth, of bodily parts).

Hartmann (1939) made this interesting point in regard to the early development of psychic structure: '. . . there is no ego before the differentiation of ego and id, but in the same sense the id does not yet exist either. Both are products of a differentiation process.'

He has difficulty in differentiating, perceptually, one person from another, so that he is prone to misidentify one person with another; part of this misidentifying often involves his experiencing transference phenomena not only at an unconscious level, as does the neurotic, but at a conscious level. He may *consciously* experience the therapist as being, for instance, his father or mother or brother. In the conduct of his daily life and in his communicating with other persons he is unable to distinguish between the symbolic and the concrete (Bateson, Jackson, Haley and Weakland, 1956). If the therapist uses symbolic language the patient may experience this in literal terms. On the other hand the affairs of daily life (eating, dressing, sleeping and so on), which we think of as literal and concrete, may be reacted to by the schizophrenic patient as possessing a unique symbolic significance which completely obscures their 'practical' importance in his life as a human being.

In this paper I shall make a general though necessarily brief survey of some of the aetiological factors at the basis of the schizophrenic's impairment of integration and differentiation, some of the manifestations of this impairment as shown in his ward-group relatedness and in the patient-therapist relationship, and in both these contexts I shall examine certain therapeutic measures, with particular reference to the ways in which they foster the resolution of this schizophrenic impairment.

Aetiology

This central difficulty in schizophrenia – the impairment of integration-differentiation – seems to be most fundamentally attributable to the schizophrenic's regression to the level of early infancy, at which developmental phase the infant had not yet become subjectively differentiated from the outer world; a phase in which he felt himself to be, instead, at one with all the world which came within his ken – a world much too vast for his rudimentary ego to integrate. This point has been conveyed by many writers – by Ferenczi in 1913 (1950), Nunberg (1920), Stärcke (1921), Federn at least as early as 1927 (Federn, 1952), Schilder (1935) (to mention only a few of these early investigators), and by many others in more recent years. One very recent work which illuminatingly traces this theme is the volume entitled *Chronic Schizophrenia*, by Freeman, Cameron and McGhie (1958).

In the most general terms, normal psychological development consists in successive stages of personality differentiation, each such stage being grounded in a newly won integration. Thus a reasonably healthy intra-uterine development is necessary to the earliest post-natal existence; a symbiotic relatedness between the infant and the mothering person is essential to the differentiation of the infant's own ego as distinct from the world about him; an effective level of non-verbal communication between infant and mother must be established before the beginnings of verbal communication can emerge in that relationship; and reasonably reliable verbal communication must be established, at a concrete level, between the child and those about him, before he can achieve the still more adult differentiation between concrete, literal thought and speech on the one hand, and abstract, metaphorical thought and speech on the other. In adulthood, similarly, we find that the better a person's integration, the more richly differentiated can his personality be–just as the tallest, most luxuriant tree is that with the most extensive root system, embedding it firmly in the nourishing earth.

When we look, in terms of this developmental sequence, at the life-history of the schizophrenic, we find that many writers– including Reichard and Tillman (1950), Lidz and Lidz (1952), and Limentani (1956) to mention but a few–point to the existence of a symbiotic relatedness between the patient and his mother as being the most fundamental cause of his later schizophrenia. But Benedek (1949, 1952a, 1952b, 1957) has stressed that a symbiotic relationship between infant and mother is *necessary* to the healthy development of the infant, as well as to the maturation of the mother herself. Mahler (1952) has found, in work with schizophrenic children, that the most deeply ill are those in whose relationship with their mother a symbiotic relatedness never became established; and my work with adult schizophrenics of various degrees of illness (1959) supports her observations.

What *is* pathological in this connexion, in the schizophrenic's life-history, is, as Mahler (1952) has stated, the circumstance that this symbiotic relatedness never became established, or became established but was not resolved in the normal way in early childhood.

Since the most significant traumata in the schizophrenic's life-history are generally conceded to be very early ones, I shall dwell upon the pathological circumstances obtaining in infancy and early childhood, and shall discuss further the relationship with the mother, before widening my focus to include aetiological factors in the family as a whole and, finally, in the over-all culture.

The mother is typically a deeply anxious, precariously integrated person whose chronic anxiety is probably intensified in her dealings with her young infant by reason of the symbiotic relatedness–with its concomitants of mutual incorporation

(Searles, 1951) and poor definition of ego-boundaries—which the infant needs, and therefore strives to establish with her. Thus, in the relationship with the infant her own personality disorganization is probably even greater than usual. One particularly poorly organized, changeable mother was described by her non-schizophrenic eldest son as typically coming home from the Baptist church on Sunday morning in a beatific state of religious exaltation, and the next moment furiously throwing a kitchen pot at one of the children. Her schizophrenic daughter insisted for years, in her therapy with me, that she had had not one but many mothers, and once explained to me, 'Whenever you use the word "mother", I see a whole parade of women, each one representing a different point of view.'[2]

It is not surprising that some of these precariously integrated mothers shy away from entering into the necessary symbiosis with their young infants. And to the extent that they do enter into it, the infant's needs tend to be subordinated, as Hill (1955) has beautifully described, to the personality-needs of the mother. This has been considered by Bateson et al. (1956) as being a matter of the mother's hatefully holding the growing child fast in this symbiosis, through 'double-bind' injunctions, such that he feels damned if he does, and damned if he doesn't, say or do this or that. But my own work (chapter 7) has shown that an even more powerful reason for the continuance of the symbiosis into the offspring's chronological adulthood resides in his basically loving and loyal sacrifice of his own individuality in order to preserve the mother's unstable personality equilibrium. He senses that his own sick personality functioning dovetails with hers in such a way as to keep her head above water.

Particularly does the child bear the brunt of the mother's various massive dissociations, and from our own experience in therapy we know how alone and anxious it makes us feel to be aware of powerful emotions in the other person of which he himself is unaware. It took me several years to realize that, for example, the rape which schizophrenic women fear is, above all, rape by the mother who unconsciously fantasies herself as possessing a penis—a fantasied penis, that is, which is dissociated in the mother herself.

The mother, being a far from whole person, because of the

· [2] Described on p. 306 also.

dissociation of large elements of her personality, is unable to respond to the growing child as being a whole and separate individual. Thus we find her focusing unduly much upon certain anatomical parts or personality attributes of her child, and blotting others out of her awareness – all of which greatly interferes with his developing a conception of himself as being a whole person. Hence, the adult schizophrenic patient may view himself, as one of my patients put it, as being 'a conglomeration of things'. Storch (1924) reports that one of his patients described himself similarly as being a 'conglomeration'.

The child's personality fragmentation may be heightened, further, as a defence against the inordinately strong incorporative needs of the mothering person, whether this latter be the mother, the father, a nursemaid, or whoever. One patient for example felt for years in childhood as though the top of his head were gone. This incompleteness of body-image was eventually found, in psychotherapy, to be in part a reaction to the invasive curiosity of his nursemaid. It was as though the only sure way to keep her from reading his mind were for much of his psychological life to be barred even from his own awareness, and this, translated into corporeal terms, gave him to feel that the cranial area of his head was missing.

In broadening my focus to include the family as a whole, let me stress that the normal infant, and the schizophrenic-to-be child, is not able to differentiate himself fully from his environment, either from other human beings or from the inanimate objects in it (Searles, 1959). Thus we can understand how fragmenting it is to his developing personality for him to have, as often happens, a bewildering succession of mothering figures or many changes in residence, or for him to be exposed to intrafamilial relationships or marked dissension. He cannot incorporate usefully the personality ingredients of two parents whose interpersonal relationship with one another is a very poorly integrated one – parents who seem (in some instances when one interviews both together) to function almost without any co-ordination at all, even an antagonistic one. Thus, at an intrapsychic level in the child, introjections from the mother cannot be well integrated with introjections from the father.

Further, as has been described by Wynne and his colleagues (1958), the actually great intrafamilial antagonisms are, by a kind of unspoken mutual pact, denied in the family, and a front of family oneness presented.

The paper by Wynne and his co-workers details, in an illuminating fashion, some of the means by which this family 'pseudo-mutuality' thwarts the child's differentiation—differentiation either of his personal identity or of his view of the world around him. In my experience, some of the families of schizophrenics make as great a fetish, by contrast, of what one might call pseudo-*non*-mutuality; Dr Joseph D. Lichtenberg emphasized this aspect of the matter on hearing a preliminary draft of this paper.

One of my patients, for example, came eventually to tell me proudly of 'those crazy Randalls' (her parental family), and seemed to share in a general family pride concerning the chaotic discord which overtly permeated the family, and which overlay a very deep sense of family *coherence* that, in my patient at least, had been deeply repressed at the beginning of her psychotherapy.

It may well be that the kind of family background which I detail above, and which is described in other respects by Wynne *et al.*, is especially true for those patients in whom non-differentiation is the great problem; for those who show personality fragmentation as the predominant problem, as did the woman just mentioned, this opposite kind of family mores may be more typical.

It should be noted that this tends to blur the real individual differences of the members of the family, such that the child does not find, presented to him in the family, real acknowledged individuals with whom to identify. He grows up instead thinking of himself as simply a part of the supposed wholeness of the unitary family, undifferentiated from it. He grows up assuming that it would be unpardonable disloyalty, and lack of love for 'the family', to differentiate himself from it. In such a family, the meaningful one-to-one interaction which any growing child needs with others in the family cannot flourish and be acknowledged as such, for this is again tantamount to the two individuals' mutual disloyalty to 'the family'. Thus such interaction, which lacks consensual validation, tends to be dissociated, like the existing dissensions in the family which the patient tends to introject. In the latter regard, one of my schizophrenic women patients once gave me to realize that, in the midst of a furious upbraiding of me, she was misidentifying herself as her mother, and me as the mother's son. She thus beautifully revealed her prior introjection of the conflict between her mother and her brother.

If we keep in mind that, in all this, the growing child's ego is not fully differentiated from the personalities of those around him, we see that he dare not experience his feelings of *loss* as such feelings tend to arise, for this would be, as R. A. Cohen has pointed out (in a personal communication), equivalent to loss of his own ego. Thus the pattern is set which is followed in later life, of pathological guarding against loss: the patient cannot relinquish interpersonal relationships which are incompatible with one another, cannot face the loss of any of these relationships, because he dare not face the threat to his personal identity which the attendant separation anxiety and grief would bring. Thus he moves, as he becomes adult, into a galaxy of interpersonal situations which are so incompatible among themselves that *anyone* trying to lead such a way of life *must* be schizophrenic. For example, part of his personality may be invested in a marriage, another part in an extra-marital relationship with another woman, another part in a 'friendship' with the other woman's husband; or he may try to have two fundamentally incompatible relationships with one person. For example, he may be involved with a woman co-worker in a romantic relationship which is quite fully compartmentalized from the co-worker relationship which the demands of their job require them to maintain.

What I am saying here applies especially to borderline patients. Among these persons too, one finds, not uncommonly, instances in which the patient is pulled apart, so to speak, by diverse career interests. He may be pursuing several quite different major career interests concomitantly, unable to relinquish any of them.

In the instances of more deeply ill schizophrenic patients, who are unable to form such contacts and career interests outside the family, we find, more frequently, that the patient is trying to develop and maintain fundamentally incompatible relatednesses with a family-member. This is most often, of course, with the mother or father, in whom he is trying to find, simultaneously, not only a parent but also a bosom friend, a spouse, a child, and so on. This latter kind of multifarious striving for diverse, basically incompatible kinds of relatedness is reproduced, in an intense form, in the transference-relationship to the therapist. Part of the therapist's function is now to help the patient to realize which of these strivings must be directed towards other objects; and to realize that *to a degree* these various strivings are *not* totally incompatible with one another–to realize that, at a feeling level though not in behavioural terms, loving relatedness means that each person is all persons and all things to the other.

These simplified examples illustrate what is really a much more complex pattern, in which one sees that the patient's ego is not merely *stretched* widely into diverse and mutually incompatible relationships, but that it functions as separate islands, and *must* function so in order for such a way of life to continue. And the 'relationships' to which I refer are not so much true interpersonal relationships as identifications with the other persons–investments of ego-identity in these diverse, mutually incompatible interpersonal situations, with a consequent lack of inner integrity, of continuity of identity and of the sense of being a whole person. Erikson (1956) has pointed out that normally this challenging task is met, and accomplished, in adolescence. He says that

> The final assembly of all the converging identity elements at the end of childhood (and the abandonment of the divergent ones) appears to be a formidable task. . . .
> . . . the adolescent, during the final stage of his identity formation, is apt to suffer more deeply than he ever did before (or ever will again) from a diffusion of roles. . . .

I have tried to show that the adolescent who goes on to become schizophrenic has had so little continuous relatively unanxious well-integrated interpersonal experience, that he has not now the strength to face the separation anxiety and grief entailed in the relinquishment of such incompatible (or as Erikson calls them 'divergent') identifications. He cannot make the necessary renunciations for his ego to become consolidated into a whole, well-integrated, undiffuse one. Another way of putting it is to say that he cannot therefore develop an integrated way of life.

To broaden our focus concerning aetiology to include finally pathogenic elements in the culture, we should note that a culture in which more than one-quarter of *all* hospital beds are occupied by schizophrenic patients[3] is a culture which presumably contains important schizophrenigenic elements, irrespective of the individual's particular family constellation. Fromm (1955) has described many such cultural elements in *The Sane Society*, which shows how various aspects of our technological culture foster in man a sense of alienation from himself, from his fellow man, and from the products of his work. Two of the consequences described by Fromm are what one might describe as man's inability to become subjectively differentiated as a human being, and his inability to feel a sense of deep participation in the wholeness of collective mankind. His existence is thus both fragmentary and poorly differentiated subjectively from the inanimate instruments and products of the technological culture which permeate his life.

Benedict (1938) has given a few extremely interesting examples, among many possible ones, of the ways in which our particular culture imposes psychological discontinuities upon the developing child and adolescent, discontinuities which many so-called primitive societies do not intrude upon him. She notes, for example, that whereas in our culture one is expected to be obedient and submissive in childhood, and rather abruptly become quite oppositely assertive and dominant on reaching adulthood, many cultures do not expect any such opposite behaviours at these different developmental phases. She notes, too, that many cultures do not require the marked shift in attitudes towards sexual behaviour which are required in our culture, as between the supposedly non-sexual boy or girl and the sexually competent man or woman. And by way of contrast to the attitudes towards productive work in our culture, where the individual is expected to contribute little in childhood and, suddenly, much upon reaching adulthood, she describes how the Cheyenne culture met this aspect of development:

> . . . The gravity of a Cheyenne Indian family ceremoniously making a feast out of the little boy's first snowbird is at the furthest remove from our behaviour. At birth the little boy was presented with

[3] This is based upon statistics collected in 1957, which show that slightly more than one out of every two hospital beds in the United States is occupied by a mentally ill patient, and that in New York State mental hospitals, for example, schizophrenics form about 57% of the patient population (National Committee against Mental Illness, 1957).

a toy bow, and from the time he could run about serviceable bows suited to his stature were specially made for him by the man of the family. Animals and birds were taught him in a graded series beginning with those most easily taken, and as he brought in his first of each species his family duly made a feast out of it, accepting his contribution as gravely as the buffalo his father brought. When he finally killed a buffalo, it was only the final step of his childhood conditioning, not a new adult role with which his childhood experience had been at variance.

Sociodynamics of the Hospital Ward

Turning from this brief discussion of the *aetiology* of the personality fragmentation and non-differentiation which are seen in schizophrenia, let us now look at the kind of group-relatedness which the patient fosters, by reason of these symptoms, on the hospital ward. Many writings have dealt with this, and I shall mention only a few notable ones. Stanton and Schwartz's papers (1949*a*, *b*, *c*) and their book *The Mental Hospital* (1954) describe how the patient's fragmentation increases on his exposure to hospital staff who are themselves involved in strongly felt, but not frankly expressed, differences of opinion concerning his management. Their writings understate the degree to which the patient's own personality-fragmenting anxiety fosters such dissension among staff members. An article by Perry and Shea (1957) makes up for this deficiency by showing the tremendously group-fragmenting effect upon the staff of one of the wards at the National Institutes of Health by an extraordinarily anxious and anxiety-provoking, personality-fragmented man. And Main (1957), reporting in a similar vein, has shown how surprisingly strong were the dissensions among veteran nursing staff concerning a number of such patients who had gone through stormy and therapeutically unsuccessful courses at his hospital in England.

Despite these and various other writings on this subject, however, there are a number of points which I have not found in the literature.

The kind of social situation which the ego-fragmented patient tends to foster on the ward can best be seen, I believe, as a process by which both differentiation and subsequent integration of the disparate ego-fragments must take place largely *externally* to himself, in the persons of those about him, before these processes can be taken into himself. Of interest in this connexion is Sullivan's (1947, p. 10) view, concerning normal personality development, that 'The self may be said to be made up of reflected appraisals', and Cooley's (1909) concept of the 'looking-glass self'. I shall explain this process first in terms of the process of *integration*, since it is only this process upon which, to the best of my knowledge, existing literature touches.

Such a deeply disturbed ward-integration as Stanton and Schwartz, Perry and Shea, Main, and others have described can be regarded as a kind of group symbiosis, comparable with the infant–mother symbiosis but now embracing a group of persons, including the patient and the various members of the staff and fellow-patients involved with him. We see in this group situation precisely the same elements which have been described by Bowen (1956), Wynne et al. (1958), myself (Chapter 1 above), and other writers as characterizing the symbiosis between the mother and the schizophrenic-to-be child. It is a mutual entanglement, intensely felt and deeply ambivalent, wherein the other person is sensed as indispensable to one's own existence. The conflictual needs of each of the participants keep the relationship in constant turmoil, and there is an over-all sense of maddening constriction.

In this group relatedness ego-boundaries are indistinct and the various participants function, as the anxiety in this group situation mounts, less in a truly interpersonal fashion than as a kind of unitary psychological organism. This may be crudely compared, in biology, to the human body in which the various different organs–brain, heart, liver, intestines, and so on–are indispensable to the maintenance of the over-all, unitary organism.

This means that the ward situation *looks*, at first glance, utterly unstable; but actually it represents a kind of social symbiosis which meets the neurotic, or psychotic, needs of the various participants well enough for it to endure for many weeks, or even months.

Looking at it from the vantage-point of the patient, each of the significant other persons in this group symbiosis represents not only a transference figure, but also an externalized fragment of his own ego. In this sense, the complex, previously unsorted-out, unintegrated fragments of his own self become painted on the canvas which the ward situation presents to him. Thus this situation, anxiety-provoking though it is to all concerned, is a necessary preliminary to his *intra*psychic differentiation and integration. Burnham (1956), in a valuable paper concerning misperception (misidentification) of other persons in schizophrenia, emphasizes that a patient's misperception of an aide (for example) as being a composite of figures from various areas of the patient's life, present and past, is a restitutive phenomenon—is indicative of his striving towards wholeness. Burnham likewise stresses the integrative aspects of a patient's misperceptions of the ward staff collectively. We see over and over in individual therapy that a patient becomes aware of a previously repressed fragment of his self only after seeing it first in a projected form, as being a part of the *therapist's* personality. This is the same process, occurring now in a group setting and with diverse projections operating simultaneously, from the patient to the diverse members of the staff.

The externalization goes on because the patient cannot as yet face the anxiety-laden realization that he has *within him* ego elements which are sharply conflictual. Instead, he unconsciously fosters, in the staff, diverse and conflictual views of himself. Instead of his becoming aware of the war within himself he fosters—largely unconsciously—the staff's warring with one another about him. To say that he is consciously 'playing them off', one against the other, is grossly to overestimate the degree of conscious control which he wields in the situation. It is more accurate to think of him as not yet being able to possess a whole ego within his own skin. His ego is only partial, a fragment, such that it is utterly necessary to him that others about him personify various of the other fragments; just as a heart must have lungs and a brain to go with it in order to survive. Parenthetically, we know that somewhat less ill individuals, whose fragmentation is such that they are only schizoid rather than frankly schizophrenic, feel it very important in some instances that their friends be friends also with one another. This can be seen as the schizoid person's need that the externalized fragments of his ego, which are projected upon these various friends, be a continuous ego rather than a split one.

From the staff's point of view also, this group symbiosis, anxious though it is, meets neurotic needs. For those who are in a 'Good Mother' position, or who personify 'good' aspects of the patient's ego, there are the gratifications of feeling oneself to be a warmer, more loving, better human being than one's co-workers. For those in the 'Bad Mother' position, who represent 'bad' ego-aspects of the patient, there is the opportunity to ventilate pent-up resentments towards one's fellows, resentments which may long antedate the patient's arrival on the ward scene. There is also the opportunity to feel murderous in a relatively free and unalloyed way towards almost everyone else in the situation (including the patient), without any irksome diluents of fondness, compassion, or comradeship. There is, I believe, a deep pleasure in our experiencing *any* feeling in a powerful and unconflictual way, and this social symbiosis is such as to minimize *intra*psychic conflict for all participants—such as to provide for the externalization of each one's potentially *inner* conflicts.

Each member of the staff tends to relate himself particularly to a single one among the fragmented patient's various disparate personality components—tends to see it as though this represented the totality of the patient. The nurse or attendant may assert that 'this is the way the patient *really* is', and feel that only she or he recognizes what the patient '*really* is like'. To the extent that they see the patient with this kind of tubular vision, we can surmise that such a relatedness is enabling this nurse to project upon the patient some unconscious emotion or unconscious self-image which would cause internal conflict if it were recognized as an ingredient of the staff member's own personality. And I do not mean, of course, that they are 'only projecting'. Freud (1922) long ago pointed out that we project upon that which offers us some reality-basis for the projection. But it is presumably such a projective process which causes the various staff members to have a personal stake in the group symbiosis which these patients powerfully tend to foster on the ward.

To return to the vantage point of the patient, we should realize that he needs the 'Bad Mothers' as much as he needs the 'Good Mothers', for the preservation of both 'good' *and* 'bad' objects allows for the preservation of both his loving and his hateful feelings; these feelings being wedded, as I have indicated, to the objects. Both these two broad categories of feeling are necessary to adult living. This simplified good-mother, bad-mother dichotomy is a fundamental step towards the infinite variation,

331

or differentiation, of perceived objects and felt emotions that characterizes adulthood. If the staff all realized this, there might be a lesser tendency for them–for those in the 'good' as well as those in the 'bad' roles–to become involved in guilt, which in most instances hopelessly complicates this social picture and turns what could have been a step towards the patient's growth into an unworkable ward situation which ends in therapeutic failure and undermining of staff morale.

In any case, to the degree that the staff personnel go on, week after week, in such oversimplified, stereotyped roles, participants in this social symbiosis, they inevitably feel increasingly constricted. The healthy side of them demands something more than this symbiotic functioning as a less than whole person. One wants to function as, and be recognized as, a whole individual, even though this entails one's facing one's inner conflicts. Even the 'Good Mothers' among them encounter increasing frustration within themselves in the face of their constricting social role, a role which forbids their having anything but love, solicitude, and protectiveness towards the patient. Thus there develops a great deal of frustration-rage and consequent murderous feeling among the personnel, not only towards one another but towards the major fly in their ointment–the patient. But this intense rage tends–except, perhaps, in those who occupy the extreme 'Bad Mother' positions–to be maintained largely under repression, as being too threatening to the social structure and to each participant's conception of himself.

I believe that some of the patient's increasingly destructive symptomatology represents in such a situation an acting out of the repressed destructiveness which he senses to be at work in the personnel about him, analogous to the acting out, described by Johnson and Szurek (1952), by the disturbed child who is giving vicarious expression to the mother's own repressed destructiveness. I believe that his typically mounting anxiety is to a degree based upon a realistic fear of the formidably great measure of murderousness which the other participants in the symbiosis come to feel towards him.

In the face of the increasingly intense conflictual feelings which permeate such a group symbiosis, regression deepens, not only in the patient's behaviour but in that of the staff members as well. Not only do his demands become more infantile, but the personnel's mothering, good and bad, tends to assume more and more primitive forms. Just as he tends to become a suckling, demanding infant at the breast, they tend almost literally to offer him a breast, 'good' or 'bad' as the case may be, rather than provide more adult forms of mothering. There is a nice illustration of this point, although concerning a not-yet-hospitalized patient, in one of Knight's (1953) articles on borderline psychosis. Here we see what I consider regression not only in the patient, who moves nearly into a literally sucking-at-the-breast role, but also in the therapist – a woman dean, who is a self-styled psychotherapist – who moves, concomitantly, nearly to the position of trying literally to give suck to the patient:

> . . . The dean was subject to increasingly demanding expressions of need from the student. Interviews could not be terminated, since the girl refused to leave, and sessions came to be held at the dean's home in the evening and on weekends.
>
> The student refused to see a psychiatrist or to go elsewhere for help, and the dean felt cornered. The girl demanded to use the dean's car as proof of her love and trust, and this was granted. Then she began to request that she be permitted to stay overnight in the dean's home, and when this was granted, that she sleep in the dean's bed with her. At times she expressed irrational hatred of the dean and pounded her with her fists. At other times she wanted to be held on the dean's lap and fondled, and this wish was granted also. No real limits to her regressive behaviour were set until she expressed a strong wish to suckle the dean's breasts. Here the dean drew the line . . .

In my experience, frequent and informal meetings of the various staff members who are involved in the care of these patients are of inestimable value, for at least three reasons. First, they provide an arena for catharsis of some of the powerful feelings which have been engendered, so that the emotions in the over-all social group I have described can be kept within manageable bounds of intensity, thus avoiding the total fragmentation of the group. Secondly, they help the various individual members to go on functioning *as* individuals in their work with the patient – as individuals who are relatively free to act upon their own particular feelings about the patient. Thus he is presented with genuine people of various kinds, with whom to identify constructively, rather than being faced with a staff group which is struggling to preserve some pseudo-harmony, some ostensible unanimity of attitudes towards him, in order to hide their sharply divergent true feelings about him. We see how similar this latter unconstructive ward situation is to the pseudo-unanimity so frequently found in the schizophrenic's family. Thirdly, these personnel meetings enable, again as part of the same process, a genuine collaborative integration to develop within the working group – an integration of different attitudes towards the patient. This is a process which, as I have previously indicated, must take place outside the patient before integration of his own diverse personality fragments can occur *within* him, through constructive introjection of the well-integrated staff group which is working with him.

At the beginning of this paper I described integration and differentiation as being opposite faces of a unitary process. It is useful, however, to conceive of schizophrenic patients as showing a disjointedness between these two phenomena.

This point has been touched upon by Hartmann (1939) in a paper on ego psychology: 'Precocity of differentiation or relative retardation of synthesis may disrupt the balance of these two functions.' And Hartmann, Kris, and Loewenstein (1946) noted that '. . . acceleration of certain integrative processes may become pathological'.

In the normal individual, integration and differentiation proceed simultaneously and in pace with each other as a relatively smoothly advancing unitary process of personality growth. But one can think of the kind of schizophrenic patient I have just described as showing an imbalance between these two part-processes; an imbalance wherein differentiation has temporarily outdistanced their integration, with consequent fragmentation of personality functioning, such as I have described. There is a resultant need for *integration* as the most pressing problem at the point in their development when we see them on the ward and in the therapeutic situation.

By contrast, there are other schizophrenic patients, still more deeply ill than those I have just discussed, whose emotions, attitudes, thinking-processes, and other personality aspects are not yet sufficiently *differentiated*, with the result that they are even more helpless than the former type of patients in discerning, sorting out, and communicating to others, the welter of undifferentiated thought and emotion which is within them.

Freeman *et al.* (1958), noting how relatively unvarying are their descriptions of the chronic schizophrenic patients whose therapy their book details, state, 'It is our contention that loss of individuality is a feature of the chronic patient in the refractory ward.' These are the patients who are unable to express their thoughts or feelings because they quite literally are unaware of–do not 'have'–thoughts and feelings, most of the time. One of them let me know that he felt himself to be in a 'mist'; another, when I taxed her with failing to report any thoughts or feelings and asserted that I could clearly see, from her rapidly changing facial expressions, that there was a great deal going on in her, explained, 'My face thinks, Dr Searles; but I don't think.' And these are the patients who, in their ward-life and in their psychotherapeutic sessions, are mute and motionless most of the time, and who show, at most, only stereotyped repetitive verbalizations or bodily movements. Finally, these are the patients towards whom the staff members tend to have a genuinely unanimous, stereotyped view–a view in which there is, in a sense, not *enough* of the kind of disharmony which is so overwhelmingly strong among these same staff members in reaction to the former type of patient. In other words, these patients tend to go on, month after month and year after year, in a social role on the ward which is as stereotyped, as un-rich and as unvarying as is, evidently, their subjective intrapsychic experience. Here the pressing need is for greater *differentiation* to occur.

For these patients it is well that they be exposed, over the months and years, to a relatively large procession of different staff members, even if this entails a rather rapid turnover of staff. In my experience, these patients are less likely to become further differentiated if they are taken care of by only the same few nurses and attendants, for such veteran personnel tend to stay in their rutlike, stereotyped view of the patient. More often, it is some newcomer who sees in the patient a bit of differentiation which is trying to sprout, so to speak–an additional personality facet emerging – and who therefore finds himself reacting to the patient in a way which is new and unstereotyped, thus bringing to the over-all staff attitude a welcome piece of differentiation. This is essential because just as for integration, the process must take place first externally to the patient, in the staff, before it can be established in the patient himself.

Often there is evidence that, all along, the 'new' potentiality in the patient has been evidencing itself but, being unnoticed by the staff, being therefore not interpersonally shared between any one of them and the patient, it has persisted as a dissociated aspect of his personality, for that which does not gain consensual validation from one's fellows tends to be dissociated from one's own awareness. For example, at Chestnut Lodge we have had for many years a hebephrenic middle-aged man who is quite generally regarded, by the staff, as good old 'Georgie'. The fact that good old, fawning, obsequious, doglike Georgie not infrequently evidences a loud, blood-curdlingly sadistic laugh seems simply not to be noticed by those who are most involved in his care. They apparently likewise dissociate the fact that his stereotyped 'How's everything, Lovey?' is at times said in a tone as if he were disembowelling the person whom he is greeting. If a new attendant were to take full note of this sadistic, hostile side of good old Georgie, and persistently relate himself to that personality aspect, I have no doubt that the staff as a whole would grow to have a more differentiated reaction to the patient, and this presently dissociated sadism would eventually emerge, bit by bit, into his own awareness. The result would be that he would be a more differentiated (and, at the same time, better integrated) personality, both subjectively and as viewed in the ward social setting.

Not long ago, as part of my supervisory work here, I sat in for a half-hour with a therapist, his female schizophrenic patient and the patient's husband and mother. The therapist and the patient had been meeting thus with these two relatives of hers (who were here on an extended visit) for several sessions, and I had heard from the therapist a lengthy description of how these meetings had been going. At the beginning of the session in which I participated, I was immediately struck with the patient's frequent rubbing of her genital area. This was a blatantly obvious act, and was done in a manner indicative of both sexual excitement and anxiety. I soon asked her about this and, with evident relief, she described the embarrassment this uncontrollable, repetitious act had long been causing her. After the session I learned from the therapist that this stereotyped act had characterized her behaviour in each of the preceding sessions, but he had omitted any mention of it in his lengthy description

336

of these group interviews. Until I began asking the patient about this, she and her relatives, as well as the therapist, had been functioning as though there were a silent, unanimous, pact whereby the group's abundant verbalizations would never refer to this particular behaviour of hers.

For ward staff as well as for the therapist, the highest order of skill consists, in this connexion, in the *timing* of the relating of oneself to the patient's dissociated process; in sensing *at what point* the patient is ready now to face this aspect of himself, or more accurately, in sensing at what point one's relationship with the patient is strong enough to warrant a mutual coming to grips with the dissociated material. Prior to such a time, it may be the ward staff's or the therapist's unconscious intuition which causes one not to take notice of the dissociated processes in the patient; an intuition which tells one that it would be premature as yet, to try to integrate these into one's relationship with him. But in my experience, errors are as often made on the side of postponing this intervention too long, or of never accomplishing it, as on the side of burdening the patient by a premature response to processes of which he is unaware in himself.

It is often the therapist who sees a new potentiality in the patient, a previously unnoted side of him which heralds a phase of increasing differentiation. And frequently the therapist is the only one who sees it. Even the patient does not see it as yet, except in a projected form, so that he perceives this as an attribute of the therapist. This situation can make the therapist feel very much alone and intensely threatened.

I have worked for several years with a hebephrenic man whom the staff had come to view, unanimously, as being a kind of pitiable, charming little boy, endearing with his flashes of robin-like gaiety. He was regarded as basically hopeless because he had been hospitalized constantly, in a series of institutions, for sixteen years, was now in his mid-forties, and in nine years at Chestnut Lodge had shown relatively little change in the social position I have described. But as my work with him progressed, I began to have glimpses of murderousness—of precariously controlled violence—in him. The charge nurse and others of the ward staff did not see this, and the charge nurse even went so far, in her resentment of my jaundiced view of this robin, as to declare that if the patient ever did become assaultive, he would merely

337

be acting out his therapist's own violence. This placed me in the position of not only being alone in my opinion, but in addition being held totally responsible for the patient's potential violence. And I would have looked in vain to the patient himself for any reassurance on this score, for he was meanwhile misidentifying me, in an acutely threatened fashion, as being 'Pretty Boy Floyd' (a boyish-faced gangster of the 1920's).

On the way to an informal staff conference concerning this situation, I fell downstairs and smashed my head into a wall with a much greater jolt that I ever received in four years of high-school football. It was such a jolt, in fact, that later in the day I obtained skull X-rays and a neurological examination which proved–I must for some reason add–to be negative. In any case I managed to go on to the conference, feeling marked indeed as a violent man by the ward personnel who had witnessed this fall. But the conference, consisting predominantly in the expression of intensely antagonistic feelings between the charge nurse and myself, each documenting our stand with details from our respective work with this patient, proved to be the breaking up of what had been a long-frozen ward-attitude towards him, and I lived to see the happy day when the charge nurse herself became frightened at seeing his murderous side.

What I have just described touches upon the subject of the therapeutic relationship itself, and the severe stresses which the phenomena of schizophrenic disintegration and non-differentiation place upon both therapist and patient.

The Patient-Therapist Relationship

Focusing now upon the transference relationship with the therapist, we find that the patient naturally brings into this relationship, just as he brings into the group-relatedness on the ward, the difficulties concerning differentiation and integration which were engendered by the pathological upbringing I have described. And, as in the ward situation, we find that here too, advances in differentiation and integration necessarily occur first outside the patient–namely, in the *therapist's* increasingly well-differentiated and well-integrated view of, and consequently, response to, him–before these can become well established within him.

Because the schizophrenic patient did not experience, in his infancy, the establishment of, and later emergence from, a healthy symbiotic relatedness with his mother such as each human being needs for the formation of a healthy core in his personality structure, in the evolution of the transference relationship to his therapist he must eventually succeed in establishing such a mode of relatedness. In Chapter 7 above, and in my book *The Nonhuman Environment*, I have described a few of the many clinical experiences which convinced me of this point.

This means that he must eventually regress, in the transference, to such a level in order to get a fresh start towards a healthier personality differentiation and integration than he had achieved before entering therapy. This is not to say that he must act out the regressive needs in his daily life. To be sure, the schizophrenic patient, whether in therapy or not, inevitably does so to a considerable degree; but to the extent that these needs can be expressed in the transference relationship, they need not seek expression, unconsciously, through acting out in daily life.

This symbiotic mode of relatedness is necessarily mutual, participated in by therapist as well as patient. Thus the therapist must come to experience not only the oceanic gratification, but also the anxiety involved in his sharing a symbiotic, subjective oneness with the schizophrenic patient. This relatedness, with its lack of felt ego-boundaries between the two participants, at times involves the kind of deep contentment, the kind of felt communion that needs no words, which characterizes a loving relatedness between mother and infant. But at other times it involves the therapist's feeling unable to experience himself as differentiated from the pathology-ridden personality of the patient. He feels helplessly caught in the patient's deep ambivalence. He feels at one with the patient's hatred and despair and thwarted love, and at times he cannot differentiate between his own subjectively harmful effect upon the patient, and the illness with which the patient was afflicted when he, the therapist, first undertook to help him. Thus, at these anxiety-ridden moments in the symbiotic phase, the therapist feels his own personality to be invaded by the patient's pathology, and feels his identity severely threatened, whereas in the more contented moments, part of the contentment resides in both participants enjoying a freedom from any concern with identity. In the latter connexion

339

I recall a contented silence in which a schizophrenic woman and I, lounging in adjacent chairs, were listening to the borborygmal rumblings in our abdomens. At one point, hearing some rumbling, she giggled and said she couldn't tell whether this came from her own 'stomach' or from mine, or from the first floor of the building, below. I wasn't sure either; but, above all, it didn't matter.

This same profound lack of differentiation may come to characterize also the patient's view of the persons about him, including his therapist; and at times, in line with his need to project a poorly differentiated conglomeration of 'bad' impulses, he may perceive the therapist as being but one head of a hydra-headed monster. The patient's lack of differentiation in this regard, prevailing for month after month of his charging the therapist with saying or doing various things which were actually said or done by others amongst the hospital staff, or by the family members, can have a formidably eroding effect upon the therapist's sense of personal identity. But the patient may need to regress to just such a primitive, poorly differentiated view of the world in order to grow up again, psychologically, in a more healthy way this time.

Among the most significant steps in the maturation which occurs in successful psychotherapy are those moments when the therapist suddenly sees the patient in a new light. His image of the patient suddenly changes, because of the entry into his awareness of some potentiality in the patient which had not shown itself before. From now on, his response to the patient is a response to this new, enriched view, and through such responding he fosters the emergence, and further differentiation, of this new personality area. This is another way of describing the process which Buber (in Friedman, 1955) calls 'making the other person present': seeing in the other person potentialities of which even he is not aware, and helping him, by responding to those potentialities, to realize them.

In my experience, schizophrenic patients' feelings start to become differentiated before they have found new and appropriate modes for expressing the new feelings. Thus a patient may use the same old stereotyped behaviour or utterance to express nuances of new feeling. This is identical with the situation in those schizophrenics' families which are permeated with what

340

Wynne *et al.* (1958) term 'pseudo-mutuality': 'In pseudo-mutuality emotional investment is directed more toward maintaining the *sense* of reciprocal fulfilment of expectations than toward accurately perceiving changing expectations. Thus, the new expectations are left unexplored, and the old expectations and roles, even though outgrown and inappropriate in one sense, continue to serve as the structure for the relation.'

The therapist, through hearing the new emotional connotation, the new meaning, in the stereotyped utterance and responding in accordance with the new connotation, fosters the emerging differentiation. Over the course of months, in therapy, he may find the same verbal stereotype employed in the expression of a whole gamut of newly emerged feelings. Thus, over a prolonged time-span, the therapist may give as many different responses to the gradually differentiating patient as are simultaneously given by the various members of the ward-staff to the patient who shows the contrasting ego-fragmentation (or, in a loose manner of speaking, over-differentiation) I have described earlier in this paper.

Persistently stereotyped communications from the patient tend to bring from the therapist communications which, over a long period of time, become almost equally stereotyped. One can sometimes detect, in recordings played during supervisory hours, evidence that new emotional connotations are creeping into the patient's verbal stereotypes, and into the therapist's responsive verbal stereotypes, before *either* of the two participants has noticed this.

What the therapist does which assists the patient's differentiation often consists in his having the courage and honesty to *differ* from either the patient's expressed feelings or, often most valuably, with the social role into which his sick behaviour tends to fix (transfix might be a more apt word) the therapist. This may consist in his candid disagreement with some of the patient's strongly felt and long-voiced views, or in his flatly declining to try to feel 'sympathy'–such as one would be conventionally expected to feel–in response to behaviour which seems, at first glance, to express the most pitiable suffering but which the therapist is convinced primarily expresses sadism on the patient's part. Such courage to differ with the expected social role is what is needed from the therapist, in order to bring to a close the symbiotic phase of relatedness which has served, earlier, a necessary and productive function. Through asserting his individuality here and at many later moments in the therapeutic interaction, the therapist fosters the patient's own development of more complete and durable ego-boundaries. At the same time he offers the patient the opportunity to identify with a parent-figure who dares to be an individual–dares to be so in the face of pressures which are at times great; pressures from the working group of which he is a part, and from his own reproachful super-ego. What I am describing here is, of course, to only a minor degree a consciously planned and controlled therapeutic 'technique'. It is rather a natural flow of events in the trans-ference evolution, with which the therapist must have the spontaneity to go along.

Now let us see what happens in the relationship between a therapist and a patient who is at the other end of the scale: one who is severely and overtly fragmented in his functioning, and whose urgent need at the moment is not for further differentia-tion, but for integration. Incidentally, we are dealing here not with two discretely different 'types' of patient but, perhaps more accurately, with markedly different phases of personality de-velopment. We find that a single patient can show, over the course of time, each of these two extremes–on the one hand stereotypy with a need for differentiation, and on the other fragmentation with a need for integration.

In the instance of the severely and openly fragmented patient, we find that this fragmentation places severe stress upon the therapist, fostering a sense of fragmentation in him as well. The therapist not only finds that, as one fragment of the patient's personality unpredictably replaces another quite different frag-ment on the scene of the therapeutic session, he, the therapist, finds his own responsive feelings as suddenly switching from, say, fury to compassion, or sexual titillation to loathing, or what not. A patient who suddenly, while in the midst of delicately sensuous comments about the silken draperies in the room, switches to expressions of murderous feeling, or a patient who pauses in the midst of a savage paranoid castigating of the therapist to ask him, in a calm, friendly, matter of fact way, for a light for her cigarette, tends to make the therapist feel tossed between suddenly chang-ing, intense affects within himself. And, worst of all, he sometimes finds himself having strong and utterly contrasting feelings towards the patient simultaneously. He may, for example, find himself reacting to her as being, simultaneously, a murderous woman and an appealing little child. The therapist's capacity to endure such a barrage of fragmentation-fostering experiences, from both without and within, is essential in his helping the patient to become better integrated through identification with the therapist whose personal integration can survive this onslaught.

Wexler (1952) and Hoedemaker (1955) have stressed the therapeutic value, in other connexions, of the schizophrenic patient's identifying with the therapist. I find that this holds also with regard to the integration of the previously disparate areas of his personality. I have regularly found that my own achievement of an integrated view of the patient, towards whom I have previously been responding upon two or more quite distinct and conflictual levels, is a prelude to the patient's own improved integration. It seems that the therapist needs to integrate, for example, his view of the patient as a murderous woman, with his view of the patient as an appealing child, and must respond to the patient as a unitary person who possesses both these different personality-facets, before the patient can subjectively integrate these different, heretofore more or less dissociated areas into her conception of her self.

Processes in the patient's personality which exist in a dissociated state are maintained out of awareness, basically for the reason that the affects contained in them are so intense, so conflictual, and so opposed to those prevailing in the conscious ego. Early in the therapeutic relationship the therapist, even though able to discern in general terms the type or types of affects which are being expressed in the patient's dissociated behaviour or dissociated verbalizations, usually feels these dissociated personality components to be strange, alien, and bizarre. He does not yet find himself reacting to them with any fullness of personal response, for they are too much to one side of that interpersonal relationship which he shares with the more conscious areas of the patient's personality. But as the therapeutic relationship progresses and expands, this dissociated material gradually becomes turned towards the therapist, and he finds himself having, in response to it, feelings which grow concomitantly extremely intense. His freedom to express such personal responses–whether they be in the nature of fury, contempt, tenderness, erotic feelings (these last being no more than frankly acknowledged by him, when the patient shows a need for such corroboration), is of inestimable value in helping to integrate the erstwhile dissociated components of the patient's personality.

Such integration has to take place first, or at any rate concomitantly, on an interpersonal level–namely, in the give-and-take of the therapeutic relationship–to the tune of intensely felt mutual expressions of affect, in order that the patient may become free from the dissociative compartmentalization, and become thus a more whole person. In this process, what was sensed by the therapist as alien and bizarre in the patient must come to be eventually 'taken personally' by the therapist. It must come to have the meaning of a complex of very personal communications before it can lose its alienness, its dissociated nature, for the patient as well.

Paradoxically, the experienced therapist can thus predict, on starting work with a patient, that the more queer, strange, alien, animal-like or otherwise not quite human the patient appears, the more deeply will the therapist's own most personal feelings eventually be plumbed in the course of successful therapy with the patient. He can predict that he himself will experience fury of an intensity he has experienced rarely if ever before within memory, fondness of a purity he has never felt perhaps since early childhood, compassion of a depth of which he had thought himself incapable. But he can predict, by the same token, that if the treatment is successful, he himself will emerge from it with a deepened regard for human beings and with an increased integration, in the phrase of Whitaker and Malone (1953), of his own 'multiple selves'.

To return to the kind of stress which he must endure along the way, we find that in some instances the patient's personality fragmentation is so deep that even his body image is fragmented, and his view of the world regressed to a level at which other persons are viewed not as complete physical beings but as separate anatomical parts. Klein (1946) and Scott (1955) have postulated that the very young infant presumably views the mother in this way. The therapist, in this phase of the therapy, may find it so anxiety-provoking to find the patient expressing a conviction that his (the therapist's) head or hand, for example, is not his own, that he may resort to the somewhat relieving conviction that the patient is merely being hostile, rather than facing the anxiety-provoking fact that the patient is genuinely operating at so early a level of personality development that even the patient's image of his own body, and of the bodies of other persons including the therapist, is not yet fully formed and integrated.

Further, in the transference, the patient persistently relates to the therapist as being a parent who has many dissociated components of personality, with the result that the therapist, in the face of the patient's persistently and convincedly relating to him thus, tends naturally to function accordingly, to a degree not usual for him in his general relationships with people. M. B. Cohen (1952) has made the valuable point that we inevitably respond to any patient's transference with functioning which, to a degree, is complementary to that transference. In the kind of situation which I am describing, the therapist tends naturally, in response to the patient's special kind of transference, to dissociate rage (for instance) which, in other kinds of transference relationships with other patients, he might relatively easily admit into his own awareness. For example, to put it crudely but not inaccurately, if the patient reacts persistently and vigorously and long enough to the therapist as being a mother who has intense but dissociated murderousness, the therapist will in all probability come, one day, to find himself frightened at seeing how powerful are the murderous feelings which have grown up in him towards the patient.

Coleman (1956) and Coleman and Nelson (1957) have described a psychotherapeutic technique, which the former has employed with borderline patients, termed 'externalization of the toxic introject'. This technique consists in the therapist's deliberate impersonation of–conscious and calculated assumption of the role of–a traumatic parent, or other figure from the patient's early years, the long-standing introjection of whom comprised a 'toxic introject', the core of the borderline schizophrenic illness. The authors' psychodynamic formulations are of much interest, and highly relevant to what I have said above.

The great difference between Coleman and myself, however,

is that in my experience the therapist does not express, in such situations, affects which are merely a kind of play-acting, deliberately assumed and employed as a technical manœuvre indicated at the moment. Rather, in my experience, the affects are genuine, spontaneous, and at times almost overwhelmingly intense. This differing experience can presumably be accounted for, in part, by the circumstance that whereas Coleman was dealing with borderline cases, I have been dealing with frankly schizophrenic patients. With the latter kind of patient, because his affects are so extremely intense and his ego-boundaries so very incomplete, his therapist's own feelings become more deeply and fully involved. I have discussed this subject at greater length in chapter 6 above, and in *The Nonhuman Environment*.

Both patient and therapist, in working towards the integration of the former's disparate personality components (and, as Whitaker and Malone, 1953, have pointed out, this is a mutual process, involving the therapist's own personality integration), have an inescapable resistance to overcome. Increasing integration involves, for both of them, loss. The integration of heretofore separate personality fragments inevitably alters them—they lose, in the process, their pure-culture, pristine quality upon becoming adulterated, as it were, with other areas of the personality. And correspondingly one's own responsive reactions to them lose in purity.

I think for example of a woman who was, at the beginning of our work some years ago, extremely unintegrated in her personality functioning. She behaved from one session to the next, and often from one moment to the next, like a whole galaxy of utterly different persons. She has become, over the years, partly by dint of much hard work on the part of both of us, much better integrated. Life for her now involves more continuity, less anxiety, more genuine happiness; and I feel vastly more comfortable in the hours with her. But we have lost much, too. Just how much, I tend to forget until I look back through my old notes concerning our work. The beer-hall bouncer I used to know is no more. The captured American pilot, held prisoner by the Germans but striding proudly several paces ahead of the despised prison-camp guard, is no more. The frightening lioness has gone from her den. The incarnation of paranoid hatred, spewing hostility at the whole world, has mellowed into someone unrecognizably

346

different. The endearing little girl can no longer hide the adult woman who is now part of her. The fresh-faced girl of sixteen or so has come and gone—one sees her to a degree, of course, but alloyed now with other qualities. No more is there someone who tells me that I am a murderous woman who has killed my husband and am now about to kill my patient also. No longer is there someone, so far as I know, who thinks that I am a machine, sent to her room to destroy her. No one now perceives me as being, not a living person, but a pile of corpses, and so on. It is as though a whole gallery of portraits, some of them beautiful and some of them horrible, but all of them free from diluting imperfections, have been sacrificed in the formation of the single, far more complex and many-sided portrait, the relatively well-integrated person who now exists.

What I have been saying ties in with Rosenfeld's (1950) comment that schizophrenic confusion involves an anxiety lest the destructive impulses and objects destroy the libidinal impulses and objects, and my (chapter 1 above) comment that the schizophrenic is equally afraid that the hostile side of his ambivalent feelings will be destroyed by the positive (libidinal) side.

Of interest in this connexion is a comment by Hartmann, Kris and Loewenstein (1949) regarding the normal infant:

'We start from the assumption of the existence of an undifferentiated phase of psychic structure. During this phase manifestations of both libido and aggression are frequently indistinguishable or difficult to distinguish.' Presumably the schizophrenic adult's fear lest he lose either his loving or his hateful feelings (or both) is based in *part* upon the threat of regression to such an undifferentiated phase.

The above discussion is a result of my discovering that, here again, the schizophrenic's—and the therapist's—anxiety is well founded. Something is indeed destroyed, and must be destroyed, in the process of mutual integration which takes place in the therapy. In the instance of the woman of whom I wrote above, for example, I can no longer love her and be charmed by her in quite the way I formerly could, *nor* can I hate, loathe, and fear her with quite the intensity and 'purity' which used to be not only possible, but necessary, in the progress of the therapeutic relationship. My capacity to love, hate, and so forth, in those wave-lengths is not really destroyed, but it may be a long time, if ever, before I find in my life occasions which call forth such emotions. In so far as the therapy has been successful, it has in effect, for all practical purposes, destroyed them. And though she on occasion tries to recapture, for example, her old venom, it comes out only weakly now, like a nostalgic echo. (When Wexler (1951) wrote, '. . . I have been through two years of hell-fire and heaven with a schizophrenic patient . . .', he was feeling, I surmise, a sense not only of triumph but also of nostalgia.)

What we have gained more than makes up, of course, for such losses; otherwise her integration could not have progressed so far. She now has feelings—in the realm of both healthy anger and of deep and mature fondness—and complexities of feeling of which she was clearly incapable at the outset of our work, and the relationship between us has likewise become emotionally enriched. I have discussed at some length the losses which were involved in this over-all gain, because I have seen, not only in my own work but in that of fellow-therapists, how often the patient's and therapist's mutual, unconscious *denial* of this element of loss causes an undue prolongation of the disintegrated state.

As regards the patient's advancing differentiation too, there is a similarly great resistance in both participants. Diligently though both are working towards the delineation of ego-boundaries in the relationship, so that the patient may become subjectively differentiated as a truly individual human being, both he and the therapist must endure a genuine and deep sense of loss in the process of this accomplishment. Both must relinquish, as I have described in chapter 7, the sense of oceanic contentment, felt omnipotence, and mother-infant adoration which are ingredients of the symbiotic relatedness.[4]

[4] My interest in the subject of differentiation has been fostered, in part, by stimulating remarks which I have heard in recent years from Drs Robert A. Cohen, David M. Rioch, and Otto A. Will.

Chapter 12

THE EVOLUTION OF THE MOTHER TRANSFERENCE IN PSYCHOTHERAPY WITH THE SCHIZOPHRENIC PATIENT (1961)[1]

I N chapter 7 I presented a hypothesis that deeply denied positive feelings are the most powerful determinants of the relationship between the schizophrenic and his mother, and of the development and maintenance of the patient's illness. To condense that extensive theoretical discussion, I described the mother's poorly integrated personality structure, her fear of her own love for the child, her low self-esteem, and her transference to him of a welter of feelings, consisting basically in thwarted love, from her own childhood relationship with her mother. I traced the consequent frustration of her child's–the patient's–need to give love openly to his mother, and his expressing this love in a therefore disguised, but none the less wholehearted, fashion. He sacrifices his potential individuality in a dedicated effort to preserve her precarious integration, through introjecting the dissociated components of her personality, components which become distortedly personified, and in a sense crystallized, in the schizophrenic illness.

The mutual love in the mother-patient relationship is early subjected to so rigorous and unconscious a denial in each participant that its presence is difficult or impossible to discern through history-taking from either of them; nor is it easy to detect in their interaction with one another. I became aware of the presence, and striking intensity, of this love only in the evolution of patients' mother transference to me in the course of intensive psychotherapy conducted in each case over a period of several years.

This present chapter is intended, first, to take advantage of the

---

[1] First published in *Psychotherapy of the Psychoses*, edited by Arthur Burton. (New York: Basic Books, 1961.)

opportunity to present two more case descriptions, buttressing the earlier paper's single case, in support of that hypothesis, which I regard as the most important insight I have reached in ten years of work with schizophrenic patients, and which stands, as the earlier paper showed, in marked contrast to a voluminous literature on the relationship between the schizophrenic patient and his mother.

Second, these two case descriptions will serve to underline a number of theoretical and technical points concerning the dynamics and therapy of schizophrenia. Third, they will demonstrate the marked involvement of the therapist's personal feelings, which I regard as an essential component of the recovery process and which, despite the guilt and anxiety of younger therapists on this score, is *relatively* infrequently based preponderantly on countertransference in the classical sense. I by no means wish to imply that the therapist can dispense with personal analysis; on the contrary, the degree of feeling involvement required by this work necessitates, in my opinion, that his own analysis be at least well under way before he undertakes intensive psychotherapy with patients of this degree of illness.

These case descriptions are not intended to do justice to the multiplicity of factors which go into the development, maintenance, and resolution of schizophrenic illness. They trace but one theme among many which are of significance and which would have to be included in any comprehensive report of my total experience with either of these patients. For example, I do not attempt to show fully, in either case, the importance of the father transference (although this will be touched on, more than passingly, in the second); I omit data concerning transference from other early-life figures; and I shall make only a few remarks, at the end of the paper, concerning the *new* interpersonal experience which the therapist brings to the patient, experience which must be of great significance, otherwise the transference could not evolve as I shall describe, and eventually be resolved.

The First Case

A 27-year-old woman, the mother of two children, had been overtly ill with paranoid schizophrenia for at least five years at the time I undertook intensive psychotherapy with her. There was much evidence that she had suffered from latent schizophrenia since about 8 or 9 years of age. At 24 she had finally been hospitalized in a nationally famous institution near her home, but over the course of a year there failed to show even symptomatic improvement, despite psychotherapy, sixty-five insulin coma treatments, and twenty-five to fifty electro-shock treatments. She was then transferred to Chestnut Lodge where another therapist on the staff began intensive psychotherapy with her. But he discontinued working with her after fifteen months, discouraged by her adamant opposition to treatment and by the steadily mushrooming, rather than lessening, development of her paranoid delusional system.

At the beginning of my work with her, I found her verbalizing a luxuriantly delusional experience of her life, both past and present, as being saturated with external malevolence. She was genuinely unable, evidently, to recall any experiences of fondness with anyone at any time in her life, and she spent the great bulk of each therapeutic session in paranoid tirades directed towards everyone around her—but, increasingly as time went on, focusing more determinedly upon myself—as being the same malevolent figures who had surrounded her all her life. She incessantly poured out accusations that we were raping her, performing surgical operations on her for various weird purposes, extorting money from her, and maddeningly frustrating her own efforts. She repeatedly vowed murderous revenge; she subjected me to verbal abuse of truly battering intensity; and, as the months went by and she became increasingly sure that I was the malevolent mother who was primarily responsible for the whole venomous 'master plan', her aggressiveness had to be met very firmly to dissuade her from physical attacks upon me and other persons. This was her predominant mode of functioning for about the first eight months of our work, and it remained the more or less persistent matrix of the therapeutic interaction for more than two years after that, long after the favourable changes which I shall describe had begun their development.

I acquired from her during those initial eight months, as well as from the history given to us by her youngest sister, a picture of her relationship with her mother as having contained nothing but hostility, fear, and rejection. The sister had told the admitting physician, with considerable shame, that up until the patient's late teens the mother had beaten her so brutally that it sometimes made the sister nauseated to hear the blows. A younger brother informed us that the mother had 'loved to dominate' the patient.

The patient repeatedly described in her therapeutic sessions her mother's having many times punished her by beating her or by locking her in a closet, and having incessantly blamed her for myriad occurrences, telling her harshly, 'You're evil!' or 'You're crazy!' Whenever the daughter was physically ill, she was given to feel that the illness was a sign of her own sinfulness. Whenever she revealed some of her own confused thoughts, in a search for clarifying information, she was turned away, by others in the family as well as by the mother, with an abrupt 'You're crazy!' Innumerable times in her presence her mother would say to one or another member of the family, 'She's hopeless—she'll never make it!'; and the patient tried desperately, but always unsuccessfully, to find out from the mother what it was that she, the daughter, was supposed to try to carry out. Whenever she was taken to a movie by the mother, she would be told at the beginning of the picture, 'Now, *think!*' and would then feel herself to be a hopeless failure for not succeeding in perceiving in the picture the same hidden meaning which the mother, who evidently suffered from at least a latent schizophrenia throughout the girl's childhood, perceived in it.[2]

The mother, as I got the picture at this time, incessantly rejected the daughter's femininity and her efforts to identify with the mother. When as a small child she would try to get into her mother's bed the mother would tell her harshly, 'Go and get in bed with your father; he can love you,' whereas she would accept the patient's siblings. The mother arranged a birthday costume party for the child to which her little girl friends came in dancing costumes, but the patient, as she described bitterly, had to get her hair cut short and go to the party dressed as a stagehand, in overalls. When one morning the patient awoke to find that she was menstruating, she immediately assumed that it represented the 'issue of blood' which the Bible describes as the mark of a guilty person, felt that she literally bore a 'curse', and hid in the bathroom all morning and thought of committing suicide.

Much more convincing to me than all this content—not so different, qualitatively, from that which may be obtained from hysterical patients—was the psychotic intensity of the mother-

[2] Some of this same clinical material was presented on pp. 274-5.

daughter relatedness as it was revealed in the transference relationship. I found every evidence that the often extremely upsetting tirades, of a blaming, hostile, threatening nature, with which the patient castigated me were an accurate sample of the manner in which the mother had treated her throughout her upbringing.

In the ninth month of my work with her, the patient gradually began uttering, especially towards a fellow-patient whom she misidentified as the mother who had beaten her in childhood, murderous threats which seriously worried the ward staff, and in the tenth month, after she had rushed up to this woman and had begun to choke her violently, she was transferred to the maximum security ward. She was showing a more than usually murderous hostility towards me, also, as a malevolent mother figure in the transference, at that time, and for a week or two I thought of this administrative move as having been necessitated by an intensification of murderous feelings in the transference which had partially overflowed to her ward life.

But then, in reviewing my notes, I found that it had been only eight days before this incident that she had revealed intense tender, solicitous feelings towards a third woman patient on the ward. This woman had just been readmitted to the ward from outpatient status one evening, and the next morning I found my patient red-eyed and on the verge of tears throughout the session, as she had rarely if ever been previously in my experience with her. She told of having stroked the head of this (grey-haired) woman as the latter was lying on a couch in the living room. Although she disclaimed, with great anxiety, that she had felt any fondness or solicitude towards the woman, such feelings permeated her voice as she described the incident. I now realized in retrospect that the increased disturbance which had necessitated my patient's transfer to the maximum security ward had stemmed not from a purely de-repressed murderous feeling alone, but rather from depressed *ambivalent*-tender and solicitous, as well as murderous—feelings traceable to her early relationship with her mother.[3]

She remained on the maximum security ward for slightly

[3] R. C. Bak (1954) states that schizophrenic regression is a defence against aggression. On the basis of such clinical experiences as that described above, I have developed the impression that it is a defence against, not aggression alone, but overwhelming *ambivalence*.

353

more than one year. During this period a great deal was achieved in the therapy, in terms of further de-repression of her ambivalent feelings—about, most importantly, her mother—with the consequent releasing of intense, long-repressed feelings of grief and loss.[4] A few weeks after her arrival on that ward a nurse's report contained the following item about this woman who had long been bellowing her denial that any such thing as love exists in the world: '. . . told Dorothy [another patient similar in age and similar, also, in being a mother] about "love" tonight. Then abruptly ended by saying, "There is no such thing as love. What am I talking about?" '

For the first time since her admission to the hospital she now began crying openly and wept a great deal both during her sessions with me and at other times. Her insults towards me now took on at times a friendly, teasing quality. During one hour, near the end of the tenth month of our work, we laughed together at her joking, not entirely inaccurate characterization of me as a 'Briggs ham'; and at the end of the session, as I walked up the corridor, she called after me in the friendliest departure we had experienced thus far, 'I must say, Dr Searles, that your sense of humour is improving.' During the course of this same hour she had reminisced about 'one of the fathers' in unprecedentedly friendly terms, saying at one point, 'That one really is my father,' definitely and with much feeling.[5] Heretofore she had denied ever having any real parents, and she continued for years to think of her parents—as of all other individuals in her past and present life—as being multiple persons. It is noteworthy that it was to require years of further therapy before she could become aware of equally clear-cut feelings of fondness towards her mother.

For many months, however, her overt emotional expressions showed more often than not intense hostility. But I counted it a landmark in therapy when in the thirteenth month of our work she became able to regard me, for whole sessions at a time, as being a thoroughly malevolent mother; the therapeutic relationship had not before been strong enough to withstand the degree

[4] I have presented in chapter 5 above data showing that paranoid vindictiveness is founded, in part, upon repressed grief and separation anxiety.
[5] This reference to her father, and the accompanying hints of a positive father transference at this point, show how artificial must be my present endeavour to trace the course of the *mother* transference alone.

of hostility which she now ventilated. My therapeutic conception of such a development was, and had long been, different from that of many therapists who feel it necessary in working with a paranoid patient to try somehow to avoid getting into the position of an evil delusional figure in his eyes. Hand in hand with this development came equally intense and evidently newly de-repressed depths of fondness, tenderness, and solicitude towards me as well as towards various women patients on the ward whom she often regarded as being, like me, literally the 'mothers' from her past. It became more and more obvious now that her hostility, no matter how intense and at times genuinely dangerous, was in the nature of an unconscious denial of fondness. For example, in this same month, after she made venomous threats for weeks towards a patient named Alice, whom she seemed particularly to fear and hate, she became able to confide to me, 'There is one Alice that I like.' During this same month she brought out in the sessions many touching, indirect expressions of her dependency upon me and her unconscious wishes to marry me.

In the fifteenth month there came for the first time a description from her of some childhood interaction with her mother which clearly revealed a deep fondness between her mother and herself; fondness which she as a child had concealed behind an insolent kind of defiance, and which the mother had concealed behind harsh and scathingly condemnatory words towards the daughter, and the existence of which the patient had still to deny unconsciously. The content of the dialogue she quoted was much like that which I had heard from her many times before, but this time the feeling-tone was one of obvious fondness. At the end of the hour, she demanded, in her usual paranoid fashion, why she was having to cry all night long. 'Is it because the [Baptist] Church requires it?' she demanded loudly and castigatingly. I replied, gently, 'No–it's because you miss your home and your mother so much; you've made that clear to me today beyond a doubt.' Whereas a few months before such a statement would have brought a most venomous tirade from her, she now did not deny what I had said.

By the eighteenth month, our relationship had become predominantly one of intense, mutual fondness of a mother-child sort. I consciously adored her, perceiving her varyingly as an adorable childlike person and as an omnipotent mother. For her part, she evidenced towards me a comparable adoration, which she always denied and expressed somewhat indirectly. Whether exhibiting deeply dependent or maternal fondness towards me, she had to pooh-pooh the existence of such feelings in herself. She revealed her loneliness in a most touching way: she had long voiced the delusion that 'they' literally turn people into bugs, but now she went ahead to make out a case for the desirability, instead, of 'their' turning bugs into people. 'Then,' she said poignantly, 'a person could take a bug and turn it into a person and then they'd have something to call their own.'

This same period yielded many useful results in terms of her realizing how intensely she had yearned to be literally at one with another person and how impossible of fulfilment is such a desire. In spontaneously ruminating about the possibility of her ever having someone of her very own, in this sense of genuine psychological oneness, she said that even though one turned an insect into a child and brought the child up and married him, 'there would still be hatred'. As she was saying these things, she was extending her arms as if embracing a beloved person. She listened with open interest to my response, 'Yes, if you try to hold anyone too close, they will hate you, and you will hate them as well.' She was able to tolerate a good deal of exploration of her fantasied omnipotence, a broad subject so integrally related to her long-held conviction that a mother and child can be truly at one with each other. Whereas earlier she had threatened me with physical assault when I had tried to question some of her concepts of mothering, she now listened with interest to my views.

In this same month and in the following (nineteenth) one, I had the impression that she was very near to being *conscious* of her fondness for me, as being–so she evidently perceived me at these times of apparent conscious fondness–literally her own beloved child. She berated me a great deal in a bellowing voice, called me 'degenerate', 'stupid', and complained loud and long of having to do this 'baby sitting'; but there was so much fondness in her tone that many times I could not help laughing happily, basking in this fondness while she was ostensibly insulting and browbeating me. She interpreted my laughing as a sure indication of my unrepentant malevolence, and found in it

356

food for more of this ostensible vilification. There were times when I felt nearly overwhelmed by the intense fondness, with sexual components, which the interaction with her called up within me, and I found abundant evidence that what I was experiencing at her hands was a precise replica of much that she had experienced in childhood at the hands of her mother, who had untiringly 'castigated' the daughter in just this same way. It was in this (nineteenth) month that we reached a consensus that she had long felt, and still felt, required to keep a kind of steel wall round her fond feelings; previously she had denied adamantly that any such feelings existed within her towards anyone.

But I could not long forget that her intense *ambivalence* had yet to be resolved.[*] Later in this same (nineteenth) month, for example, on one occasion she subjected me to such a prolonged, savage raging that I became filled with panic lest, if I did not get out of the room and if she kept up this raging much longer, I might lose control of myself and kill her. I managed to hold on until the end of that session, and before our next session took place she had succeeded in temporarily decompressing our relationship by getting into some relatively harmless acting out, in a way which enabled her to release a good deal of this steam.

Late in this (nineteenth) month, I saw unfolding, in her previously malignant, pathological delusional thinking, a charming, playful quality. For example, concerning another female patient whom she had previously misidentified as being some really sinister person, now in a spirit of childlike pretending she termed this woman a Vietnamese soldier. This was at the time of the warfare in Indonesia, and the patient revealed, here, a healthy, childlike pretending that she was in the midst of this exciting, much-publicized situation. Over these same weeks I heard from her unprecedentedly realistic and friendly descriptions of her family life with her husband and children, and of her psychotherapy, during the first year of her hospitalization elsewhere, with a female therapist. She made clear to me that her mother had imbued her with the conviction that she–the patient–had a life mission to fulfil, of some indefinable sort, as a

[*] It is not only theoretically sound but technically useful to conceive of ambivalence as a primitive defence against the overwhelming intensity of the love which characterizes the preambivalent phase of infancy—overwhelming, in these abnormal instances, to the mother and, as a result, to the infant also.

lieutenant of the mother,[7] and she made it clear that in her own experience as a mother she had felt it necessary to protect her children from her own genuine maternal love feelings. I found, also, a number of extremely moving indications that she had felt it necessary to remove herself, via hospitalization, from the lives of her children in an effort to protect them from the psychosis-transmitting effect upon them of her presence in the home.

In the twenty-first month, for a period of about two weeks, there reappeared in full force the hostile side of her ambivalent feelings towards me as a mother figure in the transference. She literally reacted to me as being a murderous woman who had killed my husband and was determined to kill her, and she showed such a terrible fixity in her paranoid delusions that, for the first time, I felt deeply discouraged as well as anxious in the face of her tirades. But then, when we had weathered this, unprecedentedly intense grief emerged with regard to rejections which she had suffered at the hands of her husband; in this, he was described in terms identical with those she had employed in telling, earlier in the therapy, of her mother's rejections of her.

And so it went, in the subsequent many months of the therapy, with the ventilation and exploration of her ambivalent feelings towards me as a mother figure constituting the most important thread in the continuing work. The fondness became gradually more sustained until the hostility which for so long had been the predominant theme became limited to briefer and briefer episodes. For a long time still, however, this hostility was a formidable element. There was an occasion in the thirty-seventh month when, in response to her raging insults, I again felt great anxiety lest I lose control of myself and kill her; and there was more than one occasion late in the therapy when I felt beaten by her verbal battering to a kind of hurt and helpless pulp, much as she may have felt after the physical beatings she had received from her mother. On the occasion of the incident in the thirty-seventh month which I mentioned, the intense ambivalence between us again spilled over to her 'extra-analytic' life: she

---

[7] I have found evidence, not only here but in a number of other cases, that the paranoid patient's 'mission' consists, basically, in a striving to convince the world that his mother's distorted and largely dissociated (or at least poorly integrated) views are valid. This is all part of his effort to protect both her, and himself, from the recognition that these views are tragically inappropriate, 'crazy'. (For an extensive theoretical exposition along this line, see L. B. Hill (1955).)

became disturbed in the evening and bit one of the nurses on a breast; then, while in a cold wet sheet pack later that evening, she twice asked for, and received, a kiss from another nurse. The latter nurse, telling me of that incident, had been amazed at the tenderness and dependency which the patient had revealed, and enthusiastically termed the patient 'a different person' from the hostile and suspicious one she had been a year previously.[8]

By the end of the third year of our work, I was finding myself deeply moved at seeing how full of love this woman was, not only towards me (as, predominantly, a mother figure in the transference) but also towards people in general, including various patients whom she had long vilified.

At the end of the third year, also, I began to see evidence that her long-standing and severe ego splits were in part a function of a powerful striving on her part to help other persons to become better integrated, even at the expense of her own psychological wholeness. For example, in one session, the patient, who had long been exercising her ability as an artist, set about helping me to draw in an uninhibited, imaginative way. Finding me more than a little inhibited, she spoke of the efforts she had made in childhood to help 'one of my so-called brothers' to become 'integrated' so that he could express the artistic talent which, from various indications, she knew that he possessed. She let me know that she had felt great distress and frustration at finding herself unable to help him overcome his 'pathetic' inability to give free rein to his imagination. She did not demur when I commented that I had never realized how hard she had tried, probably all along, to help other people become integrated. I began to get the hunch that her highly imaginative delusions, involving an extreme degree of ego fragmentation, had been partially in the service of an effort to help other persons whom she perceived as being tragically inhibited, helplessly cut off from *joie de vivre* (a phrase she herself used), to become at one with themselves and thus more participative in living.

Three months later (thirty-ninth month), further data along

[8] H. Stierlin (1961) has pointed out that such a temporary splitting (or diffusion) of the transference, such a diversion of it to persons other than the therapist, has a constructive aspect in terms of the preservation of the patient-therapist relationship. Ideally, perhaps, such things should never happen; but any therapist's tolerance of anxiety has some limit, and the schizophrenic patient's ambivalence may be, at times, too intense for the therapist to bear in a persistently sharply focused state.

this line emerged. When I came to her room for the session, I found her weeping, clutching her chest, and shrieking in unmistakable agony. She demanded to know whether we had taken her heart out. To my great relief, she was able within a few minutes to bring out some data which helped to explain what this was about. She told me that she had just come back from a trip to the local drugstore with a student nurse. While she was eating a sandwich at the lunch counter, 'There was a man sitting nearby who looked as though he needed a heart. What did they *do*? Did they take me outside and take my heart out?' she demanded, in great anxiety and pain. She had noticed that next to the man sat a woman whom she considered to look like an utterly unfeeling, social-climbing clubwoman, and the patient evidently had more than half suspected that this woman had somehow taken out the man's Heart. She told me, further, that while on the way back from the drugstore, 'I thought, "Don't I have a heart?" ' Thus the chest pain had been precipitated.

Although there are clear hints here of unconscious guilt, what had impressed me particularly had been her tone while describing, in some detail, the suffering man in the drugstore: she spoke with deep compassion in her voice, giving me to understand that she had regarded him as a fellow sufferer towards whom she had experienced a helpless, anguished yearning to bring relief. Although she scoffingly dismissed my suggestion that her 'heart had gone out to' the man in the drugstore in his suffering, I noticed that at the height of her agonized weeping and shrieking she said, 'This is just the way I felt all the time I was at Twin Elms Farm!' [during her childhood]. She went on, with encouragement from me, to say that there had been a person there who had complained of heart trouble and would take a drink to relieve it, but that she knew all along that he didn't really have heart trouble–knew that he was really 'a hard-boiled wool-puller' like the woman in the drugstore. The impression I developed was that she had had to repress, and was still having to repress, much of her desire to dedicate herself to the welfare of that person in childhood. As nearly as I could determine, that person consisted in the mother whom she loved, and the hard-boiled person was the mother whom she hated. I had learned long ago that she referred to her mother, more often than not, as 'he'.

Further confirmation of this reasoning came during the forty-fourth month when there came to light a long-hidden (genuinely repressed, I believe) loyalty to her first therapist, a woman whom the patient described in terms identical with those she had used to describe 'the so-called mothers'. I now realized something of the extent to which she had been carrying the torch for that therapist and for, at a deeper level, her mother. Also, she now described aspects of her mother's personality of which I had not heard before: she gave me a picture of the mother as being not so much a malignantly powerful figure as, rather, an insecure recluse with many naïvely inappropriate conceptions of the outside world. This description tallied rather well with that given me by an older cousin who had lived near the patient's home during her upbringing; he described the mother as being considered by all who knew her an eccentric, socially withdrawn person. In this same (forty-fourth) month she expressed for the first time memories of having suspected that her mother was psychotic: 'I thought she was hallucinating, and she'd tell me, "You're evil!" ' And when she referred to 'the people who used me throughout the Hoover Administration and the Second World War [periods coinciding respectively with her early childhood and with the onset of her overt psychosis in adulthood] to represent the confusion of ideologies, to amalgamate thinking', she was revealing, I felt, that her delusional thinking was based partly on an unconscious *effort to* foster the amalgamation, the personal integration, of the other family members in a home which was indeed full of personality difficulties and paradoxical behaviour.

In one of these sessions she, who for years had been convinced – and for many months yet was to remain convinced – that trees are people who have been transformed, tragically, into trees, recalled a childhood incident which constituted one of the sources, I felt, of this particular delusion. The family was living on a farm, and they needed some firewood. The patient, as she recounted it, had made a simple and practical suggestion to her mother, 'Why don't we get a power saw and cut down the trees [which had died long before] in the orchard?' At this, the mother had gasped and said, 'Good heavens, no!' and had shown every indication of being utterly horrified. This reaction of her mother had made the child suspect that the trees must really be people, for only through some such interpretation could she find her mother's reaction to be a sensible one. This proved to be the first of several detailed accounts of childhood experiences with her mother's highly eccentric and inscrutable reactions which had fostered delusional thinking in the child, who had not been able, and still in the psychotherapy was not fully able, to face the fact of her mother's psychosis. Soon after this it became clear that the patient's own psychosis had been precipitated, in adult life, in a setting in which she was re-experiencing, *vis-à-vis* her husband, the same kind of intense anxiety, ambivalence, and confusion which she had felt in childhood in her relationship with her mother.

Meanwhile, the patient had been showing impressive progress in other ways. At the end of the second year of our work she had been able to move, for the first time since her hospitalization four and a half years previously, to an unlocked building. By the thirty-seventh month, although still having to maintain denial mechanisms against her dependency upon me, she was clearly revealing, through misidentifications of myriad persons as being me, that she unconsciously felt me to have a godlike importance to her; it was as though she succeeded in avoiding a sense of missing me desperately, between our sessions, only by perceiving me all about her in the guise of various persons on the hospital grounds and in the village. And in the thirty-eighth month, having maintained previously the most adamant resistance against any frank and acknowledged collaboration with me in the psycho-therapy, she asked me to give her a schedule of our weekly sessions. It was in the same month that for the first time she used the phrase 'my friends' in recounting some incidents from her past – used it in a tone which made me realize beyond doubt that this woman who for years had violently denied that she had ever known the friendship of anyone, had really had friends. Now, too, came clear-cut evidence that she had been her mother's *favourite* child to such an extent that she had always feared her siblings' envy and had therefore had to stress the black side of her visits to the movies with her mother – visits which, it now became clear, had been by no means devoid of pleasurable aspects.

In the forty-fifth month she began reacting to me as having a head which was not my own and expressing this in such a way that I felt intensely anxious. In a session a few days later, she expressed a confused, anxious semi-conviction that the building in which she was housed consisted, in actuality, of the disjointed fragments of a human female body, and I found that she had packed all her belongings to flee 'this place' which 'is dying'. It became clear that she had experienced an identical sense of threat as a child in the family home. And she made known that her fear was that if she did not flee she would be 'turned into this building'. In this same session she spoke of 'smelling a rat' in such a context that it conjured up in my mind the concept of a rat deserting a sinking ship. She continued for several sessions to express her conviction of my being, in essence, anatomically unintegrated; the conviction still concerned the identification of my head.

This was a crucial time in my work with her. I felt that the dying building symbolized her crumbling illness system, but did not realize until later that both the perception of myself as being anatomically unintegrated and of the building as being an anatomically fragmented human being had to do with her coming closer to an awareness of the full depth of the ego fragmentation which had prevailed earlier in her mother and which had long prevailed in herself partially as a result of her having introjected that ego-fragmented mother.

In response to her intensely threatened feeling that she must leave, the administrative psychiatrist suggested that she move to a different room in the same building. Her moving out of the room which she had been occupying for nearly two years to this new room coincided with a marked diminution in her anxiety and an increasing ability to relate to other persons, including myself, on close and friendly terms. Within the first few days after this move, I found her expressing the conviction that she was now in a different building, one in which she felt relatively secure. She asked me in puzzlement, 'What is this building? Is this building supposed to be my sister Lucille?' and went from this into fond recollections of pleasurable experiences she had had in past years with this (youngest) sister. Several times in the next few sessions she expressed a puzzled semi-conviction that the building, or the room itself, was literally composed of the body of this sister, and she evidently felt warm and sheltered in proportion as she was convinced of this. Not until a week or two later did it dawn on me that this move had symbolized a shift from her identifying, until now, with her loyally-clung-to, but considerably ego-fragmented, mother to her identifying now with this sister, who in reality was a much better integrated person than the mother and whose visits, letters, and gifts were playing an increasingly valuable part in the patient's recovery.

Six weeks later (forty-fifth month) there emerged from her almost incredibly intense feelings (though still indirectly expressed and denied by her) of cherishing and adoring me, and simultaneously came a marked shift in her self-regard, from a former self-loathing to a perception of herself as genuinely precious. All this was expressed in bodily terms. She asked, looking at me, 'Is that my body you have?' in the intimately possessive way in which a person regards a beloved sexual partner. She went on to express an almost complete conviction that my body had indeed once been hers, and went on to say that 'back when I had a [i.e. that] healthy body . . . they could make rubies out of my blood, and amethysts out of my saliva. . . .' All this was said in such a tone, and with such additional verbal communications, that I felt admired in the most glowing way imaginable. There was much evidence that she was reacting to me here again as a mother figure–but one who was now not threateningly fragmented but adorably and beautifully whole. Later in this same day a colleague expressed to me his amazement and enthusiasm at having found during a hospital party that morning how warm and friendly and relatively rational this woman had been while having a lengthy conversation with him.

Space does not permit me to describe the subsequent and increasingly favourable course of her psychotherapy. In essence, with the transference evolution which I have traced here, she was now solidly on the road to recovery from an illness which at the beginning of our work had presented, by reason of its depth and chronicity, an unusually formidable therapeutic task.

The Second Case

One of the points of incidental interest in this second clinical example is the unusually clear role of displacement of positive feeling on the part of the patient–from mother to father. The case I reported in chapter 7 also showed this phenomenon conspicuously, and it has been frequent in my experience that the schizophrenic patient's deeply repressed love for the mother is hidden thus, behind an openly expressed adoration for a father who prides himself upon being both father and mother to the patient, while the actual mother remains–to *outward* appearances–rather off the scene.

This woman, 35 years of age at the time of her transfer to Chestnut Lodge, had been suffering from overt schizophrenia, with paranoid and hebephrenic features, for five years. She had been hospitalized on four occasions during these years, for periods of a few months to one year; had received a total of 175 insulin coma treatments and an indeterminate number of electro-shock treatments; had been engaged in sporadic psychotherapy throughout these five years; and had been sent to the Lodge for a two-month trial of intensive psychotherapy as a last measure to avoid her being subjected to a prefrontal lobotomy as recommended by a number of psychiatrists. She had failed– primarily because of her insidiously developing mental illness–to complete high school, and her background was also grossly deficient in the acquisition of ordinary social skills. A battery of psychological tests given upon her admission to the Lodge showed evidence that schizophrenia had 'engulfed very large areas of the personality', with unusually great–even for the Lodge–impairment of her intellectual functioning. Her full-scale I.Q. (measured by the Wechsler-Bellevue test) was only 77.

Her relationship with her mother seemed, at the outset of my work with the patient and for several months thereafter, to have been devoid of love on the part of either towards the other. Her father, who was indicated by all the family members (including the patient's only sibling, a sister two years younger) to have always been the patient's idol, told the admitting psychiatrist, 'Her mother never knew where she stood with Martha; I always felt I did.' He told me later that his mother–who had lived in a nearby village throughout the patient's upbringing–had warned him that if Martha's mother didn't stop treating the girl so strictly and critically, 'she will wind up in a mental hospital'. He obviously blamed his wife for Martha's illness, telling how punitive his wife had always been towards her, for example, by not letting the girl go to the movies for a week when she had done something which had displeased the mother. The sister, in a visit one year after the patient's admission, told me, 'There has always been some antagonism between my mother and Martha,' going on to describe the patient as having always been disrespectful to the mother.

Throughout her childhood and adolescence the girl had been much attached to her father, to her paternal grandmother, and to a nursemaid, while treating the mother with open antagonism and disdain. When she repeatedly taunted her mother with the question, 'How did *you* ever manage to get a man like Daddy?' the mother would slap her face; but otherwise the mother seemed to accept a thoroughly scorned, Cinderella role in her own household, being treated with open contempt by Martha and the husband and finding only one ally: the younger daughter. This sibling, who had evidently adopted many of her mother's views and personality traits (as I saw in successive interviews with the two women), fared much more successfully than the patient–attended college, had a number of boy friends, worked capably at a job, got married and had children, and never became mentally ill.

As the patient entered her teens her open antagonism towards her mother increased, and she now became violently competitive with her sister, towards whom there had earlier been at least a fair measure of fondness. As her psychosis became overt, she finally picked up a hammer and threatened to kill her mother with it, and repeatedly made murderous threats to her sister ('I'll get you in the back when you're not looking') which the sister found reason to regard very seriously. Even some years after the patient's hospitalization at the Lodge, the sister frankly expressed her fear of the patient's aggression, and the mother similarly continued to react in an acutely threatened fashion to any indication that the patient might be considered by the hospital staff well enough to attempt a visit home.

Throughout the first two years of her stay at the Lodge, the patient acquiesced in seeing her father during his periodic visits, but flatly refused to see her mother and showed intense fear and agitation at any suggestion of a visit from her. During this time, although she referred frequently to past experiences with her father and sister, she seldom spoke of her mother. In a psychotherapeutic session six weeks after her arrival, she said, 'I don't care for my family. I liked my grandmother. I used to care for my father,' without mentioning her mother or sister.

Within the first two months of our work, she made clear that she had become disillusioned with her father on finding unmistakable evidence that he had coached her in golf–the one area of living where she had achieved really notable success–not primarily as an expression of genuine interest in her but rather so that she would serve as an instrument to his own greater glory. She still spoke of him at times, however, with respect and even adulation. For many months, though, she devoted most of her time to ruminating about two men with whom she was autistically in love: a young man in her home city, Eddie Wilson, whom she had been idolizing for years, and, secondly, Dr Jones, the psychiatrist on our staff who had admitted her and who served as her psychiatric administrator for the first few months of what proved to be her unusually long hospitalization.

Concerning each of these three men (her father and the other two) she spoke in much the same terms, evidently perceiving each as an omnipotent father figure, and she frequently wrote letters addressed to a composite delusional figure comprised of all three as well as various additional father figures.

Within a few weeks she had settled into a pattern which endured for nearly four years–a pattern of idolizing Dr Jones and, to a lesser extent, her father and Eddie Wilson; and treating me and the nurses and her mother as though we were the dirt beneath her feet, or often as though we simply did not exist.

There were occasional hints, even within the first few months of the hospitalization, that she was reacting to me as a mother figure whose importance to her was not insignificant but rather was being subjected to a vigorous unconscious denial, and that her conspicuous infatuation with the father figure, Dr Jones, was at least in part a function of this need to deny the importance of the mother. Despite this I was cold-shouldered by her so persistently that my own feelings for her became, as I realized subsequently, subjected to a reactive denial. After the first few months of our work I mainly felt a sense of chronic irritation, dissatisfaction, scorn, and lack of interest towards her, and tolerated with Olympian detachment her conspicuous preference of my colleague to me.

It was in the eighteenth month of our work and at a time when she was now practically mute, dishevelled, and continuing to exhibit the extremely bizarre behaviour which was to keep her

367

on a disturbed ward for a total of four years, that I suddenly became aware, with astonishment and very considerable anxiety, of feelings of adoration towards her and fantasies of being married to her.[9] With considerable anxiety and embarrassment I reported these personal feelings in a staff conference which took place about two months later, and was relieved and strengthened to find that my colleagues did not abhor or despise me because of my having such reactions to the patient, and a few months later still (at the end of the first two years of the work) I began seeing with increasing clarity that *I* was far more important to the *patient* than either of us had been able to acknowledge previously. The nature of the patient's transference now became quite clear to me so that, although this transference denial of my importance was still far from resolution, I could now consciously invest much deeper feelings in our relationship without loss of self-esteem or intolerable jealousy when she conspicuously continued to show a doglike worship of my colleague and to act as though I were of less importance to her than a dog.

We had a long road yet before she became able to acknowledge consciously either my importance to her or her mother's importance. In the twenty-fifth month of the therapy, for instance, when I made some mention of her mother, she replied with utter coldness, 'I have no mother . . .', referred to her mother still only sporadically and impersonally now as 'Mrs Kennedy',[10] and on one occasion in this month while using my telephone to call her mother (her first conversation with her, to my knowledge, in about three years), spoke to her in a loud, flat, impersonal voice as if to a maid who has the status of a non-person in a household, ordering her to go out and buy and send to her *'three dark red, seductive-looking dresses'*. I had stepped out into the corridor and closed my door before this conversation started, but could not avoid hearing the patient's strident voice and getting every impression, as later information from the parents substantiated, that the mother meekly acquiesced in—and actually solicited—this kind of scornful treatment from the patient.

[9] I have discussed such aspects of the patient-therapist relationship in a recent paper, 'Oedipal Love in the Countertransference' (1959b) (ch. 9).
[10] The patient's surname (pseudonym).

THE MOTHER TRANSFERENCE

By the end of four years of work, when she was finally able to move to a ward for undisturbed patients (though still in a locked building), she had become appreciably freer in revealing fond feelings towards me, towards certain of the nurses and some of the other female patients, although not able as yet to divulge any fond memories about, or fond current interest in, her mother. A little less than one year later (at the end of four and three-quarters years of work) my patient, who throughout these years had been manifesting deep confusion as to her sexual identity—she had consistently referred to herself as 'a girl' but had misidentified other persons on innumerable occasions in terms of a projected male-female unconscious image of herself—referred to herself for the first time in all my experience with her as 'a woman'. Intense feelings of dependency, loneliness, and grief were now emerging from her in the hours as she began expressing fond memories of transitory acquaintances with various girls and women in the past both at school and in hospitals. Although still maintaining her letter-writing to the tenaciously-clung-to Dr Jones, she was now addressing these letters in such a fashion as to make it clear that they were directed as much to me as to him. In a fit of pique at feeling snubbed by Dr Jones, she expostulated, 'Why, I'd rather be married to a woman!'

By now (just one month short of five years) we had become so consciously, but as yet very shyly, fond of one another that we could not look at each other during the session without our faces revealing this fondness. I recall that I fantasied now, and continued to fantasy for many months thereafter on innumerable occasions during our highly productive hours together, that I was giving suck to her from my breast. This was a highly pleasurable experience free from either anxiety or guilt.

She came to express glowingly libidinized memories of various girl friends, expressive of feelings of adoration and sexual desire which were at least as intense as those she had long expressed, earlier in our work, with regard to various father figures. These included long-repressed feelings of intense interest in the female breast. The nurse in charge of her ward reported that she and the other nurses could now deal with Martha much more constructively than ever before; previously, every one of a long series of charge nurses had been in Martha's view a thoroughly rejecting mother figure with whom she had locked horns in endless, unproductive power struggles, maintaining a haughty, demanding demeanour towards the nurse.

By the beginning of the sixth year she had established an obviously friendly pal relationship with another young woman patient, and reported a dream in which they were living together. Her erstwhile offensively grandiose delusions had now come to be expressed in charmingly childlike terms, like the pleasurable fantasies that little girls have of being princesses, and the nurses commented to me on her looking like a little girl who is trying hard to be grown up.

In the first month of this sixth year, at a time when she was bringing out evidences of both small-child dependency feelings and genital-sexual feelings towards me, I had, one night, two dreams which show something of the personal pressures I underwent in the course of this de-repression of her warm feelings towards me as a mother figure. As a background, it should be mentioned that during her upbringing, whereas there had been an abundance of physical contact between the patient and her father, she had rarely had physical contact with her mother except at times when she succeeded in provoking the mother into slapping her. Similarly, whereas she had literally thrown herself around the neck of Dr Jones or certain other male colleagues of mine, she was extremely intolerant of any physical contact, however slight, with the nurses or me.

In the first of my two dreams, Martha and I were stroking one another in a free and sexually exciting way. In the second dream I was preparing to have intercourse with my infant daughter; at first I felt some guilt and hesitation, but then overcame these and was, when the dream ended, in a state of going ahead with this in a conflict-free spirit. I immediately felt, upon awakening, that these two dreams belonged together, and realized that Martha was inspiring much this same combination of feelings in me; one might well term her, at this time, a very sexually exciting infant. I have every reason to think, from subsequent data, that this extraordinary combination of feelings was a measure of the earliness, in Martha's relationship with her mother, of the time at which their fond feelings for one another became subjected to a mutual, rigorous, unconscious denial.

In the next month, Martha made clear in a communication

which I found extremely moving that she had long been anxious lest I 'drop' her 'like a hot potato' because of the embarrassment which she had been causing me over the years by her publicly flaunted contempt for me. This fitted exactly with the fact of her mother's having threatened, in indirect ways throughout the patient's upbringing, to 'drop you like a hot potato', completely and permanently. In the same session this young woman, who had been hospitalized off and on for the past ten years, and constantly for the past six years, and had shown, of course, a most deep-seated hopelessness for long periods of time, said determinedly, 'Some day I'm going to get out of here; I'm going to get people's recognition; and I'm going to be a worthwhile person again!'

Two months later (the fourth month of the sixth year) for the first time she reported a dream in which her mother appeared; also in her description of this dream she used, for the first time in our work, the phrase 'my mother'. In the dream her mother was rejecting her, treating her as being of less importance than a father figure who also appeared in the dream, and in so doing Martha said, 'She was not a friend of mine.' But I clearly felt that this content emphasis on the negative side was of far less significance than were the two positive aspects which I have mentioned. Over a period of several months, in several different sessions she supplied data which clearly portrayed her competitiveness with men for the mother's favour, and I learned that she regarded even the long-idolized Eddie Wilson with basic antagonism as an interloper in her earlier, more deeply cherished relationship with a girl friend whom Eddie had taken away from her. In the middle of this sixth year she reported a dream which symbolically portrayed her having rejected her mother as a person with whom to identify, and her having identified instead with her lonely, isolated father in a way which had been dangerous to herself—processes which, as I by now knew on the basis of abundant information, had actually taken place.

In the first month of the seventh year she moved to an unlocked building. She had become much surer of her identity and was able to be healthily assertive, in a basically unhostile way, towards me as well as towards other persons.

For example, in one session she was reminiscing about one of the several brief jobs she had held, as a salesgirl, between her early hospitalizations. She told of having been informed at the beginning of a week that she was to be fired at the end of that week. 'So,' she said, matter-of-factly, 'I worked to the end of that week.' I replied, in an effort to encourage her to express feelings of rejection which I assumed that this incident must have aroused in her, 'That must have been tough.' She said, 'No, it wasn't,' in the same matter-of-fact tone. To this I responded with unusual heat and insistence, 'Well, *I* should think it must have been *tough*, working there the rest of that week, knowing you'd been fired.' At this she pointed out to me, emphatically and directly, '*You're* not *me*,' and went on to make clear that she had felt 'relieved' while working there the remainder of that week, feeling that the next job she obtained would probably not require her to work as long hours as this one had.

Not long before this I had been surprised to find on awaking one morning that I had had this dream: she and I were riding a tandem bicycle; the bicycle broke down, and Martha took command of the situation, put the machine right and took over the driving. I had been surprised, that is, at seeing her in a new light, as a competent, self-assured person; this dream had occurred at a time when her confusion, which I have not tried to describe here but which was a most prominent factor throughout all these years, was still very much in evidence.

She also began revealing a rich sense of humour. She showed this, for example, in the course of an hour in which she began doing some quite practical, verbalized ruminating as to how she could obtain a livelihood in the future–commenting that probably she will inherit enough money from her parents so that she won't have to work (quite true), but that the money might not last her all her life (conceivably true), and that, in this latter event, she might then go to a state hospital. I pointed out with some amusement, 'You'd have to have a psychiatric illness to get into a state hospital, Martha.' To this she replied, emphatically, 'If I were in *that* situation I'd *have* a psychiatric illness!'

In the fourth month of the seventh year came relatively clear-cut evidence of her feeling reproachful towards me, as a mother figure, for my having failed to stop her from 'running to'– identifying with–the father figure Dr Jones, and she told in the same session of a film she had seen long ago in which a little girl, out walking in the care of a nursemaid, starts to run across the street to her father and is killed by a passing car; she expressed her feeling that the nursemaid should have stopped the child. A picture was steadily developing of the father as a remote, isolated, socially insecure individual with whom the patient had identified herself in an attempt to rescue him from his isolation, with, of course, disastrous consequences to herself.

It was becoming clear, too, that the father had long reacted to this girl as being a mother figure, and that he clung to her by, among other methods, undermining her self-confidence by treating her in a chronically belittling way; and undermining her relationship with her mother by showing a chronic derision towards that relationship. I learned, now, of his long-standing fondness for uttering such 'witticisms' as 'A woman's only a woman but a ten-cent beer's a drink', and 'You can tell a lady by the way she picks her nose'. Martha had become able by now to show a little of her fondness for her mother–to give a little acknowledgement of her mother's importance to her–by more frequent phone calls in which she asked the mother to buy various sweets and other items of food and send them to her. In an interview which I had with the two parents together and in which the mother sheepishly but fondly spoke about doing these errands for Martha, the father broke in with a cynical laugh, 'I know what Martha's up to–she just wants to save allowance money!'

A few months later, during another of their visits to the Lodge, I found that despite Martha's showing (in her diminished confusion, in her improved grooming, and so on) solid evidence of impressive progress, the father expressed an awareness only of the fact that she had refused, on this particular occasion, to go out to dinner with them. He behaved exactly like a very small boy who has been disappointed and enraged by a frustrating mother, and it became painfully clear to me that he was not primarily interested in his daughter's becoming genuinely well, but rather in her developing to a point at which she would satisfy his infantile dependency needs. It was in the fourth month of this same year that Martha provided historical data which clearly indicated that her own psychosis had become overt just as she was beginning to realize that her father, in whom she had been maintaining such a deep emotional investment after having forsaken her mother very early in life, was himself a person ridden with fragility and behavioural eccentricities.

As her disillusionment with her father became worked through—primarily in the transference to me as being a 'crazy', depressed, withdrawn father figure—there was a further freeing of constructive identifications with her mother, and the development of increasingly positive relationships with women about her in the hospital.[11] For the first time one of the nurses found this young woman, who had for so long been cold, haughty, and demanding towards the ward staff, to be 'sweet'—as I had often seen her to be in the therapeutic sessions, beginning about a year previously. Martha now revealed solicitude towards a woman patient of about her mother's age, and poignantly told of how at the time of one of her hospitalizations she had been planning to 'go to California to stay at a hotel with my mother [who had been born and reared in California]' but that—because, she hinted, of the father's interfering possessiveness towards her mother—she 'was sent to — [a psychiatric sanatorium] instead'. The long-standing displacement of her transference love for her mother, from me over to Dr Jones, had now shifted to the extent that, after telling me of some home-town girl friend who had blue eyes, she commented, 'like your eyes', and then added, *as an afterthought*, '—and like Dr Jones' eyes'.

Half-way through this seventh year she began revealing feelings of self-reproach for not having taken better parental care of her mother, for having let her mother go out dressed in such a fashion as to amount to her committing social 'suicide'. Martha recounted this in terms very similar to those in which she had told me in the first few months of the therapy of herself having destroyed irretrievably—as she then felt—her own social standing through indiscreet (actually, psychotic acting-out) behaviour towards young men. This dovetailed with evidence, which I found in my own contacts with the mother, that the older woman had an astonishingly small-child orientation towards her daughter, reacting with a kind of helpless dependency upon Martha

[11] The resolution in the transference of her still more deeply ingrained introjection of comparably 'crazy' aspects of the mother's personality came much later in our work, at a time when a basically positive mother transference (the achievement of which marks the end of the period covered by this case description) had long been established.

and feeding on the daughter's mother-hen kind of picking on her about her grooming and manners when the two were together.

But there now came up in the therapy feelings also of warm admiration on Martha's part towards her mother as displaying a kind of vigorous absorption in earthy, practical things, with an obliviousness to what Martha and her father regarded as essential niceties of high-society living. In quoting some bluntly outspoken critical assessment which the mother had made about someone outside the family, Martha laughed in a warm, merry way (for the first time in all my experience with her) and said, not with ridicule but with warm admiration, 'My mother–she's something!' A few days later she expressed the same kind of admiration for her sister, laughing in this same fashion, and now expressing a regretful wish that she herself could be as uninhibitedly 'catty' as her sister (and, I knew also, her mother) had often been. She described her sister's making the 'catty' remark in question 'with all the vermilionishness of life!' Martha, whose liberal use of neologisms I have not tried to describe here, was showing an unusual degree of 'vermilionishness of life'–of vigour and *joie de vivre*–in saying this, as a result of this freeing of a constructive identification with her more spontaneous sister and mother.

Over all these years, the most powerful pathological dynamism, or unconscious ego defence, manifested in me as well as in the patient, proved to be the denial of fondness in the mother-child relationship. This denial was predominantly a transference phenomenon which resulted from the mode of relatedness–the mutual denial of fondness–existing in her childhood relationship with her mother. To a lesser extent it was based upon countertransference phenomena traceable to my having experienced a qualitatively similar childhood relationship with my own mother. My personal analysis, which had been completed prior to my work with the first-described patient, was only half finished at the time I started with this woman. This countertransference element was undoubtedly a relatively great hindrance in the first two years of my work with Martha; but for years after my fondness for my mother had become powerfully de-repressed, the denial of mother-child fondness loomed up formidably, time after time, in this particular therapeutic relationship as a measure of the remarkably intense denial which had characterized the relationship in childhood between this profoundly ill woman and her mother. Each time this denial was broken through, I found in myself new depths of fondness for her, and she moved into a stage of fondness-towards-mother which was still a bit deeper than any she had reached before.

Near the end of the seventh year she came to a poignant realization of the finitude of life.[12] She expressed this at first with a kind of child-like, puzzled, protesting refusal to believe – not very different, probably, from some of the feelings which any human being finds in his heart as he comes face to face with this transcendental fact of his existence. But the most memorable thing of all was her expressing this – as I was both astonished and deeply moved to find – in terms of a readiness to sacrifice herself, to consecrate herself, so that scientists could overcome this barrier which, she now realized, stood between her fellow human beings and immortal life. I am paraphrasing her own words which in actuality were doubly moving because of the groping, fragmentary, neologistic manner in which she expressed them. She wondered why 'they don't take blood from me' for this purpose – expressing this wonderment not in a tone of guilty self-reproach, not in any spirit of atonement for past sins, but in a genuine eagerness to dedicate her life's blood to this supremely worthy human cause.

At one point in this first session in which she began expressing such sentiments, these feelings had clearly to do with her beloved paternal grandmother who had died a few years before her own first hospitalization. Seven weeks later – weeks in which the sessions were devoted primarily to this same theme – she brought out these feelings in clear reference to her father, who for many years, during her childhood, had suffered from anxiety about his heart. She asked now, 'Why does a person die? – their heart wears out, is that it?' and went on to express a child-like puzzlement and protest as to why 'they' don't do something about this problem, why they don't 'duplicate' the heart; 'a mirror duplicates things,' she pointed out. 'I *can't* understand it,' she said protestingly and frustratedly, and then added something which made me feel like crying: 'Why don't they take a

[12] In chapter 17 of this book I have discussed schizophrenia as being defence against – among other types of anxiety – this form of existential anxiety.

child's heart . . . [and, in essence, use that to keep the person alive]?' I asked, as calmly as I could, for I had long ago come to realize that she could express herself relatively freely only if I responded in a calm way to her communications, even the most surprising and deeply moving of them, 'Wouldn't that be kind of tough for the child, Martha?' She explained then, in a tone of wholehearted acceptance of the subjective fact of life which she now stated, 'It would be born for that purpose. Otherwise it wouldn't be born, I guess.' She made clear, further, that she felt that since the child owed its existence to the parent, there would be no reason for the child to feel any protest about this.

In ensuing months she went on to express similarly deep fondness, adoration, and dedication towards her mother, referring to her in a warm, fond tone as 'my mother'. At times her admiration for the mother was interlarded with expressions of her viewing her mother as being a delightfully impossible or idiotic, endearing child. From my own contact with the mother, I had no doubt that she felt much more comfortable at being responded to in this latter fashion by Martha than in any openly admiring way. These feelings came, as usual, through the medium of the transference: Martha would laugh in amusement at statements and behaviour traits of mine which she evidently found amusingly naïve, and at other times let me know, indirectly, that she admired and appreciated her mother-figure therapist as being 'very helpful' and 'handsome'. Interestingly, such open expressions of fondness came in a context of her overtly pressing the Director of Psychotherapy for several weeks for a change of therapist–something which I met with an open-handed, genuine readiness to relinquish her if she were determined to bring this about. Over the years evidence had appeared, recurrently, that her great anxiety was that a fond relationship with her mother would be tantamount to the annihilation of her own individuality; so I thought it no coincidence that these new fruits of psychotherapy were to be won only in a setting of my being able to brave the very real possibility of her leaving me for another therapist.

She had become well enough, near the end of the seventh year, to move to outpatient status, and during the three years which have passed since then she has not needed readmission to the hospital.

Discussion

Difficult though it is to discern the nature and progressive evolution of the patient's transference to the therapist, it is even more difficult to conceptualize that which is *new* which the therapist brings into the relationship, and which, as J. M. Rioch (1943) has emphasized, is crucial to the patient's recovery. Rioch is in my opinion quite correct in stating, 'Whether intentionally or not, whether conscious of it or not, the analyst does express, day in and day out, subtle or overt evidences of his own personality in relationship to the patient.'

I surmise that there is a companion evolution of *reality* relatedness between patient and therapist, concomitant with such a transference evolution as is described in each of the above cases. In my work with patients I have repeatedly had the impression that it is only when the reality relatedness between patient and therapist has reached, finally and after many 'real life' vicissitudes between them, a depth of intense fondness that there now emerges, in the form of a transference development, a comparably intense and long-repressed fondness for the mother.

Presumably a point which Freud (1922) made concerning projection also holds true for transference. He stated that projection occurs not 'into the sky, so to speak, where there is nothing of the sort already', but rather on to persons who in *reality* possess an attitude qualitatively like that which the projecting person is attributing to them. So it is with transference; we may presume that when a patient comes to react to us as a loved and loving mother, this phase – as well as other phases – of the transference is founded upon our having come to feel, in reality, thus towards him. M. B. Cohen (1952) stresses here the importance of the therapist's inevitable feeling response to the patient's transference; and I am suggesting that a second and equally healthy source of the therapist's feeling participation is the evolving reality relatedness which pursues its own course, related to and paralleling, but not fully embraced by, the evolving transference relatedness over the years of the two persons' work together. Of a third root, namely, countertransference (which I showed to be a significant factor in Case 2), much has already been written; but as I indicated at the outset, there is a great need for us to become clear about the sequences which the *recovery process* in the schizophrenic adult, very roughly analogous to the growth process in normal infancy, childhood, and adolescence, tends innately to follow. When we have become clearer and surer about this, and particularly about the reality-relatedness element necessary to it, then I believe that frequently—though by no means always—various manifestations of feeling participation by the therapist which in the past have been regarded as unwanted countertransference will be seen to be inevitable, and utterly essential, components of the recovery process.

What are some of these new ingredients of relatedness which the therapist brings into the situation? I shall mention only those which are of most immediate relevance to my main theme. These lie in the realm of the therapist's acceptance of the deep dependency,[13] including even—at one crucial phase of the work—a symbiotic kind of mutual dependency,[14] which he naturally comes to feel towards the patient; his acceptance of a mutual caring which amounts at times to adoration; and his being able to acknowledge the patient's contribution—inevitable, in successful therapy—to his own personal integration. In the last-mentioned regard, it is of interest that we find literature concerning the importance, for the patient's recovery, of his forming constructive, enduring identifications with the therapist, and the therapist's empathic experiencing of momentary identifications with the patient as a means of his knowing more clearly in what disturbing feeling experience the patient is now immersed; but so far as I know, there is literally no report anywhere of therapists' forming long-range, constructive identifications with various aspects of patients' personalities.

In conclusion, I want to note that the schizophrenic patient responds with great regularity to the therapist's maternal warmth as being a sure indication that the latter is a homosexual or a Lesbian. The younger therapist needs to become quite clear that this is, in actuality, a formidable resistance in the patient against the very kind of loving mother-infant relatedness which offers the patient his only avenue of salvation from his illness. I do not mean that the therapist should depreciate the degree of anxiety, referable to the deep ambivalence of the patient's early relationship with his mother, which is contained within this resistance. I

[13] See ch. 3.   [14] See ch. 8.

mean that the therapist's deep-seated doubts as to his own sexual identity—and what person is totally free of such doubts?—should not make him lose sight of the fact that the patient's contempt (or revulsion, or what not) is basically a resistance against going ahead and picking up the threads of the loving infant-mother relatedness which were long ago severed.

Chapter 13

SCHIZOPHRENIC COMMUNICATION
(1961)[1]

ALTHOUGH communication with his fellow men is one of the basic goals to which every person's life is dedicated, it is for the schizophrenic individual an even more absorbing activity. Unlike his relatively healthy fellows, who possess reliable tools of communication in both verbal and non-verbal media, tools to which they can confidently turn as the need arises, he has few if any such dependable techniques. Thus in his activities the communicational facet which is, perhaps, present in every human activity, is the facet which takes precedence over other aspects of or motives of his behaviour. Rarely, if ever, can he 'just' eat, or walk, or read, or listen to music, or whatever, immersed in this as an immediate experience having an end in itself; instead, for him, it presents itself as primarily another front in the unceasing battle for communication with others—or sometimes, for a prevention of disturbing delusional communication with others—a front on which a breakthrough may at last be achieved. The following comments by Ruesch, concerning two of the varieties of non-verbal language in human beings generally, are particularly applicable to the schizophrenic individual and, in my opinion, are proportionately less applicable to the person who has developed reliable modes of communication and who can afford, therefore, to 'just live' as a subjectively separate entity at least a fair share of the time:

. . . *Action language* embraces all movements that are not used exclusively as signals. Such acts as walking and drinking, for instance, have a dual function; on the one hand, they serve personal needs, and on the other, they constitute statements to those who may perceive them. *Object language* comprises all intentional and non-intentional display of material things such as implements, machines, art objects, architectural structures, and last but not least, the human body and whatever clothes it . . . (Ruesch, 1955, p. 323).

[1] First published in *Psychoanalysis and the Psychoanalytic Review*, Vol. 48 (1961), pp. 3–50.

In this paper, I shall describe the more overt features of schizophrenic communication; next, various aspects of the patient's psychodynamics which account for these modes of communication; and, lastly, a number of points concerning relevant psychotherapeutic technique.

Overt Features

In our attempt to pierce the obscurity and unravel the indirectness of schizophrenic communication, it is useful to become acquainted with the various forms of disguise – that is to say, mental mechanisms or modes of defence – which are commonly at work. These are the same as those which constitute the various disguises found in dreams. In my experience these are the most common:

DISPLACEMENT

Here the patient's comment has reference to a different person, and is often couched in terms of a different temporal era, than is intended by the preconscious or unconscious impulse striving for expression. For example, one of my first schizophrenic patients, a single young hebephrenic woman, ruminated for months on end, both throughout her therapeutic sessions with me and in her daily life on the ward, about the social rejections she had suffered in previous years, in her home city, prior to her hospitalization. It took a number of months for me to realize that, though she was consciously thus immersed in events which had happened years ago and hundreds of miles away, innumerable of her comments could be understood, now, as preconscious or unconscious responses to events in her current life in the hospital. For instance, when she pressed her psychiatric administrator for an explanation of 'Why did those two men give me the go-by?', I now understood this to mean, 'Why are you and Dr — [another member of our staff; she showed indications of being romantically interested in each of them] giving me the go-by?' And, after approximately two more years, I developed the necessary courage to see that there was still another level of displacement involved in such comments: her remarkably intense libidinal feelings had been intended, evidently from the first, primarily for me as a father-figure in the transference, but had been almost totally displaced, in their overt expression, on to the young men in her history, and more recently, on to my colleagues on the hospital staff.

This woman loved to wear unconventional and ever-changing costumes, and I had some reason to think that she found me boringly unimaginative in my attire, though she had never made as yet any direct statement to this effect. One day, after I had worn the same plain brown suit for many days in succession, she glanced at me as she came in and, to my amusement, said with annoyance, 'I had a dream last night about Dr — [one of the above-mentioned colleagues]. He was wearing that damned brown suit.'

This was one of the occasions when the displacement seemed almost consciously contrived. Another such incident occurred in an hour when, after having received some stiffening of the back-bone from one of my supervisors, I resolved to delete from my psychotherapeutic approach to this young woman certain of my more obsequious responses; this was not an easy thing to do, for there was in her not merely a recurrently jilted young thing, but also an arrogant, tyrannical *grande dame*, who was not accustomed to any trifling with her imperiousness. This time, as I went to close the door for her after she had entered my office, I behaved not like an effortless doorman but, one might say, like a well-oiled one: I said, sarcastically, 'Grace, if you ever *feel like* closing the door as you come in, feel free to—and you won't lose any status as a woman, either, as far as I'm concerned, if you do.'

Scarcely had these solicitous words ceased purring from my lips than she expostulated, in an unusually loud, outraged voice, full of scathing contempt, something about a play she had seen in New York several years previously in which 'they had Eddie Landon's [a personal acquaintance of the patient] sister come out with her hair up and powder on her face. It was *stupid*,' she exclaimed, practically spitting her contempt, 'It was *stupid* as all hell!' On hearing this, I said firmly, 'If you thought my suggestion that you close the door was stupid –', whereupon she interrupted, 'I *did* think it was stupid,' flatly and emphatically. I asserted, 'I *don't* think it was stupid,' and proceeded to bawl her out for not taking more responsibility for herself.

Here again, the displacement of her anger and contempt may have been in large part a conscious manœuvre, since it was so easily cut through with my comment. But I encountered thousands of instances with her in which the displacement was a largely or wholly unconscious operation; evidently she genuinely *experienced* the communicated feelings in their displaced context. As with all the forms of distorted communication which one encounters with schizophrenic patients, one fairly soon learns that any particular patient shows considerable variability, from moment to moment, as to whether the distorted form of communication is only a 'manner of speaking', or whether, instead, it is a faithful reflection of a distorted 'manner of experiencing'. The less experienced therapist is apt to assume too frequently that it is only a highly distorted form of *communication*, which springs out of a subjective experience on the part of the patient, not widely different from his own experience of what is happening at the moment. It seems usually to require of any therapist some years of work in this field to dare to see how remarkably distorted is the subjective experience of the patient.

In the instance of the patient I have just been describing, for example, it required more than four years for me to realize that she experienced *similar* people or things as being *identical* – a phenomenon to which Arieti (1955, pp. 186–219) has applied the term 'paleologic'. This became evident during an hour in which she commented, 'Dr Edwards and Dr Michaels [two of the other psychiatrists on the staff[2]] are the same,' after having touched upon some similarities between them; and when, later in the hour, she said in a tone first of genuine puzzlement, then of discovery, 'I always think my stockings are my glasses. Well, I don't *always* think so; but I often do.' A few days before, she had mentioned that she derived the same feeling of security from her stockings (which she wore not on her legs but stuffed, wadded up, under the soles of her feet) as she did from her glasses (which she always wore, because of severe myopia). This revelation came a few days after her eccentricity about the stockings, a symptom which had persisted for many months, had been finally relinquished. Three months later, she described in retrospect an incident during that era when her administrative psychiatrist 'told me, "You ought to get along without your stockings!" I felt just as if he'd said, "You ought to get along without your glasses!" ' It is small wonder that schizophrenic patients whose perceptual-conceptual experience is so poorly differentiated

[2] All the names used in the clinical material in this paper are pseudonyms.

would be prone, in innumerable instances, to the unconscious use of displacement.

Another young woman, whose ego-fragmentation was so extreme that she was incapable for years of more than fleeting moments of relatedness, revealed even less often any friendly feelings. I was touched, therefore, to learn that after she had been bathed by a student nurse whom she liked, she expressed her appreciation by saying, 'I love your brother.' She could not yet dare to say it–or, perhaps, even to experience it–in the direct, undisplaced form, 'I love you.' This woman used occasionally to ply me with the question, 'Do you like — —?', giving the name of some person or other from her home city, a city with which I am almost totally unacquainted. One day she asked, 'Do you like Roger O'Neill?' and, for the nth time, I wearily responded, 'Roger O'Neill? I never heard the name before. Any thoughts about him, as to how you feel about him?' She made no direct answer to this; but after some apparently unrelated, fragmentary comments from her, it dawned on me to comment, 'When you asked if I like Roger O'Neill, maybe you were wondering if I like *you*,' gently. Tears came into her eyes, and I felt confirmed in my interpretation of her meaning. I had noticed a few moments before this interchange that when I addressed her by her first name in a friendly, close way, she turned round with sudden hopefulness on her face, as if her heart had lifted.

Since then I have gradually come to see how very much of the time the schizophrenic patient is absorbed with the question whether the therapist (=mother, in most such instances) likes him; and that he ventures to inquire about this in dozens of different questions which are couched in contexts involving displacement.

One becomes impressed, even more, by the extent to which he is concerned, basically (whether consciously or unconsciously), with what is transpiring *at the moment* between the doctor and himself, although his communications may involve, persistently, so much displacement to distant persons and remote temporal eras that the therapist will be slow to realize this. One of the many incidents which helped to convey this point to me occurred in a session with a hebephrenic man. He had grown up in a beautiful home, but had been hospitalized now for a dozen years on wards which, because of the severity of his illness, were far indeed from duplicating the beauty of his home surroundings. In one session he graphically described his being in a beautiful, happy, peaceful and secure home, filled with lovely furnishings; then suddenly, with a gesture of his arm, he spoke of its being all swept away by some catastrophe which he seemingly refused to describe. At first I thought how graphic a description this was of his having been ejected, by force of circumstances, from the nest of his family home, into a world where he had become caught up in increasing rootlessness, deterioration of his personal identity, and eventual schizophrenia. But some time later—just how and when, I did not record—it dawned on me that this had been his way of experiencing the loss, probably only a moment before, of some unusually rich sense of relatedness with me, a loss attributable to some catastrophe which he could not possibly as yet conceptualize. Many times subsequently I had occasion to see that it required but a shift in my position in the chair, an ill-timed word, or a distracting gesture of my hand while speaking, to disrupt a stream of non-verbal relatedness between us, a stream in which he had evidently been happily immersed.

PROJECTION

Of this much-discussed process I wish to mention only two features: the extent to which the patient reveals, in statements based upon his projections, the feelings and ideas which are at work in his own unconscious; and the extent to which he projects his own unconscious utilization of non-verbal modes of communication. His verbalizations of his projection-ridden subjective experience often fill in, in a remarkably detailed and precise way, gaps in our knowledge of what is going on in him.

A woman suffering from chronic paranoid schizophrenia experienced her interpersonal world as being comprised not of whole persons but of anatomical and psychological fragments of persons controlled, through holes in their heads, by vaguely defined beings who held omnipotent power; and she felt herself to be likewise fragmented and victimized. She devoted the hours with me, for many months, to expressions of physical anguish, protestations of despair, and castigations of me for being responsible for the hellish state of the world in which she existed. It was largely through projection-ridden utterances of hers that I gradually became aware how much she was, at an unconscious level, enjoying all this—enjoying a sense of omnipotent power over others, and, with this, a freedom from all controls.

This revelation came in such accusations as, 'The doctors have holes put in their heads and enjoy their not having any control!' '. . . people who love to sit up in garrets and split personalities!' (said at a time when she was housed within a dormer roof, in the upper storey of one of the hospital buildings, and was speaking often, in the hours, of the persons—experienced by her as personality-fragments—she saw walking past on the road below); and, 'They [referring to the family of her childhood] wanted a dream world, and they've *got* one; how do we get *free*?', said at a time when she perceived me as being, like herself, imprisoned within the dream world which 'they' had wanted to create. These statements came, with others in the same vein, over widely scattered hours; the last-quoted one occurred long before she, subjectively the most down-to-earth of women, could admit to herself any wish to create, and confine herself to, any such dream world as the luxuriantly delusional one in which she existed.

Her positive feelings towards me first found verbal expression in this same unconscious, projective fashion. In one hour she screamed at me, 'I'm *not* going to marry you, and I don't care how many people are trying to *make* me marry you!' This, coming at a time when I had not realized that there was any such depth of positive feeling in her towards me, I found a very touching statement from this woman who generally presented herself to me as a kind of lioness encased in chain mail. Two or three weeks later these positive feelings were much closer to awareness, though not yet fully acknowledged as her own: she conjectured about the dilemma a married woman—and she was a married woman—would find herself in if a man other than her husband saved her life and she fell in love with him in the process.

Eight months later, as her infantile-dependent feelings towards me began to come to the fore, she told me scornfully, 'You live only to have an hour with me every day.' I was quite aware that the hours with her meant a great deal to me; but she could not yet acknowledge any such emotional investment in them. It was only a few weeks later that the following significant interchange occurred. I went to see her for the regularly scheduled Wednesday hour and was greeted with an abrupt, 'Why are you up here today, anyway? I don't have an hour on Tuesday.' I replied, 'This is Wednesday,' whereupon she looked puzzled and said, 'What happened to Tuesday?' I distinctly felt that she was unconsciously revealing the fact that those days in which she had no hour with me (and she had none on Tuesdays) were so desolate that they did not exist, for her, in her memory; that, in this quite striking sense, she indeed lived only for the hours with me. My impression was abundantly documented by her increasingly open expressions of dependency during subsequent months.

Lidz and Lidz (1952) call attention to the schizophrenic patient's projection on to the therapist of his own proclivity for non-verbal communication:

. . . The patient further projects, not only feelings, but his own attitudes of passive communications through symbols and indications rather than by words. Therapy is often hindered or endangered more by what the patient believes the therapist is covertly conveying than by anything actually said (Lidz and Lidz, 1952, p. 175).

I have seen innumerable instances of the phenomenon which Lidz and Lidz describe. One such instance occurred only a few days ago, during a session with a man suffering from chronic schizophrenia with both hebephrenic and paranoid features, who after several years of therapy is apparently still unable to recapture more than occasional memory-fragments of his past. Most of the hours are still spent in silence. During this particular session, in the course of a prolonged silence as we were seated in chairs rather near one another, I began drumming on my chair, lightly and unthinkingly, with the fingers on my right hand – the hand nearer to him. His eyes lit up and he promptly broke his silence by saying in a tone of discovery, 'You used to be light-fingered when you were young; I understand, Sweetie.'

On the basis of my work with other patients I had little doubt that, as his memory improved and he became able to confide more fully in me, we should discover that petty stealing was one of the aspects of his boyhood behaviour. Another of my patients, a paranoid woman, was long convinced that the people about her (including me) in the hospital were trying, by their behaviour, to 'show me' or 'tell me' that this action in which they were engaged – an action always to her offensive – or this soiled garment they were wearing, or whatever, was typical of her own upbringing. In at least one instance which I recorded, she interpreted an action of mine not as a communication about the past, but as a warning about the future: she felt that my accidental dropping of an ash-tray was my way of telling her that I was going to drop her. I was interested to find, in the subsequent course of her therapy, that she became able to recognize the great extent to which she herself, all along, had been trying in comparably indirect and non-verbal ways to convey reproach to others. For example, she told me, in one of the later sessions, that earlier in the day she had gone into the combined living-room and kitchenette where there were a number of patients and members of the staff, had seen a banana skin lying on the sink, and had put it into the waste-bin. 'I wanted to show them that they shouldn't leave things lying around,' she explained. Dozens of times in earlier years she had expressed, in a stingingly insulted tone, the conviction that I, or some nurse or aide, was 'trying to show me that . . .', and she had evidently been unaware, until recently, of the extent to which she had been projecting on to the rest of us her own non-verbal and largely unconscious reproachfulness.

Another paranoid woman expressed the conviction that various of the daily-life activities on her ward were 'tableaux' which were being presented to her for the purpose of illuminating, for her, the poorly remembered and chaotically confused events of her past life. It only slowly dawned upon me how frequently her own room, where my sessions with her were long held, could be seen to be a tableau, unconsciously arranged by her for the purpose of conveying to me some unexplored facet of her past life. For example, there was a period of some weeks in which her room, equipped with open suit-cases and little in the way of anything 'homey', was her unconscious portrayal of a time which she was struggling to remember, when she had made a coast-to-coast car journey, many years before, with her mother and brother. I eventually came to realize that her room had grown to look much like a hotel room where one stays only overnight. In a later phase of our work, there was a period of several weeks during which her room looked very like a boiler-filled basement. This was a time when memories of childhood experiences in the basement of her family home were beginning, bit by bit, to emerge into her awareness. Always, in such phases, her conscious reasons for so arranging her room were quite other and very delusional ones; and always it dawned on me only belatedly that another meaningful tableau had presented itself.

A hebephrenic woman, upon entering my office after I had rearranged some of my furniture, asked in an irritated, disconcerted, anxious tone, 'What's happened to the office?' When I explained that I had switched the furniture round so that it would harmonize better with a new picture which I had acquired, she said irritatedly, 'I don't care anything about the picture.' She was more restlessly anxious than usual throughout the hour; but near the end of it she laughed briefly and said, in a tone of realization, 'Hilda [her current room-mate] was making a take-off on me – I change my clothes a lot, so she moved her furniture around.' It was apparent that, in this displaced fashion – displaced from me to her room-mate – she was expressing the conviction that, in rearranging my furniture, I had been 'making a take-off on' her several times a day changing of her clothes – or, more accurately, costumes.

This woman, throughout the early years of her unusually prolonged therapy, seemed never to experience anyone in her current environment as *reminding her* of someone from her past; always, instead, the other person, or occasionally a pair of inter-acting persons, were, she was immediately convinced, 'doing a take-off on' some person(s) from her past. In later years of our work, it became clear that such misinterpretations had been based, in part, upon projection of what she could now acknowledge as her own zest for doing take-offs on – for mimicking in a carica-tured fashion – other persons in either her present or her past life. In one session during the fifth year of our work, for instance, she described her having 'put on a George White's Scandals show' for her administrative psychiatrist, was hurt that he had been angered rather than pleased by it, and was quite unaware, at that phase of our work, that she had unconsciously been trying to reproach him, by this 'Scandals' show, about something concerning which she seriously disapproved of him. Later in this session, significantly, she said in an incensed tone that 'it's *scandalous*' that these doctors (using her administrative psychia-trist as a prime example) 'aren't more formal than the patients'. Later in her therapy she became quite freely able to acknowledge, and enjoy, her doing take-offs, on various people, often including me, during many of our sessions. These proved, incidentally, not only great fun for her, but very instructive to me; they showed much better than could mere verbal descriptions, how I appeared to her currently, or, for example, how her parents had appeared to her during this or that significant incident in her childhood. But my main point here is that, earlier in her therapy, her projection of a then unconscious tendency to do take-offs—mimicking which involved a high degree of non-verbal communication—had been one of the causes of her misconstruing the activities of those about her in the hospital.

INTROJECTION

In chapter 6 I have described in detail some of my experiences with manifestations of introjection on the part of schizophrenic patients. I shall not repeat here what I said there. This discussion will be seen to be simply another frame of reference for viewing, or another level of viewing, those clinical phenomena which I have just been describing in terms of the patient's 'doing a take-off on' the therapist or somebody else. But in the instances discussed here, the patient's ego is so little in command, either consciously or unconsciously, of what is being expressed, that we do not sense it as his trying to show us, by caricatured mimicry, this other person. Rather, his behaviour seems so completely in command of the introjected other person, from present or past life, that his ego is quite overwhelmed by the introject which is manifesting itself, now, in the verbal or non-verbal communications we are receiving from him.

So far as the patient's subjective experience of these introjective phenomena is concerned, the more de-differentiated is his ego, the less able is he to distinguish between the introject and his own self; basically he experiences, as an indistinguishable part of his self, some quality which 'belongs' primarily in the therapist or someone else in his current surroundings, or in someone from his past.

It is not easy for the therapist to discern when, in the patient's communicating, an introject has appeared and is holding sway. One learns to become alert to changes in his vocal tone—to his voice's suddenly shifting to a quality not like his usual one, a quality which sounds somehow artificial, or in some instances, parrotlike. The content of his words may lapse back into monotonous repetition, as if a gramophone needle were stuck in one

SCHIZOPHRENIA AND RELATED SUBJECTS

groove; only seldom is it so simple as to be a matter of his obviously parroting some timeworn axiom, common to our culture, which he has evidently heard, over and over again, from a parent until he experiences it as part of him.

One hebephrenic woman often became submerged in what felt to me like a somehow phony experience of pseudo-emotion, during which, despite her racking sobs and streaming cheeks, I felt only a cold annoyance with her. Eventually such incidents became more sporadic, and more sharply demarcated from her day-to-day behaviour, and in one particular session, after several minutes of such behaviour–which, as usual, went on without any accompanying words from her–she asked eagerly, 'Did you see Granny?' At first I did not know what she meant; I thought she must be seeing me as someone who had just come from seeing her grandmother in their distant home-city. Then I realized that she had been deliberately showing me, this time, what Granny was like; and when I replied in this spirit, she corroborated my hunch.

At another phase in the therapy, when a pathogenic mother introject began to emerge more and more upon the investigative scene, she muttered in a low but intense voice to herself, 'I hate that woman inside me!' I could evoke no further elaboration from her about this; but a few seconds later she was standing directly across the room from me, looking me in the eyes and saying in a scathingly condemnatory tone, 'Your father despises you!' Again, I at first misconstrued this disconcertingly intense communication, and I quickly cast through my mind to account for her being able to speak with such utter conviction of an opinion held by my father, now several years deceased. Then I replied coldly, 'If you despise me, why don't you say so directly?' She looked confused at this, and I felt sure it had been a wrong response for me to make. It then occurred to me to ask, 'Is that what that woman told you?' She clearly agreed that this had been the case. I now realized that she had been showing me, in what impressed me as being a very accurate way, something her mother had once said to her; it was as if she was showing me one of the reasons why she hated that woman inside her. What had been an unmanageably powerful introject was now, despite its continuing charge of energy disconcerting to me, sufficiently within control of her ego for her to use it to show me what this introjected mother was like.

Earlier, this woman had been so filled with a chaotic variety of introjects that at times, when she was in her room alone, it would sound to a passer-by as though there were several different persons in the room, as she would vocalize in various kinds of voice. A somewhat less fragmented hebephrenic patient of mine, who used often to seclude herself in her room, often sounded through the closed door–as I would find on passing, between our sessions–for all the world like two people, a scolding mother and a defensive child.

Particularly hard for the therapist to grasp are those instances in which the patient is manifesting an introject traceable to something in the therapist, some aspect of the therapist of which the latter is himself only poorly aware, and whose recognition, as a part of himself, he finds distinctly unwelcome. I have found, time and again, that some bit of particularly annoying and intractable behaviour on the part of a patient rests, in the final analysis, on this basis; and only when I can acknowledge this to myself as being indeed an aspect of my personality, does it cease to be a prominently troublesome aspect of the patient's behaviour. For example, one hebephrenic man used to annoy me, month after month, by saying, whenever I got up to leave and made my fairly stereotyped comment that I would be seeing him on the following day, or whenever, 'You're welcome,' in a noticeably condescending fashion–as though it were his due for me to thank him for the privilege of spending the hour with him, and he were thus calling attention to my failure to utter a humbly grateful 'Thank you' to him at the end of each session. Eventually it became clear to me, partly with the aid of another schizophrenic patient who could point out my condescension to me somewhat more directly, that this man, with his condescending, 'You're welcome,' was very accurately personifying an element of obnoxious condescension which had been present in my own demeanour, over these months, on each of these occasions when I had bid him good-bye with the consoling note, each time, that the healing Christ would be stooping to dispense this succour to the poor sufferer again on the morrow.

Another patient, a paranoid woman, for many months infuriated not only me but the ward staff and her fellow-patients by arrogantly behaving as though she owned the whole building, as though she were the only person in it whose needs were to be met. This behaviour on her part subsided only after I had come to see the uncomfortably close similarity between, on the one hand, her arranging the ventilation of the common living-room to her own liking, or turning the television off or on without regard to the wishes of the others, and on the other, my own coming stolidly into her room despite her persistent and vociferous objections, bringing my big easy chair with me, usually shutting the windows of her room which she preferred to keep in a very cold state, and plunking myself down in my chair – in short, behaving as if I owned her room.

CONDENSATION

Here a variety of meanings and emotions are concentrated, or reduced, in their communicative expression, to some comparatively simple-seeming verbal or non-verbal statement.

One finds, for example, that a terse and stereotyped verbal expression, seeming at first to be a mere hollow convention, reveals itself over the months of therapy as the vehicle for expressing the most varied and intense feelings, and the most unconventional of meanings. More than anything, it is the therapist's intuitive sensing of these latent meanings in the stereotype which helps them to become revealed, something like a spread-out pack of cards, on sporadic occasions over the passage of the patient's and his months of work together.[3] One cannot assume, of course, that all these accumulated meanings were inherent in the stereotype at the beginning of the therapy, or at any one time later on when the stereotype was uttered; probably it is correct to think of it as a matter of a well-grooved, stereotyped mode of expression – and no, or only a few, other communicational grooves, as yet – being *there*, available for the patient's use, as newly-emerging emotions and ideas well up in him over the course of months. But it is true that the therapist can sense, when he hears this stereotype, that there are at this moment many emotional determinants at work in it, a blurred babel of indistinct voices which have yet to become clearly delineated from one another.

Sometimes it is not a verbal stereotype – a 'How are you now?' or an 'I want to go home', or whatever – but a non-verbal one which reveals itself, gradually, as the condensed expression of more than one latent meaning. A hebephrenic man used to give

[3] See chs. 10 and 11.

394

a repetitious wave of his hand a number of times during his largely silent hours with his therapist. When the therapist came to feel on sufficiently sure ground with him to ask him, 'What is that, Bill–hello or farewell?', the patient replied, 'Both, Dearie–two in one.'

Of all the possible forms of non-verbal expression, the one which seems best to give release, and communicational expression, to complex and undifferentiated feelings is laughter. It is no coincidence that the hebephrenic patient, the most severely dedifferentiated of all schizophrenic patients, shows, as one of his characteristic symptoms, laughter–laughter which now makes one feel scorned or hated, now makes one feel like weeping, or now gives one a glimpse of the bleak and empty expanse of man's despair; and, more often than all these, conveys a *welter* of feelings which could in no way be conveyed by any number of words, words which are so unlike this welter in being formed and discrete from one another. To a much less full extent, the hebephrenic person's belching or flatus has a comparable communicative function; in working with these patients the therapist eventually gets to do some at least private mulling over of the possible meaning of a belch, or the passage of flatus, not only because he is reduced to this for lack of anything else to analyse, but also because he learns that even these animal-like sounds constitute forms of communication in which, from time to time, quite different things are being said, long before the patient can become sufficiently aware of these, as distinct feelings and concepts, to say them in words.

As I have been intimating, in the schizophrenic–and perhaps also in the dreams of the neurotic; this is a question which I have no wish to take up–condensation is a phenomenon in which one finds not a condensed expression of various feelings and ideas which are, at an unconscious level, well sorted out, but rather a condensed expression of feelings and ideas which, even in the unconscious, have yet to become well differentiated from one another. Freeman, Cameron and McGhie (1958), in their description of the disturbances of thinking found in chronic schizophrenic patients, say in regard to condensation that '. . . the lack of adequate discrimination between the self and the environment, and the objects contained therein . . . in itself is the prototypical condensation' (p. 75).

395

In my experience, a great many of the patient's more puzzling verbal communications are such for the reason that concrete meanings have not become differentiated from figurative meanings in his subjective experience. Thus he may be referring to some concrete thing or incident in his immediate environment by some symbolic-sounding, hyperbolic reference to transcendental events on the global scene. Recently, for example, a paranoid woman's large-scale philosophizing, in the session, about the intrusive curiosity which has become, in her opinion, a deplorable characteristic of mid-twentieth-century human culture, devolved itself, before the end of the session, into a suspicion that I was surreptitiously peeping at her partially exposed breast, as indeed I was. Or, equally often, a concretistic-seeming, particularistic-seeming statement may consist, with its mundane exterior, in a form of poetry—may be full of meaning and emotion when interpreted as a figurative expression: a metaphor, a simile, an allegory, or some other symbolic mode of speaking.

Of such hidden meanings the patient himself is, more often than not, entirely unaware. His subjective experience may be a remarkably concretistic one. One hebephrenic woman confided to me, 'I live in a world of words,' as if, to her, words were fully concrete objects; Burnham, in his excellent article (1955) concerning schizophrenic communication, mentions similar clinical material. A borderline schizophrenic young man told me that to him the various theoretical concepts about which he had been expounding, in a most articulate fashion, during session after session with me, were like great cubes of almost tangibly solid matter up in the air above him; as he spoke I was reminded of the great bales of cargo which are swung, high in the air, from a docked steamship. Another borderline schizophrenic young man experienced the beginning stirrings of de-repression of feelings, early in his analysis when, for example, he would be strolling along the street in an unguarded moment, as though he had suddenly bumped into, or been struck by, some massive but invisible object. It proved later to be in this way that important emotional insights had first been presaged. Many schizophrenic patients, when presented with a penetrating but premature interpretation, evidently feel not that they have heard a meaningful figurative concept from their therapist, but rather that they have been struck a physical blow, or, in some instances I have seen, that they are being shot at from various quarters.

The therapist, too, may unconsciously long protect himself from seeing the poignant meanings latent in these patients' communications by hearing their statements as having purely concrete, or otherwise mundane, meanings. A paranoid man who had gradually become overwhelmed with psychosis in the course of a solitary Caribbean cruise used to bore me, in the sessions, by mentioning time and again, another and yet another of the titles of the almost innumerable films he had watched during the cruise; only after some weeks did it dawn upon me that the titles of the pictures formed symbolic expressions of the terror, the loneliness, and other warded-off emotions which had been building up in him as the cruise progressed. A therapist during a supervisory hour with me recounted, boredly, what to him seemed the almost endlessly detailed description, by a paranoid woman who had recently returned from a visit to her children, of an afternoon's hike with them in the hills along the seashore. I heard this account, as he listlessly quoted it, as constituting an allegory filled with the most poignant statements of the patient's whole life-experience with her children and her years of separation from them during her hospitalization, and larded with echoes of her own childhood. Moreover, when I called these meanings to the therapist's attention, he could immediately accept them as being indeed there. It is not uncommon for the therapist, in daily contact with the patient's great but much-concealed grief and loneliness, to need to so ally himself with the strength of a colleague in order to perceive these meanings. Recently, in a session with a hebephrenic man – about whom I have many times received this kind of help from various colleagues – he said 'Hello' to me in the middle of the session. This struck me as a bit incongruous, and I expressed to him my curiosity. He replied, simply by way of explanation, 'A friendly hello as we pass on the avenue.' At first I reacted to this as being only another of the familiar indications of his fantasying himself to be a tourist in this or that city; then the metaphorical impact of the whole statement hit me – its implications about the fleetingness of life, the impossibility for us as human beings to overcome our innate separateness from each other, the rarity with which we can enjoy a moment of simple and uncomplicated friendliness with one another.

ISOLATION

The content of the patient's speech may be descriptive of incidents or situations which seem to the listener as though these *must* be charged with intense emotion; but the words are astonishingly, and often maddeningly, isolated from–divorced from – any affective tone. Over the course of years of working with schizophrenic patients, the therapist gradually comes to realize how rarely the patient is aware, in such instances, of emotion and consciously withholding its expression. As the therapist becomes aware of this he desists from pressing the patient to express what he is unaware of, and dares to look at these various incidents and situations more and more from the patient's own point of view, a point of view from which feelings are elusive or completely shrouded in fog.

With great regularity, as I have seen it, this isolation–or, from the patient's point of view, inability to discern and experience any emotions about the subject at hand–is a defence erected primarily against the awareness of intensely *ambivalent* feelings. The comparatively lengthy discussion of ambivalence, in the next section of this paper, will serve as an extension of these brief remarks.

Various of the defences enumerated above are of course found, in actual clinical practice, *in combination with one another* more often than not, to that degree complicating the decipherment of many of the patient's communications.

For example, when I had just entered the room of a hebephrenic woman for my usual therapeutic session with her, she said, while pressing her lower abdomen searchingly, 'It feels as though there's a crazy shit in here that's going to the left.' I had already acquired, from previous sessions, enough knowledge of her distorted modes of experience and of communication to surmise that this was a much-disguised way of her experiencing this unconscious feeling and idea: 'I feel that my crazy shit of a therapist, who has just come into this room, is becoming a Communist.' Her comments during the remainder of this session, and the immediately subsequent one, strongly supported such an interpretation. Space does not allow my adducing enough of these data to 'prove' my hunch; let me say only that for many hours there had been indications that my intrusive presence in her room was experienced by her as a stubborn 'shit' that would not 'get out' of her body, and that in the session following this one she confided to me some passages in a letter from her teen-age son (whom I often represented to her in the transference) in which he described his interest, in a current course in college, in reading about the 'Communist revolution' in Russia.

Here was a triply-disguised communication in which the defences of both introjection and condensation (specifically, con-cretization) were at work. The percept of the therapist was condensed into the concrete representation of a 'crazy shit'; the room–the 'in here'–was introjected by the patient and felt as being within her abdomen; and the figurative concept of a political 'going to the left' was experienced by her in a con-cretistic, geographical sense, as the moving to the left, in her abdomen, of the 'crazy' faecal mass.

A paranoid woman whom I had been treating for several years bewildered me by saying abruptly, 'If you turned me into a gnat or mosquito, then the trees would have safe passage!' She of course behaved as though the meaning of this comment should be crystal clear to me; but she did rather impatiently give a bit of elucidation: she reminded me that the trees (on the hospital grounds outside her window) 'have been allowed to stay here so long they're about to split and divide'. My further pressing for information clarified 'split and divide' as meaning 'explode'. When I asked for further elaboration of the idea of her being turned, for example, into a mosquito, she replied, 'Then I could go around and bite everybody,' in a charming tone. I com-mented, 'That wouldn't hurt people very much, would it?', to which she agreed. In earlier phases of our work, she had been terrified of her murderousness.

Many corollary data from my long previous experience with this woman made me fairly sure that this initially so bewildering communication was a much-disguised expression of this un-conscious idea: 'My life-functioning is paralysed by my fear that I will seriously hurt other people. If only you would detoxify my destructiveness, then I could get out of the immobility of this long hospitalization, and safely get moving again as a functioning person.' Both her state of paralysis, and the powerful energy pent up by this paralysis, she projected upon the immobile trees. Further, to her at this stage of her therapy, the concept of her being turned into a relatively innocuous insect was not a figurative concept, but a process which, she was convinced, was quite concretely possible and, in fact, rife in the world about her.

A session during the following month produced from this same woman another example of a remarkably multiply-disguised communication. We were sitting on benches on the lawn near her building. She was in the midst of expressing an unusual upsurge of memories, laden with much feeling – in particular, with fondness and nostalgia – about the persons and places from a long-forgotten era of her past, when, by a seeming effort of her will, she discontinued this line of talk, saying, 'Do you know that woman over there [gesturing towards the building where she roomed; I never became sure whom she meant by 'that woman'] who has that strange head? I think it's about to explode. What do they do – do they take people out of the pipes and then put them in someone's head like that until they mature? I think it would be dangerous if the person isn't able to feel.' She explained that it would be dangerous if the person were unable to feel, because he (or she) would be unaware of the presence of these people in his head; she also elaborated enough to make fairly clear that she visualized the maturation process as a biological one, a change from an embryonic into an eventually adult state.

All this had at first an eerie, ugly, anxiety-provoking effect upon me. But data from my long experience with her delusional perceptions, coupled with the fact that she had just been manifesting anxiety in the face of the upsurge of memories, enabled me to decipher this in a way which, although met with her usual resistiveness when I verbalized the translation to her, proved durably meaningful to me. In essence, it seemed that she was communicating an unconscious protest at this upsurge of memories from her unconscious (the 'pipes', which in many preceding sessions she had located as being underground), a protest that, because she was not yet able to cope with the feelings associated with these memories, these feelings might cause her 'strange head' – projected upon 'that woman over there' – to explode. The agency of the unconscious, which of course did not feel subjectively part of her or within her control, she projected into the outer world; all this was, to her, something that 'they' do. The process of a biological maturation of these people in the host's brain, as she conceptualized it, was a symbolic representation of a psychological process at work in her unconscious–a process whereby her remembered images of these persons were becoming more filled out, richly differentiated–in a sense, therefore, matured. As in the first-described example from my work with her, the defences of both projection and condensation (specifically, here, concretization of figurative concepts) can be seen to be at work, when the communication is retrospectively analysed.

Underlying Psychodynamics

Thus far, I have been describing various forms of the overt features of schizophrenic communication; the various forms which it takes, depending upon whatever unconscious defence(s) the patient is utilizing. Next I shall try to portray something of the underlying psychodynamic state of affairs which necessitates the patient's use of these various pathological forms of communication. Both the depth and breadth of this portrayal will be limited by the need to couch the discussion in general terms; I am attempting here to describe psychodynamics which hold true for schizophrenic patients in general, whereas only a thoroughgoing account of any one individual patient's psychodynamics could clarify, reasonably deeply and fully, the nature of his particular illness and the roots of his particular forms of communication.

REGRESSION

The circumstance of the patient's having regressed to a more or less early level of ego-functioning is explanatory of many of the idiosyncrasies of schizophrenic communication. The clinical picture is complicated, in most instances, by the fact that the level of regression varies unceasingly, at times from one moment to the next, and there are even instances where the patient is functioning on more than one developmental level simultaneously.

The fact of the patient's regressed mode of psychological functioning helps to account for the 'concretization', or contrariwise the seeming oversymbolization, of his communications; these phenomena represent his having regressed, in his thinking (and over-all subjective experiencing), to a developmental level comparable with that in the young child who has not yet become able to differentiate between concrete and metaphorical (or similar forms of highly symbolic) thinking.[4]

[4] Cf. ch. 19.

Similarly, the patient may prattle in a way which gives us to know that the content of his speech is relatively unimportant to him at the moment; he is immersed in the pleasure of saying the words and hearing the sound of them, very like the young child who has not yet learned to talk but loves to babble and to hear the sound of his babbling. A non-verbal patient may usefully be regarded as having regressed even further, to the pre-verbal era of infancy or very early childhood.

The matter of regression, in various ramifications, will come up again and again in the remainder of this discussion.

LACK OF SELF-ESTEEM

A very low self-esteem, generally accepted as one of the characteristics of the schizophrenic patient, is another psychodynamic feature basic to his pathological forms of communication.

So frequently, one feels that the schizophrenic patient is making a most forceful and effective communication, but that for a healthy person so to communicate would exact an unbearable toll in self-abasement.

Ferenczi, in 'Stages in the Development of the Sense of Reality' (1913), says that during the animistic period in the developing apprehension of reality, the child 'learns to represent by means of his body the whole multifariousness of the outer world' (pp. 227-8). To just such an all-encompassing degree is the behaviour of the adult schizophrenic individual, partly by reason of his previously mentioned regression, given over to a communicational representation—a representation much more distorted, however, than that which one sees in the healthy young child—of the events of his perceived outer and inner worlds.

One patient's drooping shoulders, stubble of beard, and tramp-like mode of dress vividly convey his feeling of not-belonging, and his reproach to those about him for not making him a part of their society. A woman's idiotic laughter and simpering demeanour towards her therapist, as they walk across the hospital grounds to his office, serve powerfully to communicate her derision towards him. Another woman's freakish demeanour and her mouthing of confused and half-inaudible sentences serve, eventually, to tell her therapist graphically how grotesque in appearance, and unintelligible in speech, she perceives him to be.

Another woman's making herself up, dressing, and in general behaving like a prostitute, more than adequately communicates her
contempt for those about her, as does another man's frequent
belching, passing of flatus, and generally porcine behaviour.

But all these communicated acts are predicated upon, as well
as being expressive of, an abysmally low self-esteem. It is as
though, in fact, the regressed patient's need to communicate in
such ways—in ways which involve the use of body posturings
and other forms of non-verbal caricature—his need to communicate in such ways because more adult, verbal-symbolic
ways are not as yet available to him, forms one of the *determinants
of* the low state of his self-esteem. It is as though even greater, at
the moment, than his need for self-esteem is his need to communicate with a fellow man.

AMBIVALENCE

The strikingly intense ambivalence, another fundamental aspect
of the schizophrenic individual's psychodynamics, contributes
to a number of different typical kinds of schizophrenic communications.

(a) *Indirect communications*—A hebephrenic woman whom I had
been treating for two years managed to convey to me, in her usual
very indirect, hinting fashion, that she wanted to subscribe to her
home-town newspaper. I felt much moved when I realized the
import of this message; I sensed how poignantly left out she had
felt, throughout her stay at the Lodge, by not having received
this. I suggested to her that she ask Dr Jones, her administrative psychiatrist, to arrange for such a subscription; but she immediately said that there were several Dr Joneses, and that it was
so hard to talk to them. I felt that she could not manage, at this
stage in her therapy when any direct communicating was still
very difficult or impossible for her, to bring this up to Dr Jones
herself, and told her that I would mention this matter to him.

But no sooner had I said that I would tell him, than she proceeded to make it clear that she felt, on the other hand, that were
she to start receiving that newspaper it would be a great burden
to her, and that she would rather forget all about her home town,
and not have to worry about what this person and that were doing there. After having heard this (as usual, indirectly couched)
communication, I changed my position, telling her that I would

not speak to Dr Jones about it, and suggesting that she should do so if she wished. To this she made no, or at most a non-committal, reply.

The above incident is reminiscent of a general principle expressed by Burnham (1955) concerning the schizophrenic man with whom his paper on communication with schizophrenic patients is mainly concerned: 'The obscurity of his language could be thought of as a compromise between his intense desire for, and equally intense fear of, an extraordinarily intimate relationship' (p. 70).

(b) *Self-contradictory* verbal and non-verbal communications – On occasion, the patient may make a statement, or series of statements, in which both content and vocal tone switch suddenly in such a way as to give a self-contradictory effect. For instance, one hebephrenic woman commented to me concerning another woman patient, 'She has a beautiful face,' in an admiring tone. But then without a pause her words switched to scorn in both tone and content, 'She looks like a bulldog.' Another hebephrenic woman made to me an eight-word statement in which the first seven words were uttered in a tone of heartfelt adoration and, with no pause whatever, the eighth in a tone of equally profound contempt: 'You should have the Congressional Medal of Spit.' The person with a reasonably well-integrated ego is quite incapable of reproducing her spoken words – of making so rapid and complete a switch in expressed affect.

(c) Verbal communications in which there is a *split between content and vocal feeling-tone* – A number of examples from one hebephrenic woman will suffice to illustrate this very common type of schizophrenic communication. On one occasion she said to me, 'If you don't like it, sit down and have a drink!', in an antagonistic and defiant tone which clearly conveyed the meaning, 'If you don't like it, get the hell out!' On another occasion, after she had been struggling for some time to convey intelligible words to me, while I had been listening silently, she said disgustedly, '*You* dirty *your* hands on the candy for a while!' The word 'candy' in no way interfered with her getting across, in this, the message, 'You lazy slob – you roll up your sleeves and take a hand at this work of ours, for a change!' On an occasion when I had correctly deciphered the meaning of one of her indirectly-put communications, and succinctly 'read it back' to her, to see if this was not what she was wanting me to understand, she replied with partially irrelevant words, but with a thoroughly confirming vocal tone, by saying, 'You got the tickets!' delightedly. On still another occasion she said, 'You're such a darling!' with a peculiarly hostile vocal tone such that I felt that, despite the complimentary words themselves, she was cutting off my head.

In assessing the meaning of such communications, one soon learns to brush aside the content and attend to the feeling-tone –or, in still more complex instances, tones–in which the words are said.

Incidentally, a patient sometimes evidences a quite accurate grasp of the true import of such communications when they come from the therapist. At the end of each of the maddeningly silent sessions I spent with a hebephrenic man, I would constrain my fury and scorn towards him and politely say, as he started towards the door, 'So long, Mr Bryant–I'll see you tomorrow,' to which he would mutter a furious reply, 'Go to hell, you son of a bitch!' After this had happened several times, it dawned on me that he was very accurately expressing the covert message contained in my 'polite' parting comment to him.

(d) *Non-verbal expression of a feeling contradictory to the one being verbalized*–A paranoid woman verbalized to me, for many months, her impatient wish to have her hospitalization and her work with me completed. Meanwhile, as the months passed, she developed a deep fondness for me which was quite evident to others but, at the time of which I am writing, not yet to herself. Towards the end of one session she said, 'You know I want to live away from here more than anything in the world–you know that, don't you?' to which I made a noncommittal reply. When I indicated, a few minutes later, that the time was up, she seemed as usual reluctant to leave, and this time, as she moved towards the door, instead of opening it she turned her back to it and stretched both arms across it, exactly as if she were determined to hold me captive there, in my office, and simultaneously broke into her usual verbal demands that I should let her go. Despite her words, I had rarely felt so intensely desired by, and desirable to, anyone.

A hebephrenic woman who frequently verbalized her wish to live in the refined atmosphere of a fine hotel (such, presumably, as the one in which her wealthy grandmother had lived throughout the girl's upbringing, in the same city) said in one of her therapeutic sessions, 'I don't see any reason why I can't live in a hotel,' going on to indicate that she thought her behaviour entirely refined. Simultaneously, however, she had raised the front of her skirt and was wiping her genitals with Kleenex–as, for many months, she frequently did. In my experience it is particularly frequent for a patient to verbalize a desire to move out of the sanatorium, but simultaneously to communicate non-verbally a fear of or unreadiness for such a move.

A hebephrenic woman, in one of my earliest sessions with her, was verbally disclaiming any interest in sex, while squirming about in her chair in a markedly seductive, sexually excited manner. In a session sixteen months later she said to me, in a tone of intense loathing, 'God, you're freakish! . . . slimy . . . dopey!', pausing repeatedly to hug her pillow to her, with grief-stricken tears, long before she was to become able, eventually, to acknowledge her wishes to hug and cherish me. During the following month the daily nurses' report contained the following item written by a student nurse. '. . . She grabbed my hand and put it on her and said "Don't touch me." I said, "Judy I am not touching you." She said, "You are," and kicked me. . . .'[5]

Four years later in my work with this same deeply ill woman, I came into her room on a very warm summer day, with the top button of my shirt unbuttoned and without a coat. She soon began behaving, both in her postures and in various indirect verbal comments, in a coarsely sexual fashion. The particularly memorable instance of ambivalence occurred a little later on in the session when she sat down in a chair directly across from me, about five feet away, put her knees far apart, pulled her skirt up to the middle of her thighs and said, looking at my collar, 'Put your collar up, will you?' I asked her bluntly whether she were wishing that I would put my penis up her. To this she made no direct reply but, after some indirect references with sexual overtones, she made some quite sardonic but direct reference to my collar, harshly conveying to me that she felt that it was un-

[5] Here, as in some of the other clinical examples reported, we see the element of the patient's projecting upon the other person the feeling or attitude or behavioural act which he himself is unconsciously communicating, or doing, at a non-verbal level.

tidy. In this deeply disorganized and often animalistic woman I had seen clear evidence, on a number of earlier occasions, of a remarkably severe perfectionism concerning behaviour and particularly dress, reminiscent of each of her perfectionistically tidy parents; I had been reprimanded by her about such matters more than once before. But I was astonished to realize that her 'Put your collar up, will you?' had been simultaneously (i) a very gross sexual overture and (ii) a measure of her perfectionistic prissiness. Each of these had had as strong a feeling-impact upon me as the other.

(e) *Expression of contradictory feelings at an entirely non-verbal level*– A brief example will suffice to illustrate this kind of communication; I have already mentioned on p. 395 the two-in-one, hello-and-farewell, wave which the hebephrenic man gave to his therapist.

A woman was describing to me in detail, and in a strikingly matter-of-fact tone of voice, her having attempted to kill herself during a visit to her parental home, from which she had just been returned to the sanatorium. As her measured, precise words continued their unemotional cadence, her eyes were filled with tears of–so I distinctly sensed it–grief and despair, while her mouth was fixed in a smile of sadistic triumph–triumph, I surmised, at the anguish and anxiety which her near-suicide had aroused in others.

SUPEREGO

The archaically harsh, forbidding superego of the patient is another basic factor which helps to account for his heavily disguised and often fragmentary communications.

For example, the same hebephrenic woman who figured in the collar incident described above, during the early years of our work communicated with me in a fashion which suggested that she felt as though we were a couple of Yanks in a Japanese prison camp, or in some similarly repressive atmosphere wherein her words must be so disguised, and often so muted, that the oppressors would not overhear them and catch their meaning. Very frequently, her speech would consist of a few tersely abbreviated colloquialisms, or mention of names and places which would be meaningful (as I learned from some discussion with the members of her family) to a person from her home city, and from her social circle in that city, but to no one else. Maddeningly often, key words in her few sentences would be unsaid, or muttered inaudibly and not repeated. At times she referred uneasily to 'the woman in the ceiling' who evidently must not be allowed to overhear what was taking place between us—reminiscent to me of much earlier data, from her as well as from the other family members, indicative of a kind of pal-relationship with her father, from which the mother had been excluded.

On many subsequent occasions, when I was now a predominantly hated, despised, and feared mother in the transference, I would feel hurt when she abruptly turned from a seemingly close interchange with me to check with, seemingly, a hallucinatory image of her father, saying some variation of, 'It's O.K., Bill—I'm on to this guy.' This reminded me of the father's undisguised pleasure in telling me, at the time of his daughter's admission to Chestnut Lodge, that she always had liked him better than any of her succession of boy friends; and I came to realize that the mother, portrayed for a long time in the transference relationship as a severe person whom one must avoid provoking—by, for example, avoiding an almost infinite number of touchy subjects —had been shut out, like the boy friends, from the apparently easy-going relatedness between father and daughter.

Later on still in the therapy it became evident that this easy-going relatedness was not actually such, but could be preserved only if one avoided subjects about which the father, whose easy-going demeanour clothed a cruel rejectingness and harsh perfectionism, felt defensive. Thus this hebephrenic woman's superego, which contributed so heavily towards making communication between us desperately difficult, and was projected variously in the form of concentration-camp rulers, or 'the woman in the ceiling', or her seemingly easy-going father, 'Bill' (to mention only a few of the forms which this projection assumed), was a superego which had clearly derived a pathological harshness from *each* of her parents.

But it was particularly interesting to see, as the therapy developed still further, that this harshly forbidding superego apparatus, experienced apparently by her as something quite outside herself which interdicted any free and prolonged communicational exchange between us, resolved itself into a more and more clearly acknowledged sensitivity on her *own* part, in reaction to innumerable key words among my comments, which happened –often quite unexpectedly to me– to touch upon areas of hostility, terror, or grief in herself. It became relatively easy to discern when a word or a phrase from me had suddenly blundered into such an area, and it required much determination on my part to go ahead into, as it were, a field mined with these unseen charges of rage, grief, and so forth. Had I deferred unduly, however, to such areas of sensitivity in her as I already knew of, my speech would have been precisely as disjointed and incomplete as her own had been, earlier in our work, when she had evidently been experiencing it that, for instance, the presence of the disapproving 'woman in the ceiling' made it necessary for her to punch out many of the key words from her own sentences, and otherwise render them cryptic.

THE ATTEMPT TO ACHIEVE, OR TO PERPETUATE A SYMBIOTIC INFANT-MOTHER RELATEDNESS WITH THE THERAPIST

I have come to believe that it can be said, quite generally, that the various forms of verbal and non-verbal communication characteristic of schizophrenia are reflective of the patient's effort to foster, or to maintain, a symbiotic relatedness with the therapist (and, apart from the therapeutic sessions, with–to use Sullivan's phrase–significant other persons), a relatedness such as normally holds between the young infant and his mother, in which the participants are subjectively at one with each other. I have reported elsewhere (chapters 10, 11, 15) my experience that such a mode of relatedness marks a therapeutically essential phase in the evolution of the schizophrenic patient's transference to his therapist–that his ego-fragmentation must gradually be resolved into such an interpersonal relatedness, before a more healthy ego-differentiation can subsequently develop out of this basic healthy-infant-and-loving-mother oneness in the transference relationship. I have attempted carefully to explain that this is a mode of relatedness which it is not within the power of the therapist to wield manipulatively as a deliberate psychotherapeutic technique, but rather that it tends inevitably to *happen* over the long course of the therapy, after an earlier phase of intense and mutual ambivalence between patient and therapist has been traversed, and that the cue for the therapist is to try to see whether this is occurring, and to try not to interfere with its development, rather than to feel guilty, ashamed, or afraid about this state of affairs.

The obscurity of the patient's communications is such that his therapist tends to become the sole expert, or in any case the leading expert, in deciphering his communications. This circumstance contributes greatly to the private aura which their relationship develops, an aura of uniquely close communion as contrasted with their subjective distance from an outer world which 'does not understand'. Moreover, the therapist progressively moves into a position where he translates the communications of the confused schizophrenic patient even for the latter himself; in this, as well as in other ways, he functionally does the patient's thinking and feeling for him, to a considerable degree—he comes to personify the patient's externalized ego.

The prolonged silences which characterize the sessions foster abundant projection and introjection on the part of each participant. Thus not only does the patient maintain the quiet conviction that his therapist knows what he is thinking and feeling, without the need for any explicit communication—that, in essence, the therapist can read his mind—but the therapist also comes without realizing it to assume, much of the time, that the patient is sharing his thoughts and feelings as the quiet minutes pass. The therapist may find himself quite disconcerted when the silent patient does resume speaking, for it then becomes unmistakable, more often than not, that his thought-content has been pursuing a course, a subject, widely different from the thoughts which have been running through the therapist's mind. Each of them finds painful such reminders that they are separate beings. One of my patients said, after I had broken a silence with some words which he evidently found alien and unsharing of his own feeling-state, 'There's no friendly intuition here.' Much of the time, however, their communion is genuinely close, and it is not without reason that the therapist, as well as the patient, develops the conviction that the other knows him better and more intimately than does anyone else in the world.

In the instance of most of the chronic schizophrenic patients with whom I have worked, there has been a predominantly non-verbal phase extending over a number of (in some instances, many) months. This is evidently the phase which Eissler (1951) terms the 'phase of relative clinical muteness' in the patient's psychotherapy. Invariably, when the patient has gone on eventually to the solid establishment of verbal interaction with me, this has been experienced by me, and so far as I could determine by the patient also, as not an unalloyed triumph of increasing maturation, but a step which also involves a marked sense of loss –the loss of the subjective sense of therapist-patient (mother-infant) oneness, so akin to the infant's coming to lose, with advancing individuation as his ego-boundaries become established, his erstwhile oceanic world-self.

The transference evolution which I have outlined makes heavy demands upon the therapist's–as well, of course, as the patient's –feeling-capacities. He tends to be afraid of the intimacy involved in a genuine symbiotic relatedness with the patient; for example, he tends to be afraid of the deep communion which the silent hours often involve, and to be concerned lest the patient matters more than he should to him. And later, when it is time for both to relinquish their symbiotic relatedness, it is tempting for the therapist to try somehow to preserve this subjective oneness over-long, in order, first, not to have to experience the pain and anxiety of the sense of separateness and, secondly, to avoid facing all kinds of negative feelings, in himself as well as in the patient, against which the symbiosis can serve so effectively as an unconscious defence, just as did the pathology-ridden symbiosis in the patient's background. Whereas the therapist earlier had the task of learning to understand the patient's communications, now he must help him learn to communicate in terms which are understandable to the other people in his environment. The therapist who earlier had dared to accept a Pygmalion feeling-orientation towards his Galatea, an orientation at first awesome in its power and later deeply enjoyable, must come to accept this far humbler-seeming role in order to have the satisfaction of helping the patient to achieve a healthy and durable maturity.

Psychotherapeutic Technique

The above paragraphs have already opened up the subject to which the remainder of this paper is devoted: the therapist's technique in coping with those difficulties in communication which are a function of the schizophrenic process.

Innumerable instances of the therapist's uncertainty how to

respond to the patient's communication turn upon the question
of whether the communication is to be 'taken personally'–to be
taken as primarily designed, for instance, towards filling the
therapist with perplexity, confusion, anxiety, humiliation, rage,
or some other negatively toned affective state; or whether it is to
be taken rather as primarily an effort to convey some basically
unhostile need on the patient's part. Just as it is often essential
that the therapist become able to sense and respond to personal
communications in a patient's ostensibly stereotyped behaviour
or utterances, so too it is frequently essential that he be able to
see, behind the overt 'personal' reference to himself–often a
stinging or otherwise emotionally evocative reference–some fundamental need which the patient is hesitant to communicate
openly.

A hebephrenic woman and I had, for years, a great capacity to
rub each other up the wrong way; whole sessions would be spent
in mutually vindictive comments and non-verbal torture operations. In one period of the therapy, during which she was often
described by the ward staff as sitting in her bed, or in a chair in
the hall, crying for hours on end, her first comment as I came into
her room was, 'Do you know you're Dr Searles?' She asked this
in a matter-of-fact rather than a taunting tone; but on the basis
of abundant past experience with her taunts I felt needled, as
usual, and thought to myself, with irritation and impatience,
'Of course I know I'm Dr Searles.'

This time, however, I replied with a measure of friendliness and
matter-of-factness, 'Yes–either Dr Searles or Harold Searles,'
wanting her to know that it was all right for her to call me by my
first name if she wished. It was perhaps twenty minutes later in
the session, after much other talk–most of it fragmentary, as
usual–from her that she said, 'Thelma Foster [a name I had
never before heard] is a nice person,' in a tone of forced enthusiasm. She added, in the same tone, 'Diana Kendall [another
such name] is a nice person too.' She then added in a noncommittal tone, 'She sits and cries all the time.' I said, 'I wonder
what she is crying about.' She replied, in a tone I found very
poignant, 'She's crying because she doesn't know who she is.'

This came to me as a deeply moving revelation, for, despite
the fact that she clearly had misidentified me on innumerable
occasions, I had failed to realize that she was often unaware of

her own identity. I understood now that her initial question, 'Do you know you're Dr Searles?', indeed had not been intended as a jeering commentary on my stupidity, but had been an indirect way of trying to reveal a grief-laden but to her also humiliating aspect of her self-experience.

It continued for long after that, however, to be a difficult thing for me to sense, in the face of her remarkable facility for making me feel insulted, the painful feelings about which she was covertly asking me for help. Another of the times when I became able to sense these occurred five months later.

On this second occasion I had been feeling exasperated, anxious, and perhaps more than anything worn down, by her having misidentified me most of the time for more than two years as being one or another person–sometimes several changing persons in any one session–from Philadelphia, her home city, while mentioning in her fragmentary way innumerable names of persons and places which she evidently assumed were well known to me, but which to me were unadorned names only; she would keep looking to me to know all the background details that went with the names of these persons and places. When I went into her room for this particular session, she was sitting on her bed, looking through some sheets torn out of an advertising brochure from a famous store, sheets showing pictures of women's clothing. I commented that this store is in California; she agreed. I asked her whether she had ever been shopping there; to this she gave no clear reply. But then she asked me, 'Have you ever been shopping?' At first I started to feel derogated by this question; so many times before I had smarted at her treating me like an imbecile.

It occurred to me, however, that perhaps she was not sure she had ever been shopping; so I simply said, 'Yes.' She soon said, 'You've been shopping–I've been shopping,' but in an unconvincing tone as though reciting something. I asked, 'But do you feel so out of touch with shopping that it's hard for you to believe that you've ever *been* shopping?' She clearly agreed that this was so, and went on to say, after having just said the names of two or three New York department stores, 'Names mean me little.'

With this, the realization dawned on me that for over two years now, in the previously described kind of relatedness wherein she had been simultaneously misidentifying me and inundating me with names which I found meaningless and bewildering, actually these had been, all along, little but names to her also, and that she had been trying desperately to perceive me as someone (various persons at various times) who could fill in the details for her. With this I felt once again, of course, much more receptivity, kindliness, and patience with her.

On the other hand, as I have said, it is often crucial for the therapist to be able to sense a covert interpersonal communication in schizophrenic behaviour which seems, on the face of it, utterly stereotyped and autistic. For example, the stereotyped military salute with which a hebephrenic man greets me—just as he greets other people in his environment, including each of the passers-by who speak to him—has at times, as I have come to see and feel it, a defiant, contemptuous little additional jerk to it, after his hand has snapped up to his brow, a jerk which clearly conveys something translatable in words as, 'Up your ass, you stuffed shirt!' At other moments, the salute conveys equally strong feelings of fondness, genuine respect, and a pleading for help. In chapters 10 and 11 I have presented other clinical examples of this nature. Some comments by Ruesch, although concerned primarily with non-verbal communication, are beautifully descriptive of the process which occurs in such patients as the transference evolves over the course of the therapy:

> . . . the primitive and uncoordinated movements of patients at the peak of severe functional psychoses . . . may be viewed as attempts to re-establish the infantile system of communication through action. It is as if these patients were trying to relive the patterns of communication that were frustrating in early childhood, *with the hope that this time there will be another person who will understand and reply* in nonverbal terms. This thesis is supported by observations of the behaviour of psychotic children who tend to play with their fingers, make grimaces, or assume bizarre body positions. Their movements rarely are directed at other people but rather at themselves, sometimes to the point of producing serious injuries. *As therapy proceeds, interpersonal movements gradually replace the solipsistic movements,*[6] and stimulus becomes matched to response. Once these children have been satisfied in nonverbal ways, they become willing to learn verbal forms of codification and begin to acquire mastery of discursive language (Ruesch, 1955, p. 327).

A hebephrenic woman, in two successive therapeutic sessions,

[6] All italics mine—H.S.

made strikingly clear the presence of two contrasting feeling-states, one of helplessness and the other of hostility, which lay behind the fragmentation that had characterized her communications to me for many months.

In the first of these two sessions she helped me to see with unprecedented clarity the fact that her own perceptual world was a fragmentary, chaotically confused one. She conveyed this to me by reading aloud to me, first from a two-page typewritten letter she had just received from a home-town friend, and then from a chewing-gum wrapper. As she read from the letter, she spoke only isolated words, some of which (I later found upon reading it myself, with her permission) were actually in the letter, and many others of which were not; these latter were evidently welters of associations which certain of the words touched off in her mind, associations experienced by her not as such but rather as words on the page. In reading the gum wrapper she read, 'Wrigley's-keys-trees-,' the second and third words being clang associations, and then read the remainder of the brief sentence correctly, except for the word 'manufacturer', which she read as 'maintainer-maintainer'. The letter, in particular, evidently came through to her as utterly meaningless gibberish – reminiscent to me of the nature of most of her verbalizations to me and, I presumed, comparable with the way most of my comments sounded to her. Her demeanour throughout conveyed her anguish at finding her own mental processes so impossibly hampered. At one point she said in a low, intense voice, 'I'm crazy!', as if the stunning realization of this were coming home to her more deeply than ever before. This whole hour left me feeling unprecedentedly patient with her and devoted to helping her.

Then in the session on the following day she was her more usual antagonistic self towards me and, although not having to be propelled to the hour – as was often necessary – she came to her room most reluctantly. Her verbalizations in the first few minutes were sparse and utterly fragmentary; she addressed me by various different names; and her over-all demeanour was that which I had found, so very often in the preceding many months, hate-engendering in me. After about five or ten minutes of this she said, 'How would *you* like to see a different doctor every morning – all these *doctors*!' in utter resentment and disgust, making it very clear with this and subsequent fragmentary comments that she felt thoroughly fed up. Then she said, with unprecedented directness (so far as this particular subject was concerned), 'I hate doctors! That's why I make things [clearly referring, as I felt it, to her communications] mush!' As the hour progressed, it became very clear to me that one of the prices she was paying for 'making things mush' was that her own experience became mush in the same process. Just as I had felt nearly overwhelmed on the preceding day at seeing the depth of her helpless despair, now I felt the comparably awesome impact of her hatred.

The therapist must rely, in the far more numerous instances than the above two unusually clear-cut ones, upon his own intuition to tell him which kind of feeling is striving for expression behind the patient's utterances; but his intuition can develop the necessary breadth only in proportion as he can bear to be attuned to such intense and extremely contrasting feelings as these.

There are certain constraints under which the therapist must at times labour. Frequently, the patient's anxiety and proneness to confusion may be such that any verbal communication must be couched in a very few words; one of the patients I am treating at present, for example, can usually attend to no more than the first three or four words of a sentence.

Almost as frequently, we find that figures of speech which are in everyday use in our culture will have, for the schizophrenic individual, a bewilderingly concretistic meaning; so that for extended periods of time, with some of these persons, we learn to be sparing with the use of metaphor and allied modes of expression.

In occasional instances, we may find that the suspicious and confused patient attaches so much more significance to the nonverbal accompaniments–the manual gestures, for example–of one's speaking, than to one's words themselves, that we learn deliberately to keep such distracting physical movements to a minimum in saying something which we particularly want to get across to the patient.

Incidentally, in these last-mentioned instances it would be quite erroneous, of course, as well as technically unwise for the therapist to deny that his gestures have inadvertently revealed some significant, but to him unconscious, feeling or attitude towards the patient. The therapist, so much of whose professional activity is dedicated to helping the patient to explore the pre-conscious and unconscious realms in his personality-functioning, must be able freely to acknowledge the existence of such realms in his own personality. Thus when a patient whom I am seeing in her room notes, while I am speaking to her, that my hand has inadvertently gestured towards her nearby bed, and she, seated across the room from me, quite disregards my words and expresses her conviction that I am trying, with my gesture, to tempt her into sexual activity, I do not brush aside the possibility that she may be quite correct. For one thing, I have long since learned that schizophrenic patients are however unadept at interpreting the therapist's *conscious* communications, extremely perceptive of what is going on in his unconscious —extremely alert, that is, to communications which he is *unconcious* of conveying. To deny out of hand that such perceptions possess validity is to deny such accurate reality-testing as the ill patient does possess.

So instead I reply in such an instance somewhat as follows: 'You may be quite correct about that; all I can say is that I was not aware of trying to say that. Try to listen to my words, for my words, rather than the movements of my hands—which much of the time I don't even notice—represent what I am conscious of and am trying to get across to you.' Then I will repeat what I had earlier attempted to convey, this time deliberately avoiding the distracting gesticulations. If, by the way, the patient has pointed out something revealed by me in such a non-verbal manner, and which was so close to consciousness that I now become aware of it when it is thus called to my attention, I confirm the patient's suspicious hunch, but indicate that this matter which I had earlier begun to express verbally to her must still be explored. Such a response is reassuring rather than alarming to her: it both reassures her that she has perceived correctly a bit of outer reality, and it reassures her that the therapist dares to face his own unconscious processes and to remain responsible for them, rather than having to deny their presence in himself and burden her with the main brunt of seeing them and coping with them, as did her mother and father during her upbringing.

There is one other communicational restraint to be mentioned, and this is a quite general one: schizophrenic patients, for so many of whom the other person's non-verbal communications take precedence over the accompanying verbal communications, are themselves likely to react, when their own non-verbal accompaniments to speech are called to their attention by the therapist, only with increased anxiety. Here, even more than in the analysis of neurotic individuals, it is well for the therapist to wait until the patient has become able to reveal *in words* an at least partial awareness of this or that conflict before calling it more explicitly to his attention. That which the patient reveals by gesture and other non-verbal avenues provides the therapist, of course, with, abundant and invaluable data; but it is usually best to store up this information privately and wait for the patient's *verbalizations* to indicate that these data are now beginning to reach the level of his own consciousness. To call them to his attention earlier disturbs, in too many instances, his precarious sense of personal identity (see chapter 15).

So much for the matter of constraints upon the therapist's communications and upon his utilization of those of the patient. These restrictions upon our modes of participation with the patient are, even when taken all together, minor in contrast to the considerations which render it not only legitimate but imperative for the curative process that the therapist enjoy a relatively great measure of freedom.

Only if the forces of liberation and growth in the therapist are more powerful than those tending towards constriction, stasis, and psychological paralysis, can the patient by turn–partially through identification with the therapist–live, grow, and become progressively well. Such a statement as the following by Arieti (1955) would deny the therapist the inner freedom to experience as wide a range of feelings as possible towards the patient–the freedom to accept himself as a human being with hatred as well as love in his make-up–which in my opinion is a most essential ingredient of the therapeutic interaction: '. . . If at the beginning of the treatment the therapist has a feeling of hostility, or even a feeling of non-acceptance for the patient, any attempted treatment will be doomed to failure' (p. 451).

Similarly Hill (1955), in his book which for the most part I consider unexcelled, implies in the following passage that the therapist who works with schizophrenic patients must somehow delete any real hostility from his make-up (and, to apply this to our subject here, from his communications to his patients) in order to be genuinely qualified for this work:

> . . . Even in moments of warm appreciation and grateful co-operation, the patient may suddenly block everything because of his fear and distrust, even his strong belief that the therapist is an enemy. It may be, unfortunately, that at this moment he eliminates him forever from the company of those who can be useful to him. This may be the beginning of the end of reality for him. Some patients probably are beyond effective co-operation when first seen, but there is a painful suspicion that such a sudden rejection is usually based upon the patient's recognition of something in the doctor's or the nurse's attitude which is in psychological reality destructive to him (pp. 30–31).

Such counsel underestimates the unquenchable power of the human being's—including the schizophrenic human being's—striving to live and grow. It is reminiscent to me of a description given by Fromm-Reichmann, in one of her later papers, of how fragile the schizophrenic patient was considered to be, relatively early (1939) in the history of the work at Chestnut Lodge with these patients; and of how much more strength they were now seen, at the time of her writing that later paper (1948), to possess.

Related to the therapist's readiness to condemn himself for any strongly negative feelings he experiences towards the patient is his concern lest he make irreparable errors of technique. Here it is well to remember that, since the patient's needs are usually so deeply ambivalent, any single response on the therapist's part is apt at best to meet reasonably well one need or set of needs, while inevitably thwarting the conflicting ones. Further, I have come to think it a useful rule of thumb to assume that the deeper the patient's confusion, the more unquestioningly does he attribute omniscience to his therapist; evidently it would be intolerably anxiety-provoking to him to realize that there are many occasions when *both* persons in the therapeutic situation are feeling confused and helpless. Burnham (1955) puts it that the schizophrenic patient tends to 'assume that the therapist understands much more than he actually does . . . to the point of believing that all of his inner thoughts are known by the doctor . . .' (pp. 68–9). When the therapist comes to realize how entirely beyond human attainment is this godlike understanding which the patient needs to attribute to him, his appraisal of his own efforts becomes less perfectionistic, he no longer perceives his mistakes as being catastrophic, and he dares to rely more upon his intuition—his preconscious and unconscious processes which are his strongest tool for seeing to the heart of the bewilderingly complex interaction taking place between himself and the patient and for communicating with him. This interaction, much of the time, must switch its affective tone and ideational content too rapidly for any consciously well-thought-out verbal responses from the therapist to meet the patient's needs.

I very much like, and found occasion to quote in chapter 3, comments by Leo Berman and by Lidz and Lidz concerning the role of the therapist's mistakes in the treatment of schizophrenic patients. Berman (1949) says that the therapist's

... 'failing', if it does not become too marked, probably . . . plays a part in the therapeutic process. The patient has occasion to experience the reality of a person who dedicates himself to the task of helping him to grow up and who comes through reasonably well in spite of obvious difficulties (p. 165).

Lidz and Lidz (1952) point out that 'The strength in the therapist that must be conveyed to the patient may well derive from sufficient integrity not to need to be infallible' (p. 173).

There is still another reason why it is well for the therapist to become able to desist from a perfectionistic striving towards omniscience in response to the schizophrenic patient's puzzling or confusing communications: such a striving on the therapist's part, at some phase in the work with almost any one of these persons, plays into the hands of the patient's sadism. On innumerable occasions, as I have seen both in my own work and in that of therapists whose work I have supervised, it comes about that the therapist reaches a point of desperation in his efforts to rescue the schizophrenic damsel (female or male; this is a figure of speech) from the scaly dragon of confusion which, as evidenced by the unceasing torrent of unintelligible words which issue from the patient's mouth, has this poor sufferer in its grip. Eventually, in those instances where the psychotherapy succeeds in breaking through this deadlock, it dawns upon the therapist that the patient is not only the poor struggling victim but the dragon also, and he realizes to what a degree he himself has been impaled, all along, upon the patient's sadistic effort—usually a genuinely unscious effort—to drive him crazy with these maddeningly unintelligible utterances.[7] It seems as though in most instances this effort has been pushed within striking distance of its goal before the therapist, with his own sanity subjectively at stake, develops sufficient 'callousness' to step back and take a somewhat dispassionate look at what has been going on all along with this dragon and its victim.

The precise way in which the above-described development becomes therapeutic is, I think, as follows. The patient has indeed been in the grip of a 'crazy' introject—usually, as Hill (1955) puts it in beautifully vivid detail, an introject of a crazy mother—which disrupts his own ego-functioning with crazy utterances and malicious counsel, coming to him oftentimes in the form of auditory hallucinations. In many instances, I think, the words which the patient conveys to the therapist are a fairly faithful repetition of the confusing words which this introject showers upon the poor patient's head. But, on the other hand, this introject has long ago become the vehicle, also, for the patient's own repressed sadism, and by exposing the therapist to the destructive force of the introject he is, in the same process, venting upon the latter his 'own'—but anacknowledged—sadism. Eventually, the therapist becomes aware of the part which the patient's sadism is playing in the interaction, and thereby becomes able to shield himself against the destructive effect of the patient's communications—primarily by desisting from the self-tormenting rescue effort as described above. The result of this change in the therapist's mode of participation is that the patient's dissatisfaction with, and eventually rage against, him becomes more and more explicit and therefore therapeutically investigable. Then, through identification with the steadfast therapist who can ignore the crazy distractions, the patient in turn is able finally to ignore them and to go ahead with exercising his healthier ego-functions in spite of them. All this is no mere conjecture as to the course which psychotherapy with a schizophrenic patient should ideally follow in this particular regard, but is, rather, the course which I have actually seen it to follow in successful instances.

Closely related to the above development, and overlapping with it, is the gradual realization on the part of the therapist,

[7] Cf. ch. 8.

SCHIZOPHRENIA AND RELATED SUBJECTS

previously so caught up in a deadly serious endeavour to rescue the poor struggling patient, that all this is not so desperately serious now as he had long felt it to be; that the patient's maddeningly confusing communications, once the emergence of their sadistic 'driving-crazy' significance has helped him to see them in a different perspective, have a healthily playful quality at their root. Whereas he used to be the sober target of the patient's partially sadistic, but also partially genuinely playful, teasing *via* the bewildering communications, he becomes able instead to join the patient more and more often in mutually enjoyable plays on words, contributions of chaotically nonsensical verbalizations, and uninhibited flights of fancy. Here has become restored, I believe, what was best and healthiest in the patient's very early relationship with the mother;[8] and it is upon this kind of playful and unfettered interaction, historically traceable to the beginnings of verbal relatedness in the young child's life, that the patient's gradual development of firm ego-boundaries, and use of more logically organized, adult forms of thought and communication, can be founded. The therapist learns to his surprise that there is a kind of chaos and confusion which is not anxiety-provoking and destructive, but thoroughly pleasurable–the playful chaos which a mother and a little child, or which two little children can share, where mutual trust prevails to such a degree that there is no need for self-defensive organization.

Another way of viewing schizophrenic communication, in such a way as to help ourselves become free from undue self-demandingness, is this. We have the job of becoming more skilful at deciphering the patient's disguised communications; but *he* has the task of becoming able, over the long course of therapy, to express himself in more conventional terms. Thus we find that our therapeutic dedication is on several counts misplaced if it is persistently directed towards a sober and selfless wracking of our brains to unravel the confusing communications: not only does an unvarying orientation of that kind prevent us from assessing fully the patient's sadism, and from participating subsequently with him in a therapeutically valuable phase of playfulness with communicational devices, but also it tends to maintain him in a regressive position where he is not held basi-

[8] See ch. 7.

cally responsible for the development of increasingly mature forms of communication.

In my work with an initially highly autistic, though verbal, woman it was only after a number of years of therapy that she had become sufficiently in tune with her own emotions and ideational content, and tolerant enough of interpersonal intimacy, to be able to clarify the meanings of various puzzling verbalizations which she had been uttering, from time to time, all along. I realized, in retrospect, how utterly impossible it would have been for me to divine their meaning earlier in the therapy. Experiences of this kind, over the years during which the work with such a patient necessarily extends, help one to develop more realistic and therefore more comfortable self-expectations.

Without exception in my experience, the psychotherapy with each schizophrenic patient includes a phase, sometimes at the very outset and sometimes only after years of work, in which the whole realm of verbal communication must gradually be relinquished by both participants in the therapeutic interaction, as it becomes clear that there is a need for the establishment of reliable communication in the developmentally earlier, non-verbal, mode before really effective verbal communication can develop in the patient. I am in full accord with Ruesch's (1955) statement that '. . . the patient has to gain communicative experience in the non-verbal mode before he can engage in verbal exchange' (p. 326) and '. . . It is only through non-verbal replies that a non-verbal patient can be influenced; and once such non-verbal interaction has been established, the organization of the patient's experiences gradually can be translated into words' (ibid., p. 329).

Space allows me to give only one brief sample of this therapeutic evolution which I believe to be so generally true of the work with these patients. A paranoid woman had been in therapy with me for several years. The work had been, much of the time, stormy indeed and, during the first few years, highly verbal; she used to assert spontaneously that she could not stand, and never had been able to stand, 'the intimacy of silence'. Then gradually she became able to endure, and eventually to enjoy, more and more prolonged periods of mutual silence in the sessions. In one particular session, for instance, my words were limited to (*a*) an initial, 'Want to go outside?' (we often spent the sessions sitting on adjoining benches in the hospital grounds) to which she replied, 'Yes', the only word she spoke during the interview; (*b*) an unpressured and unpressuring question, 'What's the matter?', about two-thirds of the way through the hour, when she had winced, to which she made no reply; and (*c*) a parting, 'See you in the morning.' Throughout the course of this hour, we exchanged innumerable glances, reflective, as I experienced them, of fondness, pleasure, comfort, perplexity, at times a little tension, and so on—with, throughout, a feeling of communion on my part with her, and with her facial expressions clearly appearing to reflect such communion on her part. There had been many such predominantly silent hours, by now, in my work with her; but for the first time I experienced a deep conviction that such non-verbal communication is genuine, valid, and to be relied upon. I had little doubt that if she or I had said much, our words would not have expressed at all accurately or adequately what was being expressed non-verbally; but I realized that *even this* would not negate the validity of the non-verbal.

I was reminded, during the above therapeutic session, of a memorable passage in the writings of the philosopher, Martin Buber, in which there is conveyed with rare eloquence the author's daring to rely upon, and to experience deep meaning in, purely non-verbal communion with a fellow human being. In this passage, Buber describes the communication which can flow between two men, only recently met, who are sitting silently beside one another. One of these is psychologically there, whereas

. . . The other, whose attitude does not betray him, is a man who holds himself in reserve, withholds himself. But if we know about him we know that a childhood's spell is laid on him, that his withholding of himself is something other than an attitude, behind all attitude is entrenched the impenetrable inability to communicate himself. And now—let us imagine that this is one of the hours which succeed in bursting asunder the seven iron bands about our heart—imperceptibly the spell is lifted. But even now the man does not speak a word, does not stir a finger. Yet he does something. The lifting of the spell has happened to him—no matter from where—without his doing. But this is what he does now: he releases in himself a reserve over which only he himself has power. Unreservedly communication streams from him, and the silence bears it to his neighbour. Indeed it was intended for him, and he receives it unreservedly as he receives all genuine destiny that meets him. He will be able to tell no one, not even himself, what he has experienced. What does he now 'know' of the other? No more knowing is needed. For where unreserve has ruled, even wordlessly, between men, the word of dialogue has happened sacramentally (Buber, 1947, pp. 3-4 of 1955 edition).

To be sure, this hypothetical incident which Buber describes only in part approximates to that which took place between the paranoid woman and me, for neither of us had become, as yet, as unanxiously receptive to non-verbal communication as is one of the men–undoubtedly the philosopher himself–in Buber's portrayal. I had every impression that we were moving *mutually* towards an acceptance of the validity which inheres in deep and non-verbal communion. Moreover, recurrently there appears in Buber's writings a note of mysticism–for example, 'Speech can renounce all the media of sense, and it is still speech' (*ibid*, p. 3) which I cannot accept. But we psychiatrists have been trained for so many years to revere *words* as the prime carriers of meaning that, confronted now with the discovery that the schizophrenic patient can become well only if we can make contact with the meaning implicit in the neglected and unfamiliar realm of non-verbal communication, we can be grateful for the rare illumination which Buber throws upon this terrain.

My few remaining points concerning technique have to do with various aspects of patients' verbal communications.

I have learned slowly and painfully, at great cost to myself and even greater cost to my patients, that when one is working with a deeply-fragmented patient who vocalizes only isolated words or phrases, each of which one senses to possess multiple possible references, it is well to wait until the fragments coalesce more fully, and the referents become thereby more clearly focused and sure to one, before responding with any great frequency. The coalescence to which I refer is, of course, gradual and may require many months; but for the therapist to respond earlier, very abundantly, to these isolated words and phrases only serves to inundate the confused patient with the therapist's own free associations to these verbal fragments. In line with the already-mentioned point that the deeply-confused patient assumes the therapist to be omniscient, the former immediately assumes now that the latter is trying to tell him something, and is further

distressed at being unable to find meaning in the therapist's associations, whereas these had been intended to encourage the patient to verbalize further *his* initial, fragmentary communication.

There thus develops within a matter of seconds, a state of
affairs in which *each* person is confused—or at best puzzled—and
is mistakenly assuming that the other is trying to tell him something. It is good, of course, for the therapist's free-associational
processes to be as unconstricted as possible; but the integration
of the patient's fragmentary subjective experience, and of his
communications, will proceed relatively unimpeded if the therapist at this stage of the work keeps his free associations, his
'hunches', largely *to himself*, storing them up until these have
become better integrated within him, and until the patient
has developed a sufficiently integrated ego—primarily, I believe,
through non-verbal therapeutic interaction—to be able to make
use of more liberal verbal responses from his therapist.

I have learned, too, that in the instance of the patient who is
better integrated and more verbal, but whose experience involves a high degree of projection, introjection, or displacement,
it is well to accept his verbal communications in the frame of
reference in which he couches them—that is, in their projected
or introjected or displaced form—rather than try for example to
bring the projection home to him where it belongs. A premature
effort to cut through the particular defence will quite regularly
terminate the state of communicativeness between oneself and
the patient, whereas accepting his vantage-point will facilitate
his elaborating his views more fully, and a progressively elaborated projection, for example, may come gradually to develop a
sufficient number of ego-syntonic elements for the patient to
begin to accept the projection as a part of himself.

There are two situations in which I have found that a certain
rather specific response facilitates the differentiation of the
patient's ego:

In one of these situations, the therapist senses that what the
patient is saying comes not from his own ego but from an introject; one detects this from a cliché quality in the content of his
words or, more often, from a shift in his vocal tone such that he
sounds as though he were parroting someone else rather than
expressing him*self*. Here I have found it useful to reply, 'Who
used to say that?' At first he will probably be disconcerted by

this, and may angrily assert, 'Nobody. *I'm* saying it!' But this kind of response, persisted in over the months, helps greatly in his coming to locate, gradually, the parental figures from whom a very high proportion of 'his own'–actually introjected–views have come; and, by the same token, this facilitates his getting his parents out of himself so that he can now better experience, and explore, his *feelings towards* them–feelings which had been repressed, partially through the unconscious use of such introjects since his childhood years.

In the second of these situations, the patient has developed as yet very little of any 'observing ego'; he is so inundated by his feelings that, when these well up in him during the therapeutic session for example, he is swept up in their outpouring towards the therapist. The therapist, feeling the full and unrestrained impact of these, and finding the patient so unable to keep an open mind to the possible transference origin of any of these feelings, is himself caught up, many a time, in a comparably thoughtless feeling-response to the patient's words. For example, it is very difficult to retain much of one's own observing ego when a hebephrenic man glares at one and says, in a deeply insulting tone, 'Go to hell, you slimy son of a bitch!' A no-holds-barred retort in kind has often seemed mandatory. And comparably with a paranoid woman's argumentativeness, her power to arouse dissent in me was so great that, for months on end, I could not achieve any appreciable psychological distance from the arguments which would engage us. But in my work with each of these two patients I have learned eventually to respond to such utterances as constituting the patient's effort to *report* his thoughts and feelings to me–an effort in line with my many-times-repeated suggestion made during silent intervals in the sessions. No doubt my eventually 'learning' to respond in this new manner was, in each of these instances, in part a function of the patient's advancing ego-differentiation as the therapy progressed.[9] It seems at first more than a little incongruous, of course, to reply, in the brief pause after a schizophrenic patient's full-throated torrent of abuse, with 'Let's see what comes to mind next.' But I have found these patients readier than I had imagined to accept such a view of their own verbal productions. With such reinforcement from their therapist, they are helped in developing

* Cf. chs. 10, 11.

a growingly consistent observing ego, and one learns that a surprisingly large number of their outpourings of their 'own' feelings consist in the patient's serving as the communicational vehicle for the introjects–consist in his instantaneous and unthinking quotation to the therapist of what the 'voices' are saying to him.

Eight years before writing this paper I was taking part in a research seminar led by Frieda Fromm-Reichmann where the question early arose, concerning schizophrenic patients' distorted verbal communications, whether such communications are to be regarded as only a manner of speaking, or whether they are to be heard as reasonably accurate representations of a subjective experience which is actually distorted to such a degree. All of us, in discussing this point, found that we were in agreement that one reason why the therapy of schizophrenia is so complex is that, in the instance of any one patient, as I mentioned early in this paper, his communications are at one moment towards one end of a scale in this regard, and at another moment towards the other end. In the course of my own work during the intervening years, I have seldom found that a communication initially hard to locate on such a scale proved eventually to have been only a manner of *speaking*; recurrently, instead, I have discovered with awe that the patient's subjective experience is, in a high proportion of instances, as genuinely and terribly distorted–as chaotically fragmented, or rudimentarily differentiated, or bleak, or what not–as his words suggest. For example, I now have no doubt that a hebephrenic woman struggling against repressed jealousy really did see 'triangular pupils' in her rival's eyes; or that a paranoid woman during a phase of depression really did see things in her environment as coloured blue; or that a hebephrenic man thought, when I left his room for only a moment, that I had been away for a whole week-end; or that various of these and other patients have perceived me, and themselves, as multiple and often non-human beings.[10] Becoming able to deal skilfully with schizophrenic communication requires one, more than anything else, to become able to endure seeing, and at least momentarily sharing at a feeling level, the world in which the schizophrenic individual exists.

[10] See my *The Nonhuman Environment*.

Chapter 14

SEXUAL PROCESSES IN SCHIZOPHRENIA (1961)[1]

A VOLUMINOUS literature attests to the importance of sexual
processes in the aetiology and symptomatology of schizophrenia. Freud describes this illness as involving 'a complete
abandonment of object-love and a return to infantile auto-
erotism' (Freud, 1911, p. 77) and of Schreber's paranoia he says,
'The exciting cause of his illness . . . was an outburst of homosexual libido . . . and his struggles against this libidinal impulse
produced the conflict which gave rise to the symptoms' (Freud,
1911, p. 43). Sullivan (1953, p. 135) describes schizophrenic
panic as traceable to 'the failure of dissociations which were connected with, and made possible, the sublimation of the undis-
sociated components of the sexual drives'. Bleuler (1911), Rosen
(1953), Macalpine and Hunter (1955), and others note that
schizophrenic patients regularly show confusion as regards their
sexual identity, and Katan asserts that '. . . in its deepest nature,
schizophrenia arises from a bisexual conflict, and this bisexual
conflict eventually leads to a state where the heterosexual factor
is relinquished' (Katan, 1954, p. 121).

I, for one, would not wish to attribute such a key role to
sexual factors in schizophrenia – would not hold of lesser importance such affective components as tenderness, compassion,
grief, rage, and so on. But I have found it instructive to explore
sexual factors as comprising *one* of those major threads which,
when carefully traced through various phases of the patient's
life – his infancy and childhood; the period of onset of his illness,
usually in young adulthood; the years of his advancing schizophrenic illness; and the years of resolution of the illness in the
course of therapy – help to link otherwise patternless data and
to reveal continuity in the over-all path which he has followed.

[1] In addition to its inclusion in the Chestnut Lodge Symposium, this paper was
presented at the meeting of the American Psychoanalytic Association in New York
City in December 1960. It was first published in *Psychiatry*, vol. 24 (1961), suppl.
pp. 87-95.

My first point of discussion will have to do with the circumstance that, as the pre-schizophrenic adolescent or young adult becomes pressed by biological maturation and by social forces towards genital erotic relatedness with another person, unresolved pregenital conflicts–conflicts having to do with infancy and early childhood–emerge in so formidably threatening a fashion that they can be coped with, eventually, only by psychotic defences. Secondly, I shall describe the aetiology of these crucial pregenital conflicts; and, lastly, sketch their manifestations, and eventual resolution, in the transference developments which unfold over the course of successful psychotherapy.

The pregenital strivings are to be considered not as merely auxiliary, but rather as fundamental, to adult genital interaction. This is in line with Ferenczi's view, expressed in 1923, that orgasm arises from a blending of erotisms from all the erogenous zones. He suggests that 'genitality is a summation of instinct components . . . and of excitations of the erotogenous zones', and he points out that 'in the child every organ and every organ function subserves gratificatory strivings to an extensive degree' (Ferenczi, 1923, p. 97).

One readily sees behavioural, anatomical, and physiological similarities between genital intercourse and the nursing situation, for example–similarities which would tend to call forth, in intercourse, any repressed conflicts having to do with the nursing era. These similarities include the intense, non-verbal, mutual absorption in physical intimacy, the insertion of a fleshy appendage into a bodily orifice, and the central feature of transmission of a milky secretion from the body of one partner to that of the other. Similar, too, is the ego-state of the participants–the relinquishment of ego-boundaries at the climax of intercourse, so evocative of the undifferentiated stage of ego-development in the young infant, and of the lack of ego-boundaries between the mother and her nursing infant. As Ferenczi vividly describes it,

. . . the acts preparatory to coitus . . . have as their function the bringing about of an identification with the sexual partner through intimate contact and embraces. Kissing, stroking, biting, embracing serve to efface the boundaries between the egos of the sexual partners, so that during the sex act the man, for example, since he has as it were introjected the organ of the woman, need no longer have the feeling

430

of having entrusted to a strange and therefore hazardous environment his most precious organ . . . (*ibid.*, p. 17).

I would emphasize that it is to the extent that one's mother, in one's early months as a largely undifferentiated infant, did indeed present one with a 'strange and hazardous environment', by reason of deep ambivalence and much dissociation of feelings, that one now tends to experience such a threat in moving towards the boundaryless state of sexual orgasm. A brief examination of the Schreber case will help to clarify this point.

Freud (1911) ascribes Schreber's illness to a welling up of homosexual feeling referable originally to Schreber's relationship with his father and focused, in the illness, upon his physician, Flechsig, as a father-figure; it is striking that, in his whole lengthy account, and interpretation of Schreber's illness, Freud nowhere raises any conjecture as to the possible importance of the patient's relationship with his mother. But Robert B. White adduces formidable evidence that 'a mother-figure is prominently, though symbolically, represented [in the patient's delusional system] and . . . conflict over voracious, primitive oral impulses towards that mother-figure is an important feature of his psychosis' (White, 1961). This evidence comes primarily from his perusal of Schreber's own account of his illness–the account upon which Freud based his study, and which was not translated into English until 1955 (Macalpine and Hunter, 1955). White not only interprets this clinical material in a fascinating way, but provides a scholarly résumé of the extensive literature which is relevant to the Schreber case and, therefore, to my own subject.

After having read White's article, I, in turn, studied Schreber's memoirs–a course which, incidentally, I strongly recommend to others; so far as I know, this brilliant, articulate man's account of his own schizophrenic illness has never been equalled. In Schreber's document we find, indeed, an abundance of symbolic material indicating an unfulfilled yearning for infantile gratifications. Flechsig and God are the two most prominent figures in his delusional system; and of his subjective contacts with God, he says that 'voluptuousness streams so mightily into me, that my mouth is filled with a sweet taste' (Macalpine and Hunter, 1955, p. 250), and he rejoices at another point that he, who had no belief in God prior to his illness, should have 'sucked from his fingers' (p. 296) that unique knowledge of God which was conveyed to him in his illness.

White, in his summary, states that 'the basic defence which Schreber used . . . was that of projection – accusing God of needful, greedy, potentially destructive, oral longings for Schreber when in fact it was Schreber's jealous, possessive longing for God which . . . threatened to destroy the entire world and even God himself'. He ascribes the original frustration of Schreber's oral needs to the intervention of the father, an eminent physician and one of Germany's leading authorities on nursing, who held that babies during the first year of life must learn 'the art of renouncing', and who carried out in full, with his own infant and the nursing mother, the cruelly stern programme he had devised for teaching the infant to become stoical in face of oral needs, a programme which included deliberate tantalization of the infant when he was crying from hunger. White hypothesizes that the mother wanted to give to the infant, but was restrained by this domineering, stern father who is, indeed, remarkably easy to hate as one reads about him.

White conjectures briefly, concerning the mother, that 'she, as well as her husband, may have been highly ambivalent and inconsistent in her behaviour towards her infant', and this is one aspect of his interpretation which, in my opinion, could well be expanded. My own perusal of Schreber's memoirs leaves me in no doubt that Schreber's mother possessed, in reality, strong, repressed cannibalistic strivings towards her infant son, was greatly anxious lest uninhibited closeness with him would destroy him or her or both, and used the powerfully forbidding and intrusive father as the instrument for acting out her own unconscious negative feelings towards her son, as well as for providing a mutually protective barrier between her and the baby. There are abundant data supporting this interpretation, as well as suggesting that Schreber, in his illness, identifies with his mother's repressed destructiveness. Only brief samples of these data can be given here.

First, there is the already described intrusion by the father into the nursing situation. My clinical experience has repeatedly shown me that when an overtly dominant father thus arrogates to himself the mothering function, one ingredient in this situation is a mother who has an unconscious view of herself as potentially lethal to her infant if uninterrupted intimacy were permitted, and therefore subtly encourages the husband's intervention.

Secondly, whereas for a long time, in his delusional state, Schreber saw the father-figure Flechsig as his only real enemy, and regarded 'as my natural ally God's omnipotence' (Macalpine and Hunter, 1955, p. 77), he came later to realize that 'there is something rotten in the state of Denmark—that is to say in the relationship between God and mankind' (p. 164)—between, I would translate this, his mother and himself. And by the time he came to write his memoirs, it dawned on him that 'God Himself must have known of the plan, if indeed He was not the instigator, to commit soul murder on me . . .' (p. 77). Suggestive of his having had a deeply ambivalent mother is his description, at another point, of God (that is, his mother) as 'two distinct beings', an upper God and a lower God (p. 127), and although he says, 'I could not get myself to believe that God harboured really evil intent towards me' (p. 129), in still another place he says, 'The lower God's behaviour towards me has since been generally friendly, that of the upper God much more hostile' (p. 151). During his illness, he spends most of his time in efforts to recapture, or maintain, a voluptuous 'nerve-contact' with God, and he describes 'God's realms' as being depleted by this, and God as struggling 'to avoid the fate of having to perish in my body with more and more parts of his totality' (p. 150). To me this is as suggestive of his having indeed had a mother who was afraid of closeness with her infant, as it is of his own internal conflicts about oral needs, which are so well documented by White. My interpretation is in line with the findings concerning persecutory delusions by P. G. S. Beckett and his colleagues (1956), who show that these reflect, in a disguised but none the less accurately detailed fashion, real-life traumata which the patient has suffered at the hands of his parents.

In my experience, the child defends himself against mutual ambivalence of such degree in the relationship with the mother by the perpetuation, into chronological adulthood, of a symbiotic relatedness with her and by the retention—inherent in this same process—of fantasied infantile omnipotence. With, later on, the maturation of the anatomical and physiological sexual apparatus, a sexual differentiation comes to be required at a psychological level, too, the acceptance of oneself as *either* male *or*

433

female, which runs counter to the infantile fantasy of being *both* —of being, in fact, the whole perceived world. But such differentiation is one of the basic requirements of the over-all individuation process, and certainly only a person whose individuality has become solidly formed can dare to enter into the closeness involved in a genital-love relationship, which extends into subjective oneness during such transitory relinquishments of ego-boundaries as Ferenczi describes. The person still largely invested in a symbiotic relatedness with a parent is psychologically unready to meet this maturational demand. For him, if the advent of genital lust—which is normally a trump card in the young person's struggle towards individuation—does enable him to emerge from that symbiosis, he has to face not only the usual challenges of his chronological age, but also the previously repressed emotions, arising from the relationship with the parent, against which their symbiosis had been protecting them—for example, murderous rage, envy, and pregenital lust. Moreover, the loss of this symbiotic relatedness entails also the loss of the foundation of his sense of identity.

If the mother-infant relationship has been particularly seriously disturbed, the symbiotic relatedness may be more prominent between the girl or boy and the father. With two of my female patients it has become clear that a symbiotic relationship with an adored father was shattered when the girl's becoming, physiologically, a woman confronted her and her father with an incestuous threat too great to permit their former 'closeness'. In each instance, the girl then became psychotic in face of the evidence that the father, all along, had loved her not for herself but only as an extension of himself, and that he envied her separate femininity. She was thus thrown back, deeply confused now about her identity, into the earlier, deeper conflicts in relation to her mother, against which the symbiosis with the father had been functioning as a defence.

Typically, whether the symbiosis more discernibly involves the mother or the father, so little individuation has occurred, and pregenital erotic interest towards the mother has been so rigorously kept from awareness, that when the genital drive begins to assert itself, it has not only an incestuous object—namely, the mother—but also an incorporatively pregenital, rather than maturely genital, quality. Thus the adolescent or young adult reacts with terror to this drive, as impelling him not towards individuation, but rather towards dedifferentiation, towards being absorbed or swallowed up in a mother-infant relatedness whose emotional concomitants were long ago repressed, have not undergone subsequent maturation, and are now emerging in their original primitive form. By contrast, a healthier parent-child relationship would have permitted much freer recognition of, and in fact would have been nourished by, the participants' mutual erotic interest, as the offspring progressed from orality to genitality.[3] But in those infant-mother relationships which lead eventually to schizophrenia, the mother has to repress her erotic interest towards her offspring–which I presume even in normal instances is predominantly cannibalistic in quality–and project it on to the infant, whom she therefore comes to perceive as being glandularly over-sexed; and, in addition, she acts out this basically natural cannibalistic interest by a kind of smothering, devouring, individuality-constricting mothering of him.

For a number of reasons, he is unable to develop a realistic body image. His mother's repressed hostility towards him has a castrative or even dismembering impact upon his developing body image. Moreover, in a setting of the symbiosis with his poorly integrated mother, he introjects various of her warded-off emotional attitudes and concepts of herself; some of these introjects bear strong sexual tags or labels, as it were, and in any case they are indigestible by his own ego. Much later on, in adolescence or young adulthood, the boy's struggle to become a man is hampered by an introject of his mother's warded-off femininity or of her phallically destructive strivings; or the girl's struggle to become a woman is complicated by an introject of the phallic mother, or, in some instances, of a father who, for some of the reasons I have already suggested, early usurped the symbiotic mother role. The weaker the ego, the more likely it is that the lust will be experienced as a function not of the self but of the introject–as something alienly lustful and, further contradictory of the person's own sexual identity, such that the boy may sense a lustful female within him, or the girl, a lustful male.

A third very powerful reason for basic distortions in the body image springs from the infant's and child's counterhostility in the face of such circumstances. Stärcke in a brilliant paper (1921)

[3] See ch. 9.

435

describes weaning, even in normal development, as constituting a primal castration, since for the infant it is experienced as the loss of the mother's breasts which had been felt, erstwhile, as his own. This is undeniable, yet only in those instances where the weaning is pathologically traumatic does a castrated body image actually result. Clinically, one finds that the patient, schizophrenic or otherwise, is subjectively emasculated or 'defeminated' to the degree that he or she possesses unresolved, repressed destructiveness towards the breast and other attributes of the mother. I do not believe that in healthy development the breast is subjectively destroyed by the infant and his potential body image to that degree crippled; but rather the loss of the breast is worked through and the breast is internalized as a crucial contribution to his own developing body image–and, above all, to its sexual components.

Incidentally, as regards the matter of introjects, I have found some evidence that, for precariously integrated pre-schizophrenic adults, the experience of being possessed by sexual lust, such as is so essential to orgastic experience, is frighteningly similar to being possessed by–their behaviour uncontrollably governed by–introjects from one source or another. Further, in two of my female patients who manifested marked ego-fragmentation for years, it became clear that the concept of sexual entry was subjectively indistinguishable from the experience of feeling invaded and taken over by introjects. In each of these instances, as the patient became aware, after much progress in therapy, of the presence of these introjects–experienced by her, of course, as an actual physical presence within her–she was bewildered as to how the introjected person had got there, and could only conclude that it was somehow the result of rape.

Weiss has pointed out that, not only for the girl but for the boy, the initial identification with the mother is basic to the establishment of a sexual identity (Weiss, 1957). He has emphasized that it is necessary for the boy to externalize the mother-image, in order to attain masculinity, as the girl must externalize the father-image to attain femininity. We find that various identificatory needs, unfulfilled in childhlod years, may dominate the scene when physical maturation is occurring. Thus the youth, finding himself drawn towards male identificatory figures, develops the frightened conviction that he is basically homosexual, and the girl, finding one or another female identificatory figure more fascinating to her than any of the men she knows, is similarly horrified by what she feels to be evidence of Lesbianism in herself.

The great problem of the pre-schizophrenic person, of course, is that, in keeping with the perpetuation, at an unconscious level, of the undifferentiated mother-infant stage of ego-development, he has not achieved any deep-reaching sexual differentiation of himself and perceived others into *either* male *or* female. The struggle to achieve such differentiation is probably one of the internal causes of his conception of all possible human feelings and behaviour traits as bearing, like all French nouns, some sexual label. Such judgements have been fostered in his superego development by parents who were themselves insecure about their sexual identities, and who inculcated in the son the erroneous idea that, for example, gentleness and a love for artistic things are feminine qualities, or in the daughter the notion that assertiveness and practicality are masculine attributes. Such notions, when applied not only to these few human qualities but extended over the whole range of psychological experience, and when applied not to the moderate degree found in the background of the neurotic person but invested with all the weight of actual biological attributes, have much to do with the person's unconscious refusal to relinquish, in adolescence and young adulthood, his or her fantasied infantile omnipotence in exchange for a sexual identity of—in these just-described terms—a 'man' or a 'woman'.

It would be like having to accept, out of a whole patchwork quilt of emotions and developing personality traits, only certain scattered ones as salvageable, while having to relinquish all the rest, and to see the whole fabric ruined into the bargain. A person cannot deeply accept an adult sexual identity until he has been able to find that this identity can express all the feeling-potentialities of his comparatively boundless infancy. This implies that he has become able to blend, for example, his infantile-dependent needs into his more adult erotic strivings, rather than regard these as mutually exclusive in the way that the mother of the future-schizophrenic infant frightenedly feels that her lust has no place in her mothering. Another difficult facet of this situation resides in the pre-schizophrenic boy's conviction, based on his intrafamilial experiences, that he can win parental love only if he can become—or, perhaps, at an unconscious level remain—a girl; accepting a male identity, becoming subjectively a man, is tantamount to giving up all hope of ever being loved. And comparably, to the pre-schizophrenic girl, sexuality as a woman is equated with the abandonment of the hope of being loved.

Concerning the warped experiences these persons have had with the oedipal phase of development, I wish to call attention to two features. First, the child whose parents are more narcissistic than truly object-related is faced with the basically hopeless challenge of trying to compete with the mother's own narcissistic love for herself, and with the father's similar love for himself, rather than being presented with a competitive challenge involving separate, flesh-and-blood human beings. Thus, I recall one young man's descriptions, given in a tone of helpless jealousy, of his psychotic mother's talking adoringly with Jesus Christ—the latter being in actuality, of course, unbeknown to him, but a narcissistically adored, projected aspect of her own ego. I recall coming to feel similarly helpless jealousy of the hallucinations with which one of my hebephrenic patients enjoyed, month after month, such an apparently lively and warm intimacy, leaving me out in the cold. And I may as well add that, when I confessed to him that I felt so, he did respond to me, this time: he said, carefully, 'You're jealous of my hallucinations?' Small wonder that schizophrenic patients are convinced their therapists are crazy!

Secondly, concerning warped oedipal experiences, I would point out that in so far as the parents have succeeded in achieving object-relatedness, this has often become only weakly established at a genital level, so that it remains much more prominently at the mother-infant level of ego-development. Thus, the mother, for example, is much more able to love her infant son than her adult husband, and the oedipal competition between husband and son is in terms of who can better become, or remain, the infant whom the mother is capable of loving. And, when the infant becomes chronologically a young man, having learned that one wins a woman not through genital assertiveness but through regression, he is apt to shy away from entering into true adult genitality, and be tempted to settle for what amounts to a 'regressive victory' in the oedipal struggle.

Not infrequently the schizophrenic illness is precipitated in a setting of rejection in a love affair. I have found that more traumatic to the young person than this rejection itself has been his family's reaction to this first adultlike extrafamilial love-relationship – their shocking disregard for the meaningfulness of his love, their disillusioning inability, basically, to let him emerge from the family symbiosis. One of my patients was told by each of her parents separately, not long before the onset of her illness, that they hoped she would never marry, because the family had such good times together; and the father told me with quiet satisfaction, on transferring his hebephrenic daughter to our hospital, 'My daughter has had two love affairs that didn't materialize, I think fortunately for her. We're always surprised at the selection she makes', going on to describe one suitor as being a somewhat unsettled young man, and the other as having an inauspicious social background. Such parents minimize the mutual feeling-investment in these unhappy love affairs, and we therapists are too ready to call them 'autistic love affairs', thus precluding their ever being seen in their true significance. In a number of instances where I initially thought this label applied, I came eventually to find that the 'autistic love affair' had actually involved repeated dating, proposals of marriage, and unmistakably genuine love; but the parents had been too insecure to regard it as anything but hollow or imaginary.

Freud, in his paper (1931) entitled 'Female Sexuality', expresses his surprise at having found, behind the girl's intense attachment to the father, evidence of an earlier 'phase of exclusive attachment to her mother . . . equally intense and passionate', and he compares this with the surprise attendant upon the discovery, in archaeology, of the Minoan-Mycenaean civilization behind that of Greece. He goes on to say,

Everything in the sphere of this first attachment to the mother seemed to me so difficult to grasp in analysis – so grey with age and shadowy and almost impossible to revivify – that it was as if it had succumbed to an especially inexorable repression. But perhaps I gained this impression because the women who were in analysis with me were able to cling to the very attachment to the father in which they had taken refuge from the early phase that was in question (Freud, 1931, p. 226).

439

My impression is that Freud himself clung to this father-transference role in order to avoid facing the anxiety associated with his patient's working through their earlier conflicts in relation to him as a mother in the transference. This is a clue, I think, to why Freud considered schizophrenic patients, in whom the resolution of such conflicts is crucial, to be insusceptible to psycho-analytic therapy. Sèchehaye (1951a) and Eissler (1951), Schwing (1954), and many other therapists in the field of schizophrenia are in agreement concerning, as Hayward and Taylor say, 'the absolute necessity for a happy infantile experience with a good mother before the patient can begin to grow toward adult reality' (Hayward and Taylor, 1956, p. 35). But the anxiety for both participants in the therapeutic situation, attendant upon transference-reliving of the early infant-mother conflicts, makes the reaching of this ancient stratum as difficult as it is essential.

In the first place, the patient's libidinal strivings dating from the genital level of ego-development are poorly integrated with, rather than in coherent harmony with, those traceable to the much earlier oral phase. Thus, one of my female patients, in a car journey with a nurse and myself, seemed agreeable to my stopping for ice cream cones for each of us; but when hers was proffered to her, she showed both a hungry oral yearning for it and an anxiety as though it were a penis about to rape her. On other occasions she would approach me like a dependent little child; but suddenly I would find that our relatively comfortable parent-child closeness had switched into what felt to be a completely incompatible adult-lustful relatedness. When I finally became able, after many months of therapy, to relate myself to both the adult woman and the very young child in her, she exclaimed in delight, 'So you'll meet me on the first and fourteenth floors!'

The patient's inability to differentiate between fantasy and reality complicates matters; Sullivan has mentioned, for example, the prominence in schizophrenia of sexual dreams which are experienced by the patient as real assaults (Sullivan, 1956, p. 162). Sometimes the therapist, in the long run, loses to a degree this distinction also, and reacts to his sexual fantasies concerning the patient with as much anxiety and guilt as though they were illicit consummations in behavioural reality. One hebephrenic woman kept trying to get me to elope with her to Florida, and in various ways chided me for being so stodgy. In one session I sensed, with relief, that she was trying merely to get me to unbend and share such an experience with her in *fantasy*, whereupon I confessed, 'Well, if you're thinking of this in terms of fantasy, I've already had intercourse with you several times in fantasy so far this hour!' To this she responded, with such pleasure as I had rarely seen in our often-despair-filled years of work, 'Progress has been made in this room!'

This vignette brings up the point, too, that as the patient and therapist encounter prolonged periods of mutual despair at ever resolving the illness, both experience powerful urges to give up the difficult struggle towards a genuinely psychotherapeutic goal, and to settle for a much more primitive goal of finding sexual satisfaction in one another. One may see this phenomenon when mutually gratifying investigative work is interrupted, for long weeks or even months, by a recrudescence of the patient's defensive withdrawal. The therapist, having tasted the pleasures of carrying on a relatively high order of collaborative therapeutic investigation with this difficult patient, now has reason to feel that such gratifications are irretrievably gone, and he is apt to be preoccupied more than usual by sexual feelings towards, and fantasies about, the withdrawn patient. Such sequences suggest the extent to which the gratifications of psychotherapeutic or psycho-analytic work[4] represent sublimations of libidinal impulses, which break down, for varying periods of time, during such periods of withdrawal–more accurately described as mutual withdrawal–in the relationship between patient and therapist. Just as sexual behaviour by a schizophrenic person may represent his last-ditch attempt to make or maintain contact with outer reality, or with his own inner self–one paranoid woman described the dreaded feeling, in retrospect, of being 'completely severed from yourself'–so the therapist's sexual feelings towards the withdrawn patient may be, in part, an unconscious effort to bridge the psychological gulf between them, when more highly refined means have failed.

Further, the deeply regressed patient may have so much difficulty with communication on a verbal, or even a gestural, level,

---

[4] As described by Thomas S. Szasz: 'On the Experiences of the Analyst in the Psychoanalytic Situation: A Contribution to the Theory of Psychoanalytic Treatment' (1956).

that he tends to resort to physical contact with the therapist, in one fashion or another, as a mode of communication; and the touching which this involves, although having a much more generous place in such therapy than in the analysis of neurotic patients, does tend to arouse intrusive sexual feelings in both participants. Then, too, the therapist often has reason to feel that, even by the standards of ordinary social relations, the isolated schizophrenic patient's life, between therapeutic sessions, includes no relationship which compares in intimacy with the one which the patient has with him, so that any exploration of sexual material tends to proceed in a relatively highly charged atmosphere.

Finally, there is the formidable threat to the therapist's sense of sexual identity, arising from the patient's projection upon him of confusion or lack of differentiation in this regard; and, particularly for the male therapist, from the patient's intense reactions to him as a mother in the transference. It takes some of these patients several years to become clear about their own and their therapist's sexual identity. The patient thrives to the extent that the therapist can be unanxious when being viewed as, and subjectively being, a full-breasted, lactating mother to the nursing-infant patient, or—in keeping with the poorly differentiated mother-infant situation being revived in the transference—when feeling himself to be in the infant position, in relation to the patient as a nursing mother.[5] Loewald (1951), Bak (1953), and Katan (1954) have described how deep-seated is our fear of ego-loss—or, in the words of Bak and Katan, castration or emasculation—which arises from our unconscious wish to identify with the mother of our early, relatively undifferentiated infancy. Successful therapy with the schizophrenic patient both requires and, through repeated exposure, facilitates the therapist's becoming free from such anxiety. He is then rewarded by the full emergence of the Minoan-Mycenaean stratum of the transference, comprised basically of Good Mother-thriving infant relatedness, in which the lustful and destructive feeling components of the Bad Mother have become largely transformed into, and in any event safely subordinated to, a feeling of boundless love—the only soil, in my experience, from which the patient's healthy ego-differentiation and maturation can subsequently grow.[6]

[5] See ch. 3.   [6] See chs. 10, 11.

442

Chapter 15

ANXIETY CONCERNING CHANGE,
AS SEEN IN THE PSYCHOTHERAPY
OF SCHIZOPHRENIC PATIENTS–WITH
PARTICULAR REFERENCE TO THE
SENSE OF PERSONAL IDENTITY (1961)[1]

I T was nearly two thousand years ago that Ovid wrote, in his
Metamorphoses, that 'Nothing is constant in the whole world'
(Ovid, p. 369). Discoveries made since his day, in such sciences
as astronomy, geology, and physiology, have borne out, to an
extent which Ovid and his contemporaries could not have conceived, his words, 'The heavens and everything that lies below
them change their shape, as does the earth and all that it contains' (p. 376). '. . . our own bodies are always ceaselessly
changing, and what we have been, or now are, we shall not be
tomorrow' (p. 370). Intellectually we know this well; but the
feeling-realization of the all-pervasiveness of change is a realization which persistently arouses anxiety in us. The manifestations
and determinants of this anxiety concerning change are the
subject of this chapter.

Let us note briefly, at the outset, that to a degree such anxiety
is existential in nature: not only do we know, from our life-
experience, that change may prove harmful to us; we know,
also, that none of us can escape the final change which will rob
us of life itself. Ovid's own struggle against this anxiety is shown
in the eloquent final passage of his poem:

My work is complete: a work which neither Jove's anger, nor fire
nor sword shall destroy, nor yet the gnawing tooth of time. That day
which has power over nothing but my body may, when it pleases, put
an end to my uncertain span of years. Yet with my better part I shall
soar, undying, far above the stars, and my name will be imperishable.
Wherever Roman power extends over the lands Rome has subdued,
people will read my verse. If there be any truth in poets' prophecies,
I shall live to all eternity, immortalized by fame (p. 388).

[1] First published in the *International Journal of Psycho-Analysis*, Vol. 42 (1961),
pp. 74–85.

443

Mankind's anxiety in face of the universality of change is revealed in many areas of human activity; I shall mention only three. It is to be seen, firstly, in the dependence of so many of us upon the religious concept of a god, somewhere, who is not only omnipotent but eternal, changeless. Secondly, the history of philosophy shows that a long series of philosophers have devoted their efforts to the delineation of something eternal, enshrined in a changing world. Plato, for example, postulated in his Theory of Ideas a realm of timeless Forms or Ideas, which he considered to be the objects of true knowledge, and he regarded the perpetually changing things of ordinary life as merely the transitory manifestations of these (Bergson, 1944, p. 55; Warner, 1958, pp. 73-4). Plotinus, the last of the great Greek philosophers, went so far as to assert that only the 'spiritual' world is real, and held that the changing world of perception flows from this spiritual world like light from an unvarying, undiminishing source (Warner, 1958, p. 225). Aristotle postulated a Thought of Thought, a god who is immutable and apart from what is happening in the world (Bergson, 1944, p. 349). Spinoza stated that the essences of individual mutable things are to be sought only from fixed and eternal things (Hampshire, 1956, p. 141).

In our anxiety concerning the ubiquity of change, we may find refuge not only in religion or in the pursuit of some personal philosophy such as those I have mentioned, but, thirdly, in *scientific* endeavour. Bergson has pointed out that science, by its very nature, can work only upon what is supposed to repeat itself, and he notes that

In vain, therefore, does life evolve before our eyes as a continuous creation of unforeseeable form: the idea always persists that form, unforeseeability and continuity are mere appearance – the outward reflection of our own ignorance (Bergson, 1944, pp. 34-5).

Michael Balint (1958) notes that 'Science . . . for some time conceived both the physical and chemical worlds as consisting of firm, sharply contoured objects, mechanical points and molecules or atoms', and he states that

. . . It is easy to show that this picture of the world is based partly on . . . projection. We conceive the objects, the ultimate constituents of the world, as we wish to see ourselves, or perhaps even as we really see ourselves: firm, unchangeable, indestructible, in fact, eternal (p. 84).

444

As psycho-analysts, we need to be alert to the respects in which the concepts and technique of our particular science may lend themselves to the repression, in ourselves as well as our patients, of anxiety concerning change.

Our necessary delineation of the repetitive patterns of transference and counter-transference tends to become so preoccupying as to obscure the circumstance that, as Janet M. Rioch phrases it, 'What is curative in the [analytic] process is that in *tending* to reconstruct with the analyst that atmosphere which obtained in childhood, the patient actually achieves something *new*'[2] (Rioch, 1943, p. 151).

Our necessarily high degree of reliance upon verbal communication requires us to be aware of the extent to which grammatical patterns tend to segment and otherwise render static our ever-flowing experience; this has been pointed out by Bergson (1944, p. 340), Bertrand Russell (1900, p. 12), Benjamin Lee Whorf (1956) and others. The tendency among us to regard prolonged silences as being merely gaps in the analytic process, or evidences *per se* of the patient's resistance to it, may be due in part to our unconscious realization that profound personality-change is often best facilitated by silent interaction with the patient; hence we tend to press towards the crystallization of change-inhibiting *words*.

Further, our topographical view of the personality as being divisible into the areas id, ego, and superego, tends to shield us from the anxiety-fostering realization that, in psycho-analytic cure, change is not merely quantitative and partial—'Where Id was, there shall Ego be', in Freud's dictum—but qualitative and all-pervasive. It seems to me, that is, that in such passages as the following, Freud gives a picture of personality-structure, and of maturation, which leaves the inaccurate but comforting impression that at least a part of us—namely, a part of the id—is free from change. In his paper entitled 'Thoughts for the Times on War and Death', in 1915, he said,

. . . the evolution of the mind shows a peculiarity which is present in no other process of development. When a village grows into a town, a child into a man, the village and the child become submerged in the town and the man. . . . It is otherwise with the development of the mind . . . the primitive stages [of mental development] can always be

[2] Italics mine—H. F. S.

445

re-established; the primitive mind is, in the fullest meaning of the word, imperishable (Freud, 1915b, pp. 285–6).

In *Introductory Lectures on Psycho-Analysis*, he says that in psycho-analytic treatment,

> . . . By means of the work of interpretation, which transforms what is unconscious into what is conscious, the ego *is enlarged*[3] at the cost of this unconscious . . . (Freud, 1915–17, p. 455).

In *The Ego and the Id*, he said that

> . . . the ego is *that part of the id*[4] which has been modified by the direct influence of the external world . . . the pleasure-principle . . . reigns unrestricted by the id. . . . The ego represents what may be called reason and common sense, in contrast to the id, which contains the passions (Freud, 1923, p. 25).

Glover, in his book on technique published in 1955, states similarly that

> . . . a successful analysis may have uncovered a good deal of the repressed . . . [and] have mitigated the archaic censoring functions of the superego, but it can scarcely be expected to abolish the Id (Glover, 1955, p. 5).

In my opinion, modesty about the state of development of our science, and about our own individual therapeutic skills, should not cause us to understate the all-embracing extent of human personality-growth in normal maturation and in successful psycho-analysis. I think we have all encountered at least a few fortunate instances which have made us wonder whether maturation really leaves any area of the personality untouched, leaves any steel-bound core within which the pleasure principle reigns immutably, or whether, instead, we have seen here a genuine metamorphosis, from an erstwhile hateful and self-seeking orientation to a loving and giving orientation, quite as wonderful and thoroughgoing as the metamorphosis of the tadpole into the frog or that of the caterpillar into the butterfly.

Freud himself, in his emphasis upon the 'negative therapeutic reaction' (1923), the repetition compulsion, and the resistance to analytic insight which he discovered in his work with neurotic

[3], [4] My italics—H. F. S.

patients, has shown the importance, in the neurotic individual, of anxiety concerning change, and he agrees with Jung's statement that 'a peculiar psychic inertia, hostile to change and progress, is the fundamental condition of neurosis' (Freud, 1915, p. 271). This is, as we know, even more true of psychosis–so much so that only in very recent decades have psychotic patients achieved full recovery through modified psycho-analytic therapy. I have found it instructive to explore in detail the psychodynamics of schizophrenia in terms of the anxiety concerning change which one encounters, in a particularly intense degree, at work in these patients, and in oneself in the course of treating them. What the therapy of schizophrenia can teach us of the human being's anxiety concerning change, can broaden and deepen our understanding of the non-psychotic individual also.

When we follow the life-history of the schizophrenic patient, in its totality up to the onset of his illness, we see that change, for him, consists too little in a flowering of personal capacities and enrichment of life-experience, and too much, rather, in successive personal losses, increasing anxiety and loneliness and, very often, mounting tragedy in the family as a whole. He has much reason to assume that further change will bring, in the main, only increased loads of such suffering.

Further, we see that during his developmental years he lacks adequate models, in his parents or other parent-figures, with whom to identify in regard to the acceptance of outer changes and the integration of inner change in the form of personality-maturation throughout adulthood. Rather, these are relatively rigid persons who, over the years, either tenaciously resist change, or if anything become progressively constricted, fostering in him the conviction that the change from child into adult is more loss than gain–that, as one matures, fewer and fewer feelings and thoughts are acceptable, until finally one is to attain, or rather be confined to, the thoroughgoing sterility of adulthood. The sudden, unpredictable changes which punctuate his parents' rigidity, due to the eruption of masses of customarily-repressed material in themselves, make them appear to him, for the time being, like totally different persons from their usual selves, and this adds to his experience that personality-change is something which is not to be striven for, but avoided as frighteningly destructive and overwhelming.

447

We find evidence that he is reacted to, by his parents during his upbringing, predominantly in terms of transference and projection, as being the reincarnation of some figure or figures from their own childhood, and the personification of repressed and projected personality-traits in themselves. Thus he is called upon by them, in an oftentimes unpredictably changing fashion, to fill various rigid roles in the family, leaving him little opportunity to experience change as something which can occur within himself, as a unique human individual, in a manner beneficial to himself.

When the parents are not relating to him in such a transference fashion they are, it appears, all too often narcissistically absorbed in themselves. In either instance, the child is left largely in a psychological vacuum, in that he has to cope more or less alone with his own maturing individuality, including the intensely negative emotions produced by the struggle for individuality in such a setting. Because his parents are afraid of the developing individual in him, he too fears this inner self, and his fear of what is within him is heightened by the parents' investing him with powers, based upon the mechanisms of transference and projection which I have mentioned, whose nature he does not understand, powers which he experiences as somehow flowing from himself and yet not an integral part of himself nor within his power to control. As the years bring tragedies to his family, he develops the conviction that he somehow possesses an ill-understood malevolence which is totally responsible for these destructive changes.

In so far as he does discover healthy maturational changes at work in his body and personality, changes which he realizes to be wonderful and priceless, he experiences the poignant accompanying realization that there is no one there to welcome these changes and to share his joy. The parents, if sufficiently free from anxiety to recognize such changes at all, tend to regard them as evidence that their child is rejecting them by growing up. Also to be noted, in this connexion, is their lack of trust in him, their lack of assurance that he is basically good and can be trusted to mature into a basically good, healthy adult. Instead they are alert to find, and warn him about, manifestations in him which can be construed as evidence that he is on a predestined, downward path into an adulthood of criminality, insanity, or at best ineptitude for living.

More and more he experiences change not as something within his own power to wield, for the benefit of himself and others, but rather as something imposed from without. This is due not only to strictures which the parents place upon his autonomy, but also to the process of increasing repression of his emotions and ideas, such that when these latter manifest themselves, they do so in a projected fashion, as being uncontrollable changes inflicted upon him from the surrounding world. We see extreme examples of this mechanism later on, in the full-blown schizophrenic person who experiences sexual feelings not as such but as electric shocks sent into him from the outside world, and who experiences anger not as an energizing emotion welling up from within, but as a massive and sudden blow coming somehow from the outer world. In less extreme instances, in the life of the yet-to-become-schizophrenic youth, he finds time after time that when he reaches out to another person, the other suddenly undergoes a change in demeanour, from friendliness to antagonism, in reaction to an unwitting manifestation of the youth's unconscious hostility. The youth himself, if unable to recognize his own hostility here, can only be left feeling increased helplessness in face of an unpredictably changeable world of people.

The final incident which occurs prior to his admission to the hospital, giving him still further reason for anxiety in regard to change, is his experience of the psychotic symptoms as an overwhelmingly anxiety-laden and mysterious change. His own anxiety about this is heightened by the shock and horror of the members of his family who find him 'changed' by what they see as an unmitigated catastrophe, a nervous or mental 'breakdown'. Although the therapist can come to see, in retrospect, a potentially positive element in this occurrence – namely, the emergence of erstwhile-repressed insights concerning the true state of affairs involving the patient and his family, none of those participants can integrate so radically changed a picture at that time. Over the preceding years the family members have not been able to tolerate their child's seeing himself and them with the eyes of a normally maturing offspring, and when these repressed percepts emerge from repression in him, neither they nor he possess the requisite ego-strength to accept them as badly needed changes in his picture of himself and of them. Instead, the tumult of de-repressed percepts goes into the formation of such psychotic

449

phenomena as misidentifications, hallucinations, and delusions, in which neither he nor the members of his family can discern the links to reality which we, upon investigation in individual psychotherapy with him, can find in these psychotic phenomena – links, that is, to the state of affairs which has really held sway in the family. Parenthetically, it should be noted that the psychotic episode often occurs in such a way as to leave the patient especially fearful of *sudden* change, for in many instances the de-repressed material emerges suddenly and leads him to damage, in the short space of a few hours or even moments, his life situation so grievously that repair can be effected only very slowly and painfully, over many subsequent months of treatment in the confines of a hospital.

It should be seen, also, that the regression of the thought-processes, which occurs as one of the features of the developing schizophrenia, results in an experience of the world so kaleidoscopic as to constitute still another reason for the individual's anxiety concerning change. That is, to the degree that he has lost the capacity to grasp the essentials of a given whole – to the extent that he has regressed to what Goldstein (1946) terms the 'concrete attitude' – he experiences any change, even if it be only in an insignificant (by mature standards) detail of that which he perceives, as being a metamorphosis which leaves him with no sense of continuity between the present perception and that immediately preceding. This thought-disorder, various aspects of which have been described also by Angyal (1946), Kasanin (1946), Zucker (1958), and others, is compared by Werner with the modes of thought which are found in members of so-called primitive cultures (and in healthy children of our own culture):

> . . . in the primitive mentality, particulars often appear as self-subsistent things which do not necessarily become synthesized into larger entities . . . the natives of the Kilimanjaro region do not have a word for the whole mountain range which they inhabit, only words for its peaks. . . . The same is reported of the aborigines of West Australia. Each twist and turn of a river has a name, but the language does not permit of a single inclusive name for the whole river . . . [and he quotes Radin (1927, p. 200) as saying that for the primitive man] 'A mountain is not thought of as a unified whole. It is a continually changing entity.' . . . [and, Radin continues, such a man lives in a world which is] 'dynamic and ever-changing . . . Since he sees the

same objects changing in their appearance from day to day, the primitive man regards this phenomenon as definitely depriving them of immutability and self-subsistence' (Werner, 1957, pp. 138–40).

In chapter 19 I described the defensive function of the *de-differentiation* which is so characteristic of schizophrenic experience, and one finds that this *fragmentation* of experience, which I have just been mentioning, likewise lends itself to the repression of various emotions which are too intense, and in particular too complex, for the weak ego to endure, and which must be faced as one becomes aware of change as involving continuity rather than total discontinuity.

That is, the deeply schizophrenic patient who, when her beloved therapist makes an unkind or stupid remark, experiences him now as being a different person from the one who was there a moment ago–who experiences that a Bad Therapist has replaced the Good Therapist–is thereby spared the complex feelings of disillusionment and hurt, the complex *mixture* of love and anger and contempt, which a healthier patient would feel at that moment. And similarly, if she experiences it in tomorrow's session –or even later in the same session–that another Good Therapist has now come on the scene and the Bad Therapist is now totally gone, she will feel none of the guilt and self-reproach that a healthier patient would feel at finding that this therapist, whom she has just now been hating or despising, is after all a person capable of genuine kindness. Likewise, when she experiences a therapist's departure on vacation as being a total deletion of him from her awareness, this particular bit of discontinuity, or fragmentation, in her subjective experience spares her from feeling the complex mixture of longing, grief, separation-anxiety, rejection, rage and so on, which a less ill patient feels towards a therapist who is absent but of whose existence he continues to be only too keenly aware.

As a final example of this psychodynamic function of the 'ego-fragmentation' seen in schizophrenia, I wish to describe a glimpse which I had of this process in a schizophrenic man as the erstwhile separated vignettes of remembered incidents and situations from his past began to coalesce into a sense of *continuity-of-change*, running throughout his life.

For many months, as he tried to fit together the slowly

451

accumulating bits of past experience which he could recall, he voiced distress because he could grasp as yet only 'fragments of memory'–an incident here, a situation there, without knowing which preceded which–without seeing any link, any continuity, between them. It was not until he had provided me with enough accumulated data of this kind, over the months, for *me* to feel reasonably sure that two of these fragments represented eras of his past which immediately followed one another, that I was able to realize how much affect he had been spared, thus far, by reason of his memories, being thus fragmented.

During the first of two crucial sessions which caused me to reach this realization, he recalled a happy, though evidently brief, era of his childhood, when he lived on a farm with his mother and father and several siblings. This was a place where, he recalled, he had felt relatively free of anxiety, felt himself to be among relatively comfortable and well-intentioned people, and felt free to roam at large in natural surroundings which he loved. In the immediately following session he recalled this 'fragment of memory': he was living with two very anxious people–quite clearly, from his description, his parents–in an intolerably confining little apartment in Chicago. He was, in this remembered scene, feeling physically very ill and they were hovering anxiously about his bedside. He could not remember that the scene on the farm–which, I reminded him, he had described to me the day before–had immediately preceded this apartment scene. But over the preceding months he had supplied enough data to convince me that such a sequence had indeed occurred in his childhood; my certainty about this was further reinforced by case-history material which his father had supplied at the time of the patient's admission to the Lodge. What became clear to me now, therefore, was the extent to which his inability–as yet–to remember, the *change from* living on the farm to living in the apartment, was serving to protect him from a multitude of emotions associated with that change–emotions having to do with the *loss* of his wide-roaming life on the farm (to which he had never returned), the *loss* of the companionship of his siblings, his *fear of their envy* for his exclusive possession, now, of the parents, and so on. Such emotions came more and more into evidence as his fragments of memory, of which I have given but two examples, progressively coalesced.

452

ANXIETY CONCERNING CHANGE

As we know, the onset of psychosis involves a severe disturbance, or even total dissolution, of the sense of personal identity.
One hebephrenic woman, for example, who in the early months
of our work treated me with the most intense contempt, stung
me more than usual one day, upon my coming into her room, by
sneering, 'What's the matter, don't you even know your own
name?' but later in the session gave me a glimpse of the despair
which lay behind this contempt, when she said, weeping in-
consolably, 'There's a girl in here who doesn't even know
her own name.' It was not for years later on in her treatment
that she was able to develop any enduring sense of personal
identity.

It is less well known that over the years prior to the onset of a
schizophrenic psychosis, one of the most basic reasons for the
individual's anxiety in face of change has been the fact that
change threatened to rob him of his sense of identity which, even
then, was most tenuous and precarious. His years-long struggle
to preserve this sense of identity was a more or less completely
unconscious struggle, and we have to piece together its history
from relatively subtle data in the course of psychotherapy.

Another hebephrenic woman would quote, from time to time
over the years of our work, snatches from a song entitled 'Laura'
which had been popular before her hospitalization, a song about
an ephemeral girl who, the final line reveals, is 'only a dream'.
It gradually became apparent, from the context in which she
would quote, 'Laura is the face in the train going past', or 'The
laugh on a summer night that you can't quite recall', that she was
expressing a longing here for her self, a self with which she felt
in contact only fleetingly, and a self which was only peripheral
to the world of human beings. By contrast, one often heard from
her about persons who were 'on the inside'–on a solid footing
with other people–and during her recounting of an incident from
her teens, when she had been starting to meet with some social
acceptance–to get 'in' with people–she said wonderingly, 'I
didn't know who I was.' She had played much tennis, but never
thought of herself as even potentially top-ranking, and in one
of our sessions, describing a time when she had made a particularly difficult, winning shot during a match with a top-ranking
player, she made it clear that she had suffered thereupon a transitory loss of identity on the tennis court. When she had progressed,

453

later in her treatment, to the point of out-patient living and I
suggested that she learn to drive a car–something that in all
her life, apparently, she had never dared even to consider–she
reacted with anxiety, thought the suggestion preposterous, and
said, 'Why, I wouldn't even know myself, driving a car!' In
another session, she told how she used to wear long black gloves
'to make my arms look heavier', and many corollary data suggested that this, and other unusual modes of dress which she had
adopted in the hospital, had been due to her feeling of herself
as being insubstantial.

In course of time she corroborated my unverbalized hunch
about the song, 'Laura', by saying, 'I used to imagine that my
name was Laura.' On another occasion she told how much she
used to like the song, 'I Wonder What Became of Sally', and with
some embarrassment said, 'Maybe I used to think I was Sally,
before I was sent away, and maybe I wonder what became of
myself.'

The developments in psychotherapy with such patients show
the great extent to which their personality functioning, throughout their lives since infancy, has depended upon a growingly
complex constellation of introjects, undigested into the relatively
fragile and poorly formulated self of their own upon which the
sense of personal identity must basically depend. We see the importance of these introjects not only in discovering how much of
the patient's behaviour becomes identifiable as a conglomeration
of *en bloc* portrayals, in random sequence, of figures from his
early life, but also in the great anxiety, the evident sense of imminent personal dissolution, with which he reacts to the process
of resolution of one or another of these introjects. One patient
began to express the conviction, at a time when I found evidence
that an importantly pathogenic mother-introject was finally in
process of resolution, that the building in which she was housed
was breaking up and that it, as well as all the world visible outside her window, was in imminent prospect of sinking under
water, so that she felt a desperate urge to flee the place. Later on
in therapy she showed a similar reaction to the resolving of a
pathogenic introject traceable to an older sister who had been
important in her upbringing. This passage in the daily nursing
report is a sample of the kind of material which I, too, was en-
countering then with her:

Patient asked me, 'Is this house rotting down or is it the same house with the same boards? Is it my sister?' I told her that it was the same house. She then said her voice was like the voice of her sister and why did they give them both the same voice. . . .

The patient's confusion–confusion of herself and her sister (or mother) and the building–was extreme during such periods.

This same woman, who suffered from long-standing paranoid schizophrenia, showed strikingly how important, to the stunting of the sense of personal identity in the child who becomes a schizophrenic adult, is his own unresolved hostility and reject-ingness towards the persons important in his upbringing and to-wards the introjects derived from them. This woman refused for years, with a steely tenacity and often in a violent manner, to acknowledge her mother, father, siblings, husband, and children as being so related to her. Moreover, it gradually became clear that in so far as her thoughts, feelings, and bodily parts bore in her eyes any resemblance to those of persons important to her in past or present life, she disowned even these. This process, much more than simply consciously willed, was quite beyond her power to understand or control. At times she felt that the head on her shoulders was not her head; at other times she experienced the head as her own, but felt that the remainder of the body in which she found herself was not her own. A time came when she felt neither to be her own, and said, in anxious puzzlement, 'This head and this body are not mine. What part of this body is *me*?' In another session, in the midst of deep confusion and many vehement assertions that 'I *won't* identify myself with . . .', enumerating various persons and groups of persons at the hospital, she said, in an urgently troubled and insecure way, 'Who am I? I don't have any *identity*!'

Now, as we follow the over-all course of a schizophrenic patient's treatment, we see that a whole galaxy of clinical phenomena are determined, in part, by his anxiety concerning change. I shall describe a few such phenomena, dwelling particularly upon his struggle to preserve his sense of identity in the face of, or during the course of, personality change.

It is to be emphasized, in the first place, that the patients who are, to our view, most desperately ill, most urgently in need of personality change, are the very ones who also possess the greatest fear of change; *any* change, no matter whether in our view it be clinically favourable change, is an intense threat to their sense of identity. Moreover, this is true no matter how frantically they may demand change, not only in non-verbal ways through a terror-ridden or otherwise pathetic demeanour, but also in consciously-expressed verbal demands for relief. Here we need to realize to what a degree this anxiety-concerning-change is an *unconscious* anxiety, particularly in such deeply-ill persons. When I finally came to realize these things clearly, I became relatively free of the urgent pressure to 'cure' these patients, and to that degree able to be less pressing towards them myself. Probably there is nothing which interferes more with the psychotherapy of such patients than the therapist's anxious need to 'cure' them.[5]

Secondly, the more deeply ill the patient, the more exclusively he experiences change as being an attribute to that which is outside himself, rather than as occurring within himself. One of my paranoid women patients, for example, was objectively a remarkably mercurial person; but subjectively she felt changeless in the midst of a chaotically changing world. Instead of realizing how intense and rapidly shifting were the feelings in her towards the other person, she experienced him as being replaced, unpredictably, by a series of 'doubles' of himself. She described to me, for example, a shopping trip she had taken earlier in the day with a male attendant towards whom I knew varied responses were at work in her. She made it clear that, in her own experiencing of the trip, the 'attendants' had been changed eight or nine different times, a gentlemanly one being replaced by a boorish one, and he by another of a different type, and so on. When I suggested that one's feelings towards a single other person might undergo various changes, as a result of things which he says and does, she peremptorily dismissed this idea with the comment that a person who felt so would be a mere 'will-o'-the-wisp'. She often boasted that she had grown up at the age of eight, that her concepts of herself and the world, concepts according to which no emotion whatever had an acceptable place in adult personality functioning, had never changed one iota since then.

---

[5] See ch. 3 above, especially pp. 133-9.

Similarly in the therapeutic session itself, we can be reasonably sure when we see a deeply-ill patient in a state of chaotic change-ability, as evidenced by a shifting welter of facial expressions, verbal statements, or other changes in demeanour, that he is experiencing such changeability not as a quality in himself but as a characteristic of his surroundings, including, most particularly, his therapist. Even his own inner strivings towards growth and creativity are felt as restless demands from the therapist and other persons to produce. He may feel anxiety of near-panic proportions in response to actual changes in the therapist—even to shifts in the latter's bodily posture. One man used to demand, furiously and in great anxiety, that I 'Shut up and just sit there!' A woman told her therapist, in explanation of why it was so urgent to her that he sit still, 'When *you* move, *everything* moves.'[6]

Such early therapeutic growth as the patient experiences is apt to be felt as a change within the body alone; it seems that this is less threatening than the experiencing of change as involving the psychological self. Thus, with striking frequency the schizo-phrenic patient reacts to the development of what is really new ego with the conviction that he or she is pregnant. One of my patients, after many times expressing a conviction that she had been raped and impregnated, came to express it that 'There's something that's living and leaping inside me!' She was close, now, to realiz-ing that this was healthy personality growth pushing up through the encrustations of a remarkably rigid paranoid psychosis.

Among the many realistic fears which the process of what we call 'becoming well' arouses in the schizophrenic patient, there is one particularly pertinent to the present subject—namely, his fear that he will lose his sense of personal identity in the course of increasing closeness with the therapist. One patient expressed her anxiety about this through a fantasy of one person's giving a direct blood transfusion to another; another expressed it by wondering 'what would happen if you take two pieces of gum and chew them together', and asked if this would be 'like two clouds merging together'. I refer to this fear as realistic, and to a degree it is so, for, as I have described in chapters 6 and 8, there is a necessary phase of symbiosis between patient and doctor in the transference evolution followed by the recovering schizo-phrenic patient, a phase in which the ego boundaries between

[6] I am indebted to Dr Berl D. Mendel for supplying this clinical item.

457

himself and the therapist are mutually relinquished to a large degree. This development can occur only after successive resolutions of increasingly ancient personality-warp in the patient, and the establishment, thereby, of a hard-won mutual trust and security. In this atmosphere the therapeutic relationship makes contact with the healthy ingredients of the patient's early symbiotic relationship with his mother, thus laying the foundation for his subsequent new growth as a separate and healthy individual.

In such fashion the patient develops importance not merely as a separate object, but to a degree as a symbiotic partner, for the therapist as well as for other persons on the staff who participate deeply in his treatment. This fact accounts for some of the anxiety with which the therapist himself, as well as such other staff members, reacts to favourable change in the patient. Not infrequently, we hear from fellow-therapists and ward-personnel of how 'stunned' or even 'shocked' they were at seeing dramatic improvement in a long-ill patient, and I have felt thus many times myself. Characteristically, too, the therapist notices only very belatedly that various long-standing symptoms have dropped out of the patient's behaviour. On looking back through his records, for example, prior to a staff-presentation, he finds to his surprise that a delusion, once long familiar to him, has not been evidenced by the patient for several months. Thus his feeling of personal loss is mitigated. Noteworthy, also, even among the most technically capable of therapists, is the initial reacting with dismay and discouragement to a patient's new-found ability to express verbally the depths of his despair, loneliness, confusion, infantile need, and so on; typically, the therapist only belatedly recognizes the forward move which this development constitutes. His initial response is traceable to the unconscious loss which this development inflicts upon him–the loss of the long-familiar, and inevitably therefore cherished (*unconsciously* cherished), relatedness which he had shared with the patient.

In a series of papers in 1958–9[7] I indicated that the dependency gratifications of this symbiotic relatedness are such as to promote resistance, in therapist as well as patient, to the relinquishment of this mode of relatedness. A paper in 1951[8] had described this relatedness as lending itself readily to defensive functions–to

---

[7] Chapters 6, 8, 10 of this book.　　　　[8] Chapter 1 of this book.

the repression, that is, of such negative emotions as hostility and feelings of rejection. I wish now to postulate a third reason why both patient and therapist have unconscious resistance to their emergence from the symbiotic phase of their work: for each of them, to emerge from this symbiosis means not the resumption of his familiar sense of individual identity, but the experiencing, rather, of a *new* individual identity–an identity which has been changed by the symbiotic relationship with the other person. The impact of this process is presumably much greater upon the schizophrenic patient than upon the therapist, in view of the latter's relatively strong sense of personal identity; but for the therapist, too, the personal growth-experience involved in the symbiotic phase, and the resultant experience of an individual identity which is to that degree new, are not insignificant phenomena. I shall return to this general subject at the conclusion of this paper, in commenting on the therapist's identifying with the patient.

The patient, particularly in the symbiotic phase of the therapy but in preceding and succeeding phases as well, is notably intolerant of sudden and marked changes in the therapeutic relationship–that is, of suddenly seeing himself, or feeling that his therapist sees him, through new eyes. He rarely gives the therapist to feel that the latter has made an importantly revealing interpretation, and when he himself conveys a highly illuminating nugget of historical information to his therapist, he does so casually, often feeling sure that he has already mentioned this before. He tends to experience important increments of de-repressed material not as being earth-shaking revelations in his development, but things he has known all along and simply never happened to think of. His experience of the world about him is often permeated by *déjà vu* sensations, and misidentifications of strangers about him as being familiar persons from his past.

The forward moves in therapy, on the patient's part, occur each time only after a recrudescence in his symptoms. It is as though he has to find reassurance of his personal identity, as being really the same hopeless person he has long felt himself to be, before he can venture into a bit of new and more hopeful identity. I have been amazed to find how much of her time one of my patients devotes to proving to herself that she is, indeed, an incurably crazy patient, before she can stick her toe a little

459

farther into the unfamiliar waters of hopefulness. Earlier, she was very afraid to let me see how malevolent she felt herself to be; but whenever I now react to her as being the increasingly warm and friendly person I find her becoming, she shows equally great fear, for evidently to her, still, to lose the malevolent creature in her would be tantamount to losing her real self. With various others of my patients, I have realized that when I address a relatively newly developed area of the personality which is not yet integrated into their self-picture, they feel totally misidentified by me, with fully as much attendant anxiety as I myself have experienced when one or another deeply confused patient was totally misidentifying me.

The patient's forward moves are not only *preceded* by the aforementioned exacerbation of symptoms, but oftentimes *accompanied* by, or interlarded with, deeply regressive symptomatology. Thus the nurses' report of his 24-hour day may show an amazing conglomeration of unprecedentedly mature actions, mingled with various of the most profound symptoms to be dredged up from the whole past course of his illness. Fromm-Reichmann (1953) has called attention to the need of schizophrenic patients to cling to remnants of their illness until their new identity as a healthy person is solidly established. One of my patients, looking back over her years of profound illness and the many subsequent months of increasing health, expressed her relief that 'I'm still myself'.

Another valuable thing to realize is that the patient's forward moves are initiated, almost invariably, in such a *fashion* that they tend inevitably to evoke the therapist's rejection or opposition. The motionless and mute catatonic patient may finally make a gross physical movement, but a movement of a kind which frightens the therapist; or his first verbalization may be of a kind which so startles or puzzles the therapist that the latter can think of nothing useful to say. I could give innumerable examples of this phenomenon, from work not only with catatonic patients but with those suffering from other varieties of schizophrenic illness. Almost invariably, the therapist tends to belabour himself with guilt and self-reproach for not having made a more adroit and welcoming response to the patient. The point is that the patient, whose sense of identity is still so largely bound up in his customary behaviour, is in effect *reassured* by finding that this attempted new relatedness is, as he has long assumed, closed to him; one can postulate that he would be frightened out of his wits if it were somehow possible for the therapist to meet his first reaching-out in a warmly welcoming spirit. In my experience it is not this inevitable circumstance of the therapist's reacting against such incipient forward moves which complicates the therapeutic picture, for the patient will try again; the prolongation of therapy arises, rather, from the therapist's becoming enmeshed in self-blame about this.

Another thing which the patient tends to do, when his recovery has proceeded far enough to become a formidable threat to his personal identity, is press for a change of therapists. If he succeeds in this, he will thereby be shielded, for a considerable time longer, from the recognition of how much he himself has changed, for it will be all too easy for him to assume that any shift which he now detects in his functioning in the therapeutic sessions, and elsewhere, is due solely to the contributions of this different therapist. He feels not that he himself has become better, but that he now has a better therapist. Some thought about this will show us how much more readily subtleties of inner personality-change are obscured by such a changed outer situation, subtleties which would tend to be highlighted when seen against a background of continued relatedness with the same therapist. Change of therapist is of course indicated in some instances; but this factor should always be weighed before a change is made.

Broadening our scrutiny to include the hospital milieu as a whole, we find that, until relatively late in his recovery, the spurts of progress which he manifests are seen *either* during the psychotherapy sessions *or* during his daily life outside the therapist's office, but seldom in both these areas concurrently. It is well for us to understand that this is not necessarily an indication of incompetence on the part of either the therapist or the ward-staff, but rather the pattern which progress follows, in the best of circumstances, in an individual with a precarious sense of identity. It is as though he has to maintain one relationship, or set of relationships, relatively *in statu quo* while he is branching out a bit in other areas of his living, in order not to suffer the loss of personal identity which a theoretically possible forward move on all fronts would almost certainly inflict upon him. It is useful to keep this factor in mind, for this situation tends strongly to promote serious splits between the therapist on the one hand and the ward-staff on the other (see chapter 11). The therapist who is unaware of this factor will often be deeply hurt when, enthusiastic about new progress which he sees in the psycho-therapy sessions, he meets with a resentful, rather than similarly pleased, response from the ward-staff, who in all likelihood are not finding themselves particularly successful in their own efforts to help the patient just at this time, and are feeling personally remiss about this. And similarly, at times when he himself is seeing no forward movement whatever in his own work with the patient, he will tend to respond to glowing reports from the nurses only with jealousy and guilt, and above all will regard these reports as confirmation of his own lack of therapeutic worth.

Parenthetically, as regards the total group of patients in any chronic hospital ward, it sometimes comes through to me that here is a place permeated by deeply-submerged but explosively powerful growth-strivings, and the more static in appearance the patients are, the more anxiety-provokingly true this is. It seems to me that the ward-staff, whether consciously or uncon-sciously sensing this fact, need for the sake of their own security, individually and collectively, to have at least a few of the patients occupying the social role of people who are 'hopeless', who stay the same, to provide some continuity of identity to the group. Even for the most superficial and 'practical' reasons, one could see that this must be so: brisk forward movement on the part of all the patients simultaneously would present an overwhelming need for many more staff; even in these terms alone, the existing personnel can cope with massive improvement in only a certain percentage of the patients at any one time. But, as I have tried to indicate, there are deeper reasons for this in the psychic economy of the personnel members, comparable with the reasons why, it seems, most therapists need at least one of the patients in their case-load to remain relatively static while the rest of them are notably improving. The therapist, like the ward-staff, needs this state of affairs for the protection of his own sense of identity.

The few specific suggestions I have to make concerning perti-nent technique are already implied in what has been said. The very deeply-ill patient finds it more helpful if we respond in a relatively casual manner to evidences of improvement on his part, than if we manifest a pleased astonishment. Secondly, there may be a long phase early in our work with him during which we need not be ashamed if we sense that it is better for us to sit quite still, indeed to say nothing for very long periods of time, and in general comport ourselves in what by ordinary standards would seem a ludicrously stereotyped manner. It is unnecessary to assume, that is, that we are thereby submitting humiliatingly to his domination of us, for he may well be primarily concerned not with dominating us but with preserving a fragile identity in the face of a bewilderingly changing world, or even with achieving an identity of which at present he possesses only scattered fragments. Thirdly, in course of time and bit by bit, we can help him to *become aware of* his anxiety concerning change, and eventually assist in tracing the etiological roots of this anxiety. Fourthly, we should endeavour to keep in touch with the person he feels himself to be, consistently addressing our interpretative comments to that subjective person, for a new and healthy sense of identity can evolve only gradually, and only from the sick one which he at present possesses.

Lastly, it is essential that we become able, sometime or other, freely to acknowledge the fact that we ourself have changed to a not insignificant degree during the years of our work with him, and free even to acknowledge that he has contributed to this change. In other words, although there may be some dubious place, in psycho-analysis with the neurotic patient, for the model practitioner who himself changes not at all over the course of a patient's treatment—except, perhaps, to tidy up bits of counter-transference as they arise, and then get back on to the strait and narrow path—there is no place for him in psychotherapy with the deeply schizophrenic patient. The person afflicted with schizophrenia needs, above all, to find that there is something in him which can be not malevolently destructive, but contributive, to the growth and enrichment of a fellow-man.

We write much about the analyst's or therapist's being able to identify or empathize with the patient for the purpose of helping in the resolution of the latter's neurotic or psychotic difficulties. Such writings always portray a merely *transitory* identification, an empathic sensing of the patient's *conflicts*, an identification which is of essentially *communicative* value only. But it should be seen that we inevitably identify with the patient in

463

another fashion also: we identify with the *healthier* elements in him, in a fashion which entails enduring, constructive additions to our own personality. In the instance of each of my patients with whom I have worked intensively for years, I have encountered qualities–whether courage in the face of despair, or appreciation of such quiet things as a tree or a sun-bathed room, or an unconventional view of some sacred tenet of our society, or whatever–qualities which have led, through my identification with the patient, to expansion of my personality. Patients–above all, schizophrenic patients–need and welcome our acknowledging, simply and undemonstratively, that they have contributed, and are contributing, in some such significant way, to our existence.

Increasing maturity involves increasing ability not merely to embrace change in the world around one, but to realize that one is oneself in a constant state of change. By contrast with a woman who expressed concern to her therapist because she had two images of herself which could not quite be superimposed upon one another–like, she said, a double view of the world seen through poorly-fitting glasses[9]–the recovering, maturing patient becomes less and less dependent upon any such sharply delineated, static self-image or even constellation of such images. The answer to the question, 'Who are you?' is almost as small, solid, and well defined as a stone to the former person, but to the latter is as large, fluid, richly-laden, and shiftingly outlined as an ocean. As the individual becomes well, he comes to realize that, as Henri Bergson (1944) puts it, 'reality is a perpetual growth, a creation pursued without end (p. 261). . . a perpetual becoming' (p. 296), and to the extent that he can actively welcome change and let it become part of him, he comes to know that–again in Bergson's phrase–'to exist is to change, to change is to mature, to mature is to go on creating oneself endlessly' (p. 10).

[9] I am grateful to Dr Berl D. Mendel for supplying this clinical example.

Chapter 16

THE SOURCES OF THE ANXIETY IN PARANOID SCHIZOPHRENIA (1961)[1]

IN this description of what I have found to be the major sources of anxiety in individuals suffering from paranoid schizophrenia I shall endeavour to demonstrate how affective phenomena and structural phenomena are interrelated. Further, although I shall have to assume, during much of this portrayal, the vantage point of the observer, whenever possible I shall discuss these sources of anxiety in terms of the patient's own subjective experience of them. This latter emphasis helps to explain the apparent paradox that I shall count, among the 'sources' of his anxiety, various ego-*defensive* phenomena. We well know that to any psychiatric patient himself, the threatening affects present themselves not undistortedly as such, but in forms modified by ego-defences which, although intendedly protective, at the same time distort his experience in a strange and frightening way.

One point I wish to make at the outset is that the paranoid individual seems rarely, if ever—except perhaps in states of panic—to feel anxiety as such. I have come to believe it pathognomonic of him that he experiences, instead, an awareness of various ingredients of his surroundings—or, less often, of things within his body—as being charged with sinister meaning, charged with malevolence towards himself. A simple example of this is to be seen in the reaction of a woman to a new room to which she had been moved, after she had spent many months in a room upstairs in the same small building. Whereas I found myself feeling, in our first interview in this new room of hers, a fair amount of anxiety which I related to the unfamiliarity of these new surroundings, she seemed entirely unaware of any such anxiety, and flatly disclaimed, when I inquired, that she felt any. She asserted that a woman has no such feelings, that a woman likes to move around and, in fact, has to, in order to

[1] An earlier version of this paper was presented at Philadelphia Psychiatric Hospital on 24 March 1960. First published in the *British Journal of Medical Psychology*, Vol. 34 (1961), pp. 129–41.

keep alive. What she voiced, instead, was a threatened kind of conviction that the water in this new bathroom tasted sinister; she mentioned uneasily that some wine which a nurse had given her that day tasted like 'mahogany'; and she said that she did not like being down near the earth, indicating that this would make her more vulnerable to being turned, by 'them', into a tree.

Freud (1911), in his discussion of the Schreber case, described repressed homosexual desires as being at the root of the paranoid patient's preoccupation with the persecutory figure or figures. It seems to me a more adequate explanation to think of the persecutory figure as emerging into the forefront of the patient's concern, not primarily because of repressed homosexual interest on the latter's part, but rather because the persecutory figure is that one, among all the people in the patient's current life situation, who most readily lends himself to reflecting or personifying those qualities which the patient is having most vigorously to repudiate in himself and project on to the outer world. Whereas he is convinced that the persecutory figure is pursuing him—in one fashion or another pressing threateningly upon him—we find, in the course of his psychotherapy, that the state of affairs actually consists, basically, in the circumstance that his own unconscious feelings and attitudes, projected upon that other person, are pressing for awareness and acceptance into his conscious conception of himself.

He finds himself unable to renounce any concern with that other person, and reach a state of peace about the matter, for in actuality this would be tantamount to repudiating important components of himself; moreover, the other person is necessary to him as the bearer of these externalized (i.e. projected) emotions. But, on the other hand, he cannot find peace through a friendly acceptance of the persecutory figure, for this would be tantamount to accepting, into his own picture of himself, various qualities abhorrent to him. So an uneasy equilibrium is maintained, with his experiencing a gnawing, threatened, absorbing concern with the persecutory figure whom he cannot rid from his mind.

One sees this mechanism particularly clearly in those patients whose projections attach not to any real-life figure at all, but to a quite pure-culture *alter ego*. One such patient had changed his name, at the age of twelve, from John Costello to John Cousteau, evidently in an attempt to establish an identity more acceptable to himself. He came into one particular session, early in my work with him at a VA clinic years ago, shaking and perspiring visibly, and described how furious it had made him, a few days before, when at a pension examination the secretary had mistakenly called out his name as 'John Costello'. He became very worked up as he described this, saying: 'I don't like John Costello—he was a selfish stinker . . . the name sticks in my throat.' A woman who for years had the delusion that she had 'doubles' to whom she attributed all the feelings, attitudes, and behavioural acts which she had to repudiate from her concept of herself, came, in the course of our sessions, to express intense hatred of these 'doubles'. She said: 'I wish they'd fry. Somebody ought to shoot them. They're chisellers.' I commented, 'You seem to hate them at least as much as you hate psychiatrists', and she agreed. I went on: 'You seem to feel that the doubles are as much your enemy as the psychiatrists are.' She replied, vehemently: 'They [i.e. the doubles] *are* the enemy.'

Conspicuous as the defence mechanism of projection is in paranoid schizophrenia, I have come to believe that the complementary defence, introjection, while less easily detectable, is hardly less important. The patient lives chronically under the threat, that is, not only of persecutory figures experienced as part of the *outer* world, but also under that of *introjects* which he carries about, largely unknown to himself, within him. These are distorted representations of people which belong, properly speaking, to the world outside the confines of his ego, but which he experiences—in so far as he becomes aware of their presence—as having invaded his self. These, existing as foreign bodies in his personality, infringe upon and diminish the area of what might be thought of as his own self—an area being kept small, also, by the draining off into the outer world, through projection, of much affect and ideation which belongs to his self.

In the course of his psychotherapy we come to see the extent to which these introjects threaten the self with total abolition. One woman came to express it, after many months of therapy: 'Why, I'm not even myself! . . . Those peoples are in my bowels and in my stomach and in my heart! . . .' On another occasion she said, with urgent anxiety: '*Who am* I? I don't have any *identity*.' For several months, when an introject of a constellation of qualities traceable to her mother held sway, she showed every indication of assuming herself to be her mother, and spoke of her siblings as 'my children'. One patient came to experience herself as a 'baggage car'; another as 'Noah's ark'. Still another experienced herself as a Trojan horse filled with a hundred people; and a man portrayed in a dream his own state of being filled with introjects: he dreamt of a man with a belly so enormous that he could scarcely move about.

A woman met me as I walked towards her building, for a therapeutic session with her, and in great agitation showed me a page in a story she was trying to read, a page on which the protagonist, 'I', was describing a conversation involving several participants. She said: 'Four men and a girl—which one is "I"?—There's William and George and Peter—maybe Peter is "I" . . . Which one is "I"?' And as we walked into the building she said: 'You've got too many people here, Dr Searles. . . . I get overwhelmed by people.' She had recently been expressing a wish to 'push people away', and would say of this or that nurse or fellow-patient, 'she reminds me of several different people'. This woman, so close to a hebephrenic state involving the loss of any continuous sense of personal identity, was attributing to these other persons her own state of personality-organization, namely that of, as one patient phrased it, a 'composite personality', comprised largely of introjects.

I have found repeatedly that the individual with paranoid schizophrenia, initially so unwaveringly certain about everything, and never doubting that his views are his very own, reaches, after years of intensive psychotherapy, a point where it becomes clear not only to the therapist, but to himself also, that nearly everything he has been saying is in actuality but an ill-understood hodge-podge of the parroted—though unwittingly caricatured and otherwise distorted—utterances of his parents and other significant persons from his childhood. He comes to reveal, at long last, precisely the confusion of a small child who has been exposed to a bewildering cacophony of parental statements and who has not heretofore found anyone sufficiently trustworthy and patient to help him find his way out of his confusion. Two among the patients who have reached this point, in our work together, have come to say, quite simply and seriously and trustingly, 'I don't know anything.'

Inevitably, on the path to the establishment of such a degree of trust and openness in the transference relationship, there will be many periods when the anxiety in both participants will far exceed any mutual security they have as yet been able to find together. During these periods the unintegrated welter of emotions, memories, fantasies, somatic sensations and other perceptions, initially contained within the patient's rigidly formulated delusions, will emerge, with the result that his personality functioning becomes chaotically fragmented–so much so, oftentimes, as to constitute a formidable threat to the therapist's own personality organization. At such times the therapist can see to what a degree the patient's delusional formulation of his life has served as a substitute for any genuine and healthy sense of a pattern in living. The paranoid patient is not sufficiently in tune with his fellow-men; not sufficiently able to integrate the ever-flowing nature of life with its concomitants of change and growth, fulfilment and loss, birth and death; not sufficiently matured in his thought-processes to be able to distinguish the more significant from the less significant incidents and threads in his life; and not sufficiently loving and trusting to experience love as the ingredient which gives human existence cohesiveness and meaning; to be able to feel the wholeness, the genuine 'master plan', which the healthy individual comes to see in his life. I like to compare the description, in Noyes's (1951) text-book, of the process of retrospective falsification in paranoia, with the healthy realization of a true pattern in his life which the neurotic patient achieves in the later phases of a successful psycho-analysis: 'Incidents of the past receive a new interpretation and he discovers in them a significance which was not recognized when they occurred. . . .' (Noyes, 1951, p. 399).

The fragmentation to which I refer is not different in kind from that seen in hebephrenia. Markedly varying moods, and widely disparate levels of ego-organization, may appear in rapidly changing and random sequence. The individual's perception of the world about him is jumbled up with hallucinatory phenomena and with vivid perceptions of scenes from his past. He may experience not only other people but also himself as being unwhole, a composite of bodily fragments of persons from both current life and bygone years. He may be incapable of sequential thought and speech, and may hear only fragments of what the therapist says to him. One such patient, who at the beginning of our work had shown, for years, the rigid over-control of feeling so characteristic of paranoid schizophrenia, went through many months of fragmentation in which, for example, she would bellow at one moment that we criminals should kill her and thus end her torture, and at the next moment would be laughing warmly; would at one moment be a monu-mentally arrogant woman and, the next moment, a touchingly childlike creature; and, at times when I overestimated her capacity to share an informal friendliness in our sessions, she would become overwhelmed by deeply ambivalent feelings trace-able eventually to her relationship with her mother. Following one such therapeutic hour, she became savagely combative and, when the nurses were putting her into a cold wet sheet pack, she bit the breast of one of them; but only a short time later, while still in the pack, she asked another for a kiss, and this nurse, touched by this childlike request which the patient had never before made, gave her one. Her moods with me would change equally rapidly, and I can only mention in passing, here, the extreme fragmentation which occurred not only in her affective experience, but in all areas of her perceptual functioning, in-cluding that having to do with her body-image, before a healthy reintegration became established.

I find it helpful to think of this phase of fragmentation not simply under the global heading of regression–which is, indeed, one way of characterizing it–but, more specifically, as a reversal of the normal growth process of integration-and-differentiation (see chapters 10, 11). That is, we can see normal growth, psycho-logical as well as biological, to be a process of integration of previously separated *Anlagen* into coherent functional structures, and, concomitantly, differentiation of functional structures into more complex patterning which provides for an increasingly wide range of discriminations and specializations of functioning. In the phase of fragmentation which I have been describing, there are phenomena not only of disintegration but also of de-differentiation, a term introduced by Heinz Hartmann (1939) to describe the loss of already differentiated psychological func-tions which we find in states of regression, particularly in schizophrenia. The comparative psychologist, Heinz Werner (1940), who introduced this term independently, illuminatingly compares the states of de-differentiation seen in schizophrenia and in brain injury with the ego-functioning found in children and in members of so-called primitive cultures, as well as with the modes of sensory functioning found among a wide variety of lower animal species. Rapaport (1958) has extended meaningfully some of Hartmann's observations. Hartmann's (1950a, 1956) concept that there is, already established at birth, a rudimentary ego, which tends to follow its own autonomous pattern of maturational differentiation—a process which is reversed in schizophrenia—is another concept I have found helpful.

Thus, many of the bewildering manifestations of the paranoid patient's—or, for that matter, any other schizophrenic patient's—fragmentation can be seen to consist in such relatively obvious de-differentiation phenomena as the loss of ego-boundaries, such that the outer world and the world within the self are mixed up, as in the phenomena of projection and introjection I mentioned earlier; or the loss of distinction between present and past, such that persons in the present surroundings are misidentified as being persons from the past, and, contrariwise, vivid memories from the past are experienced as being perceptions of the here-and-now; or the loss of differentiation among thinking, feeling and acting, such that, for instance, the thought or feeling is reacted to as being tantamount to the deed.

But, as we study such patients for years, we see that the de-differentiation is, in a subtler form, far more extensive than we had thought. We see that the de-differentiation of the thought processes, or to put it another way, the loss of the higher forms of ego-organization, is such that the patient has little or no realm of *fantasy* experienced as such; whenever he experiences a new combination of thoughts or mental images he immediately assumes it to be, instead, a representation of outer reality. Further, he has little or no psychological realm of *memory*, experienced as such: people about him never *remind* him of people from the past whom he then *misses*; to him these either *are* those very people, or are those people in a disguised form, or—and this is true, perhaps, of the slightly healthier patient—they are 'doing a take-off of', or as one patient put it, 'projecting', people from the past.

Further, his inability to differentiate important from trivial, intendedly communicative from non-communicative, ingredients of the world around him may account for some of his well-known *suspicion*. He may be suspicious, that is, not only for the reason that he has been hurt too often before when he has placed his trust in someone, but also because his suspicion provokes his only mode of processing, of sifting out, the data from a world which is as bewilderingly complex as the adult world is to a little child. Many times I have seen this or that paranoid patient start to look utterly confused by the many words and, simultaneously, manual and other gestures coming from me, until his attention crystallized, after a brief moment or two, upon some word or some gesture, whereupon it clearly appeared that he had found his suspicion once again confirmed, had found his delusional simplification of experience adequate to pigeon-hole this new incident, and had found relief from his momentary bewilderment in face of perceptual data which his capacity for abstract thought was insufficient to enable him to integrate on any but this primitive suspicional basis.

I have been particularly interested to discover how frequently the fragmented patient is involved in a kind of literal and somaticized experience of what would be, to a healthy person with mature ego-differentiation, a *figure of speech*–a metaphor, for example–confined to the levels of thought and emotion, with at most an echo of somatic representation (see chapter 19). For example, one patient reacted to a harsh comment from me without any awareness that it had made her feel hurt and betrayed, but with the evident physical sensation, instead, of having been quite literally shot in the back. Upon seeing a pathetic elderly man in the nearby drug store, she remained quite unaware of the extent to which her heart had, figuratively speaking, gone out to him, as I could see in my immediately subsequent session with her; instead, she had an agonized literal experience that her heart had been torn out. Another patient, when shame and embarrassment started to emerge from repression, felt a literal, rather than a figurative, sensation of sinking through the floor. Other patients, when evidently involved in feelings of admiration or awe of me, have experienced this not as such, but as a perception of me as being gigantically tall; or, when grappling with feelings of disillusionment or contempt towards me, instead of experiencing the feeling as such, have perceived me as a midget. They may perceive their fellow-patients, or themselves, as being not figuratively sheep-like or cow-like, for instance, but as being literally indistinguishable, perceptually, from sheep or cows, or even inanimate things. Even the earliest differentiation, in normal ego-development of infancy, that between animate and inanimate, may be lost.[2]

Thus we see that the paranoid schizophrenic patient, when we begin working with him, is labouring under the threat not only of constellations of specific projections and introjections, but also of imminent disintegration and de-differentiation of his whole personality-structure—such as becomes blatantly overt later on, when his delusional defences have been undermined midway in his therapy. Our own psychodynamic understanding of this disintegration and de-differentiation, as constituting very active (though unconscious) ego-defences of a primitive sort—whereby a part of the ego's integrity is temporarily sacrificed in the interest of personality-survival[3] (Searles)—cannot serve directly to alleviate the threat under which the patient himself suffers.

Usually we can detect at least a few subtle indications, even at the beginning of our contact with a relatively rigidly organized paranoid individual, that he is struggling against such disorganization of his psychological processes. The following brief portion of a psychologist's lengthy report concerning a newly admitted woman with paranoid schizophrenia, a woman who needed hospitalization but was opposed to it and whose illness was not sufficiently overt to make possible her commitment for prolonged treatment, is reminiscent to me of various patients I have seen. After detailing at great length the many evidences of adequate personality-functioning, the psychologist says:

I did get various definite evidences of a psychotic process going on in Mrs Bennett. In the first two hours I had with her she verbalized many rather bizarre somatic symptoms, such as a feeling that her hair had all been torn out during the stay at the previous hospital, although she said that she knew quite well that this had not actually occurred. Also, she described a feeling of 'being broken in two in the middle', indicating her abdomen. Likewise, she went into great and rather bizarre length in trying to describe some chronic lower back complaint. . . . During a subsequent hour with her, I found her to be describing her distress at being in the presence of one or another of

---

[2] Cf. my *The Nonhuman Environment.*   [3] See ch. 19.

the patients here who was knitting. She said, 'It makes me feel like wool–you know.' I could get no further elaboration about this from her.

Although this paper does not deal with therapeutic technique, I must touch upon that area in order to make an additional conceptual point concerning the paranoid patient's de-differentiation. The beginning practitioner of psycho-analysis or psychotherapy learns, in the early years of his experience with neurotic patients, how very much of what the patient is saying has references, at some level of awareness or unawareness, to the immediate treatment situation itself, although the patient may be quite resistant indeed to recognizing this transference ingredient in what he is saying. After years of practice in detecting such immediate, though usually preconscious or unconscious, referential roots in what his patients say in his presence, the therapist or analyst becomes impressed, too, with the extent to which this phenomenon enters also into ordinary conversations between individuals in daily life. For instance, A is expressing to B some strongly felt attitude concerning an absent third person, C, quite unaware that simultaneously he is revealing, to a practised ear, that he holds this attitude, in some degree, towards B as well; and B, if he does not have a practised ear, is equally unaware of this quite direct communication from A to himself. But I, at least, have come to believe that such a direct referent is nearly always present in such situations.

Such ubiquity of this phenomenon would be in line with the work of Piaget (1930), whose voluminous and meticulously detailed researches concerning normal development indicate that the establishment of ego-boundaries, far from being completed in infancy or early childhood, is still far from complete as late as twelve years of age, and never reaches full completion even in adult life. He speaks of one's perception of the outer world as being distorted, even in adult life, by at least some 'adherences' –that is, projections–of ingredients which belong, properly speaking, within the boundaries of the self. Thus we might think of this circumstance which I have been describing as one in which, even among so-called normal people, A's perceptual differentiation between B and C is, at an unconscious level, not complete, so that the feelings which he is expressing about the absent *C* may adhere to, or be directed towards, *B* who is actually in his presence.

In any case, whether or not this phenomenon occurs with such a high frequency as I believe it to do, the paranoid schizophrenic patient may be thought of as being particularly acutely aware of this 'normal element of self-reference' in his contacts with people, when he is in the position of person *B*. Because his ego-boundaries are so grossly incomplete that the ingredients of the outer world, including both *A* and *C*, are reacted to unconsciously or perhaps even consciously as mere extensions of himself, he is very prone to hearing, in *A*'s remarks about *C*, *only* that level of meaning which refers to himself, and to dismiss the significance of *A*'s consciously intended meaning.

At this juncture I wish to note how heavy a penalty we have to pay for the use of such psychotic defences against anxiety as massive projection and introjection, disintegration and de-differentiation. The penalty, which has no counterpart in neurosis, consists in the experience of *weirdness* suffered, for instance, by the paranoid man who, in the struggle against repressed grief, feels that his streaming tear glands are controlled by some weirdly mysterious agency outside himself; or by the woman who, projecting her violently aggressive sexual lust, feels herself to be repeatedly raped by some eerie and invisible outside agency. The self-concept is constricted by so harsh a super-ego that the warded-off desires, in order to emerge at all, have to assume so disguised a form that the patient lives, consequently, in a nightmarishly distorted world. Data from the only quantitatively more distorted world of hebephrenic patients provide vivid examples of what I am discussing here. One hebephrenic woman, unable as yet to conceptualize her subjective unfeelingness as such, recurrently saw an eerily unhuman 'plastic man' appear, terrifyingly, at her window; another, unaware of her murderous rage as such, experienced instead an hallucination of a line of exploding teeth marching unendingly up one wall of her room across the ceiling, and down the other side; and a hebephrenic man, whose self-concept as a little girl was repressed and projected, saw in his clothes-closet an 8- or 10-year-old girl, swimming in purple liquid, and pleaded urgently for me to rescue her.

I have become interested in trying to discern in what form, if at all, the paranoid patient experiences any awareness of his own thought-disorder and, in general, of his ego-mechanisms. It required four years of therapy for one man, for example, to become able to say, 'See, this is the way I think . . .', and to proceed to lay out before me, for our mutual investigation, his distorted ways of thinking. Prior to such a development, I believe, the patient experiences his state of more or less severe de-differentiation of ego-functioning not as any disorder within himself, but rather as an indistinguishable component of the poorly delineated 'them', the anthropomorphized persecutors in his external world. We see comparable phenomena in normal development, in the little child who, only precariously established as yet in well-differentiated modes of thought, perception, and sensation, seemingly experiences his remnants of the earlier, undifferentiated level of ego-functioning not as a truly internal threat, but rather in the form of the vaguely outlined shapes which, he is convinced, lurk behind the closed doors and in the dark corners.

Tausk (1919), in his classic paper, 'On the Origin of the "Influencing Machine" in Schizophrenia', in which he introduced the concept of a loss of ego-boundaries, described the delusion of there being a fascinatingly complicated influencing machine, experienced commonly in that era by paranoid schizophrenic patients, as being in actuality a projection of the patient's own body, the whole body being unconsciously fantasied as a genital. Since I have come to see how frequently schizophrenic patients experience abstract concepts in a concretized, and often anthropomorphized form, I have come to believe that such phenomena as the influencing machine–which one of my patients experienced, for years, as a 'Watcher-Machine' protectively overseeing her daily living–represent, most significantly, the patient's own externalized, and to him fascinatingly complex, ego-functioning. Modell's (1958) paper concerning hallucinations as being related more closely to ego-functions than to superego-functions is relevant here, and much of my clinical experience is in line with his.

If there is any single most basic threat to the paranoid schizophrenic person, it is, I believe, the threat that he will cease to exist as a human individual. This threat presents itself in various forms. There is the danger that his identity will be reduced to that of only *part* of a person–most often, a genital–rather than his being a whole person. There is the danger that his individuality may be submerged in symbiotic relatedness with the other person. There is the danger that his status in the world of his fellow human beings will be reduced to that of an animal, a dead person, or an inanimate object. And there is, finally, the danger that, in the eyes of human beings, he may cease totally to exist.

Interviews with the mothers of these people suggest some of the causative factors in the patient's unsureness that he can maintain any solid place in the emotional life of his fellow human beings. These mothers appear, so frequently, remarkably overcontrolled, placid—as the late Lewis Hill (1948) termed it, impervious. One mother states of the patient's father, in the most matter-of-fact tone possible: 'He died from ulcers of the stomach and cancer of the stomach and liver.' Another says, similarly dispassionately, of her son's infancy: 'There was quite an interval, at four months, when I thought he would starve to death, when he wouldn't either eat or take the bottle.'

The degree to which various of these parents disavow, whether unconsciously or even consciously, any blood-relationship with their child, is sometimes startling. One mother, for example, in giving me an account of the background of her schizophrenic daughter, now married, commented less with scorn than with emotional detachment: 'Mrs Matthews, from a young child, was always what we called the goody girl, the Pollyanna type: tractable, obedient, of a sweet disposition; and I thought that during her childhood and adolescence I had a good contact and understanding with Mrs Matthews.' For a short time, during our lengthy session, she referred to her daughter as Alice, 'to make it easier', but soon lapsed back into using the term 'Mrs Matthews' which seemed really more in accord with the way she regarded the young woman. Several times I have been astonished to see, in the course of a patient's psychotherapy, that one or other of the parents felt that he or she had married far beneath his or her social station, to such a degree that the patient, in striving for acceptance by this parent, was met not only with rejection but with subtle reproach for trying to be a social climber.

Sometimes such attitudes are expressed quite openly. One mother, in telling me of her marriage, said: 'My father was violently opposed to it because he said it was worn-out stock. He went to some pains to prove to me that it was stock that was on

477

its last legs. He had done a lot of breeding of cattle', she explained – all in such a tone as to make clear that she had long ago come round to her father's way of thinking. She went on: 'There was so much T.B. and cancer in my husband's family that not only did three of my children have mental breaks, but one of his family had cancer and another one committed suicide. My side was stronger physically, stronger emotionally, stronger intellectually . . . ; but his was an old New England family', in contrast to her own Southern background. She commented, at another point, that her husband always wanted a big boat, such as one his own father had once had. 'But', she went on, 'we couldn't afford it; we had six children instead. Perhaps it would have been better if, instead of having the children, we had gotten the boat.'

The devaluation, by various of these mothers or fathers, of their child's emotions and ideas is often readily detectable. One mother said that her son, from the time he was old enough to hold a pencil in his hand until the age of about eight, used to draw for several hours a day. 'He drew all his ideas out in the form of cartoons, little series of pictures that followed a thing through. . . . We got awfully amused at him, his odd little ideas', she commented, which reminded me of another paranoid patient's repeated references to his childhood as 'my little life'. Another mother said, of her son's graduation from a top-level preparatory school, that 'He wasn't anything', meaning that he had won no class office or athletic award. A father, with a similarly erasing kind of scorn, said shortly, of his schizophrenic son's academic achievements, 'He's a genius; but he's no good to me being a genius in that condition', referring to the son's incomprehensible 'refusal' to apply himself to any line of work.

The mother of a very strong, and at times dangerously combative, young schizophrenic man, when asked whether her son had ever struck her, calmly replied that several times he had grabbed her hair and pulled it, and that once – a week previously, when she had been trying to persuade him to come to Chestnut Lodge – he had slapped her face. She went on, in a rather amused way, 'I knew he would', and added that at times he had pulled her hair 'not very hard, but like a child would pull somebody else's hair. I told him', she continued with a laugh, 'that I thought it was a great improvement – " At least you don't hurt

478

anybody when you pull my hair." ' A father, describing a drive he had taken with his paranoid daughter, while she had been home on a visit from the Lodge, mentioned that she had become enraged and hit his arm repeatedly, so hard that it was bruised for several days. I was astounded when he added: 'I wanted to concentrate on driving, so I acted as though nothing were happening.'

The effects of such parental responses, or lack of response, could be seen in one of my patients who, after much therapy, was able to confide to me, quite simply and resignedly, that 'nobody responds emotionally to me'. Another patient required several years of therapy to become free from her long-held, though previously unconscious, self-concept as a 'snow man in a glass' – one of those little snow men in a glass globe, with artificial snow – quite outside the realm of living human relatedness, and it was with the keenest pleasure that she finally became aware that '*I'm alive*, Dr Searles'. Another patient felt, for years, that she was a robot, and at times other types of machines, before becoming convinced that she was a human being, capable of responding emotionally and of evoking emotional responses in other human beings. Earlier, she had phrased it that her family 'used me as a thing for their amusement'.

Another patient, after much therapy, said, weeping bitterly, 'I felt as though I didn't have anything that was mine, almost', and told of how, in the course of her childhood, her mother, without consulting her, had given her doll's house to a Society for Underprivileged Orphans, her doll's carriage to someone, her favourite sweater to a younger sister, and had had the girl's dog spayed; and an older sister, on going away to college, had taken as many as she desired of the patient's books, likewise without asking. A divorced woman, the mother of two small children, said of her mother that: 'If things aren't going along the way she wants them to, it is within her power to take away my financial support and take over my babies. She has threatened to cut off my financial support since I've been ill. She sold my house and she sold her house and bought a new house with room for herself, the maid, and the two babies, and,' the patient ended with a hollow laugh, 'didn't leave any room for me.'

Always one can find evidence that one or both parents, during the patient's upbringing, have been so absorbed in *transference*-relatedness – traceable, that is, to unconscious elements in their

479

own childhood relationships – transference-relatedness to various members of the marital family, including the patient, that the patient's existence in his own right receives little acknowledgement. For example, to one mother, the patient's long-deceased elder brother, an important transference figure to the mother, was evidently still a much more alive and absorbing person to her than was her living schizophrenic son. In patients' marital family relationships, also, one sees the same phenomenon: in a number of instances, I have found that a paranoid woman's husband is so absorbed in his relationship with their daughter, unconsciously a mother-figure to him, that the patient has come to have, for all practical purposes, no place left in his psychological life, or in the marital family-structure. Another patient said, of her childhood, that when her mother and her paternal grand-mother, who lived in the home, were waging their chronic arguments, the 'tension was terrific', and 'I wasn't even given the acknowledgement of a piece of furniture in the room'.

Another woman, both of whose parents had been schizoid persons at best, and who felt convinced that she had had no single continuous home, or set of parents, said to a nurse: 'I've been in so many houses and been met with so many people behind newspapers. Either they didn't love each other or else I was to blame in some way for this. . . .' This illustrates how vulnerable is the child, who finds so little assurance of his real ability to affect other people, to the development of a conviction that he possesses some magical, inhumanly destructive, power over them. Other causes for such a self-concept lie in his uncomprehended transference significance to – and thereby power over – his parents' feelings, and in his unconscious hostility.

Out of such multiple ætiological factors, one patient felt herself to be less a human being than a 'force of evil'. Another patient confided, in a troubled tone, 'I work up the other person's destructiveness against life', and in describing her previously unsuccessful treatment, said despairingly, 'I was, and still am, impervious to any influence emanating from the psycho-analyst', and likened her own imperviousness to 'cancer'. At another point, she said, 'I felt that my little girl – as much as a child needs her mother – would be happier with her father; since I am so unhappy, couldn't help infecting her . . .'. We repeatedly find, in the course of psychotherapy with these patients, that they reveal a long-standing concern lest they convey their disease to other persons, as if it were caused by germs and communicable through physical contact.

Poignantly, in a number of instances this view of the self as being unfit for the world of human beings, by reason of some ill-understood destructive effect upon one's fellow-men, has seemed to represent an effort to account for the physical isolation in which the little child lived, the deprivation in terms of physical and emotional contact with any parental figure. The quite evident anxious disorganization with which these mothers, and sometimes the fathers, have met the patient's strivings, for intimacy with them, subsequent to his infancy, must be counted among the important factors in the child's developing conviction that his love has a destructive effect upon human beings.

Other ætiological circumstances I can touch upon only briefly. There is the parent's inability to relate to the child as being a whole person; the little son may have psychological significance for his mother or father only as a penis; and the girl may be quite literally only a pair of pretty legs, or a pair of maternal breasts, to the father or mother. Further, there is the parent's inability to differentiate the child clearly from his siblings, or from the parent himself or herself. One of my patients, who had two sisters, two and four years younger than herself, in one session started to reminisce, 'When I was six four and two . . .', as if she felt herself to be literally one person with her sisters. Nearly a year later she was able to describe how her mother 'never seemed to realize that we [girls] were different from one another'. One mother commented blandly, concerning her son: 'George objects violently if I address him in the tone I use in addressing either his father or his sister. He emphasizes [in the former instance], "I'm not Dad! I'm not married to you!".' In the symbiotic relationship with the mother or father, the child is, of course, often under pressure to express vicariously the parent's unconscious feelings. One mother, who seemed largely unaware of her own very considerable paranoid hostility, in painting a particularly malevolent picture of one among the many physicians who had, she felt, mishandled her son, commented approvingly that 'Eddie said he felt like killing him and for two cents he would have.' Another mother, who gave a similarly paranoid account of her daughter's experiences with a long series of previous therapists, including a terse comment concerning one, 'The man was a beast and did a bad job', and, concerning another, an even more terse, 'I'd like his head', seemed none the less to think of herself as a non-violent person, and, in tracing her daughter's background for me, said of a time when the young woman had been living with a lover: 'I lived in constant terror of what might happen that year; both are violent people, both are filled with hate, and anything could have happened.' It is somewhat remarkable to me that, despite such parental pressure, so many of these patients manage to avoid killing anyone.

I cannot elaborate, here, upon what might be thought of as the *internal* causative factors in the patient's fear that he may cease to exist as a living human individual. The resolution of these factors is invariably more difficult for him, and for the therapist, than is the clarification of the ways in which *other* persons have warped him. These internal factors, intimately related, of course, to the external ones, include: (a) his wide-scale repression of his emotions, which is one of the great causes for his feeling himself to be a dead person, or an inanimate thing; (b) his unconscious denial of his dependency-needs, such that he, regarding his therapist, for example, as being 'of no more importance to me than that spot on the wall there', as one of my patients phrased it, assumes, through a projection of such denial-of-dependency, that the other person considers *him* to be next to nothing; (c) the externalization of both sides of his internal conflicts, such that he feels himself to be a mere 'pawn', or 'rubber ball', buffeted about by the powerful beings upon whom these conflicts are externalized; (d) emotional withdrawal from human relatedness, as an expression of hostility, so habitually, and to such an extreme degree, that he feels himself to be, as one patient phrased it, a mere 'ghost'; and, lastly, (e) the clinging to the infantile view of other persons as being omnipotent and omniscient, which is a rather effective way for one to deal with one's feelings of guilty responsibility, but which leaves one with only the most tenuous room for existence as a functioning and significant human entity.

Any more comprehensive description of the ætiology of paranoid schizophrenia would have to include two additional factors which I shall only enumerate here: first, the presence of deeply repressed love-feelings in the mother-child relationship–a factor which, as I have detailed in chapter 7, is predominantly responsible for the child's introjection of the mother's submerged personality-fragmentation, and for the mother's–since she is convinced, at a deep level, that her intimacy is destructive to the child–becoming, early in his infancy, psychologically so aloof from him; and, secondly, the failure of mother and child to resolve their symbiotic mode of relatedness, a mode of relatedness which is normally found only in infancy. Their symbiosis is maintained into the patient's chronological adulthood, and those feelings, or other psychological contents, in either party which threaten the symbiosis are projected on to the world around the two. Not only such feelings as hatred and lust are projected on to the outer world, which therefore appears correspondingly threatening to the child; much of his own ego-capacities, also, being incompatible with the symbiosis with his mother, are projected on to various other figures, who are seen for a time as being larger than life, but always with eventual disillusionment. We might think of it that both the child and his mother have been unable to traverse successfully the ambivalent phase of his infancy–or, more accurately, the ambivalent phase of the mother-infant relationship, since this is a phase which, in normal development, is one of ambivalence not only for the child but also for the mother. In order to achieve true object-relatedness, as contrasted with symbiosis, this mutual ambivalence must be faced, accepted, and integrated into each person's concept of himself and of the other.

The threat which his genital lust poses to the paranoid schizophrenic individual can be understood most meaningfully, I believe, in connexion with the structural phenomena of symbiosis, non-differentiation, and dedifferentiation which I have already touched upon. His sexual identity is poorly differentiated, and although other areas of his personality are equally poorly demarcated, the culture is particularly punitive in regard to incomplete sexual differentiation. Moreover, his own unresolved infantile omnipotence, a facet of the unresolved mother-infant symbiosis, is directly threatened by the necessity for him to accept a single sexual identity, as either male or female, and relinquish the complementary one; he cannot be wholly a man–or she wholly a woman–without relinquishing that tenaciously held fantasied omnipotence. Further, the advent of genital lust at a time when his object-relations are at a level predominantly of symbiosis with the mother – herself poorly differentiated sexually, with a strongly, though unconsciously, phallic body-image – means that the sexual drive will be directed either towards the mother, or towards mother-surrogates, with connotations of both incest and homosexuality for the child, whether boy or girl. Another important ingredient, in the threat which lust poses for these young people, is traceable to their greatly thwarted identificatory needs; the young woman's need to identify with an adequate mother-figure is experienced as an utterly unacceptable 'Lesbian tendency', and the young man's need to identify with an adequate father-figure is experienced as an equally shameful 'homosexual tendency'.

The lust, although genital in expression, actually operates, as regards its psychological significance in object-relations, upon at best an oral level – that is, the first developmental stage beyond full symbiosis – with the result that sexual intercourse is reacted to as posing the threat that one will eat, or be eaten by, the sexual partner. Most often, I think, the cannibalistic feelings which in the healthy person are relatively readily admissible to awareness, as a natural concomitant of oral needs dating back to earliest infancy, in the paranoid individual are, by contrast, deeply repressed and projected on to the other person, so that the fear is of being devoured by the other in the sexual act. With each of the paranoid schizophrenic patients who have progressed far towards health in my therapeutic experience, it has required years of therapy for them to become aware of cannibalistic desires. Prior to such a development, their view of sexual intercourse is well epitomized by this poem, composed by an intellectually brilliant and witty, but deeply paranoid, young man. It is a parody upon Edgar Allan Poe's 'Annabel Lee', and is entitled.

Miss Cannibalee
It was many and many a day ago,
    In a city you all can see,
That a maiden lived whom you might know
    By the name of Cannibalee;
And this maiden she lived with no other thought
    Than a passionate fondness for me.

484

I was a lad and she was a lass;
  I hoped that her tastes were free.
But she loved with a love that was more than love,
  My yearning Cannibalee;
With a love that could take me roast, or fried,
  Or raw, as the case might be.

And that is the reason that long ago,
  In a city you all can see,
I had to turn the tables and eat
  My ardent Cannibalee—
Not really because I was fond of her,
  But to check her fondness for me.

But the stars never rise but I think of the size
  Of my hot-potted Cannibalee.
And the moon never stares but it brings me nightmares
Of my spare-rib Cannibalee;
  And all the night tide she is restless inside
Is my still indigestible dinner belle bride,
  In her pallid tomb, all rent free,
In her carnivorous sepulchre—me.

Although such repressed emotions as hostility and lust may readily be seen, early in our work with any one of these patients, to account for some of his paranoid anxiety, as we go on with him we find that each one of the whole range of human emotions has been, in him, long repressed as constituting an equally important source of this anxiety. It may require many months for us to see how filled he is, also, with loneliness, unfulfilled dependency, and feelings of abandonment; with fear and guilt, helplessness and despair; with disillusionment and grief; with heretofore stifled compassion and boundless love. These feelings are not easy to hear expressed, as, for instance, when a woman who, at the beginning of her therapy, had been encased for years in flintlike paranoid defences, becomes able to express her despair by saying that 'If I had something to get well for, it would make a difference'; her grief, by saying, 'The reason I'm afraid to be close to people is because I feel so much like crying'; her loneliness, by expressing a wish that she could turn an insect into a person, so then she'd have a friend; and her helplessness in face of her ambivalence by saying, of her efforts to communicate with

485

other persons, 'I feel just like a little child, at the edge of the Atlantic or Pacific Ocean, trying to build a castle—right *next* to the water. Something just starts to be grasped [by the other person], and then bang! it's gone—another wave.' And it is not entirely easy, either, to find oneself, in course of time, so important to, and adored by, the patient that he clearly yearns to be the ring on one's finger, sees one's face everywhere in people about him throughout the day, and finds that the days on which he has no therapeutic hour do not exist, in retrospect, for him, like so much time out of his life. But when he has become able to express any of these feelings, we can know that he is well in process of leaving his paranoid fortress, and joining the mainstream of his fellow human beings.

Chapter 17

SCHIZOPHRENIA AND THE
INEVITABILITY OF DEATH (1961)[1]

. . . throughout life one must learn to die.
SENECA

THE first half of this chapter will be devoted to a hypothesis concerning schizophrenia: Among the many sources of anxiety against which the illness system serves as a defence—some of these being unique to the patient's own particular existence, some of them uncommon, and some of them common to all mankind (that is, existential in nature)—is the seemingly prosaic fact of the inevitability of death. Here the role, in schizophrenia, of this one form of existential anxiety[2] will be studied.

In the second half of the chapter the focus of the discussion will be expanded to explore the meanings, to human beings in general, of this circumstance that death is inevitable—that human life is, like all other forms of life, innately finite.

Concerning Schizophrenia

Psycho-analysis and intensive psychotherapy show us how infinitely varied and complex are the emotions which activate the human personality. These psychotherapeutic techniques show us that the interpersonal situations which individuals foster with other individuals, situations in which this gamut of human feeling-capacities is played upon with such richness, are often, from this psychological point of view, truly exotic. The analyst or therapist may develop the impression, as the facts of the patient's early-life exposure to lurid feeling experiences unfold in the transference (experiences involving cannibalistic feelings, urges to dismember, incestuous feelings, and so on and on through infinite

[1] I am grateful to Drs Joseph H. Smith, Berl D. Mendel, Leslie Schaffer, and Donald L. Burnham for their helpful suggestions concerning a preliminary draft of this paper. It was first published in the *Psychiatric Quarterly*, Vol. 35 (1961), pp. 631–65.
[2] In chapter 7 of this book I have discussed another, and to my mind similarly important, existential factor in schizophrenia. There I portray schizophrenia as a function of the struggle to express one's love constructively, certainly a general human struggle.

twistings and turnings and combinations) that these most strikingly *unusual* experiences in the *past* constitute, so to speak, the most potent wellsprings of anxiety, against which the illness has become created as a bulwark, or has formed as a system of scars over these ancient traumata. He will find such abundant evidence for this impression, an impression which has more than a little of theoretical validity and clinical usefulness, that he may ignore even more significant sources of anxiety which are resident in the patient's current situation, relatively colourless though this situation may appear in some instances, by contrast to highly extraordinary family situations from long ago.

For several years I have had the growing conviction that, out of all the welter of situational factors which play upon the human being's feeling capacities, none is more potent than the simple fact that, for every individual, the whole complex business of living, this whole fascinating, agonizing, thrilling, boring, reassuring and frightening business, with all its moments of simple peace and complex turmoil, will some day inescapably end. To me this seems a fact of life so significant as to be ranked, in psychological import, alongside those which have long been accorded fundamental places in psycho-analytic theory and practice – alongside, that is, such fundamental phenomena as weaning, oedipal situations, the physiological and psychological concomitants of adolescence, and so on.

In the psychotherapy of schizophrenia it has seemed striking that, even in this overtly most exotic of psychopathological processes, the very mundane, universal factor of human mortality seemingly constitutes one of the major sources of anxiety against which the patient is defending himself – unconsciously, with his schizophrenic modes of intrapsychic experience and of interpersonal relatedness.

To be sure, schizophrenia can be considered a *result* of exotic, warping experiences in the past – predominantly in infancy and early childhood; but it can equally accurately, and with greater clinical usefulness, I think, be seen as consisting in the use of certain defence mechanisms, learned very early, to cope with *present-day* sources of anxiety. And of these latter, none is more potent than the existential circumstance of life's finitude. In essence, then, the hypothesis here is that schizophrenia can be seen, from one among various other possible vantage-points, as an intense effort to ward off or deny this aspect of the human situation. To the schizophrenic patient, this is—for reasons which will be detailed later—both more demanding of recognition, and more difficult to face, than it is to relatively well persons.

I wish to make it quite clear that, in my experience, the fact of the inevitability of death has a more than merely tangential relation to schizophrenia. That is, it is not a matter of the patient's becoming able, as he grows free here from his schizophrenia, to turn his attention yonder to that great life-circumstance of the inevitability of death—a circumstance which had previously lain inertly at the periphery of, or even totally beyond, his ken. On the contrary, my clinical work has indicated that the relationship is a much more central one than that: it is a matter, rather, of the patient's having become, and having long remained, schizophrenic (and reference here, of course, is to largely or wholly *unconscious* purposiveness) *in order to avoid facing*, among other aspects of internal and external reality, the fact that life is finite.

Only after several years of work with schizophrenic patients did I realize that—precisely as the repressed seeks constantly to find access into awareness, so that repression is maintained only at the cost of unceasing vigilance and energy expenditure—outer reality strives constantly, in a thousand and one incidents each day, to emerge into the patient's awareness. Thus, even the most deeply ill patient's delusions are under constant attack from the probing fingers of reality. To put this in unanimistic, less colourful, and more accurate terms, the schizophrenic patient's inner striving towards reality is an unceasing striving. In no instance, in my experience, is this striving so totally lacking that the reality aspect under present discussion, the fact of death's inevitability, is utterly divorced from the subjective experiences of the patient's daily life, and devoid of relevance to the psychodynamics of his schizophrenia.

At Chestnut Lodge the twice-weekly, hour-long case presentations usually have to do with schizophrenic patients, for such patients form the majority of those being treated there. When I went there, the therapists—including myself—presenting these cases often tended to paint a totally, or almost totally, black picture of the patient's childhood family relationships; the feeling-atmosphere of the presentation was one of blame of the parents more than anything else. As the years went on I found that the presentations came to convey less and less of such blame, and more and more of the tragedy of the patients' lives–tragedy which is so much of a piece with the tragedy of life for all of us that the presentation is often a profoundly grief-laden experience for both the presenter and the listeners. One feels that the staff-presentation now gives a truer picture of a patient's life, but a picture which is much more deeply shaking than was the blame-coloured picture previously often seen.

No doubt some of the change in my view was due to a degree of personal maturation over these years. But others commented on the same phenomenon; and I believe that the staff at Chestnut Lodge indeed matured, individually and collectively, beyond the level of twelve years' before.

What it is intended to emphasize here is that a prominent *part* of this existential tragedy which permeates the case history of the schizophrenic has to do with the finitude of human life. There is tragedy in many other forms–as indeed there is in all human living–tragedy in the form of personal unfulfilment, family dissolution, separation from the scenes of childhood, deeply-cherished relationships that have come to grief of one kind or another. But certainly the tragedy having to do with death's inevitability looms large here: the patient's parents are now elderly, and their deaths will obviously come before he can ever share with them a good relatedness whose years can equal those over which a predominantly pain-laden relatedness has extended. Or, in his childhood, the patient lost, through death, a parent or a nursemaid or a sibling who was obviously of the deepest value to him. Or he himself is now in middle life, and it is clear that when, even at best, his long treatment is successfully concluded, only a comparatively few of his years will remain to him. And so on.

It was several years ago, in the setting of my psychotherapeutic relationship with a certain schizophrenic man, that I sensed what depths of emotional challenge may be contained in so ostensibly simple a question as the stock one, contained in the traditional mental status examination,[3] whether a patient is reality-oriented in time, place, and person. For this particular

---

[3] An interrogatory procedure which, I am glad to say, has never held sway—to the best of my knowledge—at Chestnut Lodge, since it became a psychotherapeutic hospital decades ago.

man to be able to answer this question realistically, at a more than simply intellectual level, I realized, he would have to face the awesome tragedy involved in these circumstances of his present situation:

I am Charles Brennan, a man who is now, this being 15 April, 1953, 51 years of age; who is living here in Chestnut Lodge, a psychiatric hospital in Rockville, Maryland; who has now been living in a series of psychiatric hospitals constantly for eight years; who has been seriously ill for over 25 years, with a mental illness which has robbed me of any realistic prospect, considering my present age, of ever being able to marry and have children, and which, quite possibly, will require my being hospitalized for the remainder of my life. I am a man who was once a member of a family which included two parents and seven children, but who has seen, over the years, a crushing series of tragedies strike this family. Years ago my mother died, in a state of long-standing mental illness; one of my brothers developed a mental illness as a young man, requiring extended hospitalization; another brother committed suicide; still another brother was killed in action in the second World War; and a third was murdered only recently, at the height of his legal career, by a mentally ill client. My remaining parent, my father, is now elderly, a man pathetically far removed from the strong man he used to be, and death cannot be far off for him.

To be sure, a patient does not have to say all this in answer to the traditional mental-status question concerning orientation; but, if his answer is to be more than merely intellectually meaningful, he must be able to feel all this and, of course, much more. What I wish to emphasize, concerning the hypothetical answer from this particular man, is its permeation by the recognition of life's finitude. To be sure, this man's situation is exceptional; an extreme example has been chosen in order to make the point. But the burden of tragedy in his answer is only *somewhat* greater than that which any schizophrenic must come to face if he is to become able, as it is so glibly put, to 'face reality', and with these other patients, too, a considerable portion of the tragedy relates to the inevitability of death.

Also within the past few years, I have had the opportunity to work over very extended periods with chronic, and initially deeply schizophrenic, patients. I have been impressed at seeing that, in one instance after another, where as the patient's delusional ideas initially give one the impression of having to do with luridly exotic matters, they prove to include, inconspicuously and seemingly tangentially–as a kind of colourless rider-clause –an ingredient which represents a denial of the finitude of life. To give but one example of this, I shall cite my experience with a schizophrenic woman.

This woman was 28 when I began intensive psychotherapy with her; she had been overtly psychotic for at least $4\frac{1}{2}$ years, and had been hospitalized elsewhere for a year before her transfer to Chestnut Lodge. At her other hospital, she had had sporadic psychotherapy and several courses of insulin coma and electric shock therapy. There was no improvement in the luxuriantly delusional paranoid schizophrenia from which she was suffering. After her transfer to Chestnut Lodge, one therapist worked with her for a year and a half before quitting in discouragement at the rigidity of her resistance to therapy and at the increasing rather than diminishing course of her delusional thinking.

Beginning with my first session with her and as the therapy went on, I found abundant evidence of a richly detailed, fascinatingly exotic and complex, extremely vigorously defended delusional system, replete with all manner of horrendous concepts, ranging from brutal savagery to witchcraft, and to the intricate machinations of science-fiction. But towards the end of the first year of work, I became increasingly impressed with the fact that although her perceptual world was in many respects far more frightening, miserable, and horrible than that in which more normal persons live, it contained fewer of such qualities in many other respects. One scrutinized it in vain for any of the *innate* tragedy which sane persons find in their world–tragedy having to do with such matters as illness, poverty, aging, and, above all, inescapable death. In the sixteenth month of treatment she made her view of this quite explicit, when she stated, with vigorous protest:

There's no reason for anybody in the world to be unhappy or miserable in the world today; they have antidotes for everything. They just keep pulling the wool over people's eyes. . . . People don't die [but in actuality are simply 'changed', 'moved about from place to place', made the unwitting subjects of motion pictures, and so on]. It's a government that has girded the earth with horror and hell!

It required nearly $3\frac{1}{2}$ years of continued psychotherapy before this woman had developed a predominantly reality-oriented view of the world and of herself. To me the most memorable sign of this change was when she began to realize that life—including human life—is finite. I felt then that she was not merely taking fleeting glimpses of reality, as she had been doing increasingly during the previous 3½ years, but was at last coming to face reality fully and to accept it. During the last few months before this realization, there had been an evident intensification of her delusional defences against recognizing death's inevitability. She came to spend most of her time picking up dead leaves and the occasional dead birds and small animals which hours of searching revealed, and buying all sorts of articles from the stores in the nearby community, then, by various alchemy-like processes, attempting to bring these to one or another form of life. It became very clear (and she herself substantiated this) that she felt herself to be God, selecting various dead leaves and other things to be brought to life. Many times the psycho-therapeutic sessions were held out in the hospital grounds; the therapist sat on a bench, while she went on with her day-long scrutinizing of the lawn nearby.

But as these months wore on, towards the end of this period of denial of death, she came to express more and more openly a feeling of despair about this activity. Then there came an autumn day when, during the session, patient and therapist sat on benches not far apart and gazed together at the leaf-strewn lawn. She let it be known, mainly in non-verbal ways, that she was filled with mellowness, tenderness, and grief. She said, with tears in her eyes, in a tone as of resignation to a fact that simply has to be accepted, '*I* can't turn those leaves into sheep, for instance.' The therapist replied, 'I gather that you're realizing, perhaps, that it's this way with human life, too—that, as with the leaves, human life ends in death.' She nodded, 'Yes.'

This marked an openly-acknowledged acceptance of two great aspects of reality simultaneously: that she was not God—that she could not be held responsible for man's mortality—and that we human beings are mortal. This showed that the very foundation of her paranoid schizophrenic illness was now crumbling, an illness which had involved her years-long conviction, for example, that both her deceased parents were still living.

To cite another instance, a 37-year-old woman was suffering from a hebephrenic illness when I became her therapist. She had been hospitalized most of the time for the preceding eight years, and a lobotomy had been recommended before her transfer to the Lodge for a last-ditch trial of intensive psychotherapy. It required slightly more than six years for her to become able to accept the inevitability of death. During those six years, a kaleidoscopically-changing variety of schizophrenic manifestations revealed themselves in the therapy. These were seen, not so much in verbalizations of her delusional thinking, which was relatively undetailed in keeping with the deeply fragmented state of her ego, as they were in her non-verbal behaviour (bizarre modes of dress, weird laughter, and so on). To the extent that she was able to verbalize her thinking, it was evident that she experienced the world as being dominated by omnipotent father-figures and omnipotent nonhuman forces. I have seldom felt so moved as I did when, after her very deep confusion had steadily lessened over the years, she verbalized a poignant realization of the finitude of life. She expressed this, at first, with a kind of childlike, puzzled, protesting refusal to believe–not very different, probably, from some of the feelings which any human being finds in his heart as he comes face to face with this insurmountable fact of his existence.

She said, 'People don't live more than a hundred years,' in a tone as if to say that people say this; it doesn't make any sense, but that is what people all say. '. . . I'm going to live more than a hundred years [touching determination in her tone] . . . Why do people die? They say the heart expires. . . . Why should the heart expire? . . .' In a session not long after this, she asked, 'Why does a person die? Their heart wears out, is that it?' and went on–after I had agreed that this was the most common cause of death–to express a childlike puzzlement and protest as to why 'they' don't do something about this problem, why they don't 'duplicate' the heart. 'A mirror duplicates things,' she pointed out. 'I *can't* understand it,' she said protestingly and frustratedly.

In subsequent sessions, she made clear that the anxiety and sorrow associated with this so objectionable fact had to do not only with concern about her own existence, but also with concern for deeply-beloved persons in her life, some of whom were now dead, and some of whom were living but elderly.

The feeling-tone of the schizophrenic's eventual realization of the innate finitude of life is not different, in my experience, from that of the neurotic. I had been aware for several years that this poignant realization is a feature of the relatively late phases of neurotic patients' psycho-analyses; what I had not realized, until the last few years, is its significance in schizophrenia also. It has now become evident to me that a beautiful poem by Marcia Lee Anderson expresses a truth which is valid for us all, whether we be 'normal', neurotic, or schizophrenic:

Diagnosis

We multiply diseases for delight,
Invent a horrid want, a shameful doubt,
Luxuriate in license, feed on night,
Make inward bedlam—and will not come out.
Why should we? Stripped of subtle complication,
Who could regard the sun except with fear?
This is our shelter against contemplation,
Our only refuge from the plain and clear.
Who would crawl out from under the obscure
To stand defenceless in the sunny air?
No terror of obliquity so sure
As the most shining terror of despair
To know how simple is our deepest need,
How sharp, and how impossible to feed.[4]

In working with schizophrenic patients, one soon comes to realize that many if not all of them are unable to experience themselves, consistently, as being *alive*. I had long thought that this has to do mainly with their widespread repression of the gamut of their feelings—feelings of all sorts. But I have come to wonder whether this repression *in toto* may serve an additional defensive function: One need not fear death so long as one feels dead anyway; one has, subjectively, nothing to lose through death.

And it certainly seems to me that a second great aspect of schizophrenic symptomatology, the fantasy of personal omnipotence, ties in closely with the subject of this chapter. It is often mentioned that the schizophrenic patient views himself, and other people, as being omnipotent; but we need to remind ourselves that the companion of omnipotence is immortality. These two

[4] I am indebted to Dr Robert A. Cohen for having made me acquainted with this poem, the original source of which I have been unable to locate.

subjective qualities are, in fact, two sides of the same coin; whenever the gods are thought of they are assumed to be *immortal* gods.

Having touched upon the evidences that schizophrenia is a defence against recognizing the inevitability of death (among other anxiety-laden aspects of inner and outer reality, against which it is also a defence), I wish now to take up the central question of *why* the schizophrenic individual, unlike the normal-neurotic individual, has been unable to recognize and accept this aspect of reality.

First, it can be said that the anxiety concerning life's finitude is too great to face unless one has the strengthening knowledge that one is a whole person, and is, with this wholeness, able to participate wholly in living–able to experience one's self as a part of the collective wholeness of mankind, all of whom are faced with this common fate. A person cannot bear to face the prospect of inevitable death until he has had the experience of fully living, and the schizophrenic has not yet fully lived. (In saying this, I have in mind not only clinical experiences with patients, but also my personal experience. Not until I had had many months of personal analysis did I come to experience a sense of peace with respect to the fact of my eventual death; I remember well that at the end of a certain day, I felt that I had known for the first time, this day, what it was really to live; and simultaneously I found that I was no longer burdened by the prospect of death. I was astonished that it had required but one day of real living to work this curative result. It has been said that a man cannot bear to die without having really lived; but I found that one does not have to experience 30 years of real–i.e. relatively wholly participating–living to make up for the previous 30 years of existence as a less-than-whole person. One day, I found, was enough to enable me to face the threat of death with equanimity. This equanimity, though disturbed for varying periods in the intervening years since that day, has never been wholly lost to me, and forms what I feel to be the strongest and most basic of my feelings about death. The rest of this discussion will deal primarily with my clinical experience with schizophrenic patients who have gone on to, or–as in most of these instances–a long way towards, recovery.)

Second–and these are not separate features of the schizophrenic's past, but aspects of a single complex situation–the losses which he has already experienced have come too early in his development, and in too great magnitude, for him to have been able to integrate them. Perhaps, if it were possible for him to experience his sense of loss fully, at a phase of his life when durable object relationships had not yet been established, he would experience a feeling, not of 'loss' in the mature sense, but rather of disintegration of the total self.[5] Thus, such a person would react to these losses, because of the immaturity of his ego, with various pathological defence mechanisms–most of all, with reinforcement of his subjective infantile omnipotence, which involves his conviction that he has suffered no loss, and that it is unthinkable that he could ever suffer loss, for he is the whole world. Thus, not having been able to integrate losses in the past, he is unable now to integrate the prospect of the greatest of all losses, the loss which stems from the mortal nature of himself and of everyone he knows. He meets this supreme threat of loss with his habitual defence mechanism of subjective omnipotence–a defence mechanism which is, as already mentioned, so prominent a feature in any schizophrenic illness.

The early losses referred to are seen in any of the hundreds of schizophrenic patients' case presentations known to me through many years at Chestnut Lodge. These include, very often, the death, or otherwise physical departure from the scene, of deeply significant persons in the infant's or young child's life; or the psychological withdrawal of an erstwhile mothering figure. In the latter connexion it is of interest that Lewis B. Hill (1955) after much longer experience than mine with the psychotherapy of schizophrenic patients, states:

There is . . . evidence that many of the mothers of schizophrenics actually accepted their babies warmly and took excellent animal care of them while these babies were small and were not regarded as individuals having any will or wilfulness contrary to that of the mother . . . (p. 111).

Third, in direct line with what has just been said about early losses, the symbiotic relatedness between infant and mother, while normally found in infancy, is, in the life of the future

---

[5] A concept suggested to me, in another connexion, by Dr Robert A. Cohen in 1955.

schizophrenic, prolonged into chronological adulthood. The 'mother' in this symbiosis may be the mother herself, a nurse-maid, the father in occasional instances, or later figures in the patient's life to whom this kind of relatedness becomes transferred. The presence of this symbiotic relatedness in the schizophrenic's life-history has been described by a number of writers, including Reichard and Tillman (1950), Lidz and Lidz (1952), Mahler (1952), Hill (1955), and myself (chapters 1 and 7 of his book), and only certain aspects of it which are of the greatest relevance here will be discussed.

In such a relatedness, each person finds himself oscillating helplessly between a position of intense 'closeness' to the other person, and an utterly contrasting position of total psychological divorce from that person, the latter position being experienced as a sense of having completely *lost* the deeply cherished relatedness of a moment before. It may well be that, for the adult schizophrenic patient, the prospect of death is intolerably reminiscent of such experiences of loss—and, of course, of similar experiences in the present with parent-figures—of bleak, death-like interruptions in his sense of contact with this other person who is felt to be necessary to his very survival.

There is another respect in which such a relatedness involves tremendous loss, if one can apply the term 'loss' to something which one has not yet had: the patient's loss of the experiencing of himself as a relatively wholly-integrated person, at both intrapsychic and interpersonal levels. The symbiotic relatedness requires, for its maintenance, that neither party experience himself or herself as a whole person; instead, each needs the other's personality to complement his or her own personality, in order to achieve anything like a sense of 'wholeness'. Moreover, this symbiosis precludes a sense of wholeness, on the part of either person or of both together, with the larger world of collective mankind; typically, this is a two-against-the-world kind of relationship. This larger world, made up of all persons outside the symbiotic relationship, must be kept at a distance psychologically, rather than related to, closely and realistically, if for no reason other than the child's and the mother's need to project upon it various intensely negative affects which are engendered in both of them by the very nature of their extremely constricting symbiosis with one another.

In addition to the loss-of-subjective-wholeness aspect of this symbiosis, there is another aspect of it which militates also against the child's developing in such a way as to be able to meet, in chronological maturity, this great fact of the inevitability of death. That is, this symbiosis involves, on the part of both persons, a subjective–and repressed–infantile omnipotence, in keeping with the basically very infantile nature of this relationship, a relationship which is normally found only between the infant and the mothering figure, as has been pointed out by Mahler (1952).

The child who eventually develops schizophrenia needs, in his chronological maturing, to maintain this subjective omnipotence as a defence against various threats, internal and external, in addition to the threat involved in the recognition of human mortality. He needs it to cope with, among other lesser threats which there will be no attempt to list comprehensively, his profound, repressed sense of helplessness in the face of his mother's, and his own, very intense ambivalence. As I have described in chapter 7, he and his mother do not simply bear murderous hatred and intense rejectingness towards one another, but equally genuine and powerful love. He has a sense of profound personal helplessness in the face of his feeling his deepest hate towards the person whom he most deeply loves, and helplessness in the face of his fear of this person who is at once the most important person in his life and who loves him intensely, and is at the same time the person who above all others also hates him. It is this sense of personal helplessness which, more than anything else, requires his maintenance of the fantasy, normal only in infancy, of personal omnipotence.

Nothing else would so completely demolish this subjective omnipotence, this so desperately needed defence, as would his recognition of the inevitability of death; a human being is never more aware of his own powerlessness than he is when experiencing this recognition.

But among the many psychological prices which he pays for thus clinging to this cherished defence, this subjective omnipotence, there is a great complicating of his perceptual picture of the reality-aspect which more normal persons experience as life's innate finitude. The resultant complexity makes it inordinately difficult, then, for him to sort out perceptually, and

499

become aware of, this fact of human life, for it has become thoroughly entangled with his defensively-distorted views of himself and of the world.

Every schizophrenic person, or young person who is on the road to schizophrenia, has a great deal of repressed hatred within him, and has a view of himself—whether in consciousness or at a repressed level—as a creature bearing within himself an omnipotent malevolence. Thus what is normally experienced as realistic death which will inevitably come to embrace every human being, he tends to experience in terms of a projection of his own supposedly all-powerful destructiveness; he tends, then, to feel personally and totally *responsible for* death itself, as he is indeed responsible—more, certainly, than anyone else—for his own feelings, including his hatred, whether it be conscious or unconscious.

So, before he can face the fact of man's innate susceptibility to death, he must come to know clearly that he does not carry the seeds of mankind's destruction in his own breast. This necessitates prolonged working-through of his erstwhile repressed hostility; and, only when he can mature to a point where his love is greater than his hatred, and where he can feel convinced that this is so, can he find the assurance that mankind's mortal nature is not to be laid at the door of his own personal responsibility. Prior to that development, he tends to equate the existential fact of death's final victory with the fact that his own hatred repeatedly triumphs over the forces of love in himself.

The psychological state of his partner in the symbiotic relationship—most often his mother—is such as to add to the complexity of his problem in coming to face this aspect of reality. She, too, clings to a fantasy of subjective omnipotence and she herself also possesses deeply ambivalent feelings. One must not forget that the ego-boundaries demarcating these two persons are very incomplete. Thus, for him, existential death tends to wear the countenance of his mother's repressed and projected murderousness, mingled with his own.

His incomplete ego-integration, and his painful experience of apartness, not only from other persons (as mentioned in the description of the symbiotic mode of relatedness), but from his own self, tend to make him react to existentially normal death, with its connotations of physical disintegration and removal from the world of living beings, as tantamount to both the intrapersonal and interpersonal experiences of psychological non-integration which have caused him his most intense suffering. Thus he tends to react to existential death, as this moves towards his awareness (although as a not-yet-realistically defined perception) with feelings not only of personal guilt, but of irrational anxiety. One of my schizophrenic patients, as she started to come to grips with this aspect of reality, became obsessed for months with efforts to arrange to have her body, after death, kept indefinitely in a deeply frozen state, so that it would not 'fall apart'—the same phrase she had used, for years, in reference to her experiences of psychological disintegration.

We might say that every human being faces this dilemma: He cannot face death unless he is a whole person, yet he can become a truly whole person only by facing death. But so long as one is still schizophrenic, one is much less well able to meet this dilemma successfully; one is much *too* unwhole to do so. Only a relatively whole man can experience a sense of participation in the wholeness of mankind, a sense that is so deeply reassuring in the face of the knowledge of death, as William Cullen Bryant's poem, *Thanatopsis* beautifully conveys:

> Yet not to thine eternal resting-place
> Shalt thou retire alone, nor couldst thou wish
> Couch more magnificent. Thou shalt lie down
> With patriarchs of the infant world—with kings,
> The powerful of the earth—the wise, the good,
> fair forms, and hoary seers of ages past,
> All in one mighty sepulchre. . . .
>
> . . . .
>   . . . All that tread
> The globe are but a handful to the tribes
> That slumber in its bosom.—. . .
>
> . . . .
> So shalt thou rest—and what if thou withdraw
> In silence from the living, and no friend
> Take note of thy departure? All that breathe
> Will share thy destiny. The gay will laugh
> When thou art gone, the solemn brood of care
> Plod on, and each one as before will chase
> His favourite phantom; yet all these shall leave
> Their mirth and their employments, and shall come

And make their bed with thee. As the long train
Of ages glides away, the sons of men, –
The youth in life's fresh spring, and he who goes
In the full strength of years, matron and maid,
The speechless babe, and the grey-headed man –
Shall one by one be gathered to thy side,
By those, who in their turn shall follow them.

So live, that when thy summons comes to join
The innumerable caravan, which moves
To that mysterious realm, where each shall take
His chamber in the silent halls of death,
Thou go not, like the quarry-slave at night,
Scourged to his dungeon, but, sustained and soothed

By an unfaltering trust, approach thy grave
Like one who wraps the drapery of his couch
About him, and lies down to pleasant dreams.

From what has been described of the psychodynamics of schizophrenia two implications emerge for a therapeutic approach which will help the patient to become able to face the inevitability of death.

The first implication is an obvious one: the therapist's awareness of these psychodynamics enables him to help the patient to unravel this reality aspect from the complexities of his delusional thinking. The therapist's awareness will also help him to understand why the patient's recognition of the inevitability of death can only follow a prolonged working through of hatred, guilt, and anxiety.

The second implication is simpler, but if anything more important, than the first: it is essential that the therapist himself be well aware, at a more than simply intellectual level, of life's finitude, and that his whole therapeutic approach be conducted in the light of his recognition of it. The chronically schizophrenic individual often requires deep and genuine patience from the therapist; the latter is often required – or one might say allowed, for there is a pleasurable side to this, too – to function as though time did not exist, in order to nourish the patient's slow growth out of an ego-shattered state. Many a therapist shies away from this phase of the treatment, for it tends to be deeply frustrating-and-gratifying to infantile dependency needs, whose presence within himself he cannot acknowledge (see ch. 3). But the time comes, in every instance in which treatment is successful, when the therapist must gradually oppose, more and more firmly, a powerful tendency in the patient-therapist relationship towards becoming bogged down in the timeless, infantile-omnipotent world of the schizophrenic—a world which the therapist has had to share, to a degree, in empathizing with the patient, and a world which holds a powerful alure for the vestigial infant in each of us. Thus, although the therapist had earlier to be predominantly patient and undemanding, he can now be (and in fact it is essential that he now be) unashamedly impatient with the schizophrenic's continuing to function as though an eternity of time remained in which to carry through the mutual therapeutic task.

Concerning Human Beings in General

In my experience, any successful, long-range psycho-analysis or psychotherapy comes to involve the patient and the doctor in facing life's most basic issues together, even though the doctor may be participating little in an overt, verbal fashion. Each emerges, when the treatment is over, with a deepened and enriched understanding of life's meaning. Certainly, in working with a schizophrenic patient, the therapist must, in the course of helping him to face the fact of the inevitability of death—a facet of reality which, as has been indicated, is the focus of so much anxiety for the patient—search deeply into the meanings which this existential fact holds for *himself* also.

Thus my work with schizophrenic patients has formed one of the wellsprings of my interest in the meaning which this subject—the finitude of life, the inevitability of death—holds for human beings in general. A second major source of my interest was a series of bereavements, which occurred between six years and a year and a half before this was written. Since the most recent of these, sufficient time, thought, and working through of feelings have been expended for me to feel myself capable of bringing to this presentation both a degree of personal interest and one of considered thought.

This is a subject which present-day Western culture tends mainly to discourage us from investigating, from thinking about often or deeply. Our culture predominantly fosters in us, psychiatrists and laymen alike, a readiness to ignore it altogether. Our non-recognition of death's inevitability is encouraged not only by the prevalence of such escape-entertainment media as television, the radio, and the cinema, but also in less obvious ways. To the extent that we are kept preoccupied by the quite realistic fear that international tensions may lead to a global holocaust at any time, and thus wipe out our lives, we are shielded, paradoxically, from the ineradicable fact that, no matter whether the dim chance of international peace brightens, human life is in any case finite. And to the not inconsiderable degree that suicide is prevalent (and the tremendous toll which is exacted, annually, by road accidents suggests that unconscious suicide may be vastly more prevalent than conscious, unmistakably identifiable suicide), then, again paradoxically, a segment of the population may be thought of as having rejected the full recognition of life's innate finitude, through its members having subjectively willed–consciously or unconsciously–their own deaths. And modern medicine, with its highly publicized campaigns to lower the statistics which show us that so-and-so-many persons out of ten die of cancer, or heart disease, and so on, foster–however valuable these campaigns are in other respects–our overlooking the fact that, no matter how highly developed medical science becomes, out of every ten persons there will still die, from one cause or another, ten.

Further, to the extent that a culture is permeated–as is our own–with thinking which is couched in the frame of reference of *blame*, we tend to shield ourselves from the inescapable conditions of our existence, one such condition being the inevitability of death. In my description, earlier in this chapter, of the changed atmosphere of the staff presentations at Chestnut Lodge, the impression was noted that, in this miniature 'culture', the atmosphere of blame which had prevailed years ago had served to shield the staff from a relatively full awareness of the innate tragedy of the patients' lives. And similarly in one's daily life in the larger culture, when someone we know dies, we tend to become involved in feelings of blame, whether of other persons or of ourselves, rather than regard the death as something which is a natural part of our existence. It is not meant here, of course, that mankind should passively accept the ravages of disease, or of human suffering in any form; but the fact of our innately mortal nature must be accepted if we are to know what it is to live in peace.

I wish finally to suggest, before leaving this aspect of the subject for the time being, that our culture's whole emphasis upon the use of *verbal communication* may serve to shield us from the reality of death. Benjamin Lee Whorf, in particular, has expounded what has come to be known as the Sapir-Whorf hypothesis, which states in essence that our thinking, and our perception of the world about us, is limited by the nature of the language which our culture employs—instead of language possessing, as had previously been widely assumed, a much less significant, purely instrumental, function in our living. Edward Sapir, under whom Whorf studied, had phrased the hypothesis thus:

> Human beings do not live in the objective world alone, nor alone in the world of social activity as ordinarily understood, but are very much at the mercy of the particular language which has become the medium of expression for their society. It is quite an illusion to imagine that one adjusts to reality essentially without the use of language and that language is merely an incidental means of solving specific problems of communication or reflection. The fact of the matter is that the 'real world' is to a large extent unconsciously built up on the language habits of the group. . . . We see and hear and otherwise experience very largely as we do because the language habits of our community predispose certain choices of interpretation (Whorf, 1956, p. 134).

Langer notes that Bertrand Russell, in a philosophical work written in 1900, had pointed out the essential principle embodied in the Sapir-Whorf hypothesis (Langer, 1942, p. 55).

If we grant, then, the premise that our particular language tremendously conditions—not only consciously but unconsciously—our thought-processes and our view of 'reality', then it follows that our culture's great emphasis upon *verbal* communication results, by way of the segmentation and abstractification which are involved in discursive language, in our having not only consciously but unconsciously a segmented and abstractified experience of our existence. Such a mode of experiencing our life tends to shield us from the continually flowing rhythm of our actual existence, the essential continuity of birth-growth-decay-death. I think these would not be experienced, if we knew them face to face, in the segmented form in which they have to be presented through the limited medium of verbal language. A verbal-language view of life tends to shield us from experiencing existence as involving a concrete and continual relatedness to death.

Such cultural factors as those here mentioned may account, in part, for the relative paucity of psycho-analytic and psychiatric literature on this subject. But it is, nonetheless, somewhat puzzling to find that scant attention has been paid, in professional writings, to a subject whose importance in human living is attested by the position of great prominence which it has long occupied in the world's various religions, in myths, in general literature, and in philosophy.

In our own culture, religion is one of the very few institutions which repeatedly puts before us this basic fact of our existence, the fact of death – even though it presents a palliative at the same time, in the form of a concept of life after death, to relieve the harshness of this fact of death. Apparently religions from time immemorial have attempted, in some manner or other, to grapple with the fact of death. Suzanne K. Langer, in *Philosophy in a New Key* (1942) says: '. . . Life and life-giving, death and the dead, are the great themes of primitive religion . . .' (p. 122).

And of myths, she says:

Myth . . ., at least at its best, is a recognition of natural conflicts, of human desire frustrated by non-human powers, hostile oppression, or contrary desires; it is a story of the birth, passion, and defeat by death which is man's common fate . . . (*ibid.*, p. 143).
. . . the culture-hero [in the myth] *is Man, overcoming the superior forces that threaten him.* A tribe, not a single inventor, is unconsciously identified with him. The setting of his drama is cosmic; storm and night are his foes, deluge and death his ordeals. These are the realities that inspire his dream of deliverance. His task is the control of nature – of earth and sky, vegetation, rivers, seasons – and the conquest of death (*ibid.*, p. 150).

Likewise in most great literature, we are never far removed from facing this theme of death's inevitability. Perhaps one symptom of the relative mediocrity of much of current writing is the fact that it seldom attempts to deal with this basic facet of human existence. There is no lack, in today's literature, of accounts of death by human violence; but only seldom is a modern novel couched in terms of human existence as being quite *innately* terminated by death. It seems to the writer that the best of our novels are those which include cognizance of this theme. For example, in James Jones' *From Here to Eternity* (1953), and James Gould Cozzens' *By Love Possessed* (1957), this theme forms the ever-present background of the narrative.

Philosophy, too, of course, from its beginnings has always striven to come to terms with, among other facets of human existence, the fact of death. A brief sampling of some of the tenets of a relatively recently-developed school of philosophy which is of much interest to the behavioural sciences, Existentialist philosophy or ontology, will show that the finitude of man's life is one of the most central concerns of this system.

Concerning Heidegger's existentialism, Eissler writes:

> The cornerstone of Heidegger's ontological analysis of existence (1927) is the presence of death in each moment of life prior to the actual occurrence of death. . . . existential analysis reveals that existence is *existence (or being) toward death (Sein zum Tode)*. . . . in the system of Heidegger's ontology, dying does not mean that existence has reached an end; rather, death is a mode of being upon which existence enters as soon as it has begun (Eissler, 1955, pp. 4–6).

O. F. Bollnow is quoted, in Eugen Kahn's recent review (1957) of existential analysis, as holding that 'To exist means to be faced with death'.

Ludwig Binswanger is paraphrased by Edith Weigert (1949) as asserting similarly that 'Being-in-the-world is existence towards death'.

And lastly Paul Tillich, a theologian whose existentialist volume, *The Courage to Be* is one of the relatively few such works available in English, presents the anxiety concerning death as one of the foundation-stones of his views of man's psychology:

> . . . The first assertion about the nature of anxiety is this: anxiety is the state in which a being is aware of its possible nonbeing. The same statement, in a shorter form, would read: anxiety is the existential awareness of nonbeing. 'Existential' in this sentence means that it is not the abstract knowledge of nonbeing which produces anxiety but the awareness that nonbeing is a part of one's own being. It is not the realization of universal transitoriness, not even the experience of the death of others, but the impression of these events on the always

latent awareness of our own having to die that produces anxiety. Anxiety is finitude, experienced as one's own finitude. This is the natural anxiety of man as man, and in some way of all living beings. It is the anxiety of nonbeing, the awareness of one's finitude as finitude (Tillich, 1952, pp. 35–6).

Valuable as is the emphasis placed upon this theme, namely the psychological significance of human mortality, in existentialist writings such as the few mentioned here, one seldom gets from them a sense of the basically *uniquely individual* impact upon one's self of this fact, that one is, like all one's fellow human beings, mortal; Tillich is unusual, among such writers, in stressing, as noted here, the anxiety having to do with one's *own* individual death. Binswanger is apparently more typical of such writers, in couching his views in terms of mankind as a whole, a frame of reference which necessarily entails much dilution of individual poignancy: '. . . If we talk of human existence, . . . we *never* mean human existence as mine, thine, or his, but human existence in general, or the human existence of mankind . . . ' (Kahn, 1957, p. 217).

Weigert (1949) has called attention to this breadth of existentialism's focus: '. . . Existentialism is not interested in individual psychopathology; it describes certain basic irreducible dialectic trends like One and Self, Care and Love, which determine existence in our culture. The psychotherapist looks at trees, the existentialist at the forest as a whole . . .'

Coming now to the contributions of psycho-analytic literature concerning this subject, let us look first at Freud's writings. In 'Thoughts For the Times on War and Death' (1915*b*), written in a state of profound disillusionment about the First World War, he distinguished three different basic attitudes in us regarding death. Our own death is, he says, unimaginable to us; the deaths of our enemies are desired by us; and the deaths of our loved ones arouse ambivalent reactions in us:

It is indeed impossible to imagine our own death; and whenever we attempt to do so we can perceive that we are in fact still present as spectators. Hence the psycho-analytic school could venture on the assertion that at bottom no one believes in his own death, or, to put the same thing in another way, that in the unconscious every one of us is convinced of his own immortality (Freud, 1915*b*, p. 289).

On the other hand, for strangers and for enemies, we do acknow-

ledge death, and consign them to it quite as readily and unthinkingly as did primæval man . . . (*ibid.*, p. 297.)

Then, after describing our unconscious ambivalence towards
the deaths of our loved ones, Freud says, 'To sum up: Our unconscious is just as inaccessible to the idea of our own death, as
murderously minded towards the stranger, as divided or ambivalent towards the loved, as was man in earliest antiquity. . .'

In *Beyond the Pleasure Principle* (1920), Freud put forward
his concept of a death instinct in man, a concept which came to
form a major component of his definitive over-all theory of
human psychology. But, to my own mind at least, it tended for
many years (to the degree that this now largely-abandoned
concept was embraced by his followers) to obscure the deepest
significances of the inevitability of death. Specifically, I believe
that this concept obscures the fulness of the impact which this
fact makes upon us: the potential poignancy, terror, rage and
sorrow which it holds are all diluted in a conceptual view which
maintains that, to a marked degree each of us unconsciously
longs for this inevitable event. I believe that a longing for death
is, indeed, one among our many attitudes towards it; but I
believe that Freud's concept of a death instinct of almost unparalleled power, followed by subsequent writings in psycho-
analysis which have tended either to prove or disprove this
theory, have served to distract us from looking into the depths
of poignancy–a poignancy far more complex than some mere
two-sidedly conflictual matter–which is aroused in us by our
awareness of death's inevitability.

Eissler, in *The Psychiatrist and the Dying Patient*, subscribes to
Freud's theory of a death instinct, and even suggests that death
may always be psychological in nature–that death in whatever
form, whether or not it is *overtly* a suicide, may involve the ego's
having decided, as it were (and here Eissler is paraphrased), to
die. Although he puts this forward as a tentative hypothesis, he
dwells upon it at such length as to indicate that he is much
impressed with this possibility; the following passage merely
introduces his relatively lengthy case for the hypothesis: '. . .
There is still the faint possibility that man could die only when
the inherent forces of life have lived out their potential or when
an inner complication forces the ego to turn the balance in

favour of the ever-ready forces of internal destruction . . .'
(Eissler, 1955, p. 106).

Such a viewpoint colours much of Eissler's book, including the
bulk of it which has to do with the specific title-subject of psychotherapy with the dying patient. A major technique which, he
feels, helps the patient to endure the 'final pathway' is the
psychiatrist's helping the patient to feel that the psychiatrist is
identified with him in facing death. But we get the impression
that this is, indeed, recommended primarily as a *technique*,
something which is here of use to the patient; that the psychiatrist does not identify with the patient in a really deep sense;
and that, above all, Eissler does not appear to look upon this
situation as one in which the psychiatrist's view of his *own*
inevitable death is plumbed in its deeper meanings:

. . . A part of the therapist's ego must remain free of identification.
As has been remarked earlier, even the belief in immortality must be
activated. If the therapist's own fear of death is considerable, he will
either recoil from even a partial identification or become anxious, if
not depressed. . . . the main function of the identification is . . . to
make it possible for the patient to establish a therapeutic relationship
which is at all usable . . . (*ibid.*, p. 250).

If the author were a dying patient, and in psychotherapy, the
greatest service a therapist could render him would be, beyond
helping him to face the fact of his own coming death, that of
giving him to know that the relationship was also being of use
to the therapist in his own adjustment to the death which will
inevitably come to him as it is coming, sooner now, to the
dying patient.

Eissler expresses the troubled rumination:

. . . there was no doubt that in Case Two it would have helped if
I could have told the patient that I, too, was suffering from a disease
bringing me slowly closer to death. In this moment a community of
spirit would have been established which would have permitted an
identification on her side (*ibid.*, p. 246).

I feel that we all *do* suffer from something which brings us
slowly closer to death – namely, aging; and to the degree that a
psychiatrist need not shield himself from this fact in the deepest
levels of his being, the closer and more genuine can be the
communion felt with a dying patient. I shall not go further into

this special aspect of the subject, with which Eissler mainly deals; but, in leaving it, I wish to emphasize that this is not an aspect which is far off to one side from the everyday practice of psychotherapy and psycho-analysis. Eissler's book can help us to become clearer about philosophical matters which not only are involved in the psychiatrist's relatively rare work with patients who are close to death, but which underlie all our work with patients, for surely one criterion of maturity, which we endeavour to help patients in general to achieve, is their ability to face, and live with, the knowledge of the mortal nature of human life. Eissler devotes part of his attention to the more general aspects of this subject–the psychological significances, to man, of the fact that he must eventually die–and presents a review of the relatively sparse psycho-analytic literature on this subject, a review which need not, therefore, be duplicated here.

In addition to Freud's controversial death-instinct theory, a second characteristic of the developmental history of psycho-analysis has tended to minimize the significance of death: the preoccupation of psycho-analysis with the first few years of the patient's history. Of interest in this connexion is a comment made by Hartmann, Kris, and Loewenstein (1946). After describing the development of the superego organization in the child, they emphasize: 'The development of personality is not concluded at this point, and we feel that the potentialities of its transformation throughout latency and adolescence have for some time been underrated in psychoanalytic writings. . . .'

However essential it is that the very early period of life be focused upon strongly as of preponderant importance in the development of the personality, it should be seen that this is a period in which the individual is normally but little occupied with the reality of his own, and other persons', innate susceptibility to death. This aspect of reality tends to remain principally over the horizon until one's life course is to a very significant degree already run–that is, half-run or so. Even adolescence, which has marked the outer limit of most of the ground covered by psycho-analytic theory, knows little of the feelings which come in later years about this, when death is a clearly visible reality and we find in fact that we have already walked half-way, or much more than half-way, to it.[6] In relatively recent years writers such as Therese Benedek (1952a, 1959, 1960) have explored some of the psychological phases of life after adolescence, after 'maturity' has been reached; this paper is intended as a contribution to such studies. Incidentally, it may be no coincidence that members of that very age group, the elderly, to whom the reality of death looms largest, have been considered relatively unsuitable for psycho-analysis or intensive psychotherapy. Perhaps as analysts and therapists come more to grips with the significance of death, we shall have the personal courage and understanding to work more deeply with elderly persons, and shall find that they are better 'candidates' for therapy, or even analysis, than we had long assumed them to be. We shall be encouraged to enter into such work, for example, in proportion as we become convinced that even a single moment of deeply-felt intrapersonal and interpersonal relatedness is subjectively timeless, eternal, and 'makes up for' several decades of living as a less-than-whole person.

In psycho-analytic theory, we have too often tended to limit ourselves to thinking that a patient's preoccupation with the subject of death connotes only some pathological reaction, whether a phobia about death, or guilt-laden death wishes, or what not. Death as a great aspect of reality, an aspect whose reality needs to be recognized by the patient–and an aspect which no psycho-analysis of whatever depth and thoroughness can ever efface, but only more clearly delineate–is seldom mentioned in our professional literature. We tend to forget, for example, when a phobia about death is being discussed, that even after the *symbolic* meanings of 'death' to the patient have been brought to light, and there has been a resolution of the neurotic anxiety concerning heretofore unconscious affects

[6] But it may be that adolescence possesses a feature which psycho-analysis has largely overlooked: a *beginning* attempt to face death's inevitability. The presence of such an ingredient in normal adolescence is suggested by the fact that so many adult schizophrenic patients, who – as indicated in the first part of this paper – have such intense difficulty with this matter of life's finitude, became schizophrenic in adolescence. And the following comment by Erikson is additionally suggestive:
'In extreme instances of delayed and prolonged adolescence an extreme form of a disturbance in the *experience of time* appears which, in its milder form, belongs to the psychopathology of everyday adolescence. It consists of a sense of great urgency and yet also of a loss of consideration for time as a dimension of living. The young person may feel simultaneously very young, and in fact baby-like, and old beyond rejuvenation . . .' (Erikson, 1956).

(concerning sex, aggression, passivity, or whatever) which have presented themselves in the guise of anticipated death, there will still remain the *reality* of death itself, and the anxiety realistically associated with it.

Erich Fromm (1955), while in my opinion giving certain of man's interpersonal conflicts—such as those arising from the Oedipus situation—less than their due, accords a full and eloquent acknowledgement to the significance of human mortality; he makes it, in fact, one of the cornerstones of his theoretical system (which he calls humanistic psycho-analysis), and his views provide a valuable counterbalance, therefore, to the emphasis which classical psycho-analysis has placed upon instinctual factors:

> . . . the main thesis of humanistic psychoanalysis: that the basic passions of man are not rooted in his instinctive needs, but in the specific conditions of human existence, in the need to find a new relatedness to man and nature after having lost the primary related-ness of the pre-human stage . . . (Fromm, 1955, p. viii).

> Self-awareness, reason and imagination disrupt the 'harmony' which characterizes animal existence. Their emergence has made man into an anomaly, into the freak of the universe. He is part of nature, subject to her physical laws and unable to change them, yet he transcends the rest of nature. He is set apart while being a part; he is homeless, yet chained to the home he shares with all creatures. Cast into this world at an accidental place and time, he is forced out of it, again accidentally. Being aware of himself, he realizes his power-lessness and the limitations of his existence. He visualizes his own end: death. Never is he free from the dichotomy of his existence: he cannot rid himself of his mind, even if he should want to; he cannot rid him-self of his body as long as he is alive—and his body makes him want to be alive (*ibid.*, pp. 23-4).

Fromm's views, expressed in 1955, are similar in content, and in eloquence, to these of Langer, expressed in 1942.

> For good or evil, man has this power of envisagement, which puts on him a burden that purely alert, realistic creatures do not bear—the burden of understanding. He lives not only in a place, but in Space; not only at a time, but in History. So he must conceive a world and a law of the world, a pattern of life, and a way of meeting death. All these things he knows, and he has to make some adaptation to their reality (Langer, 1942, p. 283).

Fromm writes with a moving simplicity of aspects of our life which are seldom, if ever, acknowledged in classical psycho-analytic literature: '. . . death confronts us with the inevitable fact that either we shall die before our loved ones or they before us . . .' (Fromm, 1955, p. 201).

Psycho-analytic literature concerning grief tends to limit itself, by contrast, to a consideration of the grief which one feels over having lost a loved one; how often do we see mention of the grief one feels at the prospect of one's own death, or that of a loved one? In the latter two instances, we turn too quickly to a search for unconscious suicidal feelings or unconscious death wishes.

There is one aspect of psycho-analytic literature, beyond its long-standing emphasis, pro or con, concerning a hypothetical death instinct; beyond its time-honoured focus upon the early years of life; and beyond its preoccupation with the symbolic, as distinct from the real, aspects of 'death', which has limited its ability to do justice to the subject of death. This aspect consists in a limitation which psycho-analytic literature shares, inherently, with all literature: it must rely upon verbal communication to deal with a subject which is of extraordinary complexity, and of a complexity which very possibly lends itself better to various forms of non-verbal communication than to communication in the medium (the highly abstract and reality-segmentalizing medium) of words.

The fact that all men must die is a simple fact; but for each one of us the feeling-ramifications which flow in response to this fact are probably among the most complex, if not *the* most complex, that we can possibly experience. It may well be that the more mature a person is, the more complex are his reactions to this simple and universal fact of human existence; and surely the fabric of a person's reactions will make up a uniquely individual pattern, different from that of any other human being. Certainly such complexity is too much to be grasped by the very immature ego of a child, or by the impaired ego of a psychiatrically deeply-ill adult. Here, I am reminded of a beautiful statement made by the Irish short story writer, Frank O'Connor, near the end of a story concerning a deeply conflictual situation in his own boyhood. He says: '. . . For the first time I realized that the life before me would have complexities of emotion which I couldn't even imagine' (O'Connor, 1954).

A deeply schizophrenic woman who is unusually talkative has shown, many times, the following phenomenon. As I start to leave her room at the close of the therapeutic session, her speech becomes more rapid and, within the space of less than a minute, she recounts as many as a dozen incidents in the past involving as many different persons she has known, each incident involving a single predominant affect: one or more of the incidents clearly involve anger, others grief, others contempt, and so on. It was only after I had seen this phenomenon a number of times that I realized that this is her indirect way of expressing the complexity of her feelings, probably for the most part unconscious feelings, concerning the single *here-and-now* situation of impending separation from the analyst. I think it accurate to describe her ego as being, at present, too impaired to enable her to tolerate, within awareness, the complexity of feelings, among which are rage, grief, contempt, and so on, aroused by this stressful here-and-now situation. Instead, the feeling-complex is experienced in its separate ingredients and is spread, moreover, over 'target-persons' from various situations in past years. Thus instead of her being able to experience this as, 'I feel rage and grief and contempt (etc., etc.) toward you right now, as you are leaving,' she apparently feels it as follows: 'I was angry at A in that situation four years ago, and I was grieved in that situation with B two years ago, and I was filled with contempt in that situation with C six years ago, and . . .'

This phenomenon has struck me as being very similar to that which is reported in the literature as occurring in the experience of people who are face to face with imminent, and apparently inescapable, death: an extremely rapid reviewing, before the mind's eye, of events from their whole remembered lives. Eissler (1955), discussing Oscar Pfister's paper (1930) on this subject, says that 'surprisingly many informants report having had the feeling that their whole lives passed in stage-like manner before the inner eye . . .' (Eissler, 1955, pp. 181–2). Eissler suggests that this represents the struggle to create a new ego, in order to meet the supreme challenge of apparently certain and imminent death. Another way of looking upon this phenomenon –a view which would not exclude that of Eissler–is that this supreme moment of personality stress calls forth emotions which are too intense and too varied to be experienced simultaneously, as having to do with the here-and-now situation. This is precisely analogous to my schizophrenic patient's mode of experiencing the impact of the end-of-the-session separation from her therapist.

It seems to me very possible that such complex emotions may be conveyed better by non-verbal media than by the media of words, to which psycho-analytic literature must, of course, limit itself; a symphony, for instance, may help us to feel the complex meanings of our own personal anticipation of death, far more adequately than any words could express. Langer (1942) expresses her conviction that various forms of artistic expression – music, poetry, and other art forms – can express emotions which our much-vaunted words cannot communicate:

> . . . Just as words can describe events we have not witnessed, places and things we have not seen, so music can present emotions and moods we have not felt, passions we did not know before.
>
> . . . A composer not only indicates, but *articulates* subtle complexes of feeling that language cannot even name, let alone set forth . . . (Langer, 1942, p. 180).
>
> . . . art – certainly music, and probably all art – is formally and essentially untranslatable . . . (*ibid.*, p. 190).
>
> Because the forms of human feeling are much more congruent with musical forms than with the forms of language, music can *reveal* the nature of feelings with a detail and truth that language cannot approach. . . .
>
> . . . Liszt warned specifically against the practice of expounding the emotive content of a symphonic poem, 'because in such case the words tend to destroy the magic, to desecrate the feelings, and to break the most delicate fabrics of the soul, which had taken this form just because they were incapable of formulation in words, images or ideas (*ibid.*, p. 191).
>
> . . . I believe the 'aesthetic emotion' and the emotional content of a work of art are two very different things; the 'aesthetic emotion' springs from an intellectual triumph, from overcoming barriers of word-bound thought and achieving insight into literally 'unspeakable' realities; but the emotive content of the work is apt to be something much deeper than any intellectual experience, more essential, pre-rational, and vital, something of the life-rhythms we share with all growing, hungering, moving and fearing creatures: the ultimate realities themselves, the central facts of our brief, sentient existence (*ibid.*, p. 211).

Concerning poetry, Langer points out:

... though the *material* of poetry is verbal, its import is not the literal assertion made in the words, but *the way the assertion is made,* and this involves the sound, the tempo, the aura of associations of the words, the long or short sequences of ideas, the wealth or poverty of transient imagery that contains them, the sudden arrest of fantasy by pure fact, or of familiar fact by sudden fantasy, the suspense of literal meaning by a sustained ambiguity resolved in a long-awaited keyword, and the unifying, all-embracing artifice of rhythm . . . (*ibid.* p. 212).

In connexion with the last of these quotations from Langer, we see that poetry, though couched in words, does indeed serve more adequately to symbolize various ingredients of our complex feelings concerning the inescapable prospect of death than do words in the form of prose. I, at least, am unacquainted with any prose works which so fully convey the fear of death as does Keats' sonnet, 'The Terror of Death'.

> When I have fears that I may cease to be
> Before my pen has glean'd my teeming brain,
> Before high piléd books, in charact'ry,
> Hold like rich garners the full-ripen'd grain;
> When I behold, upon the night's starr'd face,
> Huge cloudy symbols of a high romance,
> And think that I may never live to trace
> Their shadows, with the magic hand of chance;
> And when I feel, fair creature of an hour!
> That I shall never look upon thee more,
> Never have relish in the faery power
> Of unreflecting love–then on the shore
> Of the wide world I stand alone, and think
> Till Love and Fame to nothingness do sink.

Or consider the courage of Robert Browning's 'Prospice'.

> Fear death?–to feel the fog in my throat,
>   The mist in my face,
> When the snows begin, and the blasts denote
>   I am nearing the place,
> The power of the night, the press of the storm
>   The post of the foe;
> Where he stands, the Arch Fear in a visible form,
>   Yet the strong man must go:

.   .   .   .

I would hate that death bandaged my eyes, and forebore,
And bade me creep past.
No! let me taste the whole of it . . .

Or there is the raging protest of Dylan Thomas' plea to his aged, mellowed father, in *Do Not Go Gentle Into that Good Night*:

Do not go gentle into that good night,
Old age should burn and rave at close of day;
Rage, rage against the dying of the light.[7]

. . . .

Or there is the longing for death, as epitomizing peace, which is contained in Robert Louis Stevenson's 'Requiem':

Under the wide and starry sky
Dig the grave and let me lie.
Glad did I live and gladly die,
And laid me down with a will.

This be the verse you grave for me:
Here he lies where he longed to be,
Home is the sailor, home from sea,
And the hunter home from the hill.

Discussion

What has been said in this paper concerning the effectiveness of intrapersonal and interpersonal integration in enabling us to face the prospect of death–one's own individual death, as well as that of one's loved ones–seems to me to be equivalent to what certain existentialist writers have said in a different terminology. For example, Binswanger, and in one instance Jaspers, are paraphrased by Weigert (1949) as saying, concerning love,

. . . Here is no longer the I threatened by the loss of self in the struggle for existence, nor the you endangered by isolation: I and you are merged in the we, togetherness. This we-ness is experienced as the most triumphant security and certainty of existence there is. . . .

The existential certainty of Love triumphs even over death. Not that it takes anything away from the intensity of grief. But there is not the bitterness which follows the ultimate termination

[7] Copyright 1952, 1953 by Dylan Thomas. Reprinted by permission of New Directions.

of an ambivalent relation. . . . The nature of Love is above all separations, since the selfhood of you is so deeply imprinted in me, just as mine is in yours, that the security of we-ness endures. Only an individual can die, the we-ness remains intact. This we-evidence meets life with that 'deep serenity, which dwells at the bottom of the unextinguishable grief' [Jaspers].

And Tillich emphasizes that man's sense of being an integral part, not only of humankind, but of the universe as a whole, enables one to conquer the anxiety concerning death (a point which I have elaborated in my book, *The Nonhuman Environment*):

> . . . The anxiety of fate is conquered by the self-affirmation of the individual as an infinitely significant microcosmic representation of the universe (Tillich, 1952, p. 120).
> . . . Even loneliness is not absolute loneliness because the contents of the universe are in him (*ibid.*, p. 121).

Fromm (1955) has described our culture as containing many features which interfere with the individual's developing such a sense of wholeness, and we may compare the writer's description of the schizophrenic's inability (partly by reason of his non-integration on both intrapsychic and interpersonal levels) to face death's inevitability, with Fromm's following remarks:

> . . . modern man exhibits an amazing lack of realism for all that matters. For the meaning of life and death, for happiness and suffering, for feeling and serious thought. He has covered up the whole reality of human existence and replaced it with his artificial, prettified picture of pseudo-reality, not too different from the savages who lost their land and freedom for glittering glass beads. . . .
> Another factor in contemporary society . . . is destructive to reason. Since nobody ever does the whole job, but only a fraction of it, since the dimension of things and of the organization of people is too vast to be understood as a whole, nothing can be seen in its totality . . . (1955, pp. 170–1).
> . . . man can fulfill himself only if he remains in touch with the fundamental facts of his existence, if he can experience the exaltation of love and solidarity, as well as the tragic fact of his aloneness and of the fragmentary character of his existence. If he is completely enmeshed in the routine and in the artefacts of life, if he cannot see anything but the man-made, common-sense appearance of the world, he loses his touch with and the grasp of himself and the world . . . (*ibid.*, p. 144).

I surmise that, in so far as an individual is a whole person intrapsychically, and able to participate wholly in his relatedness with other persons as well as with his nonhuman environment, he does not react to this subject of life's finitude as a separate nucleus of feelings in itself. It constitutes, rather, an ingredient of, or background for, all his life-experiences. In so far as we can dare to keep ourselves open to the recognition of the finitude of our lives, this recognition can make our pleasurable experiences more precious, our despair supportable, our work a matter not of resented drudgery but of wholehearted dedication, and so on. Just as one can be a truly whole person only through facing this harshest aspect of reality, the inevitability of death, so, too, can one become able to live fully, only if one lives in the light of this recognition.

I believe others will find, as I have, that the more one explores this whole subject of the psychological import of life's finitude— its import to human beings, whether schizophrenic or non-schizophrenic—the more one's personal philosophy of life is deepened and enriched. And we know how essential it is, for one who conducts psycho-analysis and psychotherapy, to be deeply sure that life is meaningful and worth while—even a life which at times seems meaningless and which ends, inescapably, in death.

Chapter 18

PHASES OF PATIENT-THERAPIST INTERACTION IN THE PSYCHOTHERAPY OF CHRONIC SCHIZOPHRENIA (1961)[1]

A T the end of three years of intensive psychotherapy with chronically schizophrenic patients, I found myself occupied, for a comparatively brief period, with the question whether I should go ahead and devote myself, for an indefinite number of further years—perhaps for the whole remainder of my professional career—primarily to this line of endeavour. I decided in favour of doing this, from a feeling of having found myself, in the course of my personal analysis, in the course of these early years in the crucible of the intensive psychotherapy of schizophrenia, and in the course of my developing marital-family life. The question whether I am a human being, possessed of the feeling capacities which activate human beings, had been affirmatively put to rest, and I felt able now to approach this psychotherapy in a new and workmanlike spirit, sure that the basic potential for this work was there in me, and curious to see what truly professional *techniques,* quite beyond the countertransference-ridden flounderings of the neophyte, I could develop in grappling with this remarkably complex job that clearly needed doing.

The nine years which passed between making this decision and writing this paper, while confirming for me the validity of that shift in my feeling-orientation, have none the less forcibly brought home to me the realization that the 'technique' of psychotherapy of schizophrenia is best spelled out in terms of an evolutionary sequence of specific, and very deep, feeling-involvements in which the therapist as well as the patient becomes caught up, over the course of what has emerged, for me, as—in necessarily broad and schematic terms—the 'normal'

[1] First published in the *British Journal of Medical Psychology,* Vol. 34 (1961), pp. 169–93.

and predictable over-all course of psychotherapy with the chronically schizophrenic person. This paper, then, will attempt both to highlight the crucial role of feelings in the therapeutic relationship, and to delineate what I have found to be this 'normal' over-all pattern of the psychotherapeutic course which that relationship follows over the years of the patient's treatment.

The therapist's feeling-involvement in this therapeutic work is, for various reasons, a deep one, and personal analysis does not spare him from the deep involvement which is so necessary, but rather makes his feelings more available to him for it.

First, the very length of time required for this therapy tends to foster a deep involvement on his part, such that the hours he has spent with the patient over the course of say six or eight or ten years become deeply a part of all that the years have brought for him—the joys and sorrows, the triumphs and bereavements.

Secondly, the various forms of intense transference on the part of the schizophrenic individual tend forcibly to evoke complementary feeling-responses, comparably intense, in the therapist. Mabel Blake Cohen (1952) has made the extremely valuable observation, for psycho-analysis in general, that:

> . . . it seems that the patient applies great pressure to the analyst in a variety of non-verbal ways to behave like the significant adults in the patient's earlier life. It is not merely a matter of the patient's seeing the analyst as like his father, but of his actually manipulating the relationship in such a way as to elicit the same kind of behaviour from the analyst. . . .

It is not too much to say that, in response to the schizophrenic patient's transference, the therapist not only *behaves like* the significant adults in the patient's childhood, but experiences most intimately, within himself, activated by the patient's transference, the very kind of intense and deeply conflictual feelings which were at work, however repressed, in those adults in the past, as well as experiencing, through the mechanisms of projection and introjection in the relationship between himself and the patient, the comparably intense and conflictual emotions which formed the seed-bed of psychosis in the child himself, years ago.

A third reason for the necessarily deep feeling-involvement on the part of the therapist is inherent in the nature of early ego-formation, the healthy reworking of which is so central to the therapy of schizophrenia. Spitz (1959), in his monograph on the early development of the ego, repeatedly emphasizes that emotion plays a leading role in the formation of what he describes as the 'organizers of the psyche' (which he defines as 'emergent, dominant centres of integration') during the first eighteen months of life. He says, for example, that:

> ... the road which leads to this integration of isolated functions is built by the infant's object relations, by experiences of an affective nature. Accordingly, the indicator of the organizer of the psyche will be of an affective nature; it is an affective behaviour which clearly precedes development in all other sectors of the personality by several months.

This brings us back to my other main topic, namely the phases comprising the over-all course of psychotherapy with the chronically schizophrenic person. Within recent years I have become increasingly convinced that it is possible to delineate such phases amongst the complex, individualistic, and dynamic events of clinical work. One can take heart, in this difficult effort at conceptualization, from Freud's delineation of the successive phases of libidinal development in healthy maturation, from Erikson's (1956) portrayal of the process of identity formation as a gradual unfolding of the personality through phase-specific psycho-social crises, and from Hartmann's (1956) statement, concerning the process of evolution of the reality principle in healthy development, that 'The impact of all stages of child development – the typical conflicts, the sequence of danger situations, and the ways they are dealt with – can be traced in this process.'

The successive phases which in my experience best characterize the psychotherapy of chronic schizophrenia, with each of which the remainder of this paper will deal in turn, are the 'out-of-contact' phase, the phase of ambivalent symbiosis, the phase of pre-ambivalent symbiosis, the phase of resolution of the symbiosis, and the late phase – that of establishment, and elaboration, of the newly won individuation through selective new identifications and repudiation of outmoded identifications.

The first three of these phases retrace, in reverse, the phases by which the schizophrenic illness was originally formed. To my way of thinking, the aetiological roots of schizophrenia are formed when the mother-infant symbiosis fails to resolve into individuation of mother and infant–or, still more harmfully, fails even to become at all firmly established–because of deep ambivalence on the part of the mother which hinders the integration and differentiation of the infant's and young child's ego. The child fails then to proceed through the normal developmental phases of symbiosis and subsequent individuation; instead, the core of his personality remains unformed, and ego-fragmentation and dedifferentiation become powerful, though deeply primitive, unconscious defences against the awareness of ambivalence in the object and in himself. Even in normal development, one becomes a separate person only by becoming able to face, and accept ownership of, one's ambivalent feelings of love and hate towards the other person. For the child who eventually goes on to schizophrenia, the ambivalence with which he had to cope in his relationship with his mother was too great, and his ego-formation too greatly impeded, for him to be able to integrate his conflictual feeling-states into an individual identity.

My theoretical concepts have been fostered by Mahler's (1952) paper on autistic and symbiotic infantile psychoses and by Balint's (1953, 1955) writings concerning phenomena of early ego-formation which he encountered in the psycho-analysis of neurotic patients. In 1958 (see chapter 10 above), I ventured to express my conviction that a symbiotic relatedness between patient and therapist constitutes a necessary phase in the transference-evolution of successful therapy with either psychotic or neurotic patients, although it is particularly prominent and important in the former group. I have noticed with great interest, therefore, that Mahler and Furer (1960) emphasize that 'Our first therapeutic endeavour in both types of infantile psychosis [i.e. both autistic and symbiotic] is to engage the child in a "corrective symbiotic experience". . . .' Loewald (1960a), too, reports that what I call a symbiotic relatedness occurs in the schizophrenic patient's transference to the therapist: as he puts it, '. . . If ego and objects are not clearly differentiated, if ego boundaries and object boundaries are not clearly established, the character of transference also is different, in as much as ego and objects are still largely merged. . . .'

It is now time to embark upon a description of the successive phases of therapy with the chronically schizophrenic adult patient.

The 'Out-of-contact' Phase

I do not term this the 'autistic phase', for the reason that the word 'autistic' has come to have a certain connotation, in psychodynamic theory, which I regard as invalid and therefore do not advocate. Specifically, the term 'autistic', as generally used, conjures up Freud's (1911) psychodynamic formulation of schizophrenia as involving withdrawal of libido from the outer world and its subsequent investment in the self–as involving, in other words, a regression to narcissism. My own view is that there occurs instead, in schizophrenia, a regressive dedifferentiation towards an early level of ego-development which has its prototype in the experience of the young infant for whom inner and outer worlds have not yet become clearly distinguishable as such (see chapter 16). This is in line with the formulations of Werner (1940), and Loewald (1960a) follows the same reasoning in his previously mentioned paper.

To the degree that the patient is schizophrenic, this phase predominates during the early months, and in many instances the early years, of his therapy. Characteristic of this phase is the circumstance that his feelings are unavailable to himself and are not conveyed in his interpersonal relationships; hence the therapist experiences comparatively little in the way of feeling responses to the patient's behaviour, except for a sense of strangeness, of alienness, in reaction to the bizarre symptomatology into which the patient's feeling-potentialities have long ago become condensed–the hallucinations, the delusional and neologistic utterances, the stereotyped and manneristic non-verbal behaviour, and so on. It is seldom that the therapist feels that the patient even perceives him, undistortedly enough for the therapist to sense that he as a person in the here and now is being seen, or heard, or otherwise perceived, by the patient who much more often shows, instead, every evidence of being lost in a world of chaotically disturbed and distorted perceptions. Patient and therapist, so long as this phase endures, have clearly not yet entered into a deep feeling-relatedness with one another.

The feeling-orientation in the therapist which best serves a constructive approach to the patient and his bizarre symptomatology, and best facilitates the traversing and resolution of this phase of the therapy, is a calm, neutral, investigative orientation. By contrast, the inexperienced therapist is apt to approach the patient in a spirit of urgent need to relieve the suffering of this deeply and tragically ill person. One is helped to relinquish such an attitude, which to the extent that it predominates renders constructive therapy impossible, by realizing a number of things about the patient. First, as Szalita-Pemow (Personal communication, 1952) helped me to see, the patient's individuality, his sense of personal identity, resides largely in his psychotic symptoms; thus the therapist is reacted to as threatening to rob him of his individuality, by 'curing' him of his illness. He has no conception of psychological health in our experience of this term; for him, 'getting well' is tantamount to a restoration of the state–the anxiety-ridden, unendurably boring, or what not, state–which he experienced just before he originally became overwhelmed by the psychosis. Basically, 'getting well' is, for him, tantamount to loss of his individuality through return to symbiotic relatedness, towards which he is constantly being impelled by the inner drive which never ceases to pull him back towards the world of people. Also, for him, 'facing reality' is a very different thing from the therapist's being able to face the reality of *his* life; the reality of the patient's own life, which must eventually be confronted if he is ever to become well, is a reality overfull of tragedy and loss.

We need to realize, in the same vein, that the patient is not solely a broken, inert victim of the hostility of persons in his past life. His hebephrenic apathy or his catatonic immobility, for example, represent for one thing an intensely active striving towards unconscious, regressive goals, as Greenson (1949, 1953) has helped to make clear in his papers on boredom and apathy in neurotic patients. The patient is, in other words, no inert vehicle which needs to be energized by the therapist; rather, an abundance of energy is locked up in him, pressing ceaselessly to be freed, and a hoveringly 'helpful' orientation on the part of the therapist would only get in the way. We must realize that the patient has made, and is continually making, a contribution to his own illness, however unwittingly, and however obscure the nature of this contribution may long remain.

It is particularly when the therapist sees the dimensions of the patient's hostility, of his sadism, that he realizes that, on balance, the sufferer is doing what, on the whole, he *wants* to do at the moment. When this understanding comes home to the therapist, he does not need to struggle to maintain some artificially neutral-screen façade, but comes to *feel* on the whole neutral towards the patient whom he sees to be both loving and hateful, and whom, he increasingly realizes, he himself is capable of both loving and hating.

The therapist's hand can be strengthened, in effecting this change, by his identifying with his predecessors who have reported in the literature their achievement of such an attitude towards their work. Winnicott (1947), for example, points out how inevitably hatred is a component of the therapist's, as well as the normal mother's, feelings towards the patient or the child, respectively. Knight (1940) describes his having found that, in the psychotherapy of paranoid patients, the use of such time-honoured techniques as reassurance, re-education, and tactfulness in dealing with the patient's homosexual wishes only causes him to become increasingly paranoid because, Knight saw, the patient has real hatred, and this is what the anxiety is mainly about. Heimann (1955) finds it best not to try to convince the paranoid patient of one's good will, or to avoid coming to terms with his delusional material, and clearly sees the sadism involved in her patient's suffering. Hayward and Taylor (1956) find that 'When a patient is suffering, the decision as to whether to give comfort or to attack is often very difficult', and Hayward's recovered schizophrenic patient tells him, in retrospect, 'You should never have stood by and let me torture you by crucifying myself and making you watch my suffering. You should have forced me to come down or at least thrown rocks at me,' and reminds him that 'People need practice in hating without guilt or fear, just as much as loving'.

The therapist, operating from this basic feeling-orientation, can meet usefully a wide variety of typical problem-situations; I can mention only a few. In response to the patient's manifestation of delusional thinking, he will be aware that, for the patient, the delusions represent years of arduous and subjectively constructive thought, and are therefore most deeply cherished. He will not forget that obscured in them is an indeed indispensable nucleus of reality-perception. He will not become caught up in either disagreeing or agreeing with the delusional view, but will try to help the patient explore the feelings which this delusional world-view causes him to feel–the dismay, the shock, the despair, and fear, and so on. Not only here, but in general, free from any absorbingly urgent need of his own to 'cure' the patient, he will remain attentive to what the *patient* is experiencing. He will couch his remarks in terms of the patient's own presumed point of view, and when the patient is able to express a feeling–whether of fear or loneliness or anger or what not–the therapist will usually content himself with simply acknowledging the feeling and encouraging its further elaboration, rather than rushing verbosely somehow to relieve the patient of it. Likewise, when a patient is having vigorously to disavow any feeling about a clearly affect-laden matter, the therapist will remain in tune with the patient's own feeling experience, by remarking, 'I gather you don't find yourself having any particular feeling about this',–or, better, will make no mention of feelings–rather than try to overcome the unconscious denial by asserting; 'But surely this *must* make you very angry (or hurt, or what not)'. Similarly, in responding to the expressions of an archaic, harsh superego in the patient, rather than set himself up as the spokes-man, the personification, of the repressed id-impulses, he will realize that it is in the superego that the patient's conscious self–his personal identity–mainly resides; thus he will seldom urge the patient to recognize sexual or aggressive feelings within, and will more often acknowledge how strong a sense of protest or outrage the patient feels upon perceiving these in others.

To the extent that the therapist is free from a compulsion to rescue the suffering patient, he can remain sufficiently extricated from that suffering to be able to note significant sequences in the appearance of such symptoms as hallucinations, verbalized delusions, and so forth, and thus be in a position to be genuinely helpful. Even when on a car ride with a patient, or grappling with the latter's physical assault, the therapist may on occasion be able to allow himself enough detachment to help the patient to link up this immediate experience, clarifyingly, with forgotten situations from earlier life; such 'action interpretations' may be especially important to the patient whose memory, and whose capacity for abstract thinking, are severely impaired.

In working with the patient during weeks or months of silence on the latter's part, he will not, out of a compulsion to help the tragic victim of schizophrenia, rack his brain with diligent therapeutic efforts focused upon the patient, who is already afflicted with overwhelming intrapsychic pressures. Rather, the therapist will feel free to let his thoughts roam where they will, leaf through magazines, do some serious reading of current interest to him, and otherwise see to his own personal comfort and freedom from anxiety. This may at times involve periodic letting off of steam at the inarticulate patient; but such blasts do, in my experience, the patient no harm and help one to become again, for a relatively long period, genuinely accepting of this difficult situation. Thus one places in the long run a minimum of pressure on the patient who is already paralysed with pressure, and keeps oneself in a comparatively unanxious and receptive state which, better than anything else, helps eventually to relieve the patient's anxiety and unlock his tongue. Sooner or later, like a bright dawn pushing back a long night, the patient will put his rusty vocalization capacities to work in venting reproach, contempt, and fury upon the therapist for doing, as the patient sees it, nothing to help him.

In general, while aware that the parents responded to the patient in certain ways—such as by condemnation, reproach, contempt, or what not—which promoted illness in the child, the therapist will refuse to tie his own hands with any self-imposed injunction to make his own behaviour always an antidote for such early trauma, and never to engage in such responses himself. He knows that there will be times when these are the only realistic responses to make to a given piece of behaviour on the patient's part, and he rests assured that if the patient were never able to find *anything* of the latter's mother or father in the therapist, the transference-reliving, and eventual resolution, of the schizophrenic illness would be impossible. We could postulate with some confidence that a person whose intrafamilial relationships had been so warped as to lead to schizophrenia would quite simply be at a loss to know how to relate, would have insufficient tools from past experience for relating, to a hypothetically ideally loving and mature therapist.

The therapist learns to take fewer and fewer things for granted in this work, to question more and more of his long-held assumptions and discard many of them. He learns that one does not set a ceiling upon any human being's potential growth. He finds recurrent delight in the creative spontaneity with which the schizophrenic patient pierces the sober and constricting wrappings of our culture's conventions, and he discovers that humour is present in this work in rich abundance, leavening the genuine tragedy and helping to make it supportable. While developing a deep confidence in his intuitive ability, when working with the severely fragmented or dedifferentiated patient he will not jump too quickly to attempt communicational 'closure' (in the Gestalt sense), but will leave it in the patient's hands to do, no matter how slowly and painfully, the parts of the communicational work which only he can do. Meanwhile, he will not need to shield himself, through the maintenance of an urgently and actively 'helpful' or 'rescuing' attitude, from feeling at a deep level the impact of the fragmented and dedifferentiated world, with its attendant feelings, in which the patient exists. The unfolding of such feeling experiences, which will be elaborated in my portrayal of the next phase of the therapy, the 'urgently helpful' therapist attitude is unconsciously designed to avert, comparable to the defensive function, in the patient, of the latter's schizophrenic delusions.

I hope I have made it sufficiently clear that, in describing a basically neutral feeling-orientation towards the patient, I am not thereby recommending that the therapist should assume, and hold to, any rigid professional role of 'the psychiatrist'. My experience of this coincides with that indicated by a number of workers in this field. Robert A. Cohen (1947) reports, concerning his therapy of a paranoid schizophrenic woman, 'the patient's unfavourable reception of any remark which smacked of the usual psychiatric jargon', and learned to avoid becoming so interested in the *content* of her delusions as to lose track of their *feeling*-implications for the patient. Lidz and Lidz (1952) point out that: 'More paranoid patients, in particular, can participate in treatment but cannot be treated in the sense of having another person control or manage them.' Bullard (1960) offers to the paranoid individual 'not interpretations but, rather, hypotheses for the patient to consider as possibly shedding some light on the problems he is exploring'. The basic orientation I recommend is well described in Loewald's (1960a) remarks about psycho-analytic work,

. . . Through all the transference distortions the patient reveals rudiments at least of that core (of himself and 'objects') which has been distorted. It is this core, rudimentary and vague as it may be, to which the analyst has reference . . . and not some abstract concept of reality or normality, if he is to reach the patient. If the analyst keeps his central focus on this emerging core he avoids moulding the patient in the analyst's own image or imposing on the patient his own concept of what the patient should become. It requires an objectivity and neutrality the essence of which is love and respect for the individual and for individual development . . .

The Phase of Ambivalent Symbiosis

To the extent that the therapist's basic orientation towards the patient is a neutrally investigative one, free from a compulsive need to help and to love the patient, but open, rather, to the sensing of hateful as well as loving feeling-tones in the therapeutic relationship, he comes progressively to detect the intense ambivalence which has been locked within the patient's psychotic symptomatology. He detects this, before the patient himself has become able to experience and verbally express such ambivalence, through the awareness of sudden fluctuations of his own feelings in reaction to the patient's verbal and non-verbal communications. He finds his feelings towards the patient switching unexpectedly from, for example, tenderness to contempt, or from fury to grief, or what not. He finds himself experiencing, on occasion, feeling states which are quite ineffable and foreign to his memory and which, despite whatever roots in his own preverbal childhood, can usefully be regarded as samples of the feeling states at work in the patient himself, though, more probably than not, as yet outside the latter's awareness.

The prolonged silences, or obscurity of verbal communication, or both, which characterize work with the chronic schizophrenic patient have served to foster a progressive weakening of ego-boundaries between patient and therapist. That is, in this situation of clouded communication, projection and introjection on the part of each participant is facilitated to an extent which is seldom if ever seen in an analyst's work with a neurotic patient, for in the latter instance the frequent and clear verbalizations, from each participant, tend to keep *relatively* clearly in view the ego-boundaries between the two participants. Thus there develops a generous reality basis for the symbiotic transference which the schizophrenic patient tends powerfully, in any case, to form with his therapist. The therapist's own ego-boundaries are weakened not only in reaction to the prolonged silences and in reciprocity to the patient's transference, as indicated in the above-mentioned comment by Mabel Blake Cohen, but also for the reason that regression towards symbiotic relatedness tends to occur in the therapist himself as an unconscious defence against the intense and deeply ambivalent feelings–of helplessness, fury, loathing, tenderness, grief, and so on–evoked by his relationship with the schizophrenic patient, long before that relationship has become strong enough and well-defined enough to permit his recognition of these feelings, and any full-scale expression of them, towards the patient.

As I have described in chapters 8, 10, and 11, the therapist at times will find himself in the extremely uncomfortable state of experiencing two quite different, and subjectively unrelated, feeling attitudes towards the patient simultaneously. Particularly in instances in which one or other parent was psychotic, the patient tends to form such a subjectively ego-splitting kind of transference towards the parent-surrogate therapist. The relatedness between patient and therapist comes, sometimes for several months, to bear many of the earmarks of a mutual effort to drive each other crazy (ch. 8). I have described in chapter 6 some of the manifestations of the patient's vulnerability, during this phase, to the disturbing impact of the therapist's unconscious processes.

More and more the therapist comes to feel enmeshed, as it were, in the patient's own ego-fragmentation and dedifferentiation. The therapy has a sticky feel about it; the therapist feels restrained from any decisive actions, incisive comments, or even clear-cut and unambivalent feelings towards the patient. His resentment, rage, and hatred towards the latter are tormentingly guilt-provoking in nature; and his tender and loving feelings are hardly less burdensome and guilt-provoking. He feels that he does not truly love the patient, but has only an ugly lust which will not stand the light of day; and when he does feel that his love is more of a parent-to-child order, his love feels guiltily possessive. He is painfully aware of being like a jealous Pygmalion concerning this Galatea with whom is he at once blessed and afflicted: he looks to his colleagues for succour, but deeply resents any participation from a third person–psychiatric administrator, therapeutic supervisor, nurse, or whomever–as an intrusion into his own private domain. One other simple earmark of this phase of ambivalent symbiosis is the circumstance that the relationship with this patient has assumed an absorbing, unparalleled *importance* in the therapist's life, an importance which not only jars with such relationships with other staff-members as impinge upon the situation, but which he experiences also as a competitive threat to his most personal and cherished non-professional relationships.

At its fullest intensity, this phase is experienced by him as a threat to his whole psychological existence. He becomes deeply troubled lest this relationship is finally bringing to light a basically and ineradicably malignant orientation towards his fellow human beings. He feels equivalent to the illness which is afflicting the patient; he is unable to distinguish between that illness and himself. This is not sheer imagination on his part, for the patient is meanwhile persistently expressing, in manifold ways, a conviction that the therapist constitutes, indeed, the affliction which threatens to destroy him and with which he, the patient, is locked in a life-and-death struggle. In my theoretical view, the therapist is now experiencing the fullest intensity of the patient's transference to him as the Bad Mother.

The patient's own ego-boundaries may be so unclear that it may be impossible to know whether, when he speaks, he is uttering thoughts which are subjectively his 'own', or rather giving voice to what he assumes the therapist to be thinking but not expressing. The therapist will often find it similarly impossible to know whether a predominant feeling-tone of anger, or grief, or what not is welling primarily from the patient or from within himself.

Murderous feelings arising within the therapist tend particularly, in contrast to more readily acceptable feelings, to become projected upon the patient, whose own oftentimes prominent assaultive tendencies offer a ready reality-basis for such projections. The therapist in these circumstances is prone, for various reasons some of which are quite obvious, to the development of intense murderous feelings. These result from the intense frustration of his therapeutic endeavours, the threat to his individuality arising from the symbiotic relatedness with the patient, and his residual of infantile omnipotence brought to bay during the mutual regression which this symbiosis involves, such that the therapeutic relatedness often takes the form of a raging struggle between two gods. There thus supervenes all the murderousness of the thwarted infant not only in the patient but in himself also.

Uncomfortable though it is for the therapist to feel afraid of the murderous patient, it is still harder for him to realize the full extent of his own murderousness towards the patient, and to see that the latter is unaware of feeling murderous and is experiencing, instead, intense fear of the therapist who is viewed as murderously insane. It is more acceptable to the therapist's superego to feel intimidated than intimidating, and the realization that the patient is deathly afraid of one tends, at least initially, to weaken one's own feeling of control over one's rage.

I have reported in chapter 6 a dream which I had during the course of my work with a hebephrenic man whom I had been viewing, for some months, as being a dangerous, uncontrollable person. In the dream, during a desperate struggle between us he got his hands on a knife-like letter-opener. But then *he* took *me* into custody, and at the end of the dream he was functioning as a kind of sheriff's deputy, marching me out to turn me over to the authorities. This dream was one of the developments which helped me to become aware of massive, previously repressed rage in myself which I had been projecting on the patient. A colleague reported to me in a supervisory hour, two weeks ago, the uneasy feeling that he and the patient were presently in a state of ostensible calm which was really the calm, he sensed, of the eye of a hurricane; he felt that there was some as yet undefined fury in the patient which was looming somewhere. But in last week's supervisory session he reported various intimations of a previously unsuspected quantity of rage in himself, such that he said, 'I'm not sure now whether the hurricane is in her or in me.'

More often than not the therapist is, unlike this colleague, unaware that a state of symbiosis is developing, or has long been established, between the patient and himself. This state of affairs is easier to detect in one's colleagues than in oneself. When one becomes alert to the significance of this phase of the therapy with the schizophrenic person, one is struck by how frequently one hears therapists make, in supervisory sessions or in staff presentations, such comments as 'There's been a lot of anger this past week', without specifying in *whom*; or, likewise, 'There's a manicky mood around–there's a lot of giggling'; or, 'There is a very strong dependency there', without specifying *where*. The therapist may make repeated slips of the tongue concerning the sexual identity of the patient–a response not only to the deep-seated sexual confusion in the patient which has now come to light, but a function also of the therapist's lack of differentiation between his own sex and that of the patient. He may say, 'I started seeing her in [a cold, wet sheet] pack', in such an ambiguous tone as to make one wonder momentarily whether he means that she was in pack, or he was in pack, or both were in packs. On rare occasions one may hear: 'The first period when he was my therapist was – I mean, the first period when I was his therapist was. . . .' One becomes alert to such clues in one's own presentations also.

The dissolution of ego-boundaries between patient and therapist is only a major aspect of a more general dedifferentiation and disintegration of ego-functions which occurs in both participants (although to a much lesser, and therefore more subtle, degree in the therapist, of course, than in the patient) as the symbiotic relatedness develops. Thus the therapist, losing temporarily his ability fully to differentiate between fantasy and reality, may react to various of his sexual fantasies about the patient with as much guilt as though they represented consummation in behavioural reality, and may feel jealous of the hallucinatory figures with which the patient is immersed in a seemingly lively and intimate interaction, as though these hallucinatory figures were to be compared on a par with himself (Searles, 1961c). On occasion, too, during this phase, childhood scenes have welled up in my memory with an almost overpoweringly tangible reality. One feels from time to time, too, the impact of some previously unglimpsed fragment of the patient's past, conveyed to one now by him in ways that are largely nonverbal and hard to objectify.

Before this phase of ambivalent symbiosis can give place to the succeeding one in the therapeutic sequence, the relationship between patient and therapist must gradually grow, through the resolution of innumerable and increasingly severe tests of the kind mentioned above, strong enough for the therapist to be able to endure the fullest intensity of the patient's hostility, focused directly upon him. In contrast to the warnings given by Sullivan (1956), Hill (1955), and many other writers, to the effect that such a development means that the therapy has foundered irretrievably, I have come to see this, both in my own work and in that of my colleagues, as an utterly essential therapeutic development. The patient can never become deeply a whole person unless he has this chance, in Hoedemaker's (1955) way of describing it, to identify with the therapist who survives the fullest intensity of this kind of attack to which the patient was exposed in childhood and from which he, the patient, had to flee into psychosis. And complementarily, I have found that it is an equally essential part of this phase that the therapist finds himself gradually coming, step by step, to express openly–even though not as often as he feels it within–the very fullest intensity of his own hatred, condemnation, and contempt towards the patient, expressing these in ways which are unconsciously patterned after those ways by which the parents expressed their destructively negative feelings towards the patient as a child; the therapist's responses are so moulded, in powerful degree, by the patient's transference, and it is thus that the patient is at last able successfully to cope, symbolically, with the parents' destructiveness, recapitulated in the therapist's side of the transference relatedness. The deep reassurance which therapist as well as patient derive from finding repeatedly that each can survive the other's, and his own, baring of hatred at its fullest means that the foundation for the next therapeutic phase, that of full–or, genetically speaking, preambivalent–symbiosis has now become established.

The Phase of Full, or Preambivalent, Symbiosis

This phase, which is ushered in gradually and–as in the instances of the other phases I am describing–with unceasing fluctations towards both earlier and later phases, most often makes its presence known in terms of the therapist's finding, to his surprise, that his largely silent hours with the patient are no longer predominantly a source of conflict and anguish to him, but rather mainly one of pleasureful contentment, contentment which his superego at first reacts against as being reprehensible in view of the still formidable degree of illness in the patient after the passage of these many months of treatment. Or the therapist may discover, in the course of work with a largely verbal patient, that their verbal encounters have somewhere along the way lost their disturbing, anxiety-provoking, and hurtful quality, and are now predominantly, though largely deniedly, cherished by them both.

The therapist now comes more and more unconflictedly to accept both the feelings of a Good Mother who has a godlike importance to the little infant in the patient, as well as his own equally infantile-dependent feelings towards the patient as a similar Good Mother; the therapeutic relatedness, having progressed to the preambivalent mother–infant symbiosis, oscillates between the therapist's being now in the one position, now in the other, towards the patient.

I cannot overemphasize the extent to which it is the little child in each participant upon whom mutual trust must eventually be placed, for therapy to succeed; in the Biblical phrase, '. . . and a little child shall lead them' (Isa. xi. 6). Psychotherapy with the schizophrenic patient tends naturally to involve the therapist's feelings at the level of his own early childhood experiences. He powerfully responds to the patient as being an omnipotent mother, both because the latter's history of prolonged symbiotic relatedness with the mother has fostered strongly maternal qualities in the patient, and also because the present deeply undifferentiated state of the patient's ego gives the therapist the impression of unlimited potentialities for his own gratification.

One's love for the patient is now experienced as boundless and unthreatening, no longer a threat to, for example, one's relationship with one's wife and children, but rather a confirmation of one's ability to love anyone whatever. The sexual components of the love are no longer experienced as predominant, but submerged in a kind of boundless, fundamentally maternal, *caring for* the patient. This love, experienced towards the patient of one's own sex, is no longer experienced, as it was previously, as being any threat to one's sexual identity. Such hateful feelings as do from time to time arise become progressively guilt-free and

537

actively enjoyable, on the whole much subordinate in power and frequency to loving feelings, and increasingly rapidly revealed as defensive against the intensely tender love which underlies them. One comes to see that, at this level of dedifferentiation, 'love' and 'hate' are one, and that any intense and overt relatedness is, in effect, love. One of my patients, during such a phase, expressed her realization that 'There's a very thin line between love and hate'.

The patient's formerly archaically harsh superego is now seen progressively as no longer a giant foreign body in the patient–therapist relatedness, but rather as the vehicle for the patient's expression of his most deeply denied, but at the same time most intense and intimate, love for the therapist-mother. Comparably, the therapist finds that his own vestiges of infantile omnipotence, fanned to flame by the 'struggle-between-two-gods' nature of the ambivalent phase of symbiosis, give way to a realization, and deep acceptance, of his inability to 'cure' the patient through any exercise of rageful, godlike authority–his inability, that is, to bend the patient to his will by 'curing' him. There emerges in him then a feeling-orientation which, achieving what I have experienced as a 'gentle victory' over the domineering god-infant in oneself, is felt, for all its quiet gentleness, to be awesome in its power: a loving acceptance of the immediate relatedness with the patient, founded upon the knowledge that one's now full and unswerving dedication to his recovery, mingled with the patient's own increasingly liberated striving towards health, together make up a current which is carrying the therapeutic process forward. Out of this whole-hearted commitment of feeling by both patient and therapist, we understand the accuracy of the comment made by Bak (1958), that to the degree that the adult person is truly mature, there is in him no realm of the superego, demarcated as such within the over-all functioning of the personality; and of Anna Freud's (1946) observation that '. . . our picture of the superego always tends to become hazy when harmonious relations exist between it and the ego. We then say that the two coincide. . . .'

The therapist experiences not only the above-mentioned sense of whole-hearted commitment to the therapeutic relationship, at a depth which, he now realizes, despite all his previous expenditures of effort and feeling, he never felt before; he responds to the patient, during the therapeutic session, as being of boundless personal importance to him, and becomes progressively unafraid to acknowledge this on occasions when the patient needs such acknowledgement. It is not too much to say that the therapist feels the patient as necessary, even, to complete himself; temporarily and acknowledgedly, that is, he feels towards the patient that which the 'schizophrenogenic mother' was not strong enough either to acknowledge or to relinquish: the need for the patient to complete her own personality. For years we have been accustomed to damn this phenomenon totally as wholly destructive, and productive of schizophrenia; we need to realize that the core of any human being's self esteem is traceable to the healthy infant's experience that he is indeed needed to complete the psychological wholeness of the mothering person; it is there, I have come to believe, that the core of the *raison d'être*, for each of us, is to be found.

By the same token, the therapist should not be ashamed to receive from the patient such help in personal integration as he is able to provide; in this regard I fully concur with Whitaker and Malone (1953). The healthy child's self-esteem is strengthened by the experience that, just as his mother needed him to complete herself in his infancy, she now finds him deeply helpful in fostering her personal integration, her maturing. We should be able to have the courage to see and acknowledge these aspects of the symbiotic core of therapeutic interaction, when we see that, as long ago as 1923, Groddeck (1923) had the courage to describe how, in his treatment of one of his patients:

> . . . Her childlike attitude towards me–indeed, as I understood later, it was that of a child of three–compelled me to assume the mother's role. Certain slumbering mother-virtues were awakened in me by the patient, and these directed my procedure. . . . And now I was confronted by the strange fact that I was not treating the patient, but that the patient was treating me; or, to translate it into my own language, the It of this fellow-being tried so to transform my It, did in fact so transform it, that it came to be useful for its purpose. . . . Even to get this amount of insight was difficult, for you will understand that it absolutely reversed my position in regard to a patient. It was no longer important to give him instructions, to prescribe for him what I considered right, but to change in such a way that he could use me.

The therapist, at moments when he is in the position of the mother in the mother-infant symbiosis, may have vivid fantasies of giving suck to the patient as a happily nursing infant; Warkentin and Taylor (Whitaker, 1958, pp. 79–84) have described the physical accompaniments of such fantasies, and I, too, have experienced these in my work with a number of patients. It is equally important that the therapist become able to accept his nursing-infant fantasies towards the patient, whether female or male, for otherwise the patient cannot learn deeply to accept his own desires to nurture – the primeval basis for all givingness. I find it impressive, in this connexion, that Sèchehaye (1951), Eissler (1951), Schwing (1954), Hayward and Taylor (1956), Whitaker and Malone (1953) and many other therapists are in agreement concerning 'the absolute necessity for a happy infantile experience with a good mother before the patient can begin to grow toward adult reality' (Hayward and Taylor, 1956, p. 211), and it is of additional interest that the recovered schizophrenic patient reported by Hayward and Taylor, who gave a detailed account of her therapy as she saw it in retrospect, 'stressed that the happy nursing experience was the most important single part of her therapy'. I am trying here to describe something of how this particular phase of the therapy, this 'happy infantile experience with a good mother' phase, actually manifests itself, particularly in terms of the therapist's experiences during it.

A mutual spirit of childlike playfulness is another prominent characteristic of this phase. Because the ambivalent stage of the symbiotic transference relatedness has been successfully traversed and the stratum of preambivalent lovingness attained, the lack of structure, the lack of rigidly defined boundaries between patient and therapist, or between such intra-psychic realms as those of remembered 'reality' and those of creative fantasy, or those of concrete imagery and those of metaphorical or allegorical or otherwise highly figurative imagery, is experienced no longer as a threatening kind of dedifferentiation, but rather as giving both participants the unfettered opportunity to trade places playfully with one another (and even, in one instance in my experience, imaginatively to trade various body-parts with one another), and to gambol playfully about all these various realms of psychological experience in a mix-up which is oftentimes thoroughly merry to both of them. One finds something which one had never thought possible: confusion itself, usually regarded in psychiatry as so tragically destructive to the patient and threatening to his therapist, can be actively pleasurable in an atmosphere where such a degree of mutual trust has been reached that, where hate for all practical purposes does not exist, confusion is no longer tantamount to vulnerability, and ego-structure need not be thrown up as a poorly erected bulwark against external threat, but can form at its own pace as, primarily, a growing organization for the expression of increasingly complex inner potentialities and therefore needs.

It is appropriate at this juncture to note the impact upon the total hospital environment of the foregoing phase in the psycho-therapeutic relationship, namely the phase of ambivalent symbiosis, and of this phase of full or preambivalent symbiosis. In the former phase the patient-therapist relationship tends to foster incessant and severe splits among the group of patients and personnel on the ward, pervading, at times, the social structure of the whole hospital. In the same way, the deep ambivalence in the patient, as well as the not inconsiderable ambivalence roused responsively in the therapist in the course of the therapy, tend to make their relatedness the ready instrument for the expression of already existing, latent disagreements rife in the social environment surrounding them; thus, of the ambivalence which permeates this larger social environment, their therapeutic relationship is at once cause and victim. Such ambivalently symbiotic phenomena in the larger social structure of the hospital have been well described by Stanton and Schwartz (1954), Main (1957), Perry and Shea (1957) and others; I have reported my own experience with, and interpretations of, such phenomena in chapter 11.

Many a therapeutic relationship miscarries, and therapist and patient, unable to face and resolve the intense, mutual hatred which is evoked by the symbiotic phase of the psychotherapy, repress this hatred, project it on to various figures in the surrounding social matrix of the hospital, and become locked in a relatedness in which they both share the fantasy of being lovingly at one. But this is not the truly preambivalent phase of the transference symbiosis which they are experiencing; rather it is, as those responsible for the long-run management of the hospital

541

are painfully and irritatedly aware, predominantly a *folie-à-deux* between patient and therapist, in which symbiosis is functioning mainly as a defence against the recognition of mutual hatred. This development is so common that I have come reluctantly to conclude that there is no sure criterion by which we can know, for long periods of time, whether we are involved in a genuinely preambivalent symbiosis with the patient, or rather in the predominantly paranoid symbiosis which is a defence against hatred; there is no kind of litmus paper which will definitely tell us, and we must remain open-minded to the ever-present possibility that, for example, a basically constructive, subjectively preambivalent symbiosis will be misused unconsciously from time to time, by both participants, to keep increments of particularly intense hostility out of awareness.

Even in those treatment relationships where a healthy, preambivalent symbiosis has full sway, it is not always easy for the social environment to take. The therapeutic relationship even here needs a kind of delicate handling, much as a pregnant woman needs special care from her environment even when the pregnancy is progressing well. For example, neither therapist nor patient is yet ready for any third person to come upon the scene as a consistently valued, and openly acknowledged, contributor to their mutual therapeutic work. Further, the subjectively irresponsible playfulness and contentment, so genuinely healing in itself and so central an ingredient of the preambivalent symbiosis, nonetheless strains the faith and patience of others on the hospital staff who have little or no opportunity to participate in the favourable developments I have been describing, and who are aware mainly of such conspicuous factors as the patient's already long hospitalization, his persisting manifestation of various chronic symptoms in his daily life on the ward, and perhaps, the intimations from the family that this hospitalization cannot be underwritten indefinitely.

'They were going around on a merry-go-round—no, not on a merry-go-round, because that implies movement', snorted a supervisor at a recent staff conference, concerning the therapeutic relationship between a hebephrenic woman and her therapist who were, from my viewpoint, in the midst of the phase of preambivalent symbiosis at a time when, for extraneous reasons, the therapist had had to leave Chestnut Lodge to return to his distant home country. 'Going around on a merry-go-round' is a beautiful way of describing the kind of therapeutic interaction in which it is so important for the patient and therapist to become able freely to participate, but which is so difficult for the hospital organization to permit. I myself, who 'know' these things as well as I know anything about the therapy of schizophrenia, feel, when in the role of supervisor hearing from a therapist concerning his work during such a phase, unenjoyably aware of being an 'outsider' to the intimate two-person relatedness I am hearing about at second hand, and must work against my tendency to express envious resentment to the therapist through admonitions and reproaches that he should buckle down to the business of psychotherapy with the patient—the worst possible supervisory response at this phase of the therapy. By contrast, the sheepish therapist obtains invaluable help from his supervisor's realization that what is going on in therapy is the very essence of what is good for the patient, confirming the therapist's own courage to go on doing this in the face of the reproaches of his own all too conscientious super-ego.

The Phase of Resolution of the Symbiosis

The complex individualistic needs of the two participants, and thus their respective strivings for individuality, will not tolerate indefinitely the perpetuation of the therapeutic symbiosis. The basic function of this symbiosis is, after all—despite the intense regressive gratification which it holds in itself—a maturational one: it provides the patient, and to a not insignificant degree the therapist also, with a basis for renewed, and healthier, development of individuality. Thus, after a period extending, as best I have been able to determine, from a few months to one or two years, the dynamic equilibrium of the therapeutic relatedness shifts increasingly towards resolution of the symbiotic phase. The initiative for this shift may be manifested first by either patient or therapist, and it is my impression that the resolution process—that is to say, the process of both participants' coming to be subjectively, and to function as, individual persons, rather than partners in symbiosis—proceeds by turns, with now one, and now the other, showing the greater push towards emancipation. I shall describe first the therapist's experiences when the initiative is in his hands, and then his experiences in reaction to the patient's showing such initiative.

One of the therapist's typical feelings, in the former instance, is a quiet, subjectively unaccountable, but deeply memorable sense of apartness from the patient, a feeling-realization that the patient is outside oneself–a realization that he is a person 'over there', a person afflicted with a schizophrenic illness which is, likewise, 'over there' in the patient. One facet of the therapist's realization is, then, that he–the therapist–is not the patient's illness. This shift in feeling orientation is at times experienced, also, as a sensation of now being, at long last, 'out of love with' the patient–a feeling always, for me, tinged with some guilt in those instances in which he is still showing much need for persisting symbiosis with me beyond the time when I have now 'outgrown' it.

On other occasions, the therapist experiences a resolution of the symbiosis, or at least a step in this resolution process, not in this quiet and subjectively inscrutable way, but rather with a sudden sense of *outrage*. The very word '*out*rage' is significant, and the feeling it designates is qualitatively different from annoyance, anger, or even rage. He feels outrage at this or that chronic regressive symptom in the patient, or outrage at the latter's whole regressive symptomatology, and always outrage at the unreasonableness of the demands which the patient has been making upon him these many months or years. He sees the enormity of these demands which the patient has been placing, through his illness, upon him and other persons, and sees clearly the folly of acquiescing further in these regressive demands. He is suddenly and vigorously determined to give no more of his long-time dedication, now seen as misplaced dedication, to the gratification of these demands, which he formerly saw as infant needs which it would be unthinkable to brush aside.

The therapist sees now, by the same token, the full interpersonal offensiveness of the patient's defence mechanisms, whereas he possessed heretofore a high degree of tolerance for such offensiveness in his patient and maintained a devoted effort to see, and empathize with, the anxiety, the hurt, the loneliness, and so on, against which the patient has been unconsciously protecting himself through the use of these defence mechanisms. In my work with, for example, one paranoid schizophrenic man who chronically manifested intense scorn and sarcasm in his dealings with other persons including myself, for nearly two years I had experienced increasing forbearance towards and sympathy with him as I saw more and more clearly the feelings of hurt, disappointment, and so on which the scorn and sarcasm was serving to maintain under repression. But then, with the advent of the resolution-of-symbiosis phase, it forcibly dawned upon me how genuinely obnoxious, to me as well as to others, he was being with his scorn and sarcasm, the defensive function of these notwithstanding.

In other words, one now holds the patient highly responsible for his symptoms. One now leaves in his hands the choice as to whether he wants to spend the remainder of his life in a mental hospital, or whether he wants, instead, to become well. In every instance that I can recall from my own experience, I have found occasion to express this newly won attitude to the patient himself, emphasizing that it is all the same to me. These are no mere words, but the expression of a deep and genuine feeling orientation. One cares not, now, how callous this may sound, nor even whether the patient will respond to it with suicide or incurable psychotic disintegration; and one feels and says this while casting one's own professional status, too, into the gamble, not to mention the potential feelings of lasting remorse to which one might be subject in case one's communication had such an irremediably destructive effect upon the patient. Thus, in effect, one braves the threat of destruction both to the patient and to oneself, in taking it into one's hands to declare one's individuality, come what may.

It may well be that individuation–the resolution of symbiosis–innately contains, even in the healthy maturation of the young child, this element of going ahead in the face of such a life-and-death threat. Incidentally, if this is true, we have here the primordial determinant of democracy's tenet that it is better to brave death than to live as anything other than a politically free individual.

Part of this new attitude on the therapist's part is a readiness to let the patient 'stew in his own juice', in contrast to his having often found himself, previously, vicariously expressing the patient's feelings in the symbiosis which then obtained. Likewise, he feels a new freedom to express his own individual thoughts and feelings to the patient as an individual–or, at any rate, as one whose nascent individuality is increasingly in evidence–without being hampered by concerns as to whether he is being inconsistent towards him, or is treating the latter unfairly in comparison with his other patients–a not unimportant aspect of the work when one has two or three patients on the same hospital ward.

The therapist feels a clear realization, with all this, of the fact that he himself is no longer indispensable to the patient; he realizes, that is, that he himself is not the only conceivable therapist who can help the patient complete the journey to health. He can look about him and see various colleagues, who he can readily imagine, would fill this capacity as well as, or possibly better than, he can. He feels now a lively appreciation, a genuine welcoming, of the invaluable contributions to the patient's recovery which have been, are being, and will continue to be made by nursing staff, relatives, various other patients on the ward, and so on. This is in marked contrast to the therapist's feeling earlier in the work, a grandiose feeling but, I think, a feeling quite essential to the development and maintenance of the therapeutic symbiosis, of being a God the Creator in the therapeutic situation, of being the only conceivable Pygmalion for this Galatea; that feeling was, after all, of a piece with the mother's sensing of her own god-like indispensability to her so needful infant. The therapist's subsequent realization, now, that these others are helping in major ways to meet the patient's needs, comes predominantly as a deeply reassuring one; but it has, obviously, affective ingredients of deflation and loss.

We see the loss-aspect of the therapist's experience more clearly at those junctures when the patient rather than the therapist is manifestly showing a determination to grow free of the symbiosis. One of my most frequent experiences as a supervisor is that of helping a therapist to explore his feelings of dissatisfaction and despair about a current therapeutic relatedness in which, he is consciously convinced, the schizophrenic patient is showing discouraging stasis, but is actually evidencing, as shown by various subtle clues, all too many indications of a growing, though still somewhat submerged, determination to slough off the symbiosis in which the therapist has a far deeper feeling-investment than he cares to acknowledge to himself.

The therapist paradoxically finds himself despairing, for example, just at the time when the patient has actually been opening up unprecedentedly deep areas for investigation–areas of fondness and dependency towards the therapist, areas of confusion or other disturbed subjective experience, and so on. One unconsciously employs, as therapist, the same defence mechanisms against recognizing the beginning resolution of the symbiotic phase as one employed earlier against the recognition that this phase of symbiosis was becoming more and more deeply established–namely the defence mechanisms of denial and reaction-formation: the denial of how well the work is actually proceeding, of how much the patient means to oneself, of how deeply cherished are the gratifications which one is obtaining or has been obtaining, of how deep is the sense of loss which further change will bring; and reaction-formation feelings of impatience and dissatisfaction, as part of one's struggle to maintain under repression feelings of contentment, satisfaction, and accomplishment.

I think it correct to say that the therapist, no matter how mature or experienced, inevitably reacts somewhat against any move on the patient's part into a new area of feeling, a new area of psychotherapeutic investigation. This is partly for the reason, as I have said in chapter 15, that the patient's sense of identity is so deeply invested in the old way of experiencing things, the old and familiar way of relating to the therapist, that he would experience a major threat to his sense of identity if the therapist were somehow able to welcome with unambivalently open arms this move into a new area of experiencing and interpersonal relating. But it is partly for the reason, too, that the therapist has a more or less deeply imbedded emotional investment in the familiar, more predominantly symbiotic mode of relatedness with the patient, and hence reacts against the threat of personal loss with which the patient's new growth as an individual confronts him.

I have had the experience of finding that a hebephrenic woman, with whom I had been involved for a number of years in an increasingly unambivalent and pleasurable symbiotic relatedness, had come to radiate–with disconcerting suddenness, so it felt to me–a self-containment which, by all logical standards, was a most welcome therapeutic development. Instead of

547

making unceasing efforts for me to be everybody to her and to satisfy her every need almost before it arose, she now spent the hours with me in saying little, but mainly looking at me calmly, appraisingly, and objectively. She was not being actively rejecting to me, in either word or facial expression, as she had been on innumerable occasions much earlier in our work, particularly during the phase of ambivalent symbiosis. But I felt a distinctly unpleasurable sense of being apart from her; I could not help feeling rejected in the face of a development which I knew represented, for the first time, the establishment of a genuine sense of self on her part.

For the patient to become firmly established as, subjectively, an individual person, he must come to accept that, although he can contribute to the healing of other persons'–including his therapist's–psychological difficulties, he cannot cure them in any total sense, and therefore does not have to hold himself responsible for curing them. He can proceed, therefore, with the getting-well process, the process of becoming an increasingly healthy person, without *guilt* for being, and increasingly becoming, a separate individual. This is one of the dividends which the relinquishment of infantile omnipotence yields to the patient–a relinquishment which is part of the relinquishment of the mother–infant symbiosis in the transference.

From the therapist's viewpoint, he must come to accept that, although the patient has been of deeply personal help to him, the patient cannot totally 'cure' him–that he will have to struggle towards increasing maturity, increasing personal integration and differentiation, in future courses of work with the patients who will succeed this one, and he may glimpse, now, the basic truth–if so it be, and I surmise that it is–that the ideal of 'complete maturity' is only one of the disguises worn by the persistent striving, within him, towards infantile omnipotence. Loewald (1960b) speaks of the valuable role, in superego formation in healthy development, of manageable increments of disillusionment. The successful resolution of the symbiotic phase of therapy with the schizophrenic patient requires, likewise, that each person be able to integrate his disillusionment about his own and his partner's powers, shrunken now from omnipotent to lifesize proportions.

It has seemed to me, both in my own work and in the material reported by colleagues in supervision and elsewhere, that the patient has first to demonstrate to himself that the therapist is not omnipotent, but rather–at this moment, at least–totally helpless, before he can feel it permissible to go ahead and function, capably, as an individual. This seems in part a function of the vulnerability to guilt-about-being-a-separate-person to which the schizophrenic person–and, I believe, to a lesser extent the neurotic person also–is so prone. It is as though he has to exhaust every possibility of getting help from the therapist–about whatever issue is at hand–before he can himself allow his own constructive potentialities to come to the fore, and meet the issue at hand in his own functioning individuality. Thus is it no coincidence that the emergence of the patient's individuality tends to occur in a setting of the therapist's feeling more than usually helpless in the situation. We can think of it from the viewpoint, also, that no one, whether adult patient or healthy child, would give up a therapist (or, respectively, a parent) who is, as far as can be determined, omnipotent; human beings are, if nothing else, practical, and this would be simply impractical: it would make no sense to individuate oneself from such an omnipotent being.

It is worth noting, further, that if the therapeutic relationship is to traverse successfully the phase of resolution of the symbiosis, the therapist must be able to brave not only the threats of suicide or psychotic disintegration on the patient's part, and of the professional and personal destruction to himself which might be a correlate of such outcomes; he must also brave the threat, which seems at times to be of a comparable order of magnitude, that the patient will, after these arduous years have passed and the home stretch is in sight, change therapists. It is as though the patient, by presenting the therapist with this threat of separation and finding that the latter can face it squarely without resort to panicky efforts to re-establish their erstwhile mother-infant symbiosis, gains the reassurance that the therapist will allow him to become a person in his own right, and to regard the recovery from psychosis as predominantly the patient's own achievement, rather than as a feather in the therapist's cap.

An important step in individuation for one of my patients, with whom I had been working for seven years, occurred when I allowed her to use my telephone, during one of her sessions with me, to call the Director of Psychotherapy for an appointment to discuss her desire for a change of therapists. In retrospect I have seen this as a crucial experience for her, that I freely allowed her to do this although her changing therapists would have meant a great personal loss to me, and although I felt it quite possible that she might succeed in that endeavour.

Incidentally, my readiness to face this development was, I think, one factor which enabled her to explore soon afterwards, in her sessions, her desires, repressed since childhood, for a different set of parents. This transference-development tends, I think, to occur comparatively late in treatment, when the therapist is likely to think the patient painfully ungrateful for wanting, in the transference, a different therapist. I have mentioned in chapter 12 how apt the patient is to press for a change of therapists just at a time when he is threatened with beginning to recognize how greatly he himself has changed, a recognition which tends to disrupt his still tenuous sense of personal identity; in the context of this paper, he tends to flee from the recognition of his having undergone the great change of individuation–tends, in Erich Fromm's (1941) phraseology, to flee from the freedom of individuality, by seeking a symbiotic relationship with a new therapist.

The resolution-of-symbiosis phase is always complicated, often to a marked degree, by the resistances which various persons in the patient's life between therapeutic sessions, including the family members, some of the nursing staff and, it may be, some of his fellow patients, pose to his becoming a separate person and depriving them, therefore, of such symbiotic gratifications as the therapist himself has come to know, and reluctantly to relinquish, in the transference relationship. It is by now a truism that the family members, no matter how genuinely fond of the patient and devoted to him they are at a conscious level, are particularly likely to withdraw him from the hospital just at the point when his individuation is promising to become established; and the therapist is not the only member of the hospital staff who inevitably acquires, over the years, a deep emotional investment in the patient's remaining ill and symbiotically oriented towards the more significant among his fellow human beings. But that aspect of the matter has been discussed already in the literature to a considerable extent, and any detailed examination of it would carry us beyond the intended focus of the therapeutic relationship itself with which I am here primarily concerned.

The Late Phase

This phase extends from the resolution of the therapeutic symbiosis up to the completion of the therapy. It is a long phase, for only with the resolution of the symbiotic mode of relatedness is the patient capable of genuine object-relatedness and able, therefore, to cope with the matters with which psycho-analysis of the neurotic individual ordinarily deals. Only now, that is, is he ready for psycho-analysis; thus this phase requires a number of years of continued work.

Now that his symbiotic mode of relatedness has been resolved, the patient becomes involved in a better differentiated, more selective, process of de-repression of identifications from the past, with acceptance into his own ego of those identifications which are predominantly useful to him, and relinquishment of those which have proved unuseful or pathological. He shows a similar capacity for forming, or rejecting, part-identifications with figures in current life, including the therapist. This process is well described in some of Erikson's (1956) words about identity formation, where he says that this '. . . arises from the selective repudiation and mutual assimilation of childhood identifications, and their absorption in a new configuration . . .'

The patient now evidences increasingly, not only in therapeutic sessions but in his daily life, the demeanour of a healthy child or adolescent; he belatedly evidences, that is, those normal developmental phases which, because of the severity and early onset of the schizophrenogenic personality-warp, he had barely known in his biological childhood and adolescence. From a childhood which earlier in therapy he had experienced as unrelievedly black, he now remembers, with powerful affects of love and grief, positive experiences with his parents and other figures in his childhood, and there is a consequent freeing-up of useful identifications with those persons' strengths. Thus the strength which helps him to become well derives not only from his positive identifications with the therapist and other figures from current life in the hospital; there is also, and most importantly, this ingredient of his making contact with the strengths in his own past.

To an extent far greater than in the neurotic, however, the patient is likely for at least several months to present himself–and no doubt genuinely to feel–as a naïve little child who doesn't know anything, and who therefore needs to be taught all over again, and correctly this time, how to live. The therapist, aware that so much of what the child learned from family members was indeed pathological and that a high degree of social isolation outside the family prevented his learning innumerable things about everyday life which were common currency among his age-mates, will be under extraordinary pressure to assume the function of a teacher or counsellor. I believe that the patient may benefit from, or at least not be greatly harmed by, the therapist's assuming such a function on occasion. But the therapist rapidly finds himself, here, on thin ice, in danger of losing touch with the only consistently solid function he has in the patient's life–that of psychotherapist. The words of Spitz (1959) concerning psycho-analysis are forcefully applicable here, and the therapist will do well to recall them:

> The essence of psychoanalytic treatment is that it does not direct, advise, educate. It liberates the personality and permits it to make its own adjustments. . . . No directive or educative measures in the commonly accepted sense of the terms are necessary. Indeed, they can only disturb the natural process, which is so highly individualistic as to make it impossible for the particular therapist to direct it in its minute details. Any direction required is provided actually by the transference situation. This insures a process of developmental unfolding free from the anxieties, perils, threats of the original situation.

The patient has been exposed in actuality, prior to the psychotherapy, to more of adult-life experience than he as yet realizes, and the naïve-child orientation is eventually seen in retrospect to have represented a powerful though unconscious striving to keep the therapist enshrined as an omniscient parent, while himself avoiding the fulness of his childhood disillusion-ment with the parent(s) and avoiding, thus, the responsibility for his own going on to adulthood. If the therapist persists in adhering to his psychotherapeutic function, the next unfolding of the transference consists, in my experience, in the patient's deeply disillusioned and scornful conviction that the therapist is in no measure qualified to be an omniscient general manager of the patient's life but is, quite the contrary, crazy. This is the development which Hill (1955) evidently had in mind in describing the schizophrenic patient's experience of the conclusion of therapy:

... one hears very little about gratitude from these patients. What happens is that, in the process of taking in the goodness [i.e. identifying with the good qualities of the doctor] and incorporating it actually into himself, the patient manages to make the sort of split that is comfortable to all of us. He is good, and the badness is left with the doctor. Even the illness is left with the doctor. Sometimes it is quite striking that the patient comes to believe that the doctor is thoroughly psychotic, quite in the fashion in which he himself has been psychotic.

This is a very regular development in my work with patients, as I have reported in chapter 8; but, unlike Hill, I feel it essential for the patient's future welfare that the psychotherapy be pursued far beyond this point, until the craziness has been well resolved, rather than simply left in this projected form upon the therapist. It is subsequent to this that there is a differentiation, in the transference, of those intense affects–murderousness, envy, loneliness, fear, and above all deeply denied love (cf. ch. 7)– which lay behind the parents' craziness. The added ego-strength which the patient has acquired in the course of his psychotherapy enables him to experience de-repressed feeling along these paths with a clarity of delineation, and depth of intensity, which he could not subjectively experience previously– no matter how intense were the affects which he acted out during the phase of ambivalent symbiosis. And the therapist is unprecedentedly free now to experience within himself, and on crucial occasions to express, the reciprocal feelings inherent in these transference positions in which he finds himself, with a minimum of the conflict and guilt which had been so prevalent during the ambivalently symbiotic phase.

It is during this late phase of the therapy that the onset of the patient's psychosis becomes clarified; he is finally able to experience, and integrate, the emotions which at that much earlier date had had to be repressed, and defended against by the advent of psychosis. For example, I have had the experience, at once fulfilling and somehow awesome, of finding that a patient who had become schizophrenic at the age of fifteen and had spent nineteen years predominantly in mental hospitals, had now reached a point, after ten years of intensive psychotherapy with me, where the secondary elaborations of her hebephrenic illness had been sufficiently unravelled for the material of her original delusions to be now coming to the fore, but in a way progressively understandable to both of us.

As the patient makes emotional contact with the various previously repressed areas of his past experience, bit by bit, he eventually reaches the realization that, despite all the years of illness, as one patient expressed it with great relief, 'I'm still myself'. In other words, there is eventually established a sense of continuity of identity, combining the person he felt himself to be prior to the psychosis with the emotions and attitudes manifested in the psychosis, long unacceptable to the conscious ego, but now accepted as a part of it. It is on the basis of such a newly achieved ego strength and such a firmer sense of personal identity that he is now able to take his stand and assess the personalities of figures from present and past life. I remember how impressed I was with one schizophrenic woman, for example, when after three years of therapy she became able to express, in a single breath, her realistic disapproval of certain qualities in her mother, in her father, and in me. Earlier in our work she had possessed far too little of a sense of individuality to be able to objectify these three so important figures, so clearly and simultaneously. She became, as do other patients in the late phase of the work, able to express admiration and fondness equally towards parents and therapist.

Because the therapy of these patients usually requires a considerable number of years, the therapist may find it particularly difficult to be receptive to the expression of some feelings which the patient can face only after several years of treatment. The therapist, keenly aware that, say, five or six or seven years of intensive psychotherapy has elapsed, may feel threatened and therefore impatient at the patient's finally becoming able to explore the depths of the latter's discouragement and despair, or – as I mentioned before – wish for a different parent in the transference, or regressive strivings. It is only through the therapist's being fully aware of the therapeutic progress represented by the patient's becoming conscious of these feelings, and able now to express them verbally rather than having to act them out as in the foregoing years of the treatment, that he is able to help the patient on towards completion of the therapeutic investigation, rather than towards a re-repression of these feelings for an indefinite time longer.

Similarly, because the therapist has seen the patient to be, earlier in the therapy, such a deeply fragmented person, he tends to retain a lingering impression of the latter's fragility, an impression which may interfere with his going along at the faster pace which the patient, now a very different and far stronger person, is capable of setting. But even this memory-image of the fragile patient, carried with the therapist, has a natural function in the course of the psychotherapy, for it is only very late in the work that the patient himself is able to realize how very ill, how very fragile, he indeed once was; until he becomes strong enough to integrate this realization into his self-image, the therapist has to be the bearer of this piece of the patient's identity. This process is analogous to the well-known phenomenon in which each major forward stride in the patient's therapeutic growth is accompanied, or presaged, by the therapist's suddenly seeing in the patient a new and healthier person (see chs. 10, 11); there, too, the impact of the development falls primarily, for a time, upon the therapist rather than the patient. The patient himself, because his sense of identity is still, during the earlier therapeutic phases to which I am referring at the moment, relatively tenuous, is easily overwhelmed – in one patient's words, 'knocked out' – by the realization of the extent to which he is now changed, even though this change be, in our view, a most beneficial and welcome one.

Another characteristic of the late phase – and I am not attempting to describe, here, all such characteristics – is the circumstance that many of the patient's adult strivings may be found more deeply repressed than his infantile strivings. That is, it may well prove easier for the therapist to contemplate (above, ch. 9), and easier for the nursing staff to recognize and at least partially gratify, various of the patient's infantile and small-child oral needs, than to help him face squarely his powerful adult desires, mobilized and given shape in the course of the psychotherapy but still painfully thwarted by reason of his long hospitalization – his desires to marry and procreate and bear adult responsibilities. Sometimes the patient's expression of such desires, particularly if he or she has been so long hospitalized that many of these must be accepted as losses or deprivations which can never be made up, is at least as poignant for the therapist to hear as were the earlier-expressed yearnings for infantile and childlike gratifications. He realizes to what an extent, for probably many months now, it is the more *mature* areas of the patient's personality which have been the more deeply repressed ones (ch. 12), and that, in contrast to some of the views expressed by Freud (1915*b*), the maturation process is so deep-reaching that it leaves no changeless core of the personality, no eternally infantile id, unchanged by it.

The evolution of the reality-relatedness between patient and therapist, over the course of the psychotherapy, is something which, so far as I know, has received little more than passing mention in the literature (ch. 15 above). Hoedemaker (1955), in a paper concerning the therapeutic process in the treatment of schizophrenia, stresses the importance of the schizophrenic patient's forming healthy identifications with the therapist, and Loewald (1960*a*), in his paper concerning the therapeutic action of psycho-analysis in general, repeatedly emphasizes the importance of the real relationship between patient and analyst, but only in the following passage alludes to the evolution, the growth, of this relationship over the course of treatment:

. . . Where repression is lifted and unconscious and preconscious are again in communication, infantile object and contemporary object may be united into one—a truly new object as both unconscious and preconscious are changed by their mutual communication. The object which helps to bring this about in therapy, the analyst, mediates this union. . . .

It has been my distinct impression that the patient's remembrance of new areas of his past—his manifestation of newly de-repressed transference reactions to the therapist—occurs only hand in hand with the reaching of comparable areas of feeling in the evolving reality-relatedness between patient and therapist (ch. 7). For example, he does not come to experience fond memories of his mother until the reality-relatedness between himself and the therapist has reached the point where the feeling between them has become, in reality, predominantly positive. Loewald's words, quoted above, imply to me that an increment of transference resolution slightly antedates, and makes possible, the forming of each successive increment in the evolving reality-relationship between patient and analyst. It has been my impression, by contrast, that the evolution of the reality-relatedness proceeds always a bit ahead of, and makes possible, the progressive evolution and resolution of the transference, although to be sure the latter, in so far as it frees psychological energy and makes it available for reality-relatedness, helps greatly to consolidate the ground just taken over by the advancing reality-relationship. Loewald (1960a) thinks of it that

. . . The patient can dare to take the plunge into the regressive crises of the transference neurosis which brings him face to face again with his childhood anxieties and conflicts, *if* he can hold on to the potentiality of a new object-relationship, represented by the analyst.

But it seems to me that this new object-relationship is more than a potentiality, to be realized with comparative suddenness, and *in toto*, towards the end of the treatment with the resolution of the transference. Rather it is, it has seemed to me, constantly there, being built up bit by bit, just ahead of the likewise evolving transference relationship. Pertinent here is Freud's (1922) having pointed out that projection–which is, after all, so major an aspect of transference–is directed not 'into the sky, so to speak, where there is nothing of the sort already', but rather on to a person who provides some reality-basis for the projection.

In the final months of the therapy, the therapist clearly sees the extent to which the patient's transferences to him as representing a succession of figures from the latter's earlier years have all been in the service of the patient's unconsciously shying away, to a successively decreasing extent, from experiencing the full and complex reality of the immediate relatedness with the therapist in the present. The patient at last comes to realize that the relationship with a single other human being–in this instance, the therapist–is so rich as to comprise all these earlier relationships, so rich as to evoke all the myriad feelings which had been parcelled out and crystallized, heretofore, in the transferences which have now been resolved. This is a process most beautifully described by the Swiss novelist Hermann Hesse (1951) winner of the Nobel Prize in 1946, in his little novel, *Siddhartha*. The protagonist, in a lifelong quest for the ultimate

557

answer to the enigma of man's role on earth, finally discovers in the face of his beloved friend all the myriad persons, things, and events which he has known, but incoherently before, during the vicissitudes of his many years of searching.

It is thus that the patient, schizophrenic or otherwise, becomes at one with himself, in the closing phase of psychotherapy. But although the realization may come to him as a sudden one, it is founded on a reality-relatedness which has been building up all along. Loewald (1960*a*) in his magnificent paper to which my brief references have done less than full justice, suggests, as I mentioned, something of the role which transference resolution plays in the development of this reality-relatedness. I suggest that the evolution of the 'countertransference'—not counter-transference in the classical sense of the therapist's transference to the patient, but rather in the sense of the therapist's emotional reactions to the patient's transference—forms an equally essential contribution to this reality-relatedness. This chapter has been primarily an attempt to describe the evolution of what might be called—in this special sense—the therapist's typical 'counter-transference' to the schizophrenic patient, over the course of successful psychotherapy.

Concluding Remarks

In my attempt to make clear the paramount place which emotions—emotions in the therapist as well as in the patient—hold in the psychotherapy of schizophrenia, I would not wish to leave the impression that the therapist should strive to be im-mersed continually in a kind of emotional blood-bath. On the contrary, as I described it at the outset, the emotionally charged transference evolution which has been traced here can develop, and run a relatively unimpeded course, only if the therapist is sure enough of his capacities for feeling for his basic emotional orientation to be an investigative, rather than for example a compulsively 'loving', orientation. Moreover, each of these patients—and, I think, this is true to a lesser degree of the neurotic patient also—needs in the course of the therapy to project upon the therapist the subjectively unfeeling, non-human and even inanimate, aspects of himself, and thus to see his therapist, in the transference, as the representative of the parents who were, to the child's view, incapable of human feeling, as has been the patient himself in his own view (ch. 16 above, and my *The Non-human Environment*). Only by thus re-externalizing his pathogenic introjects can the patient make contact with his own feeling-capacities and come to know, beyond any further doubt, that he is a human being. This aspect of the transference, this aspect of the healthy reworking of very early ego-differentiation, cannot be accomplished unless the therapist is able to be self-accepting while spending hour after hour without finding in himself any particular feeling whatever towards the patient. He must be sufficiently sure of his own humanness to endure for long periods the role, in the patient's transference experience, of an inanimate object, or of some other percept which has not yet become differentiated as a sentient human being.

In the course of writing this, the realization has dawned on me that the therapist recurrently experiences guilt in reaction to the arousal of one or another kind of emotion in himself, during the course of his work with the schizophrenic patient, on the basis of a rekindling of the therapist's infantile omnipotence. Such a temporary regression on the therapist's part, to the level of infantile omnipotence, is his major unconscious defence against the realization, and deep and consistent acceptance, of the fact that not only the patient but he also is in the grip of a process, the therapeutic process, which is comparable in its strength to the maturational *process* in the child–which is, indeed, this same process in a particular context, the context of psychotherapy of the adult schizophrenic person. The more experienced and confident the therapist becomes in this work, the more deeply does he realize that this process is far too powerful for either the patient or himself to be able at all easily to deflect it, consciously and wilfully and singlehandedly, away from the confluent channel which it is tending–with irresistible power, if we can give ourselves up to the current–to form for itself. When the therapist sees this, he realizes how illusory has been his subjective omnipotence, but also how groundless has been his subjective guilt.

Chapter 19

THE DIFFERENTIATION BETWEEN CONCRETE AND METAPHORICAL THINKING IN THE RECOVERING SCHIZOPHRENIC PATIENT (1962)[1]

LANGER (1942, p. 32) has called the symbol-making function 'one of man's primary activities, like eating, looking, or moving about. It is the fundamental process of his mind,' she says, and she terms the need of symbolization 'a primary need in man, which other creatures probably do not have'. Kubie (1953) terms the symbolizing capacity 'the unique hallmark of man . . . the *sine qua non* of man's highest psychological and spiritual capabilities', and he states that it is in impairment of this capacity to symbolize that all adult psychopathology essentially consists.[2]

As regards schizophrenia, we find that as long ago as 1911 this disease was described by Bleuler (1911) as involving an impairment of the thinking capacities, and in the past thirty years many psychologists and psychiatrists, including Vigotsky (1934), Hanfmann and Kasanin (1942), Goldstein (1946), Norman Cameron (1946), Benjamin (1946), Beck (1946), von Domarus (1946), and Angyal (1946) – to mention but a few – have described various aspects of this thinking disorder. These writers, agreeing that one aspect of the disorder consists in overconcreteness or literalness of thought, have variously described the schizophrenic as unable to think in figurative (including metaphorical) terms, or in abstractions, or in consensually validated concepts

---

[1] Highly abbreviated versions of this paper were presented at the Annual Chestnut Lodge Symposium in Rockville, Md., October 1958, and at the meeting of the American Psychiatric Association in Philadelphia, April 1959. It was first published in the *Journal of the American Psychoanalytic Association*, Vol. 10 (1962) pp. 22–49.

[2] The term 'symbol' which has various psycho-analytic definitions, is used throughout this paper in the sense of the following everyday, non-psycho-analytic, dictionary definition: 'That which suggested something else by reason of relationship, association, convention, etc.; esp., a visible sign of something invisible, as an idea, a quality; an emblem; as, the lion is the *symbol* of courage' (*Webster's Dictionary*, 1956).

and symbols, or in categorical generalizations. Bateson *et al.* (1956) describe the schizophrenic as using metaphor, but *unlabelled* metaphor.

Werner (1940, p. 52) has conceptualized this most accurately, in my opinion, as a matter of regression to a primitive level of thinking, comparable with that found in children and in members of so-called primitive cultures, a level of thinking in which there is a *lack of differentiation between* the concrete and the metaphorical. Thus we might say that just as the schizophrenic is unable to think in effective, consensually validated metaphor, so too is he unable to think in terms which are *genuinely* concrete, free from an animistic kind of so-called metaphorical overlay.

In so far as this paper deals with symbolic thinking it will confine itself to one variety of symbolism–namely, metaphor.[3] But if Kubie (1953) is correct in holding that there is an essential continuity in all symbolic functions, the psychodynamics to be described here possess relevance to kinds of symbolization other than metaphorical thinking alone.

Most of the writings on this subject do not attract the psychotherapist, for they possess a certain static, fatalistic quality, portraying this aspect of schizophrenia as though it, more profoundly than any other manifestation of the disease, sets the schizophrenic hopelessly apart from his fellow human beings. Rarely indeed, in these writings, is there any intimation that the therapist can have the rewarding, and even exciting, experience of seeing a schizophrenic patient become free from the chains of 'concrete'[4]–that is, undifferentiated–thinking, able now to converse with his fellow human beings in consensually validated metaphor, and able, as a result of this same double-edged process of increasing differentiation, to share their recognition of the world of concrete things as being truly concrete.

I shall describe two sample cases, among several in my experience, in whom this emergence occurred. In tracing the process of thought differentiation in the recovering schizophrenic patient, I shall focus largely upon the emergence of *metaphorical* thinking

---

[3] I use the term 'metaphor' not in a grammatically strict fashion, but as a blanket term to include such related expressions as similes and figures of speech, all of which may be considered approximately equivalent in their psychodynamic significance which will be investigated here.
[4] Throughout this paper I shall place this term in quotation marks, to distinguish it from mature, *genuinely* concrete thinking.

(that is to say, upon the acquisition of the capacity for *symbolic* thinking). But it must be remembered that this differentiation process is a double-edged or double-armed one, and I shall include a few examples of the less dramatic, though equally important, emergence of truly *concrete* thinking which constitutes the other edge or arm of the over-all differentiation process.

This paper will endeavour to demonstrate three interrelated conceptual points. First, in order for the above-mentioned differentiation to be achieved, the patient must develop reliably firm ego boundaries. Secondly, these boundaries can be formed only in proportion as he becomes able to experience various repressed *emotions*. Thirdly, these emotions have been maintained under repression by his unconscious defensive use of this very instability of ego boundaries, and similar use of the 'concrete' thinking which that instability permits.

Sample Cases

PATIENT A

The first patient is a 42-year-old man with paranoid schizophrenia, whom I had been treating at the time of writing for five years. For many years he had led an extremely lonely life at home with his schizoid father, and during those years had found much of his 'interpersonal' experience in his relationship with his cat. Upon becoming overtly psychotic at the age of 35 he had begun making philosophical observations of which his family had never suspected him to be capable. Among these observations was, 'People should love *people*, not *cats*.'

In the early years of my work with him, I found much evidence that his ego differentiation was rudimentary – much evidence that he experienced no firm ego boundaries demarcating himself, as a human individual, from the outside world; and that he was unable to distinguish clearly, at a deep psychological level, among the three great classes of objects in the outside world: inanimate things; living but non-human things such as animals and plants; and, finally, human beings.

For instance, there was abundant evidence of massive projection, not only on to human beings around him but also on to trees, animals, buildings, and all sorts of inanimate objects. Rather than experiencing his own precarious personality integration as such, he felt intensely threatened, for many months, that the building in which he was living might fall to pieces at any moment. In course of time I came to realize that his great difficulty in leaving my office, at the end of the sessions, resided in the fact that he had come to experience the office as part of himself, that departure from it threatened him with a loss of his identity. His intense, mixed, and rapidly changing feelings were for years largely inaccessible to his awareness and were projected on to the climatic elements, so that, unable to know what he was experiencing within himself, he remained fascinated for years with the changing weather, and felt uneasily somehow responsible for the rain, the sunshine, the chill winds, and so on.

His anxiety lest he lose his identity in close interpersonal relationships caused him to isolate himself, to a marked degree, from patients and personnel, of whom, and to whom, he habitually spoke with a kind of dehumanizing scorn and rejectingness, as if they were inanimate objects, so that many of them would hotly remind him that they were human beings. Much of his time he spent on solitary walks into the village, and after many months he revealed to me that he loved to stand before the store windows, feeling himself to be in vivid group interaction with the mannequins, both 'adult' and 'child' ones, which stood in the windows, and which his unconscious loneliness caused him to perceive as being more truly human than were the alien objects which constituted, in his view, the people at Chestnut Lodge. As late as three years after the beginning of our work together, he said, while looking at a picture of an empty boat on my wall, 'It looks lonesome,' with a peculiar tone precisely as if it were a human being of whom he was speaking.

He had reason to fear the loss of his identity as a human individual, for this was indeed precarious. On one occasion he said, 'I guess I'm just nothing,' in a completely literal tone, and later on said in a similarly concretistic manner, 'I'm like tissue paper'; and on a windy day he expressed a serious fear that he might be blown away by the wind. In so far as he gradually came to feel that we at times treated him fondly here, he felt that we were treating him 'like an animal', for this, it developed, was the way he had treated his beloved cat over the lonely years at home.

For nearly two years his impact upon other persons here

was somehow not quite that of a human being. A small, thin person who for several months lay flat, motionless, and nearly mute on his bed, he seemed not only to me but also to an interim therapist, who saw him during one of my vacations, like little more than an unusually large wrinkle in the bedcover. As the months wore on and he became gradually a bit more active, he would materialize in a ghostly way at my office door, and then would lie crumpled in the chair throughout the hour, like an empty sack. He took to lying thus out on the front lawn, and one of my private patients came to a session considerably shaken, reporting that she had seen what seemed to be a bundle of clothes on the front lawn, then on closer inspection had found that there was someone in it. About two years later he became able to confide to me his feeling that he was conterminous with the bed in which he was now again lying, during a brief repetition of his regressive behaviour, and to reveal to me also that he experienced me as being quite literally a part of the chair in which I sat near his bed.

Although he became able, after about two years, to communicate verbally throughout his sessions with me, I found him maddeningly and discouragingly unable to deal with any comments which I couched in figurative terms. When, for example, antagonized by his self-righteous demandingness, I told him abruptly, 'You can't have your cake and eat it, too!' I felt completely helpless when he responded to this at a literal, 'concrete' level, by saying, 'I don't want to eat any cake in this hospital! *You* can eat cake here, if you want to; *I* don't want to eat any cake here.' One can see how his concretistic interpretation of my figure of speech enabled him to avoid the affective meaning of my comment.

On another occasion, he was protesting about a prospective move to an outpatient residence of his own, apart from his family, asserting that other patients he knew had gone back to their families. I reminded him gently that, because his father had died and his brother and sisters had dispersed to other cities during his hospitalization, this was, as I put it, 'just not on the cards for you, is it?' He was able to avoid the affective implications of this metaphor—able to avoid, for example, the sense of loss implied here—by experiencing my comment in literal terms: he retorted, as though I had accused him of some immoral activity, 'I'm not playing cards!' These are but two among many hundreds of examples from my work with him.

For approximately three years he rather consistently reacted to me as being crazy, quite seriously and frighteningly crazy, on the thousands of occasions when I tried to help him see the metaphorical, or otherwise symbolic, meaning in his own verbal communications.

One incident which helped me to understand why he was as yet unable to think in figurative terms occurred during one of the many sessions when evidently he was finding me to be discouragingly unresponsive and unmoved by his helpless plight. He commented, 'Always angry—my therapist is always angry at me,' and then said, in the same tone of discouragement and exasperation, that his sister had written that she had purchased some chairs for her apartment, chairs made of iron, so heavy that one could move them only with great difficulty. I replied, 'And you feel, perhaps, that your therapist is like the heavy chairs— very hard to move?' He laughed as though my comment were ridiculous, saying, 'No, I know you're not a chair, Dr Searles. . . . There's a chair,' he said, pointing to the chair over at my desk, 'and there's Dr Searles,' he finished, pointing at me. I realized now that as yet he could just *barely* distinguish between the chair and his therapist, even at a *concrete* level; and that if he had to struggle to discriminate such perceptions at a concrete level, he was in no condition as yet to attempt the facile symbolizing of one by the other which metaphorical thinking entails.

It gradually became apparent to me that his literal mode of thought, serving as an unconscious defence against a welter of repressed affects, was a product of the tenuousness of his ego boundaries. This revealed, therefore, the defensive usefulness of his regression to a state of incomplete differentiation of ego boundaries.

A number of writers—including Ferenczi (1913), Sharpe (1940), Langer (1942, p. 100), Kubie (1953), Little (1957, 1958), and Freeman *et al.* (1958, ch. 8)—have noted that the establishment of firm ego boundaries is necessary to the evolution of metaphorical thinking. But those writers do not describe this psychodynamic mechanism which I have just mentioned, and which I have seen clearly illustrated in my work with various patients including this man. Usually the loss of ego boundaries is regarded as a final, grievous *result* of the schizophrenic process, and in a sense this is so. But I have found it of the greatest value, in my therapeutic work, to realize that this loss of ego boundaries is one of the most vigorously formidable *defence mechanisms* which comprise the schizophrenic process.[5] This latter view is not only accurate, but is particularly conducive to our approaching the chronic schizophrenic patient not as being solely a grievously broken object for our compassion, but as being also, like every other living person, a creature imbued with limitless energy and the unquenched potential, therefore, for limitless growth and change.

I shall give only one more example, especially memorable to me, among many available in my records, of this defensive functioning of the schizophrenic's literalness of thought and of the incompleteness of ego boundaries which made possible that mode of thought. This man, even after a year of living in the same single room, showed little evidence of feeling at home in it; he evidently suffered from a persistent experience of the furnishings of the room as belonging exclusively to the hospital. He seemed to feel almost no freedom at all to rearrange the furniture in the slightest degree to his own greater comfort and convenience, or to make any easeful use of it where it stood.

One day I noticed that a small rough rug, back from the cleaner's, was folded over the back of the upholstered chair in which he customarily sat during our sessions. As usual, he did nothing about its uncomfortable bulk, and only once commented, in a quiet, neutral tone, that the maid had not yet put it back on the floor.

---

[5] The nearest approximation to this point which I have found in the literature is in a paper by Hartmann (1950b), entitled, 'Comments on the Psychoanalytic Theory of the Ego':

'The autonomous factors of ego development . . . may secondarily get under the influence of the drives, as is the case in sexualization or aggressivization. To give you only one example: in analysis we observe how the function of perception, which has certainly an autonomous aspect, may be influenced – and frequently handicapped – by becoming the expression of oral-libidinous or oral-aggressive strivings. . . .

'The autonomous factors may . . . become involved in the ego's defense against instinctual tendencies, against reality, and against the superego . . .'

My point is that not merely specific ego functions, such as perception, may become sacrificed in the service of unconscious defence against anxiety (from whatever source), but that even the very boundaries of the ego itself may fluctuate, may be in large part relinquished, in the last-ditch struggle against anxiety of psychotic proportions.

CONCRETE AND METAPHORICAL THINKING

During our next session, the rug was still there. In the course of the hour, while showing relatively little anxiety and talking quite freely, he started to lean back comfortably in the chair. But he instantly caught himself and quickly leaned forward again, saying, in an anxious tone, 'I don't want–' and left the sentence unfinished. I encouraged him to say what he had in mind, and he explained, 'I don't want the rug to get into my hair.' This was said in such a tone, impossible to reproduce here, as to give me the startling realization that he was afraid not that *lint from* the rug would get into his hair, but rather that the rug *itself* would do so–as if the rug, actually several feet across, were so much smaller than his hair that the whole of it could get lost or swallowed up in it.

It was some weeks later that he became able to recognize and express some of the quite evidently deep resentment which such behaviour on the part of the maid caused him. He became able now, that is, to experience and describe it, that such things as this incident of the rug 'got in his hair', one might say, in a figurative sense–that is, they *irritated* him. Previously he had seemed genuinely unaware of any irritation and had experienced, instead, something in the realm of weird anxiety such as I had momentarily sensed.[6]

As the years went on, hand in hand with the development of firmer boundaries about his own ego and boundaries between the three broad classes of perceived objects in the outer world, he became able more and more to communicate with me in metaphorical terms. The first such incident occurred near the end of

[6] A deeply ego-fragmented woman who chronically plucked hairs from her scalp startled me in a similar way when she made clear that she was trying exasperatedly to get 'bugs' out of the inside of her cranium. It was only later on in her therapy that she became able to realize that she, in a figurative sense, 'was "bugs" ', or 'had bugs in her head', so to speak. She had left off her hair-plucking, and it was now something far more severe than exasperation which she was evidently feeling: she said to herself in a low voice, full of shock and awe, 'I'm crazy.' Previously she had been too ill – her ego had been too weak – to let this realization dawn upon her. One could see, now, that her erstwhile so-defective ego boundaries had enabled her to experience it, instead, only that these exasperating bugs were inside her brain. That had been by no means comfortable for her, but its impact was trivial when compared with that of her realization that she had a devastatingly severe mental illness.

Another deeply schizophrenic woman confided to me, 'I had a dream last night. They had taken out all my teeth and put people in place of them and then ground them down.' This dream experience was hardly more distorted than much of the waking life of this woman whose ego boundaries (including, of course, the body image) were remarkably fluid. It required years of further psychotherapy before she began to realize, in a figurative sense, what was being expressed literally in the

567

the fourth year of our work, when he returned from what had evidently been an unusually comfortable vacation of several days with relatives in St Louis. After he had described, with great interest, how many architectural changes had occurred there in recent years, dwelling particularly upon some buildings which are a blend of both old and new, I commented that perhaps he himself sometimes felt like such a remodelled building, a blend of both old and new qualities. For the first time, now, he did not say, 'You're crazy,' or 'You think funny,' or 'I don't think in comparisons,' or 'I'm not a building,' but was able to take up this comment and elaborate upon it, indicating that he felt in some ways both adult and child. After five years of work, he could communicate confidently, with rare exceptions, in metaphorical as well as literal terms, seeing both levels of meanings in his own comments and in mine.

PATIENT B

The second patient, a 38-year-old paranoid schizophrenic man whom I have been treating for four and a half years showed initially a far greater impairment of ego boundaries, and of perceived boundaries between the three classes of objects in the outer world which I have mentioned, than did the man of whom I have just been speaking. This second patient, until recent months, and even still to a lesser degree, has shown the persistent conviction that people can quite literally be turned into trees or animals or buildings or rocks, and vice versa; and has expressed, innumerable times, the conviction that he himself exists and has existed in such forms. It was approximately two years ago that, as his recovery gradually proceeded, I became able more and more readily to detect, in his almost incredibly 'crazy' talk, nuclei of figurative truth. When, as one simple example, he protested that

dream; the fact of herself having 'ground down' – so to speak – persons close to her, with an extremely powerful and persistent castrativeness. Significantly, I had been feeling unusually ground down by her during our hour on the preceding day – the day of the dream. But she was still far from being able to accept her own wish to do this to me and to others. Instead, the potential realization presented itself to her in a thrice-disguised form: (a) in a *dream*; (b) filled with *projection* – 'they' did all this; and (c) the case in point here: literalized or '*concretized*', with the people being transformed into teeth which are then literally ground down.

It is not a handful of such examples which have convinced me of the validity of the psychodynamic mechanism which I have outlined above, but rather many dozens, and perhaps hundreds, encountered over the years.

people are turned into sheep, this had a less completely literal ring to it, so that one could easily hear this in terms of modern technology's turning human individuals into herds of sheep. But for an additional year he flatly insisted, as always, that he meant this in literal, concrete terms, not in any figurative sense.

It was, then, after about three and a half years' therapy that he himself became able to see on occasion, though not yet consistently, the figurative meaning in his own perceptions and communications, and with this change, of course, not only I but other people found him less crazy, more a person with whom one could talk sensibly. Now, for example, when he was looking at his careworn face in a mirror and commented to a nurse standing nearby, 'That face is awful. It's an apartment building,' and the nurse asked him what he saw in his face that made him compare it with an apartment building, he did not bizarrely insist this time that it *was* an apartment building. Instead he explained with wry humour, 'It's white, lined, haggard, and has no life!'

I was impressed repeatedly, over the year that followed, in which his ability to communicate metaphorically grew steadily, to see how the de-repression of long-unconscious feelings was necessary to this process. For example, now when we were having session out on the lawn, as we often did, and he picked up a handful of dead leaves, showed them to me and said, 'These are people,' he was very clearly saying to me, 'This is how completely cast-off, useless, and forgotten some people, including me, feel themselves to be,' and was readily able, by this time, to elaborate upon the subject in this poignant figurative vein.

The long-repressed feelings of which he had to become aware in order to be capable, now fairly consistently, of metaphorical thinking and communication, are feelings which cover a wide range, including tenderness, erotic feelings, grief, hatred, and so on. Most memorable of all to me were the consequences of his becoming aware of the intensity and all-pervasiveness of his long-repressed murderous feelings. Such feelings proved, over the years of our work, particularly difficult for him to face. It had been his threats to murder his infant daughter which had led his family to place him in a psychiatric hospital, and in the early years of his treatment at Chestnut Lodge his convincing threats to murder a fellow patient had led to a stay of many months on the maximum-security ward. On hundreds of occasions, in the first three years of my work with him, he went into murderous rages which were frightening to everyone about him, including, at times, myself.

By about a year and a half before the writing of this paper his expressed delusional view of the surrounding world had altered, so as to make clear that now, to him, practically everything in the world which we would call non-human (animals, plants, buildings, and so on) was a human being who had been turned, through the greatest sort of *violence*, into something non-human and was waiting desperately to be liberated into a human form again. About six months later, when the roots of this delusion were being unearthed still further, I became increasingly impressed, and even awed, at the degree of murderous feeling which he possessed towards *all* his fellow human beings. Many times in preceding years I had realized that it was repressed hostility towards various individuals which in part accounted for his experiencing of them, on different occasions, as metamorphosing into for example, a tree or a rock. But I had never before seen the full intensity, and particularly the universally directed nature, of his murderousness towards *all* human beings.

It was not until this full extent of his murderous feeling had been revealed, to himself as well as to me, that there appeared, so soon as to be practically hand-in-hand with this development, evidence that he was now on the threshold of metaphorical thinking and experiencing, not simply in the form of sporadic excursions into this area, but as a consistent realm of existence–the same realm occupied by his adult fellow human beings. I shall never forget the excitement of finding, in one particular session at the apex of this development, that his utterances could now be best understood, not in the frame of reference of increasingly intense homicidal violence, but in terms of a struggle to become liberated from concretistic thought, into the realm of interpersonally meaningful symbolism, including metaphor.[7] Thus when

[7] A fellow therapist – Dr Berl D. Mendel, who kindly permits me to use the clinical item which follows – was working with a schizophrenic woman who had been, for years, dangerously assaultive, but had become appreciably less so by this time. During the course of a relatively comfortable walk together on the hospital grounds, she commented, 'They're going to kill Edna,' referring to one of her fellow patients whom she clearly valued unusually much. She said this in a comfortable tone, rather than in the tone of murderousness with which she had often referred to killing, earlier in the therapy. The therapist replied, reassuringly and in a similarly comfortable tone, 'You're not going to kill Edna.' She then went on, 'They're going to roll her up into

he now referred, in a puzzled way, to a certain chair in the near-by living room as being his younger sister Marian, of whom I knew him to be fond, I realized that, although he insisted he meant this literally, as usual, his puzzlement indicated that he was struggling to see *in what sense*–namely, a metaphorical one–this was actually true; he could not yet experience it that something about the chair *reminded him of* his sister, and that it there-fore *symbolized* her to him. But it proved to be only a short while after this that he became able increasingly often, as I have indicated, to make such a conceptual leap.

For this particular man, as I say, the de-repression of *murder-ous* feelings has been especially crucial to the evolution of meta-phorical thinking. He had to become able to look at his pervasive hatred in at least the degree which this comment of his indicates: 'Why, it's getting so you're making me hate the whole human race!' and to go on subsequently to assume greater personal ownership of this hatred, in order to achieve the evolution of thinking which I have described. For years he had transposed, in his comments, and clearly often in his actual subjective experi-ence also, the sexes of persons in his current life and in his remembered past–referring to (or in conversation addressing) a woman as a man, and vice versa. He explained, now, like a parent explaining to a child, the meaning of hatred: 'To hate means to change a person's sex,' and I realized that, by exten-sion, to hate still more intensely (at an unconscious level) meant, for him, the perceiving of the person as being changed into something non-human such as a rock or a tree.

Thus for quite some time thereafter, in applying this clinical

a Christmas tree,' saying this in a completely literal fashion, without its conveying any figurative meaning at all to the therapist. At this point he gestured towards a nearby birch tree and said, jokingly, 'Why not into a birch tree? There's a birch tree.' She replied very emphatically, 'You don't understand the Chinese metaphor!' It had long been established between them that her idiosyncratic way of communi-cating, which involved many neologisms, was 'My Chinese'.

Both he and I felt that his patient was, like mine whom he had heard me describe, at the borderline between 'concrete' – undifferentiated – and metaphorical thinking, in which she was only now becoming clear that to *symbolize* a dear person by a Christmas tree is not really equivalent to *killing* that person – equivalent, that is, to literally rolling the person up into the tree. My patient spent many months in indubitable distress and anxiety about the cherished people from her past who were, she was convinced, imprisoned within the trees, the walls of the building, the furniture, and so on, and tried desperately to devise ways to liberate them.

Werner (1957, p. 194) employs a phrase which I find very apt in this connexion: 'the domination of the concrete field'.

material to conjectures about the development of metaphorical thinking in the normal child, I felt much impressed with how important it is that he be able to be aware of his murderous feelings, be able to translate them into metaphorical thinking, to sublimate them into the kind of adult metaphor which, after all, in a sense does violence to human beings by transforming, conceptually, a faithful person into a dog, or an ill-tempered one into a bear, or an unyielding one into a rock.

But I have come to believe, subsequently, that in the case of this particular man, murderous feelings held an atypical prominence in this process for reasons in his personal life history. Dr Lyman C. Wynne at the National Institute of Mental Health, in describing to me his observation of less deeply schizophrenic patients' transitorily reverting, in the face of upsurges of anxiety, from figurative to literal communication, has helped me to become aware of the function of concrete thinking in maintaining under repression *various* anxiety-laden affects. I think it enough to conclude that the awareness of emotion–whether murderousness, tenderness, grief, or whatever; awareness of the whole spectrum of emotion–is the father to metaphorical thought and, perhaps in the same way, to all forms of the symbolic thought which distinguishes the adult human being.

Hand in hand with this man's gradually coming to experience a realm of metaphorical thought, more and more clearly differentiated as such, he became able to differentiate concrete things as being genuinely concrete, free from the metaphorical coloration which had formerly made them nebulous. For years, every object which we would call concrete had been, for him, primarily a *symbol* of some complex, vaguely defined, and delusionally distorted area of his world as he himself experienced that world. As one among many hundreds of possible examples, he once patiently explained to me, 'Whenever you see a red brick building, it's part of British investment. Whenever you see a Schlage lock or a Yale lock, it's part of the chain system.'

In another session, when I had learned from the nurses' report that he had not been able to get to sleep until 3 A.M., he complained to me that 'Those electronic creeps wouldn't let me get to sleep until three this morning,' and went on to say that during the preceding evening, when he had been 'over at the [occupational and recreational therapy] Centre, six ash trays jumped on my back. How can I do anything with those on my back?' In so protesting, he gestured in such a way as to indicate that he still felt, vaguely, that the ash trays were on his back. When I pressed him for further information about this, he said that 'All those old war veterans' were on his back. I told him that I didn't understand, and wanted to understand, what he was saying.

As often happened, I was holding a glass ash tray, and I commented, 'Now, this is an ash tray, isn't it?' He replied, tiredly, as if it were just impossible to get the point across to me, 'How many sides does it have?' indicating that he himself knew—which I felt sure he did–and simply wanted me to count them and thus get the point. I counted them and said, 'Six,' at which he nodded significantly and concludingly, as though that explained it. But as if for good measure, he emphasized in no uncertain terms that it *is* (literally) a patient, saying, 'All worn down–that's what they do to patients.' In retrospect it occurred to me that the 'six', because the word is phonetically equivalent to 'sicks', helped to give the ash tray the connotation, for him, of a patient, and its smooth surface probably symbolized the 'all worn down', 'old war veterans', the depressed and chronically ill patients of whom one almost always sees a few at the Centre. But for him, even after several years of intensive psychotherapy, the ash tray was not yet experientially differentiated into a genuinely *concrete* object which was, at the same time, a *symbol of* the patients. It *was a patient*, just as the patients themselves *were ash trays*.

But as the figurative realm eventually became separated out, more and more, as such, so also did the genuinely concrete realm. One of the simplest, and to me most memorable, instances of this development occurred towards the end of the several-months' phase, to which I have already referred, of his being preoccupied with all sorts of physical objects, both natural and man-made, as being human bodies. He had now established an unusually friendly and comfortable relationship with a woman who worked at the Centre, in the occupational therapy department. This woman, in the course of expressing her enthusiasm to me about how realistically the patient was now speaking, told me how the latter had come to respond to a woman patient's building a desk over there. She had been working on this for two or three weeks, and he had always referred to the object as a 'body'–long after its general outlines had become clearly recognizable to a normal person. The occupational therapist described it, 'But the other day he said, "Oh, you're making a desk!" Always before, he made something of things [i.e. referred to them as being the bodies of various persons]. Maybe he'll make something of the desk, too [i.e. revert to so experiencing it]; but for a moment, anyway, it was a desk.'

Discussion

The process which I have traced above in the two case descriptions can be seen, in a larger context, as one important phase of the over-all differentiation process through which human psychic experience evolves from early infancy to maturity. That is, when one reaches back still further, in investigating the subjective experience of patients who are even more deeply regressed, as best one can discern it these patients are not experiencing any thoughts at all. They are evidently immersed, instead, in a world of pictures, a world permeated by the hallucinatory wish fulfilment which Freud (1900, pp. 566–7) and Ferenczi (1913) and many subsequent writers have described as being a precursor of thinking in early ego development. They seem not to be sufficiently differentiated, or distanced, from this world of subjective perceptions in which they are engrossed, to be able to experience anything so abstract, so detached from immediate sensory experience, as *thoughts*.

Putting such clinical findings together with those which I have mentioned above, the intensive psychotherapy of deeply schizophrenic patients provides many data to support Fenichel's description of the sequences in the development of the capacity for abstract thinking: '. . . the drive to discharge tensions . . . is slowed down [by the maturing ego] . . . and the tendency to hallucinatory wish fulfilment . . . is reduced to the imagination of the prospective events and subsequently of the abstract symbols of these events' (1945).

I had worked with schizophrenic patients for several years before I came to realize that the deeply schizophrenic individual has, subjectively, no imagination. The moment that something which *we* would call a new concoction of fantasy, a new product of his imagination, enters his awareness, *he* perceives this as being an actual and undisguised attribute of the world around him. He cannot yet experience a realm of the imagination, differentiated as such, demarcated from the realm of perception of real events round about. Similarly, memories of past events are experienced by him not as such, but rather as literal re-enactments of those events by the persons around him.

Tausk's comment that the schizophrenic experiences both such preverbal pictures and later thoughts as coming from the *outside* world, rather than initially as *inner* phenomena, has been substantiated repeatedly in my work with patients:

> In the period [of infancy] here duplicated pathologically [i.e. in the adult schizophrenic patients whom Tausk studied] there are indeed no thoughts, but even thoughts are . . . regarded at first as coming from the outer world before they are accounted among the functions of the ego. . . . Freud[8] has taught us that [the stage of memory perceptions] . . ., too, is a later process, and that it is preceded by the stage of hallucinations of memory pictures, that is, a stage when the perceptions actually appear in the outer world and are not regarded as inner occurrences (Tausk, 1919).

The volume by Inhelder and Piaget (1958) entitled *The Growth of Logical Thinking from Childhood to Adolescence*, presents evidence that in the course of maturation the individual exists in a state of subjective non-differentiation from the world about him, not merely in the *earliest* phase of life but in *three* successive phases–during those phases, that is, when he is in process of achieving the successive steps in the development of adult thinking. Their terminology is somewhat difficult to integrate into psycho-analytic concepts; but in essence thay describe this non-differentiation (in their terminology, 'egocentrism') as occurring (*a*) in early childhood (and, presumably, infancy), at the 'sensorimotor' level of thought development; (*b*) in later childhood, on the 'representational' (i.e. first stages of symbolic thought) level; and (*c*) in adolescence, on the experiential level of formal thought or cognition.

Viewing such sequences in the development of thinking from an *interpersonal* viewpoint is, of course, particularly useful for the therapist who is working with the schizophrenic patient. We find that the deeply regressed patient must establish a reasonably

---

[8] Tausk does not mention where, in Freud's writings, this concept is presented; but see *Interpretation of Dreams*, p. 543.

satisfactory mode of relatedness with his therapist (and with other people) at each successive level, before the next level can be attained. We find, for example, that as Ruesch (1955) aptly phrases it, '. . . the patient has to gain communicative experience in the nonverbal mode before he can engage in verbal exchange.'

In my experience, communicating with the non-verbal patient by means of gestures, facial expressions, touching, and so on, involves a sense of *intimacy* between us to which we both, it appears, need a good deal of time to become accustomed; certainly I, at least, tend to shy away from it on this account. But I have found it quite essential that such a non-verbal mode of relatedness be shared before the next step, of 'concrete'–undifferentiatedly literal and figurative–*verbal* communication, can be achieved. It is noteworthy, also, that as this next phase becomes established, we feel not only that a new world has opened up before us, but also that another world, a deeply cherished one–namely, the world of a kind of oceanic non-verbal relatedness–must be largely relinquished as we enter this new and more structured realm of communication.

Once the verbal phase of therapy has become firmly established at a 'concrete' level, it becomes clear–in work with such a person as Patient A, whose course of treatment I described earlier–that, before the patient can enter the metaphorical realm of communication, he must first become sure that he can make himself understood at the literal level of meaning. Thus, I have learned painfully and slowly that, when a patient makes an intendedly concrete communication, it is a mistake to respond in terms of its potential metaphorical meaning without first acknowledging its validity as a statement of literal fact. It is as though the patient–and analogously, the healthy young child–must first become assured of his ability to make contact with the therapist (or parent) at the more primitive levels of relatedness, before he can face the greater sense of apartness which must be braved, in successive degrees of intensity, in attaining successively abstract modes of thought and interpersonal relatedness.

With certain of my patients, I have seen evidence that when in childhood they had reached the threshold of figurative thinking, they did not receive from their parents the necessary help in sorting out figurative from literal meanings. When

CONCRETE AND METAPHORICAL THINKING

Patient B, for example, would go to his mother in puzzlement and say, 'I feel as though I'm walking on quicksand,' his mother would abruptly reply, 'You're crazy!' being herself too anxious and guilt-ridden to help the child verbalize his anxieties. Such responses, received thousands of times on such occasions, reinforced the boy's feeling of being a creature apart from his fellow men, a creature who lived in a different world from them and who, he evidently often felt, *literally* walked somehow on quicksand.

One of my women patients, who as a child had often taken care of several of her younger siblings, described to me how, at about twelve years of age, she had gone to her parents and said, 'I know that I'm a mother and that I've had babies.' She told me that her doing this had been precipitated by a 'dream' or 'realization' to this effect–she was not sure which–and she emphasized how pleased she had felt at this discovery. The response she obtained from them was as follows: her father turned back to the book he was writing, began writing rapidly and shuffling papers about; her mother said sharply, 'You're crazy–you couldn't have had babies if you haven't had any association with boys–then you must have had associations with boys,' and began blaming the patient. 'So I wished I hadn't said anything,' she concluded. It is conceivable that a more comfortable mother might have helped the child relate this discovery to the fact of her daily care of the younger children–and, hopefully, might even have been able to help her see it in terms of her identifying with, and wanting to emulate, her often pregnant mother from whom a succession of babies had come. It would seem that such parental responses as those she actually received would tend to throw a child repeatedly back into a world felt as unrelievedly concrete, and a world increasingly grotesque because of the figurative meanings which come more and more, over the years, to permeate this world but unacknowledged as figurative by the persons around her.

In the instance of Patient B, I found that many of the responses of the nurses and aides, responses to this man when he had come to the phase in therapy of needing to sort out figurative from concrete meanings, provided a welcome contrast to the kind of parental responses I have noted above. Time after time, in an unplanned but patient, warmly welcoming spirit, they

577

sensed and responded to the accurate figurative meanings latent in his crazy-sounding concretistic concepts, and thereby helped him to become able to function on this level of figurative thinking and communication.

It was a memorable occasion when he had developed sufficient trust in me to say, 'See, this is the way I think: . . .,' and proceeded to supply, for my examination, an unusually candid sample of his undifferentiated, delusional thinking. It was this degree of trust in the other person, this degree of reassurance that the other had time for him and could tolerate this level of closeness with him–and, when we consider it, we see that it calls for an extraordinary degree of closeness with another person to be able to discuss these things together–which he had evidently been unable to obtain in his relationship with his anxious and guilt-ridden parents.

In some instances a patient may function in such a way as to render his immediate interpersonal world devoid of anyone who is able to catch the potentially figurative meanings of his communications. This state of affairs may first become detectable to the therapist's supervisor, who is far enough removed from the immediate impact of the patient's anxiety to be able to perceive these more covert meanings. Until some such development occurs, the patient may go on living in a world as deaf to figurative meanings as was the world of childhood, and as unable to help him make the differentiation between metaphorical and concrete thinking on his own part.

When a patient's thinking processes have matured, in the course of successful therapy, to the point where he is now *close to* the awareness of clearly differentiated metaphorical meanings, but not yet quite aware of them, the therapist oftentimes has the stressful experience of sensing poignant metaphorical meanings in the patient's remarks, messages which the patient is as yet unaware of conveying, messages having an affective impact with which the therapist must therefore cope in a state of felt aloneness. This kind of experience did not confront the therapist earlier in the relationship, when the patient's thinking was so very undifferentiated that only quite 'concrete' communications were the order of the day. But now he finds himself experiencing at first hand, as it were, the kind of isolation which the child who later becomes schizophrenic must feel in so far as the latter starts to grasp metaphorical meanings in a family where the parents have unconsciously to deny any such meanings.

I recall, for example, a schizoid young woman who, when she had reached this phase in the differentiation of her thinking, commented scornfully in passing, during one of her sessions, that the elderly grandmother of a girl friend had written to the latter, from California, 'that she's afraid because the leaves are falling so fast this autumn'. Although my patient's only conscious affect seemed to be one of scorn about this statement as having to do with a 'silly' fear, her communication evoked in me a poignant picture of a lonely old woman who, frightened because death was taking so many of her contemporaries and could not be far off for her, was trying to reach out to her young granddaughter.

Another patient, in the comparable phase of therapy, was describing the sewing ability of a woman in a neighbouring room, a woman who, as she had mentioned in an earlier session, had been separated from her son and daughter for several years. In a context purely of interest in describing to me this woman's sewing skill, my patient commented, in a puzzled tone, 'Mrs L told me the other day that she hasn't put any hem in the skirt she made for her daughter, because she didn't know how long to make it.' Again in this instance, the patient seemed entirely unaware of the wealth of metaphorical meaning which she was conveying to me – the wealth of meaning as to how out of touch a mother comes to feel towards her growing children, when she is separated from them by years of severe mental illness and, in this instance, many hundreds of miles distance.

It is no wonder that therapists often seem, to the supervisor, slow to sense metaphorical meanings when, as in such instances as the two I have just given, their discovery of such meanings only exposes them to volumes of meaning and affect of which the patient is as yet quite unaware, and which the therapist must therefore put on file, as it were, while going on conversing with the patient in the only terms – namely, literal terms – which as yet have meaning for the latter.

It is, of course, correct to view the schizophrenic's thought disorder as being attributable to, or at least worsened by, the *regression* involved in schizophrenia – although one encounters patients who, one feels, never had attained (even before the schizophrenia became overt) any full differentiation between

579

metaphorical and concrete thought. The role of regression has
been mentioned by Werner (1940) and Beres (1960), among
others. Werner (1940, p. 330), for example, says that 'In all
those cases where there is a regression to a more primitive form
of behaviour as a result of some mental disturbance, it will be
found that the reasoning process itself becomes undifferentiated.'

While accepting, of course, the concept of regression, I find
that Hartmann's (1939) synonym, 'dedifferentiation',[9] evokes a
clearer and more detailed picture of the process. Along with
Hartmann's (1953) use of the over-all term 'dedifferentiation' to
describe the regression which one sees in schizophrenia,[10] and
with the subordinate term 'de-animation' which Mahler (1958)
employs to designate the phenomenon, seen in early infantile
psychosis, of one's experiencing living things as being inanimate,
I wish to place the term 'desymbolization'. By this term I refer
to a process, seemingly at work in the schizophrenic patient,
whereby the illness causes once-*attained* metaphorical meanings
to become 'desymbolized'; and in the grip of the illness, the
individual reacts to them as being literal meanings which he
finds indeed most puzzling. This would seem to be one of the
important respects in which the thinking of the regressed schizophrenic adult differs from that of the normal child. The former
has been exposed, over the years since early childhood, to
thousands upon thousands of metaphorical communications, and
many of these–unless, as relatively seldom happens, his schizophrenia was prominent even in his childhood–he was once able
to grasp, to at least a fair degree, in their intendedly metaphorical meaning. But now this mass of communications has
undergone the process of desymbolization, so that they come
back to him, from bygone years, as being among the importantly
confusing 'crazy' thoughts he finds in his head–particularly so
when the communications came from the most significant
people in his past.

I first came to suspect the existence of this process of 'desymbolization' when, in my work with Patient B, I found him
trying confusedly to 'make' a body, literally, out of all sorts of

[9] Used also by Werner (1940, p. 188).
[10] In chapters 10 and 11 I have described the development of schizophrenia, and
the psychotherapy of it, in terms of the growth processes of integration and differentiation.

materials. Many data from that phase of our work suggested that the 'make' had a metaphorical–erotic–connotation; but he was entirely unable consciously to acknowledge any sexual feelings, and kept trying literally to *make* a body somehow. Further, I felt convinced that this man, who had led quite an active social life for many years before his hospitalization, had once been quite aware of the erotic, metaphorical meaning of the slang phrase, to 'make' somebody–i.e. to make a sexual conquest. Similarly, when part of his confused talk, for months, included references to 'their' planning *literally* to 'take up the land' somehow–as if all the visible land were about to be somehow 'taken up' by a giant machine–I sensed that this unconsciously referred to property deals in which his father had engaged, in which he had 'taken up' pieces of land, metaphorically speaking, bought them up. Again, I had no doubt that he had once been familiar with this term in its metaphorical usage. I realized, now, that dozens upon dozens of such phrases–many of which I no longer recall–had become the foci of confusion on his part, and the impetus for symptomatic behaviour which had persisted for many months.

A point which I cannot make too strongly is that for the deeply dedifferentiated schizophrenic patient, the *perceptual experience itself* is grossly distorted. That is to say, the distortion–the non-differentiation–is not limited simply to the realm of *thought* alone, in any mature meaning of that term. My findings from my work with adult schizophrenic patients are very much in line with an assumption of Werner (1940, p. 89):

> I do not believe that many of the so-called metaphors so common to children–that is, those in which a word denoting the one sensation is used to describe an unrelated sensation–are actual metaphors springing from any inadequacy of exact verbal expression. It is quite reasonable to assume that they are often rooted in an *actual undifferentiated experience of sensation* [my italics].

For example, when a schizophrenic patient told me of her recent conversation with a Catholic priest, a conversation during which she evidently had thoroughly bewildered him with delusional material of a teasingly anti-Catholic variety, and she commented to me that 'his ears looked like strange–they looked like a monkey's', I felt sure, from my long experience with her, that this was not simply an indirect way of communicating to me a conscious feeling of her having figuratively 'made a monkey of' him. I felt convinced, rather, that she genuinely had *perceived* him so, and I felt equally convinced by her expressed unawareness—in answer to this suggested explanation from me—that she had figuratively turned him into a monkey. There were, indeed, times when I felt that comparable statements from her were merely indirect modes of *communication*; but this was one of the many times when her anxiety level was so very great, and her ego organization so greatly dedifferentiated, that I felt sure this had been a genuine perceptual distortion.

Likewise, on various occasions when she looked much depressed, and seemed genuinely unaware of feeling so, I did not doubt that various things about her indeed 'looked blue' to her, as she said they did, and that she was genuinely unaware of feeling, figuratively speaking, 'blue'. Similarly, upon my making a comment which, I realized retrospectively, tended to be hurtful to this woman who could not permit herself to realize that she cared enough for me to be susceptible to my hurting her feelings, and her response was an agonized physical sensation that a bullet had been shot into her heart, I was left in no doubt whatever that this was, in truth, her way of experiencing my having *figuratively* pierced her to the heart. She evidently experienced it not as a figurative thought-concept, but purely as a somatic sensation. Another patient, while deeply psychotic, evidently experienced her own intense ambivalence, through a combined process of somatization and projection, as a distorted perception of the other person—a perception of him or her as being 'torn apart', physically dismembered. It was nearly two years later on in therapy that she was able meaningfully to agree with my comment that when we have strongly conflictual feelings, we feel 'torn apart' emotionally.

If space permitted, I could present such examples, from various patients of mine, by the dozen. Pathological though such experiences are on the part of schizophrenic adults, it seems to me that they give us a sample—albeit a warped one—of the extent to which somatic sensations participate in the development of metaphorical thinking in the normal child. As a crude example, one can surmise that before the child can come to understand such phrases as 'gives me a pain in the neck', or 'turns my stomach', or 'tears at my heartstrings' in their metaphorical meaning, relatively devoid of any somatic concomitants, he must first have *felt* their meaning as a partially, or perhaps even predominantly, somatic experience. Such clinical experiences as those I have mentioned have clarified, for me, Kubie's comment that

every symbol refers simultaneously to concepts which are derived from body needs and images, and to concepts which are derived from percepts of the outside world. Consequently, every symbolic unit hangs like a hammock between two poles, one internal or bodily (the 'I') and one external (the 'Non-I') (Kubie, 1953).

Thus, although it is correct to say that without the establishment of firm ego boundaries, a differentiation between metaphorical meanings and literal meanings cannot take place, it would seem equally correct to say that metaphor, at least, could never develop if there had not once been a *lack of* such ego boundaries—if there had never been, as we believe there always has been, in infancy, a relatively unimpeded flow between the areas of experience which come, later, to be felt as inner world and outer world.

Mendel (personal communication, 1959) makes the point that as a rule the schizophrenic is unaware of the richness of metaphor for the reason that, although what he says is often heard by us as being metaphorical, he himself is unaware of the distinction between the concrete and the metaphorical, and it is this distinction which gives metaphor its richness. To this, I would add the conjecture that perhaps the reason why so many metaphors have a peculiarly poignant beauty is because each of them kindles in us, momentarily a dim memory of the time when we lost the outer world—when we first realized that the outer world *is* outside, and we are unbridgeably apart from it, and alone. Further, the *mutual sharing* of such metaphorical experience would seem, thus, to be about as intimate a psychological contact as adult human being can have with one another.

Chapter 20

PROBLEMS OF PSYCHO-ANALYTIC SUPERVISION (1962)[1]

THE typical student who comes for supervision, early in his psycho-analytic training, has developed a considerable degree of confidence in himself as a *therapist*. He feels himself to be imbued with qualities of human warmth, spontaneity, and actively participative therapeutic dedication which, he is privately convinced, enable him to help suffering human beings. But, typically, his personal analysis is still far from completion and his view of psycho-*analysis* is greatly distorted by his unresolved negative transference to his analyst. He sees psychoanalysis as being, in essence, a personification of the harsh and depriving superego. He feels that psycho-analysis interdicts one's participating, at all freely, at an emotional level with the patient; an analyst must be instead, he believes, remote and ungiving, titrating any personal responses with careful precision.

He senses that a major shift in his personal identity will be involved if his psycho-analytic training is to be more than a veneer to be worn for the sake of increased professional prestige. He feels faced with the threat that he will be forced to exchange a professional identity which he has achieved over years of arduous clinical experience, and which he cherishes–namely, a sense of identity as a psychotherapist–for an identity which will be not only very different but, so he is convinced, far more constricting–namely, an identity as a psycho-analyst. If he is relatively young, inexperienced, and unsure of himself, he will approach the supervision in a spirit of guardedness and of shame and embarrassment about his own style of personal responsiveness to his patient. If he is relatively experienced and sure of himself as a therapist, he will come for supervision in a spirit more of open defiance and thinly-veiled contempt and disdain or the supervisor as a psycho-analyst–as being one of that breed

[1] First published in *Science and Psychoanalysis*, Vol. 5, edited by J. H. Masserman. (New York: Grune & Stratton, 1962.)

who hold themselves apart and are afraid to be 'really giving' to patients. The supervisor's very designation, as 'supervisor' or 'control analyst', tends all the more to give him the significance, to the student, of a feared, hated, or despised superego.

Unless we take fully into account such attitudes which the student brings into supervision, there is real danger that he will go through his analytic training and become an analyst in name only, privately convinced that there is an unbridgeable gulf between therapy and analysis, privately feeling himself to be a therapist still, and with unresolved hostility and contempt for what he conceives to be psycho-analysis, the essentials of which he has never become really open to learning.

Although such neurotic attitudes on the part of the student must be coped with predominantly in his personal analysis, the way in which these are met by his supervisors may make a crucial difference. The supervisory orientation which I have found most effective and realistic is predominantly a lateral, rather than a vertical or hierarchical, orientation: I am not literally a supervisor, in the ordinary sense of the term, who is endeavouring to control the student's treatment of the patient. I am, rather, a comparatively experienced colleague to one side, to whom he turns for help with his work. I am quite clear that I am working with him, not with the patient, and that I can be of maximal help to him to the extent that I can discover, with him, a larger and deeper understanding of what is going on between the patient and himself. This often entails, and requires, our achieving a fuller awareness of the processes taking place between ourselves, but this too is in the service of our understanding more adequately what is taking place in his relationship with the patient. These things I do not say to him; rather, they are implicit in the spirit with which I respond to him. One of the basic discoveries he will make, in the course of our work, if he has not previously discovered it, is that the gradual shift in identity, from therapist to analyst, involves personal growth rather than constriction. He will find that his already developed therapeutic capacities are basically good and useful, and that these will form part of the foundation of his new identity as analyst.

Very early I endeavour to become clear, in my own mind, how the student himself views his work with the patient, and what he himself is endeavouring to do in the treatment. The indispensable value of the supervisor's attentiveness to this point is comparable with the necessity, in analytic treatment itself, for one to attune oneself, as far as possible, to the patient's own subjective experience. I endeavour to keep to a minimum any interference with the student's own individual style of treatment; comparable again to the treatment situation itself, the other person must be left free to find that road to Rome which is most in keeping with his own capacities and interests. One is often tempted to try to indoctrinate the student with one's own individual style of conducting treatment; but respect for the other person's individuality is, in the long run, the only basis on which supervision, like analysis itself, will succeed.

I try to become clear very early, in my own mind, whether the student is coming for supervision primarily because he feels required to by higher authority, or whether his prime need is for help from me. I have had the painful experience, more than once, of a student's dropping his supervision at the moment when he had put in the number of hours required by the analytic institute; only then did I realize to what a degree he had been feeling coerced, rather than personally involved, in supervision, and I endeavour now to detect this situation early and clarify it with the student. Likewise, if he gets into a rut of simply mechanically reporting his sessions with the patient, in sequence, without venturing to tell me his own formulations of all these raw data, and without focusing upon any particular problem areas of the week's work, I encourage him to do so. Otherwise, he will tend to attribute his own best capacities to me, sit in more or less open-mouthed awe at my oracular formulations, mechanically try to apply my ideas and techniques to his work with the patient, without having made them genuinely his own, and thereby demonstrate, through the patient's adverse responses, that my views are asinine. This common problem can be seen as an evidence of the student's acting out his negative feelings by making a mockery of the supervisor; but I think it springs more fundamentally from a stubborn and healthy determination to be allowed to use his own best capacities, and to have them acknowledged as *his*.

In achieving his own potential larger self, he will on innumerable occasions need affirmation from the supervisor that the feelings he is having are 'all right' for him to be having, and that his responses to the patient are 'all right', too, or at any rate probably not irremediably destructive. Very often, he is hesitant to report to us his most therapeutically effective responses to the patient, for fear we shall think them not sufficiently 'analytic' – not in keeping, that is, with his view of classical psycho-analysis. We need to see how vulnerable he is to feeling caught between the patient's intense criticism on the one hand and the supervisor's disapproval on the other, so that his beleaguered areas of healthy self-esteem very much need our support and encouragement.

But the mellowing of the student's own neurotically punitive superego derives not only from such responses of encouragement and affirmation from us, but also from his finding that we are able to withstand, and assert ourselves in the face of, his own increasingly undisguised periods of criticism of, and dissatisfaction with, his supervisor. A too conscientious concern with making each supervisory hour useful to the student betrays the extent to which we have become intimidated by his own superego-reinforced infantile demandingness, and really postpones the day when he can find the strength and courage to hold firm in the face of the patient's demands. Here no amount of perceptive supervisory formulations will help, but rather one must become able to be reasonably unperturbed at the student's leaving one's office with a quite evident feeling that he is getting nothing from the supervision.

A fundamental tenet of my supervisory orientation is that my potential usefulness springs in large part from the simple fact that I am at a greater psychological distance than is the student from the patient's psychopathology–specifically, from the patient's anxiety and ambivalence. This greater distance leaves me *relatively* free from anxiety and able, therefore, to think relatively clearly and unconstrictedly. This position is mine, and this potential usefulness is mine, irrespective of whether, for example, in other situations the student may prove himself more intelligent than I, and a more effective practitioner than I. By the same token, the fact that I perceive some aspect of the treatment relationship which he has not seen does not mean that he is stupid and I am intelligent, when one takes into account the so important factor of our relative distances from the patient's anxiety and ambivalent feelings. All this is, again, highly comparable with the circumstance that an analyst or therapist is potentially useful to a patient simply because the former is 'outside' the patient's shoes, and can therefore bring to bear a different perspective upon the patient's life-experiences.

Early in supervision, the student often needs to realize that it is all right for him to let his thoughts stray, for example during minutes of silence, away from the patient; he needs to realize, in fact, that a maximal degree of inner freedom to think, fantasy, and feel, is essential to the exercise of his intuition, for unless he can achieve such an inner freedom from his compulsion to help the suffering patient, he will be unable to achieve sufficient distance to note, for example, significant sequences in the patient's associations. His need to 'cure' the patient is so urgent that he cannot easily sit back, as it were, and notice what the patient himself is feeling; the supervisor's hunches concerning the patient's subjective experience are often very illuminating to him. As I shall have occasion to detail later on, the supervisor's private noting of how he himself responds to the student's personality, and to the variations in the latter's demeanour during supervisory sessions, helps him to form hunches as to how the patient, too, may be reacting to the student, and many countertransference problems can be called tactfully to the student's attention through this avenue, while being left to the training analysis for their long-range resolution.

The student learns to his surprise that even the most intensely affective statements from the patient can be viewed in their significance as free associations. A gradual process takes place, over the months and years of supervision, of the student's identifying with the supervisor's own distance from the patient's psychopathology, a process which enlarges the degree of observing ego which the student can bring to bear in his work with patients, and which in turn he can help the patient himself to acquire. The student who is initially prone to become submerged in a desperately serious effort to rescue the patient who is viewed as simply suffering, comes to see the great extent to which the patient's 'suffering' is expressing unconscious sadism. Often it is first in the supervisory sessions that the student comes to find sufficient surcease from the desperation of all this to see that, in this arena tributary to the treatment relationship, something

PSYCHO-ANALYTIC SUPERVISION

about it can be actively enjoyable: he acquires enough freedom from the patient's anxiety to be able to enter into enjoyable discussions of psychodynamics with the supervisor, and he becomes able to see, increasingly, enjoyable and even amusing aspects of his work with the patient.

Whereas he and the patient were previously enmeshed unwittingly in making retaliatory demands on one another—the patient, demands for relief from suffering; and he, demands for a greater degree of self-awareness in the patient than the latter has come as yet to possess—he now comes to see the extent to which this mutual demandingness has been a defence, on the part of both himself and the patient, against a growingly fond contentment with one another. I have described these phenomena (chs. 10, 18) as having to do with the symbiotic phase in the transference-evolution, a phase early charged with the most intense ambivalence and later giving place to a full, oceanic kind of symbiosis (or, in Little's (1960) more apt term, undifferentiatedness), which I consider the core-phase in the treatment of either neurotic or psychotic individuals. The importance of this phase in the treatment situation itself is mirrored in the important place it comes to have in the course of the supervisory relationship. The distance inherent in the supervisor's position can enable him, if used rightly, to help the student himself to achieve a sufficient degree of psychological distance from the patient's anxious ambivalence for this so essential phase of full (or, genetically speaking, preambivalent) symbiosis to usher itself in.

One of my most oft-repeated experiences is that when I point out to the student how he should have responded, without helping him to discover what factors in the patient's psychopathology made it difficult for him so to respond, I do not actually help him; rather, I only leave him feeling more wrong, stupid, and inadequate than ever. Here again, the matter of distance from the patient's ambivalence is a crucial factor. Typically in these instances, careful investigation by student and supervisor together will reveal that he was responding, in the treatment incident in question, to one aspect of the patient's ambivalence, and was so absorbed in that as to be unaware of another aspect of that ambivalence which struck a particular chord in the supervisor. My assumption, in doing supervision, is

589

that in a high proportion of instances the therapist possesses sufficiently good judgement to have provided the 'right' response himself, had he not been hampered by some comparatively subtle factors deriving, in significant degree, from the patient's ambivalence. Looking for those factors, in supervision, is roughly analogous to the important 'analysing of the resistance' in the psycho-analytic treatment situation itself. This regularly entails a larger recognition by the student of the extent of his own ambivalence, not unnaturally evoked by the intensity of the ambivalence which the patient brings into the relationship with him.

For example, one student recently saw, quite readily, that he had been responding as a taskmaster to his patient, a college girl who was evidencing indifference about her studies. But it was only when I helped him to see that her indifference was part of an ambivalence which also included an intense degree of interest in her work, and only when I helped him to see that this intense interest had its counterpart in an intensely erotic but outwardly indifferent transference relatedness towards him, that he realized why, in his unconscious fear of the intensity of her feelings for him, he had been accepting her 'indifference' towards her studies as a whole picture of her feelings about her college work. We discovered, further, that his anxiety in reaction to her erotic transference was traceable, in part, to the threat of separation which she kept always before him, in, for example, her significant references to her, as she put it, '*current* boy friend'.

The teaching *per se*, in supervision, of the essence of psycho-analysis can occur only in so far as this kind of 'analysis of the supervisory resistance' can be successfully achieved. Further, we need to see that this so precious essence of psycho-analysis is very elusive. I have had the experience, for example, of undertaking supervision of a very skilled psychotherapist who had just begun his analytic training, and of realizing only after a considerable number of supervisory sessions that, despite his admirable knowledge of psychodynamics in many regards, and despite his patient's many quoted comments about a wide variety of clearly significant psychological problems in living, (*a*) the patient was neither employing, nor being encouraged by the student to employ, a free-associational mode of reporting, and (*b*) the student and the patient, for all their active investigation of the latter's positive and negative feelings about a variety of people outside the treatment situation itself, were doing nothing in the realm of analysis of the transference. Meanwhile, the patient's presenting symptoms had subsided quite dramatically, and both he and the student were happily, and with great determination, bent upon a transference cure. Typical also, in such instances, is the student's overestimation of the patient's sphere of awareness; he is afraid to see how helpless and dependent the patient actually is, in face of the power and inscrutability of what is repressed.

If I had to select any one supervisory problem as most important, it would be that of how one helps the person under supervision to discover the extent to which his own previously unconscious ambivalence has been contributing to a prolonged stalemate in the relationship between the patient and himself. Typically, the student comes to the supervisory hour, week after week and month after month, in a state of chronic boredom, exasperation, dissatisfaction, discouragement, and despair concerning the treatment; he presents, each time, data which contain hints, impressive to the supervisor but unnoticed by himself, strongly indicative of subterranean growth in the patient and of a surprising degree of mutual fondness and contentment in this reportedly unsatisfactory treatment relationship; and he proves tenaciously resistive to, if not actively resentful and derisive of, the supervisor's efforts to point out to him these evidences of analytic progress. It gradually becomes quite clear to the supervisor that the student-analyst's genuine striving to help the patient to grow and progress is matched by an unconscious determination to keep him ill and thereby to avert the loss of a mode of relatedness which is yielding deeply cherished, but deeply denied, infantile gratifications to analyst as well as to patient. It requires all one's skill, tact, persistence and, at times, forthrightness, to help the student to see, in essence, how fond he is of this patient and, behind all the dissatisfaction, how afraid he is of losing him through the latter's recovery from illness. The student must be able to find, with the supervisor's help, the courage to see that his dissatisfaction and despair supervene at just those junctures when the patient is showing the most solid evidences of progress towards health, precisely as the patient's relatives, impelled by unconscious separation anxiety, have opposed the treatment most vigorously just at those times when it is yielding, or beginning to yield, the most marked growth in the patient.

· All this is, as the student needs to become aware, basically natural and innate in any analyst's response to the unfolding of the patient's transference; it is of a piece with the ambivalence with which any parent must in some degree cope, concerning the child's individuation and subsequent growth. In the treatment situation, this ambivalence emerges in greatest intensity from the patient's necessary return, in the transference evolution, to the symbiotic mother-infant relatedness; and before the genetically earlier symbiotic phase, of full symbiosis or undifferentiatedness, can be reached, a phase of intensely ambivalent symbiosis–the phase in which the traumatic seeds of later neurosis or psychosis were sown–must be traversed. Whereas Little (1960) describes such an undifferentiated state as characteristic of the transference specifically in psychosis, I have found it to be the core-phase of the treatment process in both neurosis and psychosis; and whereas she refers to this undifferentiated state as being a heretofore unconscious delusion in the patient, and says that 'the delusion, although accepted as true for the patient, is not shared by the analyst (unless, unfortunately, he has something of a counter-transference psychosis)', I find that the analyst inevitably shares, in subtle but significant degree, this relatedness with the patient. The student needs our help in seeing that, naturally enough, he has become, at a deep level, one with the so ambivalent patient; that for the latter's recovery it is not only permissible but essential that he be able to enter increasingly into a fond, mutually dependent, playful and contented oneness with the patient, now functioning in the transference as a healthy infant or young child; and that, in course of time, this pleasurable symbiosis must give place, with very real feelings of mutual loss as well as fulfilment, to a new and healthier individuation.

So long as the ambivalent part of this symbiotic phase prevails, the student does not react well to our offering encouragement, and our pointing out the subtle evidences of therapeutic progress, as an antidote for his despair. His despair is genuine, and only if we hear him out will he be more receptive to exploring the other, more positive, side of his ambivalence about the treatment situation. If he is thinking seriously of stopping work with the patient, and we actively encourage him to continue, he quickly gets to feeling that we are inflicting him, *via* the patient's pathology, with this tormenting ambivalence and despair from which he yearns for surcease. He must be helped to realize that no one is forcing him to continue the work, and that the basic responsibility for the treatment rests in his and the patient's hands, for successful individuation requires the assumption of personal responsibility for one's feelings, no matter how intensely ambivalent they may be.

The supervisor has his own problems of ambivalence at fostering the growth, in the treatment relationship, of a deeply pleasurable, preambivalent symbiosis which he, as predominantly an outsider, cannot share. Typically, in this phase, the essence of what is going on in the treatment is unverbalizable by the student, so that the supervisor is given, in each hour, comparatively little verbal material to work with; and in response, consciously concerned with earning his pay but unconsciously sensing that he is becoming dispensable, he is apt to try to think of all possible psychodynamic meanings contained in each of these few data, and eagerly offer these hypotheses to the person under supervision. This tends to make the latter feel that he should be doing more standard psycho-analytic work. It is in such ways that the supervisor unwittingly interferes with the evolution of the treatment symbiosis. One must become able to tolerate a high degree of ambiguity, as well as a paucity of readily workable data, from the student; to be tolerant of his discussing his work with other patients and only thus tangentially getting to less readily objectifiable work with this patient; and to enjoy chatting about such light matters as the weather, the latest cocktail party, the likelihood of hydrogen warfare, and what not.

One supervisor, describing in retrospect a student's work in a treatment situation in which the essential phase of preambivalent symbiosis was in full sway between patient and doctor, snorted, 'They were going around on a merry-go-round—no, not on a merry-go-round, because that implies movement.'[2] In the comparable phase of my work with one of my students, feeling thoroughly an outsider and helpless to influence the fate of the complex but so evidently pleasurable relationship between him and the patient, I laughingly exclaimed to him, 'I feel as though

---

[2] Described also on p. 542.

593

I were watching the mating ritual of a couple of exotic tropical birds!' I did not detect that he felt particularly consoled, strengthened, or illuminated by this contribution from me; but such a comment can be warmly recommended as an adequate means of expressing supervisory hostility at this crucial juncture.

In chapter 4 I have emphasized the extent to which not yet verbally reported problems in the treatment relationship are unconsciously brought by the student into the supervisory situation, and reflected in faithful detail in this latter relationship. Such a 'reflection process' is at work throughout the course of supervision, and my supervisory experience during the years since then has shown me, innumerable times, how significant a role it plays in supervision. The lack of mention of such a process, elsewhere in the scanty literature concerning supervision, represents to my way of thinking a failure to take cognizance of one of our most powerful supervisory tools. Ekstein and Wallerstein, in their volume, *The Teaching and Learning of Psychotherapy* (1958), and Ekstein, in a paper (1960), describe a parallel between the problems being evidenced in the treatment situation on the one hand, and the learning-problems being manifested by the student in supervision on the other. But these writers do not describe the patient's anxiety as being a paramount factor in making for this parallelism, nor do they describe the supervisor as being caught up to any degree, along with the student, in the effects of what I have described as a truly interpersonal reflection process in the supervisory relationship, one in which the supervisor, by considering his own unusual and private emotional responses as relevant data, can learn much about the more subtle modes of interaction between the student-analyst and his patient.

This reflection process is, not surprisingly, at no time in the course of supervision more in evidence than in the core phases of ambivalent, and preambivalent, symbiosis, when patient and doctor are in such significant degree, though so subtly, one. During these phases the student may function, in the supervisory relationship, with a degree of ambivalence comparable with that which the patient is manifesting towards him in the treatment. He may show, for example, a mixture of deep dependency upon, and intense competitiveness with, the supervisor. In some instances the dependency is quite overt and clearly verbalized, while the covert competitiveness sabotages his own efforts to make use of the help which the supervisor offers. In other instances the student analyst's competitiveness is easy to discern, in his routine reporting of each week's treatment in a spirit of demonstrating that he does not need the supervisor's participation, while subtly and unwittingly revealing (in his eager punctuality, his trying to prolong the supervisory session until the very last moment, his reaction to the cancellation of a supervisory hour, and so on) that actually his dependence on the supervisor is no less than that of the poorly integrated patient on his analyst, as described in the following words by Winnicott:

An example of unintegration phenomena is provided by the very common experience of the patient who proceeds to give every detail of the week-end and feels contented at the end if everything has been said, though the analyst feels that no analytic work has been done. Sometimes we must interpret this as the patient's need to be known in all his bits and pieces by one person, the analyst. To be known means to feel integrated at least in the person of the analyst. This is the ordinary stuff of infant life, and an infant who has had no one person to gather his bits together starts with a handicap in his own self-integrating task, and perhaps he cannot succeed, or at any rate cannot maintain integration with confidence (Winnicott, 1945).

During the preambivalent phase of the transference symbiosis, the student analyst needs above all to have the privacy and freedom to feel the intimate and individualistic work, during this phase, to be *his*, very much as a happily nursing mother needs the opportunity to be uninterruptedly at one with the suckling infant. His actual dependence on the supervisor is, however, as I have tried to convey, unprecedentedly great—analogous, perhaps, to the dependence of the nursing mother upon her husband—and the greatest supervisory task, at this stage, is to be able to see clearly how dependent the student-analyst is on oneself, without pressing him for conscious acknowledgement of this dependence.

In my other chapter (ch. 4) concerning the frequency with which subtle modes of interaction in the treatment situation are reflected in the supervisory relationship, I was focusing upon relatively limited temporal segments of the over-all course of treatment. Since then, I have had occasion to see something of the extent to which the transference evolution of the course of treatment as a whole is paralleled by an unfolding in the supervisory relationship, over the years of the supervisor's and student-analyst's work together, in a richness, a subtle intensity, and a specificity for the particular patient under discussion (irrespective of the student's level of experience) which are quite beyond the following mundane description by Keiser, in his report of the panel discussion on problems of supervised analysis, held at the December, 1955 meeting of the American Psychoanalytic Association:

> . . . The progress of the candidate is recognized by his greater ease and facility in presenting to the supervisor, a diminution in blocks to his listening, his acceptance of supervision, a sharpened capacity to observe, an awareness of his typical mistakes which he learns to avoid, and his application of well-timed interpretations. To this I would add a lessened dependence on the supervisor and a greater assumption of responsibility toward his patient (Keiser, 1956).

Though Keiser's comments well describe the progress of the student in the supervisory relationship viewed simply as a learning situation, which at one level it of course is, the situation will not yield its richest information to either student or supervisor unless they notice and explore its subtle resonances to the progressing treatment situation.

A student came to me for supervision concerning his analysis of a severely obsessive-compulsive woman of whose controllingness, outside the treatment situation itself, he rapidly became aware. But, as month after month went by, he presented at each of the weekly supervisory hours a remarkably cheerful, un-complaining, confident, and above all indefatigably enthusiastic, demeanour, without any hint of the negative feelings which one would expect to see in his work with so interpersonally controlling an individual. Towards me also he seemed unaware of any save friendly, appreciative feelings, although I was aware that, not infrequently, he would totally forget about our supervisory appointments. The patient's symptomatic relief was so marked that I found no solid basis for criticism of the analysis; but I could not get away from the growing conviction that any analysis is bound to be more difficult than such seemingly steady and tranquil progress would indicate. It became increasingly evident to me that the patient's transference was not being explored adequately; but when I began repeatedly conveying this impression to the student, week after week, it was as if the treatment situation were hermetically sealed against my influence, and the analytic sessions evidently continued on an unvarying course.

It was only after I had come to voice my dissatisfaction most firmly and repeatedly that, some 15 months after my having first tried to point out this situation to the student, he suddenly realized with a severe jolt, in an interim between supervisory sessions, how intolerably bored he had long been feeling, at a previously unconscious level, with this patient. Within two weeks after this de-repression on his part, the woman began to voice her own long repressed, deeply ambivalent feelings of lust, murderousness, and so on, towards her analyst, whom he and I now could clearly see to have been occupying, in the transference over the preceding months, the position of her mother; during those earlier months, whenever the patient had tried to visualize her mother, she could think only of 'a house at 72 degrees'. In sum, it was only after I had come to express open and intense dissatisfaction with the supervisory 'house at 72 degrees' that the student-analyst, and subsequently the patient, discovered the volcanic feelings within this so tranquil-seeming house. All this is particularly memorable to me because I happen to have had detailed experience with this student's work both before and after his work with this particular woman, and he has shown in these other instances no such degree of difficulty in the delineation and resolution of these patients' negative and erotic transference reactions to him.

Another student-analyst came to me for supervision of his work with a borderline psychotic woman whose object-relations were initially very tenuous; who was preoccupied throughout most of each analytic session with her own largely unverbalizable ambivalent desires for, and fear of, closeness with her analyst; who at times was clearly hard put to it to contain her urges to attack him physically; and who quickly developed a habit of arriving outrageously late for the analytic sessions. Early in the course of supervision, the student typically arrived quite late for each supervisory hour, filled with a kind of inarticulate exasperation about the analysis and conveying simultaneously an intense demand for me to supply him with something and an equally intense walling off of any such efforts on my part. The moments when I felt in any close person-to-person contact with him were of a rarity comparable with that of such moments in the relationship between the patient and himself. Each of these problem aspects of the analytic relationship was resolved only after the comparable aspect of the supervisory relationship had been successfully resolved between us. I particularly recall our gradually becoming less afraid of person-to-person closeness with one another after I had managed, despite rageful fantasies on my part of physical violence towards him—fantasies which are quite unusual in my supervisory work—to set firm limits upon his habitual lateness; following this latter supervisory development, he was quite promptly able to impose equally successful limits on the patient's own outrageous tardiness, and genuine closeness between them grew steadily thereafter.

In a third instance, a female student came for supervision of her analysis of an emotionally cold, obsessively controlling man who, it quickly became evident, had much repressed hostility and, above all, repressed separation anxiety of unusual severity. In the course of my work with the student I was recurrently chilled, for months, by her own emotional coldness and annoyed by her controllingness. Only after her negative feelings had come more and more openly into expression, through the avenue of a compulsive and increasingly angry 'politeness', did the patient's hostility become accessible to analysis, and notable interpersonal warmth supervene in both supervisory and analytic relationships. Likewise, the patient's severe separation anxiety was finally resolved, in a successful termination of the analysis, only after the student-analyst and I had been able to face and integrate, in our relationship, a degree of mutual separation anxiety concerning the termination of the supervision, which has been quite unusual in my experience.

In a fourth instance, in which a student-analyst was consulting me concerning his work with a woman who suffered from recurrent amnesia, both he and I were struck recurrently at the extent to which we kept losing all sight, for months on end, of those historical areas of her living for which she herself suffered a recurrent amnesia. It was only in proportion as he and I became able to hold these at all steadily in focus over the course of the supervision, mutually enduring the extraordinary degree of anxiety and doubt of our own grasp of reality which these incidents and situations from her past engendered in us as we explored them, that she became more and more able to explore her own feelings about them without fleeing into amnesia.

A fifth analytic student began receiving supervision from me concerning her work with a hospitalized, chronically paranoid, middle-aged woman who presented a formidable demeanour of almost incessant condemnation and reproach, interlarded with sudden eruptions of lustful interest, expressed with a shocking kind of vulgarity, towards the student-analyst. It quickly became apparent to me that the latter reacted to the older woman as being an intimidating parent figure and that in supervision she seemed likewise, during the early months of our work, to feel intimidated by me as an authority figure. In these early months I was indeed considerably critical and depreciating of her, feeling inclined to write her off as being in all respects too much of a lightweight, too insipid, to cope adequately with the formidable patient.

But I resisted the powerful temptation to take her, figuratively speaking, by the scruff of the neck, and urge her to be more firm in response to the patient's demands and verbal attacks. I sensed that there was something going on between these two women which was very good, despite my not being able to visualize it clearly, for the patient quite early began to show a degree of indubitable improvement quite beyond what one could expect this apparently insipid and intimidated young student-analyst to be able to foster. Whatever this nurturing quality in the treatment relationship was, I sensed, was something in the realm of maternal tenderness which it was all too easy to disparage as weakness; and as the months of supervision went by, I felt increasingly able to place my trust in the student, unable though she was to formulate what was 'working' in the treatment.

Meanwhile, she became increasingly unthreatened and confident during the supervisory hours, so that I no longer felt myself to be in the position of an awesome authority to whom she had to report, but rather in that of a colleague with whom she could share her increasing pleasure about the treatment situation. She now began finding that, whereas she used to leave each of the analytic sessions with a headache, she was looking forward to these sessions with enjoyment, and was having more of both confidence and pleasure about her work with this woman than with any of her other patients. During her supervisory hours she came to reveal an excellent grasp of psychodynamics; I no longer found her to be in any sense insipid. When after two years of treatment the patient was given a routine second Rorschach test for comparison with that at the time of admission, I thought it no coincidence that the diminution of the authoritarian tendency, and the increase of mutual trustfulness and closeness, in the supervisory relationship proved to have counterparts in the treatment situation. But I was surprised, nonetheless, to see this additional evidence of how very far this deeply ill patient had come in this comparatively short time. Here are a few excerpts from the report:

'The present test shows striking improvement in ability to cope in a controlled and resilient way with emotion-arousing events.

'The patient is now able to deal first with the most salient characteristics of a situation, and then to turn to the more emotion-arousing or more threatening aspects and respond to them both with feeling and with realism. Before, she often could respond only with denial, or with a spurious, label-attaching intellectuality, or with an instant retreat into private preoccupations.

'. . . the world she lives in is simply pleasanter than it was, more varied, softer, more feminine. The sternness, the rage and despair have abated. Instead of ruptured sexual flesh spouting blood, she now conceives of an arm around a waist, of a cane to help a person to walk, of peppermint-stick candy.

'. . . The patient is even able to laugh at herself; during the test she quipped in effect that she saw something as ballet dancers because she was trying to be refined, but probably in another year they would be can-can girls instead.'

Various problem aspects of the complex interrelatedness among student, supervisor, and training analyst have been described by Kovacs (1936), Gitelson (1945), Blitzsten and Fleming (1953), Ackerman (1953), Keiser (1956), Sloane (1957), Ekstein (1960), Lewin and Ross (1960), and other writers. I shall add only a few points which I have not encountered in these writings.

First, in the student's development of a sense of identity as an analyst, he may well find, for a prolonged period during his training analysis, one or another supervisor to be more available as an analyst with whom to identify than is his own analyst. This is not only because the supervisor enjoys, in the supervisory situation, a relative freedom to reveal his own reactions; a probably greater reason lies in the as yet unresolved negative transference, only in part displaced to the supervisor, which in the training analysis situation renders the analyst essentially unavailable to the analysand, for the time being, as a person with whom to identify.

Second, the supervisor is apt to displace upon this or that student-analyst some degree of friendly or unfriendly feeling, which he is relatively constricted in experiencing and expressing to one of his analysands during a current difficult phase of the latter's analysis.

Third, the supervisee-as-therapist, or as potential therapist, to the supervisor, is an important ingredient in the supervision. The supervisor responds to the student's therapeutic (and increasingly analytic) interest and ability, particularly if these are of an unusually perceptive and skilful quality, as offering him the chance, to a degree tabooed and not fully realizable by reason of the formal aspects of the situation, for help with his own unresolved conflicts. The observations of Whitaker and Malone (1953) concerning 'therapist-vectors' in the typical patient and 'patient-vectors' in the typical therapist, are relevant to this point. Supervision early involves an inarticulate kind of competition as to which of the two participants is to be the therapist for the other; subsequently, as the tensions in the relationship diminish and as the mutual and more explicit work concerning the patient proves increasingly successful, there develops an increasingly free give-and-take at this deeper level also. Not only does the student form constructive identifications with the supervisor; but the latter identifies with the former in those areas where the student manifests professional skills, and areas of emotional openness, beyond those which the supervisor has previously achieved. It may well be that such a deep 'acceptance' of the student by the supervisor is one of the essential aspects of a successful course of supervision.

Incidentally, competitiveness in the more usual sense of the word, in the supervisory relationship, has at times appeared to me as a defence against the student's and my being drawn together in compassion for the human being whose tragedies, so much of a piece with all human tragedy, we are trying to help him face and somehow integrate. The analytic training which we supervisors have received has presumably helped to free us for compassionate interaction; but almost the sole explicit teaching to which we have been exposed, concerning this kind of emotion, has taught us that we should regard it with suspicion as being merely a clue to a much more real and powerful underlying sadism. Thus the supervisory situation, which by its very nature tends so strongly to promote bonds of shared compassion between the participants, tends to be somewhat bewildering, and we resort to long familiar modes of reaction such as intellectual competitiveness in order to find relative comfort.

It has become rather widely agreed that the supervisor had best attempt any analysing of the student's countertransference sparingly if at all, and I have already included myself among the majority who hold this view, although I think that, within *somewhat* wide latitudes, this is a highly individual matter for which such general rules are of dubious value. In any case, even though explicit analysis of countertransference be eschewed, this should not lead us to the erroneous conclusion that the supervisory relationship is thereby kept at a superficial level in contrast to the depths which training analysis reaches. The supervisory relationship is rendered no less intense, no less deeply integrative for both participants, by reason of its being less verbally and explicitly 'analytic' than is the training analysis. Here a comment by Ekstein concerning the historical shift in our view of the training analysis is of interest:

> I believe that the original notion which looked at the *personal analysis* of the candidate as a *Lehranalyse*, a didactic analysis, is no longer a point of serious discussion. There is general agreement that this analysis, the emotional preparation as it were for the learning of psychoanalytic technique, is to be a thorough therapeutic analysis and is to be considered a training analysis only inasmuch as it is a required part of the total training experience . . . (Ekstein, 1960).

I strongly surmise that we are moving towards the day when there will be equally general agreement as to the essentially therapeutic significance, for both participants, of psychoanalytic supervision. Such a realization will require us to discover that *any* human interaction which is at all intense and prolonged is, in a very real sense of the word, mutually therapeutic (or anti-therapeutic). Throughout the writing of this paper, for which I have carefully perused my files on past supervisory experiences, I have recurrently found myself having to understress, partly for reasons of confidence, the true intensity of the mutual emotional involvement which characterizes psycho-analytic supervision. As yet, our relative non-acceptance of this degree of intensity as 'normal' to the supervisory relationship tends towards vicarious eruption of the underlying intense affects in other arenas of the two participants' lives – above all, in the arena of the treatment situation itself which is being discussed in supervision.

Recordings of the treatment sessions have proved to be, for me, of only sharply limited value. Used only sporadically, they can be very illuminating and can be integrated into the kind of deeply personal experience which I feel that psycho-analytic supervision must be, to be successful. When used frequently and when the bulk of the supervisory hour is spent in the two human participants' listening to the recording, there develops an interpersonal distance, a distraction of the supervisor's attention from the student's needs of the moment, and above all a further burdening of the elusively human essence in the patient by this intrusively non-human element, which all are quite antithetical to the development of the necessary depth of intimacy between the two participants. I fully concur with the more detailed reservations about recordings which have been expressed by Ekstein and Wallerstein (1958).

Concerning the termination phase of supervision I shall make no attempt at comprehensive description, but only two observations which, like the foregoing points, I have not encountered in the literature. The supervisor must accept, among other gratifications real and potential, the loss of, the chance to go on deriving further therapeutic help, no matter on how subterranean a level, from this student-analyst who has by now developed a very considerable level of competence and perceptiveness. And, finally, the supervisor realizes, as the time for termination of the mutual work draws increasingly near, that his too long continued participation in the situation will become not merely less and less helpful, but more and more of an active hindrance to student-analyst and patient in a treatment situation which must be trusted to find its resolution in the two participants' own highly individual manner. This latter point is comparable with the father's need to realize and accept that his son's individuality can never find its highest realization under the family roof. Thus I have found that, even in those instances where a supervisory relationship has been most successful, the separation has left me with some feelings of disappointment and disapproval contaminating my appreciation and approval of the student. Such 'contaminants' are, I think, inevitable to our acceptance of the fact that effective supervision helps the student to become not a carbon copy of one's professional self, but rather an individual man among men.

Chapter 21

SCORN, DISILLUSIONMENT AND ADORATION IN THE PSYCHOTHERAPY OF SCHIZOPHRENIA (1962)[1]

THIS paper is designed primarily to portray the role, in the psychotherapy of schizophrenia, of three interrelated feeling-states—scorn, disillusionment, and adoration. Their relation to the aetiology of the illness will also be stressed. In focusing upon the vicissitudes of these particular emotions, I do not imply that other affective states are of less importance in the aetiology and psychotherapy of schizophrenia; but the interesting connexions among these affects, in regard to both ego development and adult-life ego functioning, have come to constitute, for me at least, one more useful source of illumination of this complex illness. I must explain further, at the outset, that the psychodynamics to be examined here are not considered—except in a few regards which should be obvious enough—as confined to, and specific for, schizophrenia. Rather, I regard these psychodynamics as being at work, in varying degrees of affective intensity and psychopathological significance, in psychosis and neurosis in general, and I shall give considerable attention to the role of these emotions in healthy personality development.

Early in my work at Chestnut Lodge, I came to see that *scorn* holds a far more formidable place in the psychodynamics of schizophrenia than the literature concerning this illness would lead one to expect. In retrospect, this does not seem surprising, when we consider how effectively scorn serves to defend a deeply troubled human being against a whole gamut of more distressing emotions. That is, to the extent that he can hold the other person in scorn, the latter is perceived as incapable of evoking terror, fear, or uneasiness in oneself; of evoking feelings of inferiority and humiliation; of arousing positive feelings—such as fondness,

[1] An earlier version of this paper was presented at the Forest Hospital, Des Plaines, Ill., 28 June, 1961. First published in *Psychoanalysis and the Psychoanalytic Review*, Vol. 49 (Fall, 1962), pp. 39-60.

erotic interest, and dependency needs–with the attendant threat that these will remain unfulfilled; and, finally, incapable of inflicting, through his leaving us, such feelings as rejection, abandonment, separation anxiety, and grief.

Thus it is no coincidence that the predominant feeling which is in evidence at the beginning of psychotherapy with many schizophrenic patients, or which they become able to express first as therapy progresses, is scorn. This is true not only of the comparatively verbal individual suffering from paranoid schizophrenia; I have been startled at the intensity of the scorn attending the first verbalizations of previously mute catatonic patients, and equally startled to discover how much scorn is seething in hebephrenic patients who themselves tend so powerfully to evoke scorn in all persons round about. One of the latter individuals, when her own idiotic behaviour began to diminish, confided to me such thoughts as, 'That laugh speaks of an empty mind' (referring to another patient's laughter), and 'People are big blobs of nothing'. One particularly animalistic-looking hebephrenic woman came to speak with withering scorn of all the persons about her as being filled with pus; and another such woman revealed how 'slimy' and 'freakish' she found me, and said, 'You're so ugly I can't *stand* you!'

I have come to believe that one of the most nagging concerns of the schizophrenic patient, whether borderline or more deeply psychotic, is a fear lest he reveal the scorn with which he is subjectively filled. Erikson makes the point that 'The loss of a sense of identity often is expressed in a scornful and snobbish hostility toward the roles offered as proper and desirable in one's family or immediate community'. (Erikson, 1956, p. 146). The schizophrenic person's relatively healthy fellows tend to reject him not merely on account of their often mentioned unenlightened prejudice against mental illness, but also on account of their sensing quite accurately, when they come into his proximity, how intensely scornful he is towards them and all they represent to him.

Several years ago, in the course of my work with a deeply paranoid woman, it occurred to me that her seemingly limitless scorn, cynicism, and distrust were the qualities one would expect to find in a person who was fixed in a state of unresolved–that is, in complete–*disillusionment*. Crudely put, the complete disillusionment process involves one's seeing the other person as wholly good, then—with the appearance of an unlovable side of him—as wholly bad, followed by one's integrating both 'good' and 'bad' percepts of him into a realistic appraisal of him. By contrast, this woman was, I saw, as if fixed in the second stage of this process: she apparently saw the world about her, and all persons in it, as almost unrelievedly bad.

Since then I have grown alert to sensing the disillusionment implicit in many of the schizophrenic patient's expressions of scorn, antagonism, and active hostility. When one detects this note of disillusionment, one finds oneself having a quite different view of him, for one senses that his hostility, taken altogether, is a reaction to underlying positive feelings which are striving for expression, but have long been repressed because of disillusioning experiences which came too early, and in too overwhelming an intensity, for him to integrate them. Unable at that early time to carry through a successful disillusionment, with the complex feelings of hurt, painful disappointment, contempt, thwarted adoration, and eventual compassionate acceptance which such a process requires if it is to be successful, he experienced instead a splitting of the disillusioning object into two—or in some instances many—disparate objects; or, if the process occurred very early, the original disparate percepts of the mother failed ever firmly to coalesce into an integrated percept of his mother as a single and whole person.

The adult patient's fixation in this 'all-black phase' of the dis-illusionment sequence is thus not only a reaction to unassimilated traumata in the past, but also a formidable unconscious defence—analogous to, but at a somewhat deeper level than, the scorn which tends to hold sway earlier in his treatment—against the recognition of his repressed positive feelings in his current living.

Freud, in his paper entitled, 'Further Remarks on the Defence Neuro-Psychoses' (1896), emphasizes the role of self-reproach as nuclear in paranoia, but says nothing of the role of dis-illusionment with oneself or others. In his paper concerning the Schreber case (1911), although at one point he notes that 'The person who is now hated and feared as a persecutor was at one time loved and honoured,' nowhere in his lengthy discussion does he mention explicitly the role, in Schreber's illness, of dis-illusionment as such. Heimann, in her paper (1955) entitled, 'A

Combination of Defence Mechanisms in Paranoid States', gives a vivid description of the infant's conflict of feelings, with splitting of the mother into separate objects; and mentions the patient's *guilt* about the change in him from love to hatred of the object; but she does not mention disillusionment. Also, she mentions 'The triumph which the paranoid person shows when convincing his persecutor of incompetence, stupidity, cruelty, and so on,' but does not suggest that this may be essentially a triumph, at an unconscious level, over his unmanageably painful, and therefore repressed, feelings of disillusionment with the persecutor.

On the other hand, we find in the papers of Helene Deutsch (1942) and Annie Reich (1953) concerning the patient who relates to others in an 'as if' fashion–as if he were experiencing a deep emotional involvement, when he is really incapable of relating except on the basis of primitive identification of an imitative kind, traceable to his superficial identification with a narcissistic mother–a sweeping acknowledgement, by implication, of the aetiological importance of disillusionment in schizophrenia. We find this acknowledgement emerging, by implication, from (a) Deutsch's stating that such patients justify the designation 'schizoid', and Reich's similarly classifying them among the borderline states; (b) Deutsch's stressing the role of disillusionment in these 'as if' conditions; and (c) Deutsch's reporting her impression, based upon her observations of schizophrenic patients, that 'the schizophrenic process goes through an "as if" phase before it builds up the delusional form'.

In a similar vein, Robert A. Cohen (1947), in his paper concerning the management of the anxiety in a case of paranoid schizophrenia, shows the patient's development of a delusion as part of a struggle to preserve an idolized-father image of a former therapist. Likewise, C. V. Ramana (1956), in his paper concerning borderline states, emphasizes the aetiological importance of severe disappointment in the histories of these patients.

Schreber's memoirs, upon which Freud based his study, translated into English by Macalpine and Hunter (1955) clearly show what I have come to consider the typical importance which disillusionment holds in paranoid schizophrenia. These memoirs constitute no mouldy document of merely historical importance, but a vivid, abundantly detailed, ready source of clinical data which I have found to be of the liveliest similarity, in fundamental psychodynamics, to the experiences which have been conveyed to me by paranoid individuals whom I have treated and am treating. One finds the translators fully justified in their assertion that 'Schreber's name is legion' (Macalpine and Hunter, 1955, p. 25).

Throughout Schreber's account of the course of his illness, we find that among the complex determinants which this illness– like any other instance of psychosis or neurosis–possesses, one of the major determinants consists in his persistent struggle both to ward off, and to come to grips with, evidently intense repressed feelings of disillusionment concerning each of the various figures who were most important to him: God (predominantly, in my opinion, a delusional representation of his mother); his wife; his physician, Flechsig; and so on. I can present but a few brief samples of the many relevant passages from his narrative.

After having described his almost endless torments in the form of efforts at 'soul murder' which he is inclined to lay at God's door, he none the less asserts that, 'I must not omit to add that my own faith in the grandeur and sublimity of God and the Order of the World was not shaken' (p. 59).

His inability to face his disillusionment with his wife is reflected at a point where he quotes a poem which she brought to him, a poem which begins, 'Ere true peace can embrace you–God's still and silent peace–. . .' which the reader can clearly see to convey, in its entirety, her apparently unconscious death-wishes and violent rage towards her suffering but to her arrogantly aloof husband. Just before introducing this poem, Schreber describes how he 'repeatedly had the nerves belonging to my wife's soul in my body . . . These soul parts were filled with the devoted love which my wife has always shown me, they were the only souls who showed willingness to renounce their own further existence and find their end in my body . . .' (pp. 115–16).

His struggle against disillusionment with his physician, Professor Flechsig, is reflected in such comments as these: 'It seems to me in retrospect that Professor Flechsig's plan of curing me consisted in intensifying my nervous depression as far as possible, in order to bring about a cure all at once by a sudden change of mood. At least this is the only way I can explain the following event, which I could otherwise only attribute to malicious intent . . .,' (p. 66) and referring to his experiences of being persecuted by Flechsig's soul, he emphasizes that he must recognize the possibility 'that what I reported . . . in connexion with the name Flechsig, refers only to Flechsig's soul as distinct from the living human being Flechsig. . . . It will be appreciated that I do not wish in any way to attack the honour of the living Professor Flechsig in my intended publication' (p. 243).

It must have been a particularly bitter irony for Judge Schreber that the very court, the highest court in Saxony, of which he himself had been appointed president of the panel of judges shortly before the onset of his psychosis, was the court which concluded the report of his commitment proceedings—during which proceedings Schreber had argued forcibly in support of his own sanity—with the words, 'The Court is in no doubt that the appellant is insane' (p. 342). Schreber, whose inability to cope successfully with feelings of disillusionment must have had much to do with his inability to exercise successfully the illustrious professional position which he had attained, is pathetically unable to dethrone, in his own view, the court-appointed psychiatrist who holds him to be insane: he interrupts his vigorous case in support of his own sanity to tell the Court, 'I would be genuinely sorry if Dr Weber felt insulted by any of my words, for I have the highest regard both for his character and professional and scientific capacity' (p. 289). We could, of course, look upon such statements as indicative of the paranoid individual's effort to avoid experiencing the full intensity of his *condemnation* of the other; but my clinical work has indicated repeatedly that interpretations couched in terms of the avoidance of feelings of painful disillusionment are in much better accord with the patient's own feeling experience.

Although the importance of repressed disillusionment is relatively easy to discern in persons suffering from paranoid schizophrenia, it is my impression that its importance may be equally great in other varieties of schizophrenia also. One hebephrenic woman, for example, who for many months showed that her body-image was fragmented and very incomplete, had long idolized her father, an eminent and much-honoured lawyer. He paid a visit to the hospital just at a time when she had begun to recognize, through the medium of the transference relationship, a dependent-little-boy aspect of her father. After her visit to him, she started to describe to me some spoiled-small-boy behaviour he had exhibited, when she suddenly seized her forehead and said, with every evidence of terror and unbearable physical anguish, 'My whole forehead is shattered!' It seemed to me that she was introjectively experiencing in terms of a shattering of a portion of her own body-image, what a healthier individual would have been able to experience as the shattering of an idol in the outer world – namely, her formerly idolized father. This incident left me wondering whether the extremely fragmented ego so characteristic of hebephrenia may regularly be traceable to the infant's or young child's very early introjection of such a smashed-idol parent-figure in the outer world, due to disillusioning experiences which occurred too early in life for the child's own ego, including his own body-image, to have become solidly established. My experiences with hebephrenic processes in other patients have been such as to support this impression; but I have not sufficiently succinct data to document it in this brief space.

Before taking up more explicitly the role of adoration, disillusionment, and scorn in the aetiology and psychotherapy of schizophrenia, it is useful to see something of the part which these affective phenomena play in normal ego development.

Concerning very early ego development, psycho-analytic writings widely agree with Freud (1923) that, as Fenichel phrases it, '. . . When the child is forced through experiences to renounce his belief in his omnipotence, he considers the adults who have now become independent objects to be omnipotent, and tries by introjection to share their omnipotence again' (Fenichel, 1945, p. 40).

I have growingly become convinced, through accumulated clues as to how the deeply regressed schizophrenic adult experiences his world – namely, with perceptions of the subjectively *outer* world antedating his ability to perceive, with comparable clarity, his subjectively *inner* world – that the sequence Fenichel describes should be reversed to give a more accurate picture. That is, I surmise that the infant first becomes aware of omnipotence as a function of the mother, and later, through introjection of her, experiences himself as omnipotent. But I think it still truer to life to conceptualize this as a mutuality of mother's and infant's experiencing a subjectively omnipotent oneness, during the early or preambivalent phase of the normal mother-infant symbiosis. In the later ambivalent phase of their symbiosis, ushered in by the increasing complexity, and therefore less ready satiability, of the maturing infant's needs, both mother and infant must undergo a successful disillusionment process—disillusionment with the self as well as with the other participant in the erstwhile symbiosis—in order that the omnipotent phase may be relinquished, and the foundations of individuality in the infant established.

Whichever be the correct sequence here, or whatever the better frame of reference for viewing this earliest ego differentiation, let us note that just as successful disillusionment is a necessary ingredient of the later phase of it, mutual *adoration* is the necessary emotional climate for the earlier phase—what I call the preambivalently symbiotic phase (1961). Winnicott (1945) convincingly describes the 'primary unintegration' of the world of the infant of less than five or six months, a world in which 'bits of nursing technique and faces seen and sounds heard and smells smelt are only gradually pieced together into one being to be called mother', and one realizes that mutual *adoration* is the necessary medium not only for the infant's primitively identifying with the mother but, even more basically, for his developing an integrated picture of her as a whole person. His coming to see as flowing from this one source all the meaningful things of his life is the prototype for all his subsequent experiences of adoration later on in life.

Winnicott (1945, 1948), Milner (1952), and Rycroft (1955) have all described illusion and disillusion as normal processes playing an essential part in the infant's establishment of a creative relation to the world. I wish to note that the earliest phases of integration—'illusionment'—and disillusionment represent the infant's prototypical experiences with the synthesizing and desynthesizing of percepts, and that if those earliest experiences are attended by too painful an *affect* of disillusionment, there will result a proportionate impairment of the subsequently developing ego's whole ability to synthesize and resynthesize psychological data; here it is well to keep in mind that daily living, even in adulthood, involves continual increments of illusion and disillusion, and, in successful maturation, in increasing 'skill' in experiencing illusionment and disillusionment, as one develops an increasingly confident and creative approach to one's environment, and as one's ability to appraise outer and inner reality becomes increasingly accurate. Loewald, (1960b) incidentally, has pointed out the integral role which manageable increments of mutual parent-child idealization and disillusionment normally play in the child's superego formation – that is, in his internalization of parental expectations and demands.

Both in his first establishment of a sense of his own separate individuality, and in such later phases as adolescence which are critical for the reaffirmation and further elaboration of his ego autonomy, it is crucial that the individual be able consciously to experience, rather than be obliged to repress, scorn towards others, including his parents and parent surrogates. So long, instead, as he perceives the parents as omnipotent, he cannot possibly differentiate himself from them; it is inconceivable that one could sunder oneself from another who is perceived as all-powerful. Scorn, temporarily carried to a disproportionate extreme, helps the child to reduce to tolerable proportions the loss involved in his psychological differentiation from the parent who has heretofore been sensed as omnipotent, and helps him similarly to feel an enhanced appreciation of his own separate, developing powers. And later on in his adolescence or young adulthood, an accentuation of this outer-directed scorn helps him similarly to feel able to make his way into an adult world which might otherwise seem awesomely, constrictingly powerful in face of his own still largely unproved capacities. Incidentally, it is not infrequent, I believe, that one's autonomy is 'sealed' in a setting of one's having found the courage to repudiate something – some idea, belief, or custom – which is held sacred by the person (parent or parent figure) most important to oneself.

Not only at such critical phases in ego development, but continually throughout life, one needs to be free to experience scorn as well as adoration, not only to reach realistic evaluations of outer reality, but also to perform the kind of selective identifying – the taking into oneself of desirable qualities which one sees in others, and the barring away from oneself, or ridding from within oneself, of undesirable personality traits – which Erikson (1958) describes as being intensified during the identity crises of normal adolescence. Adoration and scorn come to be numbered among one's reliable affective tools for coping with outer and inner reality, with part-aspects of others and oneself; above all, perhaps, that which is uniquely individual in others and in oneself comes to be seen as deserving of adoration–of cherishing and nurturing–and that which tends to interfere with this essence as deserving of scorn.

In the childhood development of the individual who later succumbs to schizophrenia, a multiplicity of circumstances prevent him from experiencing the above-described sequences of infantile and early childhood adoration, later childhood scorn and disillusionment and the establishment of ego autonomy, and subsequently increasing skill in evaluating inner and outer reality through an increasing effectiveness in 'using' adoration and scorn (as well as other emotions) in an unceasing process of illusionment-disillusionment-reality relatedness. These unfortunate childhood environmental circumstances have essentially to do with his parents' low self-esteem and their precarious ego integration. I shall describe the mother, because she is the more immediately important in the earliest phases. The described deficiencies must exist largely in the father also or, from what I have seen, the child will never become schizophrenic.

The mother, because of her low self-esteem, is unable to accept the adoration, the idealization, which the infant and little child needs to direct towards her, for the sake of his developing both an integrated percept of her and a sense of his own wholeness through identification with such a perceivedly whole mother. Such a view of her is too widely at variance with the feelings of worthlessness which make up a major share of her personal identity; she reacts then, in the mothering role, with increased anxiety and loosened personal integration.

The mother, instead of possessing within herself a solid and mature sense of her personal worth, directs towards the child an unrealistic kind of adoration, based upon transference of unworked-through adoration of her own mother, and preservative of an unconscious, unresolved narcissism residing in this mother of the child in question. Just as the mother's view of herself is a poorly integrated dualistic one–with conscious feelings of personal worthlessness overlying her unconscious, unresolved narcissistic omnipotence–her view of the infant is comparably poorly integrated, with an unrealistic adoration directed towards those aspects of the infant which give any promise of gratification of her narcissistic transference strivings, alongside a depreciatory lack of acknowledgement of the infant as a real person–above all, of any developing rudiments of individuality in him. Thus, as he develops an awareness of how his mother responds to him, he finds a hopelessly wide gap between her idolizing, on the one hand, something which she sees in him but which to his view is not really part of himself, and, on the other, utterly scorning those attributes which he experiences as himself. He lives under the chronic threat that the parent will become destructively and irrevocably disillusioned with him; the mother of one of my patients kept before her such a threat, indirectly expressed in the warning that 'People [sic] will drop you like a hot potato!' if the girl started to fall short of the mother's expectations.

The child is thus given to feel that disparate emotions and percepts are separated by a hopeless gulf, and that one can only strive to keep these apart, rather than synthesize them in the fashion which the healthy child finds it possible to do with his disparate percepts of the adored mother and the scorned mother, and as the mother of this latter child finds it possible to do with her disparate percepts of her child. In the former instance, it should be noted that the child is looked to not only to realize the mother's grandiose, narcissistic ambitions, but also fully to satisfy her unresolved regressive demands–to spare her from coming to terms with her infantile frustrations–which would imply something approaching omnipotence in the child.

Even in normal circumstances, the young child's struggle to achieve individuation must be a deeply ambivalent struggle: to establish himself as a separate individual, with his own powers apart from her, he must prove that she is not omnipotent; but on the other hand he must brave his inevitable feelings of disillusionment and loss at finding that she is less than all-powerful. I hope I am making it clear that the child who eventually goes on to schizophrenia has not only less freedom than has the healthy child to express scorn–and therefore less freedom to allow himself consciously to feel such an emotion–but also greater cause for feeling scorn, a greater 'quantity', or intensity, of this emotion fostered within him.

It should be noted further that the mother who consciously experiences herself as worthless overtly demands an exaggerated respect from the child but covertly demands scorn from him, the latter to confirm chronically her sense of identity as a person worthy of scorn. This produces intense guilt in the child in reaction to the scornful feelings which he thus covertly supplies to her.

The child's too early, too great 'disillusionment'–a repressed and incomplete process, rather than a completed one–with the mother, occurring before differentiation between inner and outer reality has solidly occurred, leaves him with the unconscious conviction that the emotion of disillusionment, if one permits oneself to feel it, destroys the other person. One schizoid man, for example, said of his current one among a long series of briefly enshrined girl friends, 'If I could only see her as she really is, rather than sugar-coating her or annihilating her!', entirely as though such changes in his *percept of* the other person changed the real person to that same degree. Rycroft (1955), describing a woman who idealized her love objects, mentions that 'She felt, she once told me, as though she had murdered all her lost objects.' One of my patients, who had shown borderline schizophrenic symptoms at the beginning of our work, after two years of treatment came to reveal that, 'I'm afraid that if I express all the scorn that's in me, people will shrink to nothing and I'll be all alone.'

This young child's experience of *loyalty* is proportionately warped; he develops loyalty not to an admired, strong leader, but rather to a tragically crippled and weak one. He senses that his mother is utterly dependent upon this loyalty of his. In his effort to preserve a necessary adored and admired figure in outer reality, he introjects her deficiencies, experiencing these as ingredients of himself, rather than of her. He carries out this introjection–or one can see it as his perpetuating their symbiotic non-differentiation–as, basically, an expression of his literally self-sacrificing love for her (chs. 7, 12), as well as a defence against experiencing overwhelming feelings of scorn towards and disillusionment with her. This process of introjection, beginning even before the formation of his body-image, is one of the factors responsible for the incompleteness of body-image in the schizophrenic adult.

For example, repressed feelings of scorn about a parent's stupidity have been found, in a number of instances I have seen, to be among the roots of a patient's experiencing his head as grossly deformed and incomplete; repressed scorn towards the mother's breasts has been a major element in various patients' feelings of incompleteness or deformity in the genital area and other areas of the body; and we may recall the hebephrenic woman's 'shattered forehead' in this same connexion.

A number of writers have described the borderline schizophrenic individual's unconscious use of illusionment and disillusionment as *defences* against various emotions. Helene Deutsch (1942), in her classic paper describing the patient who relates to others in an 'as if' fashion, makes clear that his idealization of the objects in his adult life serves to protect him from facing the affective emptiness of his relationships with people. Annie Reich (1953) confirms Deutsch's finding that this disorder rests upon the patient's primitive identification with an idealized mother figure, an identification which is projected upon the succession of briefly enthroned 'love objects' in adult life. This is a sample of Reich's vivid descriptions of the kind of mother who fosters such faulty object relatedness in the child: '. . . the mother completely dominated the family and created in them the conviction that she was the most beautiful, elegant, efficient, and all-around most wonderful person in the world. She was predominantly concerned with the impression she made on people . . . ' (Reich, 1953).

I wish to point out, in this connexion, how a series of unsuccessful disillusionments tends over the years to accelerate. Increasingly, as a result of these, one's faith in one's reality-testing ability is undermined–rather than, as in normal maturation, one's becoming increasingly confident of one's increasingly discriminating and therefore reliable ability to appraise reality. Thus one's need for an omnipotent other person, upon whom one can wholly rely, is intensified, with the result that one's selection of such potential persons becomes increasingly unrealistic.

In the volume *The God That Failed* (Crossman, 1950), made up of six eminent writers' personal accounts of why they eventually became disillusioned with Communism, an additional related point emerges. A number of these writers rejected the bright new vision of Communism at the point when they discovered at work in Russian society the very social injustices they had come to despise in the capitalistic society they had long known. It is, I think, a mark of unsuccessful, incompleted disillusionment that one cannot accept the presence of such old elements, elements from a despised past, in a brighter, newer view of the present and future. But some acceptance, some amalgamation, of these old and new elements, taken together, must be effected in order to develop a deep sense of *continuity* between past and present. Such a sense of continuity is essential, in turn, to being able to envision, and work towards, a desirable *future* state of affairs as emerging out of one's present circumstances. Thus, the person who has not 'learned' to complete the disillusionment sequence needs all the more to idolize unrealistically other persons, in each of whom he can find an 'omnipotent' strength to lean upon, for this further reason that there has not developed within his own ego a mature sense of continuity of time, so necessary to one's own coping progressively with reality.

The above-mentioned volume also serves to bring out the role which illusionment, or idealization, plays as an unconscious defence against *confusion*. When we consider how confusing is the family environment of the child who eventually develops schizophrenia, we see how powerfully his deep-seated confusion tends to subvert the normal idealization-disillusionment maturational sequence to defensive purposes. Rycroft's paper (1955) serves to illuminate further defensive functions of illusion and idealization; he shows these as defensive against the withdrawal of cathexis from real objects, against ambivalence, and against a sense of despair and futility.

The mother whom I have been describing is not only unable to accept the young child's genuine adoration of her, but more-over tends unwittingly to thwart his need to find someone else whom he can idolize; she does this by encouraging him to act her own unconscious defiance of, and contempt for, authority-figures. The resultant chronically defiant, iconoclastic behaviour on his part she proudly views as being a degree of 'spontaneity', or 'independence', which she feels that she failed to achieve, or was denied, in her own upbringing. Such an attitude on the child's part tends to cut him off from any likely people who could, through their acceptance of his adoring feelings, foster the necessary early identifications with healthy adults.

SCORN, DISILLUSIONMENT AND ADORATION

Before turning to a discussion of the place of scorn, disillusion-ment, and adoration in the relationship between the schizophrenic individual and his therapist, it is to be noted, finally, that the schizophrenic illness first becomes manifest, typically, in a setting of the individual's coming face to face with overwhelming dis-illusionment. Specifically, he is no longer able to maintain a symbiotic relatedness with a parent, a relatedness perpetuated into chronological adulthood, long past the time when the mother-infant symbiosis is normally resolved, perpetuated partly in the service of maintaining intense scorn, and other negative emotions, under repression. He now becomes confronted with a weight of evidence which can no longer be denied, evidence showing that the parent's ostensibly altruistic interest in him has been basically narcissistic in origin—that this interest has been invested not in him as a real and separate person, but in him only as an extension of the parent's self; as one freshly dis-illusioned schizophrenic woman disappointedly put it, 'People are only interested in themselves.' This weight of evidence also points to that very parent's possessing not only grievous person-ality weaknesses, but also a degree of hatred towards him which gives him much reason to see this erstwhile adored person as being, instead, his most mortal enemy. Such feelings are too painful to be more than momentarily glimpsed, particularly because, for lack of validation from other family members, he has to face these feelings alone; and the illness system of schizophrenia mushrooms as a set of defences—with its ingredients of misidenti-fication, delusional misinterpretations, massive denial, and so on— to provide him with an endurable 'reality'.

Over the course of the patient's psychotherapy, the feelings which are under discussion here predominate, in both patient and therapist, in a sequence which is, in broad outline, predictable: first, scorn; later, disillusionment; and later still—during the phase which in chapter 18 I have termed that of therapeutic symbiosis—adoration.

Because scorn is far from being one of the traditionally accept-able feelings in a physician towards his patient, the young therapist tends to repress his scorn, and act it out in various ways, rather than be aware of it. In working with chronically schizo-phrenic patients it is essential that he should become able to experience such a feeling towards them: not only is much schizophrenic behaviour realistically deserving of scorn, but such scorn is an important part of the necessary armour preserving his self-esteem in the face of one patient after another who are themselves evidencing, in many instances unremittingly for many months, a demeanour of loathing, disdain, cold antagonism or utter ignoring of him. A feeling of scorn on his part towards such behaviour is a humanly necessary self-protection against the inferiority feelings and the sense of chronic, impotent rage which patients, during this phase of the therapy, tend to kindle in one. The more insecure therapist, unable to face his own feelings of retaliatory scorn, will tend to foster a 'prematurely idolozed' transference role–will promote the patient's viewing him as an all-knowing mentor, in an unconscious effort to avoid the transference role, utterly necessary to the patient's eventual recovery, of the crazy, stupid parent (ch. 18). The patient tends to collaborate with such a development, in order to avoid facing his own scorn which is being so abundantly acted out in his demeanour. It takes much courage for both patient and therapist to face, more and more squarely, the mutual scorn which is the first phase of the sequence I am describing.

But for patient and therapist to cling indefinitely to a relatedness of *either* defensive (premature) idolization *or* chronic scorn will preclude their coming to terms with the phase of disillusionment; for this second phase to be traversed, both the feelings of idolization and of scorn need to be *brought* near to each other–to be experienced simultaneously, in progressively intense degree, in each participant.

The therapist's own unworked-through disillusionment, dating from his early childhood symbiosis with his mother, is a countertransference factor upon which psychotherapeutic progress, in many instances, now founders. Only to the degree that the therapist has plumbed, or proves able to plumb, the depths of such disillusionment can he help the patient to work down through this transference stratum to the next phase, that of the mutual, boundless adoration typical of the very early mother-infant symbiosis. Otherwise, the therapist will avoid like the plague any such omnipotent-mother transference position, or will cling chronically to a *defensively* 'omnipotent' position which he dare not let the patient seriously question.

SCORN, DISILLUSIONMENT AND ADORATION

It is, quite simply, technically very useful when we become able to detect the emotion of disappointment, of disillusionment, trying to break through a paranoid patient's seemingly endless, caustic blamingness. But in order to be able to detect this, we must be able to empathize with the disappointed patient, and many a therapist may feel less uncomfortable even at being blamed endlessly than at sensing this disappointment. The patient himself may unconsciously defend himself, at first, from feeling this emotion as such; instead, he may experience strange, concretistic, symbolic derivatives of it. One paranoid woman, for example, first experienced her disillusionment with her husband, who had divorced her during her hospitalization, in the delusional conviction that there were bits of him scattered all about Chestnut Lodge; and she let me know that at moments in our person-to-person exchanges when I would suddenly become what I would call stuffily 'psychiatric', instead of feeling disillusionment *per se* she would literally feel as though we had been riding in an aeroplane together, and she had suddenly been dropped down into the bottom of the ocean. Her many-months-long flushing of sundry items down the toilet proved eventually to be in part an acting out of her disillusionment with various people, including myself–people whom these items unconsciously symbolized to her.

Through the experiencing of progressively severe feelings of disillusionment towards one another, both patient and therapist reach progressively deep feelings of a loving, adoring, wholehearted acceptance of each other, and each of himself in the relationship, as human beings. Part of this process is the therapist's coming deeply to accept both the fact that the patient cannot be for ever more an omnipotent mother to him, and the fact that the patient, while having fostered the therapist's own personality-growth to a memorable degree, cannot make him into the person he would ideally like to become.

Humour is one of the great avenues by which disillusionment is sublimated in normal development, and the appearance of humour in the therapeutic relationship is one of the signs that patient and therapist have begun to integrate, to master, the disillusionment in that relationship.

Even before the defensive contempt has been entirely resolved, the patient's deepest feelings of adoration may appear in an acted out form, in, for example, his finding occasion to sit or even lie on the floor, so that he can literally–if not yet consciously, at an emotional level–'look up to' the therapist. One hebephrenic woman began to feel, in a largely somatized way, 'knocked out' by her mother-figure therapist towards whom she had developed, after years of intense scorn and antagonism, feelings of small-child adoration. Later on, as such feelings come into his awareness, he feels for a time that the parent-figure therapist must not see these, lest they frighten him; the therapist may now be surprised to discover the verbally scornful patient to be casting at him, at unguarded moments, glances of glowing adoration.

Several years ago, an initially catatonic young woman left therapy with me against my expressed wishes, after having achieved marked improvement but not thoroughgoing recovery. In retrospect, I realized something of the extent to which I had collaborated, unconsciously, with her avoidance of continuing the therapeutic investigation. In one of her final sessions, she produced newly remembered material about how, as a little child, she used to look up to her mother; she vividly recalled playing on the floor about her mother's feet, and the feet, as she described them, were those of a giant. I felt sure, in retrospect, that I had unconsciously avoided her coming to express towards me such a degree of dependency, which at the time I found awesome in its depth.

By contrast, in more recent years I have found patients expressing towards me, in the transference relationship, feelings of the deepest reverence and adoration, seeing me as the majestic Lincoln whose statue, in the Lincoln Memorial, is so evocative of worshipful awe; seeing me, for months on end, as God, as the very sun and the sky; seeing me comfortingly everywhere about them, in various disguises, in the people in the nearby village, on television, and in the movies; seeing me as not only all-powerful but wholly adorable. Whereas the patient suffering from paranoid schizophrenia, for example, has narcissistically felt convinced that the universe revolved about him, to just such a degree does the therapist, in this adored-omnipotent-mother phase of the transference, come to stand at the centre of the patient's universe, at the centre of his life.

How can the very human therapist fill such an adored-God role in the transference; will this not inevitably lead to disastrous disillusionment? I have found, for a number of reasons, that it does not. First, the deepest intensity of the stratum of scorn and disillusionment has already been traversed; such emotions no longer hold any terror for either participant. Secondly, I have learned that what the patient requires is not omnipotence-in-action but, rather, *the acceptance of the patient's feelings of adoration.* Through such acceptance, the therapist enables the patient to integrate the latter's own deepest strengths and deepest love, through identification with the therapist to whom these are at first attributed. In the same process, the patient makes contact not only with the therapist's own basic strengths, but also with those of parental figures from the past, strengths heretofore maintained on an introjected level and projected, in the transference, on to the therapist. Most importantly, the patient makes contact, through the medium of the transference, with the heretofore repressed, but powerful and genuine, mutual love between his mother and himself (see chs. 7, 12).

The outcome of this development is not an unprecedentedly disastrous disillusionment but, rather, the patient's now becoming able, after having thus made truly part of himself the strengths from these various sources, to venture increasingly into autonomous functioning as an individual differentiated from the former symbiosis with the therapist (ch. 18). Such increments of disillusionment as still present themselves are coped with in a spirit of the patient's 'disillusioning himself' at his own pace, rather than being thrust—as had been the case in his early childhood—into overwhelming disillusionment combined with isolation, through the parent's having psychologically withdrawn in the face of his adoration. Here, instead, the therapist remains available and accepting of the patient's dependent adoration whenever the patient, while still in the toddler-stage of establishing his autonomy, needs to return to such a relatedness.

The relationship of unbounded adoration which makes this development possible is, I emphasize, one of *mutual* adoring oneness (ch. 3). Ramana (1956), referring in his paper on borderline states to Freud's injunction against the analyst's taking the role of prophet, saviour, and redeemer to the patient, asks, '. . . but may we not—indeed, must we not—become the lover of the material projected by the patient and make it our introjected "good object"?' Milner (1952), in her beautiful account of her therapy of an 11-year-old boy who had found outer reality mechanized and soulless by reason of its unaccept-ingness of his own spontaneous creation, a difficulty she found traceable to a premature loss of belief in a self-created outer reality, describes how she helped him to achieve a healthy reality-relatedness through her acceptance of his treating her as being part of himself–as being his own malleable, pliable, 'lovely stuff', his chemicals, which he had created. Surely the therapist here must be able to experience something of an adored God-the-Creator in the patient. Winnicott, out of his extensive experience with pediatrics as well as psycho-analysis, plausibly conjectures how the healthy mother helps her baby towards an acceptance of external reality, through helping him to experience this reality not as something alien to himself, but as something self-created:

> . . . at the start a simple *contact* with external or shared reality has to be made, by the infant's hallucinating and the world's presenting, with moments of illusion for the infant in which the two are taken by him to be identical, which they never in fact are.
> For this illusion to be produced in the baby's mind a human being has to be taking the trouble all the time to bring the world to the baby in understandable form, and in a limited way, suitable to the baby's needs . . . (Winnicott, 1945).
> . . . by fitting in with the infant's impulse the mother allows the [nursing] baby the *illusion* that what is there is the thing created by the baby; as a result there is not only the physical experience of instinctual satisfaction, but also an emotional union, and the beginning of a belief in reality as something about which one can have illusions.
> . . . In the course of breast feeding a mother may repeat this perform-ance a thousand times. She may so successfully give her child the capacity for illusion that she has no difficulty in her next task, gradual disillusioning, this being the word for weaning in the primitive setting which is my interest in this paper (Winnicott, 1948).

Winnicott's description of this first establishment of feeling-contact with outer reality is fully analogous with the mutually adoring oneness which I have been describing as typical of the therapeutic symbiosis phase of therapy with the schizophrenic adult. Likewise reminiscent to me of my therapeutic experiences, and those of colleagues which I have sometimes heard recounted in supervision, are Winnicott's further comments:

SCORN, DISILLUSIONMENT AND ADORATION

... It took me years to realize that a feeding difficulty could often be cured by advising the mother to fit in with the baby absolutely for a few days. I had to discover that this fitting in with the infant's needs is so pleasurable to the mother that she cannot do it without moral support. If I advise this I must ask my social worker to visit daily, else the mother will wilt under criticism and feel responsible for too much.... she is scared to do as she deeply wants to do... (Winnicott, 1948).

In my experience, such lovingness in the transference relationship rapidly permeates the patient's feelings towards all the persons in his life. An additional reason why there is no subsequently catastrophic disillusionment is that he does not perceive the therapist as the one idolized figure in a hostile world; rather, he very shortly comes, to his astonishment and considerable embarrassment, to experience deep feelings of loving everyone. However much his later discriminations may modify such universally directed, wholehearted love, an essentially loving basis for his interpersonal relationships has become established. He does not emerge from these therapeutic developments with the kind of incompleted disillusionment which Richard Wright expresses, near the close of his account of his enchantment and disenchantment with Communism:

... I knew in my heart that I should never be able to write that way again, should never be able to feel with that simple sharpness about life, should never again express such passionate hope, should never again make so total a commitment of faith (Crossman, 1950).

The patient who has been able to resolve, in the transference relationship with the therapist, the schizophrenia-engendering early childhood disillusionment dares, on the contrary, to extend continuingly his deepest love, his most passionate hope, and his total commitment, for he has learned to brave any disillusionment which may ensue.

Chapter 22

THE PLACE OF NEUTRAL THERAPIST
RESPONSES IN PSYCHOTHERAPY WITH
THE SCHIZOPHRENIC PATIENT (1963)[1]

Introduction

IN this paper I shall first detail the results of various sensory-deprivation experiments, as reported in the literature, and shall then compare the experience of the normal subject in these experiments with the experience of the person who is suffering from chronic schizophrenia. Next I shall show that although there are many similarities between schizophrenic experience on the one hand, and sensory-deprivation experience on the other, this does *not* mean that the therapist in working with the schizophrenic patient should endeavour, consistently and vigorously, to provide him with abundant sensory experiences–by being, for example, consistently 'active' and emotionally responsive to him –for, as I shall attempt to demonstrate, the patient's subjective sensory deprivation has a *defensive* function, and it therefore will be meeting one of the patient's real emotional needs if the therapist, while being in general more emotionally responsive than he generally is with the neurotic patient, will none the less supply the patient, not infrequently, with emotionally *neutral* responses.

I wish to emphasize that this paper is not an attempt to prescribe to my fellow-therapists how they *should* react in working with the schizophrenic patient; it is an attempt, rather, to help them to become freer, as I have gradually by dint of hard struggle become freer, to react in the ways in which the psychotherapeutic process, between therapist and schizophrenic patient, *inherently tends to require* the therapist to become free to react, as that process unfolds. It is often hardest of all for us to allow ourselves to

[1] Abbreviated versions of this paper were presented at a December 1961 meeting of the Association for Psychoanalytic Medicine, and a December 1962 meeting of the American Psychoanalytic Association, both held in New York City. It was first published in the *International Journal of Psycho-Analysis*, Vol. 44 (1963), pp. 42–56.

react in an 'unfeeling' way, and it is with that particular sector of the therapist's overall feeling-participation, in the treatment of schizophrenia, that this paper deals.

The Relevance of the Sensory-Deprivation Experiments to Schizophrenia

The extent to which the schizophrenic individual is living in a state of sensory deprivation, and the implications for psychotherapeutic technique which arise from this state of affairs, began to interest me three years ago, in the course of my work with a schizophrenic man who, despite a demeanour of moderately good contact with outer reality, recurrently surprised me with indirect revelations of the profound degree to which he was suffering from a state of sensory deprivation. Thus alerted, I subsequently came to perceive a previously unsuspected intensity of sensory deprivation in the subjective experience of various other schizophrenic patients.

For many years there have appeared random reports of observations by explorers, shipwrecked sailors, aviators, prisoners in solitary confinement, mystics, and philosophers concerning the marked changes in personality functioning which arise in these various situations of marked isolation with attendant deprivation in terms of sensory stimuli from the outer world. But only during the last decade and a half, with the increasing number of studies of experimentally-induced sensory deprivation pioneered by Hebb (1937a, b, 1949), have such random reports in the general literature become the focus of our specific interest, and have the effects of sensory deprivation been studied systematically.[2] These effects include, in so-called normal subjects, many transient changes of the kind more durably evidenced in persons suffering from schizophrenia–deterioration in ability to think and reason, perceptual distortions, gross disturbances in feeling states, and occurrence of vivid imagery, sometimes in the form of bizarre hallucinations and delusions.

The experimental techniques of reducing evironmental input have included (a) absolute reduction of sensory stimulation, as in the experiments of Lilly (1956) and Camberari (1958),

[2] Miller (1962) has provided a splendidly comprehensive bibliography both of relevant writings in the general literature and of relevant studies and conceptual formulations in the scientific literature.

whose subjects were immersed in a water tank, nude except for a blacked-out face mask through which they breathed; (b) reduced patterning of sensory input, as in the work of Bexton, Heron, and Scott (1954), in which translucent goggles permitted light but no patterned vision, patterned sound was also minimized, and kinesthetic and tactile stimuli were interfered with by the use of cardboard cuffs and gloves; and (c) imposed structuring or monotony of sensory environment without reduction of stimulation, as in the experiments of Kubzansky and Leiderman (1961), who utilized a tank-type respirator with the vents open so that the subject breathed for himself, while vision was normal but restricted to a very limited field, and auditory and tactile-kinesthetic cues were dealt with as in the second technique, thus structuring sensory inputs in a monotonous, unchanging way.

The schizophrenic patient is often living in an environment which is, to the observer's view, deceptively rich in providing sensory stimulation, at least as contrasted with such experimental situations as those just outlined. But the hypnotic situation, helpfully included by Rapaport (1958) in his review of the various situations which are characterized by sensory deprivation, provides a particularly meaningful analogy to the experience of the schizophrenic patient in this regard: there may be no lack of environmental stimuli physically within reach of the hypnotic subject, yet for psychological reasons he is effectively cut off from them.

The relevance of sensory-deprivation experimental findings to clinical work with schizophrenic patients, no doubt already widely apparent to clinicians, was explicitly discussed by Rosenzweig (1959), and I have noted[3] that the impoverishment of the perceived world for some adult schizophrenic individuals approximates to that of the subject in these isolation experiments. Stanley Cobb (1961), in his introduction to the largely laboratory-oriented symposium entitled *Sensory Deprivation*, suggests that 'the symptoms of the deprived child with "atypical" and "autistic" reactions are without doubt related to the phenomena seen in adults after experimental sensory deprivation'. Pious (1961), in a careful clinical study of a schizophrenic patient's progressive changes in behaviour and inner experience, says, 'I have defined

[3] *The Nonhuman Environment.*

the precipitating circumstances [i.e. of the patient's moments of loss of psychological contact with the therapist] as psychological deprivation. This suggests a connection with such current ideas as sensory deprivation, sleep deprivation, etc., and I have a hunch that there may very well be such a connection.' Arieti (1961b), after commenting upon the sensory deprivation experiments, notes that 'In schizophrenia too we have some kind of psychological isolation. . . .'

I find certain of the data from these experiments to be particularly suggestive. The reported disturbances in body image in some subjects are identical with those which I have found in some of my most deeply disturbed patients, and which, with the exception of reports of LSD-induced psychoses, one rarely sees reported; Freedman et al. (1961), for example, mention that to four of their subjects 'the arms seemed to be dissociated from the body; the body seemed to become smaller; there was a sensation of floating in the air; the body seemed to become rigid and could not move'; and Cohen et al. (1961) report that one of their subjects 'became unsure of his body position and feared that his body parts would disappear and disintegrate'. Vernon et al. (1961) report that under the conditions of sensory deprivation the skin resistance goes down, and express their belief that sensory deprivation generates a great need for socialization and physical stimulation; one is impressed with the relevancy of their findings to the well-known clinical observations of schizophrenic patients' intense hunger for, and equally frequently seen dread of, physical contact.

Riesen's (1961) finding, in both cats and apes, that 'Stimulation that would be ordinary for the species in nature or in the laboratory can, at the end of sensory deprivation, produce paroxysmal fear' has helped me to understand better some of the intense startle-reactions among my patients, as being due to their having suddenly become aware of my presence after having been experiencing–unbeknown to me at the time–a period of sensory deprivation during which, although their eyes may have been upon me, they had, I subsequently realized, been unaware of my presence. One has a new appreciation of the long-known empirical finding that the patient in tenuous contact with reality reacts badly to sudden physical movements on the part of the therapist.

Finally, the 'white noise' (a random mixture of all frequencies), which Freedman *et al.* (1961) report to be extraordinarily effective in evoking the phenomena of sensory deprivation, seems to me to have a strikingly close analogy in the experience of the severely fragmented and dedifferentiated schizophrenic individual, whose subjective experience is, as best one can determine, a comparably discoordinate welter of fragmentary sensory impressions, fantasies, memories, and so on. In this connexion I find of interest Pious' (1961) impression that 'there is no diminution of the quantity of sensory intake in schizophrenic behaviour no matter how it may be restructured at any level', a view comparable with Rosenzweig's (1959) earlier-stated hypothesis that 'The critical factor in schizophrenia is . . . the inability to establish the relevance of sensory experience for ongoing processes.'

The severity of the sensory deprivation suffered by chronically schizophrenic patients has repeatedly surprised me. I refer, here, not to the patient who is obviously so 'out of contact' as to be manifestly living in a predominantly hallucinatory world, but rather to patients who seemingly possess a fair measure of reality-contact. One such woman let me know that, in her more disturbed periods, she was unable to perceive the heads of other persons, including myself, because of a 'vapour' which concealed them. On many occasions she let me know, always indirectly and with much apprehension, that she was at the moment quite unable to perceive me, and was perceiving instead, in my place, her daughter or her son, or a sister, or a death's head, or various other human or non-human forms. On one occasion she let me know that during various of our sessions, she saw in me her children, for example, more clearly than she could perceive them during the actual visits which she made to them on infrequent occasions. A man confided to me that he felt himself to be 'in a mist', and another woman repeatedly made as if to run through me, as though unsure that I existed. She was reminiscent of the 10-year-old boy described by Bonnard (1958) in 'Pre-Body-Ego Types of (Pathological) Mental Functioning', of whom she writes, '. . . his 2-year-old brother was repeatedly walked through and over, as if non-existent'. There was a period of some months during which I feared that this woman would seriously injure herself by hurling herself into the walls of her room, and I am now convinced that this was not on the basis of a conscious suicidal urge, but rather the expression of a need to make contact with an outer reality the existence of which she could not surely perceive visually, auditorially, or even tactually. Even this very ill woman only rarely and indirectly divulged the extent of the sensory deprivation in which she chronically lived; patients feel as ashamed, humiliated, and apprehensive about revealing this aspect of their experience as they do about revealing the fact that they suffer from hallucinations.

The schizophrenic individual suffers from sensory deprivation to a far greater degree than does the normal subject who is merely exposed, as in the sensory-deprivation experiments, to *external* surroundings which provide minimal sensory input, for the former has to a large degree lost his *inner world* also; unlike the normal subject, he cannot turn to an inexhaustible and well-integrated inner world of fantasy to provide him with 'sensory data' of a sort, and thereby fill the void in his sensory experience.

One hebephrenic woman, for example, asked me, 'Are there any stores?', in such a way as forcefully to convey to me her experience of the world as one so desolate that there may exist no stores anywhere in it. Later in the same hour, after much fragmentary talk, she made mention of a particular hospital (the one to which she had been taken when she had initially become psychotic) and a particular store (where, whether during that same era or not, she had evidently gone to buy gramophone records), and she made it quite clear to me that, in her subjective experience, these were the only two places in the world as she could at present conceive it; all this reminded me very much of how the world might look after nuclear warfare, with only a few scattered places left standing. A man described his total experience as a candle flame that kept flickering down and going out, and a woman dreamed of herself as a bombed-out building. Van der Heide (1961), in his paper 'Blank Silence and the Dream Screen', describes, from his work with a woman suffering from a severe ego disorder, her loss of an internalized mother image as manifested by her dream of the caving in of a house near an ocean. This is a sample of the dedifferentiation which affects the inner, as well as the outer, experiential world of the schizophrenic person. It has required years of intensive psychotherapy, in the instances of some of my patients, for them to be able to achieve any fantasy-life whatever, differentiated by them as such, in

631

contrast to their erstwhile immersion in a chaotically dedifferentiated amalgam of experience in which memories, fantasies, somatic sensations, and perceptions of the outer world had not been separable from one another.

The mechanism of unconscious *denial* accounts, of course, for, much of the patient's sensory deprivation; when, for example, one endeavours to convey to him some communication which runs counter to his superego, he may show an astonishingly concrete adherence to the principle of 'speak no evil – hear no evil – see no evil': one is left feeling not consciously ignored, but literally unheard. Of interest in this connexion are Warren M. Brodey's (1959) observations, from his studies of the interaction of schizophrenic patients with their families, vividly portraying that, in the upbringing of the child who later develops schizophrenia, only those ingredients of what we call outer reality which are significantly supportive of, or significantly threatening to, the mother's 'inner workings' comprise the effective outer reality of the child; evidently the remainder of outer reality, for all practical purposes, simply does not exist for him.

But important though unconscious denial is – and I shall give a number of additional instances of it – the already mentioned defence mechanism of dedifferentiation is, I think, equally important in giving rise to sensory-deprivation phenomena.[4] Many writers have described a loss of ego-boundaries as being among the fundamental chacteristics of schizophrenia; this symptom involves, by definition, the patient's relating symbiotically to the persons in his environment, as well as his inability, similarly, to distinguish clearly between himself and the non-human ingredients of his surroundings[5]. My point here is that to the degree that such symbiotic or 'oneness' experience of the world prevails, the patient is not provided with any subjective experience of sensory input from an outside world, for he has no outer world, experienced as such. Martin Buber (1957) has pointed out that 'entering into relationship' presupposes a 'primal setting at a distance'. One could say that to the degree that the unconscious

---

[4] I hope it is clear that I am using the term 'sensory deprivation' here in a phenomenological sense only, as a means of attempting to describe some aspects of the patient's experience, rather than putting forward 'sensory deprivation' as a separate and special psychodynamic defence mechanism, on a par with such mechanisms as denial and dedifferentiation.
[5] Searles, *The Nonhuman Environment*.

defence of dedifferentiation has the schizophrenic individual in its grip, he is unable to set anything of the potential outer world sufficiently at a distance to be able to experience it with his sense-organs. In my opinion, the state of 'psychological deprivation' which Pious (1961) describes as the most archaic level of behaviour in his schizophrenic patient, is a state in which the patient's experience has become dedifferentiated to a level of symbiotic relatedness with the therapist–a state in which the therapist does not exist for the patient, because in the patient's subjective experience the therapist is so much a part of him as not to exist in outer reality. Significantly, Pious mentions that 'The schizophrenic's "mental image" of the investigator seems to function to strengthen the threshold against psychological deprivation', and I gather that his patient lost that image at the moment, in the behavioural sequence, of what he calls the 'nadir event' of the psychological deprivation. Pious says that it 'is an event which seems to me to be completely enigmatic. . . . The insufficiency of the observations of this event stand in contrast to my estimate of its importance.'

I have seen much of what I believe to be this 'nadir event', or in my terms symbiotic relatedness, in my work with a hebephrenic woman who has been struggling for many months to achieve a separation between inner and outer worlds. In one hour, for example, she said roughly, in a tone as though she wished I would disappear, 'Why don't you be a piece of cake and eat it?' Then, following several minutes of comments which I found unintelligible, she said, 'Then you'd have your cake and eat it–. . .', and after another several minutes' interlude of comments which I again found undecipherable, she asked, 'Did you ever have a piece of cake there and then it *wasn't* there?' This was said in a tone clearly implying that this is what happens, or has happened, in her experience, and she looked reproachfully and accusingly at me as she asked this. Data from subsequent hours, too detailed to reproduce here, indicated that the cake symbolized (among, no doubt, other meanings) myself, whom she recurrently 'ate' and disgorged, in varying states of, respectively, symbiosis and object-relatedness in the transference. In another hour, her wish for us to have hamburgers revealed itself as her wish for us to eat one another; and in still another hour a lollypop which she kept trying to push down her throat and make it stay down inside her represented, for her, her therapist who kept leaving her.

Concerning normal subjects' reactions to experimental sensory deprivation, Freedman *et al.* (1961) advance the hypothesis that 'it is the absence of order or meaning rather than the specific nature of the stimulus field which tends to degrade perceptual organization', and suggest that 'The auditory and visual "hallucinations" . . . may be thought of as the result of an attempt to order such stimuli as are available because of the need to find meaning in the environment.' Similarly, Ruff *et al.* (1961) state, in the conclusion of their report of their studies, 'Our formulation . . . is that isolation "destructures" the environment. The subject responds by restructuring to create a sense of continuity with his previous existence. He thus restores meaning to the situation.' This is in interesting contrast, but certainly not contradiction, to a hypothesis I put forward in 1960, namely that the schizophrenic patient's unconscious denial of outer reality has a restitutive aspect, in that it provides him with a more or less blank screen upon which a necessary reprojection of pathogenic introjects, an externalization of internal conflicts from the past, can now be effected – akin to the function of the neutral screen atmosphere fostered by the analyst in the treatment of the neurotic individual[6]

One can think of it that such a 'neutral-screen' perception of his outer world permits the schizophrenic individual to utilize, as a necessary defence against overwhelming affects, the kind of primitive denial of which Jacobson (1957) writes, when she says, '. . . clinical observations leave no doubt that denial is a more archaic, more primitive, and historically earlier mechanism than repression – in fact, its forerunner . . . denial presupposes an infantile concretization of psychic reality, which permits persons who employ this defence to treat their psychic strivings as if they were concrete objects perceived'. A person who possesses a normal clarity of perception of the actual concrete objects in his environment is thereby barred from utilizing such a defence; to use it, outer reality needs to be one's own mass of plasticine. Of aetiological interest, here again, are Warren Brodey's (1961) observations. Emphasizing the importance of the mechanism of externalization, which he defines as projection plus the selective

[6] *The Nonhuman Environment*, p. 167.

use of reality for verification of the projection, he reports that 'This selective use of reality was extreme in all the families observed. . . . Each family member appears to cathect with interest and meaningfulness only a limited aspect of his environmental surroundings–that which validates expectation; the remainder of the reality available for perception is omitted.'

Dement's (1960) dream-deprivation experiments, the results of which suggest that a relatively generous opportunity to dream is essential to healthy psychological integration, even for the normal individual, are relevant here. So, too, is Macalpine's (1950) paper, 'The Development of the Transference', in which she points out that transference–the development and evolution of which is so essential to psycho-analytic cure–does not simply arise spontaneously in the patient in the psycho-analytic setting, but that, rather, 'Psychoanalytic technique creates an infantile setting, of which the "neutrality" of the analyst is but one feature among others. To this infantile setting the analysand–if he is analysable–has to adapt, albeit by regression. In their aggregate, these factors, which go to constitute this infantile setting, amount to a reduction of the analysand's object world and denial of object relations in the analytic room.' Gill (1954) expresses his concurrence with Macalpine's view in this matter and expresses his own conviction that 'The [psycho-analytic] technique itself exerts a nonspecific, steady unremitting regressive pressure.' It is of further interest that, in Macalpine's list of fourteen ingredients of the analytic situation which so formidably foster the development of transference on the part of the patient, heading the list are, '1. *Curtailment of the object world.* External stimuli are reduced to a minimum. . .', and '2. *The constancy of environment,* which stimulates fantasy.'

Sèchehaye (1956, pp. 109-10) comments that one function of a psychosis consists in 'scotomatizing all sectors of reality related to the frustrations. . . . For this reason, Renée came to believe that the world did not exist and that she herself was only a shadow.' This observation reminded me that one schizophrenic woman's functional environment, about the hospital grounds, proved to be a complexly restricted one, interlaced with forbidden areas which were effectually barred from her existence, because for her to enter into these *geographical areas* would involve her being assailed with the repressed emotions–of, most prominently, grief—which were related, by associational memories, to the various corresponding areas of her past life; by living in a thus restricted environment, she preserved her protective areas of amnesia. Similarly, I realized that when a hebephrenic woman walked about the floor of her room, near me, in a highly complex pattern, for all the world as if walking on steel beams set about yawning gulfs at her feet, this intricate pattern corresponded to her anxious avoidance of innumerable feeling-laden topics in our therapeutic investigation; but I do not doubt that she genuinely experienced this, instead, in the form of the multiple mouths of an abyss at her feet, such that she must not stray off the narrow and complex path along which she was teetering.

With a somewhat less deeply ill woman I was able to delineate, piecemeal but quite specifically, various of the affects which one of her former denial-symptoms had served to keep repressed. She described her never having seen any men during her trips from her suburban parental home into Philadelphia. It developed that this scotoma had at least the following determinants in various different areas of her unconscious: (*a*) her parents had ingrained in her the deep-seated conviction that it is immoral for a young woman to 'see men'; (*b*) she was so fully, though at a deeply denied level, absorbed in unworked-through feelings of loss of various girls and women she had known in the past, that men did not exist for her; (*c*) she was afraid, at another unconscious level, that if a man's face registered in her perception, she would lose control of her rage-towards-men and hit him on the jaw (for, as she felt it, robbing her of her feminine friends); and (*d*) the sight of a man's face would bring before her, also, the unresolved grief over the death of a young male cousin whom she had loved.

The Important Role of Neutral Therapist-Responses in the Psychotherapy of Schizophrenia

All that I have been saying here has implications concerning the schizophrenic patient's need for a readily available neutral response from his therapist.

Many of the writings in recent years concerning the psychotherapy of schizophrenia, including my own, have emphasized that the therapist must be able to provide in generous measure an intensity of emotional response which goes far beyond Freud's (1912) injunction to the analyst: 'The doctor should be opaque to his patients and, like a mirror, should show them nothing but what is shown to him.' Sèchehaye (1961), noting that even in the analysis of the neurotic patient the analyst must at times 'depart from his absolute neutrality and from his role of the reflecting mirror', emphasizes the psychotic patient's need for personal involvement. Perry (1961) says that, in the psychotherapy of schizophrenia, 'the ideal situation would be one in which the patient feels that anything he reveals is found meaningful by the therapist, who then responds to it with genuine resonance'. Arieti (1961a), in setting out to list the necessary components of the 'therapeutic attitude' for work with schizophrenic patients, emphasizes, 'First, the therapist must have an attitude of *active and intense intervention*. He comes to participate in the struggle which goes on and not to listen passively to ideas which cannot be associated fully.' Jackson's (1961) scorn for the neutral response is apparent in his following comment, concerning the historical development of this area of psychotherapy: 'Perhaps because the therapist had a mother himself he could identify with the almost unverbalizable horrors that stemmed from the schizophrenic's longing, despair, and hate. When a therapist became a part of these feelings he was more able to become aware of his own responses, since it was unlikely that any mortal could sit inscrutable amidst these emotional barrages.'

But I wish to emphasize here that, although it may indeed severely threaten our sense of humanness, the schizophrenic patient needs from us not only the kind of intense emotional responsiveness which makes for comparatively dramatic clinical papers, but an equally liberal measure of neutral, and related, responses: responses of inscrutability, imperturbability, impassivity and, on many occasions, what can only be called indifference.

Only by a comparatively unanxious acceptance of such responses, or such lack of response, in ourselves can we help the patient to erode through the areas of 'as if' pseudo-emotion, ostensibly intense emotion which is not truly an indication of deep inner experience but rather a superficial imitative phenomenon, which has been described by Helene Deutsch (1942), Reich (1953), Eissler (1953), and Greenson (1958) in patients with ego-disorders of various degress of severity, and which I have found to be very prominent, indeed, in deeply and chronically schizophrenic persons.

Early in my work with a hebephrenic woman – to give but one typical example – I at times felt troubled, and doubtful of my capacity for human feeling, at finding myself utterly unmoved to sympathy despite her being apparently in the grip of intense and wordless grief: her body was convulsed and wracked by sobs, her face appeared ravaged by grief, and she showed a little child's helplessness to cope with the tears which streamed copiously down her cheeks. Only after many months did it become clear that such behaviour arose from introjects of her mother and her maternal grandmother, with whose controlling-ness-through-weeping the girl had never been sufficiently 'hard' to cope successfully.

On other occasions in the early months of the therapy, she showed a seductive woman-of-the-world demeanour to which I fell to reciprocating, at the level of a kind of mutually 'knowing' repartee filled with sexual allusions. In the course of several weeks she became increasingly anxious in this setting, finally cowering away from me, at the opposite side of her room, and calling out desperately, like a little girl who had got into water well above her head, 'You take the men, Mommy!'. This erotic kind of interaction, convincing though it had seemed as evidence of a well-established level of maturation, proved to be but a brittle kind of 'as-if' defence against her deeper and more genuine infantile needs for mothering, which were to occupy us subsequently for years.

In one session which occurred after we had been working together for several years, she began imitating the various laughs of some six or eight student nurses who were playing and watching tennis on a court outside her window and who, on the eve of their return to their distant home-hospital after having completed their difficult psychiatric affiliation at Chestnut Lodge, were evidently filled with relief and exuberance. The silence of our session was punctuated only by her imitating, from time to time, one or another of the wide variety of laughs which came from the nurses. Her early laughs were done with such 'skill' that I thought her genuinely happy, found her laughs often infectious, and laughed with her. But then, as she went on laughing from time to time, the eeriness of what she was doing grew more and more upon me: it became increasingly clear to me that this woman was momentarily hiding her massive despair by imitating laughs for which she, unlike their original authors, had at the moment no correspondingly genuine wellspring of happiness; I hasten to emphasize that I had many times seen this woman in scattered moments of joy which I had found no reason to question. It was this session which helped me to realize, in retrospect, how very much of this woman's behaviour over the years, including the period of her erotically-knowing, woman-of-the-world demeanour, had consisted in very complex, remarkably skilfully woven fabrics of just such imitative behaviour of which she had been showing me, in this session, a few comparatively simple threads.

A neutral type of the therapist participation proves to be essential to the resolution of the schizophrenic patient's basic ambivalence concerning individuation—his intense conflict, that is, between clinging to a hallucinatory, symbiotic mode of existence, in which he is his whole perceived world, or on the other hand relinquishing this mode of experience and committing himself to object-relatedness and individuality—to becoming, that is, a separate person in a world of other persons. Will (1961) points out that just as 'In the moves toward closeness the person finds the needed relatedness and identification with another; in the withdrawal (often marked by negativism) he finds the separateness which favours his feeling of being distinct and self-identified', and Burton (1961) says that 'In the treatment, the patient's desire for *privacy* is respected and no encroachment is made. The two conflicting needs war with each other and it is a serious mistake for the therapist to take sides too early.' The schizophrenic patient has not yet had the experience that commitment to object-relatedness still allows for separateness and privacy, and where Sèchehaye (1956, p. 181) recommends that one 'make oneself a substitute for the autistic universe which alone offered some morbid satisfaction' to the patient, I find it more helpful to—primarily by my presence—*offer* myself as such a substitute; the choice must rest in the patient's hands. This I regard as the primeval area of applicability of a general comment by Burton (1961) that 'In the psychotherapy of every schizophrenic a point is reached where the patient must be confronted with his *choice* . . .', and of Shlien's (1961) comment that 'Freedom means the widest scope of choice and openness to experience. . . .'

The Ambivalence Concerning the Relinquishment of Autism-and-Symbiosis and the Acceptance of Object-Relatedness; Borderline States; Early Ego-Development in the Healthy Infant

When the therapist conveys to the patient such a freedom to choose, he fosters by the same act an atmosphere in which the patient becomes exposed to a mounting inner *necessity to choose*, a mounting realization of the necessity to commit himself to either an autistic-symbiotic mode of existence on the one hand, or on the other to genuine object-relatedness – to existence as a separate individual among individual other persons. This conflict is, I believe, beyond being of major importance in any instance of schizophrenia, of specifically central importance in borderline states; it is, in my experience, one conflict which quite precisely characterizes these latter states, which in other regards are so vague and difficult to describe.

The borderline patient is one who literally lives on the borderline between autism-and-symbiosis on the one hand, and object-relatedness on the other. It is as if he were trying to have the gratifications of both modes of relatedness, without relinquishing either mode; trying to work both sides of the street; trying, in an almost literal sense, to eat his cake (i.e. the other person, or whatever ingredient of the outside world) and have it too – to make it part of him, and yet simultaneously to make it available there in the outside world also. In actuality, he gets less than his share of either kind of gratification, and is far from feeling possessed of any conscious ability to manipulate these processes, however prone the therapist is to attribute such power to him.

The therapist in working with the borderline patient is often made to feel helpless in face of the seeming facility with which the patient, when faced with frustration during the course of genuine interpersonal relating (as when the therapist is persistently and firmly putting forward an unpalatable interpretation) will shift into an inaccessible autistic state, or into symbiotic relatedness permeated by so much projection of part aspects of himself upon the therapist, and so much of a regressive, concretistic perception of the therapist's words that the latter suddenly finds his efforts at verbal, genuinely interpersonal relatedness to be totally ineffective. Similarly, the therapist finds that the patient is, for a long time, equally bafflingly and maddeningly defended against healthy symbiotic experience which the therapy must come to include, in order to be successful: the patient recurrently flees from the intimacy of any such developing oneness-experience into a defensive, and therefore unproductive, kind of object-relatedness which is only ostensibly mature.

Only in a therapeutic setting where he finds the freedom to experience both these modes of relatedness with one and the same person can the patient become able to choose between psychosis and emotional maturity, and he can settle for this latter only in proportion as he realizes that both object-relatedness *and* symbiosis are essential ingredients of healthy human relatedness—that the choice between these modes amounts not to a once-for-all commitment, but that, rather, to enjoy the gratifications of human relatedness he must commit himself to either object-relatedness or symbiotic relatedness, as the changing needs and possibilities of the human interaction require and permit.

I surmise that the basic therapeutic development which occurs in this setting is that the patient develops the ego-capacity to move, on his own initiative so to speak, from one mode of relatedness to the other. In contrast to the state of affairs we see in the borderline patient, whose switches from one mode of relatedness to another are actually made in the face of a patient-ego more helpless than the therapist feels himself to be, and are dictated by the urgent need to avoid overwhelming anxiety, it is now a matter of there having developed, in the patient's ego, two powerful arms—one the arm of symbiosis, and the other the arm of object-relatedness—to meet and express a personal existence which is sensed as predominantly good and inviting rather than bad and anxiety-arousing.

Spitz (1957, p. 122) tells us that not until about the eighth month of life does the infant become able to discriminate between animate and inanimate in the surrounding world, and the adult schizophrenic patient shows us, in his rageful disapproval of any signs of aliveness in the therapist during this phase of ego-differentiation in the transference, how frustrating it is to the infant to recognize the mother's separate and inner-directed

641

aliveness; the adult schizophrenic patient makes it quite clear that the therapist is supposed to be an inanimate instrument-a Coke machine, as one patient put it-which exists only for the automatic gratification of the patient's needs.

A hebephrenic woman clearly expressed the grief and feelings of rejection which are entailed in the resolution of the symbiosis with the mother-therapist-entailed in, that is, the recognition of an outside world in which the therapist exists. In one session, after I had recently relieved my intense frustration, arising from my long and arduous work with this deeply fragmented woman, by expressing intense hatred and contempt towards her, I came up to her room feeling more than usually accepting of the difficult situation. She was lying in bed sucking her thumb and looking confused and fragmented, as usual, when I came in, and after greeting her I sat down contentedly several feet from her bed and made myself comfortable. During the first few minutes she made a number of efforts at vocalization, but these were garbled and half inaudible, and I said nothing until, after several minutes had elapsed, I asked in a semi-sardonic tone, 'How are things in your world?' She replied, 'I can't see much of it.' This was itself something of a revelation to me, although I had remembered her saying on an occasion several weeks before, while sucking her thumb, 'The harder I suck the more I can see.'

In saying, 'I can't see much of it', she was looking at one of the two bedposts at the foot of her bed, and she went on, 'Do you see anything wrong with that bedpost?' She agreed with my expressed hunch that it did not look like the other one to her, and then her usual fragmentary comments contained repeated pleas to 'give me the key . . . the key to the bedpost'. She then glanced over at the fly of my trousers, and said, 'She wants to see it-do you know what I mean?' She often referred to herself in the third person. I replied, 'It *sounds* to me as though maybe she wants to see my penis.' She clearly rejected this comment, saying, 'She wants to see the outside world. Some people do,' she added with a bereft expression on her face. I replied, 'You don't see much of the outside world, I guess, do you?—And you'd like to be able to see more of it.' She responded harshly, antagonistically, and scornfully, 'I don't *care* about the outside world! I care about the *inside*!', and then during the next few moments she was looking rejected and making brief comments conveying her rejected feeling. I said then, kindly and firmly, 'Now you get feeling rejected; you very quickly get feeling rejected, don't you?' She replied, feelingly, 'It's hell, isn't it?'

At another point in the hour she was looking over at my shirt, and said, with love and grief in her voice, 'That's a nice shirt . . . I like to sit and look at the shirt.' It was as if her rare and cherished seeing of my shirt was itself a realization of our separateness from one another. Soon after this she asked, 'Do you know what my mother feels?', in a tone as if she were asking, 'Do you know whether she feels anything?', and went on, 'Do you know what she feels about sitting?' On an earlier occasion, she had said, after one of her mother's hurried and hectically gay visits to the Lodge, 'I've seen the flight of the bumble-bee.' Her own introject of this incessantly active, superficially gay but inwardly despairing and unrelated, mother had required years of therapy, earlier, to resolve. She now went on about her own head, saying that she guessed that it 'needs a lot of fixing', and later commented, 'I should have sat!', agreeing that she thought this might have prevented the trouble with her head.

In *The Nonhuman Environment* I included many separate instances of the schizophrenic patient's reacting to the therapist as being an inanimate object. Since then, I have come to see what I feel to be a more adequate total picture of the process of psychotherapy with the schizophrenic or borderline schizophrenic patient, as a process in which there is first a gradual dedifferentiation of the patient's confusingly complex but 'autistic' experience, into a phase analogous to the dream screen described by Lewin (1946, 1953) a phase of relative blankness as far as content is concerned by reason of the deeply undifferentiated symbiosis with the therapist. It is, I have come to see, in this phase that the whole of the patient's former 'reality', including the whole non-human realm in aggregate, is as it were poured into the symbiosis with the therapist, and it is out of this symbiosis that the patient's 'reality' becomes more deeply cathected with feeling and therefore with a genuine sense of reality, and he correspondingly becomes more deeply able to distinguish among such realms as human and non-human, animate and inanimate, through rediscovering them in the therapist-mother. In a sense, the therapist mediates the re-creation of the patient's world in a way that at moments can only be felt as godlike; but a new world is created for the therapist, too, out of such deeply symbiotic experience. One experiences, in the symbiotic phase of this mother-infant transference, the validity of Sèchehaye's (1956, pp. 58, 165) comments, concerning the child's relationship with the mother, 'Does not the child . . . through her establish his early relations with the outside world? . . . In a way, the mother is the child's first ego . . .' and, '. . . to the small child, is his mother not the whole universe? When the first object relations develop amid insecurity and aggression, the individual never succeeds in creating stable and positive relationships with the world around him . . .', and the validity of Spitz's (quoted by Sèchehaye, 1956, p. 58) terse comment, 'The nursling's ego is his mother's ego.'

Rycroft (1951) reports that, in analysis, 'the occurrence of a blank dream marks . . . a turning point, namely, from a narcissistic state toward a recatexis of the external world and a thrust in ego development', and Van der Heide (1961) while regarding his borderline patient's transitory blank silences as defensive in nature and, in one instance, stating that 'the very matrix of transference, the early mother-infant relation of the preverbal stage, became exposed' as a result of an interpretation which 'shattered the actual ego-defences and a functional ego regression took place', none the less indicates cautiously that these blank silences were, as in the instance of Rycroft's experience, followed by clinical improvement. Although I cannot approve of the technique of Azima, Vispo, and Azima (1961), who promote the patient's regression to a state of infantile dedifferentiation through exposing him to an experimental-type situation of sensory deprivation, I am convinced, as I have mentioned in earlier papers (1959A, B, 1961), that a naturally occurring, and to a significant degree mutual, phase of symbiotic relatedness in the transference, holding sway not merely for moments but for months, is the core phase in the psychotherapy of schizophrenia. A form of neutral participation by the therapist is essential to the development, and successful traversing, of this phase; too much activity from him, whether verbal or non-verbal, interferes with and may thwart this evolution.

NEUTRAL THERAPIST RESPONSES

The Therapist's Face

The therapist's *face* has a central role in this symbiotic interaction. In each of several instances in which deeply and chronically schizophrenic patients have progressed far towards recovery in my work with them, the symbiotic phase has been characterized by, among other manifestations, his or her sitting and staring at my face, in session after session, with all the absorbed wonderment, and responsive play of facial expressions, of a child immersed in watching a fascinating motion picture. I can now fully believe Spitz's (1945) comment that 'The child . . . learns to distinguish animate objects from inanimate ones by the spectacle provided by his mother's face in situations fraught with emotional satisfaction.' It is thus, in fact, that the child – or the adult schizophrenic patient – becomes aware of his own limitlessly varied emotional capacities, and even of his very aliveness, seen first as attributes of the mother-therapist. Freud, in *The Ego and the Id* (1923), stated that 'anything arising from within (apart from feelings) that seeks to become conscious must try to transform itself into external perceptions . . .'; from what we now know of normal infants and of adults recovering from schizophrenia, we can include feelings also within that principle. The deep significance of the face is emphasized in another statement by Spitz (1957, pp. 127–8): 'The inception of the functioning of the reality principle is evident at the three-months level, when the hungry infant becomes able to suspend the urge for the immediate gratification of his oral need. He does so for the time necessary to perceive the mother's face and to react to it. This is the developmental step in which the "I" is differentiated from the "non-I"; in which the infant becomes aware of the "otherness" of the surround.'

Papers by Greenacre (1958), Almansi (1960), and Elkisch (1957) have served to stress further the significant role of the face in early ego-development and in the establishment and maintenance of object-relatedness. Greenacre (1958), in her paper 'Early Physical Determinants in the Development of the Sense of Identity', states that

The body areas which are . . . most significant in comparing and contrasting and establishing individual recognition of the body self, and that of others, are the *face* and the *genitals*. While some response

645

to the mother's or nurse's face occurs very early, there can be no comparison of this with the own face until relatively late. . . . They are obviously of basic importance in the sense of identity. At the same time they are the areas which are at least easily visible to the individual himself. As no one ever sees his own face, the nearest he approaches this is the reflection of his face in the water or a mirror. . . .

. . . It would appear that even at a mature age the individual is in need of at least one other person, similar to himself, to look at and speak to, in order to feel safe in his own identity, i.e. that there is a continual reinforcement of the sense of the own self by the 'taking in' of a similar person without which an isolated individual feels first an intensification and then a diminution of the sense of self and of identity. . . .

Almansi (1960), in his paper 'The Face-Breast Equation', refers to Spitz's (1955) (a) postulation that, from a visual standpoint, the Isakower phenomenon and Lewin's dream screen do not represent the breast but rather the visually perceived human face; (b) observation that the nursing infant's gaze is constantly fixed on the mother's face; and (c) studies on the importance of the infant's recognition of the Gestalt of the human face first, and later identification of the mother's face, in the development of object relations and in the early mental life of the child. Almansi offers clinical evidence in support of his own speculation that the fusion of these two percepts (i.e. the percept of the breast and the percept of the face), the screening of one by the other, and their equation may occur more frequently than we have realized. Of especial interest in his presentation of evidence, from various cases, that the percept of the face has been even more deeply repressed than the percept of the breast. He writes,

. . . clinical experience indicates unequivocally that on a primitive perceptual level the face may be equated with the breasts, and that there is a particularly strong correlation between the nipples and the eyes. . . . It is also apparent that this phenomenon is not rare, as I have noted its occurrence in four patients, and shortly thereafter three other cases were called to my attention. The delineation of this [face-breast] equation confirms Spitz's hypothesis, i.e. that under conditions of deep regression the percept of the face may re-emerge from its condensation with the breast image, which may be said to act as a screen for the face. It is interesting to note that in this condensation it is the percept of the face which is most repressed and most strongly cathected.

Elkisch (1957), in 'The Psychological Significance of the Mirror', describes the significant role of mirrors in the symptomatology evidenced by three psychotic patients in her experience. Each of these patients, when faced with panic during or apart from his psychotherapeutic session, would rush to stare prolongedly at his face in a mirror, and one took to seizing frantically his therapist's hand and staring into her eyes in a similar manner. Elkisch follows Frazer (1947) and Róheim (1919) in emphasizing the connexion between mirroring and death:

> . . . This idea of death with regard to mirroring or reflecting one's image in the water is essentially connected with the idea of losing one's soul. 'When the Motomuto of New Guinea first saw their likenesses in a looking-glass, they thought that their reflections were their souls.' [Frazer(1947)] Man's mirrored image first must have appeared to him as something graspable, real. But since actually it was unreal, namely, not made of stuff he could lay his hand on, he obviously felt he was faced with his soul. And this soul being externalized might leave him and that would mean death. Contrariwise, the psychotic individual whose mortal fear of loss of self takes place inside of him seems to turn to the mirror as if it could protect him against such a loss. He 'uses' the mirror in order to externalize, alias project, his impulses and conflicts (which in reality he denies). And since the act of projection means throwing on to someone or something outside what actually belongs inside, namely to oneself, such an act amounts to a loss of psychic content. Thus, metaphorically speaking, one could say that through projection a person 'loses his soul'.
>
> It has been my impression in the three cases cited that these patients tried to retrieve, as it were, in their mirrored images what they felt they had lost or might lose: their ego, their self, their boundaries. . . .

Three schizophrenic women whom I have been treating for several years have shown a great deal of the kind of mirroring activity which Elkisch describes. My work with them and with other psychotic patients has suggested to me that the therapist (and, in particular, his face) comes to serve as a kind of mirror image to the patient–as, that is, an alter ego–preliminary to the patient's identifying with the increasingly emotionally-responsive therapist who confirms, by his increasingly rich responses, the patient's own re-differentiating emotional capacities. This is in line with a concept which I have presented in chapters 10 and 11 to the effect that, in the process of recovery of the severely fragmented and dedifferentiated schizophrenic patient, the growth process of integration and differentiation occur first outside the patient – in the realm of the therapist's developing responsiveness to him, and in the realm of the responsiveness to the patient which is engendered among the group of patients-and-personnel on his ward, and elsewhere – before the patient, by the process of identification with the increasingly richly integrated responsiveness of these others, makes the advancing growth process an integral part of himself.

Where Elkisch describes the psychotic patient's use of the mirror as representing his panicky endeavour to cling to his identity, I think of this act as expressing *ambivalent* desires on his part, both to cling to *and to lose* (through externalization upon the mirror) his identity. The invaluable work of Erikson (1956, 1958) concerning identity crises and other aspects of the struggle for identity has tended to highlight, by its very beauty and perceptiveness, the sense of ego-identity as something to be cherished so that we tend to underestimate how ambivalent are one's feelings – particularly, the psychotic individual's feelings – about this matter of identity. Until comparatively late in his treatment, the psychotic person's precarious sense of ego-identity, is, I believe, predominantly negatively toned; to be the person he feels himself to be means, more than anything else, to be a malevolent, lonely, and tortured outcast. It is small wonder that his anxiety lest he lose any sense of personal identity is balanced by his yearning to give up so painful an identity as this only one which he at all enduringly knows. Fromm's comments in his *Escape from Freedom* (1941), pointing out some of the psychological costs entailed in the development and maintenance of a sense of individuality, emphasize a facet of this subject of ego-identity not to be forgotten in our appreciation of Erikson's work which has had so great an impact upon our thinking in more recent years.

In these comments about the role, in therapy, of the therapist's face, I have been trying to describe something of the manner in which, in the evolution of the patient's transference to the mother-therapist, the patient becomes able to detect, and make increasingly part of himself, the whole realm of emotion which was too inaccessibly hidden behind the inscrutable face of the actual mother of his infancy and early childhood, and which, consequently, has heretofore been walled off, within himself, to a comparably impenetrable degree, so that his own emotionality –an emotionality for these very reasons not yet at all well differentiated, not yet maturely elaborated–has been heretofore as inaccessible to him as was the realm of feeling in his mother. One hebephrenic woman repeatedly told me that she had never been able to 'meet' her mother, and for a long time reacted to me, in the transference relationship, as a stranger-mother who would not come forth to meet her. A paranoid woman described her sense of divorcement from her own feelings as an experience of 'being completely severed from yourself'.

Discussion

Sèchehaye (1956, p. 186) beautifully describes how the person suffering from schizophrenia 'needs time, time to learn to believe again in living, to renew his confidence in others; slowly to describe a silhouette, the therapist, which gradually detaches itself from chaos and takes form in his opaque, unstable, disorganized universe'. The therapist facilitates this best by silence; here a comment, from analytic work, by Arlow (1961) is relevant: 'The magnificence of silence in interpersonal relationships is its very ambiguity.'

Emotions in the therapist have their crucial place in this work; but they cannot and need not be forced. In the overall evolution of the transference relationship, the therapist goes through, in actuality, a succession of very different 'neutral' orientations towards the patient. At first there prevails in him a kind of neutrality which is the manifestation of a lack of much feeling of any variety towards the predominantly narcissistically oriented rather than object-related patient. Later, his orientation shifts to a kind of neutrality towards the patient who is now immersed in object-relatedness, but of a deeply and pathologically ambivalent kind; the therapist sees and hears the patient's conscious and genuine efforts to make contact with him in a loving and constructive way, but is simultaneously equally aware of, and emotionally distanced by, the equally intense antagonism which the patient is as yet unaware of possessing and conveying. Still later, the therapist feels a kind of neutrality which is the manifestation of an unlimited multiplicity and variety of emotions. The patient now comes to see with fascination, in this phase of 'therapeutic symbiosis' (chs. 10, 11, 18), the varied and changing feelings on the therapist's face not only through the mechanism of the patient's attributing his own re-differentiating emotions to the therapist, but also because the totality of the therapist's feeling-capacities have indeed been called into play, over the preceding months and years, in the development of this relationship which is so deeply significant to each of the two participants.

Seen retrospectively in terms of this progression, the therapist's inscrutability is an externalized representation of the patient's limitless feeling potentialities. As a therapist, just as I have found on innumerable occasions that an emotional response from me, of one kind or another, is vital to the patient's developing related-ness with me, I have seen equally often how a premature re-sponsiveness on my part amounts to a kind of premature closure of a Gestalt in the patient-therapist relationship, with a conse-quent shutting off of an area of potential ego-development in the patient.

As a simple example of what I mean here, I came to see more and more clearly, through a series of incidents, that I was in effect acting out the rage which existed at an unconscious level in a hebephrenic woman I was treating; she seemed genuinely unaware of rage in herself, but through symptomatology which I found enraging would eventually promote such a degree of fury in me that I could no longer contain myself. Most often, I would then explode verbally at her, but on one occasion hurled my cigarette lighter at her coat which, at the beginning of the session, she had deposited on my couch. After each such eruption on my part, the relationship would be, as it were, decompressed; her infuriating symptomatology would be decreased for a time. It became increasingly clear to me that the moments when I would erupt would be junctures at which she was being in-creasingly hard put to it to avoid the recognition of her own fury, and that she would then 'succeed'–although not on the basis of any such conscious manipulation as this term might sug-gest–in getting me to express the anger for her, as it were. And now we come to the point I am attempting to illustrate here: it was only when I had come to see this process clearly, and when I had become able–only after two or three more such incidents, for my intellectual insight did not at once bring the necessary emotional capacity–to preserve, in the presence of my anger, a sufficient admixture of genuine objectivity, that I could as it were let her grow sufficiently to become aware of, and express, her own anger as such. This kind of development, this kind of acquisition of genuine neutrality and separateness on the part of the therapist, is crucial to the resolution of the therapeutic symbiosis and the patient's attainment, thereby, of ego-wholeness. My major theme in this paper is not intended to invalidate, but only to provide a necessary counterbalance for, the equally essential therapist-responsiveness, valuably stressed by many writers and advocated in particularly appealing terms by Perry (1961):

> The individuation process probably takes place only, or comes to fruition only, in relationship . . . when a patient in an acute turmoil is at some level trying to formulate a self-image, this stands in acute need of affirmation. . . . Such a self tends to take shape best in such a mutually animated emotional field. . . .

I know of no simple answer to the question which emerges from this discussion: namely, *when* is it therapeutic for the therapist to respond neutrally, and when non-neutrally? This is a question which is always before the therapist, and which can only be decided from moment to moment on the basis of his intuitive –i.e. primarily preconscious and unconscious, unthought-out- sensing of the patient's changing needs. There are, I believe, broad fluctuations in the therapist's level of emotional responsiveness corresponding with broad phases in the overall course of the therapy. In chapter 18 I have suggested that the earliest, or 'out-of-contact', phase of treatment involves a less active feeling-responsiveness on the part of the therapist than do the subsequent phases of ambivalent and pre-ambivalent (therapeutic) symbiosis; and I implied that the next phase, that of resolution of the symbiosis, and the final (essentially psycho-analytic) phase are characterized by, once again, a less overt feeling-responsiveness on his part, although his inner feeling experience is, of course, very different from that which obtained in him during the first phase of the treatment which I mentioned. Not only in such broad terms are there variations, but obviously also in any one session the therapist's necessary feeling-responsiveness may vary markedly, over a wide range, from moment to moment. I can offer no formula to apply to so changing and complex and living a situation, but have attempted here only to draw attention to some of the dimensions of the patient-therapist interaction.

A man suffering from chronic paranoid schizophrenia with prominent depressive features became, in response to relatively active therapeutic responsiveness on my part, progressively silent and inactive, until eventually he was lying, for months on end, mute and motionless on his bed throughout our sessions. Nor was he more alive between sessions in the rest of his 'daily life' on the ward; it became necessary for the staff to tube-feed him, and there were many indications that he was hovering on the brink of death itself. During the therapeutic sessions I came then, progressively, to desist from all forms of therapist 'activity'; I had tried everything I could think of, and nothing had worked, and I concluded that he could emerge from this border-of-death state only through the expression, basically, of the life which one must rely upon as existing somewhere behind his inanimate demeanour. His emaciated form, lying face down on the bed, looked more like a rather large wrinkle in the bedcover than the outline of a living human body.

I found myself saying less and less as these sessions went on, until I reached the point where I was simply bringing in my chair and placing it in a stereotyped location several feet from his bed, saying, 'Hello, Mr ——', as I sat down; sitting silently and comparatively unmoving (but comfortably so) throughout the session; and saying, 'Goodbye' or 'I'll see you tomorrow' as I got up and took my chair out at the end of the session – with, still, no discernible response, either verbal or non-verbal, from him.

Then came a session in which I simply brought in my chair and sat down, as usual, but without saying anything, and at the end of the session, as I got up and was starting out with my chair, again without any words to him, he suddenly raised up on an elbow, looked at me and asked, in a loud, clear, astonished tone, 'Aren't you even going to say goodbye?' It was this session which, in retrospect, marked the turning-point, for this man, from moving towards lifelessness to movement into living. He went on, subsequently in our work, to evidence far more of a rich aliveness than any one, whether among the hospital personnel or among the members of his parental family, had thought could possibly exist in him, and I found abundant evidence to indicate that my contribution to this recovery process sprang from, as much as anything else, my having become able to tolerate, not only during these months I have been describing, but on many occasions in the subsequent years of the therapy, the transference role of, in essence, an inanimate object—the embodiment of the patient's subjectively unalive, inanimate personality components, now safely externalized and susceptible to resolution in the transference analysis. This is not the only instance in my experience which has underlined, for me, the lesson that the neutral response is no mere luxury which the therapist can allow himself, no mere form of self-protection behind which he is enabled to hide from frightening feeling-participation with the patient, but rather is an immensely hard-won, and hard-maintained, state of feeling on his part which, in extreme instances, is of literally life-saving value to the patient.

Chapter 23

TRANSFERENCE PSYCHOSIS IN THE PSYCHOTHERAPY OF CHRONIC SCHIZOPHRENIA (1963)[1]

AFTER some five years of my work at Chestnut Lodge, developments in the therapy of various of my patients brought home to me the realization that even the most deep and chronic symptoms of schizophrenia are to be looked upon not simply as the tragic human debris left behind by the awesome holocaust which this illness surely is, but that these very symptoms can be found to have—or, perhaps more accurately, in the course of therapy can come to reveal—an aspect which is both rich in meaning and alive, one now sees, with unquenched and unquenchable energy. That is, these very symptoms now emerge to the therapist's view as being by no means inert debris but as, rather, the manifestations of an intensely alive, though unconscious, effort on the part of the patient to recapture, to maintain, and to become free from, modes of relatedness which held sway between himself and other persons in his childhood and which he is now fostering unconsciously in current life, most importantly in his relationship with his therapist. When the therapist sees and feels this aspect of the therapeutic situation, not only does much that has been bewildering, in his previous months or years of work with the patient, become coherently meaningful; but he senses, even more hearteningly, how great are the patient's potential capacities for growth, capacities which are, it is now evident, far from dead, but, rather, congealed in the perpetuation of these unconscious transference patterns of relatedness.

This realization came to me most memorably in two treatment situations in particular, in my work with a middle-aged hebephrenic man in whom severe apathy was for years a prominent

[1] Excerpts from this paper were presented at the Georgetown University Conference on the Psychotherapy of Schizophrenia, Washington, D.C., Oct. 29, 1962. It was first published in the *International Journal of Psycho-Analysis*, Vol. 44 (1963), pp. 249–81.

symptom, and a hebephrenic woman of about 30 who manifested, likewise for years in our work together, a degree of confusion which I often found overwhelming and deeply discouraging. I did not find it strange that a man who had been hospitalized constantly, whether on a back ward of a veterans' hospital or on a locked ward at Chestnut Lodge, for more than ten years, should show a great deal of apathy; nor did it seem remarkable that a woman who had been hospitalized for a similar length of time, and whose records showed that she had been subjected, over the years prior to her admission to the Lodge, to approximately 140 insulin coma treatments and an indeterminate number of electroshock treatments, should be severely and persistently confused. More often than not, when I contemplated, and persistently tried to help, each of these two persons, I found solid reason to feel appalled and helpless in the face of the havoc which chronic schizophrenia, and the diverse efforts to treat chronic schizophrenia, had wrought upon these two human beings.

It therefore came as a tremendous change of view for me to hear the man, who was lying silently on his bed as usual, say one day, with a chuckle, 'If my grandmother was still alive I'd be a *real* lounge-lizard,' and find the evidence accumulating, during subsequent months and years, that his ostensible apathy was that of a person who had felt it necessary to bank the fires of his own ambitions and devote himself to staying by a grandmother, and much more importantly, before that, a psychotically depressed father, whose needs—needs to be protected from the daily cares of the world by the patient's more or less constant reassuring presence—took priority over the patient's own life as a boy and as a young man.

Now, ironically, I, who had formerly looked with dismay upon this hopeless vegetable of a patient, found myself in the position, as his transference towards me became more richly and openly elaborated, of a 'papa' to whom he reacted, with persistence and conviction, as being a mere shell of a person, a person with a long-burnt out mind, a relic given to unpredictable moods of deep depression punctuated by explosive rages. All these qualities had marked his own illness in the preceding years, as a fuller case description would clearly show; and I do not doubt that major ingredients of his illness were originally derived from the introjection of similar qualities in his father. As his transference to me became increasingly coherent and powerful, his own personality functioning became proportionately liberated from illness; but I must say that there were times, during the ensuing months and years, when the transference role which he not so much pinned on to as more or less instilled into me, made me feel somewhat less than my usual robust self.

In the instance of the woman patient, it gradually became clear to me that her deep and persistent confusion consisted basically in an unconscious and ambivalent effort, manifested with especial coherence and clarity in the relationship with me as a father in the transference, (a) to get me to do her thinking for her, as her father had been accustomed to doing throughout her childhood and adolescence until her hospitalization at the age of 19; (b) to prove me incapable of doing this–a motive which could be called, and certainly often felt to me to be, a castratively hostile motive, but one which, as I shall subsequently state more fully, is at heart in the service of the patient's determination to be, and function as, an individual in her own right; and (c) to require me to acknowledge openly the extent of my own confusion, confusion such as had indeed been present in the father during her upbringing, and against which he erected as a defence a borderline psychotic degree of subjective omniscience.

Despite these two therapeutic experiences, and others nearly as memorable to me, when some years later a fellow seminar-member at Chestnut Lodge raised the simple question, 'What part does transference have in this work?', I shared in the general floundering which we all, despite our analytic training and our considerable experience in the modified psycho-analytic treatment of schizophrenic patients, felt in trying to answer this question.

To be sure, we have long ago outgrown the position, in this regard, of Freud (1911a, 1914) and Abraham (1908), who held that the schizophrenic patient has regressed to an auto-erotic level of development and is therefore incapable of forming a transference. Furthermore, the concept of transference psychosis, while not yet the subject of a voluminous literature, is not a new one. We have, for example, some cogent statements by Rosenfeld (1952a) to serve as a reliable avenue of entry into this subject:

. . . If we avoid attempts to produce a positive transference by direct reassurance or expressions of love, and simply interpret the positive and negative transference, the psychotic manifestations attach themselves to the transference, and, in the same way as a transference neurosis develops in the neurotic, so, in the analysis of psychotics, there develops what may be called a 'transference psychosis'. The success of the analysis depends on our understanding of the psychotic manifestations in the transference situation.

. . . It has been found that the psychotic manifestations attach themselves to the transference in both acute and chronic conditions, so that what one may call a 'transference-psychosis' develops. The analyst's main task in both acute and chronic schizophrenias is the recognition of the relevant transference phenomena and its communication to the patient . . .

Some of these chronic schizophrenic conditions seem often quite inaccessible until the relevant facts of the transference-psychosis are understood and interpreted . . . (Rosenfeld, 1954).

But, for a variety of reasons, it is not easy to discover this transference psychosis–or, as Little (1958) terms it, delusional transference–dimension in the patient's schizophrenic symptomatology.

To analyst and analytic student alike, the term 'transference psychosis' usually connotes a dramatic but dreaded development in which an analysand, who at the beginning of the analysis was overtly sane but who had in actuality a borderline ego-structure, becomes overtly psychotic in the course of the evolving transference relationship. We generally blame the analyst for such a development and prefer not to think any more about such matters, because of our own personal fear that we, like the poor misbegotten analysand, might become, or narrowly avoid becoming, psychotic in our own analysis. By contrast, in working with the chronically schizophrenic patient, we are confronted with a person who has already become, long ago, openly psychotic, and whose transference to us is so hard to identify partly for the very reason that his whole daily life consists in incoherent psychotic transference reactions, willy-nilly, to everyone about him, including the analyst in the treatment session. Little's comment (1960) that the delusional state 'remains unconscious until it is uncovered in the analysis' holds true only in the former instance, in the borderline schizophrenic patient; there, it is the fact that the transference is delusional which is the relatively covert, hard-to-discern aspect of the situation; in chronic schizophrenia, by contrast, nearly everything is delusional, and the difficult task is to foster the emergence of a coherent transference meaning in the delusional symptomatology. In other words, the difficult thing in the work with the chronically schizophrenic patient is to discover the 'transference reality' in his delusional experience.

The difficulty of discerning the transference aspects of one's relationship with the patient can be traced to his having regressed to a state of ego functioning which is marked by severe impairment in his capacity either to differentiate among, or to integrate, his experiences. He is so incompletely differentiated in his ego functioning that he tends to feel not that the therapist reminds him of, or is like, his mother or father (or whomever, from his early life) but rather his functioning towards the therapist is couched in the unscrutinized assumption that the therapist *is* the mother or father. When, for example, I tried to bring to the attention of a paranoid schizophrenic woman how much alike she seemed to find the persons in her childhood on the one hand, and the persons about her here in the hospital, including myself, on the other, she dismissed this with an impatient retort, 'That's what I've been trying to *tell* you! What *difference* does it make?' For years subsequently in our work together, all the figures in her experience were composite figures, without any clear subjective distinction between past and present experience. Figures from the hospital scene peopled her memories of her past, and figures from what I knew to be her past were experienced by her as blended with the persons she saw about her in current life.

Comparably, in the instance of another paranoid schizophrenic woman, it required several years of therapy before she became able to remember, and give me any detailed account of, her mother, who had died shortly after the patient's admission to Chestnut Lodge, and whom I never met. She reacted to me, in the transference, in the spirit of so convinced and persistent an assumption that *I personified* one or another aspect of that mother, that it was extraordinarily difficult for me also to achieve a sufficient degree of psychological distance from the relatedness to visualize what the relationship between herself and her mother must have been, and to see the role being played, in her view of me—in her various and intense feeling reactions to me—by a transference magnification and distortion of various qualities which, in truth, reside in me. One of my notes, concerning a treatment session which occurred after two and a half years of intensive therapy, includes the following comments:

'In today's hour the realization occurred to me that Susan feels hampered in moving out of the Lodge, away from me, by transference feelings from the relationship with her mother, feelings which kept her, for so many years until the advent of her overt psychosis, from leaving her mother. She brought out much material during this hour which made it plain–without her saying so explicitly–that it had never occurred to her that she might have any choice about whether to stay on at home and take care of her mother and the home, or leave and form her own life elsewhere. It was so plain that she had felt she must of course stay and take care of her mother, and that it would be unworthy, despicable, unthinkable, even to entertain thoughts of doing anything else. I've noticed for some several months that she often reacts to me as though I were an isolated person, in the backwash of life, someone she seems to feel called upon to minister to in many ways; so often, for example, she has prefaced her remarks by saying, gently, 'Dr Searles—?', as though assuming that I am preoccupied. But never till today did this transference element occur to me at all. Today it came to me with utter conviction. I have long ago felt that she was reacting to me as a condemnatory mother, a rejecting mother, a fond mother; but never before have I realized this particular element, in which I am reacted to as an elderly, lonely, desperately needful mother.

She and I have not reached any consensus at all as to the fact that these feelings are partially on a transference basis, and I am not trying to push that upon her attention.'

On the other hand, as I have mentioned, one of the great reasons for our underestimating the role of transference is that it may require a very long time for the transference to become not only sufficiently differentiated but also sufficiently integrated, sufficiently coherent, to be identifiable. This situation is entirely comparable with, though much more marked in degree than, that obtaining in the evolution of the relationship between neurotic patient and analyst, an evolution in which, as Glover (1955) has described with great clarity, the patient evidences, in the early phases of the analysis, *fleeting* indications of positive and

negative transference in the course of development of the coherent and persistent *transference neurosis*:

> ... from the time we have ascertained that this transference situa-
> tion [i.e., the transference-neurosis proper] is developing, everything
> that takes place during the analytic session, every thought, action,
> gesture, every reference to external thought and action, every inhibi-
> tion of thought or action, relates to the transference-situation ...

A hebephrenic woman evidenced, for about three years following her admission to Chestnut Lodge, an extreme degree of
ego-fragmentation and a bewildering lack of transference identifiability in her chaotic behaviour both in her daily life on the
ward and in her functioning during the therapeutic sessions. But
gradually she developed such a degree of ego-integration that not
only did our sessions come to possess a quality of coherence of
meaning throughout each session and a comparatively ready
traceability of her reactions to childhood experiences, but also
the ward staff, previously utterly unsure of where they stood
with her, became able to see that she had reconstituted her childhood family on the ward, with this person being rather consistently misidentified by the patient as being her older sister, that
person being perceived as the mother, another as the long-time
family nursemaid, and so on.

Another reason for the therapist's slowness in feeling the role
of transference in the psychotherapy is that when, after perhaps
many months of a 'relationship building' phase of treatment
during which he has found much reason to become confident
that, at long last and after many painful and discouraging rejections, he personally has come to matter to this previously inaccessible patient, it comes as a particularly hurtful rejection to
see to what a great extent the patient has been reacting to him
not as a person in his own right but rather as the embodiment of
some figure in the transference. One may discover that even
one's physical housing, let alone one's more subtle personal feelings, is not really perceived as such by the patient. One paranoid woman, for example, used to shriek at me the anguished
accusation that I had cut off my hands and grafted there the
hands of her long-dead grandmother, in order that the sight
of her grandmother's hands, extending from my cuffs, would
tear her heart with grief and guilt about this grandmother. For

a number of years she was convinced, similarly, that the head she saw on my shoulders was not really mine, but was that of some person or other from her past. The therapist under the impact of transference of this power feels very alone indeed, with little or no confirmation of *himself* coming by way of any feedback from the patient.

To my mind, the most fundamental reason of all for our finding it difficult to discern, and to keep in view the evolving course of, the transference in the therapy of these patients is that the transference is expressive of a very primitive ego-organization, comparable with that which holds sway in the infant who is living in a world of part objects, before he has built up an experience of himself, and of his mother and other persons round about him, as beings who are alive and whole and human. Transference as we see it in the neurotic patient implies three whole persons – the patient, the therapist, and a person who figured in the patient's early life. The schizophrenic patient has never solidly achieved a level of ego-differentiation and ego-integration which will allow him to experience three whole persons, or even two whole persons, or, as yet, one whole person. The question of whether he will ever achieve such a level of ego-maturation will depend, more than anything else – in so far as the therapist's contribution is concerned – upon the latter's capacity to perform three tasks. First, the therapist must become able to function as a *part* of the patient and to permit the patient to be genuinely, at a deep level of psychological functioning, a part of himself. Secondly, he must be able to foster the patient's individuation (and, to a not insignificant degree, his own re-individuation) out of this level of relatedness, a level which is conceptualized variously by several workers in this field – by Kleinian analysts (Klein *et al.*, 1955) as being a transference phase dominated by projective identification on the part of the patient; by Little (1960) as being a phase in which the patient has a heretofore unconscious delusion of total undifferentiatedness with the analyst; and by most writers, including myself, as being a phase of symbiotic relatedness between patient and doctor. The therapist's third task is to discern, and make interpretations concerning, the patient's now differentiated and now integrated whole object, that is to say neurotic, kind of transference manifestations. With the achievement of the patient's individuation as a whole person and his capacity to perceive the therapist as a whole person, what was formerly in him a transference psychosis is now a transference neurosis.

It may be questioned whether the chronically schizophrenic person's ego-organization is, in its entirety, at every moment, and in relation to whatever person, as incompletely differentiated as my foregoing comments indicate; one recalls here the valuable papers by Katan (1954) and Bion (1957) concerning the non-psychotic part of the personality in schizophrenia. But in any event I consider it valid to conceive of the patient's *transference to the therapist* as being in the nature, basically, of a relatedness to the therapist as a mother figure from whom the patient has never, as yet, become deeply differentiated. Furthermore, I believe that this 'sickest'–least differentiated–aspect of the patient's ego functioning becomes called into play in *any* relationship which develops anything like the intensity that the therapeutic relationship develops.

Concerning the symbiotic phase in the therapeutic relatedness, which I cannot attempt to discuss comprehensively here, I should like at the moment merely to note how difficult it is to discern and conceptualize the transference in those situations where, however frequent they may be, it is always astonishing to discover to what an extent the patient is relating *to himself*–or, more accurately, to a part of himself–as an object. A hebephrenic woman, for example, often sounded, when alone in her room, through the closed door as though a castigating, domineering mother and a defiant child were locked in there in a verbal struggle. Another hebephrenic woman, trying to formulate an upsurge of jealousy at a time when she had just acquired some long-sought-for liberties to go unescorted into the nearby village, said, 'I guess I'm jealous of myself'; there was a peculiarly ego-splitting kind of pain in her voice as she said this, and with repercussions in me as I heard it, which is hard to convey in words. A hebephrenic man, who generally spent his sessions with me in silence and who was intensely threatened and furious whenever I started to speak, interrupted me at one such juncture with the furious command, 'Just sit there until ya catch yourself!', and later in the therapy was able to experience the same phenomenon in an unprojected form: when I inquired what he was experiencing, he replied, 'I'm playin' possum, tryin' to catch myself.'

Still later on in our work, when I heard him murmuring some words which by then had become stereotyped, such as, 'Take your time . . . You don't say . . . Behave yourself . . .', and I asked, 'Who are you saying that to, Bill?', he replied, 'I'm just sittin' here echoin' myself.'

Similarly Freud, in a paper which included some data from his work with a schizophrenic patient, made the comment that ' . . . Analysis shows that he is playing out his castration complex upon his skin . . .' (Freud, 1915), Szasz (1957) has reported many instances of patients' having formed transferences to various parts of their own bodies. Furthermore, the whole of Klein's (Klein *et al.*, 1955) formulations concerning the importance of internal objects in mental functioning are relevant here.

To the extent that the patient is absorbed in reacting to a part of himself, whether a part of his body or one of his internal psychic objects, what then is the nature of the transference to the therapist who is in his presence? It is, I think, most useful to think of the transference, here, as being to the therapist a *matrix* out of which the patient's ego-differentiation and ego-integration gradually develops, by successive identifications with this originally undifferentiated and unintegrated, but at some level of relatedness truly external, transference 'object'.

In *The Nonhuman Environment* (p. 352) I reported a hebephrenic woman's saying apprehensively, in clear reference to me, 'There's a weird doctor around here that doesn't make sense to me. He's metal–he's [looking uneasily at the walls of the room] everything.' I asked, 'Wooden?', thinking of the wood on the walls of her room in which we were sitting. She nodded agreement and added 'He's everywhere.' Later in the therapy, as I have detailed in chapter 18, both participants' anxiety, and retaliatory hostility, in the symbiotic phase of the transference have become sufficiently resolved for each to experience the other as comparably omnipresent, comparably pervading one's whole existence; no longer, however, is this felt as a malignant, threatening and constricting presence, but rather as a benign and nurturing one.

The British analysts who embrace Klein's theoretical concepts have written more than anyone else about transference psychosis and its therapeutic management. Their approach is based upon her concept of projective identification. The most relevant of her views are to be found in her 'Notes on Some Schizoid Mechanisms' (1946):

I have often expressed my view that object relations exist from the beginning of life, the first object being the mother's breast which is split into a good (gratifying) and bad (frustrating) breast; this splitting results in a division between love and hate. I have further suggested that the relation to the first object implies its introjection and projection, and thus from the beginning object relations are moulded by an interaction between introjection and projection, between internal and external objects and situations . . .

. . . With the introjection of the complete object in about the second quarter of the first year marked steps in integration are made . . . The loved and hated aspects of the mother are no longer felt to be so widely separated, and the result is an increased fear of loss, a strong feeling of guilt and states akin to mourning, because the aggressive impulses are felt to be directed against the loved object. The depressive position [in contrast to the earlier, above-described paranoid position] has come to the fore . . .

. . . in the first few months of life anxiety is predominantly experienced as fear of persecution and . . . this contributes to certain mechanisms and defences which characterize the paranoid and schizoid positions. Outstanding among these defences is the mechanism of splitting internal and external objects, emotions and the ego. These mechanisms and defences are part of normal development and at the same time form the basis for later schizophrenic illness. I described the processes underlying identification by projection [i.e. projective identification] as a combination of splitting off parts of the self and projecting them on to another person . . .

Rosenfeld, a follower of Klein who has contributed several highly illuminating papers concerning schizophrenia, writes (1952a),

. . . I have observed that whenever the acute schizophrenic patient approaches an object in love or hate he seems to become confused with this object. This confusion seems to be due not only to phantasies of oral incorporation leading to *introjective* identification, but at the same time to impulses and phantasies in the patient of entering inside the object with the whole or parts of his self, leading to '*projective* identification'. This situation may be regarded as the most primitive object relationship, starting from birth . . . While projective identification is based primarily on an object relationship, it can also be used as a mechanism of defence: for example, to split off and project good and bad parts of the ego into external objects, which then become identified with the projected parts of the self. The chronic schizophrenic patient makes ample use of this type of projective identification as a defence . . .

In another paper, he presents detailed clinical data which serve to document the implicit point, among others, that whereas the schizophrenic patient may appear to have regressed to such an objectless auto-erotic level of development as was postulated by Freud (1911a, 1914) and Abraham (1908), in actuality the patient is involved in object-relatedness with the analyst, object-relatedness of the primitive introjective and projective identification kind. For example, Rosenfeld concludes his description of, the data from one of the sessions as follows:

. . . The whole material of the session suggested that in the withdrawn state he was introjecting me and my penis, and at the same time was projecting himself into me. So here again I suggest that it is sometimes possible to detect the object-relation in an apparently auto-erotic state.

. . . only at a later stage of treatment was it possible to distinguish between the mechanisms of introjection of objects and projective identification, which so frequently go on simultaneously (1952b).

We find, among the writings of the Kleinian analysts, a number of interesting examples of delusional transference interpretations, in all of which the keynote is the concept of projective (or introjective) identification. For instance, Rosenfeld writes at one juncture (1952a),

The patient himself gave the clue to the transference situation, and showed that he had projected his damaged self containing the destroyed world, not only into all the other patients, but into me, and had changed me in this way. But instead of becoming relieved by this projection he became more anxious, because he was afraid of what I was then putting back into him, whereupon his introjective processes became severely disturbed. One would therefore expect a severe deterioration in his condition, and in fact his clinical state during the next ten days became very precarious. He began to get more and more suspicious about food, and finally refused to eat and drink anything . . . everything he took inside seemed to him bad, damaged, and poisonous (like faeces), so there was no point in eating anything. We know that projection leads again into re-introjection, so that he also felt as if he had inside himself all the destroyed and bad objects which he had projected into the outer world: and he indicated by coughing, retching, and movements of his mouth and fingers that he was pre-occupied with this problem . . . I told him that he was not only afraid of getting something bad inside him, but that he was also afraid of taking good things, the good orange juice and good interpretations, inside since he was afraid that these would make him feel guilty again. When I said this, a kind of shock went right through his body; he gave a groan of understanding, and his facial expression changed. By the end of the hour he had emptied the glass of orange juice, the first food or drink he had taken for two days . . .

In another paper (1954) Rosenfeld writes, concerning his work with an acutely schizophrenic girl who was intermittently overwhelmed with confusion and unable to speak,

. . . She then looked at me for quite a time and said: 'Why do you imitate me?' I interpreted that she had put herself into me and that she felt that I was her and had to talk and think for her. I explained to her that this was the reason why she felt so shut in when she came to my house and why she had to escape from me. She was now looking much more comfortable and trusting, and said: 'You are the world's best person'. I interpreted that because she felt I was so good she wanted to be inside me and have my goodness.
. . . Following the interpretations that the patient felt she was inside me, she was able to extricate herself out of me which lessened her con-fusion. She then became more aware of me as an external object and was able to talk . . .

Bion (1956) defines projective identification as

. . . a splitting off by the patient of a part of his personality and a projection of it into the object where it becomes installed, sometimes as a persecutor, leaving the psyche from which it has been split off correspondingly impoverished.

The following brief example of his use of verbal interpretations comes from his work with a schizoid man:

. . . As the silence continued I became aware of a fear that the patient was meditating a physical attack upon me, though I could see no outward change in his posture. As the tension grew I felt increasingly sure that this was so. Then, and only then, I said to him, 'You have been pushing into my insides your fear that you will murder me.' There was no change in the patient's position but I noticed that he clenched his fists till the skin over the knuckles became white. The silence was unbroken. At the same time I felt that the tension in the room, presumably in the relationship between him and me, had decreased. I said to him, 'When I spoke to you, you took your fear that you would murder me back into yourself; you are now feeling afraid you will make a murderous attack upon me.' I followed the same method throughout the session, waiting for impressions to pile up until I felt I was in a position to make my interpretation. It will be noted that my interpretation depends on the use of Melanie Klein's theory of projective identification, first to illuminate my counter-transference, and then to frame the interpretation which I give the patient.

It seems to me that the above instances of verbal transference interpretations can be looked upon as one form of intervention, at times effective, which constitutes an appeal for collaboration to the non-psychotic area of the patient's personality, an area of which, as noted previously, both Katan (1954) and Bion (1957) have written. But, particularly among long hospitalized chronically schizophrenic persons, we see many a patient who is too ill to be able to register verbal statements; and even in the foregoing examples from Rosenfeld's and Bion's experiences, it is impossible to know to what extent the patient is helped by an illuminatingly accurate verbal content in the therapist's words, or to what extent that which is effective springs, rather, from the feelings of confidence, firmness, and understanding which accompany these words spoken by a therapist who feels that he has a reliable theoretical basis for formulating the clinical phenomena in which he finds himself.

In trying to conceptualize such ego-states in the patient, and such states of relatedness between patient and doctor, I find of additional value the concepts presented by Little in her papers, 'On Delusional Transference (Transference Psychosis)' (1958) and 'On Basic Unity' (1960):

. . . a neurotic can recognize the analyst as a real person, who for the time being symbolizes, or 'stands-in' for his parents . . .

Where the transference is delusional there is no such 'stand-in' or 'as-if' quality about it. To such a patient the analyst *is*, in an absolute way, . . . both the idealized parents and their opposites, or rather, the parents deified and diabolized, and also himself (the patient) deified and diabolized . . .

The transference delusion hides a state in the patient which he both needs and fears to reach. In it subject and object, all feeling, thought, and movement are experienced as the same thing. That is to say there is only a *state of being* or of experiencing, and no sense of there being a *person*; e.g., there is only an anger, fear, love, movement, etc., but no person feeling anger, fear or love, or moving. And since all these things are one and the same, there is no separateness or distinction between them. It is a state of undifferentiatedness, both as regards psyche and soma, experienced as chaos.

To reach this state is a terrifying thing, as it means losing all sense of being a person, and all sense of identity. The patient who reaches it becomes for the moment only a pain, rage, mess, scream, etc., and is wholly dependent on the analyst for there being anywhere a person who feels or acts. There is in fact, identification with the analyst of a primary kind, but the patient cannot be aware of it.

This state has to be reached so that the unreality of these identities can be recognized, but the reaching of it is felt as utter annihilation – hence the need to maintain the delusion in the transference . . .

[Concerning] the state of undifferentiatedness which the delusion hides . . . The terms 'primary identification' and 'primary narcissism' to my mind do not fit it, nor does 'paranoid-schizoid position'. I would rather describe it as a state of primordial undifferentiatedness, or of *basic unity*, in which a primitive identification might be said to be included. What I want to convey is that the undifferentiatedness is absolute, in both degree and extent. Nothing exists apart from anything else, and the process of differentiation has to start from scratch (1958).

Little not only takes issue with various of the Kleinian theoretical concepts, but stresses the importance of physical movement and contact in helping to resolve the delusional transference:

Rosemary has never sorted herself out from her sister Joyce, who is 2 years older. All childhood happenings, ideas or feelings are told of the entity 'we'; ('We did this, We hated that'). She and Joyce are indivisible; she 'never feels a person', but is often 'two people', and sometimes 'half a person'. At the beginning of a session she frequently doesn't 'know how to begin' . . .

. . . Rosemary was functioning separately on at least two different levels, and I am understanding the separateness as being due to a failure of fusion, rather than to the action of a splitting mechanism . . .

Throughout her analysis she has continued to be paralysed with terror, and unable to find any starting-point other than something happening in me. . . . Her silence and immobility can remain total for weeks on end, and only when I show signs of life in some explicit way (for anything merely implicit is useless) can she begin to tell me what has been going on . . .

In the light of this idea of absolute identity between patient and analyst I think we have to reconsider our ideas of such mental mechanisms as projection, introjection, condensation, displacement, and all that Freud included in the term 'dream work'.

. . . we can see here how what we have considered to be condensation becomes instead a regression to the primordial undifferentiated state. Similarly, . . . what appeared to be projective identification turned out to be an assertion of absolute identity with me (1960).

I have worked with patients so deeply dedifferentiated that only after several years of intensive therapy did they become able to distinguish between an 'outside' and an 'inside'. Until such a development has occurred, one may find Little's formulations helpful in approaching the patient; subsequently, the formulations of Klein and her followers, which imply both a far higher degree of psychic structure (differentiation) and a far greater reliance upon verbal interpretations, are in my experience oftentimes pertinent. It is not a matter, I believe, of our having to choose between irreconcilable theoretical concepts, but rather to determine in which phase of the patient's ego-development each is more useful for us.

Four Varieties of Transference Psychosis

Transference psychosis—or, in Little's (1958) phrase, delusional transference—may be defined as any type of transference which distorts or prevents a relatedness between patient and therapist as two separate, alive, human and sane beings. In what follows here, I shall present a variety of examples of such transference, examples which I have encountered in my clinical work and each of which I consider useful as being typical of clinical situations with one patient after another. The theoretical framework which I shall use as a vehicle for presenting clusters of these typical situations is one of which I feel much less than sure; but, beyond providing some presentational coherence, it represents the clearest theoretical integration of these seemingly dissimilar clinical phenomena which I have thus far been able to formulate. I should explain also, by way of prefacing these descriptions, that any one patient will be apt to show, over the course of treatment and perhaps in any one therapeutic session, all four of the different varieties of transference psychosis which I shall describe.

(i)

Transference situations in which the therapist feels unrelated to the patient. In these situations, the therapist may find the patient reacting to him as being an inanimate object, an animal, a corpse, an idea, or something else not essentially human and alive. I have included many examples of such situations in *The Nonhuman Environment* (1960), and here I shall merely enumerate a few sample situations which are not described there. My present understanding of such situations is that they are genetically traceable to the part-object world of infancy and very early childhood–the era during which the child has not yet achieved a differentiation between animate and inanimate, between human and non-human, in the surrounding world and in himself, and has not yet built up, through accumulated part-object relatednesses, an image of himself and of his mother as whole and separate objects. I have termed (ch. 18) the phase of therapy in which such transference relatedness–or 'unrelatedness'–predominates the 'out-of-contact phase' and have indicated that the early-life era which is aetiologically pertinent is that from which, as Mahler (1952) describes it, autistic childhood psychosis stems, as contrasted with the developmentally later symbiotic childhood psychosis; the former type found, by Mahler, in the child who had never become firmly involved in the mother-infant symbiosis typical of later infancy and early childhood in healthy maturation, and the latter type found by her in the child who had become involved in a symbiotic relationship with the mother, but had never outgrown this mode of relatedness.

The patient's misidentification of the therapist is a typical clinical situation in point here, in addition to the varieties mentioned in my book. One paranoid schizophrenic man, reared as a devout Catholic, would attend Mass at the local church each Sunday, and then when I arrived for the Monday hour he would regularly misidentify me as a priest; this he would do with a degree of certainty which I found quite uncomfortable, despite my soon coming to realize that, in all probability, he was thus repressing, through this delusional misperception of me, feelings of disloyalty to his church which were aroused by his receiving treatment–however unwillingly–from a psycho-analyst, a situation to which he thought his church adamantly opposed, and one to which his deceased mother had been in any case unswervingly hostile.

The transference position of one who is continually and at times bizarrely misidentified can be a very stressful position for the therapist to endure. One hebephrenic woman misidentified me continually, for months on end, as a succession of dozens of different persons from her past, so that I found the lack of confirmation of myself, as I know myself, to be almost intolerable. I have already described the paranoid woman who used to shriek with anguish and condemnation, while gazing over at my hands, that I had cut off the hands of her grandmother and fastened them on to myself in order to turn a knife in her heart; and who upon innumerable occasions reacted to my head as being, not my own, but the decapitated and grafted-on head of one or another person she had known. On one occasion she said to a nurse, 'Even your voice can be changed by wiring to sound like the voice of a person that I know.' She once declared to me, with chilling conviction, her certainty that I was a machine sent to kill her; and, at another time, that I was a woman who had killed my husband and was likewise about to kill her.

Similarly, the delusional transference may consist in the patient's feeling misidentified by the other person. A paranoid woman, when responded to fondly and at length by a nurse who had known her for a long time, confided, as the nurse reported it, that 'she felt when I was talking to her that I was actually talking to a third person outside her window'. This 'third person' she said was 'angels' . . . A spinster, when in one therapeutic session I tried to promote our mutual exploring of sexual conflicts which were emerging from repression in her, protested, 'Why do you talk to me like that, Dr Searles?', sometimes this was said with a warm, pleasurable laugh, but at other times in such a way as to make it clear that she felt, as she said, 'uncomfortable'. At one such point she seemed to go completely out of contact, and when I asked her what she was experiencing, she replied, 'You make me uncomfortable when you talk like that, Dr Searles.' I asked her how she felt I talked, and she replied, 'As if I were an old married woman.' I then asked her if she felt I was not talking to *her* on such occasions, and she agreed. I then suggested that naturally enough she felt removed from the situation, and she agreed with this also. There were a number of similar occasions when she behaved as though not psychologically present in the situation, evidently feeling totally misidentified by me, when my remarks were too widely at variance from her own self-concept.

In much the same vein are the instances of a patient's misidentification of himself, such that, in the instance of one paranoid woman, she assumed for many months that she was her own mother, and her children were not the two actual children I knew to be hers but were, rather, her three adult siblings. This had an utterly literal reality for her, quite beyond any figurative implications apparent enough to an observer; so, for weeks on end, I felt quite cut off from the person I knew her to be. Another paranoid woman would, one might say, literally become her mother at times of increased anxiety; another way of saying it is that a pathogenic introject derived from her mother would take over and dominate her behaviour and her sense of identity, such that one could only wait at such times for her paranoid tirades to run down until that which one knew as her real self became accessible and able to hear one's comments. The hebephrenic woman I have already mentioned, who in each hour misidentified me as being dozens of different persons from her past, from the movies, and so on, misidentified herself just as continually. On rare occasions she would ask, pathetically, if I had seen Louise (her own name) lately; it had evidently been a long time since she had seen herself, even fleetingly. Even this rare use of her own name was an indication that she felt more nearly in touch with herself than she usually did.

Also to be mentioned in this same category of phenomena are instances where the patient reacts to the therapist, in the transference, as being but one among his myriad hallucinations, or as possessing even less reality than do the hallucinatory figures. A childless hebephrenic woman, when I came into her room, would experience me as '1500 men' who were interfering with her relationship with her daughter. It appeared that she was misidentifying herself as being her mother, and was experiencing herself-as-a-child in the form of the hallucinatory daughter outside herself, a hallucination towards which she was far more absorbed in attempted relatedness than she was with the hallucinatory men into which her perception of me devolved. In another instance later on she explained, exasperatedly, while ripping her clothes—a symptom of hers which, for many months, was maddeningly and discouragingly difficult to control—that she was trying to 'get through' me as, she made clear, the personification of her father, in order to 'reach my mother' experienced by her, apparently, as an hallucinatory presence in the room apart from either of us. In the instance of a hebephrenic man, for months I felt reacted to by him as being no more than part of the woodwork, a mute and non-participative onlooker to his lively interactions with a group of hallucinatory figures in the room—a group which, as the months wore on, assumed more coherence and identifiability as his childhood family. Later on there was a phase during which I felt that he now registered me in his awareness as comparable with, and invested with something like as much feeling as, the hallucinatory figures with which he had for so long been immersed, and now I found myself feeling competitive with, and often jealous of, his hallucinations. Still later I reached a point where I felt sure that I mattered to him far more than did his hallucinations, so that whenever he began to hallucinate I could readily see this as subsidiary to—that is, as an unconscious defence mechanism related to some event in—his relatedness with me as a real person.

Another form of psychotic transference which causes the therapist to feel strikingly unrelated to the patient is that in which the patient is reacting to *him* as being psychotic. Hill (1955) has noted that '. . . Sometimes it is quite striking that the patient comes to believe that the doctor is thoroughly psychotic, quite in the fashion in which he himself has been psychotic . . .'

In my experience, this is an integral part of the transference evolution seen over the course of therapy with chronically schizophrenic patients. Each such patient has had at least one parent who evidenced borderline schizophrenic ego functioning, if not openly psychotic behaviour, during the patient's childhood, and it will then be in the nature of his unfolding transference to his therapist that he will come to regard the therapist, convincedly and, in many instances, for months on end, as being emotionally inaccessible (out of contact), delusional, and given, perhaps, to unpredictable and potentially murderous outbursts.

Hill describes it that it is thus, in the schizophrenic patient's view, that at the end of his treatment

... He is good, and the badness is left with the doctor. Even the illness is left with the doctor ... (1955).

In earlier papers (chs. 8, 14) I have given detailed examples of this form of delusional transference, and have emphasized the need for treatment to be pursued far beyond this phase, until the craziness has been well resolved, rather than simply left in this projected form upon the therapist. But here I wish simply to note how important it is that the therapist be able to endure the explicit emergence of such a transference on the part of the patient towards him. Bion makes some interesting comments concerning–by contrast–the aetiological significance of the patient's projection of his own *sanity*, which help to highlight this point concerning the necessary transference evolution:

I spoke of Melanie Klein's picture of the paranoid-schizoid position and the important part played in it by the infant's phantasies of sadistic attacks on the breast. Identical attacks are directed against the apparatus of perception from the beginning of life. This part of his personality is cut up, split into minute fragments, and then, using the projective identification, expelled from the personality. Having thus rid himself of the apparatus of conscious awareness of internal and external reality, the patient achieves a state which is felt to be neither alive nor dead ...

Projective identification of conscious awareness and the associated [i.e. consequent] inchoation of verbal thought is the central factor in the differentiation [in any one schizophrenic person] of the psychotic from the non-psychotic personality ... (1956).

... patients will use the mechanism of projective identification to rid themselves of their 'sanity'. If the analyst appears by his conduct to condone the feasibility of this, the way is open to massive regression ... I am absolutely in agreement with Maurits Katan (1954) in his views on the importance of the non-psychotic part of the personality in schizophrenia (1955).

The therapist who cannot endure the patient's reacting to him as insane–who cannot stand the projection of the insane part of the personality upon him, but unwittingly fosters and as it were insists upon the patient's projection of his own sanity upon him –cannot succeed in helping the patient to distinguish between the sane and insane ingredients of the patient's own personality, and in helping him to resolve the insanity.

These considerations have shed, for me, additional light upon the psychodynamics at work in the borderline or schizoid patient who is described by Helene Deutsch (1942) and Annie Reich (1953) as relating to others in an 'as if' fashion–as if he were experiencing a deep emotional involvement, when he is really incapable of relating except on the basis of a primitive identification of an imitative kind, traceable to his superficial identification with a narcissistic mother. I find that the nascently genuine emotionality is kept under repression in such a patient, originally out of a need to shield his mother from such real and spontaneous emotion. Comparably, I find it typical of borderline patients in general that not only their emotionality but their ego-perceptions in general are held subjectively in great doubt, and hence their sense of reality is impaired, for the reason that one's parent–or, in the therapy session, the therapist–must be spared from the reality of those perceptual data which the patient *tends* to see or hear or otherwise sense full well and accurately; but in the transference he has reason to doubt that the therapist-mother or father can stand exposure to it, by reason of the near-psychotic narcissistic brittleness of ego functioning which he attributes to the therapist, traceable to his experience with such a narcissistic mother as Deutsch and Reich describe.

Thus in the treatment sessions the patient tends to feel 'like a bull in a china shop', as various patients have expressed it, severely constricted in thought and feeling with, perhaps, their psychic productions taking shape, in their own view, only fuzzily like indistinct images on a TV screen. One of my patients regularly prefaces, or immediately afterwards tries to undo, her most penetrating observations, concerning either myself or her parents or whomever, with the apologetic statement, 'I know I'm crazy . . .' Another borderline woman patient at the Lodge, who shows a remarkably accurate perceptiveness as to what is going on in me, as indicated by either verbal or non-verbal communicational nuances, regularly gives me a way out of facing the reality of these by qualifying her comments with 'I sort of got the impression just then that . . .' or 'It seemed to me as if . . .', or 'I don't know, but I just had the thought that . . .' I now understand a little better why a schizoid patient whom I treated years ago once went to the extent of putting it that, 'A sort of a half an idea just crept into my unconscious: . . .' On the basis of a lifetime of experience with an extremely brittle mother, he was, as I now realize in retrospect, putting it thus tentatively on the assumption that I could not stand more direct exposure to the thought and feeling which he was conveying. These matters do not involve, I wish most strongly to emphasize, merely forms of communication on the patient's part; they extend into, and to a high degree permeate, his subjective experience, his perceptual functioning in general, so that he may feel quite out of touch indeed with thoughts and feelings which, in the transference, he unconsciously senses to be too threatening to the parent-therapist.

Brodey's (1959, 1961) papers, reporting his observations and theoretical formulations concerning the family therapy of schizophrenia, have been very helpful to my discovering the transference meanings which I have just mentioned. Brodey describes how greatly the schizophrenic patient's awareness of reality is constricted by reason of a need to be attentive to the mother's inner workings, and he says that, for example,

. . . One patient while psychotic seemed alive, vibrant, and was most discerning in her relationship with the mother; but she was psychotic and her behaviour unpredictable to the extreme. As she moved from this position back to what would be called by the mother 'reasonableness', she returned to being a puppet dancing with every mo·ement of her mother's hand with lifeless accuracy . . . (1961).

(ii)

The second category of *instances of transference psychosis* is that comprising those situations *in which a clear-cut relatedness has been established between patient and therapist, and the therapist therefore no longer feels unrelated to the patient; but the relatedness is a deeply ambivalent one.* My theoretical concept of such situations is that the transference evolution has unearthed that era of the patient's ego-development in which the mother-infant symbiosis had come to possess too high a degree of ambivalence for him to have been able to follow the healthy sequence from identification with the mother to the subsequent establishment of successful individuation; the ambivalence had been too intense for him to develop an integrated ego, and his ego-development had been turned, instead, into a defensive autism which left him vulnerable to the later development of schizophrenia. Thus, in the transference evolution to the therapist, he deeply hungers for, and must have if he is to become born as a real person, a symbiotic relatedness with the mother-therapist which is comparatively free from ambivalence—a phase analogous to the preambivalently symbiotic phase of the healthy mother-infant relationship. But he fears this, too, as being equivalent to the annihilation of himself, or the mother-therapist, or both.

Such theoretical concepts have been arrived at largely empirically, 'after the fact' as it were, emergent from the accomplishment of difficult clinical work.

I worked with a luxuriantly and most persistently delusional paranoid woman, for example, for four years before discovering, in the course of the next few months, two of the transference determinants (various additional ones became clear to me in later years of the therapy) which had been forming the fountainheads of all her bewildering delusions. I consider it significant that these revelations of the nature of the transference came to light only after her previously tenacious fear and hostility had given way to a considerable degree of positive feeling in the transference.

One of these approximately concomitant revelations came to light in an hour in which she said, with a striking amount of fondness, in reference to the female therapist who had worked with her at a previous hospital, 'If I had that doctor to talk to every day, I could even tolerate life here at Chestnut Lodge.' She went on to describe this therapist in terms strikingly similar to those she had applied, over the years, to 'my so-called mother'. What emerged in essence, during this hour and over the subsequent few months, was a revelation of the intense loyalty she had felt, all along, towards the earlier therapist, such that I now understood in retrospect why, over these four difficult years, in her loud defiance of and manifold resistance to therapy, she would often loudly proclaim that she was 'upholding the standards of the medical profession'. She had been upholding what she believed, with an incredible degree of confusion and distortion, to be the standards of Dr X, the former therapist, who was so little differentiated, in her perception, from her own mother.

Actually, both her mother and Dr X were remembered by her as being multiple figures, of varying sexual identities. I felt little inclination to be critical of the former therapist, for every critical implication which the patient's words bore towards that therapist, she had long made, and for a long time yet would make, towards me also, during periods when I was, for her, such a mother-figure–or, more accurately, such mother-figures–in the transference.

To return to my point here, I wish simply to emphasize what a revelation it was for me to see how greatly, for her, any positive feeling towards me, any achieved bit of collaboration in the therapy with me, conflicted with her sense of loyalty to the former therapist, and, by the same token, to what a great degree her discouragingly persistent delusions comprised, *en bloc*, a formidably massive effort to fend me off so that she could preserve her loyalty to the former therapist, in turn so transparent a screen for her own mother who, as her father told me and as I found abundantly documented in the events of the transference relationship, 'loved to dominate' the patient as a child and demanded the patient's loyalty to her views, no matter how conflictual, divergent, self-destructive, nonsensical, and simply crazy those views in fact were.

The other of these concomitant revelations can perhaps be best conveyed by quoting my notes concerning an hour approximately two months after the hour alluded to above:

The work with her has gone extremely well, and very collaboratively, again ever since about 12 March [three weeks ago]. In today's hour she was dressed in a very cute dance-costume, looking both very cute in a small-girl way and very seductive in a mature-woman way, with many flirtatious raisings of her skirt as she dissertated about theology, philosophy, and the complex workings of the world in general. Very early in the hour she accused me, in an unstinging way, of having 'lustful', 'erotic' desires. It actually was, much of the time, a quite anxious hour for me, with my feeling that she and I were interacting at two quite separate levels: (1) debating (she was doing the great bulk of it); and (2) a non-verbal sexual level, what with her sexy posturings and skirt-liftings. My discomfort consciously related to my feelings that the sexy business on her part was dissociated; so I felt, as it were, alone in having to deal with it. But late in the hour I chided her lightly, telling her, 'You've been giving me a difficult time, prancing around in that outfit looking cute as can

678

be, and accusing me of having lustful, erotic desires.' She laughed in a pleased way; so I guess her own erotic feelings can't be too heavily repressed at the moment.

But there was an additional very significant development in this hour: it became more apparent to me than ever before–I've seen it before but never realized the influential strength of this particular dynamism–that she not only loves to debate actively (which I've long known) but that she almost certainly greatly misses, unconsciously, the probably hours-long debates she used to have with her mother–at least I'm pretty sure it was her mother [confirmed by abundant data subsequently in the therapy]. She herself always refers to it as 'they' who used to say so-and-so; she was quoting to me, during this hour, much of the debates they used to have–quoting what she used to say and then telling me what 'they' used to say. The point of all this is that today I realized, better than before, that all this delusional thinking, *en bloc*, provides a *way of relating* which she greatly enjoys, a way of relating which I'm very inclined to think characterized a relatedness with her mother which she greatly misses, unconsciously. It became quite clear to me today that her behaviour is not oriented towards any satisfactory *resolution*, contentwise, of the arguments, the debates. As I told her, I feel that she would say that a tree is a dog, if necessary, to start a good argument; I said this in a friendly way, feeling friendly. I feel sure that she does not realize the dynamics of this as yet.

In the final section of this paper I shall discuss the matter of *interpretations* of transference psychosis. At the moment, I wish to note that one of my great difficulties in the work with this woman had to do with my susceptibility to being drawn into arguing with her delusional utterances. On innumerable occasions I could no longer sit silent while the most basic tenets of my concept of reality were being assaulted, not merely by the content of her words but by the tremendous forcefulness of her personality; on these occasions, the preservation of my sanity demanded that I speak. On other occasions, I would argue in an effort to rescue her from a degree of delusional confusion which was, on such occasions, indubitably genuine and indescribable here; to say that a tree is a dog would be only the tiniest measure of her confusion at such times. On still other occasions, when her anxiety was much less and there was little of any urgent help-lessness or threatening domineeringness on her part, she would simply make it irresistible fun to argue with her.

No matter in what spirit the arguments ensued, they always served, for her, as a way of simultaneously relating me, emotionally and psychologically, to herself and yet keeping me safely separate from herself, outside herself. These arguments were so difficult to deal with successfully in the therapy because they were the expression of her ambivalently symbiotic relationship with her mother. She needed so much for us to be psychologically one person – an experience which had not been successful in her early relationship with her mother – and yet, for very good reasons in her history, she felt that this would amount to the annihilation of both of us. The subsequent months and years of the therapy included a clear-cut preambivalently – that is, relatively non-ambivalently – symbiotic phase, the culmination of which she experienced as a literally becoming born; but at this phase which I am describing, her arguing – and my reciprocal arguing – represented a mutual deferring of that phase. She held it off partly by the defence mechanism of arguing; others of my patients have shown other types of defences used for the same purpose.

It is significant that this woman came to describe, eloquently and feelingly, how intensely exasperating she used to find it when her older brother – who for a long time in her treatment she insisted was 'my mother' – 'got into my mind' in the course of arguments between them, rather than, as I would put it, maintaining his position in outer reality. She clearly conveyed how utterly helpless she would feel on such occasions, when she would experience him as a physical presence 'in my mind', where, so her words and gestures conveyed, she could not get her hands on him, and therefore could not reach him.

A hebephrenic woman came to express her ambivalently symbiotic relatedness, or one might say her need for, and avoidance of, symbiosis, in a way more primitive than the arguing of which the paranoid woman I have just described was capable. She came to maintain for years, on the one hand, a demeanour of stony and silent antagonism towards me, seeming genuinely not to see me much of the time; yet on the other hand this demeanour would be interlarded with moments when she would make urgent pleas for oneness with me. Her history indicated that her relationship with each of her parents had been, until she became overtly psychotic in her early twenties, ambivalently symbiotic in nature. A note made concerning an hour in the sixth year of our work, at a time when I had become comparatively free from enmeshment in an ambivalently symbiotic relationship with her —at a time when I had come to feel, with predominant relief but with some guilt and concern, that I had 'fallen out of love with her'—suggests something of her striving to regain the symbiosis with me:

The work with Ellen continues to show, most prominently, her making clear her ambivalent effort to achieve, and to avoid, a symbiotic relatedness with me as a representative of her father. It seems to me of late that, because of my sense of separateness from her which is so much greater than that of a few years ago, her emphasis is mainly on the efforts to achieve [i.e. to regain] such a relationship.

Thus, for example, in yesterday's hour she indicated her doubt that she could survive if I stepped out of the room for a moment to get a cup of coffee, which I did. I cannot overemphasize how poignantly she expresses this kind of anxiety, such that in retrospect I am not surprised that I had such tremendous difficulty in going ahead years ago and functioning freely in the face of her anxiety and pleas in this direction [i.e. pleas for symbiosis].

This woman had once confided to me, 'My father lives when he gives to me', and the years of our therapeutic collaboration provided abundant evidence that one of the major aspects of her delusional transference to me was as a father whose own life demanded the perpetuation of a symbiotic relationship wherein he 'gave' incessantly to her, 'solicitously' lived her life for her, and so on.

(iii)

The third category of instances of transference psychosis are those in which *the patient's psychosis represents, in the transference, an effort to complement the therapist's personality, or to help the therapist-parent to become established as a separate and whole person.* These clinical situations, which appear quite diverse, all represent the patient's living out, in the transference, of the difficulty he has had since early childhood with a parent who has not proved strong enough, on his or her own, to accept the resolution of a symbiotic relationship which should have predominated only in the patient's infancy and early childhood. Because the parent is able to relate *only* symbiotically to the child, the child is given to feel that the resolution of the symbiotic mode of relatedness will mean the death of the parent, and his own potentially individual self is thus experienced by the patient as an inherently murderous self. The anxiety defended against by the schizophrenic symptomatology may be looked upon as springing from the simultaneous conviction that (*a*) the desperately needed symbiotic experience (no matter how formulated, or incapable of formulation, in the patient's mind) is tantamount to death as an individual, the erasure of individuality; and (*b*) the goal of fully achieved individuation is seen as equivalent to the murder of the parent.

These are far from being simply delusional notions on the patient's part, without any basis in reality. I have been struck, for instance, with the highly significant circumstances in which fatal or near-fatal cardiovascular accidents, quite beyond the much more frequent upsurges in anxiety of sometimes psychotic proportions, have occurred among parents of recovering schizophrenic patients. Several such incidents have occurred in the families of patients with whom I have been working; but this statistically insignificant sampling grows to sobering proportions when one sees it supported by similar incidents which have occurred in the course of my 14 years of work at Chestnut Lodge, in the collective experiences of, in cumulative total, perhaps 50 therapists who have worked with hundreds of patients here over the years. Such patients have had much solid historical reason to sense their own growth impulses as being inescapably murderous in nature, and therefore as being necessary to contain at all costs.

Comparatively early in my experience here, in my work with a catatonic young woman, I came to see that one of the determinants of various kinds of helplessness on her part consisted in an unconscious effort to promote her father's becoming a man; her persistent hope evidently was that he would find himself as man in the course of rescuing her from the situation in which she was floundering. This determinant became clearly revealed in the unfolding of her transference to me, and evident to both of us; the working through of her disappointment in her father, in this connexion, was one of the solid achievements in her therapy. Since then I have found the same unconscious 'motive' in various other schizophrenic patients, in one form or another.

A 45-year-old hebephrenic woman, for example, given for years to maddeningly fragmented and semi-audible speech, and equally maddening physical contrariness and unmanageability, came eventually to make clear that this represented, in the context of the transference relationship to me as a father, her effort to promote my making myself more firmly delineated, as it were —more explicit, more decisive, more firm. I had met her father, who died of a coronary occlusion a few months after her entry into intensive psychotherapy at the Lodge, and I had found him to be a remarkably inscrutable man. She had evidently found him so, too, and she made clear, in the transference, that she had found him to be, as well, a maddeningly indecisive person, who had as it were driven her out of her mind with his tantalizing indecisiveness and his crushingly disappointing failure to see things through. As she once put it, he 'always gave up two-thirds of the way up the mountain'; their symbiotic relatedness had consisted in her regarding him, overtly, as an adored pal, with whom she hiked, played tennis and golf, went horseback riding and sailing, and shared her experiences (by detailed subsequent reports) with boy friends whom she always compared unfavourably with him. They also played musical instruments together.

In the transference relationship, I early found that she was trying not simply to seduce me sexually, but was trying to get me to become a man by having intercourse with her. Once, for example, she wiggled her bare buttocks at me suggestively and, when I failed to make the apparently desired response, she quickly began showing increasing exasperation and said to herself, with great annoyance, 'Charlie [her father's nickname, which she generally used in referring to him and often used in referring to me] never did know how to play the bass clef!'

But comparable realizations on my part, concerning other manifestations of this same motive of father-building in the transference, were arrived at only with the greatest difficulty. It was only after several years that I discovered that one of the major determinants of her deeply schizophrenic mode of communication, which as I say was maddeningly fragmented and semi-audible, consisted in an effort on her part, an evidently genuinely unconscious effort, to foster my declaring myself, delineating myself, through my responsive efforts at filling in and clarifying which this mode of speech tended powerfully to evoke from me. Such schizophrenic speech tends to function in a way analogous to a Rorschach test, inviting the therapist's own projective self-revelations. Similarly, it was only after years of the most maddeningly indecisive and unmanageable behaviour on her part, whether during attempted walks in the hospital grounds with me or with various other personnel members, or when asked to perform any physical act, however ostensibly simple, that I realized that *her* extreme indecisiveness represented, in part, her effort to promote the other person's (in the therapeutic sessions, my) becoming decisive through his or her eventually becoming completely out of patience and cutting through all indecisiveness in the situation by a furiously impatient and unequivocal command.

Other more verbal and better integrated patients have come to make clear that their delusional utterances represent, in part, an effort to get the therapist to make clear where he stands – to determine how crazy or how sane he is, to find out what is his view of the people and events and things with which the patient is concerned. It has often come to me as not only a useful but also as an amusing realization to discover that my supposedly delusional, confused patient is now involved in trying the delusions upon me for size, or is otherwise involved in doing a kind of mental status examination of me. Recently a long-hebephrenic and genuinely disoriented woman murmured haltingly to me, 'What's the date?', and I started patiently to tell this poor benighted soul the date, when I suddenly realized that, from her view, it was I whose psyche was in question, and that she was trying cautiously to discern whether *I* knew the date. Space does not allow for an attempt to document conclusively that this is what her seeming disorientation, earlier in our work quite genuine indeed, had come to mean; all I can ask is that one does not forget that this is what one's patient may be doing with one. When this dimension of the transference relationship comes into view, it comes to one's attention that an astonishing number of bits of behaviour on the patient's part are interpretable in this light, as being evidence of a persistent, unending watchfulness for, and when opportunity affords itself, a brief and covert investigation of, data which indicate that the parent-therapist is sane or insane. It makes sense that this must have indeed been an important dimension of the patient's childhood—an important concern to him as a child—when we consider how afflicted has been the ego functioning of at least one, and often both, of his parents.

Similarly, I have found, and reported elsewhere, that a schizophrenic patient's expression of genuinely confused and delusional utterances may represent an unconscious effort to foster the creative imagination of the other person—the therapist, for example, the therapist perceived in the transference as being constricted, unimaginative, uncreative. I have seen this motive become clear and conscious in various of my patients. But in the instance of a hebephrenic woman it did not become clear to me until she physically loosened my too-tight shirt collar, which brought home to me the realization, in retrospect, of how many were the ways in which she had been trying, so to speak, to loosen my collar—trying to promote my living a freer and less obsessionally constricted life. I might add, parenthetically to any considerations about transference, that she has helped me greatly on this score. The schizophrenic patient's need to cure the therapist may dovetail in a useful way with the therapist's determination to become free from characterological obsessiveness.

Quite analogous is the schizophrenic patient's effort—a largely unconscious effort until it emerges from repression during the course of therapy—to relieve, by his crazy utterances and behaviour, depression in the other person. Depression is an important dimension in any schizophrenic patient; only after much therapy is he strong enough to feel it as his own, and until such time as he can, he has to project it upon the therapist (and other persons), and thus feels impelled to relieve it by schizophrenic symptoms which the other person may find infuriating, puzzling, or perhaps delightfully diverting, but in any case a way out of depression. Another way of viewing this phenomenon is to see that depression was prominent in the patient's parent(s) in his childhood, and in some instances oppressively permeated the whole family's life together; in the transference this becomes carried over to the therapist, who is often viewed as being on the verge of suicide. The suicidal feelings which are present,

685

whether actively or latently, in every person (except those individuals who are too deeply schizophrenic for such feelings to be accessible to them) become mobilized in the therapist, making for one of the genuinely great difficulties in carrying on successful therapy with these patients. Seen in the over-all context of the hospital, some of those patients who are most severely 'stuck' in their ego-development, year after year, are the hospital's well-known colourful characters, living legends, whose crazy antics, past and present, have served the function of relieving depression in the collective patients and personnel about them in the hospital community.

I personally have never felt more powerfully impelled towards suicide than I was during some months when a previously hebephrenic woman was working through her feelings towards me as being the personification, in the transference, of her long-depressed father. She had made clear to me that, at one time or another, each of her three other family members had been withdrawn, weeping, and 'yelling around about suicide'; but this had evidently been most severe in the father. He, a person much older than his wife, had fondly (though also enviously) told his daughter that she had 'all the vermilionishness of life', as she had once put it during the hebephrenic, highly neologistic earlier period of our work together. One of the ways in which she complemented him was by functioning as his own lost youth. She was both young, as he no longer was, and the girl he had never been and could never be. It was in part out of poignant experiences with her that I wrote chapter 17 of this book. The working-through of this aspect of her transference symbiosis with me took years to accomplish.

For years she habitually went about looking like a little girl dressed up in vivid but miscellaneous and out-of-style clothing, often reminiscent of the 'flapper era' chronicled in, for example, the cartoons by John Held, Jr., in the *College Humour* magazine of the 1920s and '30s. I was often annoyed by her attire, and embarrassed by it as an advertisement of the therapeutic capabilities of the man, namely myself, who had been her therapist for an embarrassingly long series of years; she often went to unstinting and at times highly creative efforts to constitute such an advertisement of herself. All this had, of course, a transference root derived from her experience in 'advertising', by her schizophrenic symptoms, her parents who were painfully conscious of matters of social position. Her older brother once confided to me his concern lest the patient, who had shown no little murderousness during her life both at home and in the sanatorium, might be released from the hospital prematurely and might murder somebody. This was a reasonable concern; but I was startled when the brother went on to explain that he would not wish such a thing to happen, for the reason that it would 'embarrass the family'. I was both determined that my vulnerability to personal embarrassment should not lead me into trying to dictate what the patient should wear, and recurrently touched, moreover, by the little-girl delight which she evidently found in her own attire, so that I could not bear to hurt her feelings by going beyond comparatively gentle suggestions that, yes, the attire is pretty but the orange doesn't go very well with the purple; or, yes, the hat is pretty but the dress looks a bit out of style, say thirty years or so.

Then one day, a few weeks after we had found that we had each chanced to see and like the film, 'The Sweet Bird of Youth', she came into the hour wearing, among other miscellaneous adornments (such as a black, scalloped slip and dramatic, blue-lensed eyeglasses) a taffeta skirt covered with giant splashes of colour, a skirt such as would be unlikely to be found anywhere but in a child's dream. She asked me eagerly, gesturing towards her skirt, 'Don't you think this looks like the sweet bird of youth?' It was this development which brought home to me the realization that, whereas all along I had felt that *I* was being tender to *her* in not bluntly opposing her wearing of such attire, she evidently was wearing it out of, in part, a tender concern for *me* – a concern to provide me, as a father in the transference, with Youth. I replied something like this, 'Alice, as a little boy I used to wear an aviator's helmet that buttoned down under the chin, like this –. As I say, I liked it, and I might for example come in here wearing it, some day. I might want you to admire it – and possibly you would; but I think you might have *some* feeling that my aviator's helmet, buttoned down under my chin, would be a *bit* out of place.' She took this well, and I believe it was not so much the expressing of a gentle correction as, rather, the conveying to her that I could accept the loss of my own youth which helped her eventually to get over this particular symptom.

(iv)

The fourth variety of transference psychosis is manifested at a phase in therapy in which *the deeply and chronically confused patient, who in childhood had been accustomed to a parent's doing his thinking for him, is ambivalently (a) trying to perpetuate a symbiotic relationship wherein the therapist to a high degree does the patient's thinking for him, and (b) expressing, by what the therapist feels to be sadistic and castrative nullifying or undoing of the therapist's efforts to be helpful, a determination to be a separately thinking, and otherwise separately functioning, individual.* During my years of work at Chestnut Lodge, I have successively seen the basically transference nature of schizophrenic confusion; the intense though largely unconscious sadism which is being expressed in this confusion, by the subjectively helpless patient whom the dedicated therapist is trying to rescue from the confusion; and, lastly, the striving towards individuation which is at the core of those aspects of the patient's functioning which have seemed, heretofore, primarily intended sadistically to torture, and in one fashion or another to castrate, the therapist.

One chronically confused hebephrenic woman, who for years in her therapy evidenced much idiotic behaviour and on repeated psychological examinations was found to have a subnormal I.Q., had been trained by her father throughout her upbringing how to think. As a natural extension of this, he had coached her as to what to say in various social situations, and had taught her to memorize various witticisms which amused him and which she found essentially meaningless. She became schizophrenic during her teens, at a point where it had become evident that this idolized-father symbiotic partner of hers had, in actuality, feet of clay. She then oriented her life, for several years, round a delusional omnipotent figure, a kind of composite of powerful persons, real and imagined, from past and present life, and addressed hundreds of pleas for rescue, from the hospital, to, for example,

> My Father, Zirey Edward Butcher
> Head of the Marshall Airfields
> All over the Place
> or
> My Old Man . . .
> Head the Boss of Radio City

TRANSFERENCE PSYCHOSIS

Head of General Motors
The World's Fair
Head of Standard Oil
Head of the Conferences . . .
    or, in at least one instance,
. . . Head of Those Things.

A tiny sample of the vast extent to which her functional imbecility came from emotional, transference sources became evident in an hour when she was describing–as usual against massive confusion–her struggle to hold a job as a secretary, years ago, during an interim between two of her long successions of hospitalization. She managed to bring out her conviction that the customary salutation in a business letter, 'Dear Sir', is indicative of both promiscuity (as regards the 'Dear') and of boot-licking (as regards the 'Sir'). I had long ago found much evidence to indicate that her possessive father had forbidden her participation in either 'promiscuity' or 'boot-licking' to such an extent that it had been impossible for her to develop more than the rudiments of any friendships with other young people. It had long ago become clear that she had been given to feel that she must have no other gods before him–before him who, she had quite literally believed up until her schizophrenic break, was omniscient.

In the transference relationship with me she would recount, with hebephrenic laughter, meaningless fragments of jokes that 'were going around New York' years before–always meaning, so I came to know, idiosyncratic jokes which she had heard from, specifically, her father. Always my failure to laugh in response to these unfunny 'jokes' was taken by her as confirmation that I was, like the mother upon whom she and her father had habitually heaped scorn, devoid of a sense of humour and therefore incapable of functioning upon the high plane occupied by that symbiotic twosome. For fully three years I was, in the transference, predominantly this scorned mother.

But then she began reacting to me as being, more and more clearly, the know-it-all father, and her confusion gradually took form as representing on the one hand a desperate effort to get me to clarify the awesome confusion with which she was genuinely afflicted, and on the other a mocking, sadistic, eroding kind of nullification of my efforts to be helpful to her in this very regard.

More than anything, I was patient; with seemingly endless

689

patience and solicitude I tried to help this pitiably confused girl, and only later on did I realize that she had construed my overt calmness, gentleness, and patience as being evidence of the same maddeningly aloof, know-it-all quality she had come to hate – as therapy had by now established – in her father. It was characteristic of her to deny the fact of her own confusion; she had, no doubt, too little ego-strength to be able to face this awesomely helpless aspect of herself.

A turning-point came near the end of an hour filled with the usual inundatingly confused verbalizations from her. I had recurrently commented, 'That was puzzling, wasn't it?,' or 'It's confusing to you, isn't it?'. Each time she had flatly denied that she was confused – had denied it in a way which I found progressively exasperating, since I felt very much confused most of the time myself, and since her tone, as well as her verbal content, was clearly one of confusion and puzzlement.

Finally, near the end of the hour, when for the *n*th time she had flatly disclaimed being confused, I burst out sarcastically and very exasperatedly, 'Well, if it's clear to *you*, congratulations, Louise! It sure as hell isn't clear to *me*; *I've* been confused by about 80 per cent of what you've been saying this hour. But if it's all clear to you, *congratulations*! You know, it's one thing to be confused and to *know* you're confused, and it's another thing to be confused and not even know you're confused. At least if you *realize* you're confused, that's a *beginning*!' Previously, I had been concerned to protect her from the realization of how very confusing I had long been finding her desperate efforts to convey her thoughts to me.

Significantly, it was in the very next day's session that she told me, more clearly than ever before, how exasperating it had been to her during her upbringing that her father would never admit that he was wrong about something, would never admit that there was something he didn't know. It was at this point that I realized in retrospect that one determinant of her years-long confusion had been an effort, apparently largely unconscious, on her part to thwart, and prove fallible, me as the know-it-all father in the transference. Subsequently she was much more accepting of my efforts to help her in the resolution of her severe and chronic thought-disorder.

Another hebephrenic woman, who had likewise participated,

until the onset of her schizophrenic psychosis, in an overtly idolizing but covertly competitive symbiotic relationship with her father, for several years placed me under extreme pressure—by reason of her manifest helplessness, despair, terror, and often mutely abandoned and unloved demeanour—to get me to do her thinking for her, as her father had evidently done in bygone years. Incessantly I was kept under pressure to guess aloud at the meanings which were supposedly nascent in her fragmentary, ambiguous, and half-inaudible speech, or in her oftentimes odd non-verbal communications. Despite the fact that she would almost invariably react with an undermining sneer when I did manage, by dint of flights of intuition, to guess correctly, I kept trying with dogged devotion—and, as became increasingly evident, I was trying overmuch, as she phrased it, to 'put words in my mouth'.

It was such infringement on her striving to think for herself, and to become free from the transference symbiosis, that brought forth her most sadistic responses to me. In chapter 8 I have conceptualized such responses as an effort to drive the other person crazy. She eventually came to make this sadistic motive quite explicit, in such statements as—near the end of an hour in which she had made clear, on the one hand, how much she suffered from genuine fragmentation of all her perceptual functions—'I hate doctors! That's why I make things mush!'

This was the same woman who had said, earlier in our work when I was trying, as usual, to rescue her from her despair-filled fragmentation, 'There's a weird doctor around here that doesn't make sense to me. He's metal—he's—everything', while looking uneasily about.

Rosenfeld (1954) states that

> In the acute schizophrenic state the patient tends to put his self so completely into objects that there is very little of the self left outside the object. This interferes with most ego-functions, including speaking and understanding words . . .

And Bion (1956) presents some extremely stimulating concepts, to the effect that one of the essential features of the schizophrenic personality is a hatred of reality, which is extended to all aspects of the psyche that make for awareness of it, such that his own perceptual ego-functions, as well as his attempted collaborativeness with the analyst, is subjected to hostile splitting mechanisms.

It seems to me that the concepts of both Rosenfeld and Bion do not take into adequate account a factor inherent in the early family life of the patient, wherein the invasiveness of the symbiotic parent(s) was such as to prevent the child from meeting a genuine reality either outside himself or within himself as an individual. We need to see that it is not reality as such which the patient hates, but rather the only 'reality' which he has so far known, a symbiosis-derived pseudo-reality, a reality derived, in Brodey's (1959, 1961) terms, from the mother's (or, I would add, the father's) 'inner workings'. It is this 'reality', this facet of the pathogenic symbiosis, which the patient is healthily—though seemingly so sadistically and castratively and destructively—determined to shed, in order to emerge and be born as an individual.

A chronically paranoid woman, whose mother, in the words of an uncle who gave us an admission history, had 'loved to dominate' this child and had given the girl, from her own isolated eccentric, ambulatory schizophrenic social position, unequivocal but remarkably contradictory edicts as to how to think and behave in various situations, came to reveal, in the course of our several years of work together, various of these psychodynamics with unusual clarity.

Like one of the foregoing hebephrenic women, this patient became able to acknowledge the fact of her own confusion, defended against for years by vociferously uttered delusional certainties, only after I had come to experience, and openly reveal, a deep confusion in myself in reaction to her forcefully and tenaciously expressed delusions, which I came eventually to feel as seriously eroding all the underpinnings of my sense of identity, all the things about myself of which I had felt most sure: namely, that I am a man, that I am a psychiatrist, that I am engaged in fundamentally decent rather than malevolent work, and so on and so on. She now became able to say, simply and seriously, 'I don't know anything', and to evidence a steadily diminishing resistance to my therapeutic efforts.

I knew that the death of her mother had been one of the circumstances, if not the centrally significant circumstance, attending the onset of her paranoid schizophrenia several years ago. A time came in our work when, in a spirit of unusually positive transference, although as usual she was delusional and confused, she was struggling unusually hard to try to understand and convey to me what she was experiencing during the course of the session. At one point she explained to me, 'You see, my mother was my mind', and this was said in such a tone as poignantly to convey the implication, 'and when I lost her, I lost my mind'. It was painfully clear during the hour to what an awesome extent she had indeed lost her mind, as measured by the incredible depth of her confusion, quite unreproducible here.

As far as her transference to me during this same session was concerned, I felt that all her productions, taken together, amounted to a vigorous effort to induce me to provide her with guidance, direction. She did make quite explicit her struggle at present to, as she put it, 'build a world', and was clearly trying to persuade me to work with her in figuring this out, or hopefully to show her how do to it. Part of the time she was working with pencil and paper, drawing a diagram of a very tall H, a turtle, an ark, a saucer, and one or two other items. Included in the notes I made subsequent to this session was the comment, What makes this so terribly difficult is that her competitiveness, her castrativeness, which is so much out of her awareness, is so strong as largely to nullify such efforts as I do make to respond to her indubitably sincere collaborativeness.

But it gradually became very clear to me, and confirmed by her, that the 'getting well' I sought to help her achieve was to her synonymous with getting castrated. This concept she acted out in various ways, in schizophrenic symptomatology which sometimes made one's flesh creep, as when – to mention but one among many diverse incidents–she stripped all the leaves off some luxuriant plants which she had been carefully nurturing in her room. She began to reveal more and more clearly that, in performing these various crazy acts, she was obediently following the directions which she heard coming from 'that woman in my head', who was evidently an introject, no matter how distorted by the patient's own anxiety and hostility, of the crazy mother of her childhood.

In one of the more amusing of our sessions, she suddenly reported to me, 'That woman in my head just said, "Don't have anything to do with that frump out there".' She confirmed my amused assumption that 'that frump' referred to me. At another point in the hour, she protested vigorously, when I had suggested, as had long been my custom, 'Let's see what comes to your mind next', 'You keep asking me what's in my *mind—she's* in my mind; but she has nothing to do with *me!*' She went on to make it evident that she herself felt utterly ignored and un-related-to by me, whenever I endeavoured, with those words, to encourage her to express herself. Usually we think of the person's mind as the locus and very core of his self; but she showed me that this was by no means true for her. It was evident, in retrospect, that when, all along, I had been endeavouring to help her explore and elaborate what was in her mind, she had been reacting as though my effort had been to stamp out finally her upward-struggling autonomy, to castrate finally her individuality, so to speak, by rendering permanent and total the sway which the introjected symbiotic mother already held over her ego functioning.

Before leaving this discussion of the forms in which transference psychosis is manifested, it should be noted that just as all these various forms may be shown by any one patient, at one time or another in the course of his psychotherapy, so is it impossible to demarcate clearly between transference psychosis in general, on the one hand, and transference neurosis on the other. Freud (1911b) made the comment that

We have long observed that every neurosis has as its result, and probably therefore as its purpose, a forcing of the patient out of real life, an alienating of him from reality . . . Neurotics turn away from reality because they find it unbearable—either the whole or parts of it. The most extreme type of this turning away from reality is shown by certain cases of hallucinatory psychosis which seek to deny the particular event that occasioned the outbreak of their insanity. But in fact every neurotic does the same with some fragment of reality . . .

Bion, in his paper in 1957 concerning the differentiation, in any one schizophrenic patient, between what he calls the psychotic personality and the non-psychotic personality, concludes the presentation of his theoretical formulations with,

. . . Further, I consider that this holds true for the severe neurotic, in whom I believe there is a psychotic personality concealed by neurosis as the neurotic personality is screened by psychosis in the psychotic, that has to be laid bare and dealt with.

And chapter 9 above, where I describe a phase of symbiotic relatedness in the transference relationship between the schizophrenic patient and his therapist, as being at the core of the resolution of the schizophrenia, I include the general statement that

... My experience indicates, further, that such a [symbiotic] relatedness constitutes a necessary phase in psycho-analysis or psychotherapy with either neurotic or psychotic patients, respectively ... (Searles, 1959b).

The 'Technical Management' of Transference Psychosis

Bion conveys in his paper entitled 'Language and the Schizophrenic' (1955) a warning of the patient's tendency to project his own sanity upon the analyst, and of the massive regression which follows if this is condoned by the analyst. He says:

... I have no doubt whatever that the analyst should always insist, by the way in which he conducts the case, that he is addressing himself to a sane person and is entitled to expect some sane reception ...

And Rosenfeld (1952b), in his paper concerning his analysis of an acute catatonic patient, writes,

... My own approach was analytic, in so far as a great deal of what I was able to understand of the patient's words and behaviour was interpreted to him, and whenever possible, and that was frequently, the analytical material was related to the transference situation ...

In principle, such an approach seems unassailably valid, and we recall some of the examples of the apparently dramatically beneficial results which follows from verbal interpretations of transference psychosis, as reported by Rosenfeld and others.

But in practice I, at least, seldom find it suitable to make verbal transference interpretations to the patient who—in contrast with the borderline-schizophrenic individual, for example—is still deep in chronic schizophrenia. Typically, such a patient is too unable to employ, or even hear, verbal communications to be able to make use of verbalized transference interpretations. Moreover, it is my experience that he actively needs a degree of symbiotic relatedness in the transference, which would be interfered with were the analyst to try, recurrently, to establish with him the validity of verbalized transference interpretations. I do not feel that the recognition of the patient's need for a relatively prolonged period – lasting, say, for several months – of predominantly non-verbal, symbiotic relatedness with the therapist is tantamount to one's fostering the patient's projection upon one of his own sanity. And I wonder whether such frequent, verbalized transference interpretations as Rosenfeld employs, as indicated in his reports of his work, are not suggestive of his own unconscious resistance to the development of the predominantly silent 'therapeutic symbiosis' phase which, in my experience, the patient so deeply needs in the course of the transference evolution. I presume that what is needed is for the therapist to be so attuned to the patient's needs as to be able to maintain a dynamic balance between, on the one hand, some considerable degree of participating in symbiotic relatedness with him and, on the other, helping him at appropriate times to see the transference meanings in what is transpiring, or has been transpiring, between the two participants.

In a session with a paranoid schizophrenic woman, after I had just endeavoured to call her attention, verbally, to something that had been going on between us, she looked greatly disconcerted, and told me, 'When you say things like that, I feel as though I had been riding with you in an airplane, and that I had just been dropped down into the bottom of the ocean.' Later on in the therapy, at a time when she had been trying for many months to make a body for herself out of all sorts of materials, she protested to me on one occasion, 'The minute I start to say something, you say something about, "Does this remind you of your mother, or does this remind you of your father, or somebody else?" – so naturally I don't feel that *I* exist!' I felt that she was making a valid and important point here, although by any ordinary standards I had not been overdoing such comments. I felt that she was clarifying a central determinant in her years-long lack of a sense of personal identity, which extended into her experiencing her body as not actually her own.

A hebephrenic man met, for a number of years, nearly every one of my comparatively infrequent verbalized questions with an antagonistic retort, 'I don't know you', or 'I'm a stranger', or 'I just got here'. It eventually dawned upon me, and was subsequently confirmed, that he heard each of these questions as conveying the covert, rejecting message which he himself spoke. That is, it became evident that to him the very fact that I asked him a question–concerning either what he was experiencing at the moment, or some past event–was taken by him as a denial on my part that I knew him, was close to him, and had a great backlog of shared experience with him.

It was true that, as much as two years before I realized this, he had once replied to one of my questions with the disappointed and disgusted comment, 'There's no friendly intuition here!', in such a way as to make me realize that, if the degree of friendly intuition existed between us that he was hungering for, no words would be necessary. But one reason why I was so slow to make this later discovery is that this hebephrenic man would habitually tell not only me, but various other persons about him when they made overtures, 'I'm a stranger', and so on; hence I missed the personal significance of it in our relationship. This is all another way of stating the patient's need for a predominantly silent, basically symbiotic relatedness with the therapist.

I might mention that in a later predominantly wordless 'therapeutic symbiosis' phase of my work with the previously mentioned paranoid schizophrenic woman, we were sitting in her room during one of the sessions, in a comfortable, fond silence and she was peacefully knitting. I started to say something, and she interrupted me with, 'What's the matter–aren't you satisfied with what you're getting on your radar?' I started to protest, 'Yes, but–', whereupon she said, in the way a fond mother would firmly but gently admonish a little child, 'Then be *quiet*.'

I did not then attempt a transference interpretation, nor do I feel, in retrospect, that one was in order. Many times, earlier in our work, she had shown great pressure of speech, and had protested against my comparatively silent participation with the statement that she couldn't stand 'the intimacy of silence'. This I regard as an instance of the frequent situations, with these very deeply ill patients, when it is essential for the therapist to be able not only to endure, but also to enjoy, a wide variety of transference positions in relation to the patient, before the patient can become able, acknowledgedly and explicitly, to accept him as a *therapist* to such a degree as to be able to attend to verbalized transference interpretations from him. To try to do this prematurely, before the therapeutic symbiosis phase has been allowed to develop and has come towards the end of its usefulness to the patient, is tantamount to the therapist's using the concept of transference as a kind of shield to protect himself from the necessary degree of psychological intimacy with the patient, in a way quite analogous to the patient's own unconscious use of his delusional transference as a kind of shield to protect himself from experiencing the full reality of the therapist as a person in the present.

There is widespread agreement that it is inherent in therapy that the therapist functions as an auxiliary ego to the patient in the patient's struggle with inner conflicts, until such time as, by identification with the therapist's strength, he becomes able to make this greater strength part of his own ego. To the extent that the schizophrenic patient does not possess an observing ego of sufficient strength to permit the therapist usefully to make transference interpretations, to that degree the therapist must be able to endure–and, eventually, to enjoy–various part-object transference roles, until such time as the patient, *via* increasing ego-integration, becomes able to see the delusional-transference nature of this view of the therapist. Another way of saying this is that the patient develops ego-strength, in the face of his own id impulses and pathogenic superego retaliations, *via* identification with the therapist who can endure, and integrate into his own larger self, the kind of subjectively non-human part-object relatedness which the patient fosters in and needs from him.

Several writers have made clear that interpretations of transference psychosis must extend beyond the merely verbal level. Bion (1955), for example, comments: '. . . for a considerable proportion of analytic time the only evidence on which an interpretation can be based is that which is afforded by the counter-transference.'

He evidently uses the term 'counter-transference' to refer to the analyst's feeling-reactions to the patient's transference. He illustrates the role of the analyst's feelings in this regard by a description (quoted earlier here) of a successful transference interpretation derived, initially, only from Bion's own awareness of a fear in himself that the patient was contemplating a murderous attack upon him, without there having been at that moment any discernible outward change in the patient's demeanour.

Little, in one of her papers concerning patients in whom she finds a delusional transference to exist, emphasizes, concerning these patients, 'the supreme importance for them of body happenings', and says, albeit in somewhat tantalizingly vague phraseology,

> . . . the body events may become the interpretations. Verbalization then becomes the second stage in a two-stage process, both stages being necessary for real insight to be attained, but the second only effective as a result of the first, i.e. of the body happening.
>
> . . . Discharge, and consequent differentiation [out of the delusional basic unity], comes through some body event—a movement, a scream, salivation, etc.—by means of which some kind of bodily contact with the analyst occurs. Through repetitions of such events the patient comes gradually to recognize the difference between his body, his sensations, and his emotions, while those of the analyst are discovered as separate from his. The event has concerned two people, and the patient discovers himself as a person who has moved, screamed, etc., in relation to another person, whose separate existence, experience, movements, and responses can also be recognized. The delusion breaks up, recovery begins, and relationship becomes a possibility.
>
> The importance of these body happenings lies in the fact that in those areas where the delusion is operative the patient is to all intents and purposes literally an infant, his ego a body ego. For him, in these areas, only concrete, actual, and bodily things have meaning and can carry conviction . . . (Little, 1960).

The following comments by Little show how important she considers it to be, to the patient, that he be as it were free to feel at one with the analyst—in line with my own views; but she evidently feels less sure than I do that the analyst inevitably participates in this in reality, and that this mutuality of what I call the therapeutic symbiosis is indeed essential to a successful therapeutic outcome. That is, where I would say that the patient's 'delusion' of basic unity with the analyst needs to become a mutually shared reality between the two partici-pants, she comments, variously, that

> [Concerning one particular woman] . . . Her recovery has been based on this delusion of total identity with me, which has had to be gradually broken down, as far as factual reality is concerned, while

the psychic reality of it has had to be preserved with the greatest care . . .

. . . the delusion [of unity with the analyst], although accepted as true for the patient, is not shared by the analyst (unless, unfortunately, he has something of a counter-transference psychosis).

. . . The underlying principle [of relevant analytic technique] . . . is that of acceptance by the analyst of the truth *for the analysand* of his delusion of absolute identity between them, his entering into it, and demonstrating both its psychic truth and its objective untruth.

. . . If the analyst is sufficiently one with his patient psychically, he experiences him, at times, as himself, or himself, at times, as the patient. But because of his unity with himself he also experiences what he says or does to be himself . . . (Little, 1960).

Boyer has reported upon his use of a modified analytic technique, in his office practice with schizophrenic patients, which apparently conforms more nearly to classical psycho-analysis than does any other reported approach by anyone treating such patients. Even he, while not making mention of any use of physical contact between himself and the patient in the course of his interpretations of delusional transference, does call attention to the crucial significance of physical phenomena in these patients:

It is to be remembered that with inadequate differentiation of ego and id, tensions are often fixated to physical phenomena . . . In a previous report (Boyer, 1957) I have recorded a fragment of the history of a schizophrenic whose analysis was given tremendous impetus through repetitious direction of his attention to physical tension and movements . . .

. . . preverbal communications are of signal importance with many, if not all, regressed patients. The analyst's understanding of them and communication of their meanings enables patients not only to break through resistances and to help them to learn about realities, but to restore body-ego deficiencies and to separate self from non-self. In addition, their interpretation helps analysands to progress in ego growth to where they can accurately communicate in *words*. It is not unusual . . . that the words being *said* may have little importance as messages in themselves, but constitute the contributions of a decathected part of the self, while the meaningful cathexis is invested in the posture and movements of the moment (Boyer, 1961).

In general, while my own approach is far from being as abstemious as Boyer's appears to be, I cannot wholeheartedly accept Little's enthusiastic endorsement of physical contact; I have seen a number of clear-cut instances in which my declining to provide physical contact has been as helpful, in promoting the resolution of delusional transference, as has been my touching of the patient on other occasions. In chapter 22, concerning the role of neutral therapist responses in the therapy of the schizophrenic patient, I have emphasized that if one is to help him to become subjectively alive, one must be unafraid of functioning as the transference representation of the subjectively unalive parts of the patient's self, or as the very early perceived attributes of the mother, before she had emerged as a whole and alive and human being in the perception of the infant. Prior to such a development the mother, and comparably the therapist in the transference situation, is so very important to the patient— as one chronically paranoid patient phrased it, a Coke machine for the automatic gratification of his needs–that, from his viewpoint, the mother or the therapist must not have a separate aliveness. A therapist who is neurotically afraid of physical contact with people, including schizophrenic patients, to that degree complicates the recovery process in the patient; but so does the therapist who recurrently needs to reassure himself of his own living humanness, his own capacity for feeling, by a dramatically 'curative' employment of physical contact with the patient. In the latter instance, it is only ostensibly the trembling and frightened patient who is being helped by the therapist's reassuring touch; covertly the patient is thereby reassuring the therapist of the latter's own capacity for life and lovingness.

Milner (1952), in her beautiful account of her therapy of an 11-year-old boy who had found outer reality mechanized and soulless by reason of its unacceptingness of his own spontaneous creation, a difficulty she found traceable to a premature loss of belief in a self-created outer reality, describes how she helped him to achieve a healthy reality-relatedness through her acceptance of his treating her as being part of himself–as being his own malleable, pliable, 'lovely stuff', his 'chemicals', which he had created. Winnicott (1945, 1948), in the same vein, has conjectured that the healthy mother helps her baby, in the nursing situation for example, towards an acceptance of external reality through helping him to experience this reality not as something alien to himself but as something self-created. I have described the patient-therapist relatedness during the 'therapeutic symbiosis' phase of therapy as being of essentially this same nature. We see here that what might be called a form of 'delusional transference'–the patient's reacting to the therapist as being an inanimate, or at least not separately alive, product of the patient himself–is really, in its nucleus, the primeval form of healthy, creative relatedness to external reality, and that this development could not occur if the therapist were unable to become comfortable with this 'inanimate' role in the transference.

A 32-year-old woman patient who had by now progressed far towards recovery from her chronic schizophrenia produced, in a number of sessions over the course of a month, material which illustrated memorably, for me, the point that a person can come to relinquish the oceanic ego-state, and to experience outer reality as such–can bear the loss involved in this development–only by finding an essential sameness between self and outer reality; her experience is, I think, closely comparable with that of Milner's boy-patient.

In the first of the sessions I wish to mention, she was talking about her recently acquired room-mate, a woman whom I by now knew to personify, in many respects, my patient's own sicker–more paranoid, more self-absorbed–former self, as she had been earlier in her treatment. She spoke with much feeling, including a particularly memorable, childlike naïveté. She told of having been for a walk with another woman patient and of how in the course of their walk they had come upon a little feather lying on the ground, which my patient, Edith, picked up. It so happened, she mentioned to me in her narrative, that her room-mate, an artist, had hung up a work of art she had done, a montage which had on it, among other things, a feather.

When Edith subsequently came into their room, her room-mate, Mrs Simmons, was in there and saw Edith coming in, wearing the little feather on her blouse. Mrs Simmons immediately said, 'Did you take my feather?', accusingly. Edith explained to me that this was typical of Mrs Simmons–that is, it was characteristic of her to think of everything in terms of herself. Edith described how, in essence, she then had patiently but firmly pointed out to Mrs Simmons that no, this was not the latter woman's feather–that Mrs Simmons' feather was there on the montage, and that this was a different one which she, Edith, had just picked up in the hospital grounds.

From here on in her account to me, Edith's tone took on a kind of childlike naïveté and hesitancy; but she went on determinedly, though finding it hard to express her thoughts in words. 'When I first came here, I was a little that way,' she said, and this made me smile a bit inwardly, because it was such an understatement. 'Then,' she went on, 'I sort of woke up, and said, "There are so many people here–could be somebody else–we all have almost the same".' She explained that it had been her seeing, in a department store window, dresses which were the same as one she was then wearing, and the same, likewise, as she had seen on various other women at that time during her trips into the community, that was the context in which she had awakened to this realization.

She then added that, in contrast to Mrs Simmons (who had been here in the sanatorium for only two months, in contrast to the several years of Edith's own residence here), when she, Edith, first came here, 'I didn't have anyone to tell me they had a feather.' This was said in a tone of painful deprivation, and I felt pained on hearing it, although this did not seem to be said with any aim of reproaching me for not having made clear to her that I, too, have a feather.

In a session near the end of that same month, she told me, 'Dr Searles, you know I've told you that I very seldom dream. But I had a dream the night before last. You remember that purse I have with flowers on the side of it? I dreamed that I rushed around so much that I lost the flowers from my purse, and I saw another woman pick them up and put them on *her* purse, and I said, [tone of strong protest] "*She's* taking *my* flowers!" '

She then went on, with much interest, to contrast the feeling she had had in the dream–describing it now in the following way: a sharp intake of the breath, with 'I lost my flowers!'–to the feeling she had had a few weeks previously when, while downtown shopping, she had seen a woman with a purse almost like her own, except that the other woman's purse had flowers on the top, whereas Edith's purse had flowers on the side. Edith described her feeling on that earlier, real-life occasion with a tone of pleasure, 'She has almost the same as mine!' In saying how different from this had been the feeling in the dream, she said, 'I guess I do feel that something has been taken away from me.'

It did not become established in that hour what the 'something' might be, and I was left with this as an unanswered question in my own mind. In the earlier years of our work, she had very often indeed expressed her conviction that she had been robbed; she had been unable for years to express a feeling of *loss* as such, but instead had felt deliberately robbed, of this or that person or thing, by maliciously inclined other persons including myself.

Then, in a session a very few days later, she described how the previous evening she had been in the nursing office, typing up the minutes of the recent ward-meeting, and Mrs Simmons had felt convinced, erroneously, that the paper Edith was using was from Mrs Simmons' art-tablet. Edith showed her that this was not the case—showed her that the tablet she was using was her own, with some of her own drawings in it, and went on, emphatically but not unkindly, 'Mrs Simmons, you have an illness, and I want you to get over it right this minute! You think everything is yours. I know, because I've been through it myself; I used to think that everything was—well, that everything concerned me, and was mine, and [here Edith's voice, in her telling me, became filled with a sense of loss] was gone.'

I felt that this material revealed how the paranoid person, involved as she had been, years earlier in her treatment, in a state of not-yet-completed ego-differentiation from the outside world, feels robbed of *everything*, and that this process of individuation can go on to completion, and the outside world be found acceptable and no longer made up of one's own stolen former contents, only upon one's finding an essential sameness between self and outer world—symbolized by the feathers, the flowered purses, and the identical women's dresses. By the same token, the patient can become individuated *vis-à-vis* the therapist only after she has come to find that the therapist possesses in reality essentially the same qualities which she has come to know in herself—that her various transferences to him, her various projections upon him, are not devoid of nuclei of interpersonal reality.

We begin to discover that this whole realm of various kinds of delusional transference, or transference psychosis, can be seen by the therapist to be, and needs to be responded to by him as being, an effort on the part of the patient to build up whole-project interpersonal relationships and a whole-object ego-identity. All these can be seen as part-object phenomena through which the patient successively builds up, bit by bit, through processes of both projection and introjection, a psychological feeling-image of both himself and the mother-therapist as whole persons. One borderline patient experienced this process most explicitly in displaced terms in his relationship with his wife, clearly a mother-figure to him. In the course of his being absorbed successively with various parts of his wife—her genitals, her breasts, her nose and so on—each part being the object of his fascinated attention when he was with her, over a period of months he built up to the realization that she was a whole person, and that he, no doubt partly through identification with these various part-attributes of her, was also a whole person.

The extent to which the therapist feels a genuine sense of deep participation in the patient's 'delusional transference' relatedness to him during the phase of therapeutic symbiosis—wherein the patient is reacting to him as being the personification of the Good Mother—is difficult to convey in words; it is essential that the therapist come to know that such a degree of feeling-participation is not evidence of 'counter-transference psychosis', but rather is the essence of what the patient needs from him at this crucial phase of the treatment. A hebephrenic woman who had evidenced intense antagonism towards me for several years eventually came to see me as the personification of the loving potentialities of her mother, and when, one day, as I was leaving her room at the end of a therapeutic session, she said fondly, 'Goodbye, Mother,' I simply replied, with like fondness, 'Goodbye, Betty.' This exchange had no quality of ungenuine role-playing about it; but on the other hand I felt that neither was any pathological misidentification involved. She could as well have said, 'Goodbye, Harold', without any shift in the emotional genuineness of this brief exchange. I felt it then, and have subsequently regarded it, as a landmark in terms of my deeply accepting the 'transference role' of mother to her, and in terms of her acceptance of me in that capacity.

A paranoid woman, who had reached the therapeutic-symbiosis phase of the transference after several years of comparably intense negative transference, suddenly asked in the midst of a highly productive session, 'You mean I own you?' I was not aware that I had been making any comments which could be so translated; but I had seen on a number of recent occasions how in the midst of fond exchanges about whatever subject, she would suddenly ask, 'Are you proposing to me?', or 'Are you making love to me?' This time, when she asked, 'You mean I own you?', I replied, 'Well, I'm very much attached to you—if you call that owning me, then you own me.' I had never acknowledged so candidly how much a part of her I had come to feel, and it is noteworthy that this woman, who several years earlier in our work had shown an intensely paranoid reaction against feelings of fond intimacy, showed no such anxiety now. In the course of the next few months she came to express feelings of glowing adoration of me, viewed as an inexpressibly beautiful mother whose body was, the patient felt, interchangeable with her own; and now for the first time I began to get from her a picture of her mother not as multiple, suddenly changeable, and predominantly malevolent figures, but rather as having been, on at least some occasions during the girl's upbringing, a single, whole, healthy, and fond mother to her.

It has been my recurrent experience that one of the necessary developments in a long-delusional patient's eventual relinquishment of his delusions is for these gradually to become productions which the therapist sees no longer as essentially ominous and the subject for either serious therapeutic investigation, or argumentation, or any other form of opposition; rather, the therapist comes to react to these as being essentially playful, unmalignant, creatively imaginative, and he comes to respond to them with playfully imaginative comments of his own. Nothing helps more finally to detoxicate a patient's previously self-isolating delusional state than to find in his therapist a capacity to engage with him in a delightfully crazy playfulness—a kind of relatedness of which the schizophrenic patient had never had a chance to have his fill during his childhood. Typically, such early childhood playfulness was subjected to massive repression, because of various intra-familial circumstances which I shall not try to elaborate upon here.

One of the ingredients of schizophrenia—in my experience, one of the regular ingredients—is a basically healthy and normal small-child playfulness which, for various reasons referable to the early environment, was early subjected to repression and has long been acted out in manifold ways, often highly destructive ways, by the patient, who is quite unaware of the extent to which he has come to play, in a destructively irresponsible spirit, with the irreplaceable and therefore to-be-cherished-and-preserved relationships and situations in his life. In essence, the therapist has to become able to adapt to the patient's fiddling while Rome burns; at first the therapist endures this, later he comes to be quite comfortable in this setting despite its tragically wasteful aspects, and still later comes to enjoy the music and to share in producing it. At this juncture the patient, having gained the realization that he is not at heart a malevolent being for wanting to play, becomes interested at long last in putting out the fire, clearing away the rubble, restoring what can be restored, and building anew.

For the therapist thus to succeed, in the long run, in enlisting the patient's active co-operation in the therapy, he must be able to cope along the way with feelings of guilty irresponsibility on his own part. For example, not long ago I felt a good deal of guilt at discovering that I actually had come to regard with aesthetic appreciation the abundant delusions of a paranoid woman with whom I had long been working. I found myself drinking in, as it were, with appreciation and admiration, productions which my professional conscience told me I should continue, as I had for years, to struggle manfully to investigate with her, or somehow to counter. But as the sessions went on, my enjoyment became less and less tinged with guilt, and it was in this context that the patient came, for the first time, to speak with healthy pride of her own lifelong imaginativeness. I no longer reacted to this imaginativeness as being in any sense an enemy; I could now enjoy it, and participate in it with my own verbalized imaginatively 'crazy'–childishly playful–associations. For a number of years, earlier in her treatment, during what I term the ambivalently symbiotic phase of the therapy, when she had shown a high degree of anxiety and hostility of at times near-murderous proportions, I had surely done much of what Bion, in the following illuminating passages, describes his patient as having 'felt'—supposedly a transference phenomenon without any basis in reality–that Bion had been doing:

. . . Throughout the analysis the patient resorted to projective identificaton with a persistence suggesting it was a mechanism of which he had never been able sufficiently to avail himself; the analysis afforded him an opportunity for the exercise of a mechanism of which he had been cheated. . . . There were sessions which led me to suppose that the patient felt there was some object that denied him the use of projective identification. In the illustrations I have given, . . . there are elements which indicate that the patient felt that parts of his personality that he wished to repose in me were refused entry by me . . .

Associations . . . showed an increasing intensity of emotions in the patient. This originated in what he felt was my refusal to accept parts of his personality. Consequently he strove to force them into me with increased desperation and violence. His behaviour, isolated from the context of the analysis, might have appeared to be an expression of primary aggression. The more violent his phantasies of projective identification, the more frightened he became of me. There were sessions in which such behaviour expressed unprovoked aggression, but I quote this series because it shows the patient in a different light, his violence a reaction to what he felt was my hostile defensiveness . . . (Bion, 1959).

It is particularly in the realm of playfulness that I have seen clearly before me the technical choice, whether to make a verbalized transference interpretation, or to accept, as it were, the transference role which the patient is needing me to occupy. Repeatedly I have found that transference interpretations prove to be jarring and stultifying and essentially anti-therapeutic until such time as the patient's experience of shared playfulness with me has become so customary that we can easily regain it, and the more clearly investigative 'work' aspects of what we are doing have become accepted as part of a basically enjoyable enterprise.

Delusional Identification

In this final section of the paper I attempt to illustrate the point that, just as the schizophrenic patient's symptomatology comes in the course of treatment to be revealed as consisting in manifestations of psychotic transference, so does this very symptomatology, or at any rate large increments of it, come to reveal an even deeper meaning as evidences of what might be called 'delusional identification'. That is, the patient's crazy behaviour needs to be seen as possessing, along with the psychotic transference root, a root in the form of an expressed identification with the therapist–an identification which, no matter how psychotically distorted, possesses a kernel of reality in terms of the therapist's real personality functioning. It is essential for us to see this identificational determinant of the patient's illness, for only in so far as we can acknowledge and confirm these nuclei of reality in his identifications with us (no matter how reluctant we may be to discover, or scrutinize with unprecedented directness, the pertinent aspects of our own personality), can we foster his reality-testing ability and his confidence in that ability.

By way of contrast, Rosenfeld, in his in many respects excellent paper, 'Notes on the Psycho-Analysis of the Super-Ego Conflict in an Acute Schizophrenic Patient' (1952), to my mind discounts the very real evidences of this particular mother's murderous possessiveness towards her son, the patient, and by the same token Rosenfeld seems unaware of the possibility that he himself was capable of murderous feeling in response to the patient's transference to him as a mother. We see no hint of Rosenfeld's awareness of such a possibility in his treatment of such data as the following:

... Once he said: 'How can I get out of the tomb?' I felt here that he implied that in projecting his self, his depression, into me, he felt enclosed by me and so I became a tomb from which he wanted my help to be released ... (Rosenfeld, 1952a).

In a footnote in the same paper, he expresses a point of view which certainly contains a valuable reminder of the essential importance of the intrapsychic realm in the patient–the realm which I stress in the next chapter of this book, concerning the family therapy of schizophrenia. But this passage is also a sample of his tendency to underestimate the aetiological significance of early family-environmental factors, as well as the extent to which the schizophrenic patient in therapy is responding to real personality ingredients which the therapist is feeding, inevitably and constantly, into the patient-therapist relationship:

In some papers on schizophrenia particularly by American writers like Pious and Fromm-Reichmann the mother's hostile and 'schizophrenogenic' attitude has been stressed. ... In our analytic approach we know that it is futile and even harmful to the progress of an analysis to accept uncritically the patient's attempts to blame the external environment for his illness. We generally find that there exists a great deal of distortion of external factors through projection and we have

709

to help the patient to understand his phantasies and reactions to external situations until he becomes able to differentiate between his phantasies and external reality (Rosenfeld, 1952a).

In another paper (1952b) Rosenfeld writes

. . . In my opinion the schizophrenic has never completely outgrown the earliest phase of development to which this object-relation [i.e. the patient's relating to the object by projective identification] belongs, and in the acute schizophrenic state he regresses to this early level . . .

I consider it essential for us to realize that no one ever does completely outgrow this (or, for that matter, any other) phase of development. When we realize this, we shall no longer overlook the extent to which we too share in the patient's projective-identification mode of relatedness—or, in my terms, we shall be able to see and accept the fact of our own participation in the symbiotic mode of relatedness between the patient and ourself.

Bion never acknowledges the possibility of his making, or having made, a real contribution to his patient's psychotic transference; typical is the passage, in his 'Attacks on Linking' paper (1959), concerning

. . . *what he felt was*[2] my refusal to accept parts of his personality . . .

It is in line with this viewpoint that he says, concerning the origin of the patient's pathological attitude towards linking,

. . . On the one hand there is the patient's *inborn disposition to excessive destructiveness, hatred, and envy*[2]: on the other the environment which, at its worst, denies to the patient the use of the mechanisms of splitting and projective identification . . . (Bion, 1959).

When we see the extent to which the environment contributes to the patient's difficulty—when, in particular, we discover the extent to which he is reacting, in his psychotic transference to us, to real and intense sadism, murderous feeling, and so on in ourselves—we find little need, I think, to conjecture that as a newborn baby he possessed some inordinately great, inborn disposition to hostility. Whereas Bion (1959) refers to the patient's '*belief that*[2] the analyst strives . . . to drive him insane', I have

[2] Italics mine—H.F.S.

found much evidence, not only in my own work but from various colleagues' reports of theirs, that such a striving is indeed at work in the therapist, among various other intensely conflictual feelings towards the patient, during the very difficult ambivalently symbiotic phase of the therapy. It seems to me that relatively abundant transference interpretations might be used by the therapist in an unconscious effort not only to protect himself against symbiotic relatedness with the patient, but also to deny the extent to which his own sadism, so much at odds with his genuinely therapeutic intent, is playing a part in shaping and maintaining the patient's psychotic transference – to deny specifically the extent to which, at the deeper, symbiotic level, he is cruelly and destructively denying the patient access into himself.

In chapter 6 I have described a number of instances of patients' acting out as being partially traceable to my own previously unconscious urges in the same directions, and mention the previous reports concerning this kind of phenomenon by Schroff (1957) and Barchilon (1958). In chapter 12, concerning schizophrenic communication, I have noted:

Particularly hard for the therapist to grasp are those instances in which the patient is manifesting an introject traceable to something in the therapist, some aspect of the therapist of which the latter is himself only poorly aware, and the recognition of which, as a part of himself, he finds distinctly unwelcome. I have found, time and again, that some bit of particularly annoying and intractable behaviour on the part of a patient rests, in the final analysis, on this basis; and only when I can acknowledge this, to myself, as being indeed an aspect of my personality, does it cease to be a prominently troublesome aspect of the patient's behaviour . . .

It is only more recently that I have become better aware of the *identificational* significance of these events: when, for example, the therapist is able to become aware of the relevant aspect of his personality to which the patient's acting-out behaviour has been a kind of caricatured reaction, he is thereby accepting the patient's struggle to identify with him. Earlier I noted that the schizophrenic patient tends to identify first with those aspects of the therapist's personality which are least acceptable to the latter.

I have already given several instances of a variety of transference psychosis in which the patient endeavours ambivalently
to get the therapist to do the patient's thinking for the latter–in
line with a family background of a 'know-it-all' parent's doing
the thinking during the patient's upbringing. Typically, such
a parent has to maintain such a 'know-it-all' demeanour as a
defence against inner confusion. I have described the beneficial
result of my coming eventually to acknowledge freely my own
confusion in response to such patients' extremely and often
sadistically confusing verbalizations; and I believe that here
again we can see in retrospect that the patient's confusion has
had, among other determinants, a transference root in the form
of a delusional identification with the very real confusion in the
parent-therapist. The therapist's becoming able to be aware of
and to acknowledge his own confusion helps to resolve the delusional, crazy quality of the patient's confusion. Particularly does
it help to resolve the mocking, caricaturing, sadistic, or otherwise destructive aspects of the patient's efforts to identify with
the therapist.

In one hour with a hebephrenic man, who was generally either
utterly ignoring of me or openly furious at me, and of whose
yearning to identify with me I was quite unaware, I once put
out my cigarette inside the top of his plastic wastebasket, after
having first noted that it was empty. During the following session
I was startled when, during one of the customary long silences,
the wastebasket caught my eye: there was a black ring around
the inside of the top of it where this heavily-smoking man, who
had never done so before, had been using the wastebasket as an
ash tray as he had seen me do. The potentially destructive nature
of his identification startled me, for I felt no assurance that he
took care, as I had, to make sure that the wastebasket was not
full of paper.

Incidentally, I did not attempt a transference interpretation
at this point, for from long experience I knew that it would be
like talking into the wind; but the incident had a long-run usefulness in helping me to be more alert to his need and his efforts
to identify with this therapist of whom ostensibly he wanted no
part whatever.

In my book on *The Nonhuman Environment* I presented, as an
instance of the schizophrenic patient's inability to distinguish

clear boundaries between his self and his non-human environment, the following incident from my work with a hebephrenic
woman:

> ... [She] shockingly conveyed to me the statement that the whole
> left side of her head 'is gone . . . caved in', speaking as if in reference
> to an inanimate object; one sensed her own horror and despair about
> this . . . (p. 148).

In the years that have passed in my work with this woman since
the above-noted incident occurred, two additional significances
of this same symptom have come to light. About five years later,
at a time when she had long since become—both subjectively, so
far as one could determine, and objectively, as measured by my
and other persons' responses to her—fully human, I made the
following note:

The work with Pauline continues to show [as had been true,
by that time, for many months], most prominently, her making
clear her ambivalent efforts to achieve, and to avoid, a symbiotic
relatedness with me as a representative of her father . . . [For
example] about three weeks ago when I came up on the fourth
floor to see another patient there, and stepped into Pauline's
room for just a moment while the other patient was getting
ready, Pauline once again made some reference to the left side
of her head's being gone, or some similar terrible organic defect
which I cannot precisely remember at the moment. This was
almost exactly the kind of thing which she had expressed not
very long after her admission here, and I found now that I
reacted to it privately with a completely different connotation:
I saw it as a very formidable effort to draw me into a kind of
solicitude and a kind of taking over her life for her in a symbiotic
fashion. Actually I did feel solicitude for her, but saw it, much
more this time than I initially did, as a transference manifestation.

My different reaction this second time was probably due more
to the change which had occurred in her—in terms of increased
'humanization'—than to an increase in insightfulness on my part
over the intervening five years. At that earlier time such communications had emerged from such a 'non-human' over-all
demeanour, and in such a vocal tone of horror and other-worldly
despair and eeriness, as to make the listener (whether myself or

other staff members) draw back in shock, and be quite blinded to any potential interpersonal transference significance.

 Slightly more than three years later still in our work, she was sitting nearby and looking at my face with a kind of private amusement, as I was saying something – I can't recall what. She asked, 'Is it all going to fall off? – Is it that bad?', rubbing her forehead and the top of her head as she spoke in such a way as to convey the idea that they – these areas of her body – were all crumbling. Her tone in asking this was a semi-serious one, and to this extent conveyed a genuine delusional experience; but her tone was also a semi-amused one. I replied, 'You do feel that I'm awfully *serious*, eh?' She said, with warm and open amusement and without any tinge of delusional anxiety, 'Yes.' I had been aware for many years that among the eccentricities which survived the ravages of my personal analysis are a chronically worried look and a tendency to take everything too seriously, but I had not been aware that some of this patient's delusional behaviour was a reaction, in part, to this aspect of my personality. Each of her parents possessed this quality in abundance, which no doubt was relevant here; but I felt it better simply to acknowledge this real aspect of myself. To have made some transference interpretation at that juncture would, I think have placed needless distance between her and me, and would have vitiated my corroborating her own reality appraisal of the here and now situation.

 The sequence which I have described, as occurring over the years of my work with this woman, is but one among many analogous ones which emerged as she became progressively human and progressively able to distinguish between literal and metaphorical meanings. As another brief instance, whereas there were occasions relatively early in our work when she seemingly perceived me as being inanimate – once, for example, looking at me in a kind of uncanny astonishment as I smoked a cigarette, and exclaiming to herself, 'What makes it smoke?' – several years later this bizarre perception of me devolved into a querying of me, clearly at this time as a transference representative of her compulsive father, as to whether I considered the way I lived to be really living. Her seeing me as being, in this figurative way, 'dead', contained, despite the element of transference distortion and exaggeration, a sufficiently realistic view of some of the aspects of my own compulsively work-oriented life for me to acknowledge the validity of the view of me which she was expressing.

At the end of one of the sessions during this same later period in our work, when I was about to go on a week's vacation, I commented, 'Well, I'll see you a week from Monday.' She replied in an ironic tone, as I was then starting out of the door of her room, '*Try* again.' My first thought was that she meant by this that in her opinion our efforts during the session had been futile–as she had been indicating in many ways, both verbal and non-verbal, for years. But then another possibility occurred to me, and I asked, 'Do I sound defeated when I say that?', which she corroborated in a tone of delighted warmth and closeness. I had long known that she had viewed her father as being a disappointing quitter; but she had finally got the message across to me as to how defeated I, as I now realized in retrospect, often appeared and indeed felt, though I characteristically tend to repress such feelings. I believe it correct to think that the tremendous despair which this woman had shown during the first several years of our work, and which she acted out in myriad hebephrenically fragmented forms of personality functioning, consisted in large part in a delusional identification with the despairing aspects of her father, her mother and, as the treatment relationship developed, myself.

A few months ago, a paranoid schizophrenic woman said to me, in reply to a verbalized interpretation I had just suggested to her, 'When you talk to me like that, I feel that I'm going to be led to the edge of the world and the people are going to decide whether I'll have to jump off or not.' I had known her to be living for years in a chaotically and terrifyingly delusional world, and when she said this I was momentarily awed, once again, by this glimpse into the vastly terrifying world in which she lived. But then this other viewpoint, concerning the possibility that I had unwittingly contributed to such a degree of delusional experience on her part, occurred to me, and I asked simply, 'Do you mean that I sound so portentous?', and she replied, even more simply, 'Yes.' Even more recent developments in our work have suggested that her having been living for so long in a terrifying psychotic world has been due, in part, to her delusional identification with what she has now come to call her 'fraidy-cat' therapist, who tends somewhat–as did her mother to a very great degree–to hide his own fearfulness behind the demeanour of the strong, calm parent-therapist.

In summary, it is my experience that even the most other-wordly, even the most 'crazy', manifestations of schizophrenia come to reveal meaningfulness and reality-relatedness not only as transference reactions to the therapist, but, even beyond this, as delusional identifications with real aspects of the therapist's own personality. When we come to see such meanings in the schizophrenic individual's behaviour, we come more and more to realize not only that he is now in the human fold but that, if only there had been someone all along wise and perceptive enough to know, and brave enough to acknowledge, he has never really been out of it.

Chapter 24

THE CONTRIBUTIONS OF FAMILY TREATMENT TO THE PSYCHOTHERAPY OF SCHIZOPHRENIA (1964)[1]

M Y qualifications for writing about this subject are in some regards slender indeed: I have participated in only about forty family therapy sessions. But I have had the privilege of working as a consultant, over a period of more than two years, to a research group engaged in such family therapy at the National Institute of Mental Health. To Dr Lyman C. Wynne, head of that project, I am indebted for this experience, as well as for the rare opportunity to engage in this actual form of treatment itself. Fourteen years of experience with the individual therapy of schizophrenic patients, at Chestnut Lodge, has inevitably involved a sufficient number of direct and indirect contacts with families – contacts occurring, in the instances of several families, over a span of ten years or more – for me to have had reason to become interested in the potentialities, as well as the difficulties, of family therapy. A two-year period of experience with group psychotherapy, at a Veterans Administration out-patient clinic prior to my coming to the Lodge, early helped me to see somewhat beyond the dyadic frame of reference. But the principal reason for my temerity in presenting my thoughts about this subject springs from my conviction that this is an important new field which the great majority of my fellows in individual therapy have not yet entered, and in which those persons who can count themselves really experienced authorities are few indeed.

Partly, I think, because of the dyadic context of our training analyses, we have been slow to recognize the importance in psycho-analysis and psychotherapy of the *family* frame of reference. It came to me as a surprise, in the course of working with my first supervised case, to detect that, for a brief portion of one analytic hour, the neurotic patient was reacting to me not as

[1] Also published in *Family Treatment of Schizophrenia: Theoretical and Practical Aspects*, ed. I. Boszormenyi-Nagy and J. L. Framo (New York: Harper & Row, 1964).

being a single transference figure, but rather as being both parents simultaneously–as being, specifically, her mother and father in sexual intercourse with one another. I later found an example of this very phenomenon described in the psycho-analytic literature;[2] but any such forms of more-than-one-other-person transference phenomena, any such kinds of *family* transference, are rarely to be found in the literature of psycho-analysis. Somewhat later on, I found that an initially catatonic woman had come to manifest, in her transference to me, a kind of *family-wide* sense of common helplessness, a conviction that there was not a strong figure in the whole family, and a sense of helpless waiting for some strong person to come upon the family (i.e. in the transference, to come upon the analytic session) scene. This had a distinctly different quality from the kind of two-person, mutual helplessness which is encountered so frequently.

When my father died, ten years ago, many were the people whose lives he had enriched, in the Catskill village where he had lived out his life from birth onwards, and who came to offer consolation to my mother and sister and myself and to share with us their own sense of loss. But one woman struck a chord which none of the others, however deep and genuine their feelings, touched upon: she spoke, in a single simple sentence, of the special loss involved when, for the first time, a family loses one of its members. This disclosed in me a kind of *family*-oriented feeling which, simple and obvious though it may sound, had been evoked neither by the other visitors, nor by the several years of my nearly completed personal analysis, in the course of which there had been abundantly detailed exploration of my feelings for *each* of my parental family members.

In recent years, in the course of working on committees concerned with various matters in the local psycho-analytic Society and Institute, I have wondered, of course, how many of our typical problems arise from the acting-out of neurotic conflicts on the part of various students and Society members, conflicts which have escaped, or are escaping, resolution in their respective training analyses. After having begun to think intensively about the subject of this paper, I have come to wonder whether the problem-student, for example, is simply displacing upon the class instructor some negative feeling which needs to be experi-

[2] I have not been able to locate this reference.

718

enced towards his training analyst, or rather whether these problem-situations do not arise in part because, by tradition, the training-analysis relationship is accepted as being, not only in actuality but also at a fantasy level, a dyadic frame of reference, such that various of the analysand's *family*-oriented conflicts seek, for their expression, an arena–such as the analytic classroom session, or the analytic society or committee meeting– which is in reality more similar to the family setting in which the particular conflict had its origin.

Approximately the first half of this chapter will be devoted to a topic which, as I shall try to show, is of fundamental importance in the family therapy of schizophrenia: the distinction between processes which are predominantly intrapsychic and processes which are predominantly interpersonal.

In the remainder of the chapter I shall deal with various manifestations of positive feelings in the family background and in the family-therapy interaction, and with various countertransference phenomena.

Intrapsychic Processes and Interpersonal Processes in Psychotherapy

In working 14 years ago with my first psycho-analytic patient, an obsessive compulsive man, it came to me as a surprise to realize that I had become, for him, more the personification of the mother of his childhood than was his own biological mother, who was living in the same small community and with whom he was interacting almost daily. That is to say, it came to me as a surprise to see that the real mother, as a denizen of outer reality, was less central to his neurotic functioning than was the intrapsychic early-mother imago, the early-mother introject, which had become reprojected upon me in the evolution of the transference relationship.

From this similarly early era of my psycho-analytic work, I vividly recall the relief evidenced by a phobic man who had long since become aware, in the treatment, of his murderous fury towards his father, when I realized, and pointed out to him, that he was dealing basically not with urges to kill his father as a flesh-and-blood person in outer reality, but rather with a determination to rid himself of, to destroy, an unwanted and neurotically crippling *identification with* his father.

Since then I have seen many times the neurotic, or psychotic, individual's confusion of intrapsychic processes with interpersonal processes (or, in other words, confusion of narcissistic processes with true object relations). Late in my own analysis, the analyst helped me to realize that the resolution of the transference does not mean the destruction of the analyst himself.

To continue in the same vein, I was interested in the two contrasting reports I received of a vacation trip made by a paranoid man I was treating, with an older brother, a father surrogate with whom my patient had had a symbiotic relationship. The intended vacation had soon been disrupted by a severe argument between the two men, and they returned without their differences having been patched up. Upon their return, the brother confided to the administrative psychiatrist that he had been afraid the patient, white with fury, might kill him. By contrast, the patient expressed to me no awareness of wanting, or having wanted, to kill his brother; but he repeatedly and emphatically stated to me, 'He's not my father!', spoke resentfully of the brother's trying, domineeringly, to 'father' him, and spoke of the brother in such a tone, in fact, as to make it clear that he, the patient, had psychologically ejected this brother from the family altogether. Previously, the patient had had a symbiotic experience of his whole parental family, such that when, for example, I once asked if he were not perhaps quite angry with the other members of his family, he showed genuine astonishment and replied, 'Why, no, Dr Searles; I'm not angry at *them*–they're *family*!', as if to be angry at one's family were inherently impossible, like reacting to one's right hand as separable from one's self. In short, what I felt to have been in progress, during that vacation trip, was a process of long-overdue individuation on the part of the patient (and, I would assume, to some significant degree on the part of the overtly less ill brother also), a process of resolution of their erstwhile symbiosis–an event in which neither of the two participants could clearly see both the murderous (i.e. interpersonal) and individuation (i.e. intrapsychic) dimensions simultaneously. In my subsequent work with the patient, I recurrently saw his fear, at successive steps in his individuation, lest I be destroyed by the deepening separation between us.

We not infrequently see evidence in a schizophrenic person's parent, similarly, of his or her fear that to function as a separate individual *vis-à-vis* the patient would mean the latter's death. One mother, for example, described to me her reason for having retained, for several years longer than she had meant to, an over-indulgent nursemaid for her now schizophrenic son: she said that the nurse had reported one day that while she was walking along the street with the patient on one hand and an older brother on the other, the patient had suddenly let go of the nurse's hand and darted across the street. Somewhat later in the same interview, the mother was describing her sense of helplessness to go ahead and speak her mind to her son, who, it had become clear to me (largely, of course, through my own first-hand experience with the patient), characteristically reinforced his regressive demands upon his mother and other people with implied threats of suicide. When I endeavoured to find out why she kept feeling a need for prescriptions from me as to what she should say to her son, the mother explained that 'If I say something wrong, Bill might *do something*.' The vagueness of this wording, and the dread in her tone, left me in no doubt that she was chronically afraid to be herself with her son, lest he commit suicide. I found abundant evidence, on many occasions in addition to this one, that the mother was struggling with repressed murderous feelings towards the patient; but my main point here is her readiness to assume that if she allowed herself to reveal to this son the degree of hurt and anger and genuine concern which she could relatively freely express to me about him, he would somehow be destroyed. It was evident, further, that he exploited her fearfulness on this score by exacting infantile gratifications from her, in their basically symbiotic relationship, to an extent which had long impeded his own maturing.

In a number of married patients who were bent on divorce, I have seen that the patient's determination to 'get a separation from' the marital partner consisted basically in a striving, long unrecognized as such by the patient, to achieve a separation at an *intra*psychic level, to achieve a genuine individuation *vis-à-vis* a wife or husband with whom a symbiotic mode of relatedness had been existing. In such instances, the marital partner had been responded to not predominantly as a real other person, but rather as the personification of the unacceptable, projected part-aspects of the patient's self, or, one might say, as the personification of his own repressed self-images. Thus the patient does have a need, however unrecognized as such, to achieve a separation between those repressed and projected aspects of himself, on the one hand, and the marital partner as a real and separate person on the other. The achievement of a 'separation' at *this* level is essential both for his own becoming a whole, integrated individual, as well as for the achievement of a healthy object relatedness in his marriage. It may well be that many instances of marital separations or divorces take place on the basis of such an unformulated, unconscious effort at individuation, an effort which fails because it is not seen in its true light, and which leads instead simply to a subsequent unrecognizedly symbiotic marriage, in which this next partner is reacted to, similarly, not as a real person but as the personification of unacceptable aspects of the self. In chapter 1 I have conjectured that some instances of murder may represent, similarly, a miscarried and unrecognized effort at individuation.

I assume that there is no relationship between persons in which true object relations hold sway to the exclusion of any ingredients of projection (and introjection), or any relationship so symbiotic (so dominated by projection and introjection) that no increment of real object relatedness has been achieved. These clinical examples are intended to show the distinction between those relationships which are *predominantly* on a truly interpersonal, and those which are predominantly on a symbiotic (projective and introjective) basis.

These considerations are relevant to the onset of the schizophrenic psychosis which, as I have indicated elsewhere (ch. 12), seems typically to occur in a setting of the rupture of an identity-sustaining symbiotic relationship with a parent or parental figure. The patient is suddenly faced thereby with the overwhelming realization that the parent has been responding to him not basically as a person in his own right, but rather as an extension of the parent. One patient expressed it as a realization that 'People are only interested in themselves'. To paraphrase this and analogous comments I have heard, the patient, who has felt heretofore that he was in the very centre of the parent's concerns, is suddenly faced with overwhelming evidence that the parent is really so self-absorbed as to be unaware even that the son or daughter, as a separate individual, exists. Thus, the 'he' which the patient has been ceases to exist in his subjective experience also (since his sense of identity has been so largely bound up with this now severed symbiosis with the parent) and there ensues a schizophrenic experience of himself-and-the world (dedifferentiated, jumbled up together, and distorted in additional ways which I need not here elaborate), out of which, if he is to become a new and healthy person, a new sense of identity must eventually grow.

In the individual-therapy relationship, this distinction between intrapsychic processes and interpersonal processes is often difficult to detect. For example, in an hour with a paranoid man, I was listening to his description of a TV programme in which Bob Hope, comedy script in hand, had had as his guest an Army sergeant who was an aspiring amateur comedian. The patient clearly implied that Hope had reacted competitively to the sergeant, and he described how, when the sergeant had asked Hope for some of the script so that he could have a chance to show his own ability as a comedian, Hope had torn off a little corner of one sheet and given it to him. The patient spontaneously related this to our relationship, likening me to Hope and saying, in a pleading tone, 'Give me a break, Dr Searles.' I had long seen abundant evidence of his competitiveness with me, and my first reaction was to think of this as a plea from him to be given a fair chance in the competition with me. But then I realized that the more pertinent striving being evidenced here was his need and desire to *identify* with me–just as, I saw in retrospect (despite his clear emphasis, not reproduced here in detail, upon the competitive features of the relationship between the two persons on the TV programme), the aspiring amateur must indeed have been hungry to identify with the accomplished Bob Hope.

On innumerable occasions, in my supervisory work as well as in my own therapeutic sessions with patients, I have seen that basically identificatory strivings are being defended against by competitive strivings which are, I think, more comfortable to therapist as well as patient than are the early ego-building identificatory needs, whose gratification is essential for any healthy object relatedness, including a healthy ability to compete appropriately with one's fellow-men. By the same token, I have come to see that the deeply-repressed cannibalistic urges, of which the schizophrenic patient becomes aware in most instances only after prolonged therapy, are expressive basically not of a truly interpersonal destructiveness, but rather of primitive but healthy identificatory needs.

The tangibly real quality of introjects in the subjective experience of the schizophrenic patient (whether experienced as being within the confines of his own body, or, in reprojected form, as attributes of the outer world) is often startling for the therapist to discover. One cannot work long in this field without realizing the great service which has been performed by Melanie Klein (1932, 1955) and her followers (irrespective of the validity or lack of validity of some aspects of Kleinian theory) in stressing the significance, in psychotic personality functioning, of such internalized objects. Several years ago, for example, it dawned on me that the schizophrenic woman's fear of rape is not basically a fear lest she be raped by a man, but rather a fear lest she be raped by a phallic mother-figure–by one or another woman round about, to whom she reacts as possessing a very real and terrifying penis–the projection of the penis which, at an unconscious level, she herself possesses on the basis of identification with the mother who, during the child's upbringing, in various ways acted out her unconscious conviction that she, the mother, possessed such a penis. It is often striking, too, to sense the biological literalness with which the patient perceives the male therapist as having female breasts and a vagina. Further, two of my six schizophrenic patients currently express their experience of both their own body and of mine as being peopled with myriad persons, expressing this in such a way as to leave no doubt that they do not perceive and conceptualize this as a figurative or symbolic phenomenon, but as a quite tangibly concrete one. One woman experiences these 'persons' (a changing multitude of figures from current and past years, whom she often identifies with considerable conviction) as being confined within her shoulder, or her leg, or as being distressingly active within her head just above her eyes; or one among them is struggling to get free just below one of her scapulae; and so on.

The extent to which the schizophrenic patient possesses an introjected *family*, before he is brought to us for treatment, is sometimes seen in the patient who is able fairly rapidly to reproject such internalized (and no doubt greatly distorted) family members upon a collection of real persons about him on the hospital ward, such that his childhood family milieu, and typical family interactions, become reproduced with a fidelity of detail which is sometimes remarkable.[3] Similarly, in the still more deeply ill patient who is less capable of forming object relations and less capable, therefore, of thus unconsciously moulding his current interpersonal world on the ward into the childhood family pattern, one sometimes sees to what a remarkable extent a hallucinated family is serving to perpetuate, for him, the familiar environment of his childhood family as (distortedly, no doubt) he perceived that family. Thus, whereas in the instance of the former patient, the ward staff may be able quite readily to see that one of them is perceived by the patient as mother, another as father, another as sister, and another as Cousin Jeanne, in the instance of the latter it may become clear to the therapist that he rather durably experiences his mother as being in the ceiling and his father in the radiator – or, in some instances, there is no structural embodiment for the hallucinations which is perceivable to the therapist with any consistency.

I have been discussing this subject at such length because it is of central significance to the family therapy of schizophrenia, and yet its significance is most easily overlooked in that very setting. When, for example, the schizophrenic patient reacts in the family setting to his mother as being cold and depriving, or to his father as being maternally warm but sexually provocative, it is all too easy for us as observers to be convinced that the patient is responding realistically to the parents as real persons, for we can see them indeed to possess these qualities; moreover, we know that these people have been most instrumental in the childhood development of the character traits which the patient is evidencing. It is comparatively seldom that the patient's reactions are sufficiently distorted or off-key or ill-timed to reveal that his central problem, here, lies not in the real mother and father whom we are perceiving, but rather in an *introject*, formed many

---

[3] In chapter 11 I have presented some of my observations about this point; and just before the other volume (Boszormenyi-Nagy and Framo, 1964) in which the present paper is published, went to press I discovered that Boszormenyi-Nagy and Framo in their paper 'Family Concept of Hospital Treatment of Schizophrenia' (1962) give a most interesting presentation of similar concepts at which they also have arrived.

years ago, of the cold and depriving early mother, and an *introject* of the maternally warm but sexually provocative father—introjects which he has been able to externalize upon the real mother and father, to whom such qualities seem so naturally to 'belong', rather than perceiving these qualities as attributes of himself also and achieving an integration of these various qualities within his own ego.

A paranoid woman, married and the mother of three children, for several years in the course of her individual therapy maintained so tenacious and so vociferous a conviction that her husband was impotent and worthless, that he finally grew unwilling to wait longer for her recovery, divorced her, and married another woman. Although I was quite aware, all along, that she was abundantly delusional, such contacts as I had with her husband coincided sufficiently with her view of him, as did her parents' expressed estimates of his worth, for me to accept her views of him as comparatively realistic. It was only later on that I felt I had erred grievously in not seeing the extent to which her view of her husband had been, all along, a sick and distorted one. Likewise, all through these years she had castigated me, very similarly, for my impotence in manifold regards; my own sense of helplessness in face of her massive pathology was intense enough for me inwardly to accept her view of both me and her husband as being less than real men. It was only after several years of therapy, and after her husband had divorced her, that the therapeutic investigation had proceeded deeply enough to reveal the extent to which she had been projecting upon both him and me, as well as upon many other people round about, an unconscious castrated-male image of herself. Significantly, as this image became resolved, she came to realize for the first time in all our work that she (who had continually been sexually misidentifying herself and other people) is a woman and that I am a man. Now, when she was psychologically ready to relate herself to the real man (whatever his weaknesses) in her former husband, and to respond to this real man affirmatively rather than castratively, it was too late.

In an experience I had, in company with another therapist, with one schizophrenic young woman and her parents, it was striking to discover to what a degree various interactions in which strongly oedipal ingredients were readily apparent, were being determined at a deeper level by pre-oedipal processes— processes of a symbiotic, early-ego-formation, nature. For example, the father, although at one level greatly concerned to establish his dominance as father and leader in the total group situation, was concerned at a deeper level with conflicts relevant to the matter of ego boundaries: specifically, his deep need for masculine identification with the co-therapists, versus his anxiety lest such identification lead to the loss of his symbiosis with his daughter, reacted to by him, at this deep level, as the Good Mother. When I endeavoured to help him recognize the erotic components in his feelings towards his daughter, com- ponents which I described as natural to any father's feelings towards his daughter and which I readily acknowledged as part of my feelings for my own daughter, he was horrified, reacted to me as something untouchably alien and unhuman, and declared, in a voice shaking with feeling, '. . . If you know she's your flesh and blood, nothing like that pops into your mind!' and, empha- sizing the unbridgeable gulf between himself and me, shouted, 'That's *my* name, *Davis*—not *Searles!*' This was only the culmina- tion of a series of incidents illustrating his anxiety lest he lose his sense of union with the Good Mother image which he attributed to his daughter, and become fused instead with the horrifyingly evil parent-image which he externalized upon me, upon his wife, or, at times, upon both of the therapists.

It is especially because the family members themselves are so unaware of this realm of projected (and introjected) intrapsychic content, so unaware of any boundaries between intrapsychic and genuinely interpersonal realms, so unaware that they are not reacting primarily to the other people in the room as flesh-and- blood persons in outer reality but primarily as the personifica- tions of repressed and projected self-images, that the therapist himself must be alert to these separate, or potentially separate, realms.

A number of writers have emphasized the importance of dis- tinguishing between these realms of experience. Warren M. Brodey's (1959, 1961) stimulating concepts, derived from the family therapy of schizophrenia, concerning the distinctions among what he calls image, object, and narcissistic relationships, are of the most fundamental value in this connexion. Rather than attempt to paraphrase his views, which are rich indeed, I

727

shall give only two brief quotations to show the relevance of his work to the present chapter:

> . . . *In the image relationship,* the inner image of the other person takes precedence: the emphasis is on *changing reality to fit with expectation* rather than expectation to fit reality. . . .
>
> . . . the *narcissistic relationship* is . . . descriptive of two people *each making an image relationship to the other and each acting within this relationship so as to validate the image-derived expectation of the other* . . . (1961).

Arieti (1961), in discussing the question whether or when a non-hospitalized schizophrenic patient should leave his family to live by himself, asks,

> First of all, is it advisable? On the one hand we may think that it is in the family that the troubles of the patient started, and there, probably, that they are maintained. On the other hand, we may feel that to remove the patient from his family would not really be helpful because *this would be merely a removal from the external situation, not from the introjected conflicts.* As a matter of fact, one might even think that this separation might re-exacerbate the symptoms. We remember, for instance, Geraldine, who started to hallucinate again when she was separated from her mother.[4]

Lidz and Fleck (1960) report that, among the traits which recur frequently among the mothers of schizophrenic patients is a tendency on the mother's part to confuse the child's needs with her own needs projected upon the child, a failure to recognize ego boundaries between herself and the child. Bowen (1960), from his experience with the family therapy of schizophrenia, describes that

> . . . the subjects of the mothers' overconcerns about the patients and the focus of their 'picking on the patients' are the same as their own feelings of inadequacy about themselves. This point is so accurate on a clinical level that almost any point in the mothers' list of complaints about the patient can be regarded as an externalization of the mother's own inadequacies.

A number of writers have described the parents in these families as being still so much a part of their own parental families that they are not really psychologically a part of their marital family. Lidz and his colleagues (1957), reporting data

---

[4] Italics mine – H.F.S.

from 16 families of schizophrenic patients studied by them over a period of several years, state that in five of these families the parents' loyalties remained in their respective parental homes, preventing the formation of a nuclear family in the marital home. The cardinal emotional attachment and dependency of one or both partners in these five families, the authors found, remained fixed to a parental figure and could not be transferred to the spouse. Wynne and his colleagues (1958) point out that

. . . going into the Army, moving to another city, even getting married and having children of one's own, may in some cases mean going through the motions of following social conventions as part of familial expectations, without a genuine sense of identity apart from the [parental] family system.

It is worth noting that such an attachment to the parental family is, basically, but one form of an emotional investment in *internal objects* which I have been describing as so necessary to distinguish from an investment predominantly in genuine interpersonal relationships. A paper by Towne, Sampson, and Messinger (1961) helps to show the importance of this intrapsychic realm. Reporting upon a group of 17 young women who had become schizophrenic within a relatively few years after marriage, they suggest that

. . . these women foundered upon two broad tasks presented by participation in the marital family: detaching themselves from the claims of parental ties, and synthesizing conflicting childhood identifications within a workable adult identity. . . .

Thus, in the crisis preceding hospitalization, Mrs White [for example] was confronted with various identification fragments (and defences against them) which had previously remained in partial dissociation. These images of herself—as a confused little girl in possession of secret and terrible information; as a long-suffering, neglected and betrayed wife and mother; as a frustrated, masculine careerist; as an oedipally victorious daughter, and as a promiscuous philanderer— were related to earlier identifications formed in relation to a frustrating and martyred mother, a prepossessing male mother-substitute, and a seductive, jealous, oedipal father.

What I have been trying to bring out is the fact that, in the family-therapy-of-schizophrenia session, the patient (as well as the other family members) is so often successful in externalizing (unconsciously) upon one or another of the others in the room such repressed self-images as Towne *et al.* describe, that it is extraordinarily difficult, however essential, for the therapist to keep clear that it is not basically the mother or father, for example, who is central to the patient's illness, but rather the patient's introject, distorted and unintegrated into his ego, of that parent. I am putting this in extremely over-simplified terms, of course, simply to make this principle clear.

I have wondered whether it is possible that, just as an individual family member has what one might call 'unconscious selves' or unconscious self-images, there may perhaps be, in the family, a *somewhat* integrated 'unconscious family' which is determining, far more than meets the eye, what transpires in the family-therapy interaction. My experience with the ward-group relatedness, as well as with the parental and marital family relatedness, of patients with whom I have worked in individual therapy suggests that there are indeed such 'unconscious families', however poorly integrated and shifting, and that it may therefore be crucial, in conducting family therapy, to try to determine who, at the moment, is really (at an unconscious level in the family) being the father, who the mother, who the son, and so on – quite irrespective of the sociological and biological realities of the situation. A comparatively simple example comes from the marital-family situation of a paranoid woman with whom I worked for several years. Among herself, her husband, and her teen-age daughter, it was evidently *generally* agreed upon, though at an unconscious level in all three (until this came more into the open in the patient's 'delusional' material), that the husband occupied the role of wife and mother in the family, and that the daughter had succeeded in displacing the patient from the husband and father role. It is, I believe, towards the de-repression of such 'unconscious family' modes of relatedness that one's family therapy efforts must be directed.

When we consider that projection and introjection must be among the basic psychodynamic processes by means of which object relatedness is achieved in the normal development of the child, it is striking to see the extent to which the products of such processes, occurring among the members of the schizophrenic patient's family, are *in competition with* genuine object relatedness. The real mother in the room, for example, must carry on a quite real competition with her own, and the father's, introjects of the Good Mothers of their respective childhoods, and the schizophrenic son or daughter who is present is reacted to as living evidence of the mother's failure in that competition. That is, the fact that this son or daughter, sitting there, is afflicted with schizophrenia, is testimony of the mother's having failed to fulfil the mothering role in the way in which these idealized and internalized Good Mothers would presumably have done.

One of my schizophrenic patients said to me during an individual therapy session, 'I want you to know that I don't come here because I'm interested in seeing *you*; I just like to hear myself talk.' This reminded me of an incident when I was talking with her father in a corridor of the sanatorium at the time of her admission. As we talked, he showed no interest in me at all, but was admiring himself in a mirror which happened to be located above my shoulder.

Dr Leslie Schaffer has commented, ironically but very perceptively, after observing a family therapy session through a one-way screen, 'I had a thought that if someone were standing sufficiently far out, it might look as if these people were talking with each other.' The spuriousness of the 'object relatedness' in these families consists, I believe, in the fact that, taken as a whole, they are defensive and premature. Specifically, they are defensive against the threat of symbiotic undifferentiatedness, and they are premature because such undifferentiatedness needs to hold sway, at a deep level, between any two persons, needs to hold sway and be faced and accepted, before genuine object relatedness can mature from this undifferentiatedness.

I have been helped, in reaching the above concept, by a statement made by Hendrick (1931):

We are suggesting that cannibalization (ingestion, introjection, scotomization) is not the skeletal mechanism of autism, but that the refusal of the primitive ego to perform this function is. Renunciation of the outer world appears actually to be equivalent to 'vomiting' instead of normal ingestion, to ejection of the tentatively introjected object.

Additionally illuminating has been a comment by Havens (1961), in a recently presented paper which I had the pleasure of discussing. In describing the maternal relationships of hallucinated schizophrenic patients, Havens (in support of the above-quoted statement by Hendrick, which is included in Havens' paper) reports that

> ... The mother is neither differentiated from the patient nor completely absorbed. The relationship appears to have been one not of symbiosis but of *siege* and the state of siege represented by the object's [i.e. the mother-hallucination's] distance from the patient is the extension into imaginary life of the long-term family condition. When this is true, the hallucination does not represent the externalization of a previously 'absorbed' mother-figure but the substitution of an imaginary object for a real one that was never identified with.

A healthy family may be thought of as being, at an unconscious level of participation, a fermenting mixture of projected and introjected part-aspects of the personalities of the various participants, out of which the children in the family develop individual beings, and out of which the parents, as well, achieve a deepening and refashioning of their selves which had already become established during their respective childhoods. The family which includes a schizophrenic member may be likened more, in this regard, to a seething cauldron, in which such pseudo 'object relatedness' as one observes is largely defensive against the inordinately great primitive identification needs of a collection of persons none of whom has successfully traversed this era of early ego-formation, and in all of whom there is a basically healthy need, therefore, for undifferentiated (or, at a somewhat later developmental level, incorporative) relatedness, but a correspondingly great anxiety lest their tenuous object relatedness, which is so largely spurious and ill-established, be dissolved into such primitive undifferentiatedness. It can be seen that the striving towards symbiosis, here, is not merely a striving to complete an interrupted developmental phase in the past, but is also a striving to overcome the gulf which, as the participants must at some deep level be painfully aware, separates them from one another, despite their ostensible object relatedness (or, in the phrase of Wynne *e al.*, their pseudo-mutuality). It is the intensity of this *conflict between* the more primitive, versus the more adult, modes of relatedness which is, I believe, pathognomonic of the family of which the schizophrenic person is a member.

Bowen is one of the persons who has pioneered not only in the development of the family therapy of schizophrenia, but also in calling attention to the importance of symbiotic relatedness in these families. In a recent article (1960) tracing the development of his orientation to this mode of therapy of schizophrenia, he writes that

The family unit is regarded as a single organism and the patient is seen as that part of the family organism through which the overt symptoms of psychosis are expressed.

Wynne *et al.* (1958) use comparable phraseology in describing their approach to the family therapy of schizophrenia:

In this programme a case is regarded as consisting of an entire family unit, including both parents and offspring.

The more deeply one comes to perceive the psychodynamic processes which hold sway in these families, the more startled one is to discover to what an extent the family is not truly a family at all, in the sense of a group of individuals, but comprises in aggregate what might be thought of as one symbiotic individual. Wynne *et al.* (1958) have described perceptively and in vivid terms a kind of 'rubber fence' which one discovers in these families, and which serves to provide the family with a sense— however false—of mutuality and complementarity in their relationships with one another:

The shared, familial efforts to exclude from open recognition any evidences of noncomplementarity within the pseudo-mutual relation become group mechanisms that help perpetuate the pseudo-mutuality. In the families of schizophrenics these mechanisms act at a primitive level in preventing the articulation and selection of any meanings that might enable the individual family member to differentiate himself either within or outside of the family role structure. Family boundaries thus obscured are continuous but unstable, stretching, like a rubber fence, to include that which can be interpreted as complementary and contracting to extrude that which is interpreted as noncomplementary.

I think of this rubber fence, so beautifully described by the above writers, as serving basically to preserve, for the family, what might be thought of as a family-wide, symbiotic ego. Individuation poses such a great threat, in this family, because were individuation to occur in a family where so little ego-structure has become established in any of the individuals and where there is so great a dependency upon a family-wide, shared or symbiotic ego, this would be tantamount to ego-fragmentation. Thus the 'rubber fence', hypocritical though its manifestations appear to the therapist who works with the family, represents the family members' largely unconscious attempt to cope with, and conceal, their pathetically genuine lack of collective ego-structures.

It is notable, in this connexion, that this rubber fence forces each family member towards greater *freedom*, in their behaviour towards one another, than the extrafamilial culture will allow. Specifically, the danger of incest is heightened in a family where a potential incest-partner cannot be renounced for fear of renunciation of the so necessary underlying symbiotic attachment to that person. The rubber fence forces the family member to turn his emotional needs towards tabooed goals–towards sexual involvement with, and aggression against, the very people whom the extrafamilial culture–with which the family member is in *some* degree of contact–decrees it most forbidden to have such impulses: the parents and siblings. Another way of putting it is that the need of the family members to serve as partial egos for one another, as part objects for one another, intensifies the incest-and-murder threat attaching to such rudimentary whole-object relationships as are getting formed–within, by decree of the family symbiosis, the family itself.

But, while any developing genuine person-to-person closeness, within the family, involves such intense taboos from the extra-familial culture, any genuine moving apart involves, as I have noted, a comparably intense threat of collective ego-fragmentation. Wynne *et al.* (1958) comment that

. . . both parents have frequently emphasized their vulnerability to cardiovascular disaster if they should become upset. . . .
. . . The social organization in these families is shaped by a pervasive familial subculture of myths, legends, and ideology which stress the dire consequences of openly recognized divergence from a relatively limited number of fixed, engulfing family roles.

The longer I have worked with schizophrenic patients, the more I have come to respect the intensity of the anxiety, so apt indeed to produce ego-fragmentation and/or psychosomatic disaster, which is represented by such 'myths, legends, and ideology'. A schizophrenic man with whom I once worked for a long time had a history in which each of his parents had died of coronary occlusion at times when the patient's symbiotic attachment to them was in danger of resolution; an older sister had a severe though non-fatal coronary occlusion precisely at a point when the patient's symbiosis with her had started to shift markedly; the patient lingered almost at death's door for several months in reaction to severe threats to his own symbiotic attachments; and for my part I had, on more than one occasion, 'countertransference' reactions which I had never felt before in my work with anyone – acute anxiety lest I drop dead, occurring during phases of intensified growth on the patient's part, and evoked partly by his anxiety, based on repeated past experiences in his family, lest this indeed happen to me. I am citing here only the most striking among many hardly less sobering experiences from my work and from colleagues' reports of their work at Chestnut Lodge.

From this viewpoint, then, the 'rubber fence' can be looked upon as the family's collective and unconscious dynamic equilibrium between their intense need, on the one hand, to maintain a collective ego, the only at all reliable ego there is in the family, and on the other hand their ceaseless strivings, respectively, for individuality. The emergence of psychosis in the patient represents, therefore, not only his own heretofore thwarted striving towards individuality, but also the vicariously expressed strivings of a similar nature on the part of the other family members. It is probably more adequate to conceptualize this advent of psychosis as a shift in the total family's mode of dealing with their unresolved, conflicting needs for symbiosis-and-individuation.

Positive Feelings

As I have reported earlier (see chs. 7, 12) I have become deeply impressed with the intensity of the schizophrenic patient's positive feelings, and I believe that many of the therapists who are exploring this comparatively new field of the family therapy of schizophrenia are underestimating, perhaps out of their eagerness to demonstrate the other family members' contribution to the patient's illness, the real and deeply significant role of positive feelings in the family interaction as a whole. A number of my patients, after several years of individual therapy, have become able to reveal the warm delight which they, and the family as a whole, found in just such kinds of family craziness as are portrayed, in the literature in this field, as bearing an exclusively malignant connotation. A number of my women patients came to express anguish at their childless state, anguish related in part to their inability to perpetuate the family name; such communications have been filled in each instance with a sense of deeply human tragedy. In the instance of a schizophrenic man with whom I have worked, intensively, for thirteen years, I have come to realize that his parents' devotion to this long treatment endeavour has not been based primarily, as I long thought, upon guilt but rather upon affection–or, to put it more bluntly, love–of a degree of intensity which I have found both moving and humbling to behold. Their hatred for their son, of which I long ago saw much solid evidence, was in a way easier for me to discover than was this underlying love, which only the passage of the years has brought before me in a way which I can no longer ignore or minimize.

It is essential for us to realize that the kind of family loyalty which we find in these families has, for all its constrictingly pathological aspects, a nucleus of genuinely positive feeling which is, for the family members including the patient, most highly cherished. However tragically warped and turned in upon itself, there is locked up here one of the highest aspirations of the human spirit. On occasion, when I have seen the anguish experienced by a schizophrenic patient at finding himself torn between his newly developing self on the one hand, and his family loyalty on the other, I have been reminded of the words of the Psalmist: 'If I forget thee, O Jerusalem, let my right hand forget her cunning' (Ps. 137:5).

Even the brief experience which I have had with the family therapy of schizophrenia has been replete with evidence of positive feeling, though this is often less dramatically evident than are the many manifestations of real and pervasive hatred. I have been greatly struck by the degree of trust implied in a father's exposing not only himself but his whole family to the efforts of the family therapist. I have seen something of how hungry are the family members for more real family relatedness, for more of the real interpersonal closeness which they are at some level aware of missing; the power of this striving to become genuinely a family is, I think, of a piece with every neurotic or psychotic human being's striving towards health as an individual.

In evaluating a family's potential strength and capacity for growth as a family, it is well to keep in mind that we are working with a family which has decompensated, which has become disorganized, and is not functioning at the level at which it was functioning in earlier and better years. That is, just as regression is one feature of the psychosis which has become overt in the patient himself, at least some significant degree of regression has occurred in the over-all family relatedness; so not merely the patient, but all these persons, may possess more maturity, collectively and as a family, than is apparent in the present state of decompensation or regression in their family life. The above-mentioned paper by Lidz and Fleck (1960), describing the serious disorganizations which occur in the families of schizophrenic patients, has helped me to see this aspect of the family therapy situation.

Along the same line, if the mother (for example) as we currently see her in family therapy is significantly different from the *early* mother (the mother of the patient's early childhood), and still more widely different from the patient's distorted and introjected early mother-*images*, then this has some important implications. Part of the mother's ego identity must be having to remain at this earlier level, to meet the primitive needs of her psychotic son or daughter. It would follow that part of her resentment towards the offspring is related to this thwarting of her own maturation, and that among the beneficial results of family therapy will be her becoming freer to be her more mature self. Benedek's (1959) paper, 'Parenthood as a Developmental Phase', helps us to realize that not only childhood and adolescence, but also adulthood, is a time of continuously unfolding development; so we can surmise, in approaching the family therapy of schizophrenia, that not only was the patient's childhood development thwarted 'by' the mother, but also the mother's development as a mother is being thwarted 'by' the schizophrenic offspring.

In the first family therapy session in which I participated, I found myself enjoying greatly the interaction in which I was

737

taking part, and realized that I very much wanted it not to change; this gave me a first-hand sample of the positive gratifications which the family members themselves may be deriving from the *status quo*. It stands to reason that the family must be harbouring much more of positive feeling towards one another than they reveal at all openly and early in treatment, or else–in the light of the severity of the clashes which occur among them during the sessions–they would kill one another, or otherwise destroy their ties to one another, in the intervals between the sessions. The fact that they do not thus act, between sessions, upon such feelings as they have verbalized during the therapeutic interaction, may be taken as a very significant, though non-verbal, acknowledgement by all of them as to the important role of transference, projection, introjection, and other distortions in their therapeutic session reactions to one another.

It is essential for therapy that we make contact with the positive strivings in the family, for without an awareness of these we cannot understand the historical development of psychosis in the patient and disorganization in the family as a whole; in this development the factor of unassimilated grief (over the loss of cherished relationships) has a fundamental role. Furthermore, without an appreciation of the strength of the love-feelings, no matter how repressed, we cannot appreciate the absolutely key role of *ambivalence* in the pathology with which we are trying to cope. I have reported earlier my finding that schizophrenic regression is a defence not against aggression alone, as is stated by Bak (1954) and others, but rather against ambivalence–against, that is, intensities of both hatred and love which, without the benefit of psychotherapy, tear apart the individual's attempts at more mature ego-integration (see ch. 12). Those writings which detail only the hateful aspects of the relatedness among the members of the schizophrenic patient's family bypass altogether the central tragedy in these families: the extent to which the family members are being crippled and paralysed by their inability to face the fact that they *both* intensely hate *and* deeply love one another. Only in so far as the therapist can help them to face both their love and their hatred can they relinquish the symbiotic mode of relatedness which is serving as their family-wide unconscious defence against this ambivalence, but which is thwarting, by the very nature of this relatedness, their development of ego maturity and genuine object relatedness with one another.

I wish to make only a few more comments concerning the family aetiology of schizophrenia in the patient, beyond this matter of positive feelings, before turning to the topic of counter-transference.

Loss, or the Threat of Loss, of Membership in the Family

It is to be noted that, in these families, the matter of *membership in the family* is, for each member, not something biologically given, but is to be maintained only through participation in the family symbiosis. The patient, as a child, has had only two choices: (*a*) to be part of the family symbiosis, or (*b*) to be reacted to as a non-member of the family and, at the same time, as 'crazy'. Ironically, since one must have a successful experience with the symbiotic phase of ego maturation in order to avoid autism (craziness), and since the family offers the patient his only *available* chance for symbiotic experience (unless a therapist comes along and offers him such an experience), it is tragically true that, for him, non-membership in the family is indeed tantamount to craziness. Long before the onset of his psychosis, the patient has laboured under the chronic threat of psychological banishment from the family, should he fail to fulfil his role as the personification of the warded-off part-aspects of his parents', and other family members', personalities. It is significant, too, that when and if he eventually recovers from his schizophrenia, he may find that the rest of the family presents a closed corporation aspect to him; they have no place, here, for a whole person.

During the prodromal phase of the patient's schizophrenia, his progressive withdrawal from the other members of his family is so conspicuous that we may underestimate the mutuality of this withdrawal—the extent to which the other family members have lost interest in him and have barred him progressively from functional membership in the family. The observations by Schwartz and Will (1953) concerning the degree to which ward staff participate in, and contribute to, the therefore mutual withdrawal involving the progressively withdrawing schizophrenic patient, help us to realize what the patient has experienced, prior to his hospitalization, *vis-à-vis* the members of his family.

In many of these families, the ego-state of *not knowing*—of seeking for clarification – is considered equivalent to being crazy, which in turn means being considered hopelessly apart and ineligible for membership in the family. The child has long ago learned not to question seriously the blandly pointless and dis-coordinated discussions which are so typical of these families. None of the members dares seriously to question these, for to feel, and reveal, confusion is to run the risk of being considered crazy for questioning what is tacitly agreed to be obvious and unquestionable. The previously mentioned paper by Wynne et al. (1958) deals perceptively with matters relevant to this point. Particularly with each of the paranoid schizophrenic patients I have treated, it has been a most welcome and hard-won development for him to become able to reveal his deep and previously repressed confusion; growth is possible only to the extent that one can endure confusion and uncertainty.

The patient has been reacted to conflictually, in the family, by the various others not simply as a whole person but, even more ego-disruptively, as a part object for the maintenance of their respective psychic economies. One of my patients expressed this in somatic terms, saying that one 'faction' always controlled her lungs, another her stomach, another her heart, and so on. Normally, I presume, a mother protects the little child, mainly through her own comparatively unambivalent symbiosis with him, from such complex and conflictual 'usage' by the various family members.

One of my paranoid patients, telling how in high school his brother had condemned him as being a 'force of evil', gave me some glimpse of how devastating it must be, for a child who has no solid whole person relationships to which to cling, to be thus reacted to as a part object – as, in this instance, the embodiment of the brother's repressed and projected hostility.

The increasingly formidable impact upon the other family members of the progressively anxious and hostile child who is on the way to schizophrenia is itself an aetiological factor of great importance. Whereas I used to feel scorn for those parents who are always seeking prescriptions as to 'what to say' to their schizophrenic son or daughter, I have come to realize that the patient, with his deeply hurtful and anxiety-provoking verbal and non-verbal behaviour, stirs up such powerful and conflictual feelings in the parents that it would be difficult for any one, under these circumstances, to be able unaided to *find words to express* the welter of hurt, grief, rage, and so on, which – as the therapist learns at first hand – is evoked. Because the parents cannot integrate such deeply ambivalent feelings in reaction to the patient's communications, their front of bland denial-of-feeling tends to become intensified. So the patient finds himself progressively deprived of any real and accessible person to whom to relate; this in turn throws him more and more back upon functioning, towards the other family members, as a projected part object.

In general, the nature of the family symbiosis, with its spurious (though defensively so essential) atmosphere of 'family oneness', places a taboo upon any meaningful one-to-one relationships within (or outside) the family. But one-to-one relationships represent the highest order of interpersonal complexity which the young child (or the adult schizophrenic patient) can integrate successfully, and are utterly essential to the formation of healthy identifications and the healthy emergence (in contrast to an autistic flight) from symbiotic relatedness.

Countertransference

In approaching the subject of countertransference, we should take the full measure, first, of the emotional burdens which are *inherent* in the family therapy of schizophrenia, and which will evoke deeply conflictual feelings, and anxiety often of severe degree, in any therapist no matter how well analysed he may have been. He will inevitably experience much conflict and anxiety with respect to his role in relationship to the family group, as a reflection, or sample, of the anxiety and ambivalence which was aroused in the patient himself in earlier years with regard to the matter of membership or non-membership in the family. The acute sense of isolation which I have at times experienced in this situation, when I felt shut out by all others in the room, was reminiscent to me of one of the most severe kinds of pressure which is encountered in the individual therapy of a hospitalized schizophrenic patient: the sense of deeply anxious isolation experienced on occasions when one feels that the patient, the members of the ward staff, the psychiatric administrator, and others all share a completely harmonious view as to one's own malignant unacceptability.

741

When, on the other hand, the therapist is feeling himself to be part of the family, he experiences a different kind of pressure which is again, I believe, a sample of that to which the patient himself has long been exposed in the family—namely, a feeling of acute conflict as to which of the family members is most in need of support at the moment. In earlier papers I have reported evidence of the patient's basically therapeutic efforts on behalf of his mother (chs 7. and 12 above), and this therapeutic attitude is, I believe, his most basic attitude towards the family members collectively.

Following one family therapy session, it occurred to me that I had had, during it, some goals in mind with reference to each of the family members, but that it had been impossible to think in terms of a goal for the family as a whole. This was presumably a reaction on my part to the discoordination which holds sway in these families behind the pseudo-mutuality which has been described by Wynne *et al.* (1958). Such a reaction gives one a clue to the extent to which this 'family' is not really a family in the socio-dynamic sense, but rather a group symbiosis in which the part-object roles of the various participants are constantly shifting. That is to say, we react emotionally less to the rigid outward structure in the family, than to the underlying fluidity of ego-boundaries, so that, characteristically, there is no one in the room with whom we feel a continuing sense of reliable contact. The rapidly changing transference patterns which I encountered in this therapeutic situation were in marked contrast to my experience in doing group therapy with a group of out-patients comprised largely of neurotic individuals, with a relatively few schizoid or borderline schizophrenic individuals; there, the transference patterns were comparatively easy to trace as they unfolded week after week and month after month. In the family therapy of schizophrenia, not only the sense of emotional relatedness but also that of meaning is, of course, markedly disrupted and discoordinate, so that it is difficult or impossible to find any one thread of meaning running throughout the typical session.

Bowen (1960), after describing the early difficulties which therapists and ward staff encountered in terms of becoming embroiled in the various family members' different emotional points of view, reports that

. . . When it was possible to attain a workable level of interested detachment, it was then possible to begin to defocus the individual and to focus on the entire family at once. . . . Once it was possible to focus on the family as a unit, it was like shifting a microscope from the oil immersion to the low power lens, or like moving from the playing field to the top of the stadium to watch a football game. Broad patterns of form and movement that had been obscured in the close-up view became clear. The close-up view could then become more meaningful once the distant view was also possible.

It would seem that both the close-up and the distant views are equally essential, and that the family therapist needs to become able to shift from one mode of participation to the other, as the needs of the moment require. It is such an integration of these different vantage-points, such a ready communicability between them, which the patient himself (and to a significant degree the other family members also) has not been able to acquire. For him, closeness or participation with the other family members has meant enmeshment in a conflictful symbiotic relatedness, and extrication from this state has meant isolation and unrelatedness.

It should be seen how intensely and basically ambivalent is the reaction of the family (including the patient) to the therapist as a representative of threatening extrafamilial reality. They all strive unconsciously either to render him non-existent, psychologically, or to mould him into one or another (constantly changing) part-object role (that is to say, into the personification of one or another of their repressed self-images). If they cannot succeed in so moulding him or obliterating him, the family members collectively lose their fantasied omnipotence. I have described this moulding as representative of a basically healthy need to ingest—primitively to identify with—a healthy mother-object. But here this basically healthy need is being expressed—until such time as a predominantly hateful orientation has given place to a predominantly loving one—in the service of maintaining the infantile fantasy of grandiosity, the fantasy that there is no durable external world which will not be plastic in the hands of one's own needs and desires. Yet, on the other hand, the family members desperately need the therapist to remain solid and whole, for otherwise they cannot become well and mature. So the therapist is inescapably buffeted by the family's ambivalence towards him.

Apart from such difficulties, which are inherent in family therapy, there is a truly countertransference factor of the therapist's not having adequately worked through, in his own analysis, those personal conflicts on which this kind of therapy specifically impinges. As I intimated at the outset, our dyadically oriented training analysis leaves us, typically, with a realm of comparatively unexplored (repressed) *family*-oriented feeling which tends to emerge in the form of countertransference reactions in our attempting to carry on this family therapy. Some papers on family therapy seem to be written in a spirit largely of childish glee at the writer's having 'got something on' the family of the patient; there is a close similarity between this emotional tone and that of the analytic student who, too early in his analysis to have come face to face with his feelings of love and grief with respect to his mother and father, eagerly volunteers the evidence of their blameworthiness for his personal psychopathology. I surmise that the de-repression of our feelings – especially those of love and grief – about our *families* has lagged behind our grasp of the feelings which have been formed within the two-person context with our mother, or with our father, for example. The defensively symbiotic front of 'harmony' which prevails in the family of the schizophrenic patient tends so powerfully to obscure the participants' own feelings of genuinely human loyalty, tragedy, nobility, and other basically positive feelings, that this makes it extraordinarily difficult for the therapist, also, to perceive such emotional ingredients in the family interaction; thus it is all the more incumbent upon him not to be content with a cataloguing of the negative aspects of the family relatedness – a cataloguing of, that is, their psychopathology. It becomes incumbent upon him to try to perceive the basically human family struggles and tragedies against which their psychopathology is defending these family members.

One is tempted to sneer at the so hypocrisy-laden loyalty, for example, which we find in these families; but this suggests that we have not worked through our own feelings of early loss of the Good Objects with whom we were once so deeply and symbiotically affiliated. In general, I believe – as I have devoted the whole first third of this chapter to showing – we tend to overestimate the degree of true object relatedness which is transpiring in the family, out of our need to keep from realizing the degree to which part-object (symbiotic) relatedness held sway in our own parental family, during our childhood, and the degree to which part-object introjects hold sway within us still. That is, it would be deflating to us to realize to what an extent our family members as a whole reacted to us not as a person in our own right, but rather as the externalization of their own Good or Bad Objects; and to what an extent our own reactions to them have been comparably intrapsychic in nature. There is such a degree of genuine loss attached to this realization that we tend unconsciously to perpetuate this symbiotic parental family of ours, in the realm of our repressed introjects. It is to be emphasized here that it is not the loss of our parental family members as separate and whole objects against which we are thus defending ourselves, but rather the loss of the symbiotic Family Oneness, so boundariless that all are felt to be, literally, of one heart and mind and soul.

The nature of the family therapy setting tends to evoke, then, in us, these unintegrated introjects which have thus far escaped detection in our dyadic training analysis. But I cannot overemphasize how effectively this family therapy setting tends not only to evoke the therapist's countertransference reactions, but also to keep obscured their nature *as* countertransference, rather than predominantly reality, reactions. The therapist's unconscious feelings can find vicarious expression, on the part of one or another of the family members, all too readily, because it is in such a symbiotic fashion that these persons customarily enter into, and maintain, 'interpersonal' relatedness. The subtle role of the therapist's unconscious hostility or reproachfulness, for example, towards one or another of the participants in the family drama, is all too apt to be overshadowed by the blatant reality of the hostility personified by the mother or father, and the reproachfulness which is being manifested by the patient towards them.

I wonder whether, in a setting where there is not only so ready but even eager a set of 'targets' for the therapist's introjects, he may not feel threatened lest he lose his introjects, and thus become helplessly apart from what is going on in the session. And, although introjects are subjectively experienced as being in opposition, rather than as contributing, to ego-identity, they do contain significant increments of potential, or latent, ego-identity;

745

thus, I surmise that this sense of threat may become experienced as a fear lest one lose one's self, one's identity. Such thoughts, admittedly highly speculative, seem permissible when we consider how acute is the sense of isolation and anxiety which the therapist at times experiences.

It is well to explore the personal sources of one's own interest in carrying on therapy in this field, for any unrecognized and acted out personal needs must have a great influence upon our 'technique'. If, for example, the therapist is unaware how hungry he is for participation in parental family life, he will find it difficult to disengage himself from a deeply participative role and move into a more detached-observer position at moments when this is indicated. Likewise, he will have unconscious resistance to the family's developing an increasingly healthy relatedness among themselves–a relatedness which he cannot biologically share–analogous to the individual therapist's resistance to the patient's becoming well and thereby lost to him.

The literature in this field is liberally sprinkled with examples of the therapist's assuming the task of rescuing or protecting the patient from one or both parents, on the basis of an unconscious avoidance of the transference role, *vis-à-vis* the patient or parents or both, of the personifier of these family members' 'bad intro-jects'. A genuine working-through of the patient's, and other family members', difficulties would involve the therapist's being able to endure, for whatever period of time is required for such working-through, his own being regarded by these persons as the embodiment of Bad Mother or Bad Father malevolence. But it is deceptively easy to regard oneself as a potential saviour, by definition devoid of hostility, and to regard the patient as an equally unhating victim of parental hostility. Also, the active gratifications of the role of Good Parent (or Good Child, for that matter), if only we can sustain it, are great indeed. When, for example, a paranoid father who usually regarded me in the family group as being the personification of evil, saw me for a time in an utterly contrasting light and said to me, smiling benignly, 'If you're innocent, you're innocent,' I felt quite simply blessed, with a sense of purity and goodness which I sensed to have been one of the feeling experiences of an early childhood now lost beyond remembering.

The dramatic 'interpersonal' confrontations which family

therapy promotes are very apt to keep obscured the central role of such introjects. Burton (1961), reporting his therapy of a schizophrenic woman, says that

> ... Her improvement was not matched by the growth of her family, who had considerable unconscious investment in the maintenance of her illness. In family therapy she was able, for the first time, to confront her father and husband with her needs as a person and to point out logically the part they themselves played in her illness. At this point the husband told of his ambivalence about resuming his life with her outside the hospital and began drinking again. ...

In a similar vein, Jackson (1961) observes that '. . . Perhaps the most important aspect of family psychotherapy is that the patient has to see his parents as real people . . .'

My point, here, is that we are all too apt to accept such confrontations as being genuinely and exclusively interpersonal events, and to miss the centrally significant aetiological role of the patient's own pathogenic introjects, projected here upon spouse or parents.

It seems evident that, in order that the therapist may work effectively in the family therapy of schizophrenia, his identity as a parent must be as acceptable to him, as well elaborated and established, as is his identity as a child, for otherwise he will tend unduly much to identify with the patient-as-child, and unconsciously to wreak revenge for his own childhood grievances upon the patient's parents. It would seem that, to meet the therapeutic needs of the family, as these needs shift moment by moment, he must be able to shift his identification, in a ready and fluid way, from child to parent and vice versa. We sense here that, no matter how limited as a therapeutic method this form of therapy may eventually prove to be, one of its enduring values will spring from the maturity which it requires, and therefore fosters, in the therapist—a maturity which can only enhance his therapeutic results in individual psychotherapy also.

Concluding Remarks

In our enthusiasm about this promising new therapeutic approach to schizophrenia, we should not forget that the patient himself is typically—no matter how great the other family members' aetiological contributions—the most deeply ill individual in the family.[5] Thus, while this new field is eminently deserving of vigorous exploration, we should not enter into it in a spirit of flight from facing the full depth of the patient's own psychopathology—from facing, for example, the awesome depth of his hostility, his despair, his grief, and his need to give and receive love; and the no less awesome depth of, for instance, one's own ambivalent love and hatred, and therefore despair, concerning him. It is all too easy to become convinced, with him, that his own illness is now effectively resolved, and his only remaining difficulty consists in his being afflicted with a malignant wife or mother or father, so that, if only these can be dragged into the therapeutic situation and the extent of their destructive contributions revealed for all to see, this basically well and loving patient can then function as such.

It is especially important for us to realize that these family-oriented problems can be worked through in the individual therapeutic relationship, and need to be worked through there in order that the patient may achieve the deepest possible level of personal integration. It is quite possible that we shall come to view family therapy as a most worthy companion to such individual therapy; but I doubt whether it can ever come to replace, in integrative value, the patient's working through, in the transference relationship to the individual therapist—no matter that this relationship is *ostensibly* a dyadic one—of his intrapsychic conflicts referable not merely to single other persons, but to all family members simultaneously. That is, just as we have learned that a patient can form an adequate mother-transference to a male therapist, and an adequate father-transference to a female therapist—without, that is, requiring for

---

[5] This statement is an accurate summation of my own clinical experience which is, as I acknowledged at the outset, heavily weighted on the side of individual therapy with—I should further explain—chronically schizophrenic patients. When I term the patient himself typically 'the most deeply ill individual in the family', I refer to the various family members' respective ego functioning as individuals.

The validity of this statement has been challenged by people with vastly more experience than I in the family therapy of schizophrenia. I respect their differing and in this regard much greater experience, and it is not difficult for me to believe that if one has the opportunity to work with a number of families containing at the outset of treatment a young person who has only recently come to manifest an acute schizophrenia, and with one or another parent evidencing, say, a long-existing ambulatory schizophrenia, one may come to the conclusion that it is the parent, as often as the 'schizophrenic one'—the son or daughter who in the individual therapist's viewpoint wears the label of patient—who is, all things considered, really the more heavily burdened with psychopathology.

this stage of the therapy a transfer to another therapist of the opposite sex–so, my experience suggests, the transference can find the necessary *multiplicity* also as directed toward the individual therapist, even though at a biological level he is but one person. The patient who can find mother and father and siblings in the therapist, simultaneously, and who can, through identification with his therapist, make these projected internal images into truly integrated parts of himself, becomes thereby, I believe, a more deeply integrated single individual than does the patient whose transference relationship is diverted and dispersed upon the various real members of the parental family in an exclusively family therapy approach.

Space will not allow me to detail more than a few examples of the 'family transference' which I have come to see in individual treatment relationships, and which have convinced me that individual therapy can and should be extended down into this realm–that the family *in toto* comes upon the individual therapy scene, and should not bodily be brought into it as more than an adjunct to our focus upon the individual himself. A paranoid woman, complaining to a nurse about me, demanded, 'Who the hell does he think he is? He's not my mother and father!' Later on in her treatment, during the course of one session she said, 'You–[that is,] Edgar and Dad and Louise–. . .' Edgar and Louise were the names of two of her siblings; at this stage of the therapy she saw all other persons, including me, as multiple persons, and on innumerable occasions I was, to her, several members of her parental family simultaneously. She had not been visited for years by any of her three children and steadfastly disclaimed that she had any children. I felt baffled and despairing as to how this great real-life gulf could possibly be bridged; but my concern lessened as I began to see to what degree she was able to perceive me, in the transference, as being one or other of her children, and to work through in this setting her anxiety, hostility, grief, and so on, with respect to her five-year-old daughter, or her seven-year-old daughter, or her three-year-old son–now, in actuality, several years older than that. Such transference developments helped greatly to pave the way for the real-life resumption of her relationships with her children.

A hebephrenic man lived, for years, in a predominantly hallucinatory world. Gradually, the chaotic, discoordinate

749

quality of this 'interpersonal' world in which he lived assumed, more and more consistently, the identity of his parental family; but I was still reacted to, by him, as having much less of a flesh-and-blood substantiality than did these hallucinatory family members. As the treatment progressed still further, I felt myself to be no longer an onlooker in this family scene; I was now on a par with these hallucinatory figures towards 'whom' I had more than once felt jealousy, because of the liveliness of the patient's interactions with them and the sparsity of the crumbs of emotional responsiveness which had come my way. Still later, he gave me to know that I was now more important to him than these hallucinations, the appearance of which, in his world, could now more and more readily be traced to the vicissitudes of the real and identifiable relationship between him and me. Once when I was trying to understand how he viewed me, he explained, in a compassionate tone, 'I look at you as a father. They've all gone. Martin [the patient's own name] has gone, and Leonard [a brother who was killed in Korea] has gone, and Ethel [a sister who had long ago moved to a distant foreign country] has gone, and you're the only one who's left.' I cannot adequately convey the depth and vividness of the feeling of *family* which was conveyed in his words, in his transference to me as the personification of his lonely and aged father, of whom this view was indeed so true.

A hebephrenic woman with whom I am currently working experiences both herself and me as respective *crowds*, and I expect that it may be a long time yet before her ego-integration proceeds far enough for the comparatively simple and identifiable family transference to emerge, with some consistency, as it did in my work with the above-described man. Such multiple transferences tend, of course, to be stressful for the therapist, as threatening him with ego-fragmentation.

An exploration of the family therapy of schizophrenia enriches and enlivens our concept of the healthy family also. It suggests that, just as in *individual* ego-development there is normally a symbiotic phase which gives place, later, to individuation, there is a family-symbiotic phase in the existence of the healthy family, a phase which, if the family is to live out its healthy destiny and be psychologically successful as a family, must give place to the achieved (or, in the instances of the adults, the deepened) individuation of the several participants. That is, the very conspicuous symbiotic, projected and introjected part-object phenomena which we see in the family of the schizophrenic patient have less conflict-laden counterparts in healthy family development. As seen at any one moment in time, a family is a *group of persons*; but as viewed over the years of the family's evolution, a family is a *process of individuation out of symbiosis*.

It may well be that the most mature form of interrelatedness among the healthy person's introjects can be characterized best by the term 'family of introjects', or family-relatedness among his introjects. It is notable that the schizophrenic family as a whole, like the schizophrenic patient himself, is barred by their isolation, *vis-à-vis* other families, from learning more healthy family relationships; and it hardly seems feasible to employ a healthy family in the service of meeting this troubled family's identificatory needs. But in those fortunate instances where the family therapist has matured sufficiently for a family-inter-relatedness among his introjects to have been achieved, the family can find *in him* the healthy family with whom they hunger to identify. In this sense he can constitute a bridge for them to traverse, out of their family isolation and into the world of the healthier families about them.

BIBLIOGRAPHY

ABRAHAM, KARL (1908). 'The Psychosexual Differences between Hysteria and Dementia Praecox.' In: *Selected Papers of Karl Abraham.* (London: Hogarth, 1927; New York: Basic Books, 1953.)
(1924a). 'The Influence of Oral Erotism on Character-Formation.' *ibid.*
(1924b). 'A Short Study of the Development of the Libido.' *ibid.*
ABRAHAMS, J., and VARON, E. (1953). *Maternal Dependency and Schizophrenia.* (New York: International Universities Press.)
ACKERMAN, N. W. (1953). 'Selected Problems in Supervised Analysis.' *Psychiatry*, **16**, 283–90.
ALLEN, C. (1935). 'Introjection in Schizophrenia.' *Psychoanal. Rev.*, **22**, 121–37.
ALMANSI, R. J. (1960). 'The Face–Breast Equation.' *J. Amer. Psychoanal. Assoc.*, **8**, 43–70.
ANGYAL, A. (1946). 'Disturbances of Thinking in Schizophrenia.' In: *Language and Thought in Schizophrenia*, ed. J. S. Kasanin (*see* KASANIN, *below*).
ARIETI, S. (1955). *Interpretation of Schizophrenia.* (New York: Brunner.)
(1961a). 'Introductory Notes on the Psychoanalytic Therapy of Schizophrenics.' In: *Psychotherapy of the Psychoses*, ed. A. Burton. (New York: Basic Books.)
(1961b). 'The Loss of Reality.' *Psychoanal. Rev.*, **48**, 3–24.
ARLOW, J. A. (1961). 'Silence and the Theory of Technique.' *J. Amer. Psychoanal. Assoc.*, **9**, 44–55.
AZIMA, H., VISPO, R., and AZIMA, F. J. (1961). 'Observations on Anaclitic Therapy during Sensory Deprivation.' In: *Sensory Deprivation*, ed. P. Solomon *et al.* (*see* SOLOMON, *below*).
BAK, R. (1949). 'The Psychopathology of Schizophrenia.' *Bull. Amer. Psychoanal. Assoc.*, **5**, 44–9.
(1953). 'Fetishism.' *J. Amer. Psychoanal. Assoc.*, **1**, 285–98.
(1954). 'The Schizophrenic Defence against Aggression.' *Int. J. Psycho-Anal.*, **35**, 129–34.
(1958). 'The Role of Aggression in Psychic Conflict.' Presented at the November 1958 meeting of the Washington Psychoanalytic Society.
BALINT, M. (1948). 'On the Psycho-Analytic Training System.' *Int. J. Psycho-Anal.*, **29**, 163–73.
(1952). *Primary Love and Psycho-Analytic Technique.* (London: Hogarth, 1952; New York: Liveright, 1953.)
(1955). 'Friendly Expanses–Horrid Empty Spaces.' *Int. J. Psycho-Anal.*, **36**, 225–41.
(1958). 'The Concepts of Subject and Object in Psycho-Analysis.' *Brit. J. Med. Psychol.*, **31**, 83–91.

BIBLIOGRAPHY

BARCHILON, J. (1958). 'On Countertransference "Cures".' *J. Amer. Psychoanal. Assoc.*, **6**, 222–36.

BARRY, M. J., Jr., and JOHNSON, A. M. (1957). 'The Incest Barrier.' Read at the May 1957 meeting of the American Psychoanalytic Association, Chicago.

BATESON, G., *et al.* (1956). 'Toward a Theory of Schizophrenia.' *Behavioral Science*, **1**, 251–64.

BECK, S. J. (1946). 'Errors in Perception and Fantasy in Schizophrenia.' In: *Language and Thought in Schizophrenia*, ed. J. S. Kasanin (*see* KASANIN, *below*).

BECKETT, P. G. S., *et al.* (1956). 'Studies in Schizophrenia at the Mayo Clinic: I. The Significance of Exogenous Traumata in the Genesis of Schizophrenia.' *Psychiatry*, **19**, 137–42.

BENEDEK, T. (1949). 'The Psychosomatic Implications of the Primary Unit: Mother–Child.' *Amer. J. Orthopsych.*, **19**, 642–54.
—— (1952a). *Psychosexual Functions in Women.* (New York: Ronald Press.)
—— (1952b). 'Personality Development.' In: *Dynamic Psychiatry*, ed. F. Alexander and H. Ross. (Chicago: Univ. of Chicago Press.)
—— (1959). 'Parenthood as a Developmental Phase–A Contribution to the Libido Theory.' *J. Amer. Psychoanal. Assoc.*, **7**, 389–417.
—— (1960). 'The Organization of the Reproductive Drive.' *Int. J. Psycho-Anal.*, **41**, 1–15.

BENEDICT, R. (1938). 'Continuities and Discontinuities in Cultural Conditioning.' *Psychiatry*, **1**, 161–7.

BENJAMIN, J. J. (1946). 'A Method for Distinguishing and Evaluating Formal Thinking Disorders in Schizophrenia.' In: *Language and Thought in Schizophrenia*, ed. J. S. Kasanin (*see* KASANIN, *below*).

BERES, D. (1960). 'The Psychoanalytic Psychology of Imagination.' *J. Amer. Psychoanal. Assoc.*, **8**, 65–90.

BERGSON, H. *Creative Evolution.* (New York: Modern Library, 1944.)

BERMAN, L. (1949). 'Countertransferences and Attitudes of the Analyst in the Therapeutic Process.' *Psychiatry*, **12**, 159–66.

BEXTON, W. H., HERON, W., and SCOTT, T. H. (1954). 'Effects of Decreased Variation in the Sensory Environment.' *Canad. J. Psychol.*, **8**, 70–6.

BIBRING, E., *et al.* (1937). Discussion on Control Analysis. Reported in *Int. J. Psycho-Anal.*, **18**, p. 369.

BION, W. R. (1955). 'Language and the Schizophrenic.' In: *New Directions in Psychoanalysis*, ed. M. Klein, P. Heimann, and R. Money-Kyrle. (London: Tavistock; New York: Basic Books.)
—— (1956). 'Development of Schizophrenic Thought.' *Int. J. Psycho-Anal.*, **37**, 344–6.
—— (1957). 'Differentiation of the Psychotic from the Non-Psychotic Personalities.' *Int. J. Psycho-Anal.*, **38**, 266–75.
—— (1959). 'Attacks on Linking.' *Int. J. Psycho-Anal.*, **40**, 308–15.

BLEULER, E. (1911). *Dementia Praecox or the Group of Schizophrenias.* (New York: Int. Univ. Press, 1950.)

BIBLIOGRAPHY

BLITZSTEN, N. L., and FLEMING, J. (1953). 'What is a Supervisory Analysis?' *Bull. Menninger Clinic*, **17**, 117-29.

BONNARD, A. (1958). 'Pre-body-ego Types of (Pathological) Mental Functioning.' *J. Amer. Psychoanal. Assoc.*, **7**, 581-611.

BOSZORMENYI-NAGY, I., and FRAMO, J. L. (1962). 'Family Concept of Hospital Treatment of Schizophrenia.' In: *Current Psychiatric Therapies*, Vol. 2, ed. J. Masserman. (New York: Grune & Stratton.)

(1964). (eds.) *Family Treatment of Schizophrenia*. (New York: Harper.)

BOWEN, L. M. (1956). In a transcript of the Combined Clinical Staffs of the National Institutes of Health, Clinical Center Auditorium, 29 March 1956; mimeographed by the Dept. of Health, Education, and Welfare; Nat. Institutes of Health, Bethesda, Maryland.

(1960). 'A Family Concept of Schizophrenia.' In: *The Etiology of Schizophrenia*, ed. D. Jackson. (New York: Basic Books.)

BOYER, L. B. (1957). 'Uses of Delinquent Behavior by a Borderline Schizophrenic.' *Arch. Crim. Psychodyn.*, **2**, 5415-71.

(1961). 'Provisional Evaluation of Psycho-Analysis with Few Parameters employed in the Treatment of Schizophrenia.' *Int. J. Psycho-Anal.*, **42**, 389-403.

BRODEY, W. M. (1959). 'Some Family Operations and Schizophrenia.' *Arch. Gen. Psych.*, **1**, 379-402.

(1961). 'The Family as the Unit of Study and Treatment–Workshop, 1959. 3. Image, Object, and Narcissistic Relationships.'

BRODY, E. B., and REDLICH, F. C. (eds.) (1952). *Psychotherapy with Schizophrenics*. (New York: Int. Univ. Press.)

BRUCH, H. (1947). 'Psychological Aspects of Obesity.' *Psychiatry*, **10**, 373-81.

BRYANT, W. C. (1794-1878). 'Thanatopsis.' *See: A Treasury of Great Poems, English and American*, ed. L. Untermeyer. (New York: Simon & Schuster, 1942.)

BUBER, M. (1947). *Between Man and Man*. (New York: Macmillan, 1948; Boston: Beacon Press, 1955.)

(1957). 'Distance and Relation.' *Psychiatry*, **20**, 97-104.

BULLARD, D. M. (1960). 'Psychotherapy of Paranoid Patients.' *Arch. Gen. Psych.*, **2**, 137.

BURNHAM, D. L. (1955). 'Some Problems in Communication with Schizophrenic Patients.' *J. Amer. Psychoanal. Assoc.*, **3**, 67-81.

(1956). 'Misperception of Other Persons in Schizophrenia – A Structural View of Restitution Processes, Reality Representation, and Perception.' *Psychiatry*, **19**, 283-303.

BURTON, A. (1961). 'The Quest for the Golden Mean: A Study in Schizophrenia.' In: *Psychotherapy of the Psychoses*, ed. A. Burton. (New York: Basic Books.)

BYCHOWSKI, G. (1930). 'A Case of Oral Delusions of Persecution.' *Int. J. Psycho-Anal.*, **11**, 332-7.

(1952). *Psychotherapy of Psychosis*. (New York: Grune & Stratton.)

BIBLIOGRAPHY

CAMBERARI, J. (1958). *The Effects of Sensory Isolation on Suggestible and Non-Suggestible Psychology Graduate Students.* Doctoral Thesis, Univ. of Utah.

CAMERON, N. (1946). 'Experimental Analysis of Schizophrenic Thinking.' In: *Language and Thought in Schizophrenia,* ed. J. S. Kasanin (*see* KASANIN, *below*).

COBB, S. (1961). Foreword to *Sensory Deprivation,* ed. Solomon *et al.* (*see* SOLOMON, *below*).

COHEN, M. B. (1952). 'Countertransference and Anxiety.' *Psychiatry,* **15,** 231–43.

COHEN, R. A. (1947). 'The Management of Anxiety in a Case of Paranoid Schizophrenia.' *Psychiatry,* **10,** 143–57.

COHEN, S. I., *et al.* (1961). 'Problems in Isolation Studies.' In: *Sensory Deprivation,* ed. Solomon *et al.* (*see* SOLOMON, *below*).

COLEMAN, M. L., (1956). 'Externalization of the Toxic Introject.' *Psychoanal. Rev.,* **43,** 235–42.

COLEMAN, M. L., and NELSON, B. (1957). 'Paradigmatic Psychotherapy in Borderline Treatment.' *Psychoanalysis,* **5.**

COOLEY, C. H. (1909). *Social Organization: A Study of the Larger Mind.* (New York: Scribner.)

COZZENS, J. G. (1957). *By Love Possessed.* (New York: Harcourt Brace.)

CROSSMAN, R. (1950). *The God that Failed.* (New York: Harper, 1950; Bantam Books, 1959.)

DEFOREST, I. (1950). 'The Self-Dedication of the Psychoneurotic Sufferer to Hostile Protest and Revenge.' *Psychiatric Quart.,* **24,** 706–15.

DEMENT, W. (1960). 'The Effect of Dream Deprivation.' *Science,* **131,** 1705–7.

DEUTSCH, H. (1942). 'Some Forms of Emotional Disturbance and their Relationship to Schizophrenia.' *Psychoanal. Quart.,* **11,** 301–21.

DUHL, L. J. (1951). 'The Effect of Baby Bottle Feedings on a Schizophrenic Patient.' *Bull. Menninger Clinic,* **15,** 21–5.

EISSLER, K. R. (1943). 'Limitations to the Psycotherapy of Schizophrenia.' *Psychiatry,* **6,** 381–91.

(1951). 'Remarks on the Psycho-Analysis of Schizophrenia.' *Int. J. Psycho-Anal.,* **32,** 139–56.

(1953). 'Notes upon the Emotionality of a Schizophrenic Patient and its Relation to Problems of Technique.' *Psychoanal. Study Child.,* **8,** 199–251.

(1955). *The Psychiatrist and the Dying Patient.* (New York: Int. Univ. Press.)

EKSTEIN, R. (1960). 'A Historical Survey on the Teaching of Psychoanalytic Technique.' *J. Amer. Psychoanal. Assoc.,* **8,** 500–16.

EKSTEIN, R., and WALLERSTEIN, R. S. (1958). *The Teaching and Learning of Psychotherapy.* (New York: Basic Books.)

ELKISCH, P. (1957). 'The Psychological Significance of the Mirror.' *J. Amer. Psychoanal. Assoc.,* **5,** 235–44.

BIBLIOGRAPHY

ERIKSON, E. (1956). 'The Problem of Ego Identity.' *J. Amer. Psychoanal. Assoc.*, **4**, 56–121.

(1958): *Young Man Luther.* (New York: Norton; London: Faber) (1959).

FAIRBAIRN, W. R. D. (1952). *Psycho-analytic Studies of the Personality* (London: Tavistock); American edition: *An Object-Relations Theory of the Personality* (New York: Basic Books, 1954.)

FAULKNER, W. (1939). *The Wild Palms.* (New York: Random House.)

FEDERN, P. (1952). *Ego Psychology and the Psychoses.* (New York: Basic Books.)

FENICHEL, O. (1945). *The Psychoanalytic Theory of Neurosis.* (New York: Norton.)

FERENCZI, S. (1913). 'Stages in the Development of the Sense of Reality.' In: *Sex in Psychoanalysis.* (New York: Brunner, 1950.)

(1923). *Thalassa, A Theory of Genitality.* (New York: Psychoanal. Quart., 1938.)

FLEMING, J. (1953). 'The Role of Supervision in Psychiatric Training.' *Bull. Menninger Clin.*, **17**, 157–69.

FRAZER, J. G. *The Golden Bough.* (London and New York: Macmillan, 1947.)

FREEDMAN, S. J., GRUNEBAUM, H. U., and GREENBLATT, M. (1961). 'Perceptual and Cognitive Changes in Sensory Deprivation.' In: *Sensory Deprivation*, ed. Solomon (*see* SOLOMON, *below*).

FREEMAN, T., CAMERON, J. L., and McGHIE, A. (1958). *Chronic Schizophrenia.* (London: Tavistock; New York: Int. Univ. Press.)

FREUD, A. (1937). *The Ego and the Mechanisms of Defence.* (London: Hogarth, 1937; New York: Int. Univ. Press, 1946.)

FREUD, S. (1896). 'Further Remarks on the Neuro-Psychoses of Defence.' *Standard Edition*, 3.

(1900). *The Interpretation of Dreams. Standard Edition*, **4–5**.

(1907). 'The Sexual Enlightenment of Children.' *Standard Edition*, **9**.

(1909). 'Notes upon a Case of Obessional Neurosis.' *Standard Edition*, **10**.

(1910). 'The Future Prospects of Psycho-Analytic Therapy.' *Standard Edition*, **11**.

(1911a). 'Psycho-Analytic Notes on an Autobiographical Account of a Case of Paranoia (Dementia Paranoides).' *Standard Edition*, **12**.

(1911b). 'Formulations on the Two Principles of Mental Functioning.' *Standard Edition*, **12**.

(1912). Recommendations to Physicians practising Psycho-Analysis.' *Standard Edition*, **12**.

(1915a). 'A Case of Paranoia Running Counter to the Psycho-Analytical Theory of the Disease.' *Standard Edition*, **14**.

(1915b). 'Thoughts for the Times on War and Death.' *Standard Edition*, **14**.

(1915–17). *Introductory Lectures on Psycho-Analysis, Standard Edition*, **15–16**.

(1920). *Beyond the Pleasure Principle. Standard Edition*, **18**.

(1921). *Group Psychology and the Analysis of the Ego. Standard Edition*, **18**.

BIBLIOGRAPHY

FREUD, S. (1922). 'Some Neurotic Mechanisms in Jealousy, Paranoia, and Homosexuality.' *Standard Edition*, **18**.
— (1923). *The Ego and the Id. Standard Edition*, **19**.
— (1931). 'Female Sexuality.' *Standard Edition*, **21**.
FRIEDMAN, M. S. (1955). *Martin Buber – The Life of Dialogue.* (Chicago: Univ. of Chicago Press.)
FROMM, E. (1941). *Escape from Freedom.* (New York and Toronto: Rinehart; London: Kegan Paul – under title *The Fear of Freedom.*)
— (1955). *The Sane Society.* (New York and Toronto: Rinehart.)
FROMM-REICHMANN, F. (1939). 'Transference Problems in Schizophrenics.' *Psychoanal. Quart.*, **8**, 412–26.
— (1948). 'Notes on the Development of Treatment of Schizophrenics by Psychoanalytic Psychotherapy.' *Psychiatry*, **11**, 263–73.
— (1950). *Principles of Intensive Psychotherapy.* (Chicago: Chicago Univ. Press.)
— (1952). 'Some Aspects of Psychoanalytic Psychotherapy with Schizophrenics.' In: *Psychotherapy with Schizophrenics*, ed. Brody and Redlich (*see* BRODY, *above*).
GILL, M. M. (1954). 'Psychoanalysis and Exploratory Psychotherapy.' *J. Amer. Psychoanal. Assoc.*, **2**, 771–97.
GITELSON, M. (1948). 'Problems of Psychoanalytic Training.' *Psychoanal. Quart.*, **17**, 198–211.
GLOVER, E. (1955). *The Technique of Psycho-Analysis.* (London: Baillière; New York: Int. Univ. Press.)
GOLSTEIN, K. (1946). 'Methodological Approach to the Study of Schizophrenic Thought Disorder.' In: *Language and Thought in Schizophrenia*, ed. J. S. Kasanin (*see* KASANIN, *below*).
GREENACRE, P. (1958). 'Early Physical Determinants in the Development of the Sense of Identity.' *J. Amer. Psychoanal. Assoc.*, **6**, 612–27.
GREENSON, R. R. (1949). 'The Psychology of Apathy.' *Psychoanal. Quart.*, **18**, 290–302.
— (1953). 'On Boredom.' *J. Amer. Psychoanal. Assoc.*, **1**, 7–21.
— (1954). 'The Struggle against Identification.' *J. Amer. Psychoanal. Assoc.* **2**, 200–17.
— (1958). 'On Screen Defenses, Screen Hunger and Screen Identity.' *J. Amer. Psychoanal. Assoc.*, **6**, 242–62.
GRODDECK, G. (1923). *The Book of the It.* (London: Vision Press, 1950.)
HAMPSHIRE, S. (1956). (ed.) *The Age of Reason – The 17th Century Philosophers.* (New York: New American Library.)
HANFMANN, E., and KASANIN, J. S. (1942). *Conceptual Thinking in Schizophrenia.* (New York: Nerv. & Ment. Dis. Pub. Co.)
HARTMANN, H. (1939). *Ego Psychology and the Problem of Adaptation.* (New York: Int. Univ. Press, 1958.)
— (1950a). 'Psychoanalysis and Developmental Psychology.' *Psychoanal. Study Child*, **5**, 7–17.
— (1950b). 'Comments on the Psychoanalytic Theory of the Ego.' *Psychoanal. Study Child*, **5**, 74–96.

(1953). 'Contribution to the Metapsychology of Schizophrenia.' *Psychoanal. Study Child*, **8**, 177–98.

(1956). 'Notes on the Reality Principle.' *Psychoanal. Study Child*, **11**, 31–53.

HARTMANN, H., KRIS, E., and LOEWENSTEIN, R. M. (1946). 'Comments on the Formation of the Psychic Structure.' *Psychoanal. Study Child*, **2**, 11–38.

(1949). 'Notes on the Theory of Aggression.' *Psychoanal. Study Child*, **3–4**, 9–36.

HAVENS, L. (1961). 'Hallucinations, Object-Placement and Melancholia.' Read at December 1961 meeting of American Psychoanalytic Association, New York.

HAYWARD, M. L., and TAYLOR, J. E. (1956). 'A Schizophrenic Patient Describes the Action of Intensive Psychotherapy.' *Psychiatric Quart.*, **30**, 211–48.

HEBB, D. O. (1937a). 'The Innate Organization of Visual Activity: 1. Perception of Figures by Rats Reared in Total Darkness.' *J. Genet. Psychol.*, **51**, 101–26.

(1937b). 'The Innate Organization of Visual Activity: 2. Transfer of Response in the Discrimination of Brightness and Size by Rats Reared in Total Darkness.' *J. Comp. Psychol.*, **24**, 277–99.

(1949). *The Organization of Behavior*. (New York: Wiley.)

HEIMANN, P. (1950). 'On Counter-Transference.' *Int. J. Psycho-Anal.*, **31**, 81–4.

(1955a). 'A Contribution to the Re-Evaluation of the Oedipus Complex – the Early Stages.' In: *New Directions in Psycho-Analysis*, ed. M. Klein, P. Heimann, and R. E. Money-Kyrle. (London: Tavistock; New York: Basic Books.)

(1955b). 'A Combination of Defence Mechanisms in Paranoid States.' *ibid.*

HENDRICK, I. (1931). 'Ego Defence and the Mechanism of Oral Ejection in Schizophrenia.' *Int. J. Psycho-Anal.*, **12**, 298–325.

HESSE, H. (1951). *Siddhartha*. (New York: New Directions.)

HILL, L. B. (1955). *Psychotherapeutic Intervention in Schizophrenia*. (Chicago: Univ. of Chicago Press.)

HOEDEMAKER, E. D. (1955). 'The Therapeutic Process in the Treatment of Schizophrenia.' *J. Amer. Psychoanal. Assoc.*, **3**, 89–109.

HORNEY, K. (1948). 'The Value of Vindictiveness.' *Amer. J. Psychoanal.*, **8**, 3–12.

INHELDER, B., and PIAGET, J. (1958). *The Growth of Logical Thinking*. (London: Routledge; New York: Basic Books.)

JACKSON, D. (1961). 'The Monad, the Dyad, and the Family Therapy of Schizophrenics.' In: *Psychotherapy of the Psychoses*, ed. A. Burton (*see* BURTON, above).

JACOBSON, E. (1954a). 'Contribution to the Metapsychology of Psychotic Identifications.' *J. Amer. Psychoanal. Assoc.*, **2**, 239–62.

759

BIBLIOGRAPHY

JACOBSON, E. (1954b). 'On Psychotic Identifications.' *Int. J. Psycho-Anal.*, **35**, 102–8. (1957). 'Denial and Repression.' *J. Amer. Psychoanal. Assoc.*, **5**, 61–92.

JOHNSON, A. M. (1951). 'Some Heterosexual Transference and Counter-transference Phenomena in Late Analysis of the Oedipus.' Read at March 1951 meeting of Washington Psychoanalytic Society.

JOHNSON, A. M., and SZUREK, S. A. (1952). 'The Genesis of Antisocial Acting Out in Children and Adults.' *Psychoanal. Quart.*, **21**, 323–43.

JOHNSON, A. M., *et al.* (1956). 'Studies in Schizophrenia at the Mayo Clinic – II. Observations on Ego Functions in Schizophrenia.' *Psychiatry*, **19**, 143–8.

JONES, J. (1951). *From Here to Eternity.* (New York: Scribners, 1951; New American Library, 1953.)

KAHN, E. (1957). 'An Appraisal of Existential Analysis.' *Psychiat. Quart.*, **31**, 205–27.

KASANIN, J. S. (1946). 'The Disturbance of Conceptual Thinking in Schizophrenia.' In: *Language and Thought in Schizophrenia*, ed. J. S. Kasanin. (Berkley and Los Angeles: Univ. of California Press.)

KATAN, M. (1954). 'The Importance of the Non-Psychotic Part of the Personality in Schizophrenia.' *Int. J. Psycho-Anal.*, **35**, 119–28.

KEISER, S. (1956). Panel Report: 'The Technique of Supervised Analysis.' *J. Amer. Psychoanal. Assoc.*, **4**, 539–49.

KLEIN, M. (1932). *The Psycho-Analysis of Children.* (London: Hogarth.)
(1946). 'Notes on some Schizoid Mechanisms.' *Int. J. Psycho-Anal.*, **27**, 99–110.
(1955). 'The Psycho-Analytic Play Technique: Its History and Significance.' In: *New Directions in Psycho-Analysis.*

KLEIN, M., HEIMANN, P., and MONEY-KYRLE, R. (1955). *New Directions In Psycho-Analysis.* (London: Tavistock; New York: Basic Books.)

KNIGHT, R. P. (1940). 'The Relationship of Latent Homosexuality to the Mechanism of Paranoid Delusions.' *Bull. Menninger Clinic*, **4**, 149–59.
(1946). 'Psychotherapy of an Adolescent Catatonic Schizophrenia with Mutism.' *Psychiatry*, **9**, 323–39.
(1953). 'Management and Psychotherapy of the Borderline Schizophrenic Patient.' *Bull. Menninger Clinic*, **17**, 139–50.

KOVACS, V. (1936). 'Training- and Control-Analysis.' *Int. J. Psycho-Anal.*, **17**, 346–54.

KUBIE, L. S. (1953). 'The Distortion of the Symbolic Process in Neurosis and Psychosis.' *J. Amer. Psycho-Anal.*, **1**, 59–86.

KUBZANSKY, P. E., and LEIDERMAN, P. H. (1961). 'Sensory Deprivation: An Overview.' In: *Sensory Deprivation*, ed. P. Solomon *et al.* (*see* SOLOMON, *below*).

LANGER, S. K. (1942). *Philosophy in a New Key: A Study in the Symbolism of Reason, Rite, and Art.* (New York: New American Library.)

LEWIN, B. D. (1946). 'Sleep, the Mouth, and the Dream Screen.' *Psychoanal. Quart.*, **15**, 419–34.

BIBLIOGRAPHY

(1953). 'Reconsideration of the Dream Screen.' *Psychoanal. Quart.*, **22**, 174-99.

LEWIN, B. D., and ROSS, H. (1960). *Psychoanalytic Education in the United States.* (New York: Norton, 1960.)

LIDZ, R. W., and LIDZ, T. (1952). 'Therapeutic Considerations arising from the Intense Symbiotic Needs of Schizophrenic Patients.' In: *Psycotherapy with Schizophrenics*, ed. Brody and Redlich (*see above*).

LIDZ, T., and FLECK, S. (1960). 'Schizophrenia, Human Integration, and the Role of the Family.' In: *The Etiology of Schizophrenia*, ed. D. Jackson. (New York: Basic Books.)

LIDZ, T., *et al.* (1957). 'The Intrafamilial Environment of Schizophrenic Patients. II. Marital Schism and Marital Skew.' *Amer. J. Psychiat.*, **114**, 241-8.

LILLY, J. C. (1956). 'Mental Effects of Reduction of Ordinary Levels of Physical Stimuli on Intact, Healthy Persons. *Psychiat. Res. Rep.*, **5**, 1-9.

LIMENTANI, D. (1956). 'Symbiotic Identification in Schizophrenia.' *Psychiatry*, **19**, 231-6.

LITTLE, M. (1951). 'Counter-transference and the Patient's Response to it.' *Int. J. Psycho-Anal.*, **32**, 32-40.

(1957). ' "R" – The Analyst's Total Response to his Patient's Needs.' *Int. J. Psycho-Anal.*, **38**, 240-54.

(1958). 'On Delusional Transference (Transference Psychosis).' *Int. J. Psycho-Anal.*, **39**, 134-8.

(1960). 'On Basic Unity.' *Int. J. Psycho-Anal.*, **41**, 377-84, 637.

LOEWALD, H. W. (1951). 'Ego and Reality.' *Int. J. Psycho-Anal.*, **32**.

(1960a). 'On the Therapeutic Action of Psycho-Analysis.' *Int. J. Psycho-Anal.*, **32**, 16-33.

(1960b). 'Internalization, Separation, Mourning and the Super-ego.' Read at the December 1960 meeting of the Amer. Psychoanal. Assoc., New York.

MACALPINE, I. (1950). 'The Development of the Transference.' *Psychoanal. Quart.*, **19**, 501-39.

MACALPINE, I., and HUNTER, R. (1955). *Daniel Paul Schreber – Memoirs of My Nervous Illness.* (London: Dawson.)

MAHLER, M. S. (1952). 'On Child Psychosis and Schizophrenia – Autistic and Symbiotic Infantile Psychoses.' *Psychoanal. Study Child*, **7**, 286-305.

MAHLER, M. S., and FURER, M. (1960). 'Observations on Research regarding the "Symbiotic Syndrome" of Infantile Psychosis.' *Psychoanal. Quart.*, **29**, 317-27.

MAIN, T. F. (1957). 'The Ailment.' *Brit. J. Med. Psychol.*, **30**, 129-45.

MEERLOO, J. A. M. (1952). 'Some Psychological Processes in Supervision of Therapists.' *Amer. J. Psychotherapy*, **6**, 467-70.

(1956). *The Rape of the Mind – The Psychology of Thought Control Menticide, and Brainwashing.* (Cleveland and New York: World Pub. Co.)

BIBLIOGRAPHY

MILLER, S. C. (1962). 'Ego-Autonomy in Sensory Deprivation, Isolation, and Stress.' *Int. J. Psycho-Anal.*, **43**, 1–20.

MILNER, M. (1952). 'Aspects of Symbolism in Comprehension of the Not-self.' *Int. J. Psycho-Anal.*, **33**, 181–95.

MODELL, A. H. (1958). 'The Theoretical Implications of Hallucinatory Experiences in Schizophrenia.' *J. Amer. Psychoanal. Assoc.*, **6**, 442–80.

NATIONAL COMMITTEE AGAINST MENTAL ILLNESS (1957). *What are the Facts about Mental Illness?* (Washington: the Committee.)

NOYES, A. P. (1951). *Modern Clinical Psychiatry.* (Philadelphia and London: Saunders.)

NUNBERG, H. (1948). 'The Course of the Libidinal Conflict in a Case of Schizophrenia.' In: *The Practice and Theory of Psychoanalysis.* (New York: Nerv. Ment. Dis. Mono. No. 74.)

O'CONNOR, F. (1954). *More Stories by Frank O'Connor.* (New York: Knopf.)

OVID. *The Metamorphoses,* trans. Mary M. Innes. (Harmondsworth: Penguin, 1955.)

PERRY, J. W. (1961). 'Image, Complex, and Transference in Schizophrenia.' In: *Psychotherapy of the Psychoses,* ed. A. Burton (*see* BURTON, *above*).

PERRY, S. E., and SHEA, G. N. (1957). 'Social Controls and Psychiatric Theory in a Ward Setting.' *Psychiatry,* **20**,

PFISTER, O. (1930). 'Schockdenken und Schockphantasien bei höchster Todesgefahr.' *Int. Z. f. Psychanal.*, **16**, 430–55.

PIAGET, J. (1930). *The Child's Conception of Physical Causality.* (London: Routledge; New York: Humanities Press, 1951.)

PIOUS, W. L. (1961). 'A Hypothesis about the Nature of Schizophrenic Behavior.' In: *Psychotherapy of the Psychoses,* ed. A. Burton (*see* BURTON, *above*).

RADIN, P. (1927). *Primitive Man as Philosopher.* (New York: Appleton.)

RAMANA, C. F. (1956). 'Preliminary Notes on Transference in Borderline Neurosis.' *Psychoanal. Rev.*, **43**, 129–45.

RAPAPORT, D. (1958). 'The Theory of Ego Autonomy: A Generalization.' *Bull. Menninger Clinic,* **22**, 13–35.

REICH, A. (1953). 'Narcissistic Object Choice in Women.' *J. Amer. Psychoanal. Assoc.*, **1**, 22–44.

REICHARD, S., and TILLMAN, C. (1950). 'Patterns of Parent-Child Relationships in Schizophrenia.' *Psychiatry,* **13**, 247–57.

REIK, T. (1949). *Listening with the Third Ear.* (New York: Farrar, Straus.) (1952). *The Secret Self.* (New York: Farrar, Straus.)

RIESEN, A. H. (1961). 'Excessive Arousal Effects of Stimulation after Early Sensory Deprivation.' In: *Sensory Deprivation,* ed. P. Solomon *et al.* (*see* SOLOMON, *below*).

RIOCH, J. M. (1943). 'The Transference Phenomenon in Psychoanalytic Therapy.' *Psychiatry,* **6**, 147–56.

RÓHEIM, G. (1919). *Spiegelzauber.* (Vienna: Int. Psychoanal. Verlag.)

BIBLIOGRAPHY

ROSEN, J. N. (1953). *Direct Analysis.* (New York: Grune & Stratton.)

ROSENFELD, H. (1950). 'Note on the Psychopathology of Confusional States in Chronic Schizophrenia.' *Int. J. Psycho-Anal.*, **31**, 132–7.

(1952a). 'Notes on the Psycho-Analysis of the Superego Conflict of an Acute Schizophrenic Patient.' *Int. J. Psycho. Anal.*, **33**, 111–31.

(1952b). 'Transference-Phenomena and Transference-Analysis in an Acute Catatonic Schizophrenic Patient.' *Int. J. Psycho-Anal.*, **33**, 457–64.

(1954). 'Consideration regarding the Psycho-Analytic Approach to Acute and Chronic Schizophrenia.' *Int. J. Psycho-Anal.*, **35**, 135–40.

ROSENZWEIG, N. (1959). 'Sensory Deprivation and Schizophrenia: Some Clinical and Theoretical Similarities.' *Amer. J. Psychiat.*, **116**, 326–9.

RUESCH, J. (1955). 'Nonverbal Language and Therapy.' *Psychiatry*, **18**, 323–30.

RUFF, G. E., LEVY, E. Z., and THALER, V. H. (1961). 'Factors Influencing the Reaction to Reduced Sensory Input.' In: *Sensory Deprivation*, ed. P. Solomon *et al.* (*see* SOLOMON, *below*).

RUSSELL, B. (1900). *A Critical Exposition of the Philosophy of Leibniz.* (London: Cambridge Univ. Press.)

RYCROFT, C. (1951). 'A Contribution to the Study of the Dream Screen.' *Int. J. Psycho-Anal.*, **32**, 178–85.

(1955). 'Two Notes on Idealization, Illusion and Disillusion as Normal and Abnormal Psychological Processes.' *Int. J. Psycho-Anal.*, **36**, 81–7.

SAVAGE, C. (1955). 'Variations in Ego Feeling induced by D-Lysergic Acid Diethylamide (LSD-25).' *Psychoanal. Rev.*, **42**, 1–16.

SCHILDER, P. (1935). *The Image and Appearance of the Human Body.* (London: Kegan Paul.)

SCHROFF, J. (1957). 'Acting Out in a Patient with a Character Neurosis.' Unpublished paper submitted to the Education Committee of the Washington Psychoanalytic Institute.

SCHWARTZ, C. G., SCHWARTZ, M. S., and STANTON, A. H. (1951). 'A Study of Need-Fulfillment on a Mental Hospital Ward.' *Psychiatry*, **14**, 223–42.

SCHWARTZ, M. S., and WILL, G. T. (1953). 'Low Morale and Mutual Withdrawal on a Mental Hospital Ward.' *Psychiatry*, **16**, 337–53.

SCHWING, G. (1954). *A Way to the Soul of the Mentally Ill* (New York: Int. Univ. Press.)

SCOTT, W. C. M. (1955). 'The Psycho-Analytic Concept of the Origin of Depression.' In: *New Directions in Psycho-Analysis*, ed. M. Klein *et al.* (*see* KLEIN, *above*).

SEARLES, H. F. (1960). *The Nonhuman Environment in Normal Development and in Schizophrenia.* (New York: Int. Univ. Press.)

SECHEHAYE, M. A. (1951a). *Symbolic Realization.* (New York: Int. Univ. Press.)

(1951b). *Autobiography of a Schizophrenic Girl.* (New York: Grune & Stratton.)

BIBLIOGRAPHY

SECHEHAYE, M. A. (1956). *A New Psychotherapy in Schizophrenia.* (New York: Grune & Stratton.)

(1961). Introduction to *Psychotherapy of the Psychoses,* ed. A. Burton (*see* BURTON, *above*).

SHARPE, E. F. (1940). 'An Examination of Metaphor.' *Int. J. Psycho-Anal.,* **21**, 201–13.

SHLIEN, J. M. (1961). 'A Client-Centered Approach to Schizophrenia: First Approximation.' In: *Psychotherapy of the Psychoses,* ed. A. Burton (*see* BURTON, *above*).

SILVERBERG, W. V. (1953). Paper read at the March 1953 meeting of the Washington Psychoanalytic Society.

SLOANE, P. (1957). Panel Report: 'The Technique of Supervised Analysis.' *J. Amer. Psychoanal. Assoc.,* **5**, 539–47.

SOLOMON, P., *et al.* (1961). *Sensory Deprivation.* (Cambridge, Mass.: Harvard Univ. Press.)

SPITZ, R. A. (1945). 'Hospitalism – An Enquiry into the Genesis of Psychiatric Conditions in Early Childhood.' *Psychoanal. Study Child,* **1**, 53–74.

(1955). 'The Primal Cavity.' *Psychoanal. Study Child,* **10**, 215–40.

(1957). *No and Yes: On the Genesis of Human Communication.* (New York: Int. Univ. Press.)

(1959). *A Genetic Field Theory of Ego Formation.* (New York: Int. Univ. Press.)

STANTON, A. H., and SCHWARTZ, M. S. (1949a). 'The Management of a Type of Institutional Participation in Mental Illness.' *Psychiatry,* **12**, 12–26.

(1949b). 'Medical Opinion and the Social Context in the Mental Hospital.' *Psychiatry,* **12**, 243–9.

(1949c). 'Observations on Dissociation as Social Participation.' *Psychiatry,* **12**, 339–54.

(1954). *The Mental Hospital.* (New York: Basic Books.)

STÄRCKE, A. (1921). 'The Castration Complex.' *Int. J. Psycho-Anal.,* **2**, 179–201.

STAVEREN, H. (1947). 'Suggested Specificity of Certain Dynamisms in a Case of Schizophrenia.' *Psychiatry,* **10**, 127–35.

STEINFELD, J. I. (1951). *Therapeutic Studies on Psychotics.* (Des Plaines, Ill.: Forest Press.)

STIERLIN, H. (1961). 'Individual Therapy of Schizophrenic Patients and Hospital Structure.' In: *Psychotherapy of the Psychoses,* ed. A. Burton. (New York: Basic Books.)

STORCH, A. (1924). *The Primitive Archaic Forms of Inner Experience and Thought in Schizophrenia.* (New York: Nerv. Ment. Dis. Pub. Co.)

SULLIVAN, H. S. (1925). 'The Oral Complex.' *Psychoanal. Rev.,* **12**, 31–8.

(1947). *Conceptions of Modern Psychiatry – The First William Alanson White Memorial Lectures.* (Washington: Wm. Alanson White Psychiatric Foundation.)

BIBLIOGRAPHY

(1953a). *The Interpersonal Theory of Psychiatry*, ed. H. S. Perry and M. L. Gawl.) (New York: Norton.)

(1953b). *Conceptions of Modern Psychiatry*. (New York: Norton.)

SZASZ, T. S. (1957). *Pain and Pleasure—A Study of Bodily Feelings*. (New York: Basic Books.)

SZALITA-PEMOW, A. (1951). 'Remarks on Pathogenesis and Treatment of Schizophrenia.' *Psychiatry*, **14**, 295–300.

(1952). 'Further Remarks on the Pathogenesis and Treatment of Schizophrenia.' *Psychiatry*, **15**, 143–50.

TABOR, E. (1950). *The Cliff's Edge*. (New York: Sheed & Ward.)

TAUSK, V. (1919). 'On the Origin of the "Influencing Machine" in Schizophrenia.' *Psychoanal. Quart.*, **2** (1933), 519–56.

THOMAS, DYLAN (1952). *The Collected Poems of Dylan Thomas*. (London: Dent; New York: New Directions.)

TILLICH, Paul (1952). *The Courage to Be*. (New Haven: Yale Univ. Press.)

TOWER, L. E. (1956). 'Countertransference.' *J. Amer. Psychoanal. Assoc.*, **4**, 224–55.

TOWNE, R. D., SAMPSON, H., and MESSINGER, S. L. (1961). 'Schizophrenia and the Marital Family: Identification Crises.' *J. Nerv. Ment. Dis.*, **133**, 423–9.

VAN DER HEIDE, C. (1961). 'Blank Silence and the Dream Screen.' *J. Amer. Psychoanal. Assoc.*, **9**, 85–90.

VERNON, J. A., *et al.* (1961). 'The Effect of Human Isolation upon some Perceptual and Motor Skills.' In: *Sensory Deprivation*, ed. P. Solomon *et al.* (*see* SOLOMON, *above*).

VIGOTSKY, L. S. (1934). 'Thought in Schizophrenia.' *Arch. Neurol. Psychiat.*, **31**, 1063–77.

VON DOMARUS, E. (1946). 'The Specific Laws of Logic in Schizophrenia.' In: *Language and Thought in Schizophrenia*, ed. J. S. Kasanin (*see* KASANIN, *above*).

WARNER, R. (1958). *The Greek Philosophers*. (New York: New American Library.)

Webster's New Collegiate Dictionary (1956). (Springfield, Mass.: Merriam.)

WEIGERT, E. (1949). 'Existentialism and its Relations to Psychotherapy.' *Psychiatry*, **12**, 399–412.

(1952). 'Contribution to the Problem of Termination of Psychoanalysis.' *Psychoanal. Quart.*, **21**, 465–80.

(1954). 'Counter-Transference and Self-Analysis of the Psycho-Analyst.' *Int. J. Psycho-Anal.*, **35**, 242–6.

WEISS, E. (1957). 'The Phenomenon of "Ego Passage".' *J. Amer. Psychoanal. Assoc.*, **5**, 267–81.

WERNER, H. (1940). *Comparative Psychology of Mental Development*. (New York: Int. Univ. Press.)

WEXLER, M. (1951). 'The Structural Problem in Schizophrenia: Therapeutic Implications.' *Int. J. Psycho-Anal.*, **32**, 157–66.

BIBLIOGRAPHY

WEXLER, M. (1952). 'The Structural Problem in Schizophrenia: The Role of the Internal Object.' In: *Psychotherapy with Schizophrenics*, ed. Brody and Redlich (*see* BRODY, *above*).

WHITE, R. B. (1961). 'The Mother-Conflict in Schreber's Psychosis.' *Int. J. Psycho-Anal.*, **42**, 55–73.

WHITAKER, C. A. (1958). *Psychotherapy of Chronic Schizophrenic Patients.* (Boston: Little Brown.)

WHITAKER, C. A., and MALONE, T. P. (1953). *The Roots of Psychotherapy.* (New York: Blakiston.)

WHORF, B. L. (1956). *Language, Thought, and Reality – Selected Writings of Benjamin Lee Whorf*, ed. J. B. Carroll. (Cambridge, Mass.: Technology Press; New York: Wiley; London: Chapman & Hall.)

WILL, O. A. (1961). 'Process, Psychotherapy, and Schizophrenia.' In: *Psychotherapy of the Psychoses*, ed. A. Burton (*see* BURTON, *above*).

WINNICOTT, D. W. (1945). 'Primitive Emotional Development.' *Int. J. Psycho-Anal.*, **26**, 137–43.

(1947). 'Hate in the Counter-Transference.' *Int. J. Psycho-Anal.*, **30**, 69–74.

(1948). 'Paediatrics and Psychiatry.' *Brit. J. Med. Psychol.*, **21**, 229–40. (These three papers are included in Winnicott's *Collected Papers* (London: Tavistock, 1958).)

WYNNE, L. C., *et al.* (1958). 'Pseudo-Mutuality in the Family Relations of Schizophrenics.' *Psychiatry*, **21**, 205–20.

ZUCKER, L. J. (1958). *Ego Structure in Paranoid Schizophrenia.* (Springfield, Ill.: Thomas.)

INDEX

INDEX

Angyal, Andras, 450, 560, 753
Animals
  role of, in childhood of schizo-
    phrenic patients, 260
Animate and inanimate, non-dif-
    ferentiation between (see also
    Non-human . . .)
  in normal infancy, 323, 641, 645
  in schizophrenic patients, 473,
    580, 670
    resolved in course of therapy,
      29–31, 479, 652, 713
    the self experienced as unalive,
      311, 479, 495, 713
Anxiety
  castration-, 289, 442, 726
  concerning change (see Change,
    anxiety concerning)
  concerning death's inevitability
    (see Death)
  existential (see Change; Death)
  maternal, effect of upon infant, in
    perpetuating symbiosis, 46–7,
    325, 433, 483, 498–9, 721
  rational basis for schizophrenic
    patient's, 150, 347, 457–8, 563
  separation –
    in schizophrenic patients, 325,
      ch. 17
    in supervisory relationship, 598
    in therapist (see Countertrans-
      ference)
    vengefulness as defence against,
      ch. 5
Apathy
  as aspect of pathogenic symbiosis,
    49, 655–6
  as active striving towards uncon-
    scious goals, 526
Arieti, Silvano, 254–5, 266, 384,
  418, 629, 637, 728, 753
Arlow, Jacob A., 649, 753
'As-if' phenomena (see Pseudo-
  emotion)
Autism (see also Autistic phase of
  therapy; Symbiosis, mother-
  child . . ., failure of establishment of) ch. 1

dynamics of, 731
expressive of need for individua-
  tion-oriented part-object relatedness, 31
in adult schizophrenic patients,
  19, 143, 229, 423, 630–1
  relation to anxiety concerning
    death, 500
in childhood psychosis, 218–9,
  628, 630, 670, 701
in 'love affairs' of pre-schizophrenic patients, 439
in parents of schizophrenic
  patients, 447
nascent personal communications
  in patient's, 414
need to choose between symbiosis
  and, 639
on part of therapist in supervision, 167
symbiosis as effort to overcome, 732
Autistic phase of therapy (see also
  Autism; Transference, evolution of . . ., out-of-contact
  phase), 523
Awe
  in schizophrenic patients, 128
  in therapist (see Countertrans-
    ference)
Azima, Fern J., 644, 753
Azima, Hassan, 644, 753

Babbling, 402
Bafflement
  as defence against various emo-
    tions, ch. 2
  on part of therapist (see Counter-
    transference)
Bak, Robert C., 119, 353, 442, 538,
  753
Balint, Michael, 9, 158, 308, 444,
  524, 753
Barchilon, José, 194, 208, 754
Barry, Maurice J., Jr., 286, 288–9,
  754
Bateson, Gregory, 217, 235, 257,
  305, 319, 322, 561, 754
Beck, S. J., 560, 754

768

'word salad', 101, 211
verbal
as facilitating denial of death's inevitability, 505
normal element of self-reference in, 474-5
therapist's over-use of, as manifestation of his resistance to personality-change, 445
Compassion (*see* Pity)
Competitiveness
in schizophrenia
as defence against dependency, 128
as defence against striving for identification, 723
towards introjects, 730-1
in supervisory relationship, 158, 601
in therapist (*see* Countertransference)
Condensation (*see also* Non-differentiation)
in dreams and delusions, 109
in schizophrenic thinking and communication, 394-7, 399
Conformity
fear of, in schizophrenia, 119
Confusion
as defence against various emotions, ch. 2, 493
contained within paranoid delusions, 468-9, 692, 740
equated with craziness in schizophrenic family, 740
idealization as defence against, 618
in normal ego-development, 73
mutual, in patient-therapist relationship (*see also* Countertransference), 426, 540-1
of intrapsychic processes with interpersonal processes (*see* Non-differentiation between introject and person in outer reality)
schizophrenic
as expressive of ambivalent de-

sires for individuation-and-symbiosis, 656, 688-95
fostered by free associational procedure, 78
fostered by premature interpretations, 425
healthy playfulness at core of, 422, 540
patient's subjective experience of (*see also* Subjective experience of the patient), 171, 664
relation to therapist's own (denied) confusion, 712
role of desymbolization in, 581
Rosenfeld's conception of, 73, 347
transference-origin of, 656
Conversion neurosis
vengefulness as defence against grief and dependency in, 188-190
Cooley, C. H., 329, 756
Cornelison, Alice R., 728
Coronary occlusion (*see* Psychosomatic crises)
Countercathexis
in schizophrenic estrangement, 73
Countertransference* (*see also* Symbiosis in patient-therapist relationship), ch. 6, ch. 12, ch. 18
absence of feeling in (*see also* Technique, . . . neutral responses) 525, 559
achievement of new identity in, 338-9, 459, 543
adoration in, 87, 239-40, 355-6, 368, 623, 705
anger in (*see also* Countertransference, rage in), 79
anxiety in, 114
lest one become psychotic, 258, 307-8, 661, 674, 679, 750
lest one drop dead, 735
regarding change, ch. 15
regarding 'non-human' ego-states, 637-8

---

* For convenience in indexing, all feeling-states in the therapist, irrespective of their predominant mode of origin, are included under this heading.

Ego—*contd.*
-development
autonomous factors of, 566
emotion as playing leading role
in early, 26, 28, 523, ch. 19
role of Oedipus complex in,
ch. 9, 302
-differentiation (*see* Differentiation, ego-)
-fragmentation (*see also* Hebephrenic patients), 170, ch. 10,
ch. 11
as a function of patient's giving
therapy to others, 359
as contributing to anxiety concerning death, 500–1
as defence against anxiety in
schizophrenia, 32, 316, 451–
452, 473, 524
as defence against mother's incorporative needs, 323
effort to foster
in context of ward group (*see*
Ward group)
in etiology of schizophrenia,
ch. 8
in patient-therapist relationship, ch. 8
in schizophrenic family, individuation equivalent to,
733–4
our culture as fostering, 327, 519
paranoid delusions as defence
against, 350–64, ch. 16
patient's symbiosis with therapist as refuge from, 308
-identity (*see* Identity)
-loss (*see* Dedifferentiation)
Eissler, Kurt R., 114, 148, 154, 212,
440, 507, 509–11, 515, 540,
637, 756
Ekstein, Rudolf, 594, 600, 602–3, 756
Elkisch, Paula, 645, 647, 756
Enthusiasm
as defence against hostility, 162–3
consuming, as indicator of incorporative countertransference,
63–4

Envy
as defence, 72
fear of, in schizophrenia, 452
Erikson, Erik H., 9, 326, 512, 523,
551, 606, 613, 648, 757
Errors in therapy, 78
potential usefulness of, 155, 420
Estrangement, 72
Etiology of schizophrenia (*see*
Family; Grandparents; Father;
Mother; Precipitating factors;
Siblings; Symbiosis)
Exhibitionism, 92
Experimental psychosis (*see* LSD
psychosis)
Externalization (*see also* Projection)
by patient upon therapist, as de-
fence against inner conflict, 330
of family's craziness, in etiology of
schizophrenia, ch. 8

Face
-breast equation, 646
of other person as mirror for use
in one's ego-integration, 558,
645–50
schizophrenic patient's perception of his own, in mirror, 569
therapist's, as viewed by schizophrenic patient (*see* Subjective
experience of patient)
Fairbairn, W. Ronald D., 227, 757
Family
effect of schizophrenic member
upon rest of, 740–1
healthy
psychodynamics of individuation in, 732, 750–1
introjected, in schizophrenic
patient, 724–5
loss, or threat of loss, of membership in, 262, 739–41
loyalty, 324, 736, 744–5
of introjects, in healthy individual, 751
-oriented feeling, 718
resistance on part of, to patient's
progress in therapy (*see also*

INDEX

Grief—*contd.*

in schizophrenia, 20, 75–6, 88, 91, 99, 100, 223, 325, 358, 369, 447, 452, 485, 526, 551, 636, 738

concerning death's inevitability, 397, ch. 17

perplexity as defence against, ch. 2

universal, concerning death's inevitability, ch. 17

vengefulness as defence against, ch. 5, 350–64

Groddeck, Georg, 539, 758

Group therapy (*see also* Family therapy), 219

Growth-process in recovery from schizophrenia (*see* Transference, evolution of . . .)

Grunebaum, Henry H., 757

Guilt

in schizophrenia

concerning hostility, 116

concerning need for love, 140–143

concerning striving for individuation, 549

in therapist (*see also* Countertransference)

relation to unresolved subjective omnipotence, 559

Hadley, Ernest E., 10, 18, 19, 216

Haley, Jay, 319

Hallucinations, 242, 475

as expressive of primitive wish-fulfilling precursor of thought, 574, 694

as perpetuating childhood-family environment, 268, 271, 449–50, 725, 749–50

as response to therapist's unconscious feelings, 196, 200–7

in persons living in sensory deprivation, 630, 634

libidinal cathexis of, as compared with that of therapist, 248, 268, 672–3, 749–50

of influencing machine, 476

of maternal introject, 268, 408, 421, 662, 693, 728, 732

of paternal introject, 408

on part of mother, 361, 438

patient's inability to differentiate between memories, fantasies, and, 305, 316, 319

Hampshire, Stuart, 758

Hanfmann, Eugenia, 758

Hartmann, Heinz, 319, 334, 347, 470–1, 511, 523, 566, 580, 758–9

Hatred (*see* Hostility)

Havens, Leston L., 731–2, 759

Hayward, Malcolm L., 440, 527, 540, 759

Hebb, Donald O., 627, 759

Hebephrenic patients (*see also* Subjective experience), 201–5, 241–253, 259, 293, 306–7, 315, 364–377, 402–9, 440–1, 547–8, 554, 606, 655, 660, 662, 684

disillusionment in, 439, 610

murderousness in, 337–8

psychodynamics of apathy in, 201–5, 526

psychodynamics of laughter in, 314, 395, 689

sadism in, 336

superego in, 480

ward group's reaction to, 336–8

Heidegger, Martin, 507

Heimann, Paula, 9, 160, 227, 285, 299, 527, 607, 759–60

Helplessness

feelings of, in schizophrenic patients, 415

family-wide, 718

feelings of, in therapist (*see* Countertransference)

Hendrick, Ives, 731, 759

Heron, Woodburn, 628, 754

Hesse, Hermann, 557, 759

Hill, Lewis B., 9, 195, 208, 214–15, 217, 231, 255, 265–6, 271, 304 317, 322, 358, 418–19, 421, 477, 497–8, 536, 553, 673–674, 759

Hirsch, Stanley I., 729

778

as primitive form of identification, 39, 732

in patient-therapist relationship, 40, 62–9, ch. 6

Individuation

achievement of, in therapy, 458, 642–3

role of patient's demonstrating therapist's helplessness, 549

role of therapist's free expression of feelings, 309, 651

role of therapist's neutrality, 639

role of therapist's 'non-human' transference position, 643, 653, 701–5

castrativeness in service of, 25, 688–95

child's desire for, experienced as equivalent to desire to kill mother or drive her crazy, 271, 682, 720–1

child's sacrifice of, to preserve mother's ego-integration (see Therapeutic strivings . . .)

confusion as expressive of struggle towards, 656

divorce as attempt to achieve, 721–2

equated with becoming psychotic, 272

in normal development, 46

need for mutual mother-child ambivalence to be integrated, 483, 524

role of freedom to experience scorn, 613

patient's struggle to achieve, vis-à-vis mother, 49

-process in healthy family, 732

psychosomatic crises in family members precipitated by patient's, 682–3, 734–5

struggle to achieve, in schizophrenic family, ch. 24

tantamount to ego-fragmentation in schizophrenic family, 733–4

therapist's unconscious resistance to patient's (see Symbiosis . . .,

therapist's unconscious perpetuation of)

thwarting of, in childhood, by mutually incorporative processes in child-parent relationship, 40, 42

vengefulness as result of thwarting of, 178

Infant

needs of the normal, 226–9

presumable subjective experience of, 344

undifferentiated phase in development of psychic structure in (see also Non-differentiation), 319, 323, 347, 430

Inferiority feelings

maternal, role of in pathogenic symbiosis, 45

Influencing machine, delusion concerning

as representing projection of patient's ego-functioning, 476

Tausk's explanation of, 476

Inhelder, Barbel, 575, 759

Integration as part of recovery-process in schizophrenia (see Transference, evolution of . . .)

Intellectualization

in schizoid patients, 47

Intercourse (see also Orgasm)

similarities with nursing situation, 430

Internal image (see Introjects)

Interpretations (see also Technique)

'action', 528

concerning transference psychosis, 665–7, 695–716

premature

as indicator of anxiety in therapist, 99, 134

as indicator of incorporative countertransference, 64–5, 311, 315

concrete impact upon patients of, 396–7

disturbance of patient's sense of identity by, 256, 418, 462

781

INDEX

Interpretations, premature —*contd.*
increase in patient's confusion
due to, 425
Intrapsychic processes and interpersonal processes, importance of distinguishing between (*see* Non-differentiation between introject and
person in outer reality)
Introjection (*see also* Identification;
Incorporation; Introjects; Symbiosis; Therapeutic strivings in
the patient)
by both patient and therapist,
fostered by silence in therapy,
410–11, 531
by patient, of therapist's unconscious aspects, ch. 6
in service of idealization of other
person, 399
of parental craziness, in etiology
of schizophrenia, 233, 265, 349,
ch. 23
oral, 39
role of, in development of object
relations, 664
Introjects (*see also* Introjection)
as vehicles for patients' sadism, 421
confusion of, with persons in outer
reality (*see also* Non-differentiation between introject and
person in outer reality), 47,
268, 324–6, 615–16, 647
derived from parental craziness,
265, 421
giving rise to disturbances in ego-
identity, 213, 324–5, 363,
391, 455, 467, 662, 672, 724
as regards sexual identity, 435,
724
giving rise to hallucinations (*se*
Hallucinations)
healthy-family interrelatedness
among, 751
pathological interrelatedness
among, 323
patients' communicational use of
20, 26, 391–4, 454

patients' reaction to loss of (*see
also* Symbiosis, . . . resolution
of), 454, 631
re-externalization of pathogenic,
559
regressive transformation of
schizophrenic superego into
parental, 304
role of, in paranoid schizophrenia,
ch. 16, 680
subjective experience of, compared with possession by sexual
lust (*see also* Subjective experience), 436, 724
technique of externalization of
toxic, 345–6, 426–7, 638
therapeutic technique in relation
to (*see* Technique)
traceable to dissociated components of therapist, ch. 6, 393–
394, 711
Intuition
supervisor's, ch. 4, 578–9
therapist's, 130, 138, 145, 152–4,
420
in detecting what feeling is
striving for expression, 315,
416
in timing of interpretations, 337
Isakower, Otto, 646
Isakower phenomenon, 646
Isolation
as mechanism of defence in
schizophrenia, 398–401
feeling of (*see* Loneliness)

Jackson, Don D., 319, 637, 747, 759
Jacobson, Edith, 301, 304, 318, 634,
759–60
Jaspers, Karl, 518–19
Jealousy
in therapist (*see* Countertransference)
oedipal, ch. 9
of one's self, in schizophrenia, 662
Johnson, Adelaide M., 194, 208,
218, 254–5, 260, 286, 288–9,
332, 754, 760

Murder
  as attempt to break free from symbiosis, 61–2, 720–2
  disillusionment equated with, 616
  individuation experienced as equivalent to, 271, 682
  liberation from concretistic thought experienced as equivalent to, 570
  psychological equivalent of, 261, 263
  resolution of unwanted identification, or introject, experienced as equivalent to, 719–20
  Schreber's delusion concerning soul-, 433
  (   )ous feelings among ward personnel towards patient, 331–2
  as factor in patient's acting out, 332
  (   )ous feelings, dissociated, in therapist (*see also* Countertransference), 345, 533
  (   )ous feelings in schizophrenia, 263, 295, 309, 353, 569
  derepression of, necessary to differentiation between concrete and metaphorical thinking, 570–1
  family-etiology of (*see also* Family-symbiosis), 101, 353, 482, 687
  in hebephrenic patients, 100, 337–8, 366
  patient's projection of upon therapist, 338, 347, 358, 673
  patient's terror of his own, 399
  role of mother's symbiotically-conveyed murderousness, 482
Music
  better able to express complex emotions than are words, 516
Mysticism, 425
Myths
  as expressions of man's feelings concerning death's inevitability, 506

Narcissism (*see also* Autism)
  primary, 228
  schizophrenic regression to, 72, 429, 525, 665
  unresolved, in parents of schizophrenic patient, 447, 614, 731
Negative therapeutic reaction (*see also* Symbiosis . . ., therapist's unconscious perpetuation of), ch. 15
Nelson, Benjamin, 345–6, 756
Neologisms (*see* Communication)
Non-differentiation (*see also* Confusion; Differentiation; Infant)
  among other members of one's family, in schizophrenia, 312
  as characteristic of a 'type' of schizophrenic patient, 311–16, 334–8
  as defence against anxiety in schizophrenia, 32, 316
  between animate and inanimate (*see* Animate and inanimate)
  between emotions and somatic sensations, in schizophrenia, 305, 319, 469
  between fantasy and reality, in schizophrenia, 316, 440, 469, 574–5, 631–2
  between feeling and action, in schizophrenia, 121, 132, 305
  between hate and love, in schizophrenia, 221
  between human and non-human, in schizophrenia (*see also* Non-human), 323, 361–3, 428, 472–3, 477–8, 597, 632, 641–642
  as manifestation of repressed murderous feelings, 570
  between introject and own self, 391
  between introject and person in outer reality (*see also* Introjects), 32–4, 225, 305, 329–30, 363, 466, 647, 662, 719–35
  between memories and perceptions, in schizophrenia, 305, 318–19, 469, 658

always present in healthy adult-hood, 474

as shaping 'scientific' view of world, 444

by both patient and therapist, fostered by silence, 313, 410–11

by patient, of his own utilization of non-verbal modes of communication, 386, 388–9

by patient, upon therapist, of repressed aspects of self-image, 215, 306–11, 330

by symbiotic mother, of her id-impulses, 447

in paranoid schizophrenia (see also Paranoid schizophrenia), 119, 350–64, ch. 16

informational value of patient's verbalizations containing, 386–391

of hostility in schizophrenia, 120, 306

of inner change in schizophrenia, 456

of oral needs in schizophrenia, 119, 432

of positive feelings in schizophrenia, 121

role of, in development of object relations, 118, 664

role of, in supervisory relationship, 175

upon non-human surroundings (see also Non-human . . .), 399, 465, 562

Pseudo-emotion in schizophrenic patients, 392, 608, 637–8, 643, 675, 731

Pseudo-mutuality in family of schizophrenic patient, 324, 341, 732–4

Psycho-analysis, role of comparatively orthodox, in therapy of schizophrenic patient (see also Transference, evolution of, . . . late phase), 551

Psychosis, transference (see Transference psychosis)

'Psychosis wishes', 264

Psychosomatic crises, 682–3, 734–735

Radin, Paul, 762

Ramana, C. V., 608, 623, 762

Rapaport, David, 471, 628, 762

Rape
fear of, in schizophrenia
by phallic mother, 322, 724
role of repressed oral yearning, 440
invasion by introjects experienced as, 436, 724

Reality
of outer world subjectively nullified by infantile omnipotence, 46
principle, evolution of, 523
-relatedness between patient and therapist (see also Transference, evolution of), 378, 556
schizophrenic patient's sexual behaviour as effort to contact, 441

Redlich, Fredrick C., 114, 147, 755

Reference, normal element of self-, 474–5

'Reflection process' (see Supervision, 'reflection process' in; Communication, non-verbal, in supervisory relationship; Identification, therapist's, with patient – communicational value of, in supervision)

Regression (see also Dedifferentiation)
as defence against
aggression, 353
ambivalence, 316, 353, 738
as reversal of integration-and-differentiation, 316, 320, 347, 470, 658
family-wide, 737
fear of, 116, 363
fostered by analytic setting, 635
fostered by auxiliary devices, 144, 644

Schwing, Gertrud, 114, 147–8, 156, 440, 540, 763

Science
projection as determining the concept of reality held by traditional, 444

Scorn
importance, for individuation, of freedom to experience, 613
in schizophrenic patients, 66, 76, 81, 398, 689
as defence against positive feelings, 66, 128, 181–3, 294–5, 356, 413, ch. 21
in therapist (see Countertransference)

Scott, T. H., 628, 754
Scott, W. Clifford M., 344, 763
Sèchehaye, Marguerite A., 9, 114, 141–3, 440, 540, 635, 637, 639, 644, 649, 763–4

Self, fear of the, in schizophrenia (see also Hostility, schizophrenic patient's fear of his own), 447, ch. 16, 500

Self-esteem
role of maternal deficiency in, in etiology of schizophrenia, 233, 249
schizophrenic patient's low, 246, 257
in relation to technical question of therapist's denial of, versus acknowledgment of, feelings, 293
in service of regressive modes of communication, 402–3

Sensory deprivation
experimental, 626–35
fostered by analytic setting, 635
schizophrenic patient's subjective 627–31
defensive function of, 626, 635

Separation-anxiety (see Anxiety, separation-)

Sex
anxiety concerning, 96, ch. 14

identity disturbances in regard to (see Identity, sexual . . .)
( )ual behaviour as effort to contact reality, 441
( )ual feelings in supervisory relationship, ch. 4
( )ual feelings in therapist (see Countertransference)
( )ual 'labelling' of everything, by pathogenic superego, 437

Shakespeare, William, 190–1
Sharpe, Ella Freeman, 565, 764
Shea, Gertrude N., 328–9, 541, 762
Shlien, John, 639, 764

Shock
feelings of, in schizophrenia, 98

Siblings
role of, in schizophrenic patient's development, 96, 102, 262–3, 324–5, 363–4, 366, 680, 687, 740, 749

Silence
blank, 631, 644
in therapy with schizophrenic patients (see also Communication, non-verbal; Symbiosis, . . . therapeutic), 311, 668–9
anxious, 75, 134, 212
as fostering a loosening of ego-boundaries in patient and therapist, 410–11, 531
fond, comfortable, 88, 100, 145, 293, 423–4, 528, 536–7, 548
personality-change often best facilitated by, 144, 445, 649, 652, 669, 695–7

Silverberg, William V., 125, 764
Sloane, Paul, 600, 764
Smith, Joseph H., 487
Solomon, Philip, 764
Spitz, René A., 28–9, 523, 552, 641, 644–6, 764

Splitting (see Ambivalence; Ego-fragmentation)
Staff, group dynamics of (see Ward group)

Symbiosis, mother-child—*contd.*
  failure of establishment of (*see
    also* Autism), 218–19, 321–2,
    731–2
  failure of resolution of, 321,
    524, 728, 734–5
  as defence against various
    threats, 46–7, 325, 433,
    483, 498–9, 721
  pathogenic ambivalence in (*see
    also* Ambivalence), 21, ch.
    8, ch. 10, ch. 11, ch. 14,
    470, 499, 524, 614–15, 727
  relation to anxiety concern-
    ing death, 499
  patient's struggle to resolve, 49
  murder as effort to break free
    from, 61–2, 720–1
Symbolic realization technique,
  141–3
Symbolism, schizophrenic (*see also*
  Communication, schizo-
  phrenic), 93–103, 111, 305
Szalita (-Pemow), Alberta B., 114,
  116, 168, 272, 304, 318, 526,
  765
Szasz, Thomas S., 441, 663, 765
Szurek, Stanislaus A., 194, 208, 332,
  760

Tableaux, schizophrenic patients'
  use of, in communicating
  (*see also* Communication,
  schizophrenic, non-verbal),
  389
Tabor, Eithne, 123–4, 765
Tantalization
  in etiology of schizophrenia, 256–
    257, 302, 432
Tausk, Viktor, 476, 575, 765
Taylor, J. Edward, 440, 527, 540,
  759
Technique in psychotherapy with
  schizophrenic patients (*see also*
  Countertransference; Interpretations; Intuition; Symbiosis in
  patient-therapist relationship;
  Transference), ch. 18

emphasis upon process (i.e.
  sequence) versus emphasis
  upon content, 161
'externalization of toxic introject',
  345
importance of therapist's ability
  to relinquish patient, 377
in dealing with
  ambivalence, 282, 310
  anxiety concerning change,
    309–10, 462–3
  anxiety concerning homosexu-
    ality, 527
  archaic superego, 528
  'bad mother' transference, 354–
    355, 536
  confusion, suspicion, uncer-
    tainty, 105–8
  delusions, 527–8, 530
  denial, 97–8, 528
  dependency, 21, 139–56, 379,
    540
  distorted communication, ch.
    13, 576
  dreams, 284
  ego-fragmentation, 309–10
  erotic transference, 292
  feelings concerning death, 502–
    503
  hallucinations, 528
  introjective manifestations,
    196–213, 426–7
  pseudo-emotion, 637–8
  silence (*see* Silence)
  stereotyped (non-differenti-
    ated) patient, 311–16, 338–
    342
  tenuous ego-identity, 310
  transference psychosis, 695–716
potential value of therapist's
  errors, 420
resolution of phase of therapeutic
  symbiosis, 341, 503
role of neutral responses, 421, 427,
  ch. 18, 525–31, ch. 22, 701
therapist's expressing his feelings
  to patient, 25, 36, 79, 83–4,
  292–3, 309, 344, 350, 440–1,

529, 536, 637, 650–1, 656, 690, 692, 705–6, 712
timing of interpretations, 337
use of 'action interpretations', 528
use of couch, 284
use of free associational procedure, 284, 588
  private, by therapist, to clarify countertransference, 86, 169
use of meeting with other team-members, 333, 368
use of transference interpretations, 310–11, 315
value of leaving up to patient the choice between health or continued illness, 545
value of therapist's corroborating realistic elements in patient's view of him, 393, 417
value of therapist's freedom to acknowledge the therapeutic help he receives from patient, 379, 539
Temper-tantrum behaviour in schizophrenic patients, 75
Tender feelings (see also Pity), 100
Termination of treatment (see also Transference, evolution . . ., late phase), 285, 558
Terror in schizophrenia, 397
of own murderousness, 84–5, 87, 500, 571
Terry, Dorothy, 728
Thaler, Victor H., 763
Therapeutic process (see also Transference, evolution . . .)
dynamics of
  as regards integration and differentiation, 214, ch. 10, ch. 11, 595
  mutuality of growth in patient and therapist, 316, 344, 346
  as regards symbiosis and individuation (see Symbiosis)
  patient's necessary projections upon therapist, 330

patient and therapist seen as mutually immersed in, 36–7, 538, 559, 626
Therapeutic strivings in patient (see also Positive feelings in schizophrenia; Symbiosis), 37, 199, 214, ch. 7, 269, 379, 539, 601, 675
delusions as a function of, 359, 685–6
ego-fragmentation as a function of, 359–60
sacrifice of individuality to preserve parent's equilibrium, 220, 233–4, 265, 322, 349, 374, 376, 616, ch. 23
towards each of the other family-members, 492–5, 742
Therapists, change of (see Change of therapists)
Thomas, Dylan, 518, 765
Thought processes
as influenced by our language (Sapir-Whorf hypothesis), 505
development of, in normal infancy and childhood, 320–1, 574–5, 581
in animals, 471
in children, 471, 476
in depression, 183–6
in members of primitive cultures, 450–1, 471, 647
in patients with brain injury, 471
in persons living in sensory deprivation, 627, 634
in schizophrenia, 335, ch. 13, 475–6
  in contrast to thought processes of normal child, 471, 580
  non-differentiation between more and less significant perceptual data, 112
  non-differentiation between symbolic and concrete, 112, 305, 320–1, 394–7, 472, ch. 19
  projection of the thought-disorder, 476
  role of regression in, 401–2, 450, 471, ch. 19

Printed in the United Kingdom
by Lightning Source UK Ltd.
105813UKS00001B/19-51

9 780946 439300